CREATIVE PROBLEM SOLVER'S HANDBOOK

FOR NEGOTIATORS AND MEDIATORS

CREATIVE PROBLEM SOLVER'S HANDBOOK FOR NEGOTIATORS AND MEDIATORS

A PRACADEMIC APPROACH

Volume One

A Guide for Practitioners, Academics, and Students of Creative Problem Solving

By John W. Cooley

Published by the American Bar Association Section of Dispute Resolution

with the generous support of the Association for Conflict Resolution

Editor:	Gina Viola Brown
Executive Editor:	Ellen M. Miller
Managing Editor:	Kyo Suh
Assistants:	**Jamie Jung**
	Lisa Lagos
	Emily Liddle
	Allison Rachel List
	Dave Moora
	Steve Roach
	Jonathan Weinstein
Cover Design:	**Plan B Design**

Published by the American Bar Association Section of Dispute Resolution

with the generous support of the Association for Conflict Resolution (www.ACRnet.org)

ABA Section of Dispute Resolution
740 15th St. NW, Washington, DC 20005
(202) 662-1680
Fax (202) 662-1683
dispute@abanet.org
www.abanet.org/dispute

The materials contained herein represent the opinions of the author(s) and should not be construed to be the action of either the American Bar Association or the Section of Dispute Resolution. Nothing contained in this book is to be considered as the rendering of legal advice for specific cases, and readers are responsible for obtaining such advice from their own legal counsel. This book and any forms and agreements herein are intended for educational and informational purposes only.

Support from third-party sponsors of American Bar Association publications does not imply an endorsement or promotion of the sponsor, nor its content, products or services.

While the American Bar Association Section of Dispute Resolution and the Association for Conflict Resolution acknowledge the diversity of thought and approaches to mediation, both organizations recommend to their memberships that mediation be conducted in accordance with the *Model Standards of Conduct for Mediators* and the *Model Standards of Practice for Family and Divorce Mediation*.

© 2005 American Bar Association. All rights reserved.
Printed in the United States of America.

ISBN: 1-59031-381-X

Discounts are available for members of the ABA Section of Dispute Resolution and the Association for Conflict Resolution and for books ordered in bulk. For book orders, inquire at the American Bar Association Service Center, 321 North Clark Street, Chicago, IL 60610. 1-800-285-2221. www.abanet.org/abastore   Or contact the Section of Dispute Resolution, (202) 662-1680.

For reprint inquiries, contact ABA Copyrights, copyright@abanet.org

Table of Contents

Volume One

Preface ix

Acknowledgements xiii

About the Author xv

Complete Table of Contents – Volume One xvii

Complete Table of Contents – Volume Two xxix

CHAPTER ONE: An Introduction to Creative Problem Solving 1

1.1	Purpose, General Overview, and Orientation	1
1.2	Introduction to Pracademics	3
1.3	Basic Definitions and Descriptions: Creative Problem Solving in Negotiation and Mediation	6
1.4	Role of Inductive and Deductive Reasoning in Creative Problem Solving	51
1.5	Principles of Effective Decision Making in Creative Problem Solving	62
1.6	Orientation of Creative Problem Solver	64
1.7	Principal Barriers to Effective Creative Problem Solving	66

CHAPTER TWO: Generic Strategies for Creative Problem Solving 73

2.1	Long-term Strategies for Creative Problem Solving	73
2.2	Generic Strategies for Solving Discrete Problems Creatively	74

CHAPTER THREE: Generic Tools and Techniques of the Creative Problem Solver and Sample Applications 89

3.1	Generative Tools and Techniques	89
3.2	Analytical, Evaluative, and Decision Making Tools and Techniques in Creative Problem Solving	103
3.3	Seeing the Forest (and the Trees) of Creative Problem Solving	123
3.4	Off-the-Shelf Solutions for Creative Problem Solving	138
3.5	Miscellaneous Tools and Techniques	140

CHAPTER FOUR: Creative Approaches to Process Design in Alternative Dispute Resolution 149

4.1	Designing Multiple-Hybrid Processes for Resolving Complex Disputes	149
4.2	Robert A. Creo: Other Creative Approaches to Process Design in Complex Cases	153
4.3	Rodney A. Max: Designing the Mediation	163
4.4	Rodney A. Max: Multiparty Mediation	167
4.5	Rodney A. Max: New Age of the Para-Mediator	179

CHAPTER FIVE: Creative Approaches to Overcoming Impasse in Negotiation and Mediation... 183

5.1 Peter S. Adler: Leadership, Mediation, and the Naming, Framing, and Taming of Type-II and Type-III Problems 183
5.2 Steven J. Brams and Alan D. Taylor: Use of Fair-Division Procedures in Resolving Disputes.. 194
5.3 Robert A. Creo: Breaking Impasse 196
5.4 Robert A. Creo: From No Man's Land to Common Ground: Establishing the Bargaining Model 203
5.5 Hon. Morton Denlow: Breaking Impasses in Settlement Conferences – Five Techniques for Resolution 212
5.6 Robert H. Mnookin, Scott R. Peppet, and Andrew Tulumello: Creating Value in Negotiation and Mediation 218
5.7 Rodney A. Max: Breaking the Impasse: The Unique Mediation Opportunity 221
5.8 V. Michelle Obradovic: Preventing Deadlock, Stalemate and Impasse in Mediation 224
5.9 John W. Cooley: Formula for Estimating Fair Settlement Value 227

CHAPTER SIX: Advanced Pracademic Strategies for Creative Problem Solving in Negotiation and Mediation 231

6.1 Joke Think 231
6.2 Magic Think 237
6.3 Math Think 242
6.4 Music Think 249
6.5 Robert D. Benjamin: The Physics of Mediation: Reflections of Scientific Theory in Professional Mediation Practice 252
6.6 Robert D. Benjamin: Guerilla Mediation: The Use of Warfare Strategies in the Management of Conflict and the Pursuit of Peace 255
6.7 Robert D. Benjamin: The Strategic Use of Cognitive Art in Problem Solving 263
6.8 Robert A. Creo: Mediator 2004: The Art and the Artist 270

CHAPTER SEVEN: Teaching Creative Problem Solving to Negotiators and Mediators 279

7.1 Introduction 279
7.2 Professor Linda Morton: Teaching Creative Problem Solving 280
7.3 Professor Lynn Cohn: Northwestern University School of Law; Lawyer as Problem Solver Program 285
7.4 Professor Kimberlee K. Kovach: The Hat Exercise 287
7.5 Professor Beryl Blaustone: "Broken Squares: An Exercise Designed to Demonstrate the Shift from Individual to Cooperative Problem-Solving 288
7.6 John W. Cooley: Tools and Techniques for Teaching Creative Problem Solving 294

EPILOGUE 307

INDEXES 309

A. General Index 310
B. Index to List of Sources 313

*FOR JOHN AND CHRISTINA --
AND IN LOVING MEMORY OF MARIA,
THE BEST CREATIVE PROBLEM SOLVER
I EVER KNEW*

PREFACE

This two-volume work, the *Creative Problem Solver's Handbook for Negotiators and Mediators*, is a project co-sponsored by the American Bar Association Section of Dispute Resolution and the Association for Conflict Resolution.

The model chosen for this work concerning creative problem solving in negotiation and mediation is the figure of the architect – a functionary with the vision and imagination of an artist and the practicality and precision of an engineer. The negotiator, mediator, and mediation advocate (collectively "negotiator") on the one hand, and the architect on the other, share many characteristics and attributes. They are both concerned with design. The creative negotiator designs problems, processes, and solutions and the architect designs an object to fill physical space and to satisfy both the aesthetic and the functional interests of the viewers and/or users. For the architect, design consists of two stages: conception of the idea and expression. Similarly, for the negotiator as creative problem solver, the design function also consists of two basic stages: the generative stage (conception of ideas) and the decision making (determining and expressing the solution(s)). The creative negotiator and the architect anticipate problems and attempt to convert them into opportunities and are willing to "go back to the drawing board," if necessary; they both seek the effect of synthesis, are able to work on several design levels at once, are constantly inventive, and understand that each step in the design process has the potential of modifying the next step.

Apart from the figure of an architect, this Handbook takes a pracademic approach to creative problem solving in negotiation and mediation. "Pracademics" (initial cap.) is a term that I coined in the late 1980s to describe the art and science of translating the theory of creative problem solving into practice, and conversely, converting the practice of creative problem solving into theory. It encourages an interdisciplinary approach to problem solving and seeks to draw upon the expertise of one discipline to enhance the problem solving effectiveness in another. It is particularly attentive to the areas between disciplines – the interstitial areas of overlap and ambiguity – because it is that territory that is often fertile with discovery, surprise, and insight.

As mentioned above, this Handbook consists of two volumes and both volumes should be of interest to both lawyers and laypersons. This Volume One is primarily geared to serve as a guide, generally, to practitioners, academics, and students in the practice, teaching, and study of creative problem solving methods, tools, and techniques. Because my approach is eclectic and because the literature on creative problem solving generally is replete with varying and sometimes seemingly contradictory ideas regarding proper methods and approaches, Volume One provides the practitioner with a panoply of potential ideas with which the practitioner can experiment in ways that satisfy his or her personal experiences, skills, and talents.

Volume Two of the Handbook is focused on specific creative problem solving techniques and tools that practitioners have found to be effective in negotiation and mediation and have submitted to me for inclusion in the Handbook. These submissions constitute the core of Volume Two and provide a truly phenomenal example of member-to-member, cooperation, collaboration and professional sharing. I am the editor of the Handbook but in truth, Volume Two has been largely written by practitioners for practitioners. The Table of Contents of Volume Two is included in this Volume One to facilitate your reference to it, should the need arise.

Organized into seven chapters, Volume One of the Handbook provides a full range of features geared to assist practitioners in systematically applying creative problem solving techniques in both dispute and transactional negotiation and mediation. Volume One should be of invaluable assistance to the experienced and novice negotiators and mediators alike. Chapter One provides basic information regarding the nature of creative problem solving, including definitions and descriptions of basic thinking processes (vertical, lateral, critical, creative, whole-brain, etc.), the basic techniques and skills involved in creative problem solving, as well as the appropriate orientation for creative problem solvers. A central message of Chapter One is that creative problem solving has both generative and analytical aspects. Generation of ideas is important to a successful, creative result, but just as important is the analytical aspect during which the creative problem solver (and others he or she is assisting) analyzes and evaluates the options and ultimately selects (decides) which option or options are most appropriate. So, the realization that emerges is that effective creative problem solving is, in fact, effective decision making.

Chapter Two describes generic strategies for creative problem solving and applications that are based primarily on the strategies explained by Edward de Bono in his landmark book, *Lateral Thinking: Creativity Step by Step.* Complementing the problem solving strategies described in Chapter Two, the information in Chapter Three includes more than twenty-five generative and analytical tools and techniques from the problem solving literature that serve to implement those problem solving strategies.

Chapter Four focuses on creative approaches to designing ADR processes. That chapter will become quite helpful as you, in your capacity as an advocate, negotiator, or mediator, are increasingly called upon by clients or parties to design processes for resolving complex disputes.

Among other helpful information, Chapter Five contains creative approaches to overcoming impasse in negotiation and mediation. Chapter Six describes advanced Pracademic strategies for creative problem solving in negotiation and mediation, including JokeThink, MagicThink, MathThink, MusicThink, Guerilla Mediation, and the Strategic Use of Cognitive Art in Mediation.

Finally, Chapter Seven presents several ideas regarding effective techniques for teaching creative problem solving to negotiators and mediators.

Volume Two of the Handbook consists of five chapters. Chapter One of Volume Two is a condensed version of Chapter One of Volume One. It provides basic information regarding the nature of creative problem solving, including definitions and descriptions of basic thinking processes (vertical, lateral, critical, creative, whole-brain, etc.), the basic techniques and skills involved in creative problem solving. Similarly, Chapter Two of Volume Two is a condensed version of Chapter Two of Volume One and it describes generic strategies for creative problem solving and applications that are based primarily on the strategies explained by Edward de Bono in his landmark book, *Lateral Thinking: Creativity Step by Step*. These two condensed chapters are included in this portable Volume Two because the two volumes can be purchased separately and the information can be useful to the practitioner when referring to Volume Two in the field.

Chapter Three, Four, and Five of Volume Two contain in the range of one hundred or more creative problem solving techniques that were submitted by the members of the ABA Section of Dispute Resolution and the Association for Conflict Resolution. Volume Two consists, in part, of multiple submissions contributed by two well-known and highly respected ADR practitioners. Robert Creo has provided approximately thirty original techniques, tools, or tactics that he has used successfully as a mediator. In addition, N.D. John Settle, a lawyer, mediator, and trainer in the Washington, D.C. area, specializing in workplace dispute resolution has provided a compilation of 66 tips and techniques for helping parties move ahead and overcome roadblocks in mediation. I am grateful that these highly respected professionals have agreed to share their excellent techniques with their colleagues in the field.

One highly useful feature of Volume Two of the Handbook is its multiple indexing. The creative problem solving tools and techniques are indexed by practitioner-contributor, short title, practice area (commercial, family, etc.), primary use (break impasse, emotion handling, etc.), and stage of use (premediation, joint session, caucus, etc.).

Another feature of the Handbook that I believe is helpful is the method of citations to sources. I have intentionally avoided the use of footnotes, because they are often distracting and because they also lend an air of formality that would not be conducive to attracting readers who are either not lawyers or who are not academically oriented. The method of citation is simple. At the back of each volume of the Handbook appears a "List of Sources" in alphabetical order by author. If the author has more than one publication, a number appears in parentheses behind the author's name. Thus, consider this example citation appearing in the text of the Handbook: (Jones, 343-345). This signifies that the author – Jones –

only has one publication in the List of Sources, and the material being described in the text may be found on pages 309-325. Consider this example citation appearing in the text of the Handbook: (Smith (2), 224-234). This signifies that the author has more that one publication in the List of Sources, and the appropriate one on the List is the one that in part reads "Smith (2)".

I have written this Handbook with several separate audiences in mind. First and foremost, I have written for practicing negotiators and mediators. I have deliberately written this book generically so that it will be useful to a wide variety of experienced and novice negotiators and mediators, lawyers and nonlawyers alike, serving in all types of negotiator and mediator roles in a wide variety of litigation or litigation-related disputes. This is a Handbook to use, not simply to read and to place on the shelf. Volume Two (A Portable Primer for Practitioners) is specifically designed to be used by mediators during the preliminary stages of negotiations and mediations and to be brought to the negotiation or mediation session or conference for use as an idea generator and as a quick reference tool or guide.

The next audience for whom I have written consists of the organizers of and participants in continuing legal education ("CLE") programs in the United States and in other countries around the world. The step-by-step approach, analyses of sample problems, and the succinct presentations of useful information in chart form, and the analyses of critical process and procedure issues, make it an ideal teaching resource for negotiation, mediation, mediation advocacy and creative problem solving seminars.

A third audience for which this publication has been geared consists of the teachers and students of law school courses on creative problem solving, negotiation, mediation, or ADR in general. At this writing, there are very few comprehensive law student textbooks available providing detailed "hands on" instruction on creative problem solving. This book seeks to fill that gap in ADR literature currently available for law school instruction and for the teaching and learning of creative problem solving in any academic or practice discipline.

In creating this Handbook, I have made every effort to use a personable and personalized writing style, as if I were having a face-to-face conversation with you. I hope you find this style to be friendly and engaging, as intended. Finally, I sincerely hope that this book will, in some significant way, enhance the quality of creative problem solving in negotiation and mediation both nationally and internationally for many years to come.

ACKNOWLEDGMENTS

I welcome the opportunity to thank the people who, over the years, have played significant roles in shaping my experience in the fields of alternative dispute resolution and creative problem solving, culminating in the development of this book. Particularly, I want to thank Senior Circuit Judge Thomas E. Fairchild, U.S. Court of Appeals for the Seventh Circuit, and Circuit Executive Collins Fitzpatrick, who in the late 1970s, gave me what I now realize was an opportunity of a lifetime to chair a Court-sponsored subcommittee to study possible alternatives to litigation in the federal court system. It was in that role that I was given "the freedom to be creative," an exhortation which I took seriously. I was given the opportunity to educate myself on the arbitration and mediation processes and on the courts and organizations around the country which – even at that early period – were administering the use of court-annexed and private dispute resolution. It was also during that subcommittee work I came in contact with the then Regional Director of the U.S. Justice Department's Community Relations Service, Richard A. Salem, who was then actively engaged in mediating the Nazi-Skokie conflict in Chicago, and who had previously participated in the mediation of the Kent State war protest matter, and the Wounded Knee incident in the early 1970s. Dick willingly shared his vast knowledge of mediation with me and soon we co-designed and co-taught, at Loyola University of Chicago School of Law, one of the first law school ADR courses ever offered in the country. We taught this course for several semesters together, and, even though I was a teacher, I profited immensely from Dick's insights and inspiration concerning effective mediation methods and techniques. I am grateful to Dick for his selfless sharing of his accumulated skills and experience. Especially I am thankful to him for modeling the skill of listening and for teaching me the indispensability of this tool in mediation. It was Dick who taught me early on that the most creative results in mediation and negotiation reside in the minds of the disputants and their lawyers. Part of the mediator's challenge is to help them find the creative solutions.

I also want to thank the unknown librarian who, in the early 1980s when I began to explore the subject of creative thinking, put me onto the book by Dr. Edward de Bono entitled *Lateral Thinking: Creativity Step By Step*. That book in fact changed my life in a significant way. It helped me look at creative problem solving from a fresh perspective, and provided me the incentive over the next nearly twenty-five years to acquire extensive knowledge about creativity and creative problem solving. I began to successfully incorporate de Bono's lateral thinking techniques not only in the mediations that I conducted, but also in traditional lawyering roles of client advisor, litigator, advocate, and brief writer. Of course, I also used the techniques in solving the problems that routinely presented themselves in everyday life. Eventually, through further research and study, I discovered many other creative problem solving techniques that proved very beneficial to many problem solving activities in which I engaged, both professionally and personally.

Other leaders in the fields of dispute resolution and creative problem solving have, over the years, shared with me their extensive knowledge of those topics and/or supported and encouraged my efforts to merge the two disciplines. For that I'm indeed grateful. Among these colleagues are Robert Benjamin, Peter Adler, Robert A. Creo, Howard L. Stone, Nancy Peace, Morton Denlow, James Alfini, Eric Galton, and Kim Kovach. I also wish to especially acknowledge Professor Lynn Cohn, who supervises the ADR and "Lawyer as Problem Solver" Programs at Northwestern University School of Law, where I teach. She is a brilliant teacher and a valued professional colleague, and I am additionally grateful to her for bringing me into contact with California Western Law School Professors Katharine Rosenberry and Linda Morton, who, along with their colleagues, were the first in the country to establish in a law school a full-fledged, highly acclaimed, award-winning Center for Creative Problem Solving. I would also like to recognize Lynn A. Gaffigan who unselfishly contributed many hours of her time to collaborate with me in the design of a creative problem solving seminar for lawyers and laypersons. It was during that collaboration that I learned so much more about creative problem solving – a topic which I thought I knew best.

Additionally, I particularly want to acknowledge with gratitude the insights about creative problem solving that Dr. Petronio Muniz, President of Instituto Arbiter, Recife Brazil, has shared with me over the years. Similarly, I appreciate the insights that architect Keila Porto of Recife has shared with me about the relationships between the mediator and architect functions.

Finally, but certainly not least, I want to thank the leaders of the American Bar Association Section of Dispute Resolution and the Association for Conflict Resolution for giving me the opportunity to author and edit this Handbook. I wish to thank Gina Viola Brown and Kyo Suh for their excellent editing work in shepherding the two volumes of the Handbook to publication.

John W. Cooley
Chicago, Illinois
August 2005

ABOUT THE AUTHOR

John W. (Jack) Cooley is a former United States Magistrate, Assistant United States Attorney, Senior Staff Attorney for the United States Court of Appeals for the Seventh Circuit, and a litigation partner in a Chicago law firm. He is a past Chair of the Mediation Committee of the ABA Section of Dispute Resolution and a current Council Member of that Section. Mr. Cooley has been a member of the Society of Professionals in Dispute Resolution (now the Association for Conflict Resolution ("ACR")) since 1983 and was an ACR Board Member and served in the office of Secretary of the organization in the early 2000s. Additionally, he served on the ACR Task Force on the Authorized Practice of Mediation and the ACR Task Force on Mediator Certification. He is a Fellow of the American Bar Foundation, the International Academy of Mediators, and the Chartered Institute of Arbitrators, London, England.

Currently in private practice in the Chicago area, he serves as a neutral on the JAMS panel of mediators and arbitrators. He has served as a Special Master for federal judges and as an arbitrator and mediator in a wide variety of complex, multi-million dollar commercial disputes, both domestic and international in character.

An Adjunct Professor of Law at Northwestern University School of Law, he teaches a course in negotiation and mediation. In addition, he is the principal designer and instructor of a "Mediation Advocacy" cybercourse that was developed by Northern Illinois University in cooperation with the American Bar Association Section of Dispute Resolution. He is the author of *The Mediator's Handbook: Advanced Practice Guide for Civil Litigation* (NITA, 2000); *Mediation Advocacy* (NITA, Second Edition, 2002), *Arbitration Advocacy* (NITA, Second Edition, 2003), *The Arbitrator's Handbook* (NITA, Second Edition, 2004), and more than sixty articles on litigation, judicial, and ADR topics. The first editions of *Mediation Advocacy* and of *Arbitration Advocacy* have been published in the Portuguese language by the University of Brasilia in Brazil.

Mr. Cooley has studied creative thinking and creative problem solving and their application to negotiation, mediation, and litigation for the last twenty years. His first book-length publication, Callaghan's *Appellate Advocacy Manual: A Design and Decisionmaking Approach* (1989) contained a chapter on "The Thinking Function" and described how lawyers could use lateral and vertical thinking skills effectively in a creative problem solving process to design issues and arguments on appeal. He has since published or has in process a number of articles he calls collectively the "Pracademic Series," which explore the territory between many disciplines vis-a-vis negotiation and mediation. In this series, metaphors of art, music, magic, humor, mathematics, physics, psychology, philosophy, and rhetoric, among others, are used to discover the essence of the art and science of effective problem solving in negotiation and mediation settings. These articles are cited in the "List of Sources" in the back of this Handbook and excerpts of four of them appear in Chapter Six of this Volume One. The present two-volume publication, *Creative Problem Solver's Handbook for Negotiators and Mediators* represents, in part, the culmination of many years of studying the creative problem solving process and of experimenting with and applying creative problem solving techniques to achieve optimum, and sometimes super-optimum, solutions in negotiation and mediation.

Mr. Cooley, a Vietnam War veteran, is a graduate of the United States Military Academy at West Point and the University of Notre Dame Law School, receiving a year of his legal training in international and comparative law at the School's Centre for Legal Studies in London, England.

Table of Contents (Complete)

(References are to sections.)

Volume One

CHAPTER ONE: An Introduction to Creative Problem Solving

1.1 Purpose, General Overview, and Orientation
    1.1.1 Background, purpose, and general overview of Handbook
    1.1.2 Orientation: The creative problem solver as architect

1.2 Introduction to Pracademics
    1.2.1 Definition and description
    1.2.2 Use of metaphor

1.3 Basic Definitions and Descriptions: Creative Problem Solving in Negotiation and Mediation
    1.3.1 Negotiation
    1.3.2 Mediation
    1.3.3 Thinking modes
        1.3.3.1 Vertical (Convergent) thinking
        1.3.3.2 Lateral (Divergent) thinking
        1.3.3.3 Whole-brain thinking
        1.3.3.4 Abductive
        1.3.3.5 Abstract
        1.3.3.6 Active
        1.3.3.7 Analogical
        1.3.3.8 Analytical
        1.3.3.9 Automatic
        1.3.3.10 Body (kinesthetic)
        1.3.3.11 Conscious
        1.3.3.12 Creative
        1.3.3.13 Critical
        1.3.3.14 Deductive
        1.3.3.15 Dialectical
        1.3.3.16 Dimensional
        1.3.3.17 Heuristic
        1.3.3.18 Holistic
        1.3.3.19 Inductive
        1.3.3.20 Integrative
        1.3.3.21 Reflective
        1.3.3.22 Synthetic
        1.3.3.23 Systems
        1.3.3.24 Transformational
        1.3.3.25 Unconscious
    1.3.4 Thinking mechanics

1.3.5 Thinking skills
1.3.6 Thinking styles
1.3.7 Types of problems
1.3.8 Types of processes
    1.3.8.1 High-low arbitration
    1.3.8.2 Baseball arbitration
    1.3.8.3 Med-Arb.
    1.3.8.4 Co-Med-Arb
    1.3.8.5 Arb-Med
    1.3.8.6 Binding mediation
    1.3.8.7 Co-mediation
    1.3.8.8 Mini-trial
    1.3.8.9 Simulated juries
    1.3.8.10 Special masters
    1.3.8.11 Early neutral evaluation
    1.3.8.12 Fact finding
    1.3.8.13 Expert panels
    1.3.8.14 Summary jury trial
1.3.9 Types of solutions
1.3.10 Designing the problem
1.3.11 Designing the process
    1.3.11.1 Your goals when designing a negotiation, mediation, or other ADR process
    1.3.11.2 Designing the appropriate hybrid ADR process using the Hybrid Selection Chart
1.3.12 Designing the solution
1.3.13 Types of problem solving
    1.3.13.1 Problem solving in general
    1.3.13.2 Individual problem solving
    1.3.13.3 Group problem solving
1.3.14 Creativity
1.3.15 Creative problem solving
    1.3.15.1 Creative problem solving process
    1.3.15.2 Favorable conditions for creative problem solving
    1.3.15.3 The problem finding skill
1.3.16 Creative Skills
    1.3.16.1 Communication - general
    1.3.16.2 Listening
    1.3.16.3 Learning
    1.3.16.4 Understanding
    1.3.16.5 Remembering
    1.3.16.6 Ability to recognize and form patterns
    1.3.16.7 Ability to abstract
    1.3.16.8 Ability to analogize
    1.3.16.9 Speaking/questioning
    1.3.16.10 Empathizing
    1.3.16.11 Intuitive and insightful
    1.3.16.12 Perceptive
    1.3.16.13 Imaginative
    1.3.16.14 Ability to model, play, transform, synthesize

- 1.3.16.15 Possess multiple intelligences
- 1.3.16.16 Tolerant of ambiguity
- 1.3.16.17 Capacity for risk taking
- 1.3.16.18 Preference for disorder
- 1.3.16.19 Perseverance
- 1.3.16.20 Courage

1.4 Role of Inductive and Deductive Reasoning in Creative Problem Solving
- 1.4.1 General
- 1.4.2 Inductive reasoning
- 1.4.3 Classical structures of deductive reasoning
  - 1.4.3.1 The syllogism in general
  - 1.4.3.2 The categorical syllogism
  - 1.4.3.3 The disjunctive syllogism
  - 1.4.3.4 The conditional syllogism
  - 1.4.3.5 The enthymeme
  - 1.4.3.6 Chain of enthymemes
  - 1.4.3.7 Formal validity and material truth
- 1.4.4 Fallacies of reasoning
  - 1.4.4.1 Extension
  - 1.4.4.2 Arguing in a circle
  - 1.4.4.3 Ignoring the issue
  - 1.4.4.4 Baiting an opponent
  - 1.4.4.5 Repeated assertion
  - 1.4.4.6 Structured Response
  - 1.4.4.7 Substituting bombast for argument
  - 1.4.4.8 Denying a valid conclusion
  - 1.4.4.9 Straw Man
  - 1.4.4.10 Appeal to ignorance
  - 1.4.4.11 Pseudo questions
  - 1.4.4.12 Appeal to tradition
  - 1.4.4.13 Non sequitur
  - 1.4.4.14 Post hoc

1.5 Principles of Effective Decision Making in Creative Problem Solving
- 1.5.1 Elements of good decisions
- 1.5.2 Basic characteristics of decisions
- 1.5.3 Pitfalls obstructing good decision making

1.6 Orientation of Creative Problem Solver
- 1.6.1 Optimistic
- 1.6.2 Initially non-critical
- 1.6.3 Open-minded
- 1.6.4 Flexibly perceptive
- 1.6.5 Tolerant of ambiguity
- 1.6.6 Improvisational
- 1.6.7 Analytical
- 1.6.8 Seeks to achieve quality decision making

1.7 Principal Barriers to Effective Creative Problem Solving
- 1.7.1 Informational barriers

  1.7.2 Perceptual barriers - the illusions of conflict
    1.7.2.1 Illusions of the first type
    1.7.2.2 Illusions of the second type
    1.7.2.3 Illusions of the third type
  1.7.3 Communication barriers
    1.7.3.1 Individual communication barriers
    1.7.3.2 Group communication barriers.
    1.7.3.3 Principal communication barriers in negotiation and mediation

CHAPTER TWO: Generic Strategies for Creative Problem Solving

2.1 Long-term Strategies for Creative Problem Solving

2.2 Generic Strategies for Solving Discrete Problems Creatively
  2.2.1 Suspend judgment
  2.2.2 Brainstorm
  2.2.3 Challenge assumptions
    2.2.3.1. Theory of challenging assumptions in general
    2.2.3.2. A personal example of a failure to challenge assumptions
  2.2.4 Generate alternatives
  2.2.5 Fractionate/Reframe
  2.2.6 Visualize; Imagineer
  2.2.7 Reverse thought
  2.2.8 Use analogies, metaphors, similes
  2.2.9 Welcome random ideas

CHAPTER THREE: Generic Tools and Techniques of the Creative Problem Solver and Sample Applications

3.1 Generative Tools and Techniques
  3.1.1 Reconsider your starting point.
  3.1.2 Restate/redesign the problem
    3.1.2.1 Paraphrase: Restate the problem using different words without losing the original meaning
    3.1.2 2 Flip 180 degrees: Turn the problem on its head
    3.1.2.3 Broaden Focus: Restate the problem in a larger context
    3.1.2.4 Redirect the focus: Boldly, consciously change the focus
    3.1.2.5 Ask "Why" repetitively until the essence of the real problem emerges
  3.1.3 Reconsider your goals at any time
  3.1.4 Distinguish between intermediate goals and final goals
  3.1.5 Consider indirect approaches to reach your intermediate and final goals
  3.1.6 Consider prioritizing multiple goals
  3.1.7 Express negative goals as positive goals
  3.1.8 Try pulling instead of pushing
  3.1.9 Inverse Brainstorming
  3.1.10 Try the SCAMPER tool
  3.1.11 Consider role playing to find a solution
  3.1.12 Focus on similarities
  3.1.13 Think visually and sketch visual representations

3.1.14 Imagine what someone else might suggest
3.1.15 Use Fishbone Diagram
3.1.16 Use Why-Why Diagram
3.1.17 Distinguish between dimensional independence, dependence, and relationships
3.1.18 Use Interest-Resource Table to generate new ideas
3.1.19 Use storyboarding
3.1.20 Conduct an organized random search
3.1.21 Stimulate ideas by viewing pictures
3.1.22 Use a verb checklist
3.1.23 Try Synectics
3.1.24 Mind maps
3.1.25 Use multiple matrices for idea generation purposes

3.2 Analytical, Evaluative, and Decision Making Tools and Techniques in Creative Problem Solving
    3.2.1 Use a checklist
    3.2.2 Use storyboarding in critical thinking sessions
    3.2.3 Sketch simple matrices for analysis and evaluation purposes
    3.2.4. Consider using sorting and chronologies
    3.2.5. Choose by elimination
    3.2.6 Pros-cons-and fixes.
    3.2.7 Imagine exaggerated specific cases to test creative solutions
    3.2.8 Weighted ranking
    3.2.9 Hypothesis testing
    3.2.10 Causal flow diagramming
    3.2.11 Blind bidding
    3.2.12. Pie chart
    3.2.13. Blind trust
    3.2.14. The utility matrix
        3.2.14.1 Utility analysis – general
        3.2.14.2 Conducting a utility-matrix analysis
    3.2.15 Advanced utility analysis
    3.2.16 Test the validity, quality, utility and durability of your solution(s)

3.3 Seeing the Forest (and the Trees) of Creative Problem Solving
    3.3.1 Decision trees
    3.3.2 Opportunitrees
    3.3.3 Probability trees
    3.3.4 Utility trees

3.4 Off-the-Shelf Solutions for Creative Problem Solving
    3.4.1 Structured settlement or payment in installments
    3.4.2 Future business arrangement
    3.4.3 Portion of the settlement to be paid to a mutually acceptable charity
    3.4.4 Payment in kind instead of in dollars
    3.4.5 Substitution of goods
    3.4.6 Apology
    3.4.7 Change in title, label, or description
    3.4.8 Extra-dispute resources for satisfying a party's extra-dispute interests
    3.4.9 Confidentiality agreement
    3.4.10 Propose a change in language or in the interpretation of language
    3.4.11 Split the difference

3.5 Miscellaneous Tools and Techniques
    3.5.1 Neuro-linguistic Programming
    3.5.2 The Enneagram
    3.5.3 Whole-Brain thinking applied
        3.5.3.1 Determining the brain preference of others
        3.5.3.2 Your dealings with co-counsel
        3.5.3.3 Your dealings with senior or subordinate counsel on the case
        3.5.3.4 Dealing with opposing counsel
        3.5.3.5 Dealing with mediators, judges, or former judges

CHAPTER FOUR: Creative Approaches to Process Design in Alternative Dispute Resolution

4.1 Designing Multiple-Hybrid Processes for Resolving Complex Disputes
    4.1.1 Classic co-mediation
    4.1.2 Classic mini-trial procedure
    4.1.3 Modified mini-trial procedure
    4.1.4 Blind bidding enhancement
    4.1.5 Location of settlement meetings

4.2 Robert A. Creo: Other Creative Approaches to Process Design in Complex Cases
    4.2.1 Creo Pie Chart Tool
        4.2.1.1 Case study
        4.2.1.2 Dividing the pie
        4.2.1.3 The pie chart method
        4.2.1.4 What happened in mediation
        4.2.1.5 12 Steps to settlement
        4.2.1.6 Another case study: employment insurance claims
        4.2.1.7 Facts
        4.2.1.8 Methodology
        4.2.1.9 Potential case-study settlement options
    4.2.2 Creo Blind Trust Method
        4.2.2.1 Mission
        4.2.2.2 Charge to the defendants
        4.2.2.3 Tools
        4.2.2.4 Ground rules
        4.2.2.5 Step-by-step method.

4.3 Rodney A. Max: Designing the Mediation
    4.3.1 Introduction
    4.3.2 Identification of parties to conflict
    4.3.3 Nature of the conflict
    4.3.4 Identifying mediation parameters
    4.3.5 Premediation exchange of information
    4.3.6 Opening statements and negotiations
    4.3.7 Conclusion

4.4 Rodney A. Max: Multiparty Mediation
    4.4.1 Introduction
    4.4.2 The mediator(s)

4.4.3 The facilities
4.4.4 Mediation parameters identified – premediation attorneys' caucus(es)
4.4.5 The position statements
4.4.6 The opening (joint) session
4.4.7 The negotiations/caucuses
4.4.8 The reasonable ballpark
4.4.9 Homeplate -- the mediation agreement
4.4.10 Conclusion

4.5 Rodney A. Max: New Age of the Para-Mediator

CHAPTER FIVE: Creative Approaches to Overcoming Impasse in Negotiation and Mediation

5.1 Peter S. Adler: Leadership, Mediation, and the Naming, Framing, and Taming of Type-II and Type-III Problems
    5.1.1 The challenge
    5.1.2 Type-I Problems and the myth of conventional problem solving
    5.1.3 Type-II Problems and the misapplication of Type-I problem solving strategies
    5.1.4 Type-III Problems and the challenge of bringing leadership to "wicked" problems
    5.1.5 The ACWA Case
    5.1.6 Mediation and leadership

5.2 Steven J. Brams and Alan D. Taylor: Use of Fair-Division Procedures in Resolving Disputes
    5.2.1 Strict and balanced alternation
    5.2.2 Divide-and-choose
    5.2.3 Adjusted winner
    5.2.4 Criteria of satisfaction
    5.2.5 Rules and strategies

5.3 Robert A. Creo: Breaking Impasse
    5.3.1 The mediation process framework
    5.3.2 Process and personal preferences of participants
    5.3.3 Process preferences and heuristics of Robert A. Creo
    5.3.4 Some common paradigms
        5.3.4.1 Paradigm No. 1: Creo hierarchy of case values
        5.3.4.2 Paradigm No. 2: phantom negotiators
        5.3.4.3 Paradigm No. 3: settler's remorse
        5.3.4.4 Paradigm No. 4: trading body parts?
        5.3.4.5 Paradigm No. 5: time is not on your side
        5.3.4.6 Paradigm No. 6: look ahead, not backward
        5.3.4.7 Paradigm No. 7: jury justice?
        5.3.4.8 Paradigm No. 8: all lawyers are created equal

5.4 Robert A. Creo: From No Man's Land to Common Ground: Establishing the Bargaining Model
    5.4.1 The traditional demand-and-offer model
    5.4.2 How to avoid the beau geste
    5.4.3 Common sense rules for mediators
    5.4.4 Specific bargaining models – standard approaches
        5.4.4.1 The auction dossier
        5.4.4.2 Take it or leave it dossier

- 5.4.5 Specific bargaining models - soft approaches
  - 5.4.5.1 Roaming the range of the "zeros dossier"
  - 5.4.5.2 The "what if?"
  - 5.4.5.3 Anticipation
  - 5.4.5.4 Handicapping
  - 5.4.5.5 The corkscrew
  - 5.4.5.6 Double blind mediator proposal
  - 5.4.5.7 Contuzzi safety deposit box
  - 5.4.5.8 Blind trust method for multiparty claims

5.5 Hon. Morton Denlow: Breaking Impasses in Settlement Conferences – Five Techniques for Resolution
- 5.5.1 Creating a range
- 5.5.2 Recommending a specific number
- 5.5.3 Splitting the difference
- 5.5.4 Clarifying objective facts
- 5.5.5 Setting firm deadlines
- 5.5.6 Conclusion

5.6 Robert H. Mnookin, Scott R. Peppet, and Andrew Tulumello: Creating Value in Negotiation and Mediation
- 5.6.1 Ask three important questions up front
- 5.6.2 Change the rules of the game
- 5.6.3 Identify interests and search for trades
- 5.6.4 In transactions, consider creating the first draft of the agreement
- 5.6.5 In deal-making, consider changing players to break an impasse
- 5.6.6 In deal-making, look to the future and reality check all the contract provisions

5.7 Rodney A. Max: Breaking the Impasse: The Unique Mediation Opportunity
- 5.7.1 Calling on the leadership
- 5.7.2 Court decision
- 5.7.3 Conditional offers
- 5.7.4 Mediator's proposal
- 5.7.5 Conclusion

5.8 V. Michelle Obradovic: Preventing Deadlock, Stalemate and Impasse in Mediation

5.9 John W. Cooley: Formula for Estimating Fair Settlement Value

CHAPTER SIX: Advanced Pracademic Strategies for Creative Problem Solving in Negotiation and Mediation

6.1 JokeThink
- 6.1.1 Joke model of creative thinking
- 6.1.2 Mediation punchlines
- 6.1.3 Six standard joke formulas
  - 6.1.3.1 Play on words
  - 6.1.3.2 Reversal
  - 6.1.3.3 Exaggeration
  - 6.1.3.4 Visualization

    6.1.3.5 Pairs and triples
    6.1.3.6 Routining
  6.1.4 Example of application of joke formulas in the mediation of a dispute

6.2 MagicThink
  6.2.1 General
  6.2.2 Truth, deception, and magic
  6.2.3 The magician's tools
  6.2.4 Magicians as problem solvers
  6.2.5 Effects of magic
  6.2.6 Methods of magic

6.3 MathThink
  6.3.1 Descartes' Rules for the Direction of the Mind
  6.3.2 Leibniz's Geometry of Situation

6.4 MusicThink
  6.4.1 The music metaphor for mediation
  6.4.2 Sound in music
  6.4.3 Sound in mediation
  6.4.4 Tone in music
  6.4.5 Tone in mediation

6.5 Robert D. Benjamin: The Physics of Mediation: Reflections of Scientific Theory in Professional Mediation Practice
  6.5.1 Mediation practice and scientific inquiry: science and scientism
  6.5.2 Professions and professionals from a systems theory perspective
  6.5.3 Toward a theory of mediation practice
  6.5.4 Mediation as a paradigm for professional practice: the reflective practice paradigm
  6.5.5 Application of the reflective (mediative) paradigm
  6.5.6 Significance of the paradigm shift to the practice of mediation

6.6 Robert D. Benjamin: Guerilla Mediation: The Use of Warfare Strategies in the Management of Conflict and the Pursuit of Peace
  6.6.1 Introduction – conflict mediation as a fanciful or realistic option
  6.6.2 The sources and rationale for Guerilla Mediation
  6.6.3 The basic tenets of Guerilla Mediation
    6.6.3.1 Respect for human nature as it is, not as we would like to believe it could be
    6.6.3.2 A realistic understanding and acceptance of conflict
    6.6.3.3 The effective use of strategic planning
  6.6.4 Conclusion – The promise and future of mediation

6.7 Robert D. Benjamin: The Strategic Use of Cognitive Art in Problem Solving
  6.7.1 Escaping flatland
  6.7.2 Cognitive art allows and encourages the lateral thinking essential for problem solving
  6.7.3 Techniques and Applications
  6.5.4 Commotion and order

6.8 Robert A. Creo: Mediator 2004: The Art and the Artist

6.8.1 Introduction
    6.8.1.1 Experience
    6.8.1.2 Abstract and conclusion
6.8.2 State of the artist
    6.8.2.1 Two types of civil litigation impasse
    6.8.2.2 The state of my mediation art
    6.8.2.3 My common mediation modalities view
    6.8.2.4 My mediation day funnel
    6.8.2.5 My mediator values and tools
    6.8.2.6 The integration of mediation and the expanded role of mediators

CHAPTER SEVEN: Teaching Creative Problem Solving to Negotiators and Mediators

7.1 Introduction
    7.1.1 Facilitating conditions
    7.1.2 Stimulating conditions

7.2 Professor Linda Morton: Teaching Creative Problem Solving
    7.2.1 General
    7.2.2 A process for creative problem solving
    7.2.3 Six ways to jump out of a rut
        7.2.3.1 Theoretical overlay
        7.2.3.2 De Bono's 6 Hats (Edward De Bono, Six Thinking Hats (1985))
        7.2.3.3 Synectics
        7.2.3.4 Mind Mapping
        7.2.3.5 Visualization
        7.2.3.6 Incubation
    7.2.4 Creative thinking instructions
        7.2.4.1 Theoretical overlay
        7.2.4.2 Six Hats
        7.2.4.3 Random Word Analysis
        7.2.4.4 Mind Mapping
        7.2.4.5 Visualization
        7.2.4.6 Incubation

7.3 Professor Lynn Cohn: Northwestern University School of Law; Lawyer as Problem Solver Program
    7.3.1 Purpose
    7.3.2 Overview
    7.3.3 History
    7.3.4 Student response
    7.3.5 Benefits of the Lawyer as Problem Solver Program

7.4 Professor Kimberlee K. Kovach: The Hat Exercise

7.5 Professor Beryl Blaustone: "Broken Squares: An Exercise Designed to Demonstrate the Shift from Individual to Cooperative Problem-Solving
    7.5.1 General description of exercise
    7.5.2 Goals, process, and instructions for the Broken Squares exercise

7.6 John W. Cooley: Tools and Techniques for Teaching Creative Problem Solving
      7.6.1 Perspective in creative problem solving
      7.6.2 Perception in creative problem solving
      7.6.3 Word Problems (Conundrums)
      7.6.4 Puzzles
      7.6.5 The design concept in creative problem solving
      7.6.6 Games (Word Finding)
      7.6.7   Joke design
      7.6.8 Cartoon captioning
      7.6.9 Large group creative problem solving exercises
      7.6.10 Student-developed role play exercises

EPILOGUE

INDEXES

A.   General Index
B.   Index to List of Sources

Table of Contents (Complete)

Volume Two

(FOR REFERENCE PURPOSES ONLY)

CHAPTER ONE: An Introduction to Creative Problem Solving

1.1 Introduction
    1.1.1 Purpose and general overview of Volume Two of the Handbook
    1.1.2 Orientation: The creative problem solver as architect
1.2 Pracademics
    1.2.1 Definition and description
    1.2.2 Use of metaphor
1.3 Basic Definitions and Descriptions: Creative Problem Solving in Negotiation and Mediation
    1.3.1 Negotiation
    1.3.2 Mediation
    1.3.3 Basic thinking modes
    1.3.4 Problem Solving
    1.3.5 Creative Problem Solving

CHAPTER TWO: Generic Strategies for Creative Problem Solving

2.1 Suspend judgment
2.2 Brainstorm
2.3 Challenge assumptions
2.4 Generate alternatives
2.5 Fractionate/Reframe
2.6 Visualize; imagineer
2.7 Reverse thought
2.8 Use analogies, metaphors, similes
2.9 Welcome random ideas

CHAPTER THREE: Practitioners' Suggestions for Solving Problems Creatively: What Works; What Doesn't

A - F

3.1 Maxine Aaronson: "Expanding the Pie and Creating Value" in Negotiation Through the Artful Use of the Federal Tax Code
    3.1.1 Family law disputes
    3.1.2 Probate disputes
    3.1.3 Employment disputes
    3.1.4 Business breakups
    3.1.5 Contractual disputes
    3.1.6 Disputes between foreign parties and U.S. taxpayers
    3.1.7 Disputes with government agencies
3.2 Hal Abramson: "Final Offer Arbitration"

       3.2.1   What type of impasse can be overcome by using this technique? A money impasse
       3.2.2   What can a mediator do to help the parties overcome the money impasse?
       3.2.3   Description of impasse-breaking technique
       3.2.4   How can the mediator introduce this impasse-breaking technique?
       3.2.5   What are the risks of using FOA in mediations?
       3.2.6   Final offer arbitration rules
3.3   Anonymous: "Reasonable Accommodation"
3.4   Todd H. Bailey: "Dueling Time Lines"
       3.4.1   Brief description of dispute
       3.4.2   Description of creative technique
3.5   Patrick Border: "The Strategic Bathroom Break"
3.6   Rebecca A. Bowman: "Coin Toss"
3.7   Mieke Brandon: Two Creative Problem Solving Techniques
       3.7.1   "Let it all hang out"
       3.7.2   "What qualities, attitudes & beliefs do you want your children to grow up with?"
3.8   Judy Cohen: Three Creative Problem Solving Techniques
       3.8.1   "Resource Persons and Neutral Experts"
       3.8.2   "Reflective Practice Using Mediator Teams"
       3.8.3   "Convening for Mediation Success"
3.9   Richard Cooper: "Pie Charts"
3.10   Robert A. Creo: Creative Problem Solving Techniques and Tactics
       3.10.1   Blind Buyer-Seller Bid Auction
       3.10.2   Russian Roulette
       3.10.3   Utopian and Reality (or Magic Wand)
       3.10.4   Chicken Sandwich
       3.10.5   The Bends
       3.10.6   Framing Risk and Choice in Familiar Terms
       3.10.7   Settlement as Insurance
       3.10.8   Use of Personal Stories or Experiences
               3.10.8.1 Stand Back
               3.10.8 2 The Warrior Champion Vision
       3.10.9   Techniques and Tactics Easily Understood, Applied and Common
               3.10.9.1 Buy Back Case
               3.10.9.2 Play the Lottery or Take a Trip to the Casino
               3.10.9.3 Be the Bigger Person?
               3.10.9.4 Mano a Mano?
               3.10.9.5 The Riot Act
       3.10.10 Response to "Final" Offers or Demands
               3.10.10.1 The Moment
               3.10.10.2 Final, Final Offer
               3.10.10.3 Yin/Yang and Dualism
               3.10.10.4 Line in the Sand
               3.10.10.5 Etched in Concrete
       3.10.11 Challenging the Bottom Line Approach
       3.10.12 Movie Shorts
               3.10.12.1 *Schindler's List*: Discretion is Power
               3.10.12.2 *Raider's of the Lost Arc 3*: Choose Wisely
               3.10.12.3 *Raiders of the Lost Arc 1*: Be careful what you ask for, you may get it
               3.10.12.4 *U.S. Marshals*: I Do Not Negotiate

	3.10.12.5 *The Alamo* (any version)
3.11	Michael Crump: Two Creative Problem Solving Techniques
	3.11.1 " Structural reframing"
	3.11.2 "Bobby G's Silver Bullet"
3.12	Edward Dangler: "Active Listening Plus Repeated Batna Inquiry after Impasse"
3.13	William F. Day, Jr.: "Mediator Suggested Settlement Amounts"
3.14	Louise E. Dembeck: "Marginalizing Difficult Counsel"
3.15	Patrick S. De Moon: "Magic"
3.16	Michael E. Dickstein: "Double Blind Ranges"
3.17	Janet R. Eaton: "Rapport"
3.18	Noam Ebner and Yael Efron: Three Creative Problem Solving Techniques
	3.18.1 "Reframing Evidence" and "Let Everyone Play"
	3.18.2 "Interim Agreement"
3.19	Barrett W. Freedlander: "Post-mediation Pressure"

CHAPTER FOUR: Practitioners' Suggestions for Solving Problems Creatively: What Works; What Doesn't

G - P

4.1	Lynn A. Gaffigan: "Creating Optimism with Objectives"
4.2	Jennifer Geary: "Online Narrative Mediation"
4.3	Barry Goldman: "Switch Sides"
4.4	Todd R. Gomez: "Mediator Nurturance"
4.5	Jay Gottlieb: "The Professional Bypass"
4.6	Elayne E. Greenberg: "Decision Tree Analysis in Custody Conflicts"
4.7	Shawn G. Grindstaff: "Shared Media Liaison Impasse Breaker"
4.8	Alan E. Gross: "Do the Obvious – Use Flip Chart or Writing Board"
4.9	Kitty G. Grubb: "Let's All Go to Vegas with Kitty"; A/K/A "Kitty's Reality Therapy"
4.10	Fran Haug: "Silence"
4.11	Alan I Herman: "Making Partners Out of Adversaries"
4.12	Joe B. Hewett: "Listen to the Hurt"
4.13	Hobeiche Mediation Group: "Expected Value Analysis"
4.14	Eileen Charles Hyatt: "Your Best Interests: Getting to the Core of Taking Care of Self"
4.15	Deborah Isenhour: "The Source Mediation ™ Model"
4.16	Thomas R. Johnson: "Proposal and Counterproposal"
4.17	Leo J. Jordan: "Swearing in Parties" and "Putting Yourself in the Other Person's Shoes"
4.18	Ellen F. Kandell: "Push Away and Lean Back"
4.19	Sam Kaner: "Participatory Decision Making: Uses and Implications of Different Decision Rules"
4.20	Erwin Katz: "Breaking the Sibling Barrier"
4.21	John F. Kiernan: "Saving Face - Ensure Self-determination and Prioritize Principles"
4.22	Gary Kretchmer: "Getting into the World of Your Client"
4.23	Stuart Levine: "Getting to Resolution and Creating an Agreement for Results"
4.24	William F. Lincoln: Four Examples of Creative Problem Solving
	4.24.1 "A Tricky Expansion of the Pie"
	4.24.2 "Available to Meet at Any Time"
	4.24.3 "Turning the Tables (or the Other Cheek)"
	4.24.4 "Cohabitation, Forest Style"
4.25	Jon Linden: "Empathetic Persuasion"
4.26	Fay L. Loomis: "A Little Laughter Goes a Long Way"

4.27	Lela Love: "Using Quotations to Inject Aspirational Ideals into the Conversational Mix"	
4.28	Theodore Mack: "Party Discusses Strengths of Opposing Party's Case"	
4.29	Steven L. Marquart: "Best Offer"	
4.30	Elizabeth Ellyn McLaughlin: "The Compassion Exercise"	
4.31	Henry Nardi: "A Gandhian Approach"	
4.32	Michael Nathanson: Three Creative Problem Solving Techniques	
	4.32.1 "Backrounder"	
	4.32.2 "Yield to Overcome"	
	4.32.3 "Don't Ask, Don't Tell"	
4.33	Luella Nelson: "Hypothetical Bargaining"	
4.34	John K. Notz, Jr.: "Imaginative Exploration of Relationships"	
4.35	Thomas J. Oswald: "What Would It Sound Like to You If They Understood?"	
4.36	Paul D. Pearson: "Best/Worst Case Alternative to a Mediated Agreement"	
4.37	Robert S. Peckar: "Technical Mediation"	
4.38	John R. Phillips: Two Creative Problem Solving Techniques	
	4.38.1 "Premediation telephone conference"	
	4.38.2 "Double blind mediator's number"	
4.39	James Pinkney III: "Focus, Not Hocus Pocus" and "Mediating in the Shadows"	
4.40	Emanuel Plesent: "Thinking Out-of-the-Box"	
4.41	Bertrand B. Pogrebin: "Reality Check"	

CHAPTER FIVE: Practitioners' Suggestions for Solving Problems Creatively: What Works; What Doesn't

R - Z

5.1	Sarah J. Read: Two Creative Problem Solving Techniques	
	5.1.1 "Justice in Another World"	
	5.1.2 "Technical Working Group"	
5.2	Steven L. Reed: "Mediation – Yes; Shouting Match – No"	
5.3	Melanie J. Reese and Suzanne McCorkle: Three Creative Problem Solving Techniques	
	5.3.1 "Manipulating Space"	
	5.3.2 "Strategic Breaks"	
	5.3.3 "Rewriting the Past"	
5.4	Thomas Reese: "You Solve It"	
5.5	Jonathan W. Reitman: "Stories of My First and Best Trips on the Allagash"	
5.6	Max Rivers: "The Invisible Third Party"	
5.7	Stuart B. Robbins: "Breach of Contract"	
5.8	Deri Joy Ronis: "Self Mastery and Responsibility for Owning What You Co-create"	
5.9	Anita Rowe: "Working with Impatient Attorneys and Other Mediation Representatives"	
5.10	Mary Rowe: "Picture of Child"	
5.11	Anita Rufus: "Never Use Round Numbers"	
5.12	Jeffrey M. Senger: "Pie Chart Tool"	
5.13	John Settle: Sixty-six Tips and Techniques for Helping Parties Move Ahead and Overcome Roadblocks	
	5.13.1 Start gently and with generalities	
	5.13.2 Emphasize the future and de-emphasize the past	
	5.13.3 Focus on solutions	
	5.13.4 Use the "in principle" technique	
	5.13.5 Build on affirmative positive movement of the core agreement	
	5.13.6 Beware of the premature caucus	

5.13.7 Look for opportunities to use transformations
5.13.8 Help a party work through discomfort
5.13.9 Help a party reality check
5.13.10 Lead the parties in brainstorming
5.13.11 Use easel or blackboard
5.13.12 Use hypotheticals
5.13.13 Use the phrase "some folks"
5.13.14 Relieve a party of ownership
5.13.15 Help parties overcome fear of "going first"
5.13.16 Use decision analysis
5.13.17 Reflect with parties on their "bargaining model"
5.13.18 Test the margins of positions and focus on interests
5.13.19 Encourage a party to take personal ownership of his/her position
5.13.20 Be alert to discern "nickel-and-diming" and "auction" tactics
5.13.21 Explore options to setting precedent
5.13.22 Be alert to identify "reactive devaluation" and "selective perception" behaviors
5.13.23 Control your impatience
5.13.24 Maintain momentum and a positive outlook
5.13.25 Focus on relative priorities
5.13.26 Help parties take a "fresh look"
5.13.27 Suggest setting an issue aside temporarily
5.13.28 Suggest taking a break
5.13.29 Change something
5.13.30 Get parties' views on the stalemate
5.13.31 Refocus the parties on something else
5.13.32 Ask parties to describe fears
5.13.33 Clarify that parties are not "locked in" to interim issue resolutions
5.13.34 Use a global summary
5.13.35 Summarize areas of agreement
5.13.36 Suggest a trial period or plan
5.13.37 Creatively explore enforcement/resolution options
5.13.38 Translate options into a party's personal language
5.13.39 Help parties develop criteria for an acceptable outcome
5.13.40 Be a catalyst, and be creative
5.13.41 Use humor
5.13.42 Consider using homilies
5.13.43 Try a "think again" approach
5.13.44 Try role reversal
5.13.45 Let each party play "devil's advocate"
5.13.46 Use a "time-out" mini-intervention
5.13.47 Try a listening and interpretation exercise
5.13.48 Try being blunt about the parties choices
5.13.49 Use reality checking questions
5.13.50 Check to see if all necessary parties are present
5.13.51 Politely handle a dominating attorney or other representative
5.13.52 Consider caucusing with the representatives alone
5.13.53 Consider disaggregating gains and aggregating losses
5.13.54 Be aware of the parties' perceptual and emotional connections to money
5.13.55 Accentuate the positive
5.13.56 Use parallel option development

    5.13.57 Consider substituting non-monetary things of value for money
    5.13.58 Consider having the parties write their views
    5.13.59 Foster an appearance of fairness
    5.13.60 Break a whole problem into parts
    5.13.61 Let parties share the burden of the impasse
    5.13.62 Ask one or both parties if they want to end the mediation
    5.13.63 Allow parties and their representatives time to reflect on their options
    5.13.64 Consider proposing to conclude the mediation
    5.13.65 Consider asking parties to develop their "best and final" offers
    5.13.66 Present a summary and overview of the status and progress of the mediation
5.14 T'aiya Shiner: "Experiential Feedback"
5.15 Raymond Shonholtz: "Integrating Cultural Values into the Mediation Process"
5.16 Lynn Shyman: Two Creative Problem Solving Techniques
    5.16.1 "Visualizing our Parenting"
    5.16.2 "My Family Changes: The Movie"
5.17 Carlton Snow: "Give Them What They Want"
5.18 James C. Stansbury: "Dissent as Consent"
5.19 Stephen J. Stapleton III: "Controlling Counsel"
5.20 Kenneth R. Star: "Mediation, Arbitration ... or Both"
5.21 Howard L. Stone: "Use Both Sides of Your Brain"
5.22 Ian C. Szlazak: "The Mediator's Shroud"
5.23 Ellen Waldorf: "Imagining the Possibilities"
5.24 Lois Warner: "Conflict Management and Communication Workshop"
5.25 David Watson: "High-Low Technique"
5.26 Robert Wheat: "Something's Better Than Nothing"
5.27 Simon Wheaton-Smith: Five Creative Problem Solving Techniques
    5.27.1 "Appropriate Humor"
    5.27.2 "Appropriate Internalized Self Pressures"
    5.27.3 "NIMBY Situations"
    5.27.4 "Use, Rejection, and Improvement of Macro Models"
    5.27.5 "Not IBB!"
5.28 Amy E. Wind: "Orienting Parties Toward the Future"
5.29 Mardi Winder-Adams: "Child Focus"
5.30 Robert Wright: "Wanna Bet?"
5.31 Michael D. Young: "Bottom Line Negotiating"

EPILOGUE

INDEXES

  A. Index to Techniques by Names of Practitioners and Their Submissions
  B. Index to Techniques by Practice Areas
  C. Index to Primary Uses of Techniques
  D. Index to Stages of Process to Use Techniques
  E. Index to Short Titles of Techniques
  F. General Index
  G. Index to List of Sources

CHAPTER ONE

AN INTRODUCTION TO CREATIVE PROBLEM SOLVING

That far land we dream about, where every man is his own architect.

Robert Browning, *Red Cotton*
Nightcap Country (1873), II

1.1 PURPOSE, GENERAL OVERVIEW, AND ORIENTATION

1.1.1 Background, purpose, and general overview of the Handbook

Over the past half-century there has been growing interest among psychologists, educators, and behavioral researchers to study creativity and to construct problem solving models which optimize the use of creative skills and abilities of people to achieve quality solutions to problems. As a result of the efforts of many experts in these fields, several models of problem solving have been developed under the rubric of "creative problem solving" ("CPS"). In the 1960s and early 1970s, Paul E. Torrance, one of the early pioneers in the field of creative problem solving, envisioned a five-stage linear model that eventually became widely used in teaching creative problem solving. His linear model incorporated these steps: (1) sensing problems and challenges; (2) recognizing the real problem; (3) producing alternative solutions; (4) evaluating ideas; and (5) preparing to put ideas into use.

The work of Alex Osborn also led to many other developments in defining and teaching creative problem solving. His linear model suggested an inquiry and discovery ("finding") approach in which the stages were: (1) mess-finding (determining broad goals); (2) data-finding (examining all information and impressions available); (3) problem-finding (formulating problem statements); (4) idea-finding (generate as many ideas as possible); (5) solution-finding (determining the most promising solutions to the problem) and (6) acceptance-finding (deciding how most promising solutions can best be implemented). Osborn's creative problem solving model was widely used and evaluated by many creative problem solving experts including Paul E. Torrance, Sidney Parnes, and Donald Treffinger.

In 1977, Ruth Noller developed a shortened and simplified explanation of the creative problem solving model in her small book, *Scratching the Surface of Creative Problem Solving: A Bird's Eye View of CPS*. She stressed the term "finding" that, she felt, accented the hunting and searching for ideas - activities that are primary components of creative problem solving. That same year, Sidney Parnes provided guidelines for using the creative problem solving materials with gifted students. Two years later, Noller, Treffinger, and Houseman produced a short book that contained additional ideas about applications of creative problem solving in gifted education. In the 1980s, Treffinger, Scott Isaksen, and Roger Firestein created advanced resources useful in applying CPS in instructional settings. Since 1992, some creative problem solving experts (including Treffinger and Isaksen) have been advocating the use of a non-linear model, which has as its central core the component of appraising tasks.

The purpose of presenting this brief history of creative problem solving is to impress upon you that the definition of creative problem solving is not static; its meaning is different to different people and it is dynamic in the sense that the experts are still studying and experimenting with different models. This *Creative Problem Solver's Handbook for Negotiators and Mediators* reflects the definitional fluidity of creative problem solving and the state of the literature on the subject, which is generally replete with varying and sometimes seemingly contradictory ideas regarding proper methods and approaches. The Handbook provides the practitioner with a panoply of creative problem solving approaches and models with which the practitioner can experiment in ways that best satisfy or mesh with his or her personal experiences, skills, and talents.

As to an overview of the Handbook, it consists of two volumes and both volumes should be of interest to both lawyers and laypersons. This Volume One is primarily geared to serve as a guide, generally, to practitioners, academics, and students in the practice, teaching, and study of creative problem solving methods, tools, and techniques. Volume Two of the Handbook is more focused on specific creative problem solving techniques and tools that practitioners have found to be effective in negotiation and mediation and have submitted to me for inclusion in the Handbook.

This Volume One of the Handbook is organized into seven chapters. Chapter One provides basic information regarding the nature of creative problem solving, including definitions and descriptions of basic thinking processes (vertical, lateral, critical, creative, whole-brain, etc.), the basic techniques and skills involved in creative problem solving, as well as the appropriate orientation for creative problem solvers.

Chapter Two describes generic strategies for creative problem solving and applications that are based primarily on the strategies explained by Edward de Bono in his landmark book, *Lateral Thinking: Creativity Step by Step*. Complementing the problem solving strategies described in Chapter Two, the information in Chapter Three includes more than twenty-five generative and analytical tools and techniques from the problem solving literature that serve to implement those problem solving strategies.

Chapter Four focuses on creative approaches to designing ADR processes. That chapter will become quite helpful as you, in your capacity as an advocate, negotiator, or mediator, are increasingly called upon by clients or parties to design processes for resolving complex disputes. Among other helpful information, Chapter Five contains creative approaches to overcoming impasse in negotiation and mediation. Chapter Six describes advanced Pracademic strategies for creative problem solving in negotiation and mediation, including JokeThink, MagicThink, MathThink, MusicThink, Guerilla Mediation, and the Strategic Use of Cognitive Art in Mediation. Finally, Chapter Seven presents several ideas regarding effective techniques for teaching creative problem solving to negotiators and mediators.

The Handbook uses a simplified method of citations to source materials. I have intentionally avoided the use of footnotes, because they are often distracting and because they also lend an air of formality that would not be conducive to attracting readers who are either not lawyers or who are not academically oriented. The method of citation is simple. At the back of each volume of the Handbook appears an index to "List of Sources" arranged in alphabetical order by author. If the author has more than one publication, a number appears in parentheses behind the author's name. Thus, consider this example citation appearing in the text of the Handbook: (Jones, 343-345). This signifies that the author – Jones – only has one publication in the List of Sources, and the material being described in the text may be found on pages 343-345 of that publication. Consider this example citation appearing in the text of the Handbook: (Smith (2), 224-234). This signifies that the author has more that one publication in the List of Sources, and the appropriate one on the List is the one that in part reads "Smith (2)."

Having had this brief introduction to the general nature of creative problem solving and to the structure of the Handbook, we should next have some understanding as to what orientation might be most useful in approaching the subject of creative problem solving: the orientation of the architect.

1.1.2 Orientation: The creative problem solver as architect

The function of the creative problem solver finds no better analogy than in the function of the architect. Architecture includes aspects of both "science" and "art," and when logically executed, is an expression of man's needs and aspirations. An architect achieves an end product working within the fundamental meaning of science and art: "knowing" and "doing." Paradoxically, in order to practice his or her art, the architect must come to "know" by means of the methods of science ("knowing"). For the architect, the method of science is the method of research - research for principles of architecture that, once isolated, become the basis for rational design decisions. The architect seeks to coalesce the functional with the aesthetic, the utilitarian with the visibly pleasant. The architect does this through a process called design ("doing"). For the architect, design consists of two stages: conception of the idea and expression (Cooley (1), §1:07, pp. 32-35) (Cooper, 312-323).

Similarly, it is the design function that sets the creative problem solver apart from the ordinary problem solver. For the creative problem solver, the design function also consists of two basic stages: the generative stage (conception of ideas) and the decision making (determining and expressing the solution(s)). Effective creative problem solvers have a design mentality or approach to problems. The chart below contrasts a non-design approach with a design approach.

Non-design Approach	Design Approach
Problem reacting: addressing difficulties as they come along.	Problem-seeking: the designer must anticipate problems and hopefully convert them into opportunities.
Cookbook: just follow the rules and everything will be fine.	Stochastic: this means guessing about results; designers have to be prepared to "go back to the drawing board."
Serial: one step at a time.	Simultaneous-moded: seek the "all-at-onceness" of synthesis.
Atomistic-moded: concerned only with detail.	Pattern-moded: concerned with several levels at once.
Ready-to-wear: selecting.	Mindset: inventing.
Non-heuristic: all steps (and results) known in advance.	Heuristic: each step has the potential of modifying the next step.

(Cooley (1), §1:10, p. 47).

1.2 INTRODUCTION TO PRACADEMICS

1.2.1 Definition and description

"Pracademics" (initial cap.) is a term that I coined in the late 1980s to describe the art and science of translating the theory of creative problem solving into practice, and conversely, converting the practice of creative problem solving into theory. It is both deductive (theory to practice) and inductive (practice to theory) in nature. It can be applied in relation to all disciplines, but it is particularly applicable to the study of negotiation and mediation. It envisions practitioners and academics collaborating to create new and better ways to solve problems by sharing insights and experience from laboratory and field settings. It recognizes the potential of behavioral research to produce problem solving theories of benefit to practitioners in the field, and it respects the potential of practitioners' anecdotal experience in the field to provide theories of effective problem solving that can be tested by behavioral research to confirm or deny, scientifically, the extent of their utility and general applicability. It subscribes to the proper use of both lateral and vertical thinking in problem solving and it welcomes all ideas and approaches to creative problem solving. Thus, it is inclusive, not exclusive. It encourages an interdisciplinary approach to problem solving and seeks to draw upon the expertise of one discipline to enhance the problem solving effectiveness in another. It is particularly attentive to the areas between disciplines – the interstitial areas of overlap and ambiguity – because it is that territory that is often fertile with discovery, surprise, and insight.

The word "pracademic" (lower case), used as an adjective, means "of or pertaining to the field of Pracademics." A "pracademic," used as a noun, means a person who subscribes to the tenets of Pracademics, who often is both a practitioner and an academic, and who knows and understands that, to be a successful creative problem solver, he or she must be a perpetual student of creative problem solving and of the strategies, tools, and techniques, both generative and analytical, by which it can be achieved. The word "pracademics" (lower case), used as a noun, refers to more than one person who subscribes to the tenets of Pracademics.

A pracademic knows and understands that, as an architectural designer of problems, processes, and solutions, he or she must have a keen interest in and respect for use of metaphor. The use of metaphors of art, music, magic, humor, mathematics, physics, religion, warfare, psychology, philosophy, and rhetoric, among others, can be used as tools to discover and explain the essence of the art and science of effective problem solving in negotiation and mediation. Examples of these metaphors appear in the following articles whose citations can be found in the "List of Sources" in the back of this Handbook: Cooley (4) through (14) and Benjamin (1), (2), (3), (5), (6), (7), (8), and (11). Excerpts from some of these articles appear in Chapter Six of this Handbook.

1.2.2 Use of metaphor

A metaphor is an analogy in which two different universes of thought are seen to be linked by some point of similarity. To be successful, a pracademic must strive to learn about and become a master of metaphors. As Aristotle once wrote:

> ... The greatest thing of all is to be master of the metaphor. ... [I]t is ... a sign of original genius, because a good metaphor implies perception of similarity in dissimilar things (Rothstein, 167-168).

To be a master of metaphors, one must have a deep appreciation for what a metaphor is and how it can be useful in a pracademic approach to creative problem solving.

Gestalt psychologist Marc Leman has theorized that, apart from having a cognitive meaning (that is, apart from saying something literal about someone or something), metaphors have an evocative meaning (Leman, 237-250). He offers the following example. When a person says, "Sally is a block of ice," the person does not mean that Sally is a block of ice (the cognitive meaning), rather the person means that Sally is an extremely unemotional and unresponsive person (the evocative meaning). Leman believes that there are two types of evocative functions of metaphors: one to generate emotions and feelings in the hearer or the reader (an expressive meaning); and the other to generate insights (a representational meaning). There is a difference between the cognitive meaning and the representational meaning. He writes that associated with the cognitive meaning of metaphorical utterance are the corresponding truth conditions:

> In contrast, the representational meaning does not say anything about someone or something. It just consists in mental representations and mental pictures. Their representational meaning is analogical to the expressive meaning in the sense that nothing is being said but is merely evoked. This does not mean that we cannot speak about our evoked emotions and our evoked insights, although to say what precisely they are may be very difficult (Leman, 241).

Leman's central thesis is that metaphors involve dynamics that are responsible for the evocation of emotions. He writes:

> Metaphors have a dynamic nature in the sense that they involve tensions and their

reductions at different levels of their structure. This dynamic structure can be described at a semantic level as well. Both levels are responsible for the evocation of specific emotions in the hearer. This shows an analogy with the structural and semantical aspects in music ... (Leman, 244).

Leman describes the problem solving feature of metaphors as involving two kinds of emotions: a surge of excitement at the moment of discovery, followed by a calmer feeling of satisfaction. The second calmer feeling can be understood as a release from the tension created by the previous representational conflict. He writes:

> We may distinguish two steps in the interpretation of metaphors: the first step involves the conflict of two visual representations or two mental representations or a combination of both, and this may be seen as the result of the defectiveness of the literal word and sentence-meaning. ... The second step consists in the resolution of the conflict as a result of the discovery of a third mental or visual representation. This discovery of a third representation is precisely what we call *insight* (Leman, 245-46).

Insight, then, is the goal of metaphor.

Howard E. Gruber and Sara N. Davis in a chapter entitled "Inching Our Way Up Mount Olympus: The Evolving-systems Approach to Creative Thinking" (Sternberg (1), 248-268) discuss the need, for those wishing to be creative problem solvers, to review case studies of creative people at work in their own contexts. In writing the chapter, they reviewed a series of nine doctoral dissertations in which doctoral candidates separately studied how well-known creative individuals made new discoveries in science and other fields of human endeavor. One conclusion that surfaced from this review was that almost all creative products result from long periods of purposeful work and that chance events and spontaneous play sometimes have a role in new discoveries (Sternberg (1), 244). They also concluded that famous creative individuals, such as Benjamin Franklin, Charles Darwin, William James, John Locke, and novelist Dorothy Richardson, relied significantly on metaphors to achieve their creative results. For example metaphors of water flow assisted Franklin in describing electricity connected with lightning during a storm and in understanding air circulation which eventually led to his invention of the Franklin stove. Darwin, it is said, used at least eight major metaphors in developing the theory of evolution through natural selection, three of them being: a tree, wedging, and struggle (Sternberg (1), 249-252; 255).

After analyzing the dissertations, Gruber and Davis then suggested roles for use of metaphors in creative problem solving. The roles they identified are as follows:

- A metaphor can serve directly as a modality of thought.
- A metaphor may play a synthesizing role, as when it identifies a link between disparate domains.
- Metaphors can play an analytic role, as when a complex idea is broken into components, each with different metaphors.
- Metaphors may concretize abstract ideas; they may lend palpability to otherwise vague ideas.
- Metaphors may illuminate an abstract idea that connects different groups of concrete experiences.
- By highlighting the mismatch between literal and metaphoric forms of an idea, they can both stimulate production of new ideas and can function as a method of testing a system of beliefs.
- Metaphors may also serve in a theory-constitutive role, as when they directly become part of an argument being advanced.
- They may play an expressive role, as when an idea has been

developed in some other form and is then restated metaphorically for purposes of emphasis or communication.
- Finally, metaphors can play an affective role, as when the power of a metaphor charges an idea with new excitement (Sternberg (1), 254-255).

The ability to identify the appropriate metaphor to assist in creative problem solving in a specific situation is essential to the usefulness of a metaphorical tool. That ability is invariably based upon innate skill, trial and error, and extensive experience.

1.3 BASIC DEFINITIONS AND DESCRIPTIONS: CREATIVE PROBLEM SOLVING IN NEGOTIATION AND MEDIATION

1.3.1 Negotiation

Negotiation has been defined as a process by which parties try to resolve their differences or common problems in order to reach some mutually satisfactory agreement. Broadly speaking, there are two models of negotiation – the adversarial model and the problem solving model. The adversarial model, also called the "competitive" model, focuses on "winning" in a zero-sum process. It is based on four assumptions: (1) the parties desire the same goals, items, or values (usually money); (2) the parties are in conflict because they are bargaining over the same "scarce" goals, items, or values: (3) the matters being bargained for are limited to those that a court would award, whether in the form of money or injunctive relief; and (4) the best solution is predicated upon a division of and compromise over the goals, items, or values at issue (Herman, Cary, and Kennedy, 152-53).

The problem solving model, also called the "collaborative" or "principled" model, focuses on identifying the parties' underlying interests or needs to develop a broad range of potential solutions from which an agreement can be fashioned that satisfies as many of the parties' mutual needs as possible. In contrast with the adversarial model, this model of negotiation seeks to maximize the parties' joint gain. The problem solving model is based on four assumptions: (1) the usual objective of obtaining money damages is actually a proxy for more basic interests or needs of the parties; (2) the parties' interests and needs are often not mutually exclusive; (3) identifying the parties' interests and needs can produce a greater number of possible solutions to the dispute; and (4) by exploring a greater number of possible solutions, the parties are more likely to find a solution that mutually satisfies their interests or needs (Herman, Cary, and Kennedy, 154).

For further readings on negotiation, see Herman, Cary, and Kennedy. See also, Mnookin; Schoenfield and Schoenfield; Lisnek; Gifford; Nierenberg (1), Fisher and Ury; Kozicki; and Craver.

1.3.2 Mediation

The Association for Conflict Resolution defines mediation as follows:

Mediation is a process of dispute resolution in which one or more impartial third parties intervenes in a conflict or dispute with the consent of the participants and assists them without coercion or the appearance of coercion in negotiating a consensual and informed agreement. In mediation, the decision-making authority rests with the participants themselves and strongly values the parties' exercise of their self-determination. Recognizing participants' needs, cultural differences and variations in style, the mediation process allows participants to define and clarify issues, reduce obstacles to communication, explore possible solutions and, when desired, reach a mutually satisfactory agreement. Mediation presents the opportunity to express differences and improve relationships and mutual understanding, whether or not an agreement is reached.

(Definition developed by the Mediator Certification Task Force of the Association for Conflict Resolution, and adopted for ACR policy statements in January, 2004.)

For additional readings on mediation and on advocacy in mediation, see, in the List of Sources to this Handbook (Index B): Alfini, Press, Sternlight, and Stulberg; Golann; Goldberg, Sander, and Rogers; Riskin and Westbrook; Galton; Moore; Brunet and Craver; and Cooley(2) and (3).

1.3.3 Thinking modes

Thinking has been defined as "all the mental activities associated with concept formation, problem solving, intellectual functioning, creativity, complex learning, memory, symbolic processing, and imagery," among others (Reber and Reber, 748). It is a term reserved for symbolic processes and is treated as an implicit process that is not directly observable. For one to discern that another person is thinking or is engaged in a thought process, one can infer that fact from the statements of the other person or by observing behavioral acts that suggest thinking is occurring, e.g., seeing a complex problem be solved correctly (Id.). For background information on thinking modes, see, in the List of Sources to this Handbook (Index B): Mayer; Perkins; and Nadler, Hibino, and Farrell.

It is not sheer coincidence that there are two basic types of thinking processes: vertical thinking and lateral thinking. These two processes respectively reflect, figuratively if not actually, the bilateral functioning of the brain – the logical, scientific left side and the emotional, artistic right-side (Reber and Reber, 388; Gregory (1), 741-48). Most of us have had a great deal of exposure to vertical thinking. In our society, we tend to think vertically all the time; some of us believing that it is the only way to think. However, lateral thinking is an equally important way to think. These two types of thinking complement one another. A person who employs one of the two forms of thinking to the substantial exclusion of the other, will function mentally with limited, and perhaps severely limited, effectiveness. Negotiators, mediators, and advocates in mediation should strive to employ both types of thinking at the appropriate times and in conjunction with each other in performing his/her various functions. But before you can employ them, you must understand their differences. The remainder of this section provides a basic overview of the definitions of modes of thinking. The first three modes – vertical, lateral, and whole-brain thinking – have more extensive descriptions than the remainder of the definitions, because those three modes will be referenced extensively in this publication. Except where indicated otherwise, the latter definitions appear in Nadler, Hibino, and Farrell at pages 235-240.

1.3.3.1 Vertical (convergent) thinking

Vertical (or convergent) thinking is characterized by "a bringing together or synthesizing of information and knowledge focused on a [single] solution to a problem" (Reber and Reber, 748). There are several characteristics of vertical thinking. First, vertical thinking is analytical. It is also selective in the sense that from the outset it is trying to select the best approach. It must be moving usefully in some direction. The vertical thinker says, "I know what I'm looking for." The vertical thinker moves forward logically, one step at a time, and must be correct at each step. Vertical thinking uses the negative to block off certain pathways and excludes what is irrelevant. With vertical thinking, categories, classifications and labels are fixed. If something is put into a class, it is supposed to stay there. Vertical thinking follows the most likely paths in search of "the right answer." With vertical thinking, there is always "the right answer." Vertical thinking promises at least a minimum solution (de Bono (1)).

1.3.3.2 Lateral (divergent) thinking

Lateral (or divergent) thinking is characterized by a process of "moving away in various directions ... [and] is frequently associated with creativity since it often yields novel ideas and solutions" (Reber and Reber, 748). Lateral thinking is provocative and it is generative – it seeks to open up as many pathways as it can simply for the purpose of generating them. With lateral thinking one moves merely for the sake of moving. The lateral thinker says, "I am looking but I won't know what I am looking for until I have found it." Lateral thinking can take jumps and does not have to be correct at any point in the process. In lateral thinking there is no negative. The lateral thinker welcomes irrelevant or chance intrusions. With lateral thinking, categories, classifications may change. Labels are not permanent, but rather used for temporary convenience. Lateral thinking explores the least likely paths to restructure patterns or to gain a new insight. The lateral thinker believes that there may be no answer at all. Lateral thinking increases the chances of a maximum solution but makes no promises (de Bono (1)).

In his book, *Lateral Thinking: Creativity Step by Step*, Dr. Edward de Bono presents several strategies for stimulating creativity. According to Dr. de Bono, lateral thinking is closely related to insight, creativity, and humor. Whereas vertical (logical) thinking is concerned with proving or developing concept patterns, lateral (generative) thinking is concerned with restructuring such patterns (insight) and stimulating new ones (creativity). Usually, there are alternative ways of arranging available information, and a "switch over" to another arrangement can be made suddenly. According to Dr. de Bono, when the sudden switch over is temporary, it gives rise to humor; if the sudden switch over is permanent, it gives rise to insight.

Lateral thinking is a process of effecting "switch overs" of arrangements of information to achieve restructuring of the information and the stimulation of new ideas. It enhances the effectiveness of vertical thinking by challenging the arrogance and the cliche-pattern thinking associated with logic. Both vertical and lateral thinking are essential to effective problem solving. As Dr. de Bono has observed:

> The differences between lateral and vertical thinking are very fundamental. The processes are quite distinct. It is not a matter of one process being more effective than the other for both are necessary. It is a matter of realizing the differences in order to use both effectively. With vertical thinking one uses information for its own sake in order to move forward to a solution. With lateral thinking one uses information not for its own sake but provocatively in order to bring about repatterning (de Bono(1), 44-45).

In his book, Dr. de Bono describes the following lateral thinking strategies:

- Suspending Judgment
- Brainstorming
- Challenging Assumptions
- Generation of Alternatives
- Fractionation
- Visualization
- Thought Reversal
- Using Analogies
- Random Stimulation

These thinking strategies are discussed in more detail in Chapter Two. Below is a chart, which shows the basic differences between vertical and lateral thinking.

COMPARISON OF VERTICAL AND LATERAL THINKING

Vertical Thinking	Lateral Thinking
Analytical	Provocative
Sequential	Can Make Jumps
Selective	Generative
Correct at Every Step	Need Not be Correct at Every Step
Uses Negative to Block Pathways	There Is No Negative
Excludes What is Irrelevant	Welcomes the Irrelevant
Categories and Labels May Not Change	Categories and Labels May Change
Follows Most Likely Paths	Explores Least Likely Paths
Seeks the Right Answer	Seeks Restructuring of Patterns
There Must Be a Right Answer	There May Be No Answer at All

1.3.3.3 Whole-brain thinking

More than forty years ago, Roger Sperry and his colleagues at the California Institute of Technology performed what is now commonly known as the split-brain experiments, which were eventually honored by award of the Nobel Prize. The results of the experiments revealed, in much more detail than previously known, that the left and right hemispheres of the brain house specific functions. These results led to other important research efforts and experimentation, through which scientists have identified as many as five functional areas of the brain and have invented mechanisms to actually observe brain functioning.

Currently, brain research generates more than a half-million scientific papers a year. Books on practical applications of the results of this research into problem-design, problem solving, and decision-making abound. Since negotiators and mediators, as a matter of course, are particularly concerned with such situations and the proper handling of them, they should become and remain students of the whole-brain approach to thinking throughout their careers. Even if you do not place faith in the research concerning the bilateral functioning of the brain, the concept of whole-brain functioning can serve as a useful metaphor for application of vertical and lateral thinking in creative problem solving. This section provides a brief overview of whole-brain thinking. It is an introduction to some basic facts about the human brain, its bilateral characteristics and functions, lateral dominance and preference, and determining brain preference of yourself and others (Cooley (1) §2:02, 5; and cited sources). Applications of this knowledge in negotiation and mediation are discussed in Section 3.5.3.

(1) Some facts about the human brain. Of all the earthly animals, the human being is the only animal whose brain is aware of its own existence. Not only is it conscious of its existence but it has the unique capacity of learning about the intricacies of its own capabilities and functions, and thereby learning how to put itself to better use. The brain of a bee is about the size of a grain of salt and contains approximately 900 neurons. Yet this microscopic natural computer inside a bee's head can perform amazing functions. It provides an accurate guidance system and, compensating for wind direction, the rapid beating of four tiny wings, allows bees to land their encapsulating little bodies at the center of a waving flower. If a bee's brain is capable of this, what then can be expected of the human brain which contains between ten to

twelve billion neurons, and which is many billion times as complex? Although, over the last fifty years, academic knowledge of the human brain has grown at a prodigious rate, we do not have a clear picture of the brain's ultimate capabilities. What has been determined, however, is that (1) structural development of the human brain continues throughout life, and (2) human beings on the average use less than 0.1% of their full mental potential. If your brain is functioning effectively right now it is probably asking itself why its 3-1/2 pounds mass of cells – perhaps the most complex system of any kind known in the universe – is used only to a minute fraction of its potential. A major reason is that as children we were not taught mental functions. We were taught to remember various facts, but we were not taught how the memory works or how best to remember. We were told to study, but we were not taught how to approach a book in order to optimize the learning experience. We were told to read, but not taught how the eye and brain work during reading. We were told to observe but not taught about the processes of attention. We were told to make notes, but we were not taught in what form information is most easily assimilated by the brain. But most importantly, when our teachers or parents told us to "use our brains," we were never told to "use both sides of it" (Cooley (1), §2:02, 5-6; and cited sources).

(2) The bilateral functioning of the brain. The division of the human brain into left and right hemispheres is not a new discovery. Outside the skull, the brain's natural division is obvious to the naked eye, the left half having more gray matter relative to white matter than the right. The difference transcends mere appearance. Each half seems to have developed specialized functions, the left side appearing to be better at certain tasks, the right side better at others. The most obvious task differentiation is that the left side of the brain receives sensations and controls the right side of the body, and vice versa. The ancient Egyptians were the first to discover this crossover effect, called "contralaterality." They noticed that injuries to one side of the brain caused a corresponding paralysis to the opposite side of the body. By the year 1900, researchers knew that damage to certain areas of the left hemisphere resulted in the loss of speech, poor reading, and a general deterioration in logical thinking, whereas damage to corresponding areas of the right hemisphere resulted in deterioration of visual and spatial functions, such as recognition of faces and ability to dress oneself. The theory now widely accepted among scientists and researchers is that the left hemisphere of the brain is more specialized in serial processes, i.e., analysis that involves processing information one bit after another; whereas the right hemisphere is more specialized in parallel processing, that is, forming a synthesis of several bits of information (Cooley (1), §2:02, 7; and cited sources).

In solving a problem using an algebraic formula, for example, the brain inserts numerical values for letters in the formula and then performs certain set mathematical "operations" according to directions given by the formula. The mathematical operations usually themselves involve fixed sequential procedures or rules. This is the serial or analytical (left brain) process. On the other hand, the brain's recognition of a face does not require step-by-step analysis of the facial image, feature by feature. The brain takes a large number of elements simultaneously and synthesizes them into a whole. This is parallel, or synthetic (right brain) processing. (Cooley (1), §2:02, 8).

Research has disclosed that: (1) the left and right hemispheres of the brain are connected by a massive bundle of nerves called the corpus callosum, through which the two halves communicate, and that (2) the functioning brain shifts back and forth between the hemispheres as it and the body change activities. The human brain's two halves house different specialized functions or characteristics as shown in the chart below (Cooley (1), §2:02, 8-9) (J. Wonder and P. Donovan, 24):

Left-Brain Functions	Right-Brain Functions
Analytical Rational Logical Linear Certain Goal-Oriented Concrete Sequential Explicit Serial Processing Mathematics Language	Generative Intuitive Emotional Visual Artistic Holistic Spontaneous Playful Symbolic Parallel Processing Synthesis Pattern Recognition
Vertical (Convergent)	**Lateral (Divergent)**

(3) Lateral dominance and preference. The discovery through cognitive science that the two hemispheres of the brain are specialized for different modes of thought has led to the concept of lateral dominance (also called lateral preference) or hemisphericity – the idea that a given individual relies more on one mode or hemisphere than on the other. This unconscious preference for using a particular side of the brain is thought to be reflected in the individual's "cognitive style" – the person's orientation and approach to problem solving. Other research suggests than an individual's cognitive style cannot so easily be stereotyped as left- or right-brain *directed*; rather, some individuals' cognitive style can be said to be laterally *differentiated*. For example, an individual who consistently and reliably shows good performance on "left-hemisphere tasks" but poor performance on "right hemisphere tasks" is said to be directionally left-lateralized. A laterally *differentiated* individual, on the other hand, tends to use the right hemisphere for tasks for which the right hemisphere has an advantage and also to use the left hemisphere for tasks for which the left hemisphere has an advantage (Cooley (4), 258-60; and cited sources).

Verbal analytic thinking associated with the left-brain is no more important than the aesthetic-synthetic thinking characteristic of the right brain. However, in Western culture, the faculties associated with the left-brain have historically taken a more dominant position in our lives. Money, technology, efficiency and power are viewed as the rewards of left-brain planning. Our culture tends to place a greater emphasis on verbal expression and rational and analytical thinking rather than spatial ability, artistic appreciation, creative processes, and intuitive thought. This tendency to left-brain dominance is reflected in our educational systems, which have traditionally placed undue emphasis on left-hemisphere processes. Because of our culture and our immersion in left-brain oriented education, many of us tend to prefer using our left-brain functions in our interactions with people in problem design and problem solving. In order to do these things more efficiently, many of us who are not "mixed dominants" by nature must make a special effort to use the less preferred side, to become whole-brain thinkers, to seek balanced use of our brains. The first step (logically) in making that effort is to determine which hemisphere we naturally prefer to use (Cooley (1), §2:02, 10; and cited sources).

(4) Determining your brain preference. Hold a pencil or other straight object perpendicular to the ground at arm's length centered in your line of vision and lined up with a vertical object, such as a frame, board, or door. With the pencil so held, close your left eye. Did your pencil appear to move? Remember how much. Now, open your left eye and close your right eye. Did your pencil appear to move? Remember how much. The eye that was open when your pencil stayed most still is your dominant eye. If your right eye is dominant, then you are apt to be a left-brained dominant. And conversely, if your left eye is dominant (i.e. left eye open when pencil stayed still), you are most likely a right-brained dominant. However, as with

most tests, this one is not conclusive as to all persons (Cooley (1), §2:02, 10-11 and cited sources).

Let's try another indicator of brain preference. Sit in a relaxed manner and clasp your hands comfortably in your lap. Which thumb is on top (right or left)? Unlike the pencil test, there is a direct correlation rather than an opposite one. If your right thumb is on top, it indicates right brain dominance; vice versa for left thumb (Cooley (1), §2:02, 11; and cited sources).

Here's a third indicator. Consider these two lists and check all behaviors or activities in which you engage typically:

When problem solving, I write down the alternatives, prioritize and pick the best alternative.	When problem solving, I usually wait to see if the situation will correct itself.
I have a place for everything and a system for doing things.	I daydream to plan my future.
I express myself well verbally.	I have strong hunches and frequently follow them.
I am goal-oriented.	I like to move my furniture and change the decor of my home and office frequently.
I can usually accurately tell how much time has passed without looking at my watch.	I like spontaneous social situations.
I preferred algebra over geometry in school.	In notetaking, I frequently print.
I like to plan the details of a trip.	I enjoy taking risks.
I enjoy research and study.	I have frequent mood changes.
I enjoy puns.	I prefer working in a group.

I enjoy:
 	
   Collecting
   Writing
   Chess
   Bridge
   Debating
	I enjoy:
	
	   Swimming
	   Fishing
	   Bicycling
	   Walking
	   Running

If you checked significantly more activities/behaviors on the left list than on the right list, the chances are that you are left-brained dominant. Conversely, if substantially more of your checkmarks appear on the right list, then you are apt to be right-brained dominant. If your responses are mixed equally or nearly so between the two lists, then there is a reasonable likelihood that you are a "mixed dominant" (Cooley (1), §2:02, 11-12; and cited sources).

Split brain theory should make you more keenly aware of your own thinking style which may predispose you to seeing only a limited number of solutions in decision-making if you are left-brain oriented. Alternatively, if you are right-brain oriented you may see too many potential solutions and unable to confidently select the most appropriate one. If you are left-brain dominant, you should experiment with right-brain mental behaviors. Behaviors for right-brain dominant thinkers who want to experiment with left-brain functioning and behaviors for left-brain dominant thinkers who want to experiment with right-brain functioning appear in the chart below:

Behaviors for Right-Brain Thinkers Who Want to Experiment with Left-Brain Functioning	**Behaviors for Left-Brain Thinkers Who Want to Experiment with Right-Brain Functioning**
• Be less prone to take command of the conversation.	• Enter into situations without firm goals, expectations.
• Be alert to how others structure their time.	• Let other persons lead and establish tone.
• Agree to proceed cautiously and timely, then honor your agreement.	• Reveal your knowledge of both pluses, minuses to current "game plan."
• Be more discreet in advancing your views in meetings, etc.	• Use visual presentation of ideas: charts, etc.
• Address issues as specifically as possible.	• Keep your options, facts, observations to yourself for a time.
• Keep your curiosity to yourself when it is obvious that it alarms or discomforts others.	• Invite long-range assessment, projections.
• Let others seek you out.	• Take the risk of talking about feelings.
• Put more information, less personality and emotion, in presentations.	• Give others room to succeed.
• Cite beliefs in context of facts, not appeals to tradition, authority, "righteousness."	• Listen for long periods; reply in brief.
• Demonstrate that you are knowledgeable about all sides of an issue.	• Explore mutually instead of debate.
• Use spontaneous feelings strategically.	• Enjoy the enthusiasm of others.
	• Take others' opinions in good humor.
	• Focus on persons, not on opinions.

Your long-range goal as a creative problem solver should be to become more whole-brain, more balanced in your general approach to problem design, problem solving, and decision-making. This will not happen overnight, but with serious, consistent self-improvement effort you should be able to make significant progress toward your goal (Cooley (1), §2:02, 13-14; and cited sources).

Now that we have extensively addressed vertical, lateral, and whole brain thinking, the remaining modes will be briefly defined below.

1.3.3.4 Abductive

A thinker using this mode reasons from the result and a generalization to propose a specific case. Although it is more closely aligned with deductive rather than inductive thinking (see Subsections 1.3.3.14 and 1.3.3.19, below), it sometimes involves both deductive and inductive thinking when the task involves finding causes. It is also used in fields of inquiry, such as artificial intelligence.

1.3.3.5 Abstract

This mode of thinking consists of the process of singling out one feature of a real object that is considered by the thinker to be particularly important in relation to the object's other properties. This process often reveals a surprising essence of the object (Root-Bernsteins, 72-73; 90).

1.3.3.6 Active

The active thinker sees situations differently and experiments with novel responses. It is sometimes called "reflection-in-action" when it is used by thinkers to question the assumption-structure behind their actions.

1.3.3.7 Analogical

The analogical thinker uses analogies and metaphors to determine or explain that which is not clearly known or understood by comparing it with what is known (Root-Bernsteins, 156).

1.3.3.8 Analytical

This type of thinking is used to dissect a whole into its component parts. An analytical thinker seeks to discover the characteristics of those parts and their relationship to each other and to the whole. It is the basis of the research approach to problem solving.

1.3.3.9 Automatic

This type of thinking occurs without conscious thought. It permits thinkers to act swiftly and effectively in a wide variety of situations, on the basis of relatively permanent cognitive structures known variously as mental maps, scripts, schemata, belief structures, or theories of action.

1.3.3.10 Body (kinesthetic)

The body thinker uses sensations of muscle movement, body feeling, and touch, individually or together, to serve as a tool for imaginative thinking. Also called kinesthetic thinking, body thinking is defined in terms of the body's motor images or remembered movements (Root-Bernsteins, 164).

1.3.3.11 Conscious

This mode of thinking is regimented, linear, and single-channeled. Conscious thinkers prefer complete information, but they may be limited by the nature of the information processing involved.

1.3.3.12 Creative

When you use this type of thinking, you are engaged in the generation of ideas: that are unusual, or original, and also satisfy some standard of value. It is a new combination of what is already known in order to achieve a desired result. Creative thinking is exploratory, and it is a thinking process that ventures out from the accustomed way of considering a problem, to find a new way that might work (Weinsten & Morton, 837-38, and cited sources); (Patrick, 92-109); (de Bono (2), 77).

1.3.3.13 Critical

This thinking mode has been described as "a cognitive strategy consisting largely of continual checking and testing of possible solutions to guide one's work" (Reber and Reber, 748). It is conscious, directed, controlled thinking in which each link in a chain of reason is closely scrutinized to assess the accuracy and validity of each inference.

1.3.3.14 Deductive

The deductive thinker reasons from the general to the specific. This mode proceeds from existing theories and facts to specific facts or solutions.

1.3.3.15 Dialectical

Using this mode of thinking, a thinker goes from an established thesis to an antithesis, and if successful, to a resolving synthesis. A synthesis can be viewed as a solution to a problem or merely a resolving stage in an unending cycle of dialectic evolution. Dialectical thinking assumes polarity, a conflict between two defined positions, and is often used in resolving disputes.

1.3.3.16 Dimensional

This mode of thinking involves moving from two-dimensions or three-dimensions or vice versa; mapping, or transforming information provided in one set of dimensions to another set; scaling, or altering the proportions of an object or process within one set of dimensions; and conceptualizing dimensions beyond space and time as we know them.

1.3.3.17 Heuristic

A heuristic thinker responds intuitively, based on past experience. Heuristics are various learned shortcuts that humans apply in stressful or complex decision-making situations.

1.3.3.18 Holistic

The premise of holistic thinking is that even if each part of something is perfect, the whole may not be perfect. This mode of thinking presupposes: (1) the whole is more than the sum of the parts; (2) the whole determines the nature of the parts; (3) the parts cannot be understood if considered in isolation from the whole; (4) the parts are dynamically interrelated or interdependent.

1.3.3.19 Inductive

The inductive thinker reasons from the specific to the general. Scientific theories are created through this mode of thinking. The goal of inductive thinking is to arrive at a single broad generalization that includes and adequately explains many specific observations in a realm of interest.

1.3.3.20 Integrative

The integrative thinker frames differences and problems so that a group of participants focuses on what is to be gained, rather than on what is to be lost, by following a particular path of action.

1.3.3.21 Reflective

Reflective thinking is an active, contemplative mode of serious thought. It aids learning and the judicious consideration of various alternatives. In addition, it is quite useful in conditions of ambiguity and threat.

1.3.3.22 Synthetic

Using synthetic thinking, a thinker puts parts together into a whole. This mode of thinking is at the core of the process of design. Its purpose is to achieve a construct that satisfies a goal. Synthetic thinkers proceed from a statement as to the purpose of something to statements about the something's form and use. Synthetic thinking is usually an ally of vision, whereas analytical thinking can be vision's enemy. Synthetic thinking is related to the concept of synesthesia from the Greek word "syn" (union) and "aesthesis" (sensation) – a feeling together, a union of the senses. Synesthesia may be described as idiosyncratic manifestations of interfused sensations (Root-Bernsteins, 300).

1.3.3.23 Systems

Closely allied with holistic thinking, systems thinking favors looking at all factors or perspectives, while tending toward the dissection and decomposition of conventional thinking.

1.3.3.24 Transformational

This thinking mode consists of a serial or simultaneous use of multiple imaginative tools in such a way that one set of tools acts upon another set. A mnemonic device, such as "every good boy does fine" describing the notes on the treble clef in music, is an example of transformational thinking (Root-Bernsteins, 273; 277).

1.3.3.25 Unconscious

This mode of thinking is uninhibited, faster, and more flexible than conscious thinking. It incorporates previous experience to foster new insights, it serves as the well spring of intuition and the foundation of the elusive quality known as "judgment." It fosters creativity by permitting unconscious ideas and associations to flow into consciousness, thereby providing a basis for the integration and redirection of thought.

1.3.4 Thinking mechanics

Studying how people think, or the mechanics of thinking, is an important step in determining how to improve thinking skills. History credits Aristotle as being the first person to analyze his own thinking. His method consisted of extensive self-observation, leading to general hypotheses, which he then evaluated by further self-observation. As Ericsson and Hastie report:

> His goal was to induce the general laws describing thought from these instances of self-observation... [He] excluded perceptions (experiences reflecting the current external world) and reproductive memories of specific past experiences from the category of thinking. He also distinguished between contemplation, thought directed at the attainment of new knowledge, and deliberation, thought directed toward practical action...

> Aristotle concluded that thinking, in particular recall, corresponded to a sequence of thoughts... This led to further reflections on the relations between consecutive thoughts

and the discovery that these relations could be described by a small number of associations, such as similarity, contiguity, and contrast. Hence Aristotle went beyond a recording of recalled sequences of thoughts primarily by his extraction of the relations between thoughts (Ericsson and Hastie: Sternberg (3), 39-40).

In the latter half of the nineteenth century, philosophers began to challenge whether detailed introspective analysis of thought was possible. With the progress toward a laboratory-based science of psychology, researchers turned to experimental methods of studying thinking (Ericsson and Hastie: Sternberg (3), 41). They gave well-defined tasks to highly motivated subjects whose successful performances were measured. Successful performance implied productive thinking. Investigators studied thinking behaviors in controlled, artificial tasks and used arbitrary stimulus materials to minimize the effects of pre-experiment experience of the subjects. The results of these behavioral experiments in a laboratory-type setting revealed definitions of various types of thinking, such as concept formation, reasoning (logic proof problems), and problem solving (brain teasers) (Ericsson and Hastie: Sternberg (3), 70).

For the last few decades, the information-processing method, based on early electronic computers, has become a standard approach to the study of thinking. There are three fundamental assumptions of the information-processing method, as explained by Ericsson and Hastie:

> First, thinking can be described as a sequence of identifiable knowledge states or thoughts separated by some processing activity that determines the transition from one state to its successor. Second, each state can be described by a limited number of activated Working Memory structures and thoughts that represent the primary input to the processes that produce the next state. Third, except in rare conditions, the basic processes operating to transform one knowledge state into another and the basic processing capacity limits (e.g. working memory or attentional capacity) are fixed and constant across healthy adult individuals (Ericsson and Hastie: Sternberg (3), 48).

A popular alternative approach to the study of the mechanics of thinking starts by examining thinking performance in everyday life in order to identify stable and reproducible phenomena. Of particular interest to researchers is the study of expert performance. After identifying an important phenomenon of an expert's out-of-laboratory thinking performance, the researchers attempt, in a laboratory setting, to design tasks to allow the expert thinking performance to be reproduced under standard laboratory conditions. An important result from this alternative approach is that:

> ... the thinking of expert performers is not merely the accumulation of more knowledge about appropriate actions that can be directly accessed by perceptual patterns. Instead, expert performance reflects acquired domain-specific representations and working-memory skills that support specialized planning, reasoning, and evaluation, which are essential for the high levels of performance (Erricsson and Hastie: Sternberg (3), 71-72).

The ultimate goal of the researchers of thinking – to fully understand thinking, its mechanics, and its acquisition – while far from being attained, will ultimately be achieved only through the application of a wide range of different approaches to the subject (Sternberg (3), 72).

1.3.5 Thinking skills

In his book, *de Bono's Thinking Course*, Edward de Bono defines "thinking" as the "operating skill with which intelligence acts upon experience for a purpose" (de Bono (6), 3). This definition, he says, focuses attention on three elements: operating skill, intelligence, and experience. As to operating skill, he believes that it is "possible to devise simple and usable frameworks for the practice and development of thinking skills" (de Bono (6), 8). With respect to the experience element, knowledge can be acquired by new and different experiences which can help improve the way we think and problem solve. Intelligence is the curious element of the definition of thinking. As de Bono points out, "[h]ighly intelligent people may turn out to be rather poor thinkers; [t]hey may need as much, or more, training in thinking skills than other people" (de Bono (6), 4). There are several components of what he calls "The Intelligence Trap," – the assumption that intelligent people are good thinkers. Some of them are described below.

- A highly intelligent person can construct a rational and well argued case for virtually any point of view. Such a person may become trapped into a particular view simply because he/she can support it.

- Verbal fluency is often mistaken for thinking.

- The ego, self-image, and peer status of a highly intelligent person are too often based on that intelligence. Such person often has a need to be right, clever, and orthodox.

- The critical use of intelligence – to prove someone else wrong – is always more immediately satisfying to the highly intelligent person than the constructive use of his/her intelligence.

- Highly intelligent minds often seem to prefer the certainty of reactive thinking (solving puzzles, sorting data), whereas real life more usually demands the projective type of thinking (creating context, the concepts, the objectives).

- The physical quickness of the highly intelligent mind leads it to jump to conclusions from only a few premises or signals.

- The highly intelligent mind seems to place a higher value on cleverness than on wisdom, and tends to devalue experience (de Bono (6), 4-5).

Dr. de Bono describes the characteristics of a skilled, effective thinker in part as follows:

How would I define an effective thinker? Someone who is confident of his thinking. Not confident that he is going to be right or, indeed, that he is going to find an answer to a problem: but confident that he can turn on his thinking at will and deliberately focus it in any direction he wants... He has both a clear focus and also a broad view of the situation... He is... decisive but also humble. He realizes that any approach is but one among many – most of which he has not even thought of... Even if he has not reached a satisfactory answer he learns to appreciate what has been achieved – even if it is only a realization that a great deal more thinking is required (and where to focus it).

The thinker treats thinking as a skill worth both practicing and observing. He is able to think about thinking in general and his own thinking in particular. He is objective, and notes where his thinking is being less than effective... He is constructive rather than critical... He appreciates an idea just as he might appreciate a beautiful flower, no matter in whose garden it may be growing. He treats arrogance as the major sin of thinking... (de Bono (6), 8-9) (emphasis added).

1.3.6 Thinking styles

Harrison and Bramson describe five thinking styles that are common to creative thinking:

Synthesist, Idealist, Pragmatist, Analyst, and Realist. Synthesists are open to change and seek to make connections between seemingly disparate ideas. Pragmatists are receptive to new ideas and are good at finding ways to solve problems with available resources. Analysts bring to the problem solving process a concern about having sufficient data and a focus that can be important to creating value in a new idea. Realists' concern with agreement and consensus often leads them to engage in new ways to find connections between differing views (Weinstein and Morton, 867).

Edward de Bono in his book, *Six Thinking Hats*, describes six discrete modes or styles of thinking. He has called these six thinking styles "thinking hats" and he has ascribed to each a different color. The purpose of the concept of the six thinking hats is to unscramble thinking so that a thinker is able to use one thinking mode or style at a time. As Dr. de Bono explains:

> The six thinking hats method is designed to switch thinking away from the normal argument style to a mapmaking style. This makes thinking a two-stage process. The first stage is to make the map. If the map is good enough, the best route will often become obvious...
>
> I am not suggesting that the six hats cover every possible aspect of thinking, but they do cover the main modes. Nor am I suggesting that at every thinking moment we should be wearing one of the hats.
>
> It is the very artificiality of the hats which is their greatest value. They provide a formality and a convenience for requesting a certain type of thinking either of oneself or of others. They establish rules for the game of thinking (de Bono(4), 199).

Dr. de Bono describes the six thinking hats as follows.

White Hat   virgin white, pure facts, figures and information.

> Imagine a computer that gives the facts and figures for which it is asked. The computer is neutral and objective. It does not offer interpretations or opinions. When wearing the white thinking hat, the thinker should imitate the computer.

Red Hat   seeing red, emotions and feelings, also hunch and intuition.

> The red hat covers two broad types of feeling. Firstly, there are the ordinary emotions as we know them: ranging from the strong emotions such as fear and dislike to the more subtle ones such as suspicion. Secondly, there are the complex judgments that go into such types of "feeling" as hunch, intuition, sense, taste, aesthetic feeling and other not-visibly-justified types of feeling. Where an opinion has a large measure of this type of feeling it can also fit under the red hat.

Black Hat   devil's advocate, negative judgment, why it will not work.

> Black hat thinking is specifically concerned with negative assessment. The black hat thinker points out what is wrong, incorrect and in error. The black hat thinker points out how something does not fit experience or accepted knowledge... why something will not work... risks and dangers... faults in design.

Yellow Hat sunshine, brightness and optimism, positive, constructive, opportunity.

> Yellow hat thinking is constructive and generative. It is from yellow hat thinking that come concrete proposals and suggestions... Effectiveness is the aim of yellow hat thinking.

Green Hat fertile, creative, plants springing from seeds, movement, provocation.

> The green hat is for creative thinking. The person who puts on the green hat is going to use the idioms of creative thinking. Those around are required to treat the output as creative output. Ideally both thinker and listener should be wearing green hats.

Blue Hat cool and control, orchestra conductor, thinking about thinking.

> The blue hat thinker defines the subjects towards which the thinking is to be directed. Blue hat thinker sets the focus... defines the problems and shapes the questions... determines the thinking tasks that are to be carried through.

1.3.7 Types of problems

The problems with which a negotiator or mediator is concerned are of two principal types: (1) presented problems and (2) discovered problems. Presented problems are those, which have a known formulation, a routine process for solution (known by the individual problem solver and/or others) and a recognized solution. There are two types of presented problems. Solving the first type of presented problem requires the problem solver to follow established steps to meet the requirements of the situation. An example of this first type of a presented problem would be finding the area of a rectangle whose unit width, a, is 4 and whose unit height, b, is 3. The routine process for solution is the formula: Area = a x b. The solution is easily obtained by plugging 4 for "a" in the formula, 3 for "b", and multiplying 4 x 3 to yield 12 square units. The primary thought process used in solving this type of problem is memory or retrieval of the appropriate formula. Perception and reasoning also play important roles. This first type of presented problem requires reframing assistance if the designated problem solver retrieves the wrong formula (memory error), inserts the wrong givens (perception error), or miscalculates (reasoning error).

A second, more difficult type of presented problem, is where the problem is posed, but no routine process for solving it is known by the problem solver (although a routine process is known by others). An example of such presented problem would be this question posed to a person (perhaps a child) who knows nothing about geometry: How would you go about finding the area of a rectangle? The problem solver would have to use reasoning and rationality as a primary mode of thought to solve the problem and then match his or her solution against that which is already known to others. If the designated problem solver reached an impasse and could not solve such presented problem, then another person possessing the necessary reasoning skills could assist the designated problem solver by asking questions to help reframe the impasse and to facilitate his or her reasoning to the appropriate solution. This form of dialectic (or discourse) is commonly found in the technique of Socratic method called recollection (See Cooley (2), 69-85).

The second principal type of problem is the discovered problem. A simple example of a typical discovered problem would be: Formulate a problem about a rectangle and solve it. Others would not know the method for solving the problem because they would not know what problem would be found. In this situation, the problem solver would be a problem finder, initially. The problems he or she could find (within the scope of the discovered problem) would be infinite, ranging from How is a rectangle like a circle? to Are certain dimensions of a rectangle more pleasing to the eye than other dimensions? These problems, identifiable within the scope of the discovered problem, are referred to as found problems. These interim solutions (i.e. found problems) reached by the problem solver (i.e. the problem finder) cannot be compared against a pre-determined standard of right or wrong. Rather, the interim solutions (found problems) can be rejected or accepted by the problem solver and others only on the basis of a critical, relativistic analysis. The generation of discovered problems and their progenies of found problems often lead to the identification of one or more presented problems for which there is a known, routine process for solution, or for which a solution process can be designed. The primary mode of thought required to find and solve a discovered problem is creative reframing. Identifying and solving discovered problems naturally involves the use and application of design skills hence the origin of the expression problem design.

Any given mediation situation may involve the generation of many discovered problems and found problems. In some situations a discovered problem, itself, may be an appropriate solution or resolution for the dispute. But in most situations, discovered problems may prompt the search for and perception of presented problems usually appearing as hypotheses which must be tested by known routine critical and analytical mental processes and occasionally requiring the design of a solution process. Assisting in the generation of discovered and found problems through creative reframing of disputants' mental constructs may be the mediator's most important skill. Mediators must also be able to identify disputants who possess this skill and to motivate their use of it in problem solving. A mediator can accomplish this reframing through Socratic questioning techniques (Cooley (2), 67-85).

Other sources have described the taxonomy of problem types as: simplistic, deterministic, random, and indeterminate. A simplistic problem is factual. It has only one answer, for example: who is the President of the United States? Deterministic problems have only one answer, but the correct formula must be used, for example: how many cubic feet are in a cube, each edge being two feet in length? Random problems have many different answers and all of them can be identified: Of all the candidates running for election, who will win? Indeterminate problems may have different answers, but the answers are conjectural, so not all the answers can be identified, for example: What are the prospects for U.S.-Mexican relations? (Jones, 50-51).

For other readings on types of problems, see Robertson, 3-17; and Lewis and Greene, 50-136.

1.3.8 Types of processes

It has become quite common for parties to agree to use an ADR process that is a variation of pure mediation or pure arbitration. These variations are called hybrid processes. It is important for you to understand the differences between these hybrids so that you can choose or design the appropriate process for your dispute with the help of the Hybrid ADR Process Selection Chart appearing in Section 1.3.11.2. The two primary ADR processes which are used in the hybrid ADR forms are mediation and arbitration. Mediation is defined in Section 1.3.2. Arbitration may be defined as a process in which one or more neutrals render a decision after hearing arguments and reviewing evidence. The essential distinction between mediation and arbitration lies in *who* makes the resolution decision for the parties. In mediation, the parties participate in a joint decision making process and make the decision themselves. In arbitration, the parties relinquish their decision making right to the neutral who makes the decision for them. By preagreement, the decision of the neutral in arbitration is either binding or nonbinding. If binding, the decision is final, and the winning party may enforce it against the losing party. If nonbinding, the decision is advisory in aid of settlement.

1.3.8.1 High-low arbitration

In this process, the parties negotiate to impasse and then proceed to arbitration. Plaintiff's last settlement demand and defendant's last offer establish a bracket defining the limits of the arbitrator's award in the case. The arbitrator conducts the arbitration without knowing the endpoints of the bracket. The parties preagree that: if the arbitrator's award is below the low endpoint of the bracket, the low endpoint of the bracket becomes the award; if the award is above the high endpoint of the bracket, the high endpoint of the bracket becomes the award; if the arbitrator's award falls inside the bracket, that is the award, whatever amount it is.

1.3.8.2 Baseball arbitration

This is a type of final-offer arbitration in which parties preagree that, when they have reached their last and best offers and cannot close the gap, they will submit the matter to arbitration. The arbitrator must choose one of the two last best offers, and may not award any other figure under any circumstances.

1.3.8.3 Med-Arb

Mediation and arbitration combine in the process called med-arb. In med-arb, by preagreement of the parties, the neutral first conducts a mediation to settle the entire dispute or part of it, after which a neutral arbitrates and decides any unresolved issues. The same neutral may perform the role of mediator and arbitrator, or different neutrals may serve in those roles (the preferred method).

1.3.8.4 Co-Med-Arb

The basic concept of co-med-arb is to use two neutrals, one in the role of mediator and one as arbitrator, but to have them work concurrently in the preliminary stage of an arbitration to maximize efficiency and to avoid duplicate expenses. The mediator and arbitrator review all submitted documents prior to the hearing, and at the hearing they sit as a two-person panel to hear the parties' opening statements in what is called the "open phase" of the hearing. After the completion of the open phase, the rules preclude the mediator from discussing the substance of the dispute with the arbitrator, though the two neutrals may usually confer on procedural matters. In the "confidential phase" which follows, the mediator attempts to mediate the dispute to resolution. If the parties reach impasse, they proceed to the third phase of the process and present their evidence to the arbitrator. When this occurs, the mediator is usually "on call" in the event that the parties desire to resume mediation at one or more points during the arbitration. If the parties resume mediation, the mediator sets strict time limits on the mediation conference. If the resumed mediation is unsuccessful, the parties go back to arbitration and the arbitrator issues an award at the conclusion of the process.

1.3.8.5 Arb-Med

In this process, the parties proceed to arbitration before an arbitrator-mediator who will render a binding decision. When the arbitrator reaches a decision and drafts the award, it is placed in a sealed envelope without the parties having an opportunity to review it. The parties then can negotiate a resolution on their own, or they can involve the arbitrator as a mediator to help mediate a resolution. If the negotiations or mediation are unsuccessful, the parties open the sealed envelope and, by preagreement, are bound by it.

1.3.8.6 Binding mediation

The concept of binding mediation is simple: if the parties and their counsel spend two hours in a mediation of a small-damage case with an experienced mediator, the parties can have that neutral determine the "fair settlement value" of the case and preagree to be bound by that result. This is a process of speculation and "best guess" and should normally be reserved for use, if at all, in small-damage cases.

1.3.8.7 Co-mediation

This is a process in which more than one person serves as a mediator. It involves concepts of team mediation and interdisciplinary problem solving, and it can be tailored to meet the needs of a particular dispute. Co-mediation is used in many types of disputes, but its most widespread application is in the field of family law, particularly in divorce mediation. Often a lawyer and a non-lawyer (e.g., a psychotherapist, financial or estate planner, or accountant, etc.) team up to help divorcing couples reach agreement on the property and custody issues related to their divorce.

1.3.8. 8 Mini-trial

Apparent from its name, this is an abbreviated trial or hearing. The mini-trial is most often used as a settlement tool in resolving large disputes and complex litigation. They are most successful when each party makes a genuine effort to limit discovery to only those documents and depositions that will be absolutely necessary to resolve the issues in dispute. The panel before which the attorneys will present their very abbreviated cases (one to two days of hearings) normally consists of three people: a business executive from each side with full settlement authority and a disinterested third party neutral, who chairs the panel. At the close of all evidence and arguments, negotiation commences. The third party neutral is present with the two business executives in the post-hearing negotiations to be consulted for advice or clarification. Normally, the lawyers for the parties are available for consultation, but do not actually participate in the negotiations. The business executives negotiate to achieve a reasonable business solution to the dispute.

1.3.8.9 Simulated juries

Any party may employ a simulated or mock jury in order to evaluate a case for trial or settlement. It is like a "dress rehearsal" for trial. It is also useful to choose among two or more case theory options. Watching the jury deliberate after hearing a lawyer's presentation of the case, or both sides of it, can provide the lawyer with valuable insight into the hearts and minds of an average jury panel. The experience may lead a lawyer to conclude that the case should be settled.

1.3.8.10 Special masters

Special masters are judicial adjuncts who can provide judges with specialized assistance in managing their dockets and facilitating settlement. Normally, intervention of a special master occurs pursuant to an agreement of the parties, though a court may appoint a special master without such agreement. The goal is case processing efficiency and cost reduction by eliminating costly motion practice. Typically, a judge may appoint a special master solely for the purpose of developing a case management plan expressly for settlement.

1.3.8.11 Early neutral evaluation

In this type of ADR process, a neutral evaluator who is a highly respected private attorney chosen by the court, conducts a short, usually two-hour, case evaluation conference early in the litigation process. The parties normally accompany their attorneys to such conference. There, each party presents its position within a thirty-minute time period and, afterward, the evaluator identifies areas of agreement or near agreement to allow trial counsel to limit the scope of the dispute. The evaluator encourages stipulations and discourages alternative arguments, arguments with multiple themes, or boilerplate arguments. This helps limit discovery to actual rather than perceived disputes. After this phase, the evaluator assesses for each party the relative strengths and weaknesses of their case and their opponent's case. Finally, the evaluator may offer to explore settlement possibilities with the parties.

1.3.8.12 Fact finding

This is a dispute resolution process that provides more efficient, speedy, and sensitive resolution of claims. Normally, the court appoints a fact-finder or team of fact-finders to investigate the complaint and issue a written report of findings. Because fact-finders are generally used in cases involving sensitive issues, confidentiality is a paramount requirement. The fact-finders conduct interviews with the pertinent parties and other persons who have relevant information. This is usually done outside the presence of the parties' lawyers with the knowledge and permission of the parties and their lawyers. The fact-finder's report states what the fact-finder believes happened and identifies any issues about which the fact-finder is unable to draw conclusions. Unless the parties have otherwise agreed, the report does not recommend remedies. It does, however, assess the credibility of all those interviewed. The fact-finder's report is submitted to the court and to the parties, who are given a reasonable time period to resolve the dispute on their own before the court acts on the report.

1.3.8.13 Expert panels

A court may appoint a panel of experts to help it in any number of ways, but the most typical use of an expert panel is to instruct and educate a court on complex scientific evidence in order for the court to determine the admissibility of such evidence. Scientific expert panels can be most helpful in complex cases involving difficult scientific issues. Such cases include asbestos litigation, pharmaceutical product liability cases, and tobacco industry litigation. Experts in these types of cases can help parties strip their cases of superfluous arguments, identify important issues of actual and significant disagreement, and guide parties in meaningful settlement negotiation.

1.3.8.14 Summary jury trial

A summary jury trial is an actual nonbinding trial that can usually be completed in less than one day, even in complex cases. It is an extremely abbreviated hearing designed to facilitate settlement. A party may entirely disregard the findings of the summary trial jury, but when cases that have been argued in summary proceedings go to full trial, it is quite likely that the full-trial jury will find in the same way. The parties submit pretrial briefs to the judge and the judge sets time limits on counsel's presentations. Commonly, each side is given roughly fifteen minutes for an opening-statement, one hour for its case-in-chief, one half-hour to rebut, and some time for a closing argument. Some judges permit videotapes of expert witnesses and critical occurrence witnesses to be played before the jury. In the hearing portion of the summary jury trial, counsel may use any physical evidence, exhibits, or other devices that they would be permitted to use in a full trial. Following the verdict, the jurors are debriefed by the judge and the lawyers, and sometimes by the litigants themselves. The debriefing is quite instructive, making the parties aware of the specific reasons supporting the jury's evaluation of the case. Immediately following the debriefing, settlement conferencing begins. A very large majority of the cases that go through the summary jury trial process settle. For more detailed information concerning these hybrid processes, refer to Cooley (3), pages 207-222.

1.3.9 Types of solutions

It is not enough for a mediator to know the types of problems endemic to a conflict setting; he or she must be able to recognize types of solutions achievable in the process and achieved in a resolution. The late Professor Stuart Nagel of the University of Illinois, a nationally-recognized expert in computer-aided mediation, has suggested a taxonomy of mediated solutions: super-malimum, lose-lose, win-lose, pareto-malimum, win-win, pareto-optimum, and super-optimum. In Nagel's taxonomy, the highest quality solution achievable in mediation is the creative-integrative "super-optimum solution" (Nagel and Mills (2), xi-xii). Whereas an optimum solution is one that is best on a list of alternatives in achieving a set of goals, a super-optimum solution is one that is simultaneously best on two (or more) separate sets of goals. Super-optimum solutions are better than win-win solutions. They are settlement results, which are better than the disputants' best expectations of results achievable by adjudicatory means. Nagel has identified many types of super-optimum solutions. Four examples are as follows:

1. *Solution that achieves a super-optimum goal.* A super-optimum goal is one that is far higher than is traditionally considered to be the best attainable. An example would be doing better than 0% unemployment by simultaneously eliminating or reducing traditional unemployment and greatly increasing job opportunities for those who are willing and able to work more, but who were formerly considered outside the labor force or formerly considered fully employed.

2. *Solution that resolves public policy disputes.* It satisfies liberals and conservatives in a policy dispute so that both liberals and conservatives consider the solution to be better than their original best expectations as measured by their own respective goals and priorities.

3. *Solution that resolves adjudicative or rule-applying controversies.* This is a solution that satisfies disputants in a way that is better than their best expectations. An example would be where a plaintiff demands $900,000, the defendant refuses to pay more than $300,000, and they agree that the defendant will turn over merchandise that the defendant manufactures that is worth more than $1,000,000 to the plaintiff, but whose variable cost to produce is worth less than $200,000 to the defendant.

4. *Solution that enables all sides in a dispute to add substantially to their original net worth.* An example would be in the same litigation dispute described in the preceding example, the defendant agrees to give the plaintiff a franchise for selling defendant's products and the franchise brings in a net of $1,000,000 each year, with $500,000 a year for plaintiff and $500,000 a year for defendant. This type of expanded sum solution would still be met if the total net worth of all participants substantially increased, even if the worth of some of the participants slightly decreased, provided that the decrease did not cause those participants to go below a minimum level of satisfaction (Nagel and Mills (1), 226-242).

Achieving super-optimum solutions should be the principal goal of every mediator (and negotiator) in assisting the reframing of conflict, where reframing is feasible. But even where super-optimum solutions are not achievable, the classical reframing techniques can be effectively employed by the mediator to alter mind frames of the disputants and thereby facilitating less ideal, yet satisfactory, solutions in the spectrum of solution types.

1.3.10 Designing the problem

In his book, *New Thinking for a New Millennium*, Edward de Bono asserts that design thinking is the type of thinking that creative problem solvers of the future must learn and use. Specifically, he points out:

Design thinking is very different from traditional judgment thinking. For judgment thinking, the desired output is truth. For design thinking, the output is value.

For logical thinking, certainty is essential. For design thinking, possibility is essential. Logical thinking likes to work with facts. Design thinking has to work with perception. The three most important things in design thinking are: perception, possibility, and practicality (the three Ps) (de Bono (5), 222).

A dispute is merely a problem, and it is susceptible to resolution through the application of well-known problem solving techniques. It is important for you to understand that resolution of any dispute requires the solving of three separate design problems: (1) designing (or, if you prefer, finding or defining) the problem itself; (2) designing the process for solving the designed problem; and (3) designing the solution to the defined problem by using the process you designed. Sometimes, depending on the particular situation, the mind operates to solve these three design problems in sequence; at other times it resolves the design problems simultaneously. Resolution of each of these three design problems is enhanced through the application of the lateral thinking techniques discussed in the preceding section, complemented by vertical thinking techniques.

The concept of designing a problem may be difficult for you to grasp at first. But if you think about it, you will realize that every time you attempt to solve a problem, the problem has already been designed in your mind. If the problem is a dispute, your perception of the disputants, their conduct, and related events have played a significant role in this design process; so have your assumptions, emotions, and probably, in most cases, your cliché patterns of thinking. Your interpretive *design* of the dispute may occur instantaneously; and may be only one of myriad designs available. What your instantaneous design powers produced as a problem may, in fact, if viewed or perceived from a different angle, be an opportunity for change a betterment of some kind. What is initially perceived by you as a problem may be no problem at all. Any time spent by you in solving it would be wasted.

The idea of problem design may, additionally, seem foreign because our culture and educational system (particularly mathematics and science courses) traditionally present to us single-solution problems already designed. We are rarely given an opportunity in school to design problems. Yet this is a primary task in everyday life, particularly for the lawyer. Let's take a closer look at what problem design means (Cooley (1), §2:04, pp. 46-47).

At the root of all disputes are human needs or interests which appear to conflict or which are unsatisfied to some extent. For example, consider Russ, a self-styled mechanic, who tinkers with his car late into the night and revs up the engine in the driveway under his neighbor Bob's bedroom window. Bob's problem is not Russ or Russ's car. Bob's problem is the conflict between Russ's need to repair his car at that particular time and Bob's need for sleep. This simple example can be extrapolated to the problems precipitating the most complex of lawsuits filed in any of our courts today. At the core of these lawsuits is a simple conflict of the parties' needs or interests. That is what makes the first aspect of problem solving (i.e. problem design) so important. Parties' needs or interests may, in any particular situation, be satisfied in a variety of ways, and sometimes in a way that is better than either's needs or interests could have been satisfied had the conflict or encounter not occurred (i. e. a win-win, optimal, or super-optimal solution) (Cooley (1), §2:04, 47). See Section 3.1.25 to learn how Russ, the mechanic, and Bob, the insomniac, were able to resolve their conflict.

After full consideration of all facets of a particular dispute, it may turn out that satisfaction of a disputant's needs may be best achieved by allowing a third party to determine which disputant has a right to have his needs satisfied. This requires resorting to the law. Then the problem design shifts from a needs analysis to rights analysis. There may be many problem designs possible under a rights analysis, just as there were under the needs analysis. All of these possibilities are explored and evaluated in the problem design mode (Cooley (1), §2:04, 47).

For other readings on "designing the problem" and related topics see: Taylor and Getzels, 90-117; Robertson, 49-72; Schank, 195-311; Lewis and Greene, 185-211.

1.3.11 Designing the process

1.3.11.1 Your goals when designing a negotiation, mediation, or other ADR process

After designing the problem by defining the parties' root needs and interests the next step is to design the process for solving it. The number of approaches one can take to solve a problem is limited only by the extent of one's insight and creativity. As lawyers, many of us are prone to see only one or two possible approaches to solving a problem, even though many more might exist. Normally, we try first to negotiate a solution to a problem, using methods and techniques which have succeeded for us in the past. However, depending on the parties, lawyers, and nature of the problem involved, a different negotiation approach or combination of approaches might be necessary to achieve success. Lawyers are often blind to these combined approaches because of their past negotiation ritual. In these situations, a mediator can be most helpful in adjusting the process to meet the needs of the redefined problem and in facilitating the generation of creative solutions. When designing your own negotiation, mediation, or other ADR process, or when assisting parties in designing an appropriate ADR process for a dispute, your goals should include ensuring that all parties are satisfied that:

- they have a sufficient opportunity to evaluate the design proposals;

- they have a sufficient opportunity to offer design input and to collaborate in fashioning the ultimate design;

- the ultimately selected design is fair to them individually and collectively;

- the ultimately selected design gives them a reasonable opportunity to negotiate a result for themselves rather than have a result imposed on them;

- all concerns regarding confidentiality are met;

- the ultimately selected design is a more economical alternative than court adjudication;

- the ultimately selected design will not significantly prejudice their legal positions and strategies should ADR be unsuccessful, thus requiring them to seek court adjudication (Cooley (2), 211-12).

1.3.11.2 Designing the appropriate hybrid ADR process using the Hybrid Selection Chart

This section presents a tool to assist mediators, parties, and their counsel in designing the appropriate hybrid ADR process for a particular dispute. The chart takes into account the hybrid mediation processes described in Section 1.3.8. The chart identifies special needs of a client or situation and simultaneously describes the hybrid process having features satisfying those special needs. An assumption underlying the use of this chart is that the general needs of the client are: (1) to accelerate resolution of the dispute as compared to the time required for resolution by traditional court adjudication; and (2) to lessen or minimize the costs of resolution.

Hybrid Process	Special Need(s) of Client or Situation	Process Feature Satisfying Special Need(s) of Client or Situation
High-Low Arbitration	• Desires binding result • Wants to minimize risk of aberrant adverse binding award • Does not want arbitrator(s) to be influenced by final negotiated offers and demands	• Binding award • Parties pre-agree to maximum/minimum award bracket • Parties pre-agree not to disclose bracket to arbitrator(s)
Baseball Arbitration	• Wants to limit potential losses to a known tolerable level and to maximize potential gain • Desires to maximize effectiveness of the negotiation process	• Parties preagree to limit the arbitrator's function to choosing either the high or the low end of the parties' negotiated bracket • Arbitrator's limited function influences parties to negotiate to a narrow bracket and cases often settle without need of arbitration

Med-Arb and Co-Med-Arb	• Wants to go through evidentiary hearing only if absolutely necessary • Wants to preserve relationship with other side, if at all possible • Desires to first attempt to find a creative solution • Desires to use threat of arbitration to enhance opportunity for mediated result • Desires finality • Situation appropriate for use of two neutrals • Wants to preserve option for mediated result throughout arbitration process	• Evidentiary arbitration hearing conducted only if mediation unsuccessful • Mediation can help heal and preserve relationships • Mediation can result in creative solutions • Expense or inconvenience of arbitration can influence parties to work hard to settle case in mediation • Arbitration yields a final, enforceable award if mediation is unsuccessful • InCo-Med-Arb neutral serves as mediator, the other, as arbitrator • In Co-Med-Arb the use of neutrals preserves opportunity for settlement
Arb-Med	• Does not want mediation process to taint evidentiary hearing in arbitration. • Wants an arbitrated result only as absolutely final alternative	• Arbitration award withheld pending post-hearing mediation • Arbitration award revealed only in instance where mediated result is not possible

Binding Mediation	• Does not want an evidentiary hearing (e.g., case not fully discovered; unfavorable evidence, etc.) • Wants to settle case without neutral's evaluation, if possible • Desires neutral to evaluate case based on information disclosed in mediation • Desires finality	• Mediator attempts to settle dispute by facilitative caucusing; if unsuccessful, makes binding evaluation • Mediator attempts to settle dispute, first • Mediator gives opinion of case value if mediation is unsuccessful • Binding case evaluation
Co-mediation	• Wants input of expert or person with special expertise or having ethnic, cultural, or gender characteristics matching those of parties • Wants to facilitate rapport-building and communication	• Mediator teams up with psychologist, technical expert, accountant, etc. • Mediation team relates to needs and interests of parties
Mini-trial	• Capitalize on executives' expertise in making effective business decisions • Enhance opportunities for collaboration by executives • Executives need to see evidence on both or all sides • Executives need to separate themselves from dispute to get objective view of case • Parties need to limit risk of adverse result	• Corporate executives are on panel that hears the abbreviated case presentations • A disinterested neutral facilitates negotiation between executives after case presentations • Presentations made to panel by the attorneys on both (or all) sides • Objectivity is achieved by putting executives in a temporary neutral role • Process is non-binding

Creative Problem Solver's Handbook for Negotiators and Mediators

Simulated Juries	• Party needs private rehearsal to learn strengths and weaknesses of its strategies/tactics • Need for impartial evaluation by people closely mirroring potential jury • Party needs opportunity for feedback from one or more juries • Party needs to determine whether case should be settled	• Case is presented in an abbreviated manner to pre-selected jury • Jurors deliberate and reach a verdict • Party and counsel debrief jurors • Jurors' verdict(s) and comments often lead to decision to settle
Special Master	• Need for individualized case management • Need for overseeing certain aspects of discovery process • Need for issue-framing, issue-shaping, issue reduction • Need for specialized settlement skills or experience • Need for neutral to help parties and counsel design a case-appropriate dispute resolution process or case-management plan • Court needs neutral to read pleadings, hear evidence and oral argument and report and recommend an appropriate disposition	• Court-appointed attorney or former judge can provide individualized case management and serve the other needs described in the adjacent column

Early Neutral Evaluation	- Need to minimize pretrial posturing by attorneys early in the life of the case - Need to clarify vague pleadings - Need to improve pretrial communication among counsel - Need for early evaluation of strengths and weaknesses of claims and defenses - Need to limit case to actual rather than merely perceived disputes	- Highly respected, court-appointed panel attorney conducts evaluation conference early in case, minimizes pretrial posturing, and serves the other needs described in the adjacent column
Fact-finding	- Facts needed before decision made on approach to resolution - High degree of confidentiality required - Sensitivity to parties' feelings/ reputation is paramount	- Fact-finder or team appointed to investigate and issue report - Fact-finder/team maintains strict confidentiality - Fact-finder is sensitive to others' concerns and is skillful interviewer
Expert Panels	- Judge or private neutral needs to be educated on one or more areas of complex scientific evidence - Scientific specialist needed to manage or control discovery - Parties need to explore settlement options in technically complex case	- Experts can examine complex information and translate it into simple-to-understand concepts - Technical experts are able to communicate on counsel's and parties' level - Experts' report can be used as a tool by parties to settle case

Summary Jury Trial	• Need to see jury reaction to facts in an accelerated judicial proceeding in a courtroom environment • Need to define critical legal issues and to learn how judge would rule on them • Need to know why jury ruled a certain way	• Six jurors selected by profiles; brief videotapes of expert and critical witness testimony • Comprehensive pretrial conference; evidentiary objections and jury instructions ruled on by judge • Through jury debriefing, parties learn specific reasons for jury's evaluation of case

(Cooley(3), 223-229). This chart is reproduced with the permission of the National Institute for Trial Advocacy.

1.3.12 Designing the solution

After designing the problem and the process for solving it, the next step is to design the solution. Lawyers generally feel much more comfortable with this third design problem. This is because they normally take a solution-oriented approach to a problem before they have designed the problem (given full consideration to finding or defining the problem) and before they have designed the process for solving it (explored and evaluated alternative processes). Actually, designing a solution to a problem is greatly facilitated if the first two design problems (problem design and process design) are properly solved. In most problem solving situations, there are many types of solutions possible.

1.3.13 Types of problem solving

1.3.13.1 Problem solving in general

Raymond S. Nickerson has pointed out that many writers have conceptualized problem solving as a stepwise process (Sternberg (3), 424). One of the best known of these conceptualizations was proposed over fifty years ago by the mathematician, Polya. He described the four steps of problem solving as:

1. Understanding the problem
2. Devising a plan
3. Carrying out the plan
4. Looking back

For an example of how this problem solving concept can be applied to a negotiation/mediation situation, see Cooley (7), 115-129.

In 1981, Hayes expanded Polya's concept of problem solving in three ways. First, he introduced the concept of "problem finding." Second, he included a step called "representing" (stating) the problem. And third, he divided Polya's "looking back" step into two parts: evaluating the solution(s) and learning something, on review, that would be useful in the future.

Hayes' problem solving steps contemplated the following elements:

1. Finding the problem
2. Representing the problem
3. Planning the solution

4. Carrying out the plan
5. Evaluating the solution
6. Consolidating gains (Sternberg (3), 424).

In 1984, Bransford and Stein reconfigured the Hayes concept to fit the easily remembered acronym IDEAL. Their conceptualization consisted of these elements:

I = Identify the problem
D = Define and represent the problem
E = Explore possible strategies
A = Act on the strategies
L = Look back and evaluate the effects of your activities

Nickerson observes that there are other similar step-wise conceptualizations of the problem solving process, but most of them can be viewed as variations or elaborations of Polya's original scheme (Sternberg (3), 424) (See also, Lewis and Greene, 185-230).

Much of the theoretical debate about thinking and problem solving has centered on the question of whether there are aspects of them that are independent of the content domain or context in which the thinking or problem solving occurs. Research reveals that there are many methods and strategies that are domain-content specific, but it also demonstrates that there are such methods and strategies that can be successfully applied across domains as well. The following strategies or methodologies can normally be applied across domains (Nickerson: Sternberg (3), 425-30).

1. *Problem decomposition or subgoaling.* This strategy proposes that the problem solver break a complex problem down into simpler problems and solve the complex problem by combining the solutions to simpler subproblems. The risk in using this strategy is that the nature of the problem might be changed by eliminating a critical aspect of it either by the act of breaking it down, or by the act of combining subproblem solutions.

2. *Working backwards.* Many researchers have found it useful to use the metaphor of a journey to solve problems. Sometimes when it is difficult to find a thought pathway between point A and point B, it is often helpful to try to find a pathway from point B. A problem solver may not only work backward from a final goal to the starting point, but also from identifiable intermediate goals.

3. *Hill climbing.* Another type of journey metaphor for problem solving suggests that the problem solver envision the activity of climbing a hill. The problem solver may not always have a clearly marked path to follow, but the problem solver should normally proceed in such a way that he or she is always advancing upward – closer to the goal. Occasionally, the problem solver may have to take a few steps downhill to get to the pathway that will allow upward progress. By combining the strategies of working backwards and hill climbing, the problem solver can also envision himself as being on top of the hill. From that perspective the problem solver can see all of the pathways that actually terminate at the top of the hill.

4. *Means-end analysis.* The problem solver initiates this strategy by identifying the goal state and then making a detailed listing of the differences between it and the current state. The problem solver attempts to take some action that will reduce the disparity (shorten the list of differences) between those two states. The problem solver accomplishes this by either taking a step that makes the current state more

similar to the goal state or by taking a step that, by working backward, will bring the goal state closer to the current state.

5. *Forward chaining.* Using this strategy, the problem solver begins with givens and then works directly toward the goal. It requires that the problem solver have a sufficiently deep understanding of a problem to construct an accurate representation of it. Experts are more likely to use this strategy than novices.

6. *Considering analogous problems.* This strategy suggests that one can solve a problem by finding a solution to an analogous, but easier, problem. The risk attendant to the use of this strategy is misidentifying an appropriate analogue. By using an improper analogy, the problem solver may arrive at a wholly ineffective solution to the problem under analysis.

7. *Specialization and Generalization.* This strategy is especially useful in solving mathematical problems. The term "specialization" means considering a concrete example of an abstract problem. Thus, if a problem solver is trying to solve a problem concerning the properties of triangles, he or she may find it useful to begin by considering a particular triangle, or several different types of triangles. By working with specific cases, one may obtain insights that are helpful in formulating a general solution. Solutions to specific cases may also suggest a pattern that leads to a generally applicable solution (For an example of the application of this strategy in a mediation context, see Cooley(6), 603-07).

8. *Considering extreme cases.* A strategy that is often used to advantage by negotiators and mediators is considering extreme cases. For example, assume that a possible settlement proposal in a business-to-business commercial dispute is for a supplier to provide "all of the manufacturer's parts needs over the next five years." To test the workability of this resolution, one might consider extreme cases. What would happen in the situation where material key to the supplier's fabrication of the parts became unavailable or so expensive that the supplier could not make a profit on the sale of parts to the manufacturer? What if the manufacturer negotiated new contracts with product distributors across the country that required its total production output to increase from four million units per year to forty million units annually? Could the supplier comply with the settlement provision under either of these scenarios? If not, in order to solve the problems described by the extreme cases, how should the settlement agreement language be modified?

9. *Mixing strategies.* Problem solvers should recognize that using a particular problem solving strategy seldom precludes the use of others. For example, breaking a complex problem down into subproblems often creates a situation where any of the above-described strategies can be applied to the subproblems – including further decomposing of the subproblems (Nickerson: Sternberg (3), 425-30).

1.3.13.2 Individual problem solving

There are two broad types of individual problem solving techniques: (1) the individual techniques that focus on the person, his or her personality, and cognitive characteristics; and (2) the techniques that focus on the stages of the creative process. Both of these types of individual techniques are discussed below.

(1) *Personality and cognitive characteristics.* Research has demonstrated that role-playing produces positive results in individuals as measured by psychological tests (Stein (2), 254-255). Cognitive processes consist of an individual's way of knowing, understanding, perceiving, learning, and problem solving. Some researchers have addressed the question of whether there is some way to affect an individual's cognitive characteristics so that he can behave more creatively. Their research has identified two possible ways to accomplish this: biofeedback and focusing on a person's various senses (Stein (2), 254-258).

Biofeedback is a technique in which an individual learns how to use various cues to maintain control over his internal states. This occurs when an individual becomes increasingly aware of the physiological correlates of a psychological state and he or she learns to determine when he or she has arrived at a desired psychological state and then to maintain it.

In another study involving simultaneous sensory stimulation (including high frequency signal from an oscillator, a pungent incense, a floor vibrator, and a loud percussive-type music), improved creativity resulted. In one case study with college students, divergent thinking improved with the application of simultaneous sensory stimulation, whereas convergent thinking was not affected at all (Stein (2), 258-59).

(2) *Stages of the creative process.* Individual problem solving techniques can vary depending on the stages of the creative process. Morris I. Stein has identified four processes that comprise the creative process: (1) preparatory (educational); (2) hypothesis formation; (3) hypothesis testing; and (4) communication of results.

- *Preparatory stage* this includes all formal and informal educational experiences that provide an individual with the information, training, and experience necessary for the work he will do in his chosen field; it can have a marked effect on the person's attitudes and values for creativity.

- *Hypothesis formation:* the effective problem solver can view his or her environment as if it were animated, in flux constantly and constantly in a state of becoming or evolving. He is able to be childlike in behavior, but as the occasion demands, he or she can turn such behavior off and become adult – formal and logical; he or she asks questions and continues to raise questions to produce ideas.

- *Hypothesis testing* In this stage, the role of the creative problem solver changes. She may experience self-doubt and anxiety briefly, but she knows that serendipity, discovery, trial and error, and insight will help find answers

- *Communication of results.* The creative problem solver often communicates the results of his or her efforts through intermediaries. They serve the creative problem solver by providing emotional support, at times serving as a sounding board, and also providing appropriate criticism in a non-threatening environment. The creative problem solver's role in this stage is often less developed than in the other three stages (Stein (2), 259-267).

For other readings on individual problem solving, see Maier, 110-21 and 420-431.

1.3.13.3 Group problem solving

When individuals work as a group to solve a problem or to reach a joint decision, they can either engage competitively or cooperatively. Competition occurs in group problem solving situations when it is possible to disagree about a solution, and when each individual favors his or her own solution. Competition is even more intense when the participants have committed themselves to a solution before meeting in a group. Cooperation most often occurs when a solution has to be discovered by the group and there is none apparent at the beginning of the group session (Maier, 217-218).

Maier and Solem point out that research has revealed that a group leader can upgrade a group's thinking and assist members to discover a creative solution. A leader can accomplish this by asking good questions and by influencing the direction of a group's thinking. Research has further identified three different forces operating in group problem solving conducted by a group leader: (1) the leader's contribution to the group discussion by simply allowing the minority to be heard; (2) the social pressure of the majority; and (3) the external reality or the facts which the participants supply to support their opinions (Maier and Solem: Maier, 227-228).

Certain characteristics of groups result in the inhibition of their creativity and the quality of their group decisions. Several of these are discussed below (Stein(2), 4-17):

(1) *Patterns of communication.* Faulty communication between or within groups sometimes interferes with effective group problem solving. This occurs either because appropriate individuals do not receive information that they need, or some individuals are overloaded or become burdened with information. A group's effectiveness to solve problems creatively is often a function of the available channels of communication and the patterns of communication. This topic is discussed in considerably more depth in Section 1.7.3.

(2) *Group climate.* Group creativity can be enhanced by creating a nonevaluative "group climate." If group participants are allowed to evaluate each other's ideas, the free flow of ideas will be inhibited. A freer atmosphere allows participants to take risks in problem solving, thereby expanding the possibility of creating a larger pool of ideas.

(3) *Homogeneous and heterogeneous groups.* Another important issue in group problem solving is how to compose a group in order to enhance the group's potential to produce quality results. The specific question is should the group consist of individuals who have the same personality, attitudes or abilities, or should the individuals be as different from each other as possible? Research findings demonstrate that solutions achieved by heterogeneous groups either did not differ in quality from those achieved by homogenous groups or they were definitely superior. Also, in one study, homogeneous groups never did better than heterogeneous ones (Stein (2), 10).

(4) *Group aging..* Combinations of individuals in groups develop rigidities over time, as do individuals. As a group "ages" it may become less sensitive to new ideas, processes, and creative opportunities. One antidote to group aging is the infusion of new participants, if possible, from time to time.

For other readings on group problem solving and collaboration, see John-Steiner (2), 123-51; Levesque, 193-215; Maier, 216-324.

1.3.14 Creativity

Creativity is a term used basically the same way in both technical and popular literature to refer to "mental processes that lead to solutions, ideas, conceptualization, artistic forms, theories or products that are unique and novel" (Reber and Reber, 165). One reliable source observes that "the notion of 'creativity' has... served an important function among psychologists and teachers, acting as a banner under which ideological battles have been fought; and indicating, too, a somewhat disparate body of research ..." (Gregory (1), 171).

Of all psychological constructs, few have proved more elusive to define than creativity. In 1926, Graham Wallas identified four steps in the creative process: preparation, incubation, illumination, and verification. According to Wallas, in the preparation stage, the problem is investigated in all directions; the incubation stage consists of unconscious thinking about the problem; in the illumination stage, an idea appears in an instantaneous flash perhaps after a series of tentative unsuccessful trains of thought associations varying from a few seconds to several hours; and in the verification stage, the idea is tested and reduced to exact form. The Wallas process is widely perceived as the basis for almost all of the systematic methods of creativity training in existence today. However, other experts and researchers have elaborated and refined the Wallas concept. E.P. Torrance, for example, one of the leading experts in the field of creativity, has developed several definitional formats for *creativity* including research, artistic, and survival definitions.

T. Amabile's theory of creativity hypothesizes that creativity is not best conceptualized as a personality trait or a general ability but as a behavior resulting from particular constellations of personal characteristics, cognitive abilities, and social environments. This framework attempts to describe the entire creative process from problem finding (see Section 1.3.15.3) to evaluation. The heart of her concept of creativity consists of three components: domain relevant skills, creativity relevant skills, and task motivation. These three components are discussed in more detail in Section 1.3.16.

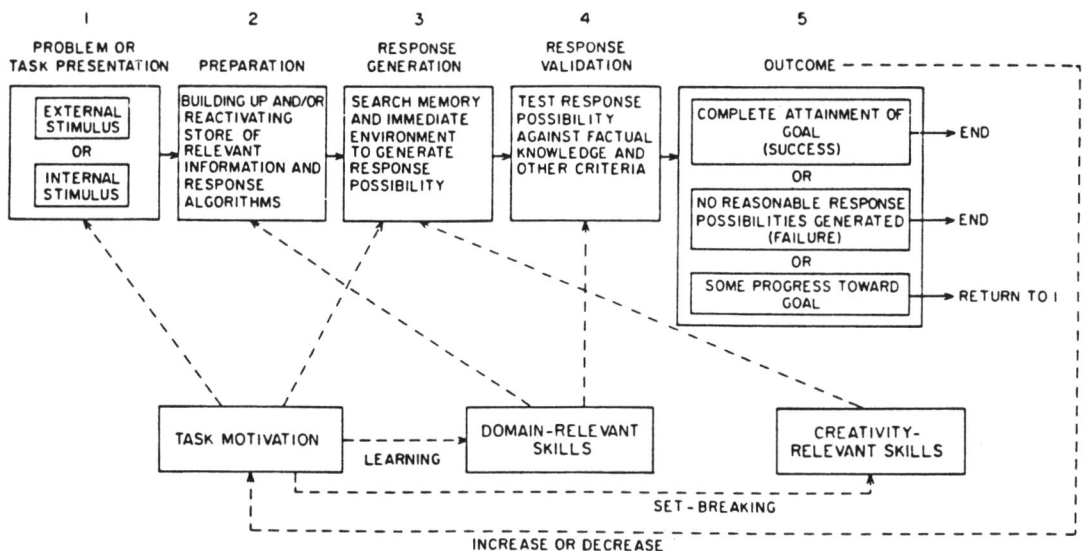

Figure 7. Amabile's componential framework of creativity. Solid arrows indicate sequence of steps in process; broken arrows indicate influences among factors. From The social psychology of creativity: A componential conceptualization by T. M. Amabile, 1983, *Journal of Personality and Social Psychology, 45*, 357–376. Copyright 1983 by the American Psychological Association. Reprinted by permission of the author and the American Psychological Association.

For other readings on creativity, see Arieti, 3-36; Csikszentmihalyi, 23-127; Runco and Albert, 61-91; Glover, Ronning, and Reynolds, 3-32; Maier, 2-81; Dacey, 3-76; Boden, 75-118; Brockman, 7-27; Mansfield and Busse, 1-84; May, 36-54; Stein (1), 3-24; and Sternberg (2), 1-124.

1.3.15 Creative problem solving

There are different theoretical positions on the definition of creative problem solving – that is, on what differentiates creative problem solving from normal or routine problem solving. Todd I. Lubart, in a chapter simply titled "Creativity" in Sternberg (3), pages 314-16, identifies four types of creative problem solving. Type I assumes that all problem solving involves certain fundamental steps: (1) defining a problem solving goal, (2) accessing relevant information, (3) building a solution from this information, and then (4) evaluating and refining the proposed solution. Type I proposes that the creative problem solving process is marked by doing one or more of the basic steps more effectively than average. Thus, according to Type I, the main difference between creative and routine problem solving is the *quality* with which each step is performed.

The Type II creative problem solving process proposes that the same basic activities are involved in creative and routine problem solving. The difference, it suggests, lies in the *amount of time* devoted to each step or the *number of times* that each activity is performed. A third theoretical position on the creative problem solving process focuses on the need for a special *sequence* of problem solving activities. Type III proponents argue that optimal creative problem solving occurs if unconstrained thinking occurs first and evaluation occurs only after several ideas have accumulated. Finally, Type IV theorists assert that what sets creative problem solving apart from mundane problem solving is the presence of a *special activity*, such as divergent thinking or reverse thinking exercises.

Other definitions of creative problem solving abound. For example, it has been said that creative problem solving in law has six facets which differentiate it from more narrow approaches to problem solving. They are: (1) a focus on underlying needs and interests, rather than positions, of individuals as well as society; (2) an analysis of values inherent in the process; (3) exhaustive and continuing investigation into disciplines and resources other than the law; (4) application of modes of creative thinking not found in legal analysis; (5) an emphasis on predicting and analyzing methods of preventing problems; and (6) conscious self-reflection and analysis (Morton, 376).

Much of the literature on creative problem solving can be distilled down to the simple reality that creative problem solving has two basic components, each having perhaps many sub-components. It consists of a generative component and decision making component. The decision making component can be further divided into three necessary sub-components: analysis; evaluation, and selection. Interestingly, each of these components and sub-components has a special and important role in designing the problem itself, the process for solving it, and the solution.

1.3.15.1 Creative problem solving process

A "problem" has been defined as a situation in which some of the attendant components are known and additional components must be ascertained or determined. "Problem solving" consists of "the processes involved in the solution of a problem ... [and] it is the area of cognitive psychology that is concerned with these processes" (Reber and Reber, 566; Gregory (1), 639-644)

Lateral thinking and vertical thinking are essential elements of effective problem solving. Both of these types of thinking must be used if problem solving is to be effective; one is not enough. It is also not enough that the problem solver knows the characteristics of the two basic thinking functions and how to employ them in problem solving. He or she must know when to employ them. This section describes a general schema or formula (also called heurism or heuristic) for solving any problem, which the problem solver encounters. It also suggests the points within the schema at which vertical and lateral thinking functions should be employed.

The schema for problem solving presented in this section is the culmination of a review of much of the literature on problem solving and decision making published over the years, and many years of experimentation with these concepts as a teacher, advocate, mediator, arbitrator, judge, and not the least, a human being involved in personal interactions of all sorts. When you view the schema, you may think to yourself, Oh I know that; that's just common sense.

However, what is most basic and obvious is sometimes most difficult to perceive until it is seen. If the schema represents the way you have always solved problems, then it will help concretize your previous approaches in conscious reality. If the schema represents a new or substantially new approach to problem solving, then I recommend it highly to you for experimentation and use. Under this schema, problem solving is a process that consists of three separate and distinct design problems (called design shells) and a generic decision making process that is specifically tailored to meet the needs of the three design problems. Each of the three design problems must be solved separately; normally (but not necessarily) in a set order. The three specially tailored decision making processes resulting from tailoring are referred to as decision-making modules. When the decision-making modules are inserted in the three design shells, three design modules are formed. If anything is revolutionary about this modular problem solving schema, it is its design orientation, which casts problems and their treatment in a positive, creative light, rather than in the traditional shadows of negativism. The philosophy underlying the schema is that every problem is really an opportunity in disguise. A problem can be anything (within certain limits) that you want it to be; and likewise so can the solution to the problem, depending on the methodology or approach you choose to reach the solution. In this design orientation to problem solving, human perception, as we shall see, is a key ingredient. Let us now take a look at the schema (Cooley (1), 40-46).

A graphic illustration appears below of a generic decision making process (module) which can be tailored to and inserted in the three design shells.

Generic Decision Making Module

A. Define Nature and Scope of Problem
   1. Collect information
   2. Interpret information
   3. Analyze information

B. Generate Alternative Designs
   In doing so:
   1. Disturb perceptions
   2. Reframe perceptions

C. Analyze and Evaluate Alternative Designs
   1. Establish criteria (primary and secondary)
   2. Weight the criteria
   3. Measure each alternative design against each weighted criterion
   4. Assess consequences

D. Verify Evaluation
   1. Incubate alternative designs
   2. Reframe designs
   3. Re-evaluate designs
   4. Refine designs

E. Select optimal design

F. Present (state) design

After tailoring, the modified generic Decision Making Module can be inserted into the three respective design shells as follows:

Problem-Design Module	**Process-Design Module**	**Solution-Design Module**
A. Define Nature and Scope of Problem 1. Collect information 2. Interpret information 3. Analyze information B. Generate Alternative Designs In doing so: 1. Disturb perceptions 2. Reframe perceptions C. Analyze and Evaluate Alternative Designs 1. Establish criteria (primary and secondary) 2. Weight the criteria 3. Measure each alternative design against each weighted criterion 4. Assess consequences D. Verify Evaluation 1. Incubate alternative problem-designs 2. Reframe problem-designs 3. Re-evaluate problem-designs 4. Refine problem-designs E. Select Optimal Problem-Design F. Present (State) Design	A. State Problem B. Generate Alternative Processes (Methods and Approaches) to Solve Stated Problem In doing so: 1. Disturb perceptions 2. Reframe perceptions C. Analyze and Evaluate Alternative Process-Designs 1. Establish criteria (primary and secondary) for process-design 2. Weight the criteria 3. Measure each alternative process- design against each weighted criterion 4. Assess consequences D. Verify Evaluation 1. Incubate alternative process-designs 2. Reframe process-designs 3. Re-evaluate process-designs 4. Refine process-designs E. Select Optimal Process-Design F. State Process	A. State Problem and Process for Solving B. Generate Alternative Solution-Designs In doing so: 1. Disturb perceptions 2. Reframe perceptions C. Analyze and Evaluate Alternative Solution-Designs 1. Establish criteria (primary and secondary) 2. Weight the criteria 3. Measure each alternative solution-design against each weighted criterion 4. Assess consequences D. Verify Evaluation 1. Incubate alternative solution-designs 2. Reframe solution-designs 3. Re-evaluate solution-designs 4. Refine solution-designs E. Select Optimal Solution-Design F. State Solution

It should be noted that a few experts have different views about what "creative problem solving" entails. In his book, *The Path of Least Resistance: Learning to Become the Creative Force in Your Own Life*, Robert Fritz concludes that there is a profound difference between "problem solving" and creating, and he believes that experts are in error when they speak of "creative" problem solving. He views problem solving as taking action to have something go away – the problem. Creativity, he argues, is taking action to have something come into being – the creation (Fritz, 31). Readers who want to explore a somewhat unusual and provocative view of this topic may find Fritz's book quite interesting.

For other readings on the creative problem solving process see Higgins, 18-27; Bransford and Stein, 19-39; Dacey, 107-134; and Stein (1), 13-39.

1.3.15.2 Favorable conditions for creative problem solving

One researcher has described the process of creativity as a system involving a person who shapes or designs his environment by transforming basic problems into fruitful outcomes facilitated by a stimulating climate. A creative climate has been defined by another researcher as the conditions that facilitate and stimulate creativity. In this sub-section, we shall explore some of the conditions that facilitate and stimulate reframing of situations.

To understand what conditions facilitate creativity in a group dynamic situation (such as a mediation) it may be helpful to focus first on those conditions that research has shown as suppressing creativity in an organizational context. Four such management behaviors have been identified as: (1) latent fear and distrust; (2) restricted flow of communication; (3) attempted imposition of motivation; and (4) attempted control of behavior. Coincidentally, these appear to be four of the conditions, which are at, work in preventing early settlements of litigated disputes. This type of management attitude tends to produce both dependent and rebellious behavior.

In contrast, behavioral research has identified four management behaviors that facilitate and promote creativity in an organization context: (1) trusting, (2) open, (3) allowing, and (4) interdependent actions. Research suggests that, in general, the more the manager creates conditions in which persons initiate, feel responsible for achieving goals, and feel free to create their own goals, the more the persons create the internal conditions which maximize the creativity potential (Gibb 23, 29-30).

Research conducted in an educational setting has suggested the following specific behaviors as facilitating and stimulating creativity:

- Rewarding diverse contributions
- Helping creative persons recognize the importance of their own talents
- Making use of opportunities
- Holding to purposes
- Avoiding equating divergence with delinquency
- Reducing or eliminating emphasis on sex roles
- Respecting unusual questions
- Respecting unusual ideas
- Showing that ideas have value
- Allowing performance to occur without constant threat of evaluation
(Taylor and Getzels, 19; 26)

A very important aspect of facilitating creativity in problem solving is using and motivating the use of the problem finding skill in ourselves and in other problem solving participants (Cooley (4))

1.3.15.3 The problem finding skill

Perhaps without knowing it, a mediator employs the skill of problem finding and assists disputants to employ it. Problem finding is an important aspect of problem design. To use this skill effectively requires creativity and the ability to reframe situations. Mediators must also be able to identify disputants who possess this skill and to motivate their use of it in problem solving. The problem finding skill is used particularly in relation to discovered problems (See Section 1.3.7). Very little theoretical and almost no empirical work has been conducted regarding discovered problems. However, because the mediator's work often entails discovering problems and dealing with them once discovered, one of the available, highly regarded empirical studies deserves comment here (Cooley (4); Runco, 69).

After completing a study with children and formulating the model of presented and discovered problems, University of Chicago researcher J. Getzels, assisted by M. Csikszentmihalyi, embarked on a substantial empirical study of creativity involving artists. The focus of their research was to observe the process of the artists drawing of pictures. As the researchers explained:

> Drawing a picture may be seen as a process of solution to a problem...It may be assumed...that if the artist begins a painting as a process of personal discovery of an aesthetic problem, his work will be relatively more original than if he begins a painting to fit a standard aesthetic problem. In a sense, in the first case he is working with what we have called a 'discovered problem,' in the second with a 'presented problem.'

The researchers thus sought to determine individual differences among the art students in problem finding at the beginning of their artistic task. The goal was to see whether systematic relationships existed between the quality of the problems and the quality of the solutions, in terms of the finished drawings.

The methodology of the study was relatively simple. A "core sample" of 179 students of the Art Institute of Chicago were permitted to select an object to draw from a table on which some 30 *still-life* objects were placed. An observer took notes and photographs of each artist's behavior. It soon became apparent that there were readily observable individual differences in the way artists behaved, even before they turned to the task of drawing. The differences observed in the pre-drawing stage fell into three categories:

- *Handling of objects (to be drawn):* Some artists handled as few as two objects; others handled as many as nineteen. The researchers assumed that in order to discover a more original problem the artist had to consider a great number of possible stimuli.

- *Interacting with objects:* Some artists simply picked up the objects, took them to a table and immediately began to draw. Others rolled the objects in their hands, threw them up in the air, held them against the light, smelled them, bit into them, felt their texture, moved their parts, turned them upside down, etc. The researchers presumed that one had to explore the greatest number and variety of problematic elements in order to discover the more original problem.

- *Selecting an object:* Popular or cliche objects, like a leather-bound book, a bunch of grapes, and a wooden ball were chosen by many of the artists. Some artists, on the other hand, appeared to seek out original objects. The researchers presumed that an artist who used only popular stimuli would be more likely to design a presented problem rather than a discovered problem, and the resulting drawing would be less original.

The researchers referred to these three distinct types of behaviors as problem finding stage or discovery orientation in problem formulation.

With respect to what the researchers referred to as the problem solution stage (behavior at the drawing board), similar sharp differences in behavior were observed among the artists. Two of these differences were as follows:

- Some artists changed their position, the material they used, and the composition of the objects. Others made no changes whatsoever.

- Some of the drawings were completely structured after as little as 11% of the total drawing time had elapsed. The final structure of other drawings was not recognized until 74% of the time had elapsed. Researchers assumed that the delay in closure was evidence that the artist was still keeping the problem open still problem finding even while the artist was drawing.

Based on the information developed in the experiment, the researchers concluded that "[e]ach of the behavioral variables of problem finding is significantly related to the ratings in originality and overall aesthetic value; [and] one of the problem finding variables is related to craftsmanship." Similar effects were found in the relationships between problem finding at the problem solution stage of the drawing and from the interviews." From this data, the researchers further concluded that "[p]roblem finding appears to be a crucial component of creativity, and what is more, it can be observed and assessed with satisfactory reliability and validity" (Cooley (4), 268; and sources cited).

1.3.16 Creative skills

It has been said that highly creative persons stress their inventiveness, independence, individuality, enthusiasm, determination, and industry. They also have a preference for cognitive complexity and for rich, dynamic, asymmetrical information as opposed to that which is simple and symmetrical. This was found to be true of creative artists as well as research scientists, architects, and writers. Creative persons also usually approve of the modern, experiential, primitive, and sensual, while disliking the aristocratic, traditional, and emotionally controlled. They also tend to reject suppression as a mechanism for the control of impulse (Taylor and Getzels, 1; 13).

As mentioned above in Section 1.3.14, T. Amabile believes that there are three primary components to being creative in problem solving: domain relevant skills, creativity relevant skills, and task motivation. These three components are defined in the chart, below.

Domain Relevant Skills	Creativity Relevant Skills	Task Motivation
Include: • Knowledge about the domain; • Technical skills required; • Special domain-relevant talent Depends on: • Innate cognitive abilities; • Innate perceptual and motor skills; • Formal and informal education	Include: • Appropriate cognitive style; • Implicit or explicit knowledge of heuristics for generating novel ideas; • Conducive work style Depends on: • Training; • Experience in idea generation; • Personality characteristics	Includes: • Attitudes toward the task; • Perceptions of own motivation for undertaking the task Depends on: • Initial level of intrinsic motivation toward the task; • Presence or absence of salient extrinsic constraints in the social environment; • Individual ability to cognitively minimize extrinsic constraints

It has also been said that creativity exists in every individual, and awaits only the proper conditions to be released and expressed. Furthermore, there are relatively low correlations between measures of IQ and creativity. In one study of creative architects, the correlation between creativity and IQ was -.08. Another study suggested that at the higher IQ levels there will be a wide range of creativity, whereas, as we go down to average IQ, and on down to lower levels, the scatter for creativity will be less and less (Taylor and Getzels, 22).

Several abilities of creative thinkers have been identified, along with these specific attributes:

- Fluency, thinking of a number of responses.
- Flexibility, seeing a number of ways circles or lines could be used.
- Originality, responding in unusual or rare ways.
- Elaboration, stating a number of details that contribute to the "story" told by the response.
- Transforming with ease from the figural to the verbal and giving expression; Synthesis or combination joining together two or more figures and making it into a coherent response.
- Unusual visualization, seeing and putting the figure in a visual perspective different from the usual.
- Internal visualization, seeing objects from the inside.
- Humor, juxtaposing of two or more incongruities.
- Extending or breaking the boundaries, getting outside the expected (also called stimulus freedom) (Torrance (2), 66-67) (Dacey and Lennon, 99-102).

In addition, effective creative problems solvers have been said to have the skills and attributes described in the following subsections.

1.3.16.1 Communication - general

In its most basic sense, communication consists of two processes: (1) receiving and interpreting information; and (2) transmitting information. The process of receiving and interpreting information consists of three component task elements:

- Receiving and interpreting verbal or auditory information (listening).
- Receiving and interpreting nonverbal information (processing sensed body language).
- Receiving and interpreting written language or visual symbols (reading).

The process of transmitting information consists of three component elements:

- Transmitting information verbally (speaking).
- Transmitting information nonverbally (use of body language).
- Transmitting information in written language or visual symbols (writing).

In creative problem solving, you perform the first three above tasks as audience; the second three tasks, as speaker or writer. If, during a negotiation or mediation for example, you consciously expend effort to accomplish each of these six tasks effectively, your chances of assisting your audiences (the other parties and their counsel) to reach a reasonable and fair settlement will be enhanced. Thus, to be an effective communicator without being imposing, domineering, or overbearing, you must concentrate on effectively: (1) listening; (2) processing sensed body language; (3) reading; (4) speaking (including questioning); (5) using body language; and (6) writing and using visual symbols (Cooley (2), 47-48).

1.3.16.2 Listening

The listening skill deserves special comment. Simply defined, listening is hearing with the mind engaged. It is both a skill and an art. As with any skill, one can improve the listening skill with practice and determined effort. As with any art, the listening art can reach a level of virtuosity through full employment of the emotional, creative, and intuitive abilities. Effective creative problem solvers normally engage in two types of listening: active and critical. Active listening involves an effort to understand and attribute meaning to the content of both the speakers' substantive concern and emotional state. Active listening requires two steps: (1) hearing and giving meaning to the content of the speaker's statements; (2) communicating the interpreted meaning back to the speaker. The reflection back is more a mirroring of what you heard rather than a parroting of what the speaker said. Critical listening occurs when you are listening to evaluate, not for pleasure. This type of listening takes effort, time, and planning (Cooley(2), 54). See also, Bergren, Cox, and Detmar, 76-90.

1.3.16.3 Learning

Lewis and Greene assert that there are two categories of learners: Groupers and Stringers. The Groupers' learning strategy involves taking a broad view of any subject they are studying. They are quick to see relationships and parallels among different areas of study, and they fare better at learning in unstructured situations that have no rigid plan. Stringers, on the other hand, prefer a systematic, methodical approach to learning. They learn best by mastering specific details before moving to more general concepts. They prefer to learn under conditions where they have to achieve a series of clearly defined goals that permit gradual accumulation of information (Lewis and Greene, 147-163).

Creative problem solvers are usually "quick studies" and they know that people have different learning styles. They know also that they have to adapt the way they present information to people so as to maximize learning possibilities. They are aware of their own learning style and they are able to identify the learning styles of the people with whom they are working. Often, creative problem solvers will organize written or verbal material to match individual learning styles. See Bransford and Stein, 163-86; Robertson, 81-104.

1.3.16.4 Understanding

Effective creative problem solvers know that there is a difference between learning certain concepts and phenomena, and being able to *understand* and apply them. They also know that there are different levels of understanding of acquired knowledge. Knowledge ordinarily can be mastered at different levels of precision, and the degree of precision depends on the uses to which the knowledge will be put. Some people acquire precise knowledge by rote, but they have no idea why they are learning it or how to imagine future uses. For example, assume that a group of people read an article about veins and arteries. After reading it, some people may feel that they have learned enough when they realize that veins and arteries are parts of a human body as opposed to parts of a car engine. Others may not feel they understand enough until they come to understand that veins and arteries carry blood rather than serve some other bodily function. Still others will not be satisfied with their understanding until they know how veins and arteries are similar and different in structure and function. Depending on the future use to which they want to apply their acquired knowledge, they may or may not have an adequate understanding of the topic of veins and arteries (Bransford and Stein, 163-185).

Lewis and Greene believe that in order for a problem solver to acquire knowledge effectively, it is essential for him or her to *understand* it first. Seeming initially to be something of a paradox, their point is that understanding is not necessarily the *result of* learning. They suggest that in order to understand something properly you must know what you are storing in your memory. They also assert that the key to adequate understanding of acquired concepts is to break those concepts into smaller and smaller parts until every confusion is resolved and all uncertainty vanishes. In their view there is no such thing as a difficult problem; there are only problem solvers who travel "too far too fast" and fail to break the problem into its simpler components (Lewis and Greene, 169).

1.3.16.5 Remembering

Effective creative problem solvers use categorization strategies to remember various items. For example, assume that someone gave you a list of 25 words and told you to study them for two minutes and then repeat the words from memory. As a creative problem solver, you would sort the words into one or more categories to remember them. Typical categories that you might use would be to remember the words that: (1) contain at least one "e"; (2) have two syllables; or (3) relate to one another as a separate concept (i.e. traffic and jam). Another strategy might be to remember the words in alphabetical order or to form mnemonics or acronyms. The strategies would vary depending on the nature of the items to be remembered (Bransford and Stein, 135-36).

1.3.16.6 Ability to recognize and form patterns

The ability to recognize visual and aural patterns enables the problem solver to make predictions and form expectations. Creative problem solvers derive general principles of perception and action from recognized patterns, and then base their expectations on those patterns. Then they try to fit new observations and experiences into these expectations. Discovery occurs when something unexpected about their observations and experiences forces them to make another pattern. The new pattern yields connections between things previously perceived as being unrelated. Psychologists call this making a new pattern a "gestalt shift" in which the same sensory information can take on two or more noncommensurate meanings (Root-Bernsteins, 92-94).

Forming patterns is essential to creative problem solving in every discipline, and it is nothing more than combining two or more structural elements and/or functional operations. The creative problem solver juxtaposes one element or operation with another in a consistent way and yields a synthetic pattern that may be much more than, and far different from, the sum of its parts. In this way, the creative problem solver uncovers new ideas and new ways of looking at things (Root-Bernsteins, 115-16; 132).

1.3.16.7 Ability to abstract

Physicist Werner Heisenberg has defined abstracting as "the possibility of considering an object or group of objects under one viewpoint while disregarding all other properties of the object. The essence of abstraction consists in singling out one feature, which in contrast to other properties, is considered to be particularly important" (Root-Bernsteins, 72-73). His definition applies to any discipline and is an essential attribute to be acquired by the creative problem solver. Knowing what abstracting is constitutes only half the battle. The other half is learning how to find the simple concepts hiding among complex expressions. To find the abstraction, the creative problem solver has to begin with reality, and then use some tool to pare away the excess to reveal a critical, often surprising essence (Root-Bernsteins, 73; 78; 90).

As one expert source teaches, "Artists do it; writers do it; scientists, mathematicians, and dancers do it. And they all do it in the same basic way. You can too... Choose your subject and your abstracting tool; think about them realistically; play around with their various properties and characteristics; get at what might be the most essential; then consider and reconsider your results from a distance of time or space" (Root-Bernsteins, 90).

1.3.16.8 Ability to analogize

This topic, so important to effective creative problem solving, is addressed in more detail elsewhere in this handbook (See Section 2.2.8). Suffice to say that, in its most general sense, analogy refers to a functional resemblance between things that are otherwise unlike. Analogies show a correspondence of inner relationship or of function between two or more different phenomena or complex sets of phenomena. Interesting analogies reveal not mere resemblances but unapparent relationships between abstract functions, one of which is understood, the other not. They are different than similes, which are resemblances between things based upon observed characteristics such as color or form. If one would say "an orange is like a grapefruit," the person has created a simile. If the person said, "an orange is like the sweetness of life," the person has created an analogy because life may be metaphorically "sweet" in that we are pleased by it even though it is not literally sensed by our taste buds. It is this ability to draw interesting analogies that enhances creative problem solving (Root-Bernsteins, 137, 142-43). See also Ward, Smith, and Vaid, 403-60; Robertson, 131-150.

1.3.16.9 Speaking/questioning

Creative problem solvers are curious and inquisitive. They continually search for the essence of things through a questioning procedure called "reframing." They accomplish reframing through the use of Socratic questioning techniques, or the Socratic Method. The technical name for the Socratic Method is the dialectic. Pure dialectic is a form of conversation, proceeding on premises supplied by one of the parties, which does not require any special knowledge on the part of either the questioner or the answerer(s). Questions are usually posited as requests for a judgment on a particular statement or for the definition of a term or object (especially in the early stages of the conversation). The answerer must always give an answer, he is expected to answer truthfully, and he is required to remain consistent with his original hypothesis (provided by the initial series of open ended questions). The following techniques of the dialectic, or Socratic Method, relate directly to creative problem solving: (1) Recollection; (2) Irony; (3) Elenchus; (4) Epagoge; (5) Analogy; and (6) Collection and Division (also called Synthesis and Division). These techniques are explained in detail in Cooley (2), 69-85.

1.3.16.10 Empathizing

In problem solving jargon, empathizing means the ability to see the world through other people's eyes. Empathy can be used to facilitate emotional and intellectual understanding in problem solving. It is a way to get into the minds of people. It can also be a kind of visual play-acting (fantasizing) with physical objects, in order to acquire a different view or perspective. To gain better insight into a problem, Albert Einstein, for example, would view the universe from the perspective of a photon. Inventor Charles Kettering, the director of research at General Motors for many decades, would reprimand engineers who came to him with complex calculations and models by saying, "Yes, but do you know what it *feels* like to be a piston in an engine?" It is said that Alexander Graham Bell was so totally absorbed in his work that he *became* the systems he studied. Thus, the creative problem solver must be able to fantasize to become one with (to empathize with) what he or she is studying (Root-Bernsteins, 187; 188; 196; 197).

1.3.16.11 Intuitive and insightful

Intuition is defined as a "mode of understanding or knowing characterized as direct and immediate and occurring without conscious thought or judgment" (Reber and Reber, 369; Gregory (1), 389). Creative problem solvers often have an intuitive sense, as they begin their creative work, about what their final product will be. Intuition is like a rough estimate that necessarily entails some margin of error. But even so, intuition can be relied on for important purposes, such as being a guide to decision making in the process of attaining creative results. Intuition is distinguishable from insight, but sometimes the two phenomena overlap. Intuition entails vague and tacit knowledge, whereas insight involves sudden, and usually clear, awareness. In the context of the creative process, intuition is thought to precede insight. Creative intuitions also serve important cognitive functions, such as setting up preliminary boundaries for exploration and preventing run-away divergent thinking (Runco and Pritzker, 89-91), (Myers, 51-63), (Gladwell).

1.3.16.12 Perceptive

Perception consists, collectively, of "those processes that give coherence and unity to sensory input ... [and it] covers the entire sequence of events from the presentation of a physical stimulus to the phenomenological experiencing of it ... [and it includes] physical, physiological, neurological, sensory, cognitive and affective components" (Reber and Reber, 519). See also, Gregory (1), 598-611; Montuori and Purser, 91-178.

1.3.16.13 Imaginative

Imagination is defined as the "process of recombining memories of past experience and previously formed images into novel constructions ... [and] [o]ften qualifiers are appended for clarity, e.g. *anticipatory* for the future, *reproductive* for the past, and *creative* for the novel." (Reber and Reber, 342). In creative problem solving, imagination often serves as a form of playful analogical thinking that draws on previous experiences, but combines them in unusual ways, resulting in new patterns of meaning. Imagination may lead to creative intuitions (Runco and Pritzker, 92), (Osborn (1), 27-38)

1.3.16.14 Ability to model, play, transform, synthesize

Creative problem solvers take advantage of an opportunity to construct a model of a problem confronted or a solution proposed. This model may be as simple as a two-dimensional or three-dimensional sketch, or as complicated as a computer program. A model could also be created in the form of a list of words that helps the problem solver to visualize and create new ways of looking at things (Root-Bernsteins, 245; Russ, 1-42).

Play is engaging in action simply for the fun of doing it – the enjoyment of doing and making without responsibility. There is no success or failure in play. It is frivolous, wandering according to the whims of curiosity and interest. Though it has no inherent goal, the whimsical nature of play may spark new ideas, new patterns, and new ways of looking at things. Creative problem solvers engage in play to allow ideas to find themselves (Root-Bernsteins, 248).

Creative problem solvers engage freely in transforming ideas and sets of data. They *try on for size* different characteristics and uses of the ideas and data. The more unexpected the transformation in problem solving, the greater the likelihood that a surprising insight will emerge. Because people who engage in problem solving have different talents and abilities, a variety of transformations on a single idea will create meaningful connections to more people than will a single formulation. This is the power of transformation. (Root-Bernsteins, 285; 289).

Effective creative problem solvers are able to synthesize easily – that is, they make associations and connections between sense and knowledge. While each of the senses perceives the world differently and discretely, they must, in fact, be coordinated for us to be able to think and act reasonably. This union of the senses are forms of synesthesia, which is defined as varied and idiosyncratic manifestations of interfused sensations. Creative problem solvers know that no difficult problem can be approached by analysis, emotion, or tradition alone. Innovation is always transdisciplinary and multimodal and the product of synthetic thinking. (Root-Bernsteins, 305; 314).

1.3.16.15 Possess multiple intelligences

As noted in the introduction to Subsection 1.3.16 above, creative people do not necessarily have high IQs. Howard Gardner of the Harvard Project on Human Potential has proposed a better way than an IQ test to identify a creative or gifted person. He has isolated seven discrete intelligences that he believes can serve as a measure of a person's overall intelligence and his or her penchant for creativity. The seven intelligences are: linguistic, musical, logical-mathematical, spatial, bodily kinesthetic, intrapersonal, and interpersonal. The higher the aptitude of a person with respect to each of these seven intelligence categories, the more likely the person will be more intelligent and a more able to be a creative problem solver (Cooley(1), Cum. Supp. § 2:04.50). See also Gardner, 73-276; Armstrong, 7-26.

1.3.16.16 Tolerant of ambiguity

An ambiguous situation has been described as one in which no framework or structure exists to help direct one's decisions and actions. In such situations, relevant facts are missing, rules are unclear, and the right procedures are unknown or unavailable. New and old behavioral research have shown consistently that the ability to remain open-minded in the face of ambiguity (and even to enjoy it) is a hallmark of the creative personality. The problem solver's inclination to find strangeness interesting or exciting, rather than frightening, fosters the ability to react creatively (Dacey and Lennon, 98-99).

1.3.16.17 Capacity for risk taking

Research has demonstrated that problem solvers who take tiny or huge risks are less likely to be successful in their efforts than those who take moderate risks. Failing to take sensible risks as a problem solver may lead to a sense of security, but often not to a creative solution (Dacey and Lennon, 103-06).

1.3.16.18 Preference for disorder

As surprising as it seems, creative problem solvers normally prefer problems having complexity and asymmetry rather than problems or situations that are simple and symmetrical. The reason why they favor disorder and complexity of information is that they have an inner desire to integrate it into a richer, higher order, yet simple synthesis. It has been said that creative persons like to create order in disorder and disorder in order (Dacey and Lennon, 106-07).

1.3.16.19 Perseverance

Much research has shown that successful creators are very perseverant in the face of frustration and even obstacles that might ordinarily be thought to be overwhelming. Invariably creative problem solvers invest intensely in their work with almost obsessive perseverance. When they encounter obstacles, they tend to go against what everyone else is doing and exhibit a great power to persevere on the path they believe to be correct. They are not afraid to suffer many failures before achieving success (Dacey and Lennon, 111-12).

1.3.16.20 Courage

Torrance stated that "after all the years he ... studied creativity and creative people, he found that courage was the most essential quality for a creator's success" (Dacey and Lennon, 112). The person who proposes an original idea must have the courage to be a minority of one. Creative problem solvers press on toward their goal, despite rejection of their ideas, ridicule, and humiliation (Dacey and Lennon, 111-14).

1.4 ROLE OF INDUCTIVE AND DEDUCTIVE REASONING IN CREATIVE PROBLEM SOLVING

1.4.1 General

Edward de Bono, in *Lateral Thinking: Creativity Step by Step* (p. 40), has said, "In order to be able to use the provocative qualities of lateral thinking one must also be able to follow up with the selective qualities of vertical thinking."

In order to fully grasp the concept of vertical thinking, we need to be acquainted initially with a few basic definitions. Vertical thinking is applied logic. Logic is the study of arguments; or, more precisely, of the quality of their reasoning. An argument may be defined as a sequence of declarative sentences, one of which called *the conclusion,* is intended to be evidentially supported by any number of others, called premises. Reasoning is the process by which the premises and conclusion are formulated or evaluated as to validity (Cooley (1), § 2:05, 49).

Every argument is either deductive, inductive, or fallacious. Traditionally, logicians defined arguments as inductive if they moved from specific premises to general conclusions and "deductive" if they moved from general premises to specific conclusions. These definitions have been generally abandoned in modern times. Now, a deductive argument is defined as a valid argument, that is – the premises, if true, guarantee the proof of the conclusion (Cooley (1), § 2:05, 49). Consider this example of a deductive argument:

All mediators think effectively.
Robert is a mediator.
Therefore, Robert thinks effectively.

In this example it is impossible for the argument's basic premises to be true and its conclusion false. Inductive and fallacious arguments, on the other hand, are invalid arguments. The inductive argument is invalid because the basic premises, if true, do not guarantee the truth of the conclusion, they only make the truth of the conclusion more likely than not; that is, its conclusion has a between fifty and one-hundred percent of being true. Consider this example:

Ninety-five percent of mediators think effectively.
Robert is a mediator.
Therefore, Robert thinks effectively.

This is an inductive (invalid) argument because it is possible for its basic premises to be true and its conclusion false. Robert may be among the five percent of mediators who do not think effectively; but the probability that Robert falls within the ninety- five percent that do think effectively is greater than fifty percent. Both of these examples demonstrate what is termed rational arguments, whose basic premises, if true, provide good evidence for their conclusions (Cooley (1), §2:05, 49- 50).

Deductive and inductive arguments are rational arguments. A fallacious argument, however, is an irrational argument. It is neither deductive nor inductive. Even if the basic premises of a fallacious argument were true, there would be a fifty percent chance or less, based on the premises, that the conclusion would be true. The probability of the truth of the conclusion of a fallacious argument lies in the interval zero to fifty percent. Consider this rather extreme example:

No mediators think effectively.
Robert is a mediator.
Robert thinks effectively.

Here, the probability of the truth of the conclusion (even if the premises are true) is zero. Thus, the argument is fallacious (Cooley (1), § 2:05, 50).

It is important not to use the terms true or false to describe the strength of reasoning of an argument. Those two terms apply only to individual statements (premises or conclusions). Again, arguments are either "valid" or "invalid." For the purposes of our discussion here, there is no such thing as a valid premise or false argument. Also, just because an argument is classified invalid does not mean it is worthless. Arguments, which are invalid, used as a term of logic, range from those whose conclusions would certainly be false even if their basic premises were true (zero percent probability) to those whose conclusions would almost certainly be true (near one-hundred percent probability). Some invalid arguments (say in the range of ninety to ninety-nine percent valid) are, in fact, very good arguments (Cooley (1), § 205, 51).

One other point should be made. As creative problem solvers, we should be interested in determining the overall strength of arguments. The question of strength consists of two component issues: (1) are the premises true?; and (2) how good is the reasoning? We have just learned how to determine an answer to issue (2) (the strength of the reasoning) through classification of an argument as deductive, inductive, or fallacious (regardless of the truth of the premises). Answering question (1) is usually not a matter of logic, but rather of science and common sense. Of course in certain instances, before an overall conclusion may be drawn in an argument, the truth or falsity of a basic premise may have to be proven. Stated more simply, the basic premise will first have to be a conclusion logically derived, before it can be a basic premise as part of a larger argument. Finally, there is one more term that is essential to insert in our logic vocabulary: sound argument. A sound argument must meet two requirements: (1) all its basic premises must be true; and (2) it must be deductive. Construction of such arguments must be a core talent of the creative problem solver in the analytical and decision making phases of creative problem solving. Because the deductive argument is one of the quintessential ingredients of sound argument, the remainder of this section will focus on the classical structure of the deductive argument. For some readers, this will be your first introduction to formal logic; for others, it will be a refresher mini-course preparing you for the broader aspects of vertical thinking (Cooley (1), § 205, 51-52).

1.4.2 Inductive reasoning

Before we proceed through the classical structures of deductive reasoning, it might be helpful to look at inductive reasoning in a little more depth. The description that follows is adapted from Jeffrey Bisanz, Gay L. Bisanz, Connie A. Korpan, "Inductive Reasoning" in Sternberg (3), 179-183.

Induction is an important function of cognition. Not only is it central to many types of problem solving and learning, but it has also long been considered as an important index of cognitive development and of individual differences in intelligence. Currently, inductive thinking processes are recognized as responsible for a person's ability to generate concepts and to provide links between concepts and actions, as well as the ability to combine sensory and memorial information in percepts.

Considering the importance of induction to cognition, one would think that there would be a vast amount of experimentation and a large body of literature on the subject. Actually, quite the opposite is true. Inexplicably, the domain of reasoning – including inductive reasoning – has been historically isolated from other domains of cognitive psychology. Presently, however, because of advances in information processing and cognitive science, the possibilities for increased studies in inductive reasoning are much improved.

Currently, there are two approaches to the study of induction, the cognitive-components approach and the pragmatic approach. These two approaches have considerable potential for linking the study of inductive reasoning with the mainstream lines of cognitive research. In the cognitive-components approach, commonly known methods from the information-processing toolbox are used to develop detailed descriptions of the processes and representations used to solve induction problems. In contrast, in the pragmatic approach, researchers have attempted to broaden the scope of inquiry to include a wider range of phenomena than have been traditionally studied under the heading of induction. This has the potential of establishing the study of induction as a vital subject in the domains of cognitive science. Creative problem solvers need to follow the growth and results of these studies as they begin to define the role of inductive reasoning in effective creative problem solving.

It is very important to the creative problem solver to understand the *interaction* of inductive and deductive reasoning. The following example is adapted from Sternberg (3), page 181. Let us suppose that a teacher presents children with a variety of small objects and a bowl of water. The children's task is to discover the characteristics of objects that float as distinguished from objects that do not float. Thus, the children must conduct research through experimentation to solve the problem. After experimenting, the children might conclude that wooden things float by the following reasoning:

P1: The cork is wood and it floats.
P2: The cube is wood and it floats.
C3: Therefore wooden things float.

P1 and P2 are "premises", and C3 is the children's conclusion. Note that C3 is an inference the children made about wooden things, and it is based on two instances in their "study." This conclusion is inductive in that it is an inference of a generalized conclusion from particular instances (or reasoning from part to whole). Note also that the children, in reaching their conclusion, engaged in precisely the type of hypothesis-generating process that characterizes scientific investigations.

The children could continue their research and conduct another experiment to test the hypothesis (C3) by finding another wooden object (toy wooden fish) and by reasoning whether it should also float. The children might conclude that the toy wooden fish floats by the following reasoning:

P4: Wooden things float.
P5: The toy fish is wooden.
C6: The toy fish floats.

This conclusion, C6, was reached by deductive reasoning. These two examples of reasoning demonstrate how inductive and deductive reasoning *interact*. It is important to note that the student's inductive conclusion, C3, becomes the first premise, P4, for deductive reasoning. This is an important principle to keep in mind in creative problem solving.

In conclusion, it should be noted that there are three core characteristics of inductive reasoning. The first characteristic is that inductive processes produce a net increase in knowledge. In the children's floatation problem above, the conclusion reached by inductive reasoning (C3) is a proposition about the nature of the world that is new to the child and thus represents a significant increase in the children's knowledge. In contrast, deductive reasoning never results in increased semantic information, although it may result in explicit statements of knowledge that are more or less implicit in the premises.

The second core characteristic of inductive reasoning is that it is risky, in the sense that it may or may not be true, even if the premises are true. For example, if the wooden cube in the children's floatation problem above would have been ebony, it would not have floated and conclusion C3 would be wrong – or more likely, the children could not have drawn the conclusion, by induction, that "wooden things float." As one cognition study reported, "induction should come with a government health warning" (Quoted in Sternberg (3), 182). Some experts say that it makes more sense to discuss the *strength* of an inductive argument, that is, how compelling the conclusion is given the premises, rather than the *validity* of an inductive argument. Inductive processes, therefore, produce new but inevitably uncertain knowledge.

Finally, the third core characteristic of inductive reasoning is that inductive processes must be severely constrained if they are to produce plausible conclusions. An infinite number of inductive conclusions, most of them irrelevant and/or trivial, can be generated from a set of premises. For example, the children in the above example could have concluded by induction that "everything floats." Thus when reasoning inductively, every effort must be made to generate only a plausible conclusion or sets of conclusions.

1.4.3 Classical structures of deductive reasoning

Two special forms of deductive reasoning are the syllogism and the enthymeme. By using these structures for the purpose of analysis, we can apply the appropriate tests of formal validity to the reasoning we encounter as we and other problem solving participants explore the problem. We will consider three types of syllogisms: (1) categorical, (2) disjunctive, and (3) conditional, followed by a consideration of the second special form of deductive reasoning, the enthymeme. But first, we will consider the general structure of all types of syllogisms (Cooley (1), § 2:05, 52-61 and sources cited there).

1.4.3.1 The syllogism in general

A syllogism is a systematic arrangement of arguments:

- A major premise, which is a proposition stating a generalization (All A's are B's)
- A minor premise, which is a proposition stating a specific instance related to the generalization (C is an A)
- A conclusion, which necessarily must follow from these premises (Therefore, C is a B)

The following statement is an example of syllogistic reasoning:

All legally insane persons are incompetent to negotiate binding agreements (major premise).
John Doe is legally insane (minor premise).
Therefore, John Doe is incompetent to negotiate a binding agreement (conclusion)

In the various examples of syllogisms that follow, assume that each premise is absolutely true (Cooley (1), § 2:05, 52-53).

1.4.3.2 The categorical syllogism

In the categorical syllogism, the major premise is an unqualified proposition. Such propositions are characterized by words like all, every, each, or any, either directly expressed or clearly implied. Some thoughtful scholars object to this aspect of the categorical syllogism, maintaining that it is very difficult to make unqualified generalizations. It might be pointed out, for example, that all legally insane persons are not alike. The nature and degree of their illnesses, the types of treatment they require, and the possibilities for their recovery are quite different. They are identical, however, in that they are all incompetent to negotiate binding agreements as long as they are legally insane. Thus, for the purpose of negotiating binding agreements, we treat all legally insane persons in the same manner. As a practical consideration, we treat many matters as identical and make unqualified generalizations about them. The problem of the creative problem solver is to determine when it is practical or necessary to make unqualified generalizations, within a specific context and when it is prudent or necessary to recognize the differences in apparently identical matters. Several tests may be applied to determine the validity or invalidity of the categorical syllogism. They are:

Test No. 1: The categorical syllogism must have three terms – no more and no less. These terms may be represented by the letters A, B, and C, as follows: Major Term: B; Middle Term: A; Minor Term: C. Consider the following example:

Major Premise: All A's are B's
Minor Premise: C is an A
Conclusion: Therefore, C is a B.

Test No. 2: Every term must be used twice in the categorical syllogism; no more and no less.

Test No. 3: A term must be used only once in any premise.

Test No. 4: The middle term must be used in at least one premise in an unqualified or universal sense. In the syllogism on legal insanity above, the middle term was correctly distributed, referring to all legally insane persons. The middle term is incorrectly distributed in the following example, because (A) is qualified (i.e. "some"). Consequently, the conclusion of this syllogism is invalid.

Major Premise: Some politicians (A) are corrupt (B).
Minor Premise: Richard Roe (C) is a politician (A).
Conclusion: Therefore, Richard Roe (C) is corrupt (B).

Test No. 5: A term may be distributed in the conclusion only if it has been distributed in the major or minor premise. The following is an example of an illicit major; a major term that is distributed in the conclusion but not in the major premise.

Major Premise: All communists (A) want the United States to cut defense spending (B).
Minor Premise: Congressman Zilch (C) is not a communist (A).
Conclusion: Therefore, Congressman Zilch (C) does not want the United States to cut defense spending (B).

When the major premise is fully stated; All communists are among those who want the United States to cut defense spending; it becomes readily apparent that the major term (B) is not used in a universal sense in the major premise and thus may not be distributed in the conclusion. Congressman Zilch might be a pacifist. The following is an example of an illicit minor; distributed in the conclusion but not in the minor premise.

Major Premise: All union presidents (A) favor the union shop (B).
Minor Premise: All union presidents (A) are members of unions (C).
Conclusion: Therefore, all members of unions (C) favor the union shop (B).

In this example, the minor term (C) is not distributed in the minor premise, but is distributed in the conclusion. When the minor premise is fully stated; All union presidents are some members of unions, it becomes readily apparent that the minor term (C) has not been distributed and that consequently the conclusion is invalid. The only conclusion that could be drawn from these premises is that some union members favor the union shop.

Test No. 6: At least one of the premises must be affirmative. Obviously, no valid conclusion can be drawn from two negative premises, as illustrated below.

Major Premise: No Democratic Senators (A) will vote for this bill (B).
Minor Premise: Senator Eliot (C) is not a Democratic Senator (A).
Conclusion: Therefore, Senator Eliot (C) will -------------?

Test No. 7: If one premise is negative, the conclusion must be negative.

Major Premise: No Republican Senators (A) voted for this bill (B).
Minor Premise: Senator Eliot (C) is a Republican Senator (A).
Conclusion: Therefore, Senator Eliot (C) did not vote for this bill (B)
(Cooley (1), § 2:05, 53-55).

1.4.3.3 The disjunctive syllogism

The disjunctive syllogism is one with a major premise containing mutually exclusive alternatives. The separation of alternatives is usually indicated by such words as either, or, neither, but, and although, either expressly stated or clearly implied.

Major Premise: Either Congress will amend this bill or the President will veto it.
Minor Premise: Congress will not amend this bill.
Conclusion: Therefore, the President will veto it.

Several tests may be applied to determine the validity or invalidity of the disjunctive syllogism:

Test No. 1: The major premise of the disjunctive syllogism must include all of the possible alternatives. Here is an example:

Major Premise: We must either have gas rationing or gas shortages.
Minor Premise: We do not want gas shortages.
Conclusion: Therefore, we must have gas rationing.

The major premise here does not include all possible alternatives. There are other ways of dealing with gas shortages.

Test No. 2: The alternatives presented in the disjunctive syllogism must be mutually exclusive. In the syllogism above, gas rationing and gas shortages were not mutually exclusive. They argued that gas rationing merely exacerbates the gas shortage by adding the problems of bureaucracy and blackmarkets.

Test No. 3: The minor premise must affirm or contradict one of the alternatives given in the major premise. If the minor premise neither affirms nor contradicts one of the alternatives in the major premise, no valid conclusion is possible, as illustrated below:

Major Premise: Congress must either raise taxes or reduce federal expenditures.
Minor Premise: Congressmen will not cut their own salaries.
Conclusion: Therefore, Congress must --------------?

Since Congressional salaries are only a minor part of all federal expenditures, the premise that congressmen will not cut their own salaries might more accurately be phrased as "Congressmen will not reduce some federal expenditures." Even though congressmen will not cut their own salaries, it is possible for them to reduce other federal expenditures; therefore, this premise neither affirms nor contradicts one of the alternatives in the major premise (Cooley (1), § 2:05, 55-56).

1.4.3.4 The conditional syllogism

The conditional syllogism, also known as the hypothetical syllogism, is a syllogism in which the major premise deals with uncertain or hypothetical events that may or may not exist or happen. The conditional event is usually indicated by if, assuming, supposing, or similar concepts, either expressly stated or clearly implied. Consider this example: Resolved: That the federal government should adopt a program of compulsory wage and price controls:

Major Premise: If the present measures have checked inflation, then we will not need compulsory wage and price controls.
Minor Premise: Present measures have not checked inflation.
Conclusion: Therefore, we will need compulsory wage and price controls.

The major premise of the conditional syllogism contains an antecedent statement, which expresses the conditional or hypothetical event under consideration, and a consequent statement, which expresses the event that is maintained as necessarily following the antecedent. In the above example, the antecedent statement begins with the word "if" and the consequent statement begins with the word "then." The "if-then" relationship is a convenient way of expressing the major premise in a conditional syllogism. Several tests may be applied to determine the validity or invalidity of a conditional syllogism, as discussed below.

Test No. 1: The minor premise must affirm the antecedent or deny the consequent. If the minor premise affirms the antecedent, the conclusion must affirm the consequent; if the minor premise denies the consequent, the conclusion must deny the antecedent, as illustrated below:

Major Premise: If the interest rate on treasury notes increases, then more of these notes will be purchased.
Minor Premise: The interest rate on treasury notes will increase.
Conclusion: Therefore, more of these notes will be purchased.

Note that, in this case, the minor premise affirms the antecedent and the conclusion affirms the consequent. The following example does just the opposite:

Major Premise: If compulsory wage and price controls are to be effective, then blackmarketing must be prevented.
Minor Premise: Blackmarketing cannot be prevented.
Conclusion: Therefore, compulsory wage and price controls cannot be effective.

Test No. 2: If the minor premise denies the antecedent or affirms the consequent, no valid conclusion can be drawn. For example:

Major Premise: If the interest rate on treasury notes increases, then more of these notes will be purchased.
Minor Premise: The interest rate on treasury notes will not increase.
Conclusion: Therefore, ---------------------?

In this example, the absence of an increase in interest rates will not lead to more of these notes being purchased; but (since a change in any of a number of fiscal or monetary policies might lead to more of these notes being purchased), one cannot conclude that more notes will not be purchased. Thus, when the minor premise denies the antecedent, no valid conclusion can be drawn. Now consider this example:

Major Premise: If compulsory wage and price controls are to be effective, then blackmarketing must be prevented.
Minor Premise: Blackmarketing can be prevented.
Conclusion: Therefore, ------------?

Even if blackmarketing could be prevented, there are numerous other factors that might prevent the effective operation of a program of compulsory wage and price controls. Thus, when the minor premise affirms the consequent, no valid conclusion can be drawn (Cooley (1), § 2:05, 56-57).

1.4.3.5 The Enthymeme

Apart from syllogisms discussed in the preceding subsections, the second special form of deductive reasoning is the enthymeme. There are two definitions of the enthymeme, both of which the creative problem solver should be aware. As a practical matter, people rarely talk in syllogisms. They are more likely to express their arguments in less than complete syllogisms. Further, there are many situations in which people must deal with probabilities rather than certainties. In these circumstances they make use of the enthymeme. The two definitions of an enthymeme are:

- The enthymeme is a truncated syllogism in which one of the premises or the conclusion is not stated.

- The enthymeme is a modified form of syllogism that deals with probability rather than with certainty.

In a debate on federal aid for higher education, we might hear the following argument: This plan would lead to federal control and is undesirable. Expressed in the form of an enthymeme, this argument would look like this:

Minor Premise: This plan leads to federal control.
Conclusion: Therefore, this plan is undesirable.

As negotiators or mediators encountering this enthymeme, we would promptly seek out the unstated major premise. If the unstated major premise were: Some forms of federal control are undesirable, we would recognize that the middle term is not distributed and that therefore the conclusion is formally invalid. If the unstated major premise were: All forms of federal control are undesirable, the conclusion would be formally valid, but we might wish to raise a question about the material truth of the major premise. Thus, when we encounter enthymemes in an argument, we should seek out the unstated premise and determine whether the conclusion logically follows that premise or whether the unstated premise is materially true. In discovering the unstated premise; we may open up important avenues of analysis.

The enthymeme, as the term is used in the second definition (a modified form of syllogism dealing with probability), may or may not omit one of the premises or the conclusion. This definition of the enthymeme is also of very real importance to the negotiator or mediator, who is often concerned with probability rather than certainty. Consider this example:

Major Premise: All plans that cause inflation should be rejected.

Minor Premise: This plan may cause inflation.
Conclusion: Therefore, this plan should be rejected.

Syllogistically, this argument proves absolutely nothing. It has a formal validity of zero. The syllogism is a logical instrument for dealing with certainty; it is concerned with all of the factors in a certain classification and with matters that necessarily and inevitably follow from certain premises. However, many problems the negotiator or mediator must consider are not subject to certainty or to absolute proof. If a negotiating party can establish a reasonable degree of cogency for its argument, if it can establish a reasonable probability that the plan will cause inflation, it might well prevail on its argument.

Enthymemes, like syllogisms, may be classified as categorical, disjunctive, and conditional. The same tests that would be used to determine the formal validity of a syllogism may be used to determine the formal validity of an enthymeme. Although the above-cited enthymemes are invalid as syllogisms, they are formally valid as enthymemes. Thus, if negotiating parties can establish a preponderance of probability to support their arguments, they may well persuade reasonable and prudent persons to accept their conclusions (Cooley (1), § 2:05, 57-59).

1.4.3.6 Chain of enthymemes

Frequently, arguments are stated in the form of a chain of enthymemes. A speaker may state only the conclusion of an enthymeme, use that as one premise of a second enthymeme, state the conclusion to the second enthymeme without indicating the other premise, and continue in this manner to build a chain of enthymemes. The omitted portion of the enthymeme sometimes will be readily evident and uncontestable; at other times, however, it may not be readily apparent or may be subject to refutation. Consequently, the advocate should recognize and analyze a chain of enthymemes, seek out the omitted portions of the argument, restructure the argument in syllogistic form, and apply the appropriate tests. A negotiating party will frequently find it advantageous to begin to build a chain of enthymemes in the minds of the listeners (Cooley (1), § 2:05, 59-60).

1.4.3.7 Formal validity and material truth

In the syllogisms and enthymemes considered above, it has been assumed that each premise of each syllogism is absolutely true, and that each premise of each enthymeme is probably true. If they are true, the conclusions drawn from the formally valid syllogisms are matters of absolute certainty, and the conclusions drawn from the formally valid enthymemes must be accorded the degree of cogency appropriate to the probability found in the premises. If, however, any of these premises is false, then its conclusion is worthless regardless of the formal validity of the construction. Consider this example:

Major Premise: Any child can make a spaceship.
Minor Premise: John is a child.
Conclusion: Therefore, John can make a spaceship.

This syllogism is formally valid; there is no question about that. It satisfies the tests for formal validity. Assume that John really is a child; the minor premise is then materially true. The major premise, however, has no foundation in fact. Obviously, the conclusion is worthless. It must be noted that a materially true conclusion is not proof that the premises are materially true or that the syllogism is formally valid. The proof of this conclusion must come from a source other than this syllogism. It bears repeating that in order to establish the material truth of a premise, the negotiator or mediator must apply the tests of reasoning and the tests of evidence. Since many premises are, in fact, conclusions from other syllogisms or enthymemes that may or may not have been stated in the argument, the appropriate tests of formal validity should be applied to them
(Cooley (1), § 2:05, 60-61).

1.4.4 Fallacies of reasoning

Negotiators and mediators constantly must be on guard to detect and to refrain from using or being a victim of fallacies of reasoning, also called pseudo arguments. The remainder of this section is devoted to defining the characteristics of pseudo arguments in order to more quickly detect them and mollify their negative effects (Cooley (1), § 2:06, 61-68).

Pseudo arguments are fallacies created, by accident or design, by distortion, confusion, manipulation, or avoidance of the matters at issue or by substitution of matters not germane to the issue. Some of the more common fallacies are described below.

1.4.4.1 Extension

The fallacy of extension carries an argument beyond its reasonable limits. For example, some opponents of right-to-work laws argued that these laws did not provide jobs for the unemployed. These laws were not intended to provide jobs, but merely to eliminate the requirement of union membership as a condition of employment. It would be just as reasonable to criticize Salk vaccine, a serum designed to prevent polio, because it does not prevent pneumonia.

1.4.4.2 Arguing in a circle

The fallacy of arguing in a circle occurs when two unsupported assertions are used to prove each other. For example: Because the death penalty is immoral, it should be prohibited. Because the death penalty should be prohibited, the practice of executing capital offenders is immoral."

1.4.4.3 Ignoring the issue

In mediation, sometimes a party will make a persuasive detailed argument in support of a settlement proposal. The opposing party then responds to the detailed argument by appealing to the emotions of the mediator or the opposing party, without addressing the details of the settlement proposal. The response is fallacious in the sense that it does not address the proposing party's argument, but rather ignores it.

1.4.4.4 Baiting an opponent

Sometimes negotiating parties will bait opposing parties by insulting them, attacking them personally, or doing anything that will cause the opposing parties to lose their tempers. Once parties lose their cool, they are very likely to lose control of the argument and make reckless statements that will expose their case to defeat. Negotiators can defend themselves against this kind of baiting only by holding their tempers during the argument; later, they may be able to blow off steam without damaging the case.

1.4.4.5 Repeated assertion

The fallacy of repeated assertion occurs when an untrue or partially untrue statement is repeated several times. Making a false statement three times does not make it true, but sometimes it seems truer the third time it is spoken.

1.4.4.6 Structured response

This fallacy is often found in cross examinations or in any situation where a negotiator has an opportunity to ask a series of questions. Using this fallacy, the negotiator first asks a series of unimportant questions of the responding negotiator, which the respondent must answer in a predetermined way, until the pattern of a response has been established. Then the critical question is asked. An old routine of insurance salespersons, for example, goes something like this: You love your wife, don't you? You love your children, don't you? You want your children to go to college, don't you? You want your wife to continue to live in this lovely house, don't you? If something should happen to you, you want your family to be provided for? You would still want your children to go to college? You want to provide protection for them? To be safe, hadn't you better write your name on this routine form today? If the prospect has been lulled into a series of yes responses, he may find that he has signed an application for insurance without fully realizing the commitment he has undertaken.

1.4.4.7 Substituting bombast for argument

When no evidence or reasoning is available, negotiators may sometimes attempt to support their argument by sheer noise and histrionics. There's an old saying that "if you have the facts on your side, argue the facts; if you have the law on your side, argue the law; if you have neither the facts nor the law on your side, ... *holler*."

1.4.4.8 Denying a valid conclusion

The fallacy of denying a valid conclusion occurs when a negotiator admits or cannot refute the premises of an opponent, yet, without evidence, flatly denies the conclusion that logically follows from these premises.

1.4.4.9 Straw Man

The fallacy of the straw man occurs when advocates set up an issue just so they can knock it down. Sometimes they attack a minor argument of their opponents and claim that they have refuted the whole case, or else they refute an argument their opponents did not advance and claim that they have thus refuted their opponents' position.

1.4.4.10 Appeal to ignorance

The fallacy of the appeal to ignorance occurs when negotiators maintain that something cannot be so because they, or the audience, have never heard of it. Appeal to ignorance is sometimes successful with an uninformed audience. The defense against this fallacy is to provide the audience with the knowledge necessary to understand the argument.

1.4.4.11 Pseudo questions

The fallacy of the pseudo question occurs when a negotiator asks an unanswerable, loaded, or ambiguous question; or a question based on a false assumption; or so many questions that an opponent cannot possibly answer them adequately within the available time. An example of this type of question is Have you stopped discriminating on the basis of race in the workplace?

1.4.4.12 Appeal to tradition

The fallacy of the appeal to tradition occurs when the advocate maintains that we should follow a certain policy because we have always done things that way.

1.4.4.13 Non sequitur

So far we have avoided the Latin names of fallacies, but this one, which simply is a conclusion that does not follow from the premises or evidence on which it is based, is best known by its Latin designation. To argue that the government program will not be successful because government bureaucracies are inefficient would be classified as a non sequitur argument. Bureaucracy does have a bad reputation, but it does not necessarily follow that all government bureaus are inefficient.

1.4.4.14 Post Hoc

This title is simply shorthand for the longer Latin phrase post hoc ergo propter hoc meaning after the fact, therefore because of the fact. The fallacy lies in assuming a causal relationship where none is proven. American history provides one of the best-known illustrations of this fallacy. Every American President elected at twenty-year intervals between 1840 and 1960 died in office (Harrison, Lincoln, Garfield, McKinley, Harding, Roosevelt, and Kennedy). A remarkable coincidence, surely, but their election in a particular year was hardly the cause of their death.

Obviously there are many fallacies, and the possibility of their being introduced into arguments is almost unlimited. As negotiators and mediators, we must be constantly on guard against these obstacles to clear thinking and creative problem solving, not only in statements of others but in our own statements as well.

For other readings in inductive and deductive reasoning, see Gilhooly; Bonevac; Moore and Parker; Baron; Holland, Holyoak, Nisbett, and Thagard; Moody; Arnold; Lewis and Greene; Billig.

1.5 PRINCIPLES OF EFFECTIVE DECISION MAKING IN CREATIVE PROBLEM SOLVING

In Section 1.3.15 above, it was suggested that creative problem solving consists of two basic components: a generative component and a decision making component (analysis, evaluation, selection). Even a mathematical computation problem involves generation of ideas and decision making, in that the problem solver must initially generate ideas about possible formulas or mathematical operations and decide which one(s) to use. After applying the formula or operation, the problem solver must decide whether the formula or operation was applied correctly and whether the solution is appropriate and accurate. It was also suggested above that the acts of designing the problem, designing the process, and designing the solution are each, usually separate decision making processes. In negotiation and mediation, good solutions are the result of both sufficient generation of ideas and good decision making. Because good decision making is such an important part of creative problem solving, it is important that we briefly explore what good decision making entails and what pitfalls may interfere with or obstruct our ability to make good decisions.

1.5.1 Elements of good decisions

In his book, *Decision Making: Proven Methods for Better Decisions*, Paul Moody identifies five elements that form the ingredients good decisions. All of these elements are present in and/or relevant to the individual and joint decision making that occurs in negotiation and mediation.

Facts. Normally, sufficient facts must be gathered on both sides of an issue, pro and con. These facts initially determine the boundaries of the problem. If detailed relevant facts cannot be obtained, it is predictable that the quality of related decision will be inferior.

Knowledge. A decision maker's knowledge of circumstances surrounding the problem, or of a similar situation, can be applied to yield a decision of higher quality. If a decision maker does not have the required knowledge, he or she must look to experts in relevant disciplines who have knowledge to share in order to produce quality decisions.

Experience. A decision maker's past experiences in decision making, good and bad, provide him or her with information useful in making decisions in similar situations.

Analysis. There are many ways to analyze a situation in order to make good decisions. Some of these analytical methods are discussed in detail in Section 3.2 below. If analysis is impossible in a given situation, then the decision maker may have to rely on intuition.

Judgment. It is judgment that synthesizes the facts, knowledge, experience, and analysis to yield a decision. Good judgment is essential for good decisions.

1.5.2 Basic characteristics of decisions

According to Moody, there are five basic characteristics of decisions (Moody, 8):

Futurity. This characteristic determines the extent to which a decision will affect future behavior, conduct, or operation. Normally, high-level decisions have long-term influence, whereas lower-level decisions customarily have a short-term effect.

Reversibility. This characteristic relates to the difficulty required to reverse a decision's effect. Normally, high level decisions are more difficult to reverse than lower-level ones.

Impact. This characteristic relates to the extent to which areas or activities are affected. High-level decisions usually have extensive impact, whereas low-level decisions have restricted impact.

Quality. Quality decisions conform to the requirements of societal norms and the law, ethical requirements, and basic principles of acceptable conduct.

Periodicity. This characteristic relates to whether the decision is made frequently or rarely.

1.5.3 Pitfalls obstructing good decision making

There are at least ten pitfalls that decision makers should anticipate and avoid when they are endeavoring to make good decisions (Moody, 9-11). These are described briefly below.

Misdirection. This is the situation of wrong question, wrong answer. An example would be where parties hired a well-known scientist to mediate a very technical, complex dispute. The scientist had tremendous knowledge in his field, but his interpersonal skills were abysmal, which caused the parties to become polarized more than they were when the mediation started. Perhaps the initial question should not have been which scientist should we hire as mediator. Rather it should have been whether we hire a scientist to be our mediator.

Sampling. Analysis and testing often requires the decision maker to obtain a sample that is both adequate and representative. Making a broad decision based only on a sample of a few items of information or events can be disastrous.

Bias. Prejudice or bias can seriously affect the quality of a decision. Thus, a decision maker must be careful to determine whether information coming from a person will inject unacceptable bias into the decision.

Ubiquitous average. Be careful of averages when decision making. Averages may hide extremes, and the extremes may be a very important consideration in the ultimate decision.

Selectivity. Using selectivity, a person can make a bad decision by rejecting unfavorable results or choosing a method that is certain to yield a favorable, but unrealistic, decision.

Interpretation. Distortion of the meaning of facts by the decision maker, either intentionally or unintentionally, can lead to a bad decision. Often people make bad decisions because they do not have the proper technical background to understand what the facts mean in the relevant discipline.

Jumped-at conclusion. This is a trap that, you as a decision maker fall into when you already are inclined to make a particular decision and the first bit of information substantiates your "gut feeling" and you immediately decide according to your inclination.

Meaningless difference. This represents the trap of not realizing that the situation you are making a decision about is in a state of change and that the impact of your decision will make a meaningless difference.

Connotation. This is the pitfall of allowing an emotional content or implication to be added to an explicit literal meaning. Connotations can mislead decision makers unknowingly.

Status. The status of people can affect the nature and quality of the decisions they make. For example in a subordinate-supervisor situation, there may be a fear of disapproval existing on the one hand, and the fear of loss of prestige on the other. Thus, the status of persons may inhibit them from sharing adequate or accurate information in aid of the decision making process.

1.6 ORIENTATION OF THE CREATIVE PROBLEM SOLVER IN NEGOTIATION AND MEDIATION

1.6.1 Optimistic

Being optimistic is a very important aspect of the creative problem solver's orientation in negotiation and mediation. Optimism has a tendency to move parties toward a mutually acceptable solution, or if they cannot find a totally acceptable solution, to see the good aspects of a lesser solution and find satisfaction in that. As one expert in creative problem solving for lawyers has said, "Optimism is complementary to perseverance; if we do not believe that a successful outcome is possible, we have no reason to persevere. Optimism may also be related to happiness, which has a positive effect on the activity of the prefrontal cortex [of the brain] where our problem solving occurs" (Weinstein and Morton, 864); (Cooley (3), 162).

1.6.2 Initially non-critical

Creative problem solving originates with an assumption of not knowing, a confession of ignorance, a kind of bafflement, and a surrender to curiosity. It was Socrates who taught that if one could convince himself that he knew nothing, he would be at the threshold of wisdom. And that is the manner in which the creative problem solver should approach a problem. It was through the recognition of his ignorance that Socrates became the greatest of all teachers. In modern times, Michael Ray and Rochelle Myers, creativity experts at Stanford Business School, suggest four heuristics of preparation for creative problem solving: (1) if you don't succeed at first, don't surrender; (2) destroy judgment and create curiosity; (3) pay attention; and (4) ask dumb questions. Zen master, Shunryu Suzuki explains it this way: "If your mind is empty, it is always ready for anything; it is open to everything..." (Kerper, 366-67; Ray and Myers; Suzuki; Cooley (1), Supp. § 103.50).

1.6.3 Open-minded

It was the Roman philosopher Epictetus who observed that "it is impossible for a man to learn what he thinks he already knows" (Cooley (1), § 103.50). "Being open to new possibilities is foundational for creative thinkers" (Weinstein and Morton, 864). As Maslow suggested, people who are very concerned with how others think of them ... and who are rigid and careful, have a difficult time being creative. They may not be in touch with their individuality, or may not allow themselves the freedom to express it" (Maslow, 82-90). Creative thinkers always are agreeable to suspending judgment.

1.6.4 Flexibly perceptive

The effective creative problem solver is flexibly perceptive. This means that the creative problem solver is willing at anytime to try a new direction, approach, or idea to solve a problem. The creative problem solver has a great capacity to tolerate ideas and suggestions from other people and to try to apply them to the problem at hand (Cooley (3), 39-40).

1.6.5 Tolerant of ambiguity

Tolerance for ambiguity, or a willingness to "remain in uncertainties," has been said to be central to creative problem solving. Such tolerance allows problem solvers to "leave the problem open" for indefinite periods of time, and increases the probability that either the problem, the process, or the solution will be redesigned (See Weinstein and Morton, 863).

1.6.6 Improvisational

The creative problem solver is continuously oriented not only *to see* problems, processes, and solutions in different ways, but also *to do* things differently to find a solution to the overall problem. In short, the creative problem solver must be oriented to improvise. In the arts, improvisers develop their skills by working with each other in a number of loosely structured contexts. Jazz musicians, for example, are conscious of the underlying form of the pieces they perform. They listen closely to each other for direction. When they sense a reaction from their audience or hear another player has taken on a more dominant voice, they call on their knowledge of rhythm, harmony, and balance to back them up. When a break occurs in the melody, if they hear that a space has been left for them, they take control. They steer the sound in new direction, developing their solo performance on the sounds and the creations of which they have been part. This goes on until another break occurs and the time comes to make space for some other member of the ensemble. All the while, they are conscious of underlying form. So too, the creative problem solver improves (Spolin; Cooley(1), Supp., §1:05).

1.6.7 Analytical

The creative problem solver needs to be able to do more than just generate ideas for potential solutions. He or she must also be skilled in analyzing and evaluating them, in placing them in an appropriate context, and determining which solution or solution(s) most optimally satisfy the needs of the problem and its parameters.

1.6.8 Seeks to achieve quality decision making

Finally, the creative problem solver realizes that his or her goal is to achieve quality decision making, working individually or in a group. The quality of the decision (result) will be directly related to the quality of the generative, analytical, and evaluative thinking, used in designing the problem, the process, and the solution or solutions.

1.7 PRINCIPAL BARRIERS TO EFFECTIVE CREATIVE PROBLEM SOLVING IN NEGOTIATION AND MEDIATION

1.7.1 Informational Barriers

Dr. de Bono describes three characteristics of information processing which affect the applications of lateral thinking techniques in problem solving:

Sequence of Arrival of Information: The mind always arranges available information in the most stable or logical way. As more information comes in, the mind adds it to the existing arrangement. But there comes a time in problem solving that the problem solver cannot proceed further without restructuring the pattern. The deadlock can only be averted by breaking up the old pattern, which has been so useful and arranging the old information in a new way. Thus, the best possible arrangement of information in problem solving is quite independent of the sequence of arrival of the pieces of information.

Choice of Entry Point: In solving a problem where the desired alternative goals (solutions) after restructuring are prescribed, but there is missing information concerning the current informational structure, entering the information at the solution end and working backwards often facilitates resolution.

Attention Area: Very often in a problem solving situation, success is not just a matter of the order in which the information is attended to but the choice of the information parts that are going to be attended to at all. To restructure the problem, one may need no more than a slight shift in attention. On the other hand, if there is no shift in attention it may be difficult to look at the situation in a different way (de Bono (1), 31-35; 175-191).

You should review these techniques in your preparation for mediation and at the negotiation or mediation conference itself. In that way, you can enhance the climate for creativity and increase the opportunities for win-win, optimum, and super-optimum solutions (Cooley (1), § 2:25, 193-98).

1.7.2 Perceptual barriers – the illusions of conflict

Human perception plays a vital role in: (1) creating informational illusions, which spawn conflict; and (2) recognizing the reality that can lead to conflict's resolution. In this segment, we shall examine three types of perceptual illusions that routinely occur in conflict settings. Knowing what the illusions are is the first step in diluting their conflict-producing influence (Cooley (4), 287-293).

It is relatively common knowledge that two people rarely perceive the same visual scenes or the same written words identically. Evidence of this, for example, is that eyewitness accounts of an automobile accident vary dramatically. One eyewitness may see something that another did not; another may see something that did not in fact exist or occur, because the eyewitness was programmed, mentally, to see it. Similarly, two people entering into a contract will think they are perceiving its terms identically, and even smile confidently as they sign the document binding themselves to its terms. Later, when events cause the parties to refer to the contracts terms for guidance, it is likely that the parties will perceive the pertinent contract provisions in somewhat different lights, interpreting the provisions, inclusively or exclusively, as best suits their separate needs. Thus, perception has at least two aspects: (1) an aspect that is totally visual; and (2) another, which involves beliefs or mental sets. Sometimes, these aspects combine to impair significantly the design of effective solutions to conflict. We will deal mostly with the first aspect, the visual aspect.

As to the visual aspect of perception, we know that sometimes the eye plays tricks on the brain, or vice versa. In childhood, we knew these tricks to be optical illusions and we normally dismissed them as being fun, or perhaps curious, but as having no substantive effect on our lives. As adults, however, we should not be so quick to dismiss them. Optical illusions in part, contribute to design impairment and, at the very least, provide a useful analogy as to how beliefs and sets can interfere with design effectiveness and efficiency.

Information provided by the eye is not always precise or uncomplicated. Nearly every cue to spatial vision and distance and thus nearly every visual situation contains potential for ambiguity. Where ambiguity arises, it is called an illusion. Visual illusions are complicated and baffling. Most geometric or spatial illusions involve one or more of several basic phenomena, and they can be classified into three broad categories: (1) those which fool all observers identically; (2) those which are perceived differently by different observers (but eventually most observers can see both shapes); and (3) those which represent impossible objects which cannot be built in three dimensional space (Cooley (4), 287-293).

1.7.2.1 Illusions of the first type

Examples of the first category of visual illusions are shown here -- those which fool all observers identically. Your brain is programmed by experience to think that two parallel lines converge in the distance and that if two objects of the same size are placed at varying distances from you, the closer one will appear larger. Thus, your brain does not accept the fact that in Figure 1, the man on the right does not look smaller, so it compensates by making the man look larger. Actually, if you measure the men, you will find that they are all the same height. This gives us some idea as to how the brain perceives in terms of background and relationships. It demonstrates how the brain does not always perceive things correctly, in situational contexts, such as here, where the men refuse to get shorter when they should.

Figure 1

Similarly, the brain tends to underestimate the size of circles and overestimate lengths of straight lines. This is exemplified by Figures 2 and 3.

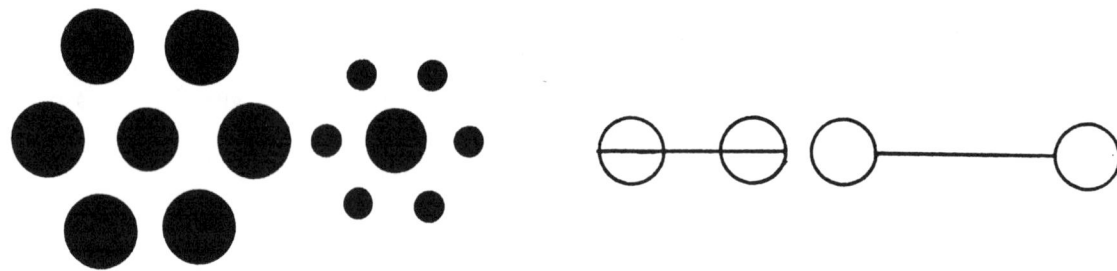

Figure 2   Figure 3

In Figure 2, the middle circles are identical in size, in Figure 3, the horizontal lines are exactly the same length. In Figure 4, the two horizontal lines are parallel, but the lines appear to be bent. In Figure 5, the circles are perfectly round, but the one seen through the spokes seems distorted. This effect is due to the fact that parallel lines and circles are perceived in terms of the relationship of the lines appearing behind them.

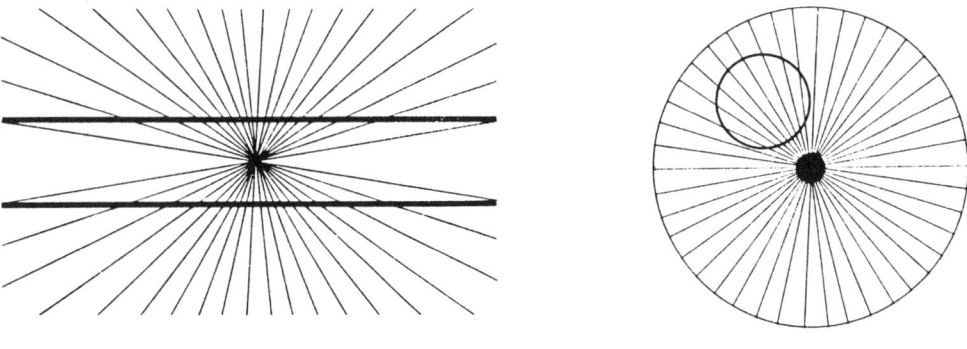

Figure 4   Figure 5

By analogy, in any interpersonal situation each party perceives events and circumstances in terms of background, relationships, and interrelationships of people and events. Sometimes the perceptions of both (or, as the case may be, all) parties to the situation are incorrect. That is, they are viewing the situation (dispute or transaction) identically, but mistakenly. This problem of perception may interfere with effective design. For example, the parties may design a problem and solution differently if they know that the men in figure 1 – being recruited as professional basketball players are all the same height, instead of thinking that one of the men is much taller than the other two. Recognition later that the men are identical in height may precipitate a hiring dispute. Usually the parties themselves with appropriate investigation and inquiry can discover their joint misperception, but sometimes the situation might require the assistance of a disinterested neutral party (and in the case of a dispute, a mediator) to detect the joint misperception. Sometimes, opposing parties in a lawsuit will have identical but incorrect perceptions of the issues in a case, and the mediator can often identify the misperception.

1.7.2.2 Illusions of the second type

The second type of visual illusions are those figures or shapes which are perceived differently yet correctly by each of the observers. With additional study, however, each observer can eventually see the figure or shape, which is perceived by the other observer (Cooley (4), 287-293). Consider the examples shown as follows.

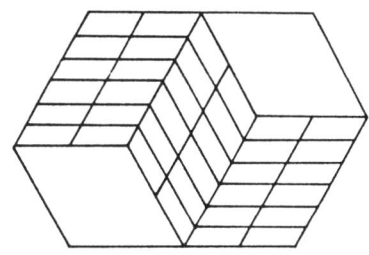

Figure 6   Figure 7

In Figure 6, what do you see? Most people who look at this figure see either a duck or a rabbit, and some can immediately see both. This second type of illusion is quite prevalent in problem and solution design situations. Oftentimes, parties enter into interpersonal situations with correct perceptions about events or circumstances, but, at the same time, they are unable to see or appreciate the correct perceptions of their opponents. This is commonly referred to as "mental set" – a person's readiness to respond to a situation in a set manner. Mental set often precipitates a standoff or stalemate when, in fact, if each side could see the problem or transaction from the other's perspective, effective (unbiased) problem and solution design could commence. Again, this process of seeing the problem or transaction as perceived by the opponent often requires the assistance of a disinterested neutral party. For example, if all parties see the situation in Figure 7 as an architect's preliminary sketch of a planned high rise, and some parties view its location to be on the left side of the plaza, while others view it to be on the right side, there is bound to be trouble down the road (Cooley (4), 287-293)

1.7.2.3 Illusions of the third type

The third type of visual illusion is impossible objects. Visual impossibilities, unknown in direct vision or reality, can be depicted on paper in such a way that at first glance, they appear to be logical. Figure 8, shown below, at first looks like it could be reproducible in three-dimensional space, but after studying it for a few seconds, it is clear that the object is nonsensical overall.

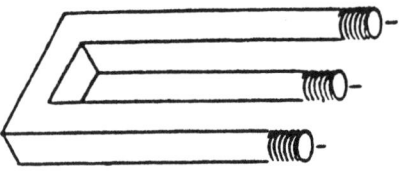

Figure 8

The brain struggles to make sense of these impossible figures, but eventually accepts them for the illusions that they are. Similarly, in some interpersonal situations, the perceptions of one or more of the parties might be consistent in some respects, but design efforts may be doomed because of an unperceived impossible objective, due to personality conflicts, uncompromising philosophies, exaggerated expectations, and ineffective or nonexistent means to attain certain goals. The earlier the impossible objective can be discovered in such situations, the better for all parties concerned. A disinterested neutral party can often be of assistance in discovering the existence of an impossible objective.

1.7.3 Communication barriers

The third type of impediment to creative problem solving consists of communication barriers. There are numerous types of communication barriers to creative problem solving, but here we will only deal with some of the individual and group communication barriers and some of the principal communication barriers that are present in the negotiation and mediation setting.

1.7.3.1 Individual communication barriers

Dr. Susan Jarboe, communications consultant and expert, has noted in her writings that there are at least five barriers within individuals that prevent them from manifesting their creativity, whether or not they are in a group setting. These individual-level barriers are described separately below (Jarboe, 338-41).

Fear of set breaking. In most cultures, even those that place a premium on individualism, compliance with social rules is valued and violation of rules is punished. For example, the mild chaos produced by brainstorming can be unsettling to the organized mind. Some people experience similar discomfort when participating in reverse brainstorming exercises where members of the group consider what would make a problem worse. A prerequisite to becoming a creative individual is to deal with rule-imposed social pressures and to overcome one's fear of set breaking.

Fear of rejection. Historically, innovators have frequently been isolated and rejected because of their unconventionality. Thus, some individuals believe that if they exercise originality, they will be perceived as odd – even deranged – and rejected because of that. Also, because many famous inventors, poets, artists and musicians had some sort of mental dysfunction, a myth has been perpetuated that anyone who thinks creatively has to have a mental quirk. This conclusion, of course, is an unreasonable application of cause and effect – a complete non sequitur. To be creative, one has to overcome any fear of being rebuffed or stereotyped as "odd."

Lack of motivation. Even individuals with significant creative talents or abilities, but who lack motivation, are not always able to engage these talents and abilities when needed. Research has revealed that motivation, interest, and effort are viewed as essential prerequisites for creative activity. Researchers also believe that some type of tension must occur to trigger creative responses. A negative stimulus, such as a problem to be solved, may trigger what is called reactive creativity. In this type of situation, the motivation for creativity is necessity (the "mother of invention") or frustration. Proactive creativity, on the other hand, is associated with a positive stimulus, such as perceptions of opportunity, reduced tension, and abundant resources which have been found to arouse pleasure and divergent thought. Closely allied to the lack-of-motivation barrier, is an individual's fear of failure. Those who fear failure lack the motivation to try something new.

Inadequate cognitive heuristics. It has been found that some patterns of thought repress creative thinking. These thought patterns are: assuming that one has the right answer; failing to challenge the obvious; and evaluating too rapidly. Other barriers to creativity that some individuals possess are overreliance on prototypes and having too much faith in past experience. To overcome these barriers, one must "train out" these biases and try new cognitive heuristics, such as casting a problem at the most abstract level at the beginning of problem solving.

Reluctance to play. Some individuals decline to engage in creative activity because they view the supporting activities of brainstorming and like techniques as frivolous or childish. They are often reluctant to engage in the supporting activities because they have a fear of looking foolish or they believe the activities to be inappropriate for their status in life. To overcome the reluctance-to-play barrier, such individuals need someone else to set the legitimizing norm that "play is okay."

1.7.3.2. Group communication barriers

Susan Jarboe has also noted in her writings that, in addition to the individual-level constraints that operate in group creative problem solving, there are at least four principal barriers at the group level that prevent groups from manifesting their creativity. These barriers are described separately below (Jarboe, 345-47).

Conformity to group norms. It is well known among behavioral researchers that conformity to the norms and customs of a particular group can suppress creativity. Thus, establishing new group norms are often necessary to stimulate group creativity. Often this occurs by engaging the members of the group themselves to work together to create changes to the existing problematic norms.

Unwillingness to collaborate. Members of a group can bring the baggage of historical experience with them that biases them against collaboration. For example, some of the group members may not have had good group experiences in the past. Some might view group meetings as unproductive, disorganized, poorly moderated, confrontational and as activities which breed distrust, disrespect, and aggression. To alter such attitudes toward group creative problem solving, members should have rewarding experiences that occur in the group. The moderator or group leader can use icebreakers at the beginning of the meeting in order to promote open, friendly, and pleasant social interaction, building the framework for later task work. The group leader can also introduce skills and interest inventories that can generate interest in fellow group members.

Differences in members' interaction styles. Research has demonstrated that conformists (adaptors) may be unwilling to collaborate with nonconformists (innovators) because they feel intimidated by more aggressive social styles. Some conformists view nonconformists as abrasive and insensitive. One way for a group to overcome this barrier is to have a trained facilitator, a neutral agent who can foster collaboration, manage interaction, and work to enlighten the group members by furnishing positive mutual experiences through creative training or problem solving sessions.

Mistrust of creative people within the group. While conformists (adaptors) often find nonconformists (innovators) irksome, the opposite is true as well. Innovators tend to see adaptors as stuffy and wedded to systems, rules, and norms. Because innovators routinely challenge the status quo, adaptors tend to mistrust them as undisciplined manipulators. To overcome these barriers, group leaders and members should recognize individual creativity, encourage freedom of expression, and defend creatively performing people from attacks by others. Group members need to realize that there is an array of important innovative roles that support creative activity in groups.

1.7.3.3 Principal communication barriers in negotiation and mediation

Many communication inhibitors exist in negotiation and mediation. Among them are fears of harm or retaliation, ego threat, result threat, role expectation, disclosure etiquette, trauma, perceived irrelevancy, and unwarranted confidence (Cooley (3), 106-110). Other conditions inhibiting communication in negotiation and in mediation are loss aversion, risk aversion, the endowment effect, reactive devaluation, and a zero-sum mindset (Cooley (3), 110-11). These communication inhibitors are described separately below.

Loss aversion. Behavioral research, in general, has shown that people are loss-averse – that is, they dislike losing money and therefore are willing to take an "irrational risk" in order to avoid a definite loss. Loss-averse defendants may choose unwisely to litigate rather than settle out of court. Loss-averse plaintiffs, on the other hand, may be more willing to accept a modest but certain settlement rather than gamble on a obtaining much larger litigated result.

Risk aversion. It has also been shown that people will give up a higher-value but riskier option to ensure they at least get something. Loss aversion and risk aversion situations can sometimes be avoided by the way a settlement proposal is framed with respect to a "gain" or "loss" interpretation.

Endowment effect. Closely related to "loss aversion" is the concept of the "endowment effect." If a person owns something that has sentimental significance, the person may ascribe to the item a greater-than-market value. That something, if surrendered, would represent a special kind of loss – the loss of an "endowment," thereby garnering, in the owner's mind, a need for extra monetary compensation.

Reactive devaluation. The theory of reactive devaluation is that a party or an advocate may automatically devalue a settlement proposal made by an adversary, whereas he or she might accept the very same proposal if offered by an ally or neutral.

Zero-sum mindset. Some people who engage in negotiation or mediation assume that these processes are purely distributive in nature – that is, if one side wins, the other side must lose. This zero-sum mindset often precludes the possibility of integrative bargaining or of value creation through consideration of non-monetary, but value-laden, possibilities.

CHAPTER TWO

GENERIC STRATEGIES FOR CREATIVE PROBLEM SOLVING

Imagination is more important than knowledge.

Albert Einstein

Famous for the above quotation, Einstein is also noted for having a knack to pose questions that no one had posed before, and then to arrive at an answer that changed for all time the way in which scientists, and eventually lay persons, construed the universe (Gardner, 149). His creative genius lay in his persistent questioning of the absoluteness of time and space. As a teenager, he pondered what his experience would be like if he were operating from the point of view of light – or, if he rode on a beam of light. By this metaphor, he eventually was able to formulate his theory of relativity. He asked himself a question that challenged the way other people might view time and space. He asked "what if" – What if I were looking at a clock, but I was flying away from it at the speed of light. He concluded that the time on the clock would be frozen because a new hour could never travel fast enough to catch up with him. On the beam of light, the time on that clock would remain perpetually the same. In this chapter, we will become acquainted with some of the thinking strategies that Einstein used (perhaps unconsciously) when he developed his theory of relativity: suspending judgment; challenging assumptions; visualizing; using metaphors; thought reversal; and seeing alternatives. Just like Einstein, you can use these and other creative problem solving strategies discussed below to achieve quality solutions in your negotiations and mediations.

2.1 LONG-TERM STRATEGIES FOR CREATIVE PROBLEM SOLVING

In his book, *What a Great Idea!*, Charles Thompson describes a four-step strategy to foster an innovative mindset for solving problems creatively in all aspects of life. The first step is to recognize that you personally, and everyone with whom you inter-relate, have the *"freedom to be creative"* (an expression I use in practically every mediation that I conduct). He suggests that people have various creative talents to contribute to the creative problem solving process. He believes that, in relation to ideas, some people are better generators of ideas, some are better promoters, some are better at designing solutions, others at implementing them, and still others, at evaluating them. He further believes that the three keys to successful creative problem solving: the ability to recognize that all of these types of talents or abilities are necessary for success in creative problem solving; the ability to see yourself as you are and as other people most likely see you; and the ability to try other creative styles on for size. The "freedom" step is an important one because it recognizes that good solutions to problems spring from a multiplicity of possible solutions. He identifies the "top 40 Killer Phrases," that stifle free flow of ideas and discourage creativity. Some of these Killer Phrases are:

- "Yes, but..."
- "We've always done it this way."
- "Don't rock the boat."
- "It'll never fly."
- "If it ain't broke, don't fix it."

Thompson's second step in his four-step strategy for an innovative mindset is freedom of expression – perhaps more accurately, freedom to ask questions. He advocates the asking of "dumb" (translation: elementary) questions. Some examples of dumb questions that he offers are:

- "Why have we always done it that way?"
- "Does anyone actually look at that form?"
- "Why do I need a hard copy of this report?"
- "Why do we need a committee to look into this?"

He believes that the question-asking process is especially powerful when joined to the Idea Mapping process described in Section 3.1.24.

The third step is creation – the freedom to play, or more precisely, to have fun. Thompson advocates a "see the future" approach to creative problem solving. The goal of envisioning the future is to return from the future, incrementally one step at a time. In doing so, picture all the moves you (or the organization, group, etc.) had to make to reach the result. In this third step, Thompson sees the obstacle to creation not to be reality itself, but rather "reality" as we *assume* it to be. The creative person, Thompson suggests, "escapes" into other realities – worlds where the future happens right now, where everything morphs into its opposite, where things we believe are true, just are not, where the normal point of view is abandoned, and everything is metaphorical.

The fourth step is action this is the phase where ideas become reality. This is the stage where innovation meets utility. Action involves the ability to effectively communicate change to foster acceptance. It is the experience of working anew, with others, in creative concert.

2.2 GENERIC STRATEGIES FOR SOLVING DISCRETE PROBLEMS CREATIVELY

The principal generic strategies for creative problem solving in negotiation and mediation derive from Edward de Bono's book, *Lateral Thinking: Creativity Step by Step* (de Bono(1)). Those strategies are described in this section, and some of the generic tools and techniques for implementing the strategies are described in Chapter Three.

2.2.1. Suspend judgment

People's need to be right all the time is the greatest barrier to new ideas. Creative problem solvers are aware of this fact and therefore suspend judgment during the generative stage of thinking and apply judgment during the selective stage. The basic principle of the suspended judgment strategy is that a wrong idea at some stage of the problem solving process can lead to a right one later on. De Bono says that suspension of judgment can produce the following effects:

- an idea will survive longer and will breed further ideas;
- other people will offer ideas, useful to others, which their own judgment
- ideas of others can be accepted for their stimulating effect rather than being rejected;
- ideas that are judged to be wrong within the current frame of reference may survive long enough to show that the frame of reference needs to be altered (de Bono (1), 110).

Several tools and techniques for implementing the strategy of suspending judgment appear in Chapter Three.

2.2.2. Brainstorm

Brainstorming is more of a setting than a special lateral thinking strategy. It encourages the application of lateral thinking strategies while providing an escape from the rigidity of vertical thinking. Brainstorming has three main features: suspended judgment, a formal (or special) setting, and cross stimulation. The advantages of suspended judgment are described immediately above. It is ironic that brainstorming is more effective in a formal setting. Intuitively, one would assume the reverse. De Bono points out that the more formal the setting the more chance there is of informality in ideas within it. Most people are so steeped in cliche pattern thinking that they feel very inhibited about engaging in lateral thinking. The more formalized the brainstorming session, the more probable the participants will jettison their inhibitions and take the risk of engaging in other lateral thinking techniques such as thought reversal and fractionation, as described below. Brainstorming fosters cross stimulation, as ideas outside one's own mind can serve to stimulate one's own ideas. An idea, even if misunderstood, may seem obvious and trivial to one person and yet it can combine with ideas in another person's mind to produce something very innovative or original (de Bono (1), 149-165).

Brainstorming is accomplished in two sessions: the brainstorming session and the evaluation session. A brainstorming session can work well with as many as fifteen people or as few as six. Larger groups can be broken down into smaller work groups that compare results periodically during the session or afterwards. It is the task of the chairperson of the brainstorming session to formulate the statement of the problem to be considered. The chairperson undertakes this task carefully because too broad a statement of the problem will evoke a variety of ideas that are too separated to bring about a chain reaction of idea stimulation. By the same token, too narrow a statement of the problem may restrict generation of ideas to a particular way of handling it instead of ideas focused on the problem itself. The chairperson moderates the brainstorming session, ensuring that all participants are allowed to speak separately and enforcing the rule that people should not evaluate or criticize the ideas of others. The chairperson normally appoints one participant to be the scrivener who records the ideas as they are generated during the session. The chairperson also suggests which lateral thinking technique to try, though any participant may suggest changing to another technique at any time. From time to time, the chairperson identifies the central problem as then defined, but encourages other perceptions of the problem and even some re-definition or refinement of it as the session proceeds. Of course, the chairperson does not normally allow a sustained flight of fancy into a wholly irrelevant direction that is unhelpful to arriving at a solution to the problem under review. The chairperson determines the appropriate point to end the session and then organizes the evaluation session and the listing of ideas. The evaluation session should yield three lists: (1) ideas of immediate usefulness; (2) ideas for further exploration; and (3) new approaches to the problem.

Generally speaking, brainstorming is a difficult activity for negotiators or mediation advocates at first. They are not used to suspending judgment, or withholding criticism, tolerating irrelevancies, or engaging in frivolity. But, in most cases, if they grant themselves the privilege of brainstorming, they are amazed at how effectively the process stimulates new or better ideas.

There are many opportunities for negotiators and mediators to employ brainstorming techniques in all three modes of problem solving (problem design; process design; and solution design). For example, brainstorming can be used initially by lawyers with their clients in the early stages of conflicts to flush out the clients' true needs in the situation. It can also be used to generate ideas for ways to develop sources of information in a particular case, and later to develop ideas for potential settlement proposals. Similarly, the process can be beneficial as an aid in stimulating ideas for designing a process or processes for resolving a particular dispute. Mediation advocates can also use brainstorming with colleagues to develop ideas and a format for a premediation statement so as to optimize its communicative and persuasive quality.

Negotiators and mediators may also consider using solo brainstorming, also referred to as "internal brainstorming." Implementation of this technique has been described as follows:

Make sure you are comfortable and in a quiet setting. You may wish to close your eyes. Lean back in your chair and let go. Now pose the problem to yourself. What answers do you hear, see, feel? Do words or pictures come to mind? If so, jot them down. If they are just fragments of glimpses of concepts, try to flesh them out a little. One idea will lead to another; some thoughts provoke several concepts or one whole solution. Keep going; let every idea come quickly, flowingly. Continue to write down cue words on your paper. Wherever they fall on the paper is fine; don't be concerned with order or sequence. If you find yourself slowing down, look at one of the cue words or concepts and go from there. After you've pursued this path for a while, look back at your notes and write down the first thought that comes to mind, starting over again, perhaps on a completely new pathway, perhaps retracing the same ground. When you retrace your steps, you will often discover some idea you sped by the first time. Continue this process for at least ten minutes. Sometimes you'll find many ideas rushing in all at once; at other times they will come more sporadically and singly. Just enjoy them as they come (Wonder and Donovan, 77-78).

It should be kept in mind that brainstorming (group or internal) can be used effectively with other strategies of lateral thinking to improve the quality of ideas. It is particularly useful in generating alternatives and in cultivating "opportunitrees," as described in Section 3.3.2. Also, several tools and techniques for implementing the strategy of brainstorming appear in Chapter Three.

2.2.3. Challenge assumptions

Alfred North Whitehead, the great American educator, once said: "It takes a very unusual mind to make an analysis of the obvious." (Albrecht, 241). To make an analysis of the obvious requires one to challenge assumptions. When using the strategy of challenging assumptions, one challenges (1) the existence of boundaries and limits in problem solving; and (2) the validity or applicability of concepts. Ask "why." De Bono teaches that a general agreement about an assumption is no guarantee that it is correct. He asserts that it is historical continuity that perpetuates most assumptions – not a repeated assessment of their validity. Even basic ideas, the cliché informational patterns, can be restructured to make better use of available information. The purposes of lateral thinking are to challenge any pattern and to try to restructure it (de Bono(1), 91-103).

2.2.3.1. Theory of challenging assumptions in general

Consider this simple problem: How many ways can a square be divided into four equal pieces? Faced with this problem, a problem solver might think of ways to cut up the square by (1) slicing it into four equal strips from left to right; (2) drawing intersecting diagonals, yielding four equilateral triangles; and (3) drawing a cross within the square, yielding four smaller squares. The problem solver may even experiment with other different solution designs, yielding other four-piece geometric figures of the same size and shape. After identifying nine or ten solutions to the simple problem, the average problem solver might reach an impasse, concluding that there might be a few more solutions, but that he or she has isolated most of them. The creative problem solver does not stop at nine or ten solutions, or even 20 solutions. The creative problem solver "keeps the problem open" and seeks other possible solutions by challenging his or her assumptions. He or she focuses on the solutions generated and then challenges his or her assumptions about the problem, the processes for solving it, and the potential solutions. In this situation, the creative problem solver would challenge the assumption that there are a finite number of rules governing ways that a square could be divided into four equal pieces. Looking again at the solutions generated, he or she would focus on the solution showing a square with intersecting diagonals as shown below:

Figure

The creative problem solver would realize that if the crossed diagonals were rotated simultaneously within the square, that rotation would produce an infinite number of solutions. Thus, the creative problem solver would challenge whether limiting rules actually exist. By eliminating the limitations imposed by non-existent rules, the creative problem solver would expand the scope of solutions infinitely.

Lawyers are widely perceived as being finders and interpreters of rules governing human conduct. Because they generally view the world through a virtual mesh of rules, they routinely tend to see rules that do not in fact exist. Their professional duty of care owed to clients intensifies this condition. They are inclined, more than the average person, to interpret the existence of nonexistent rules. While this practice of assuming the existence of rules in the interest of cautious rendering of legal advice to clients may have certain benefits, it is a handicap to those lawyers who carry over the practice in problem-solving situations generally. On many occasions lawyers erroneously assume certain "rules" limit the quantity and quality of possible solutions to a problem. These assumed "rules," if properly challenged, can be exposed as the artificial limitations they truly are, and problem-solving opportunities can thereby be greatly enhanced. The following anecdote is intended to illustrate the importance of challenging assumptions in problem solving.

There is a story told about a very famous, highly respected law practitioner who was presenting a seminar on evidence to fellow lawyers in Chicago, Illinois (Cooley (1), §2:14, 152-53). At the beginning of his presentation, without saying a word, his right hand nonchalantly removed from his trouser pocket what appeared to be a book of matches. Somewhat dramatically, he opened the matchbook, tore off a stick-like object, and held it high above his head, and asked the audience, "What is this?" Several seminar attendees in the back of the room responded in unison. "A match!" they shouted self-assuredly. Then the speaker asked this question: "Is it a match if it doesn't have a head?" A hush fell across the room. Then the speaker handed the object he had held above his head to a lady sitting in the front row, and he asked her, "What is it?" Haltingly and with some trepidation, she said, "It appears to be a match with its head removed." "Well, is it a match?" the speaker asked. "I don't think so," responded the lady. Next, the speaker handed the lady the book of matches and asked her to tear off one of the stick-like objects inside and to examine it carefully. She did so. The speaker then asked her, "What is it?" After scrutinizing the object for some time, the lady answered, "It's a match!" The speaker asked, "How could you prove that?" "By striking it against the roughened surface of the matchbook cover and seeing it ignite," she said. The speaker instructed her to do so, and when she tried, the head of the stick-like object crumbled. It would not ignite. The speaker then asked the lady, "Is it a match?" She looked puzzled for a moment, and then responded, "I don't think so." The speaker then launched into a five minute description of a "match," light years beyond the detail of an ordinary dictionary definition. He first defined the species of "match" as a nontoxic safety match. He then described the properties of the stick-like portion of the match as being composed of laminated paper products, pointing out the origin of the particular type of paper, its chemical composition, the type of laminating glue and its chemical composition, and also the particular mechanical process that is used in fabricating the paper matchstick. He then moved on to describing, with excruciating detail, the head of this particular species of match. He said that the head was composed of nontoxic phosphorus sesquisulfide, and then to the amazement of the audience, he drew the chemical structure of that igniting agent on the blackboard and then further explained in specific detail how and why the chemical on the matchhead ignited when it brushed across the roughened surface of the matchbook cover. The speaker made it clear that a principal characteristic of a match, at least the particular species he was describing, was to ignite on striking against the safety cover of the matchbook. When he was finished with his description, the audience was in awe. The speaker could have effectively concluded his seminar at that moment. With the skill of both an artist and a scientist, the speaker had taught the seminar attendees more about evidence in ten minutes than they had learned in the last five years of trial practice. They learned much about the differences between assumptions and facts; labels and proof. Specifically, they learned that it was indeed arguable that a "match" was not a "match," if it did not possess all the characteristics of a match. This lesson could of course be extrapolated to proof of facts generally. Also, they learned that assumptions can greatly interfere with a lawyer's perceptions, greatly restrict his or her ability to see alternative problem, process, and solution designs, and, indeed, impede the search for truth.

Before one can challenge assumptions, one must know what assumptions are and how to detect them. Obviously, assumptions can be very helpful to negotiators in developing arguments and to mediators in developing hypothetical questions. Assumptions, in those instances, are very useful *because they are identified as such*, and employed by people to test the strength or reliability of propositions or principles in contexts other than the specific facts of the case or situation under review. Those are not the sort of assumptions we are concerned with here. The assumptions which we need to expose through lateral thinking are those assumptions we make by accepting inferences uncritically as if they had the strength of observed facts. This type of assumption (which for purposes of this discussion we will call unconscious assumptions) is the result of cliché pattern thinking. We must constantly remind ourselves that basic ideas, even though generally regarded as true, are really patterns, which may be restructured. We should not assume that the basic ideas or statements of basic ideas are true. They may be built on assumption, misinformation, or disinformation. Let us consider another example to understand the importance of challenging assumptions in problem solving situations (Cooley (1), §2:14, 153).

The simple statement that "Columbus discovered America" is a generally accepted proposition, which some people might even regard as "fact." But if we think about it, we know that this simple statement contains multiple implicit assumptions, is quite misleading, and could, itself, reasonably be characterized as an assumption, rather than a statement of fact. The procedure that I use to test whether an idea, statement of an idea, or alleged fact is an assumption or contains implicit assumptions is as follows (Cooley (1), §2:14, 154-55):

1. Accept nothing at face value (nothing is sacred).
2. Break down the statement into its component words or phrases.
3. Nouns: ask who and what;
   Pronouns: ask who and what;
   Verbs (or verb phrases): ask what, when, where, how;
   Adjectives: ask what, what kind, how much;
   Adverbs: ask what, where, when, how, why.
   Answer these questions using other questions, which you can answer
   or which can be answered by others.
4. Note discrepancies and possible assumptions.

Let us apply this procedure to the "Columbus discovered America" statement:

Component Word: Columbus (noun)

Who:
1. Was he alone?
2. Who else was present?
3. Could someone in his party have "discovered" land first?
4. Was "Columbus" his only last name; any assumed names?

5. Did he have a first name?
6. Any chance for confusion of names?
7. Who saw him discover America?

Discussion: You could probably think of additional "who" questions. Actually, as we can see from reviewing just these seven questions, several assumptions are present. History teaches that Columbus was not the first person in his exploration party to "see" land. The captain of the Nina (Columbus was aboard the Santa Maria) claimed to have seen land on September 25, 1492, and then after several more days of sailing, a sailor named Rodrigo de Triana saw land from the prow of the Pinta two hours after midnight on October 12. Also, Columbus never used the name "Columbus," not even when writing in Latin. At various times in his life, he used the names Colombo, Colomo, Colom, and Colón. He preferred the name Colón. Thus, it is arguable that a man named "Columbus" never discovered America.

Component Word: discovered (verb)

What:
1. Does "discover" mean "see?"
2. Does "discover" mean "stand on physically?"
3. What does discover mean?

When:
1. Did any one "discover" America before Columbus?
2. Did any one "see" it before Columbus?
3. Was anyone present (natives) when Columbus landed?
4. Did they "discover" America before Columbus?
5. Should the words "was the first European to" be inserted after Columbus?"
6. Did any European discover America before Columbus?

Where:
1. Are you sure he landed in America?
2. Where did he land? Was it on mainland or on an island?
3. Was the location on a map, which pictured "America?"
4. What constitutes "America?"
5. Does what constituted America then, constitute America now?

How: See "What," supra.

Component Word: America (noun)

What: See "Where," supra.

Discussion: Again, we see the assumptions implicit in the statement. It assumes that everyone knows what "discover" means and what "America" is. Actually it can be argued, persuasively, that Columbus did not discover America at all – but rather he discovered a tiny island in the Bahamas, now known as San Salvador (then known as Guanahani). It can also be argued that Columbus did not discover this tiny island far from the mainland, until almost 500 years after Leif Eriksson, also a European, had "discovered" America by landing on the mainland of the North American continent in an area now known as Nova Scotia (Cooley (1), §2:14, 155).

Thus, we can easily see that the statement "Columbus discovered America" is not a fact, but rather a not-very-reliable inference which is based upon multiple assumptions and imprecise definitions. Unconscious assumption-making, such as that illustrated here, can inhibit effective problem-solving and, if unchecked, can permeate and debilitate the negotiator's or mediator's entire function.

2.2.3.2. A personal example of a failure to challenge assumptions

People who are extremely logical or cliché patterned in their thinking often see lateral thinkers as rule benders or breakers – even cheaters. This occurs because vertical thinkers often assume that there are rules preventing or requiring behavior. These rules often do not in fact exist. If vertical thinkers take time to challenge their assumptions, they may perceive that such rules are non-existent or inapplicable. A case in point from my personal life occurred in the mid-1980s when I was just becoming acquainted with lateral thinking strategies and their applications in both my professional and personal life (Cooley (1), §2:10, 119-121).

It was a bright, brisk day in February. My wife, son, daughter, and I were enjoying a family ski vacation in the Colorado Rockies. We were skiing the Arapaho Basin, a good part of which is above the treeline, an area generally unobstructed by trees and other obstacles. By coincidence, my daughter, Christina, who was thirteen years old at the time, and I met at the ski-lift at the base of the hill about mid-afternoon and decided to ride up the lift together. While on the lift, we decided to ski down together, which was fairly unusual because all day we had been independently going our own way, occasionally seeing each other and waving. I told Christina I would follow her down the hill. I did this for two reasons. First, I did not know her proficiency on this particular slope, and secondly, I wanted to be able to help if she ran into trouble and took a bad spill. Much to my surprise, her skiing was extremely proficient on this particular run. In fact, she demonstrated ability pretty much equal to mine, or better. I followed about fifty yards behind her all the way down the hill. There were two critical points on the run. The first point we had to get past was a boarding area for a ski-lift taking skiers to a much higher slope. I followed Christina around the far side of the boarding area and then she took a sharp left, a right angle turn, down the hill. I followed. When we got near the bottom part of the slope, Christina reached a fork. One ski-trail led to a very steep slope, with a degree of difficulty that would definitely challenge our skiing abilities. The other ski trail led to a narrow ski path winnowing through the woods near the base of the hill. Christina opted for the path through the woods, and I followed. Eventually we wound our way back to the ski-lift boarding area near the lodge at the base of the hill.

We rode up together on the ski-lift again. Being comfortable with Christina's proficiency at skiing, I challenged her to a race down the hill. She accepted with delight. We "stipulated" that at the fork near the base of the hill, we would take the winding ski-path through the woods. We got off the ski-lift and prepared to ski down the hill. "Get ready, get set, go!" We were off and skiing. I initially took the lead and headed toward the first critical point – the far side of the boarding area for the ski-lift to the higher slope – and prepared to make a right-angle turn to the left. In the peripheral vision of my left eye, I saw something I couldn't believe. I saw my daughter angling down the hill on the *near* side of the ski-lift boarding area. "She's taking the hypotenuse," I exclaimed to myself. "She's actually taking the hypotenuse!" "What nerve!" "She's cheating!" I was madder than a hatter. On making my right-angle left-turn, Christina was barely visible in the distance. I started digging my poles in the packed snow and flailing my arms up and down like a wounded pigeon. I began to pick up speed, but Christina maintained a commanding lead. When Christina reached the fork near the bottom of the hill, she took the ski-path through the woods, as we had "stipulated." Then I thought to myself, "I'll take the short-cut – it's only 'fair' since Christina had cheated on the upper slope." I therefore opted for the steeper down-hill choice, directly violating our "stipulation." I slipped and fell, thereby losing some seconds. By the time I got back on my feet and dusted off, I saw Christina come breezing out of the woods, heading for the finish line, which she crossed with a "thrill of victory" while I watched in the "agony of defeat." When I finally caught up with her near the ski lodge, I said quite pointedly, "Christina, you cheated." She said, "No I didn't, Dad, you did." "The only route we agreed to was the route to take at the lower fork, and I did as we agreed," she said. When she said that I immediately realized what had happened. I had been "topped" again by a "lateral thinker." I made an assumption that wasn't true and became a victim of my own logic. Because I followed Christina down the slope the first time, I assumed that there was a rule in our competitive second run that we would follow the identical route that we took our first time down the hill. There was no such rule, nor any agreement precluding Christina's hypotenuse route. (See figure below). In speaking with her later as to what was going through her mind at the time she took the hypotenuse route, she said that it wasn't planned. She said that she didn't see the route the first time down the hill, and that her decision to take it was instantaneous, and she believed it to be a correct and appropriate solution. She did not feel that she was cheating; she did not believe she was violating any rules.

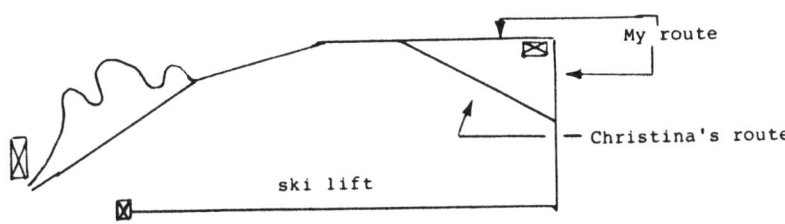

My purpose here in relating this experience from my personal life is to raise your level of awareness as to what lateral thinking is and how it manifests itself in everyday life. The example recounted here demonstrates that some people naturally think laterally. Others, such as myself, have had to work at it, and eventually lateral thinking becomes second nature. Vertical thinkers often believe lateral thinkers are "cheating," when, in fact, they are not "cheating" at all but rather they do not allow their thinking to be blocked by logic, by false assumptions as to the existence of rules, and by cliché thought patterns.

The point to be made is that in order to be creative and expand the vistas of thinking, logical thinkers must avoid the tendency to rely on old thought patterns exclusively. We must learn how to see that certain rules we assume to exist are only a mirage. We must learn how to use our imagination.

Several tools and techniques for implementing the strategy of challenging assumptions appear in Chapter Three.

2.2.4. Generate alternatives

The most fundamental principle of lateral thinking is that any particular way of looking at things is only one from among many other possible ways. Using the generation of alternatives technique, one does not search for the best approach, but rather looks for as many different approaches as possible. In the lateral search, the alternatives generated do not have to be reasonable in themselves. Even if they are not reasonable, they may spark or precipitate reasonable solutions (de Bono (1), 63-89).

Alternatives are negotiators' and mediators' best friends. They create endless opportunities for the effective design of problems, of processes, and of solutions. As noted above, problem solving is comprised of three design problems – problem design, process design, and solution design. By applying the technique of generating alternatives, each of these design stages can be infused with new ideas and new and better ways of doing things. We have learned that the number of ways that a square could be divided into four equal parts was not obvious. Or, on the other hand, maybe the solution – an infinite number of ways – was so obvious that few of us "saw" it initially. In either event, we learned that the number of possible alternative solutions in any particular problem context may be many more than initially anticipated. A person's perception plays a key role in "seeing" the appropriate solution; but so does the engagement of his or her ability and efforts in generating alternatives. This requires active engagement of mind, not merely a passive mental attitude as discussed with respect to some of the other methods of lateral thinking (e.g. brainstorming, random stimulation). The important point to be recognized here is that generation of alternatives is useful and must be accomplished at each stage of creative problem solving process – problem design, process design, and solution design. Many tools and techniques for implementing the strategy of generating alternatives appear in Chapter Three (Cooley (1), §2:12, 129)

2.2.5. Fractionate; Reframe

Using this strategy, one breaks down a situation into fractions and then restructures the situation by putting the fractions together in a new way. Ask "what if." For the negotiator or mediator, fractionation is a method of lateral thinking that is quite useful in designing settlements of disputes, either at the trial or appellate level. Any dispute situation can be broken down into "needs" and "resources" fractions and then restructured by putting the fractions together in a new way. Again, we must keep in mind that the primary aim of lateral thinking is to look at things in different ways, to restructure patterns, to generate alternatives. The mere intention of generating alternatives is sometimes sufficient. Such an intention can make one pause and look around before proceeding too far with the obvious way of looking at the situation. As one looks around one may find that there are other alternatives waiting to be considered. At other times the mere intention of generating alternatives is not sufficient. Goodwill cannot by itself generate alternatives. One has to use some more practical method. Edward de Bono explains this lateral thinking strategy by reference to a problem involving geometric shapes (de Bono (1), 131-140). [Figures for fractionation problem, copyright ©1970 by Edward de Bono, reprinted by permission of HarperCollins Publishers.]

The figure below shows a geometrical shape which could be described as an "L shape." The problem is to divide this shape into four pieces which are exactly similar in size, shape and area.

Initial attempts to do this usually take the form of the divisions as shown in the figure immediately below. This attempt is obviously inadequate since the pieces are not the same in size, even though they may be the same in shape.

Now, try to solve the problem yourself before viewing a correct solution appearing below.

  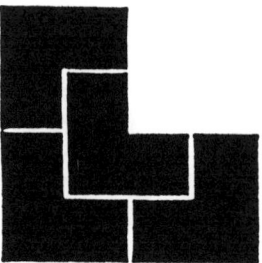

A correct solution, depicted above on the right, is seen to consist of four small L shaped pieces. An easy way to reach this answer is to divide the original shape into three squares and then to divide each of these into four pieces which gives a total of twelve pieces. These twelve pieces must then be assembled in four groups of three and when this has been accomplished as shown, the original is divided into the required four pieces. In a sense, the whole point of language is to often separate units that can be moved around and put together in different ways. The danger is that these different ways soon become established as fixed units themselves and not as temporary arrangements of other units. If one takes any situation and breaks it down into fractions, one can then restructure the situation by putting the fractions together in a new way.

An example of how this strategy of fractionation can be used in a real-real life negotiation or mediation situation appears in Chapter Three in relation to the use of multiple matrices (Section 3.1.25). Several other tools and techniques for implementing this strategy also appear in Chapter Three.

2.2.6. Visualize (Imagineer)

Edward de Bono's book, *Lateral Thinking: Creativity Step by Step*, is replete with examples of visual problem solving by use of simple geometric figures.

Several tools and techniques for implementing the strategy of visualization appear in Chapter Three. See also Section 6.7 *infra*.

2.2.7. Reverse thought

In the thought reversal technique, one takes things as they are and then turns them around, inside out, upside down, back to front, and then sees what happens – what provocative rearrangement of information results. Ask, "What's opposite" (de Bono (1), 141-47).

Comedians often use thought reversal to achieve a humorous effect. Negotiators and mediators use thought reversal to produce ideas which may not be useful in themselves, but which may lead to useful ideas. Let us consider the relationship between fractionation and thought reversal. Fractionation is a useful method for generating different ways of looking at a situation. It has certain limitations, however. The fractions selected are themselves fixed patterns and usually standard patterns. The selection of fractions is usually a vertical choice – a logical decision that follows the most natural lines of division. The result is that the fractions come together repeatedly to give a standard view of the situation. Although fractionation makes it easier to look at a situation in an alternate way, the actual choice of fractions limits the variety of alternatives that can emerge.

The reversal method is more lateral in nature than fractionation. It helps to initiate problem solving, and it tends to yield more unusual restructuring. In the reversal method one moves hard against what is there and fixed in order to move away in the opposite direction. If a person is supposed to obey the government, then the reversal would imply that the government ought to obey a person (or people). Using the reversal method as noted above, one takes things as they are and then turns them round, inside out, upside down, back to front. Then one observes what happens. In essence, it is a provocative rearrangement of information.

Any sort of reversal will do. For instance, as Edward de Bono points out, if the situation is: "a policeman organizing traffic," then the following reversals might be made: The traffic organizes (controls) the policeman or the policeman disorganizes the traffic. Which of these reversals is the better one? Either will do. It is impossible to say which arrangement will be the more useful until it has proved so. It is not a matter of choosing the more reasonable reversal or the more unreasonable one. In using the reversal strategy, one is searching for alternatives, for change, for provocative arrangements of information. As Edward de Bono has stated (de Bono (1), 143-44):

> Occasionally the reversed approach is useful in itself. With the policeman situation the first reversal supposed that the traffic was controlling the policeman. This would lead to consideration of the demand for more policemen as traffic became more complex, the

need for redistribution of policemen according to traffic conditions. It would make one realize that in fact the traffic does actually control the policeman since his behavior depends on the traffic build up in different roads. How quickly does he react to this? How sensitive is he to this? How well informed can he be of this? Since the traffic is controlling the policeman who is controlling the traffic why not organize things so that the traffic controlled itself?

The second reversal in the policeman situation supposed that the policeman was disorganizing the traffic. This would lead to a consideration of whether natural flow, traffic lights or a policeman was most efficient. If a policeman was more efficient than the lights what was the added factor – could this be built into the lights? Was it perhaps easier for the traffic to adjust to fixed patterns of direction rather than the unpredictable reactions of the policeman?

Thought reversal is an effective technique to use in individual or group brainstorming sessions to develop alternative perceptions of the needs and interests of the parties and of the issues involved. Depending on the number of people participating in the session, a "what's opposite" round may spark a new or different way of looking at a particular factual situation in one or more of the participants. Using thought reversal, you can mentally assume that you are, for example, in the shoes of your opponent and attempt to analyze the needs and rights of the parties from his or her point of view. This will help you appreciate your opponent's views and better evaluate their appropriateness.

Several tools and techniques for implementing the strategy of thought reversal appear in Chapter Three.

2.2.8. Use analogies, metaphors, similes

One can use analogies, metaphors, and similes to provide movement. The lateral thinking tool is: Ask "What's similar" (de Bono (1), 167-174).

Because lawyers are generally trained to see differences or distinctions in factual situations, the use of analogies in lateral thinking, for some, may initially be challenging. But for all, it will be stimulating. In order to restructure a pattern, to look at a situation in a different way, to have new ideas, one must start having some ideas. Two challenges associated with lateral thinking are: (1) to get going, to get some movement, to start a train of thought; and (2) to escape the natural, obvious train of thought.

The important point to remember about an analogy is that it seemingly has a "life" of its own. This "life" can be expressed directly in terms of the objects involved or it can be expressed in terms of the processes involved. Also, the analogy does not have to be long or complicated. A simple activity may suffice. As Edward de Bono explains (de Bono(1), 168):

> Analogies are used to provide movement. The problem under consideration is related to the analogy and then the analogy is developed along its own lines of development. At each stage the development is transferred back to the original problem. Thus the problem is carried along with the analogy. In mathematics one translates things into symbols and then deals with these symbols by means of various mathematical operations. One forgets all about the real meaning of the symbols. At the end the symbols are translated back and one finds out what has become of the original situation. The mathematical operation is a channel which directs the development of the original problem.

> Analogies can be used in the same way. One can translate the problem into an analogy and then develop the analogy. At the end one translates back and sees what might have happened to the original problem. It is probably more useful to develop the two in parallel. What is happening in the analogy is transferred (as a process or relationship) to

the actual problem.

It is important to note that using an analogy in this way is very different from arguing by analogy. In argument by analogy one supposes that because something happens in a certain way in the analogy then it must happen in the same or similar way in the problem situation. The use of analogies in lateral thinking is completely different. The goal is not to prove something. Analogies are used as a strategy for generating further ideas.

When choosing an analogy, it is not important that the analogy fit the situation exactly. Sometimes it is better when it does not fit, for then there is an effort to relate it to the problem and from this effort can arise new ways of looking at the problem. The analogy is a provocative device, which is used to force a new way of looking at the situation. In general, the analogies should deal with very concrete situations and very familiar ones. It can be a story, provided that the development of that story is definite.

The analogy technique can be used both in group and internal brainstorming sessions to generate additional alternatives or different ways of looking at things. In a group brainstorming session, one or two rounds can be devoted to free association of words. For example, if the propriety of a particular governmental regulation is being questioned, one or two rounds of the brainstorming session can be devoted to generating other similar governmental rules which require or proscribe similar conduct. The "closeness" of the analogies in relation to the rule in question will vary. Generation of analogous rules, or the inability to generate rules closely analogous to the questioned rule will be helpful ultimately in determining whether the questioned rule warrants being challenged. This same technique can be used in issue development. The leader reads a short statement of facts to the brainstorming group, and asks "What's similar?" The group then participates in several rounds of brainstorming offering single-word analogies or short phrases – whatever pops into mind. The group will be surprised at the variety of perceptions which will necessarily emerge. Some analogies will be humorous. But humor should not be discouraged, because even the most absurd analogy may trigger a thought in someone's mind that might otherwise be imprisoned by cliché pattern-thinking (Cooley (1), §2:22, 185).

Another method of using analogies to stimulate creative thought is to use the simile and metaphor techniques in a brainstorming session. A simile is a figure of speech using "as" or "like" in which two unlike things are compared directly and explicitly, e.g., "he's fit as a fiddle;" or "he went through it like a hot knife through butter." A metaphor is the application of a word or phrase to something that it does not apply to literally, in order to indicate a comparison with the literal usage, e.g., "autumn of one's life," "food for thought," or "screaming headlines." The basic difference between the simile and the metaphor is that in the simile the intended comparison of two things or actions is distinct, explicit, and can usually be visualized as possibly occurring or existing in real life experience. In the metaphor, the comparison is more abstract, often attributing human characteristics to inanimate objects or to natural occurrences, or vice versa. Applying the simile method to brainstorming fact perceptions and issues, the leader should first read a short statement of facts and then ask the individual participants to respond, in rotation, with a commonly recognized simile, in the format "as --------------" or "----------- like a -----------." After a round or two of commonly recognized similes, then the leader can permit the group to create their own similes. Some of these will be humorous, and humor should not be discouraged since richer and more novel ideas will be permitted to surface. A round or two of metaphors can also be conducted – both commonly recognized and participant-created metaphors. This will enhance abstract thinking and will allow the group to explore ideas that would not otherwise surface through direct comparisons spawned by the simile method. Mixed metaphors, such as "the only thing this government will listen to is muscle," should not be discouraged (Cooley (1), §2:22, 185-86).

Several tools and techniques for implementing the strategy of analogies, metaphors, and similes appear in Chapter Three.

2.2.9. Welcome random ideas

In the random stimulation strategy, one uses any information whatsoever, no matter how unrelated it may seem. No information is rejected as useless. The more irrelevant the information, the more useful it may be. Random stimulation occurs through exposure and formal generation (de Bono(1), 193-205).

For those negotiators and mediators who like to browse (through libraries, bookstores, department stores, etc.), random stimulation as a method of lateral thinking will be second nature. To others, it will be an invitation to "let go," to let your minds wander and explore. Most of the techniques discussed so far have worked from within the idea. The idea has been developed according to some routine process with the intention of allowing the information to snap together again in a new pattern. But instead of trying to work from within the idea, one can deliberately generate external stimulation, which then acts on the idea from outside. That is the key to random stimulation – any external information is useful.

The use of random stimulation differs fundamentally from vertical thinking. With vertical thinking one deals only with what is relevant. In fact one spends most of one's time selecting out what is relevant and what is not. With random stimulation one uses any information whatsoever. No matter how unrelated it may be, information is never rejected as useless. The more *irrelevant* the information the more useful it might be.

As noted above, the two main ways of bringing about random stimulation are exposure and formal generation. The division between exposure and formal generation of random stimulation is only one of convenience. If one actively puts oneself into a position where one is subjected to random stimulation, then that is part exposure and part formal generation. The following points may serve to illustrate the way random stimulation can be used. As Edward de Bono points out:

1. Accepting and even welcoming random inputs. Instead of shutting out something which does not appear relevant one regards it as a random input and pays it attention. This involves no further activity than an attitude that notices what comes along.

2. Exposure to the ideas of others. In a brainstorming session the ideas of others act as random inputs in the sense that they do not have to follow one's own line of thought even though they occupy the same field of relevance. Listening to others even if one disagrees very strongly with their ideas can provide useful input.

3. Exposure to ideas from completely different fields. This sometimes goes under the heading of "cross disciplinary fertilization." It means discussing a matter with someone in a totally different field. For instance a medical scientist might discuss systems behaviour with a business analyst or with a fashion designer. One can also listen to other people talking on their own subject.

4. Physical exposure to random stimulation. This may involve wandering around an area which contains a multitude of different objects, for instance a general store like Woolworths or a toy shop. It may also mean going along to an exhibition which has nothing to do with the subject you are interested in (de Bono (1), 194).

The core principle of the exposure method is that *one is never looking for anything*. One could go to an exhibition to see if there was anything relevant. One proceeds with a completely blank mind and waits for something to catch one's attention. Even if nothing seems to catch one's attention, there is still no effort to find something useful.

The second way of bringing about random stimulation is formal generation. In order to use truly random inputs one has to generate them deliberately. This seems paradoxical in so far as a random input is supposed to occur by chance. What one actually does is to set up a formal process to produce chance events.

Shaking a pair of dice is such a situation. Edward de Bono suggests three methods of formal generation: (1) use of a dictionary to provide a random word; (2) formal selection of a book or journal in a library; (3) the use of some routine to select an object from the surroundings (e.g. the nearest red object) (de Bono (1), 195).

Random stimulation may be difficult for lawyers at first. Lawyers are taught to be concerned primarily with that which is relevant to the problem at hand. That which is irrelevant is automatically excluded. The rules of evidence, the court system, and the lawyer's traditional immersion in the tasks of designing biased problems and biased solutions perpetuate the lawyer's near obsession to identify and select "the relevant" and to discard "the irrelevant." In order for the lawyer to effectively apply the random stimulation technique, he or she must "unlearn" the traditional concepts of relevance versus irrelevance. There is no question that determining what is relevant is ultimately an essential task in creative problem solving; but in order to expand the scope and usefulness of "the relevant," the negotiator or mediator must first explore the irrelevant by use of the random stimulation technique.

To enhance random stimulation, negotiators and mediators should maintain an open attitude when listening to the conversations of others. They should deliberately try not to be judgmental about what is being said. Whatever is said may trigger a thought or an idea that, without random input, might have never formed.

Negotiators and mediators should also seek exposure to the ideas of others, however diverse. Thus, in arranging for brainstorming sessions, you should provide for a "mix" of personalities and legal specialties. If the case you are brainstorming as an advocate in mediation is the resolution of a commercial case for example, consider not limiting the group to lawyers who practice in the field of commercial law, if you have a choice. Also invite lawyers who litigate in other practice areas – real estate, securities, domestic relations, criminal, antitrust, etc. Also invite lawyers who do not litigate at all, but rather perform corporate lawyer functions, such as drafting contracts, drawing up wills and trusts, handling incorporations, etc. In this way, you will greatly increase the probability that the random input will yield a broader array of usable ideas. In one case I mediated, the litigators on one side of a commercial case brought with them a transactional lawyer from their firm. That lawyer was of great value to the rest of us in helping to generate ideas about how the commercial case could be resolved.

Additionally, to enhance the effectiveness of random stimulation, negotiators and mediators should allow themselves to be exposed to ideas from completely different fields. In drafting a chapter on the "Thinking Function," for an appellate advocacy manual some years ago, I intentionally sought random input from fields totally outside the field of law. Musicians, artists, architects, psychologists, philosophers, game theorists, political scientists, sociologists, management experts, communication theorists, among others were consulted. Through this random input over a two-year period, it became apparent how differently the members of different disciplines think and, paradoxically, how methods used by one discipline could be effectively incorporated and used by another discipline.

Several tools and techniques for implementing the strategy of random stimulation appear in Chapter Three.

CHAPTER THREE

GENERIC TOOLS AND TECHNIQUES OF THE CREATIVE PROBLEM SOLVER AND SAMPLE APPLICATIONS

The obscure we see eventually. The completely apparent takes longer.

Edward R. Murrow

*I kept six honest serving men,
They taught me all I knew;
Their names were What and Why and When,
And How and Where and Who.*

Rudyard Kipling

It is said that Thomas Edison, the famed problem solver and inventor, was highly skilled at hiring the person best suited to perform a particular job. On one occasion, he was hiring engineers and he gave each candidate an empty flask and asked: "How much water will it hold?" Obviously, there were at least two ways to find the answer. A candidate could use special gauges, measure the surface area of the flask, and then, using mathematical formulae, calculate the volume of the flask. This usually took thirty minutes or more. The other way was simply to fill the bulb with water and pour the contents into a standard measuring cup. Time to accomplish this? About thirty seconds. Edison thanked and politely dismissed engineer candidates who used the first method. He hired those who used the second. As negotiators and mediators, we have much to learn from Thomas Edison about using a common sense approach to solving problems and resolving conflict. Oftentimes, in negotiation and mediation, the optimum problem solving approach or technique to employ is practical and obvious, but we fail to engage our common sense, and therefore we simply do not "see" it. In this Chapter we will review many generative and analytical tools and techniques that can be used to enhance creative problem solving and to implement the strategies covered in Chapter Two in any context. In that sense they are generic in nature. Of course, they can also be adapted to creative problem solving in the negotiation and mediation contexts. Many of these tools and techniques are very basic and practical, and this Chapter can be used as an idea-generator to help us apply our common sense and "see" the obvious. The creative problem solving strategies that each of the generative and analytical tools and techniques support are indicated in parentheses after the name of the tool or technique.

3.1. GENERATIVE TOOLS AND TECHNIQUES

3.1.1 Reconsider your starting point (Reverse Thought)

If you reach a solution that fails to solve the problem you have defined, reconsider your starting point. Ask yourself, "What am I really trying to accomplish?" Then consider any alternative that accomplishes this goal, even if it requires modifying the problem that you have originally designed (Fobes, 39-40).

3.1.2 Restate/redesign the problem (Generate Alternatives)

Sometimes it is difficult to solve a problem because the problem is initially ill-defined (Jones, 65-67). Here is a five-step technique for redefining the problem:

3.1.2.1 Paraphrase: Restate the problem using different words without losing the original meaning.

Initial statement: How can we limit our mediation caseload?
Paraphrase: How can we prevent our mediation caseload from growing?

3.1.2.2 Flip 180 degrees: Turn the problem on its head.

Initial statement: How can we encourage disputants to use our mediation services?
Paraphrase: How can we discourage disputants from using our mediation services?

3.1.2.3 Broaden Focus: Restate the problem in a larger context.

Initial statement: Should I change from a law practice to a mediation practice?
Broaden focus: How can I achieve job satisfaction?

3.1.2.4 Redirect the focus: Boldly, consciously change the focus.

Initial statement: How can we increase our market share?
Redirected focus: How can we cut costs of production?

3.1.2.5 Ask "Why" repetitively until the essence of the real problem emerges.

Initial statement: Should we market our in-house mediation training to the large corporate members of our association?

Why? (should we do that): Because many of our organizational members are outsourcing their mediation training to other in-house mediation training departments of national associations.

Why? (are they doing that): Because they may not be aware of our in-house mediation training offerings.

Why? (are they not aware): Because we have not marketed our mediation training to our large corporate members.

Why? (have we not marketed it): Because we have a small training staff.

Why? (is it small). Because we had only a small demand from large corporate members for our mediation training in the past.

Why? (have we had a small demand): Because we never conducted a survey of our large corporate members to determine whether they would be interested in procuring our mediation training resources.

Why? (haven't we done that before). Because we never thought about doing it until right now.

Thus, by using the restatement of problem tool, the ADR Association has uncovered a principal problem – how to determine whether its large corporate members would use the Association's in-house mediation training if the Association expanded its training staff. As you can see, restating the problem several different ways is a divergent technique that can reveal several important perspectives and issues that might otherwise be overlooked (Jones, 65-67).

3.1.3 Reconsider your goals at any time (Challenge Assumptions)

When you begin the problem solving process there may be too little information to choose a goal, or goals, wisely. Thus, you should avoid assuming that your original goals are correct and rigid. When information is developed, you may find that a new idea emerges that doesn't fit within your originally established narrow goal. If this occurs, be open to the prospect of broadening your goal to accommodate this new idea, or even to changing your goals altogether (Fobes, 41-42).

3.1.4 Distinguish between intermediate goals and final goals (Challenge Assumptions)

Often people will solve a problem and believe that they have accomplished their final goal when, in fact, they have only accomplished an intermediate goal. To ensure that your final goal is not merely an intermediate one, ask yourself, "If I accomplish this, and absolutely nothing else, will this completely solve the problem?" If you answer no to this question, you probably have set an intermediate goal for yourself. It is okay, of course, for you to set an intermediate goal in solving your problem as long as you know the difference between the intermediate goal and the final goal. But you must keep in mind that achieving the intermediate goal will not ensure that you will reach your final goal, particularly if you have limited yourself to a single pathway to your destination. You may find that there is a more appropriate intermediate goal to set for yourself, or that the achieving of several alternative intermediate goals will increase the likelihood that you will achieve your final goal (Fobes, 48-50).

3.1.5 Consider indirect approaches to reach your intermediate and final goals (Generate Alternatives)

If you meet resistance in problem solving, try an indirect approach. Work smarter rather than harder. Indirect approaches include redirection (or changing direction), proceeding step by step (slow down and seek firm footing each step of the way), amplification (procure assistance of others to arrive at a goal), and leverage (know when and how to apply power in achieving your goal) (Fobes, 51-53).

3.1.6 Consider prioritizing multiple goals (Fractionate)

Deciding the relative order of importance of multiple goals may have the effect of broadening your alternatives. If you find it difficult to prioritize your multiple goals, consider asking yourself this question: "Which goal, if it could be achieved, would make the other goals unnecessary – for now at least?" (Fobes, 54-57).

3.1.7 Express negative goals as positive goals (Reverse Thought)

Negative goals point somewhere and say "don't go there." In contrast, positive goals point in another (or opposite) direction and say "let's go there!" An example of expressing a negative goal as a positive one would be: "How do we stop racial discrimination?" (negative goal); "How do we encourage inter-racial dignity and respect?" (positive goal) (Fobes, 42-43)

3.1.8 Try pulling instead of pushing (Visualize)

If you are stymied in attempting to solve an interpersonal conflict, try pulling instead of pushing. Pulling is a type of motivation to act. To "pull" means saying, "If you do this for me, then I'll do that for you." To "push" means saying, "If you do this, then I will hurt you by doing that." Pulling, though often overlooked, usually takes less effort than pushing because it is easier to convey what you want rather than identifying the many behaviors you don't want (Fobes, 60-62).

3.1.9 Inverse Brainstorming (Reverse Thought)

Inverse brainstorming is a technique you can use when you want to make a good situation even better. Regular brainstorming begins with a problem and then seeks a solution. Inverse brainstorming works in reverse. You start with what appears to be a satisfactory situation and then you look for potential problems. By solving the problems that you find, you achieve overall improvement (Higgins, 40).

3.1.10 Try the SCAMPER tool (Generate Alternatives)

SCAMPER is an acronym useful for idea generation or idea refinement discussed in the creative problem solving literature (Ayan, 207-08). In this technique, each letter stands for a mental action you might take to test or improve upon a budding idea. The letters represent the following mental actions and related questions that you might ask yourself when creative problem solving:

- **Substitute** – What can I substitute in the material, process, approach, ingredient, appearance, etc.?

- **Combine** – What purposes, ideas, processes, ingredients, etc. can I blend?

- **Adapt** – What else is like this? What can I copy?

- **Magnify/Minimize/Modify** – What can I add? Can I lengthen it? Strengthen it? Make it thicker? Add more value? What can I subtract to make it smaller or shorter?

- **Put to other uses** – What are new ways to use what I already have?

- **Eliminate** – What can I take away? get rid of?

- **Reverse/Rearrange** – What can I transpose? Turn upside down? Turn inside out? Look at backward? Reschedule? Resequence?

3.1.11 Consider role playing to find a solution (Reverse Thought)

Role playing can be a very useful tool for the mediator in joint sessions and when caucusing. Role playing requires that the participants pretend they are someone else. Participants who put themselves in someone else's shoes, often obtain new insights into the problem situation that frequently result in potential solutions. For example, in a caucus, a mediator in a work place conflict can play the role of a supervisor and the complaining employee can vent to the mediator. This may relieve tension in the situation sufficiently to enable the employee to begin to think rationally about possible solutions. Also, in the supervisor role, the mediator can ask questions or make comments that help the employee better understand the supervisor's perspective. In a mid-mediation joint session where the disputants are amenable to role playing, the disputants each can role play in another disputant's shoes to gain useful insight to the problem. When there are multiple disputants, there can be multiple role playing in sequence so that each disputant is able to view the problem from each other's perspective. This technique enhances the opportunity for insight restructuring and for useful ideas for solutions (Higgins, 41-42).

3.1.12 Focus on similarities (Analogies, Metaphors, Similes)

Two dissimilar things can be shown through analogy to have some similarity. Analogies can be very detailed and they can assist problem solvers to gain insight into a problem. For example, creative problem solving in mediation can be analogized in some detail to the process of designing a joke. By the same token, a metaphor can be used to create new ways of viewing old realities. A metaphor is a figure of speech in which two different universes of thought are seen to be linked by some point of similarity. An example of a metaphor would be: his proposal would create a corporate Loch Ness. In one sense, all metaphors are analogies, but not all analogies – particularly complex ones – are metaphors. Similes are a specific type of metaphor that uses the words "like" and "as." An example would be: at the mediation, the plaintiff behaved "like a bull in a china shop". In group idea generating sessions, the chairperson can ask participants to think of analogies, metaphors, and/or similes to "unearth" potential "deeply buried solutions" (Higgins, 61-63).

3.1.13 Think visually and sketch visual representations (Visualize)

At the beginning of problem solving, or when you reach impasse, try thinking visually and sketch visual representations (Fobes, 126-133). Thinking in pictures and drawing images often yield different and sometimes better results than thinking in words. Consider a situation where the owner of a collection of four rare books has a dispute with her insurance company over what the insurance company should pay to settle a damage claim involving the books. The policy states that the insurance company "will pay $250 per inch of damaged pages to the listed rare books, where the damage occurs through no fault of the owner." The owner and the insurance company differ over the inches of pages damaged to the four rare books that are listed in the policy. The owner believes that the damage occurred to 4 and 1/16 inches of pages of the books. The insurance adjuster believes the number of inches of damaged pages to be much less. The facts are as follows:

> The four books were arranged on the shelf in volume order, going from left to right – i.e. Volume I, Volume II, Volume III, and Volume IV. The acid started on the first page of Volume I and ate all the way through to the last page of Volume IV. The front and back covers of the books were each one-sixteenth of an inch thick, and the pages in each book took up one inch. How many inches did the acid eat up? Sketch a picture of the problem situation and reread the statement of the problem and then come to a solution. One solution to the problem appears below.

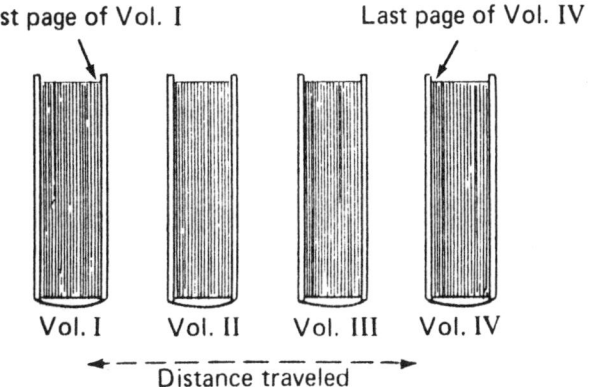

Solution: From the above figure, it is clear that the acid ate through six covers (one-sixteenth inch each) or three-eighths inches and additionally it ate through 2 stacks of pages (1 inch each), for a grand total of 2 and three-eighths inches (Albrecht (2), 36, 38). [Figure reproduced with the permission of Karl Albrecht. Visit KarlAlbrecht.com for additional resources.]

The key to solving this problem is to draw a sketch of books as if viewed on the shelf from above. Then, when you reread the problem, you pay close attention to where the first page of Volume I and the last page of Volume IV would be. They are not located where you might assume – at the extremities of the books.

3.1.14 Imagine what someone else might suggest (Generate Alternatives)

To avoid thinking in a habitual way, imagine what some other person – from some other profession – might suggest as a way to solve your problem. Suppose you are mediating a case involving an allegedly defective air conditioning system in a new high rise office building. To help overcome your cliché pattern thinking about these types of construction cases, it might be helpful to you in your planning for the mediation to systematically imagine what someone else might suggest as a solution. An architect might review the building plans to determine if the specifications for a cooling system are appropriate; an engineer might determine if the cooling system met all of the architect's specifications; a construction contractor might ask if the subcontractor that installed the system followed the manufacturer's specification and used the correct size ductwork; a cooling system manufacturer to determine if this product failed to perform properly in other high rise buildings; a building manager might determine whether the building's maintenance department serviced and maintained the cooling system in accordance with directions contained in the service manual (Fobes, 139-140).

3.1.15 Use Fishbone Diagram (Generate Alternatives)

The fishbone diagram tool was developed by Professor Kaoru Ishikawa of the University of Tokyo. The purpose of the exercise is to identify and list all the possible causes of the problem under consideration. It is primarily used in group settings, but it can also be used by individuals as well. It is called the fishbone diagram because of the way the information is gathered and arranged visually. Imagine a diagram that resembles the skeleton of a fish. The problem is written in a circle (representing the head of the skeleton) on the right side of the paper, and a straight line is drawn horizontally to the left across the page (towards the tail of the skeleton). The straight line represents the backbone of the fish. The next step is to draw the bones of the fish at a 45 degree angle from the backbone with the free ends angled toward the back of the skeleton. Causes of the problem are then brainstormed, with the least complicated written on the angled-back lines toward the head of the fish, and the most complicated near the tail. It is recommended that the fishbone diagram be brainstormed over more than one session because incubation of ideas improves the quality and success of the exercise. Normally, participants deal with the less complicated possible causes first and then move to the more complicated ones. This tool is useful, even if used in one session, because it helps problem solvers see the total problem as opposed to focusing on a narrow part of it, and it helps show the relationships between causes and the relative importance of those causes (Higgins, 45-48).

3.1.16 Use Why-Why Diagram (Generate Alternatives)

A variation of the Fishbone Diagram (see immediately above) is the Why-Why Diagram. This tool can be used to systematically identify the cause or causes of a problem. The technique involves simply asking the question "why" until possibilities are exhausted or until a sufficient level of detail has been achieved. Consider the example below:

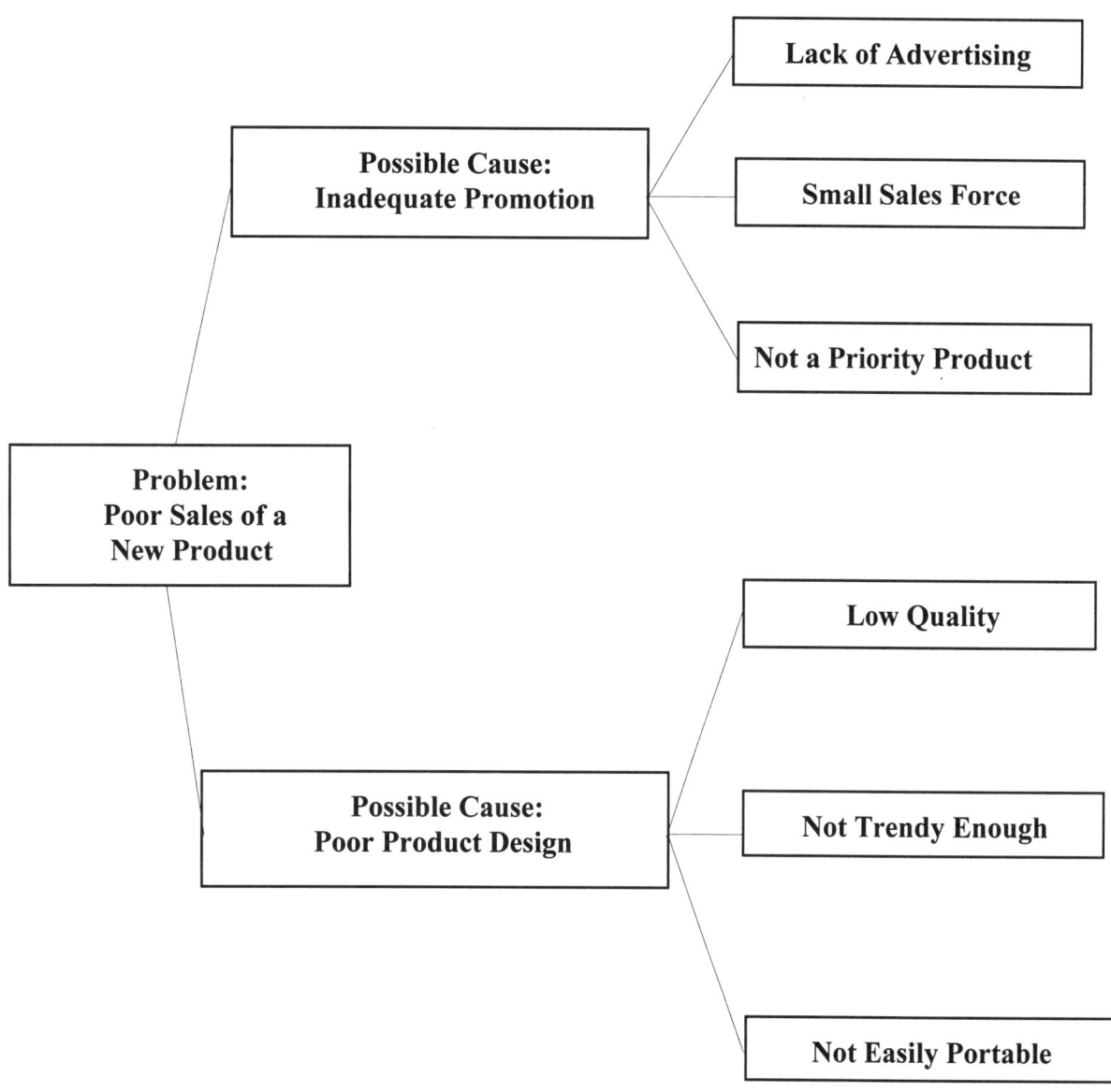

The chart above represents just a portion of a Why-Why Diagram. It only addresses two of the possible causes (inadequate promotion and poor product design). Other possible causes that could be similarly analyzed are: ineffective distribution, price too high, failed to identify market. Asking "why" concerning inadequate promotion and poor product design yielded three possible causes as to each. The process would continue by asking "why" as to the six identified possible causes, which could yield numerous additional possible causes. By continuing this process, the problem solver may be able to identify the root problem cause or causes so that possible solutions can be brainstormed (Higgins, 51-53).

3.1.17 Distinguish between dimensional independence, dependence, and relationships (Visualize; imagineer)

Often problem solvers are set to see an oversimplified single dimension where in fact multiple independent dimensions exist. It is important to perceive these other dimensions and consider how these independent dimensions relate to one another. A tool that helps reveal the other dimensions and all the interrelationships of dimensions is a simple x/y axis. Let's assume that as a mediator you have come to realize that attorneys who participate in mediations possess varying degrees of assertive behavior. Mentally you can picture a spectrum of advocate behavior as a horizontal line with 0 assertiveness at the left end and high assertiveness on the right end of the line. But that is only one dimension of advocate behavior. Another dimension is cooperativeness, which is independent of assertiveness. If you graph assertiveness in relation to cooperativeness as shown in the figure below, you can create a tool to that helps you understand the relationships between other behaviors in the mediation (Fobes, 163-177).

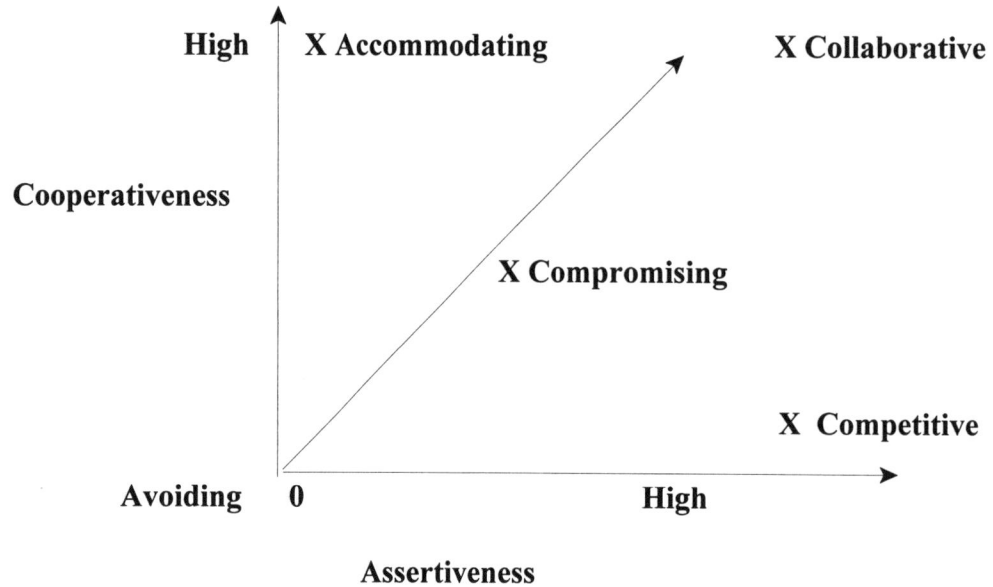

This graph reveals that when assertiveness is graphed against cooperativeness on x/y axes, other advocate behaviors can be visualized: 0 assertive and 0 cooperative -- avoiding; 0 cooperative and highly assertive – competitive; 0 assertive and highly cooperative – accommodating; moderately assertive and moderately cooperative – compromising; and highly assertive and highly cooperative – collaborative (Cooley(2), 167-172; Galvin, Bylund, and Brommel, 235).

3.1.18 Use Interest-Resource Table to generate new ideas (Generate Alternatives)

The table below provides a useful survey of possible interests and interest-satisfying resources of parties in any dispute or transaction situation. The interests may relate to different needs of the parties and may actually be overlapping or compatible, in achieving an integrative (non-monetary or combined monetary and non-monetary) in both personal and corporate disputes. Whether you are a negotiator, mediator, advocate in mediation, your pre-session analysis should include both interests and resources related specifically to the dispute, and, as importantly, general interests and resources of the parties, unrelated to the dispute. Through use of your imagination, you can expand the universe of possible interests and resources geometrically. This table can also be used, of course, at any point in the negotiation or mediation to generate alternative solutions or to obviate an impasse (Cooley(2), 221-25).

INTEREST-RESOURCE TABLE

Time	Words	Secrecy
Place	Apology	Release
Quantity	Control	Reinstatement
Quality	Persons	Assurances
Size	Nature	Procedure
Context	Structure	Opportunity
Distance	Types	Guarantee
Responsibility	Volume	Publicity
Rate	Proportion	Security
Space	Exchange	Share

For example, when preparing a case for negotiation or mediation, consider the items in the above table metaphorically – in the broadest sense possible. Thus, if you are preparing for the mediation of a business dispute, "volume" could refer to tripling a marketing effort (i.e. turning up the volume of the corporate message), or decreasing the amount of production output, or increasing the amount of storage space in a warehouse. "Rate" could refer to frequency of occurrence, or a commission or discount, or an evaluation of products, services, or performance, and so on.

3.1.19 Use storyboarding (Generate Alternatives)

Storyboarding can be used at all stages of the problem solving process, but it is especially useful in generating and selecting alternatives. Compared to brainstorming, which is normally used with a narrowly defined problem, storyboarding can be of substantial assistance in solving complex problems. Storyboarding follows the basic processes of brainstorming, but it takes brainstorming several steps farther. It uses a leader, a secretary and a group of people working together in compliance with the four rules of brainstorming.

A storyboard is organized in columns underneath major elements known as headers. There are several types of headers: topic header, purpose header, miscellaneous header, other headers related to major issues and/or solutions to the problem. There are four principal types of story boards: planning, ideas, organization, and communication boards. The planning storyboard contains all the major ideas related to solving the problem described by the topic header. The ideas storyboard is an expansion of some of the ideas on the planning board. Participants brainstorm subheadings for each of the headers, and they may add new headers during that process. The organization storyboard answers three questions: What are the tasks that need to be done? When do they need to be done? Who will be doing them? The communications storyboard answers four questions: Who needs to know? What do they need to know? When do they need to know it? What media are going to be used to convey the information? There are two types of storyboard sessions: creative thinking sessions and critical thinking sessions. These sessions take place for each of the four types of storyboards (Higgins, 161-76).

3.1.20 Conduct an organized random search (Stimulate Random Thoughts).

A matrix is a grid with as many cells as needed for whatever problem is being analyzed, and it is one of the handiest, clearest ways of sorting information (Jones, 115). The use of matrices in connection with creative problem solving techniques is discussed elsewhere in this chapter (See Section 3.1.25).

One way to stimulate new ideas is to randomly select a page from a dictionary. Then randomly choose words on that page to generate ideas by making associations regarding your problem or its attributes. A two-dimensional matrix can be used to compare the words you select from the page with thoughts about your problem or its attributes. The matrix expands the possibilities that the words selected from the page will generate useful ideas. This technique is often used by advertisers, artists, writers and others who depend on their creativity for their livelihood (Higgins, 91-92).

3.1.21 Stimulate ideas by viewing pictures (Stimulate Random Thought)

This is normally a group exercise in which the Chairperson shows randomly chosen pictures or overhead transparencies to the group. The chairperson conducts the session similar to a brainstorming session. Brainstorming occurs first; evaluation is saved until the descriptions are complete. In the brainstorming portion, without any criticism, each person in the group examines the picture and describes what he or she sees to the other persons in the group. Participants may focus on a detail or two or interpret what they believe the picture is expressing, through some of its details. A scribe records the description for later discussion. Each line of the description may trigger new insights and ideas in the participants. Often, participants are amazed at what people see in the pictures and how they interpret what they see. This realization can reinforce in the participants the importance of understanding how perception and perspectives can influence problem and solution finding. The chairperson continues this process until all the pictures have been examined, described, and the descriptions recorded. After that, the Chairperson leads a discussion to draw out any relationships between the insights and ideas generated in the exercise to the problem at hand (Higgins, 93-94).

3.1.22 Use a verb checklist (Analogies, Metaphors, Similes)

A useful tool to identify action that may be appropriate to help solve a problem is to view a pre-selected list of verbs and try to apply each one to your problem or some aspect of it. Some of the verbs will be difficult to apply, but the key to the success of using this tool is to make your best effort to apply each verb to your problem situation to see if solution ideas eventually emerge. A sample list of verbs appears below:

Multiply	Divide	Eliminate	Subdue
Invert	Separate	Transpose	Unify
Dissect	Distort	Rotate	Flatten
Squeeze	Complement	Submerge	Freeze
Soften	Fluff up	By-Pass	Add
Subtract	Widen	Repeat	Thicken
Stretch	Extrude	Help	Protect
Segregate	Integrate	Symbolize	Abstract

In a group, the chairperson can ask the participants to work separately and jot down their ideas next to each verb. The chairperson can prescribe a ground rule that requires each participant to fill out each blank – even if the "answer" does not make sense. When the participants eventually read back their "answers" in a group setting, the session can turn into a very lively, humorous experience for the participants. The answers that seemed silly or laughable to the participant sharing them may in fact be funny to the group, but they may also spark useful ideas in some participants. These useful ideas can be more fully explored in a later evaluation discussion (Higgins, 95-96).

3.1.23 Try Synectics (Analogies, Metaphors, Similes)

Synectics, created by creative problem solving expert William J.J. Gordon, relies heavily on analogies, metaphors, and association to help the imagination find relationships between seemingly unrelated objects, ideas, persons, etc. The process normally uses seven people: a problem owner, a facilitator, and five other members. Synectics is based on three key assumptions: (1) creativity is latent to some degree in everyone; (2) creativity is more closely related to the emotional and nonrational than to the intellectual and rational; and (3) the emotional elements can be harnessed through training and experience. The facilitator uses three mechanisms: (1) direct analogy; (2) personal analogy; and (3) symbolic analogy. Unlike regular brainstorming, participants are encouraged to criticize and even to be sarcastic at the appropriate time – normally in the final step of the process. A summary of the steps of the Synectics technique appears below:

- The problem is identified and defined by the owner.

- The problem is analyzed briefly by the owner.

- Participants write down personal goals and wishes for the problem which are often vague and "wild and crazy" beginnings for the solution.

- Group goals and wishes are listed by the facilitator.

- The problem owner attempts to identify a possible solution.

- The problem owner lists three strengths and three weaknesses of the possible solution.

- The group critiques the proposed solution (Higgins, 177-180).

3.1.24 Mind maps (Generate Alternatives)

A rather innovative type of self-brainstorming or note-taking is called mind-mapping. Pictorially, mind maps usually take on an organic-like structure that reflects their organized nature. They capitalize on the mind's non-linear behavior in conversation exploring the linear sequence of what is being said, but in the context of multiple subtle changes in intonation, body position, and facial expression. The technique for constructing a mind-map is as follows: (1) start in the center of a piece of paper with the major idea; (2) make the center a strong visual image and everything in the pattern must be associated with it; (3) as information is received, subcenters (topics) are recorded on the map, usually radiating from the subcenters; and (4) use visual images to enhance recall. When drawing the visual images, it is suggested that you print each key word on a line; if possible, use different colors for different topics or themes on the map; use three-dimensional shapes, where possible; use diagrams and pictures as they come to mind if they will aid memory; use arrows to associate different parts of the pattern. When constructing a mind map, you may see associations of topics or relationships of ideas that you would not have noticed if you had taken notes in a linear conventional way (Russell, 175-85).

3.1.25 Use multiple matrices for idea generation purposes
(Generate Alternatives and Fractionate)

As explained above in Section 3.1.20, a matrix is grid with as many cells as needed for whatever problem is being analyzed, and it is one of the handiest, clearest ways of sorting information (Jones, 115). The use of matrices in connection with creative problem solving techniques is discussed elsewhere in this chapter. (See Sections 3.2.3; 3.2.14.2). In this Section we will learn how to use multiple matrices to expand the scope and effectiveness of idea generation. What follows is an adaptation of Cooley (1), Section 2:16.

Let's revisit the simple example of the mechanic/insomniac dispute described above in Section

1.3.10 in relation to designing the solution to a problem. Assume that Bob (the insomniac) goes to a lawyer and after interviewing Bob, the lawyer concludes that an optimal solution to this dispute cannot be reached if he designs the problem in terms of Bob rights. While there is an ordinance in Bob's community, which prohibits residents from engaging in loud-noise activities after 11:00 p.m., the lawyer concludes that a court injunction, although obtainable, would probably not be an adequate solution. What if Bob wanted to go to bed at 10:00 p.m. on some nights? The court-injunction would probably not cover that situation. Besides, the injunction solution would further alienate these neighbors and cause animosity and other interpersonal problems in their relationship. Bob's lawyer decides to take the matter to mediation. He thinks that a mediator will be able to convince Russ to stop repairing his car at night. At this time, Bob's lawyer sees this to be the only plausible solution to the problem.

Now let's assume, further, that Russ and his lawyer agree to mediate the above-described dispute. Both sides select you to be the mediator. Through challenging assumptions, thought reversal, and brainstorming separately with the parties and counsel in caucuses, you develop additional information which opposing counsel and their clients now share:

- the mechanic has a teenage daughter who could walk the insomniac's six-year-old son to school each weekday morning;

- the insomniac attends bridge and chess club meetings two nights a week until 10:30 p.m.;

- the insomniac has a "classic car" which is in need of engine work;

- the insomniac has an extra garage behind his house which is vacant and unused;

- the insomniac has a van which the mechanic borrows from time to time to haul materials, products, and furniture;

- the mechanic and family go to their lake cottage on most weekends;

- the insomniac and family never go away on trips;

- the insomniac's teenage son stays out late most nights and sleeps "like a rock."

The goal now is for you, the parties, and their lawyers to use this information and other known information about the parties in developing a mutually acceptable, optimal solution. To accomplish this most effectively, you may want to help both sides apply fractionation, the lateral thinking technique commonly used in mediation to develop integrative (nonmonetary or combined nonmonetary and monetary) solutions.

Fractionation, as applied to mediation, is the process of disturbing perceptions, exploring options and possibilities, and then reframing and repatterning perceptions. It can be used here to disturb the perception (or assumption) of the parties' limited needs and resources, to explore the possibilities of matching resources to needs, and to repattern the needs-resources possibilities into realistic solution configurations. The discussion which follows explains how you might apply fractionation to help the disputants develop an optimal solution.

In employing fractionation, your first step is to break down the problem into the component needs and resources of the parties. You do this by listing the specific and general needs of the parties and the resources available to each to satisfy their own needs and the needs of the other party. Your use of a matrix format, as shown below, will facilitate this task. This is something you can help the parties sketch out in separate caucuses or in a joint session.

Fortunately for you, the mechanic/insomniac conflict is relatively simple because each party has a single specific need. For the insomniac, it is to substantially reduce or eliminate noise to permit sleep; for the mechanic, it is to repair his car. In other situations, each party may have multiple specific needs with multiple corresponding resources to satisfy those needs. With respect to each single specific need of the parties, there are, as shown below, multiple available resources to satisfy it.

SPECIFIC NEEDS MATRIX

INSOMNIAC

Specific Need: Substantially Reduce or Eliminate Noise to Permit Sleep

Insomniac's Available Resources to Satisfy Own Needs	Mechanic's Available Resources to Satisfy Insomniac's Needs
Sleep in another part of house	Get more effective muffler
Wear earplugs	Work on car in street
Take sleep inducing medication	Work on car on weekends
Wear stereo headset	Use rubber hammer and other rubberized tools
Wear earmuffs	Work on car earlier in the evening.
Go to bed later	
Sleep earlier in the evening	
Move to another house	

SPECIFIC NEEDS MATRIX

MECHANIC

Specific Need: Repair Car

Mechanic's Available Resources to Satisfy Own Needs	Insomniac's Available Resources to Satisfy Mechanic's Needs
Continue current behavior	Use of garage in back of Insomniac's house
See Mechanic's available resources to modify behavior in Insomniac's Specific Needs Matrix	Be out of house until 10:30 two nights per week

GENERAL NEEDS MATRIX

INSOMNIAC

General Need	Own Resources	Mechanic's Resources
Person to take 6-year-old son to school	None	1. Teenage daughter 2. Mechanic drives to work, past school
Person to repair classic car	None (except to pay for repairs)	1. Interest in classic car 2. Mechanical ability

GENERAL NEEDS MATRIX

MECHANIC

General Need	Own Resources	Insomniac's Resources
Van to transport materials	None (would have to rent)	Van
Someone to watch home and take in mail when out of town on weekends	None	Insomniac and wife never go out of town

The next step is to place all the matrices side by side and scan them simultaneously for a few minutes, either in separate caucuses or in a joint session as you deem appropriate to the circumstances. Allow everyone to see relationships and interrelationships between the various specific and general needs and available resources. Then, by using the tool "what if," begin to reframe the situation and restructure it into a new arrangement. You should attempt several "what if" repatternings until an arrangement emerges that tends to optimize satisfaction of the parties' needs and the use of available resources. No arrangement is sacred; any arrangement may at any time be repatterned in this reframing process. One possible "what if" repatterning which might emerge from your scanning of the matrices is as follows:

- Mechanic works on car in driveway until 10:30 and only on nights that Insomniac is participating in his club activities.

- Mechanic is allowed to use Insomniac's van on request in exchange for occasional repair service on Insomniac's classic car.

- Insomniac pays Mechanic's daughter a weekly stipend to walk the Insomniac's son to school.

After another "what if" repatterning, another arrangement might be:

- Mechanic can use Insomniac's spare garage to work on his car any time.

- Mechanic's daughter walks Insomniac's son to school; Mechanic gives daughter a modest increase in her weekly allowance.

- Insomniac watches Mechanic's house and takes in the mail when Mechanic's family goes to the lake on weekends.

Another repatterning might yield this arrangement:

- Insomniac and his wife switch bedrooms with teenage son who is out late most nights and sleeps "like a rock."

The matrices could, of course, yield many other arrangements through repatterning. The point of this subsection has been to illustrate how the strategy of lateral thinking particularly fractionation used in connection with multiple matrices can assist you in helping disputants develop many potential solutions to a dispute situation which initially appears to have but a single solution. If you apply the multiple matrices technique, your only problem might be the difficulty of choosing from among several good solutions. But, of course, that is a problem which you can easily tolerate (Cooley (1), § 2:16).

3.2 ANALYTICAL, EVALUATIVE, AND DECISION MAKING TOOLS AND TECHNIQUES IN CREATIVE PROBLEM SOLVING

In this Section we will be focusing on analytical, evaluative, and decision making tools and techniques that can be used in creative problem solving. A word that will frequently appear in this Section is "probability." Before describing the tools and techniques, it would be helpful to review briefly what "probability" is and how it is estimated or discerned in any problem solving situation (See Jones, 229-33).

Probability is a very difficult concept to define because, as Morgan Jones, explains:

[T]he most difficult analytic problems are of the random and indeterminate type, where, because facts are scarce, our analytic product depends heavily on subjective judgments. For that reason, *there can be no certainty* when dealing with random or indeterminate problems. No certainty at all! The moment our analysis moves from facts to judgment, we leave certainty behind and enter the arena of *estimates*. "Estimating is what we do when we run out of data. The language of estimating is probability, and the laws of probability are the grammar of that language... (Jones, 226).

There are two primary ways to determine probability: computation and frequency-and-experience. When we have all the data, such as in a deterministic problem, we can calculate probability by arithmetic computation. If we do not have all the data, we estimate probability based on frequency and experience. Frequency is defined as how often an event has occurred in the past; experience is what happened during each event. Jones gives the example of a person who drops ten light bulbs on the floor and each one breaks. What is the probability that, if the person drops an eleventh light bulb, it too will break? The probability is very high – almost 100%. The way we determined that probability was through experience. The person repeated the event (dropping a bulb) ten times, and each time there was an identical outcome (Jones, 229).

In creative problem solving, the two most common types of events whose probability we try to determine are: mutually exclusive and conditionally dependent. As Jones explains:

Mutually exclusive events preclude one another. For example, the tossing of a coin involves mutually exclusive events, or mutually exclusive outcomes. Because a coin has two sides, one outcome (Heads or tails) precludes the other. The outcomes are thus mutually exclusive events. ... *Conditionally dependent events* are those in which the occurrence of one event depends upon the occurrence of another. The events thus occur in sequence. Starting the engine of an automobile is a good example. We insert the key into the ignition switch, we turn the key, the starter rotates the engine, and the engine ignites... The first event – inserting the ignition key – conditions the second, meaning the second event occurs *on condition* that the first occurs. The second event conditions the third, and so on. (Jones, 231).

The probability of mutually exclusive events must add up to be 1.0. Let's assume that there are ninety beans in a jar. Forty-five are red, thirty-six are yellow, and nine are green. What is the probability of picking a red bean out the jar? The probability would be 45/90 or .5. The probability of picking a yellow bean would be 36/90 or .4; and the probability of picking a green been would be 9/90, or .1. The three probabilities (.5 +.4+.1) add up to 1.0 (Jones, 232).

The probability of conditionally dependent events is determined by multiplying the two probabilities that are linked conditionally. For example what is the probability of tossing two heads in a row with a coin. The probability of getting a heads on the first toss is ½ or .5. If the next toss turns up tails, the sequence concludes. We toss the second time only on condition that we get heads on the first toss. If heads turns up on the first toss, the probability of getting heads on the second toss is still .5. So there is a 50 percent probability of a 50 percent probability (.5 x .5) of tossing two heads in a row, or .25 (Jones, 236).

In summary, then, to determine the combined probability that two or more events will occur as a result of a single decision or event (the "or" situation), their individual probabilities are added together. To determine the probability that two or more events will occur in succession (the "and" situation), their individual probabilities are multiplied together. It goes without saying that a creative problem solver must carefully examine how a probability statement or question is framed to determine whether the events are mutually exclusive or conditionally dependent (Jones, 239).

3.2.1 Use a checklist (Fractionate)

Using a checklist to examine a problem situation can provide a systematic approach to problem solving, particularly when initially analyzing the situation and when evaluating a solution. Checklists can also be useful in breaking down the problem into component parts and in finding opportunities and compatible interests of the parties (Higgins, 40).

3.2.2 Use storyboarding in critical thinking sessions (Analysis and Evaluation)

See Section 3.1.19, above.

3.2.3 Sketch simple matrices for analysis and evaluation purposes (Fractionate)

To check for overlooked combinations, you can draw a simple matrix. The simple matrix can also serve as a tool to keep yourself apprised during the course of a negotiation or mediation. This can work in situations where two characteristics of a problem are independent of each other. Let's consider a simple application of this tool. Assume that you are the seller of three residential real estate parcels. The buyer is open to purchasing three styles of homes: (1) Victorian; (2) California-style; (3) Colonial. His order of preference for location is: Suburb 1, Suburb 2, Suburb 3, and Suburb 4. The problem is to come up with a means to quickly illustrate what the buyer's options are. This problem qualifies as one suited for resolution by a simple matrix because it has two independent characteristics: type of home and location. All the combinations of possibilities can be demonstrated by using the simple matrix appearing below.

	Victorian	California-style	Colonial
Suburb 1	X		
Suburb 2		X	X
Suburb 3	X	X	
Suburb 4	X	X	X

Using this matrix, the seller can quickly illustrate to the buyer that the buyer's first-preference location – Suburb 1 – has only has one residence (Victorian) that is available for inspection. His least favorite suburb – Suburb 4 – has all three styles of homes available for inspection. From this matrix, the buyer and seller can quickly determine how to schedule inspections of the homes, or which one or ones to eliminate from consideration (Fobes, 84-86).

3.2.4 Consider using sorting and chronologies (Fractionate)

Sorting is an underused analytical problem solving skill that is sometimes overlooked and underused. It is used primarily to breakdown problems and possible solutions into their component parts. It can be used both in simple or complex problem situations. A simple example of the use of the sorting tool would be a mediator's sorting of issues during the course of a multi-party mediation. Issues might be sorted in a variety of ways. Issues could be sorted according to relative priority, complexity, emotional/nonemotional, party alignment, monetary, nonmonetary, and so on. Problem sorting can facilitate resolution.

Using chronologies (or time lines) can also be helpful to problem solving. A chronology depicts, either vertically or horizontally, the timing and sequence of relevant events. It draws attention to key events and to significant time gaps, and it makes it easier to identity patterns and correlations among events. Furthermore, it enhances understanding and appreciation of the context in which events occurred, are occurring or will occur. By using a chronology we are often in a better position to interpret the significance of each event with respect to the problem at hand. Sometimes, the mere use of a chronology can point to a solution to the problem (Jones, 87-93).

3.2.5 Choose by elimination (Suspend Judgment)

In many problem-situations, it is very tempting to simply choose the alternative that you like the most and ignore the other ones. It is often a better practice to sequentially choose the alternative that you like the least and eliminate it as an option. By focusing on each alternative and carefully thinking through why you do not like it as an option, you may think of reasons why it is a better option than you initially thought. As a matter of fact, you may conclude that the alternative you initially liked best is not as good as one of the other alternatives. Consider for a moment the real estate sale scenario presented in the Section 3.3 above. If the buyer chose to inspect the residence that is most appealing to him on the basis of location and style of architecture, he would select the Victorian home in Suburb 1. However, if he focused on the least appealing Suburb – Suburb 4 – he would note that his opportunity to find his "dream home" is maximized because that Suburb has for sale all three of the style homes he prefers. When the seller also advises him that Suburb 4 is serviced by a commuter rail system that has several express trains running to the city (where the buyer works) each weekday morning, a Suburb 4 option might become most appealing to the buyer. He may even decide to inspect those homes first (Fobes, 91-95).

3.2.6 Pros-cons-and fixes (Fractionate)

It is the human condition that, when asked to evaluate the merits of something, we naturally focus on the negative to the virtual exclusion of the positive. A technique called Pros-Cons-and-Fixes is a powerful but simple technique for dealing with our strong compulsion to be critical of whatever we evaluate (Jones, 73-79).

Let's assume that you are an advocate representing a large television manufacturing corporation in a commercial dispute with a very small manufacturer-supplier company, with which the large company has had a long-term business relationship. The small manufacturer-supplier contends it had a contract to provide several thousand transistor components for televisions. After it had manufactured them, the large television manufacturing company notified the supplier that its transistor requirements had changed and that it could not use the transistors that supplier was prepared to deliver. The large company contended that the contract permitted it to change an order or cancel one, if it gave the supplier "adequate notice." The primary issue in the case is whether the large corporation's notice was "adequate." The law is on your side, but your facts are not as good as you would like them to be. Your client's executives and employees who would testify in court are very personable and credible, and would make good witnesses. However, the disputed transaction has related documents that are subject to various interpretations, with many of them being favorable to the small company. The amount in dispute is $1.5 million. The lead counsel on this case in your firm has asked you to evaluate whether a case should go to mediation or to arbitration. There are six steps in using this procedure (Jones, 78). In a nutshell, in applying this technique, the procedure will require you, separately with respect to each of the topics of mediation and of arbitration, to do the following:

Step 1: List all the Pros.
Step 2: List all the Cons.
Step 3: Review and consolidate the Cons, merging and eliminating.
Step 4: Neutralize as many Cons as possible.
Step 5: Compare the Pros and unalterable Cons for all options.
Step 6: Pick one option.

Mediation - Step 1: List All the Pros. (Divergent Thinking)	**Mediation - Step 2: List All the Cons** (Divergent Thinking)
Privacy Parties control forum Parties select neutrals Reflects concerns and priorities of disputants Flexible Process educates disputants Addresses underlying problem Often results in creative solutions High rate of compliance Relatively inexpensive	1. Neutrals have no power to impose settlement 2. No power to compel participation 3. No appeal allowed 4. Powerful party can influence outcome 5. Weak closure 6. Non-binding (unless by consent) 7. No jury to determine facts 8. No application/development of public standards 9. Outcome need not be principled 10. No court judgment (unless by consent) 11. Lacks enforceability 12. No due process safeguards

Mediation - Step 3: Review and Consolidate the Cons (Convergent Thinking)	Mediation - Step 4: Neutralize as Many Cons as Possible (Convert Cons to Pros – or Fixes) (Convergent Thinking)
Eliminate Nos. 3 and 7: "No appeal allowed;" and "No jury to determine facts" as redundant of "No due process safeguards." Eliminate No. 6: "Non-binding (unless by consent)" as redundant of "No court judgment."	Eliminate No. 1: In our case, we don't want an imposed settlement. Eliminate No. 4: In our case, we are the corporation and have the most power. Eliminate No. 8: We don't want the application of public standards – we want a confidential, practical, business solution. Eliminate No. 9: We don't necessarily need a principled result – see reason for eliminating No. 8. Eliminate No. 10: We do not want a public court judgment; we want to keep this resolution secret. Eliminate No. 12: We do not need due process safeguards – just a practical business solution.

Summary of the Analysis: Thus, only three Cons are remaining after this analysis: No. 2 "No power to compel participation;" No. 5 "Weak closure," and No. 11 "Lacks enforceability." Now we will conduct a similar analysis for arbitration.

Arbitration - Step 1: List All the Pros. (Divergent Thinking)	Arbitration - Step 2: List All the Cons (Divergent Thinking)
Privacy Expertise Parties select neutrals Written procedures Expeditious Choice of applicable norms Tailors remedy to situation Enforceability Relatively inexpensive	1. Lack of quality control 2. Neutrals unaccountable 3. Becoming increasingly encumbered by legalization 4. Relaxed rules of evidence 5. Limited or no discovery 6. No public norms 7. No precedent 8. No uniformity 9. Usually no written reasons for decisions 10. Usually no appeal of award

Arbitration - Step 3: Review and Consolidate the Cons (Convergent Thinking)	Arbitration - Step 4: Neutralize as Many Cons as Possible (Convert Cons to Pros – or Fixes) (Convergent Thinking)
Eliminate No. 1: We will control the quality of the process by carefully selecting the neutral. Eliminate No. 2: We can file a court action if arbitrator is shown to be acting in bad faith or biased. Eliminate No. 3: We can conduct ourselves more informally in this private process. Eliminate No. 4: We do not mind having relaxed rules of evidence. Eliminate No. 5: Discovery might even make our position worse. Eliminate No. 6: Public norms are not important to us in this matter; confidentiality is very important. Eliminate No. 7: We neither need nor want precedent. Eliminate No. 8: We can live with no uniformity, so long as we are strong on the case law. Eliminate No. 9: We would rather not have a reasoned decision	Nine of the ten Cons have been eliminated in Step 3.

Summary of the Analysis: Only Con No. 10 ("Usually no appeal of award") remains after this analysis. The large company is worried that it might have to pay more than a million dollar award with no recourse to an appeal. Now we can move to Step 5 of the Pros-Cons-Fixes technique.

Step 5: Compare the Pros and unalterable Cons for all options. Comparing the Pros of Mediation with the Pros of Arbitration, many of them are the same. Mediation has two Pros that especially appeal to the large company: "Addresses underlying problem" and "Often results in creative solutions." These two Pros are important to the large company because it wants to continue to do business with the disputant supplier. None of the Pros of Arbitration is an important consideration for the large company. The remaining Pros and Cons are shown in the charts below.

Mediation – Important Pros	Arbitration – Important Pros
"Addresses underlying problem" "Often results in creative solutions"	None

Mediation – Important Cons	Arbitration – Important Cons
"No power to compel participation" "Weak closure" "Lacks enforceability"	"Usually no appeal of award"

Step 6. Pick one option and provide reasons for the selection. After reviewing the remaining pros and cons, the large company opts for mediation. While in mediation there is no power to compel participation, weak closure, and a lack of enforceability, the more important considerations for the large company are to preserve its business relationship with the supplier, perhaps through creative future-oriented means, and to avoid an unappealable substantial arbitration award. Thus, mediation appears to be the most appropriate process to select for this dispute situation.

3.2.7 Imagine exaggerated specific cases to test creative solutions
(Challenge Assumptions)

When you are determining an appropriate solution from a list of generated alternative solutions, it is wise to imagine exaggerated specific cases to determine possible flaws and weaknesses in the solution(s) and ways to refine or to improve it or them. This is also called considering worst-case scenarios or anticipating possible negative consequences. This technique is particularly useful in a mediation or a negotiation in which the parties make promises to engage or not engage in specific future conduct. A simple example could be found in a typical divorce mediation. Imagine that when the child begins college, the child sends his father a room and board bill and asks his father to pay it. The father refuses to pay and tells the child to contact his mother to receive payment. The father's position is that he agreed to pay for "college education" – i.e. tuition and books – not for any extraneous costs. The father was under the impression that the mother had agreed to pay any extraneous costs. Of course, the mother assumed that "college education" included all the costs associated with her son's receiving a college education. If the mediator raises this potential flaw in the agreement during the mediation session, the mediator may be able to improve or refine the agreement so as to avoid the potential of future mediations or litigation over the college expense issue (Fobes, 111-14).

3.2.8 Weighted Ranking (Analysis and Selection)

Ranking means to assign a position to something relative to other things. This usually occurs using a one-dimensional criterion. In many problem solving situations, however, multi-dimensional criteria need to be applied. In such cases *weighted* ranking is often helpful. When using weighted ranking you first determine which criteria are most important and apply them equitably to all the items being ranked. It is a technique in which each item is ranked against every other item through what is called "paired ranking" (Jones, 139-58). Weighted ranking is particularly useful when comparing ten or more possible options. But a simple example can be helpful in understanding the weighted ranking technique in evaluating four options, as shown below. Assume that the problem is to determine the preferred way to go about resolving a commercial dispute. The options are: court adjudication, arbitration, mediation, and negotiation.

Step One: List all the major criteria for ranking. They are:

    Minimum Expense
    Minimum Time to Resolution
    Minimum Work Interruption
    Preserved Business Relationship

The processes can be displayed in relation to the criteria, as shown in the matrix below.

Process	Criterion 1 Minimum Expense	Criterion 2 Minimum Time to Resolution	Criterion 3 Minimum Work Interruption	Criterion 4 Preserved Business Relationship	Weighted Ranking	Final Ranking
Court Adjudication						
Arbitration						
Mediation						
Negotiation						

Step Two: Pair rank the criteria.

Pair ranking is a simple and reliable way to rank or measure items against each other, regardless of their subject matter. It allows the problem solver to analyze each element separately, systematically, and sufficiently. The technique for pair ranking the criteria in this problem is shown below. For simplicity we will refer to the four criteria as A (expense), B (time), C (work interruption) and D (business relationship). To pair rank in importance the criteria we first compare A with each of the other criteria (B, C, and D). We place an asterisk after the one we prefer in each pairing. For example:

      A is compared to B: A is deemed more important.
      A is compared to C: C is deemed more important
      A is compared to D: D is deemed more important.

So the voting after the first phase of pairing is as follows:

      A *
      B
      C *
      D *

The second phase in pairing is as follows:

      B is compared with A: A is deemed more important.
      B is compared with C: C is deemed more important.
      B is compared with D: D is deemed more important.

So the voting after the second phase of pairing is as follows:

      A *
      B
      C *
      D *

The third phase in pairing is as follows:

C is compared with A: C is deemed more important.
C is compared with B: C is deemed more important.
C is compared with D: D is deemed more important.

So the voting after the third phase of pairing is as follows:

A
B
C **
D *

The fourth phase in pairing is as follows:

D is compared with A: D is deemed more important.
D is compared with B: D is deemed more important.
D is compared with C: D is deemed more important.

So the voting after the fourth phase of pairing is as follows:

A
B
C
D ***

The composite votes of all four phases of pairings are as follows:

A **
B
C ****
D ******

So, A received two votes; B received zero votes, C received four votes, and D received six votes. That means that the final ranking is in this order: D, C, A, B.

Step 3. Show the pair ranking and the final ranking of the four criteria; and Step 4. Weight the criteria by assigning them percentiles according to the overall importance you assign to each criterion (their total must equal 1.0).

The pair ranking and final ranking is shown in the chart below. Note that, here, the highest final ranking is one and the lowest final ranking is four.

Criterion	Votes from Pair Ranking	Final Order of Ranking
Minimum Expense	2	3
Minimum Time to Resolution	0	4
Minimum Work Interruption	4	2
Preserved Business Relationship	6	1

The percentiles assigned to the four criteria, according to the overall importance of each in comparison to the others is shown below.

Preserved Business Relationship	.5
Minimum Work Interruption	.25
Minimum Expense	.15
Minimum Time to Resolution	.10
Totals	1.0

Step Five: Pair-rank all of the processes against each other by each of the four criteria separately and enter the number of votes that each process receives.

Let's assume that the pair-ranking of processes against each of the criteria yields the final ranking as shown in the matrix below. Note that these final rankings must be obtained similar to the way we found the final ranking for criteria, above. This may seem to be a mechanical and laborious procedure, but that is what makes the results so reliable and useful. Note also that in this particular final ranking, the highest final ranking is four and the lowest final ranking is one. Weights are inserted under the criteria headings from the results of the criteria analysis, above.

Process	Criterion 1 Minimum Expense Wt: .15	Criterion 2 Minimum Time to Resolution Wt: .10	Criterion 3 Minimum Work Interruption Wt: .25	Criterion 4 Preserved Business Relationship Wt: .50	Weighted Ranking	Final Ranking
Court Adjudication	1	1	1	1		
Arbitration	2	2	2	2		
Mediation	3	4	3	4		
Negotiation	4	3	4	3		

Step Six: Multiply the final rankings shown in the previous chart by the respective criteria weights as shown in the chart below:

Process	Criterion 1 Minimum Expense Wt: .15	Criterion 2 Minimum Time to Resolution Wt: .10	Criterion 3 Minimum Work Interruption Wt: .25	Criterion 4 Preserved Business Relationship Wt: .50	Weighted Ranking	Final Ranking
Court Adjudication	1x.15 = .15	1x.1 = .10	1x.25 = .25	1x.50 = .50	1.0	FOURTH
Arbitration	2x.15 = .30	2x.1 = .20	2x.25 = .50	2x.50 = 1.0	2.0	THIRD

| Mediation | 3x.15 = .45 | 4x.1 = .40 | 3x.25 = .75 | 4x.50 = 2.0 | 3.6 | FIRST |
| Negotiation | 4x.15 = .60 | 3x.1 = .30 | 4x..25 = 1.0 | 3x.50 = 1.5 | 3.4 | SECOND |

3.2.9 Hypothesis Testing (Evaluation and Selection)

A hypothesis is a declarative statement that has not been established as true. It is a statement accepted as true until it is proven to be false. A hypothesis is disproved by relevant, valid evidence. The validity of evidence may be established by answering four questions:

- Who or what was the source of the evidence?
- Was the source's access to the evidence plausible?
- What is the source's reliability?
- Based on everything we know, is the evidence plausible?

Oftentimes, solution evaluation and selection requires choosing among several alternative hypotheses. The technique of determining the favored hypothesis among competing ones is called hypothesis testing. The favored hypothesis is the one with the *least inconsistent* evidence, not the one with the most consistent evidence. Consistent evidence proves nothing because evidence can support more than one hypothesis. People who make judgments based only on evidence consistent with a particular course of action are frequently blindsided by unforeseen adverse circumstances (inconsistent evidence) that preclude a satisfactory outcome.

Let us consider a simple example of hypothesis testing, based on an illustration presented in Jones, 182-94. Assume that a five-star restaurant leases space from a luxury hotel to conduct its restaurant business. The restaurant's sterling reputation is based on the quality of its bakery goods and desserts, and particularly on the quality of its famed buttermilk bread. Under the terms of the lease, the hotel is required to provide three ovens for the restaurant and to keep them in good working order. The lease includes a disclaimer that relieves the hotel of responsibility for the ovens if the "restaurant's employees intentionally or negligently misuse the equipment or if defects in bakery goods result from causes completely within the restaurant's control." Two ovens overbaked ten batches of buttermilk bread and the restaurant had to close its doors for the past two days. The restaurant manager has contacted the general manager of the hotel and has demanded that the hotel reimburse the restaurant $10,000 dollars per day until the ovens are repaired. In an attempt to resolve this matter, the hotel manager engages the restaurant manager in a "joint effort" to determine, by the technique of hypothesis testing, the cause or causes of the overbaked bread. The joint effort followed these steps.

Step One: Generate multiple hypotheses. Together, the managers created a list of hypotheses to explain why the bread had come to be overbaked. Eliminating, by agreement, completely implausible ones, they narrowed the list to three: (1) sabotage by employees; (2) malfunctioning of the ovens' temperature gauges; and (3) fluctuations in the electrical power supplied to the ovens.

Step Two: Construct a matrix, permitting testing of the three hypotheses against the available evidence as shown below:

Hypotheses

Evidence	Sabotage by employees	Malfunction of the ovens' temperature gauges	Fluctuations in electrical power supplied to the ovens
Ten batches of bread were overbaked.			
Only buttermilk bread was overbaked.			
Only two of the three ovens overbaked bread.			
The hotel maintenance man found nothing wrong with the temperature gauges.			
Overbaking took place during the restaurant's busiest season of the year.			
Employees are unhappy about the lack of insurance benefits.			
Employees are angry about the restaurant firing one of the cooks after he complained about the lack of insurance benefits.			
After the firing, one of the waiters was seen talking to the fired cook in the parking lot.			

Step Three: Working across the matrix, test the evidence for consistency with each hypothesis, one piece of evidence at a time, as shown below. Determine with respect to each hypothesis whether the evidence is consistent (C), inconsistent (I), or ambiguous (A). "C" means that the evidence is compatible with the evidence (i.e., the hypothesis could be true, given the evidence). "I" means that the hypothesis could not be true, given the evidence.

Hypotheses

Evidence	Sabotage by employees	Malfunction of the ovens' temperature gauges	Fluctuations in electrical power supplied to the ovens
Ten batches of bread were overbaked.	C	C	C
Only buttermilk bread was overbaked.	C	C	C
Only two of the three ovens overbaked bread.	C	C	I
The hotel maintenance man found nothing wrong with the temperature gauges.	C	I	C
Overbaking took place during the restaurant's busiest season of the year.	C	C	C
Employees are unhappy about the lack of insurance benefits.	C	C	C
Employees are angry about the restaurant firing one of the cooks after he complained about the lack of insurance benefits.	C	C	C
After the firing, one of the waiters was seen talking to the fired cook in the parking lot.	C	C	C

There are only two inconsistencies between the hypotheses and the available evidence.

Step Four: Consider adding or rewording hypotheses. The hotel manager asks the restaurant manager whether there was anything unusual about the ingredients of the buttermilk bread at the time of the overbaking. The restaurant manager admitted that a delivery of flour was late and that it was a slightly different color than is normal. The delivery of the new flour coincided with the beginning of the overbaking and the ten overbaked batches of bread were made with the new flour. The hotel manager thus added a new piece of evidence to the matrix: "Only batches made with the new flour overbaked." He also added a new hypothesis to the matrix: "The new flour is defective."

Step Five: Test the newly added hypothesis against each piece of evidence (including the new piece of evidence), as shown below:

Hypotheses

Evidence	Sabotage by employees	Malfunction of the ovens' temperature gauges	Fluctuations in electrical power supplied to the ovens	The new flour is defective
Ten batches of bread were overbaked.	C	C	C	C
Only buttermilk bread was overbaked.	C	C	C	C
Only two of the three ovens overbaked bread.	C	C	I	C
The hotel maintenance man found nothing wrong with the temperature gauges.	C	I	C	C
Overbaking took place during the restaurant's busiest season of the year.	C	C	C	C
Employees are unhappy about the lack of insurance benefits.	C	C	C	C
Employees are angry about the restaurant firing one of the cooks after he complained about the lack of insurance benefits.	C	C	C	C
After the firing, one of the waiters was seen talking to the fired cook in the parking lot.	C	C	C	C
Only batches made with new flour overbaked	I	I	I	C

Step Six: Delete, but keep a record of, evidence that is consistent with all of the hypotheses, because those pieces of evidence have no diagnostic value.

In this example, three items of evidence remain as shown below:

Hypotheses

Evidence	Sabotage by employees	Malfunction of the ovens' temperature gauges	Fluctuations in electrical power supplied to the ovens	The new flour is defective
Only two of the three ovens overbaked bread.	C	C	I	C
The hotel maintenance man found nothing wrong with the temperature gauges.	C	I	C	C
Only batches made with new flour overbaked	I	I	I	C

Step Seven: Working downward, evaluate each hypothesis and delete any hypothesis for which there is significant inconsistent evidence.

In this situation, there is sufficient inconsistent evidence to refute three hypotheses, leaving only "The new flour is defective" hypothesis.

Step Eight: Rank the remaining hypotheses (here there is only one) by the weakness of inconsistent evidence. The hypothesis with the weakest inconsistent evidence is the most likely.

Here, the remaining hypothesis, "The new flour is defective" has no inconsistent evidence. Because consistent evidence has no diagnostic value, the hotel manager could not leap to the conclusion that the new flour caused the overbaking. However, by analyzing the relationship between the new flour and the overbaked batches and by sorting the data chronologically into matrices, the hotel manager was able to make a conclusive correlation.

The hotel manager suggested that the restaurant manager bake a few batches of buttermilk bread using flour other than the "new flour." The restaurant manager did just as the hotel manager suggested, and he discovered that none of the bread overbaked. He apologized to the hotel manager and dropped his claim for $10,000 per-day damages.

3.2.10. Causal Flow Diagramming.

Some problems can best be resolved by defining and analyzing a problem's cause-and-effect system (Jones, 94-105). There are five steps in accomplishing these two tasks:

Step 1: Identify major factors.
Step 2: Identify cause-and-effect relationships.
Step 3: Characterize the relationships as direct or inverse.
Step 4: Diagram the relationships.

Step 5: Analyze the behavior of the relationships as an integrated system.

Let's assume that the CEO of a manufacturing company has a dispute with her Marketing Director on the issue of whether the Marketing Director is responsible for a decrease in the company's profits for the previous year. The CEO believes that the Marketing Department is sloughing off. The Marketing Director maintains that the employees in his department have been working to capacity and the problem has not been caused by him or them. Let's assume further that the CEO and the Marketing Director meet to negotiate a resolution of this problem. One way that they can define and analyze this problem is to consider the principal factors that affect the profits of a company and the cause-and-effect relationships that exist between them.

Identify major factors. For simplicity, let's assume that the CEO has identified three major factors influencing company profits: sales, research and development, and the marketing of new products. In a real situation, there may be many more major factors to consider.

Identify cause-and-effect relationships. The CEO and the Marketing Director agree that there is a cause-and-effect relationship between pairs of these major factors.

Characterize the relationships as direct or inverse. They also agree that the relationship between the pairs of these major factors is direct (if one factor increases, its paired factor increases; if one factor decreases, its paired factor decreases), rather than inverse (if one factor increases, its paired factor decreases, and vice versa).

Diagram the relationships.

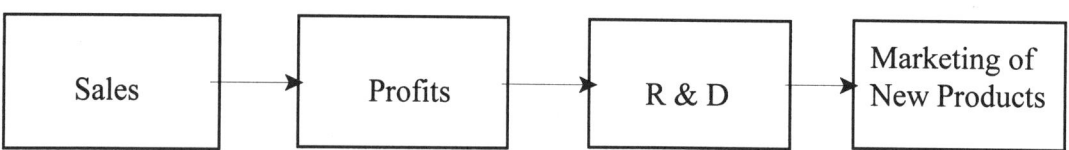

Analyze the behavior of the relationships as an integrated system. In analyzing the behavior of the integrated system, the Marketing Director notices that the CEO had left out an important factor in the causal flow diagram. He therefore re-draws the flow diagram in the form of a feedback loop, including the missing factor of the Competitors' Marketing of New Products, as shown in the diagram below.

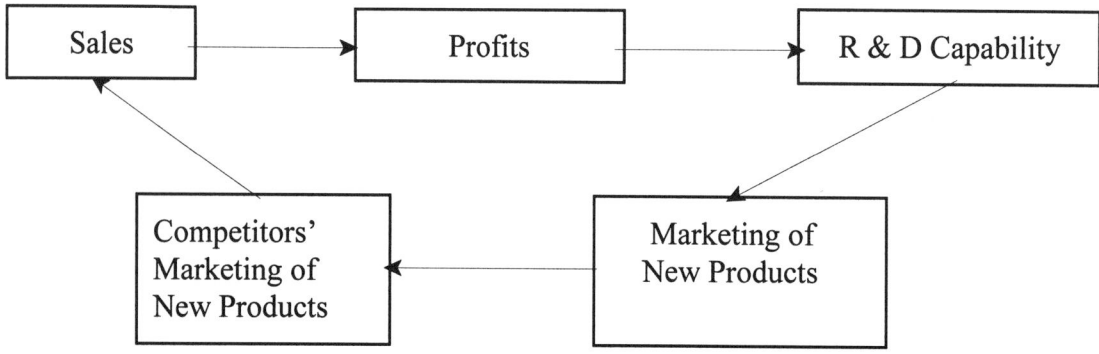

The Marketing Director knew that there are ten new competing products on the market. The CEO knew there were a few new competitors' products on the market but she did not know that there were as many as ten. Since there is an inverse relationship between the Competitors' Marketing of New Products and the sales factor, the CEO then understands that the cause for lower profits could well be the competitors' marketing of new products and not the result of a less-than-competent marketing staff. The dispute was resolved.

3.2.11 Blind Bidding

Blind bidding is a technique that can be used to close the gap in a negotiation involving money or items of value to the disputants. It has many variations, but a most common one is used routinely by mediators in reaching distributive (money) solutions in a dispute situation. In this procedure, as a last resort, each party confidentially submits a bid to the mediator. For the plaintiff, the bid represents the lowest figure that the plaintiff will accept to settle the case; for the defendant, the bid represents the highest figure the defendant will pay to settle the case. Only the mediator knows both (or all) the figures submitted. By preagreement, the parties decide what they will do depending on the outcome. For example, they can preagree that if they are X dollars apart, the mediator will disclose the numbers and they will split the difference. They can also preagree that if they are only Y dollars apart, the mediator will not disclose the actual figures, but they will continue mediating (or negotiating). Finally they can also agree that if they are more than Z dollars apart, the mediator will not disclose the figures, and they will proceed to trial. This technique and its variations can be used in connection with other creative problem solving techniques, as is explained in more detail in Sections 4.1, 5.4 and 5.5, below.

3.2.12 Pie Chart

This is a technique that a disinterested party can use to fairly allocate separate responsibilities or entitlements among several persons or entities who disagree on what the degree or extent of those responsibilities or entitlements should be. The technique envisions a process whereby each participant privately draws a pie chart allocating, by percentages, the responsibilities or entitlements of the separate participants including themselves. An example of an actual application of this technique in a complex business dispute is provided in Section 4.2.1, below.

3.2.13 Blind Trust

This is a technique that a disinterested party can use to fairly allocate separate responsibility – for example to pay money to a creditor- among several debtors. In mediation, the goal of this technique is to settle the case by raising a pot of money anonymously, without disclosing each defendant's specific amounts to the other defendants – or even the mediator. An example of an actual application of this technique in a complex business dispute is provided in Section 4.2.2, below.

3.2.14 The utility matrix

In Section 3.3 below, several different types of analysis "trees," including the utility tree, are discussed. While trees are very useful for analytical purposes, a matrix offers two important advantages over a tree for performing utility analysis. One advantage is that the utility values of outcomes are more easily perceived in a matrix than in a tree. The second advantage is that arithmetic calculations are easier to perform using a matrix (Jones, 273). Before viewing an example of how a utility matrix might be applied in a mediation or negotiation situation, we first must understand what the concept of "utility analysis" is all about.

3.2.14.1 Utility analysis – general

In his excellent book, *The Thinker's Toolkit: Fourteen Powerful Techniques for Problem Solving* (Random House, 1995), Morgan Jones describes utility analysis as follows:

> From a purely analytic standpoint, utility is the benefit that someone has received, is receiving, or expects to receive from some situation... [It] is the profit, the prize, the goal, the objective ... ...For everything we and others do, want to do, and plan to do there are reasons – and these reasons are our *utilities*... [N]ormal humans, when confronted with a choice between alternative courses of action (alternative options), choose the course that offers them the greater utility, and the person making the choice defines what that utility is... [W]e call it *self-interest* (Jones, 246-47).

Jones goes on to explain there are three basic elements of utility analysis: options, outcomes, and perspectives. He describes the elements in more detail as follows:

> **Options:** The purpose of utility analysis is to *rank* any number of options according to how they serve the decision maker's self-interest. Options are alternative courses of action. To buy or sell, to move or stay, to invest or save. Life is an endless series of choices; choices are options... When we analyze options, they must be mutually exclusive – distinctive enough from one another to permit meaningful comparisons. ...
>
> **Outcomes:** The second element of utility analysis is the *outcome*. An outcome is what happens as a result of implementing a certain course of action or selecting an option... Outcomes are the sole basis for analyzing the utility of options. We measure one option against another... In contrast to options... *outcomes as a general rule should be collectively exhaustive* – inclusive of all possible outcomes.
>
> **Perspectives:** Perspectives are "points of view" with respect to outcomes and are critical in analyzing the utility of outcomes... We, the analyst, must decide whose perspective – whose point of view – will be reflected in our analysis. If we are analyzing other people's or organizations' options, we must "role-play" their perspective, trying to view the world as they view it, to see where their self-interest lies and to understand how their choice among options would be influenced by the perspectives of others. (Jones, 247-52).

3.2.14.2 Conducting a utility-matrix analysis

Let us walk through a simple utility-matrix analysis using Jones' eight-step procedure (Jones, 272-81). Let's suppose that you are a plaintiff or a lawyer for a plaintiff in a civil case. Your complaint contains a one-count breach of contract claim for $200,000 and discovery is nearly complete. Your quandary is whether to litigate this matter to judgment, to file a motion for summary judgment, or to proceed to private arbitration. There is a lack of trust between plaintiff and defendant, and neither party wants to go to mediation. Because of the court's backlog of cases, your case will not be scheduled for trial for another year at least. The defendant has suggested private arbitration because this long-pending claim has harmed his credit status with his commercial lender and he wants closure to this matter. You don't object to arbitration because the non-applicability of the rules of evidence will enable you to get before a fact-finder much more evidence than would be admissible in a court trial. Thus, you believe the probability of victory is somewhat better in arbitration than in a court of law. What follows describes how you might use a utility-matrix analysis to determine your best course of action at this point in the litigation.

Step 1: Identify the options and outcomes to be analyzed.
Options: Litigate to judgment; file a motion for summary judgment; proceed to private arbitration.
Outcome: Win or lose.

Step 2: Identify the perspective of the analysis.
From the plaintiff's perspective, what course of action will likely produce the best dollar outcome?

Step 3: Construct a utility matrix (see below).

Step 4: Assign a utility value to each option-outcome combination. Do this by asking the question: "If this option occurs, what is the utility (self-interest; value) of this outcome from the plaintiff's perspective?

Option	Win Outcome	Lose Outcome	Total Expected Value	Rank
Litigate to judgment	$200,000	$0		
Move for summary judgment	$200,000	$0		
Proceed to private arbitration	$200,000	$0		

Step 5: Assign a probability to each outcome. Estimate this probability by asking the question: If this option is selected what is the probability this outcome will occur? The probabilities of all outcomes for a single option must add up to 1.0. The probabilities you assign for winning are .8 (litigate to judgment); .5 (motion for summary judgment); and .9 (private arbitration).

Option	Win Outcome	Lose Outcome	Total EV	Rank
Litigate to judgment	$200,000 x .8 = $160,000	$0 x .2 = 0		
Move for summary judgment	$200,000 x .5 = $100,000	$0 x .5 = 0		
Proceed to private arbitration	$200,000 x .9 = $180,000	$0 x .1 = 0		

Step 6: Determine the expected values by multiplying each utility by its probability and then adding the expected values for each option.

Step 7: Determine the ranking of the alternative options.

Option	Win Outcome	Lose Outcome	Total EV	Rank
Litigate to judgment	$200,000 x .8 = $160,000	$0 x .2 = $0	$160,000	2
Move for summary judgment	$200,000 x .5 = $100,000	$0 x .5 = $0	$100,000	3
Proceed to private arbitration	$200,000 x .9 = $180,000	$0 x .1 = $0	$180,000	1

Step 8: Perform a sanity check, to make sure that you have not omitted an important consideration and that the results make sense. In analysis presented above, the plaintiff should give serious consideration to proceeding to arbitration.

3.2.15 Advanced utility analysis

In the preceding subsection, the use of a utility-matrix analysis was demonstrated. The scenario described a situation having multiple options and multiple outcomes, but the analysis was applied from only one perspective. It is frequently necessary to assess utilities from the vantage of more than one perspective. The utility analysis process for multiple perspectives is very similar to the eight-step procedure described in the preceding subsection, except that each perspective is analyzed separately. Also, the separate perspectives can be weighted producing for each perspective a "total weighted expected value". After ranking the options from various perspectives, the one having the greatest total weighted expected value is the preferred. For examples, showing how advanced utility analysis can be applied in various factual scenarios, see Jones, 282-305.

3.2.16 Test the validity, quality, utility and durability of your solution(s)
(Challenge Assumptions.)

When you reach what you believe to be an appropriate solution, play the role of devil's advocate and ask the following questions:

- Does it solve the problem?
- Does it eliminate the problem or just eliminate the symptoms?
- Does it solve the problem permanently or just temporarily?
- Does it eliminate the problem or just shift the problem to another area?
- Does it solve the whole problem, or just part of the problem?
- Is the solution simple or is it complex?
- Does this solution benefit nearly everyone involved or only a select few?
- Are there disadvantages for the people who are supposed to benefit?
- What are the undesirable consequences of implementing this solution?
- Are you willing to accept responsibility for these negative consequences?
- Is there something about the solution you hope no one will ever find out?
- Do you have any reservations or doubts about the above answers? (Fobes, 248).

3.3 SEEING THE FOREST (AND THE TREES) OF CREATIVE PROBLEM SOLVING

3.3.1. Decision Trees

[**Editor's Note:** *The text and illustrations in this subsection are reprinted with permission of the Harvard Negotiation Law Review: David P. Hoffer,* Decision Analysis as a Mediator's Tool, *1 Harvard Negotiation Law Review 113, 134-37 (1996).*]

A decision tree is a graphical representation of a complex decision. Developed in the 1960s for use in business education, decision trees are flexible enough to be used for many types of decisions. Professionals in the fields of business, economics, medicine, public policy, engineering, and law all use decision trees when multiple uncertainties complicate the decision process.

A. *Structure*

Decision trees are organized chronologically, from left to right. They contain certain "nodes" of three different types: decision, chance, and terminal. A decision node (represented by a square) denotes a point at which the decision maker must choose between two or more options. A chance node (represented by a circle) denotes a point where the decision maker has no control over the outcome; each event following a chance node has a probability associated with it that reflects how likely it is to occur. Terminal nodes (represented by triangles) denote final outcomes, after which no events relevant to the decision are considered.

The following simple decision tree represents a situation in which a personal injury plaintiff must decide whether to proceed to trial with a chance of recovering $1,000 or settle for $500. (Fig. A.) Assume that you represent the plaintiff in this lawsuit.

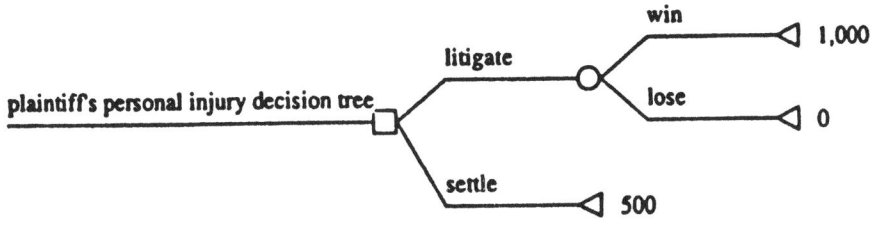

Figure A

The plaintiff faces two choices – litigate or settle – which are represented by branches emanating from the decision node at the left. If the plaintiff settles, the inquiry is complete: he gets $500 and the dispute ends. If he chooses to litigate, there are two possible outcomes: win (a terminal node with payoff of $1,000) or lose (a terminal node with a payoff of zero). For purposes of this example, all of the uncertainties associated with litigation (other than liability), as well as costs, are ignored.

To make this decision intelligently, the plaintiff must assess how likely he is to win if litigation is pursued. A $500 settlement offer may seem inadequate if the plaintiff has an excellent chance of winning $1,000; however, the offer may be very attractive if a successful outcome is less certain. In order to be more precise, we must assign probabilities to the uncertain events modeled by the tree. In this simple case, we must assess the likelihood that the plaintiff will win at trial.

Assume that, in your professional judgment, your client has a 40 percent (.4) chance of winning at trial. This probability would be displayed beneath the node labeled "win." Accordingly, a probability of 60 percent (.6) would be displayed beneath the node labeled "lose." (See Figure B.)

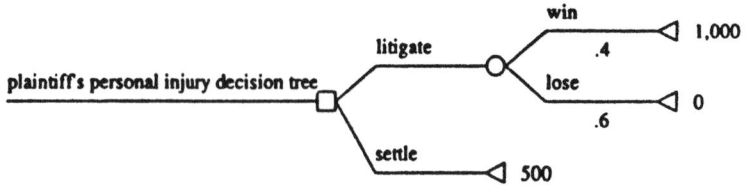

Figure B

B. *Calculation*

Settlement is apparently preferable to litigation in this case because the probability of winning is not high enough to risk the gamble of trial. This evaluation is based on a concept called expected value or expected monetary value. The expected value of a node is defined as the sum of the products of the probabilities and payoffs of its branches. In other words, the expected value of a course of action is the average value of taking that course of action many times. If one were to try cases identical to this case one hundred times, about forty would result in a victory while sixty would result in a loss. The average recovery would be forty victories at $1,000 per victory, or $40,000, plus sixty losses at $0 per loss, divided by 100 cases tried, for an average recovery of $400. Thus, the expected value associated with the "litigate" node is $400. (See Figure C.)

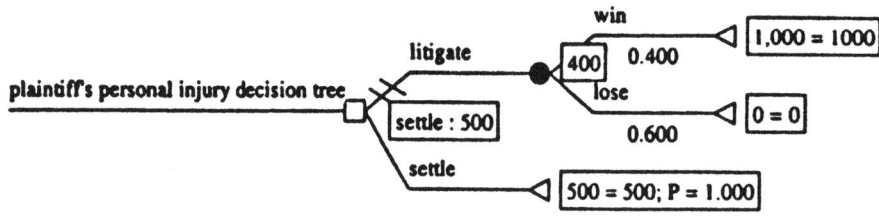

Figure C

C. *Different Kinds of Trees*

A distinction must be drawn between decision trees and chance trees. A decision tree is a tree whose first node (the "root" node) is a decision node; thus, it models a situation in which the events being modeled are triggered by an initial decision to be made by the decision maker. A chance tree (or "event tree") is a tree whose root is a chance node; in other words, no decision is required. It is used to model events over which the decision maker has no control and its value represents the value of being faced with the modeled set of uncertainties.

Chance trees are often embedded in decision trees. For example, one can examine the chance tree that represents the litigation alternative in the example above. Its expected value, $400, represents the expected value of litigation. (See Figure D.)

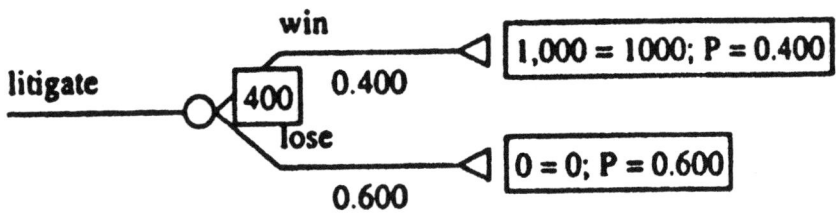

Figure D

D. *More Complex Trees*

The concept of expected value is at the core of all decision analysis. In more complex trees, the expected value is calculated in stages. In the example below, a motion for summary judgment is interposed between the decision to litigate and the outcome of the trial. (See Figure E.)

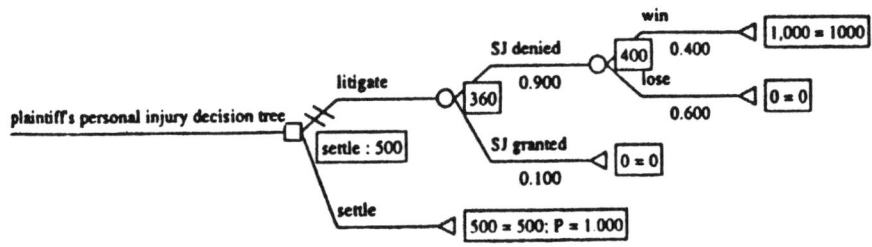

Figure E

If your client chooses to litigate the defendant will move for summary judgment, with a 10 percent chance of winning. If summary judgment is denied, the same win/lose chance tree from Figure D follows the denial of summary judgment.

To calculate the expected value of this tree, the decision analyst starts at the right side. As discussed above, by multiplying the probability of winning by the damage award, multiplying the probability of defeat at trial by the payoff, and adding the two figures together, an expected value of $400 is calculated and displayed next to the node "SJ denied." Thus the expected value of the case upon denial of summary judgment is $400.

The plaintiff's expected value of litigation must also take into account the possibility of losing on summary judgment. Thus, the expected value of litigation is calculated by multiplying the expected value associated with the denial of summary judgment, $400, by the probability that summary judgment will be denied, 90 percent. This figure, $360, is added to the product of the zero value of losing on summary judgment and the 10 percent probability of losing on summary judgment. The expected value of litigation is thus $360. The $40 difference between this expected value and the expected value in the simpler example reflects the risk that the plaintiff will lose on summary judgment. Since a $500 settlement offer is preferable to a litigation alternative whose expected value is $360, our client would be well advised to settle the case.

3.3.2. Opportunitrees

[**Editor's Note:** *This subsection is adapted from Cooley (1), § 2:12, 132-48.*]

Those familiar with decision tree analysis should have no difficulty understanding what an opportunitree is. A decision tree represents a logical analysis of how a case could be won or lost, and provides a method of determining a realistic value of a case, taking into account probability of success on critical issues and the present value of the outcome. The basic difference between a decision tree and an opportunitree is that the decision tree is issue oriented and is concerned with the probabilities of outcomes (winning or losing) on various issues; the opportunitree is information-oriented. The size of a decision tree is limited by the number of critical issues and possible realistic outcomes. The size of an opportunitree is limited only by one's imagination and creativity. The decision tree's purpose is to provide a single best answer based on probabilities – a decision. The opportunitree's purpose is to generate as much information as reasonably possible so that the quality of a decision can be enhanced (i.e. allowing selection of the best among many good solutions). Opportunitrees and decision trees can be used in tandem, but the opportunitree must be cultivated first. For example, in the problem design stage of problem solving, the opportunitree can be used to generate the possible problem design alternatives and the decision tree can be used to select the appropriate problem design. Let's use a fact scenario to better understand how the opportunitree works.

Assume the following set of facts. Mrs. Brown makes an appointment for a first interview with an attorney to discuss an automobile accident in which she was involved. During the course of the interview, Mrs. Brown tells the attorney that the vehicle she was driving on a particular day was struck broadside by an out-of-state driver. She incurred a back injury, was rushed to the hospital in an ambulance, and had to undergo emergency back surgery. She remained in the hospital for thirty days. Mrs. Brown also tells her attorney that the out-of-state driver received a citation for speeding and running a red light from a police officer who was on the scene. She also heard rumors that the out-of-state driver had been involved in two other serious accidents in his home state, but somehow managed to keep his driver's license and his automobile liability insurance. Mrs. Brown requests that the attorney represent her in the matter, and the attorney agrees to do so. The attorney's mission is to solve Mrs. Brown's problem. One place for him to start is to solve the three component problems of Mrs. Brown's problem: problem design; process design, and solution design. Assume that you are Mrs. Brown's attorney, and let us together analyze how you might solve Mrs. Brown's problem with the use of opportunitrees.

Problem Design

Our first question is to ask "how." That directs us to the appropriate design module - problem design (See Section 1.3.15.1). Part A of that module offers this guidance:

A. Define Nature and Scope of the Problem in Terms of Needs and Rights.

1. Collect Information.
2. Interpret Information.
3. Analyze Information.

Simultaneously, we ask ourselves "how much" and, for purposes of this exercise, we determine that there are no limiting factors.

The next step is to cultivate an opportunitree for "collecting information." In problem design, the steps are:

1. Ask yourself "what" at each fork of the opportunitree until no more answers come

to mind

2. Then ask yourself "who" at each succeeding fork until answers are exhausted.

3. Then ask yourself "how" at each succeeding fork until answers are exhausted.

4. Then ask yourself "where" at each succeeding fork until answers are exhausted.

5. Then ask yourself "when" at each succeeding fork until answers are exhausted.

6. *General Rule:* The "root" of the opportunitree should consist of the fewest and and most general and basic nonoverlapping categories as possible.

Now let's apply these rules in developing an opportunitree regarding "collection of information" as to Mrs. Brown's problem.

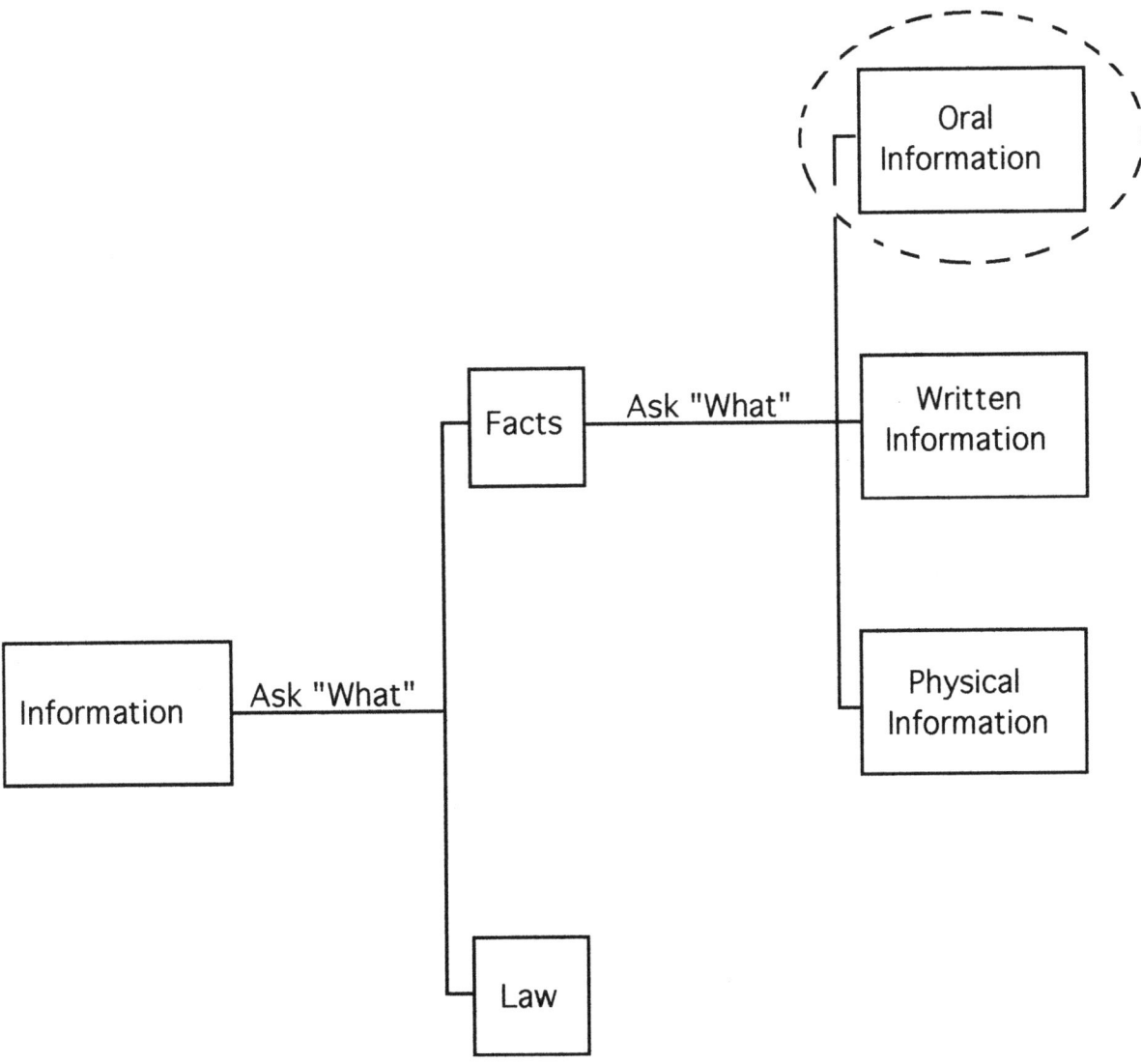

The "Oral Information Branch," as an example, is then further developed:

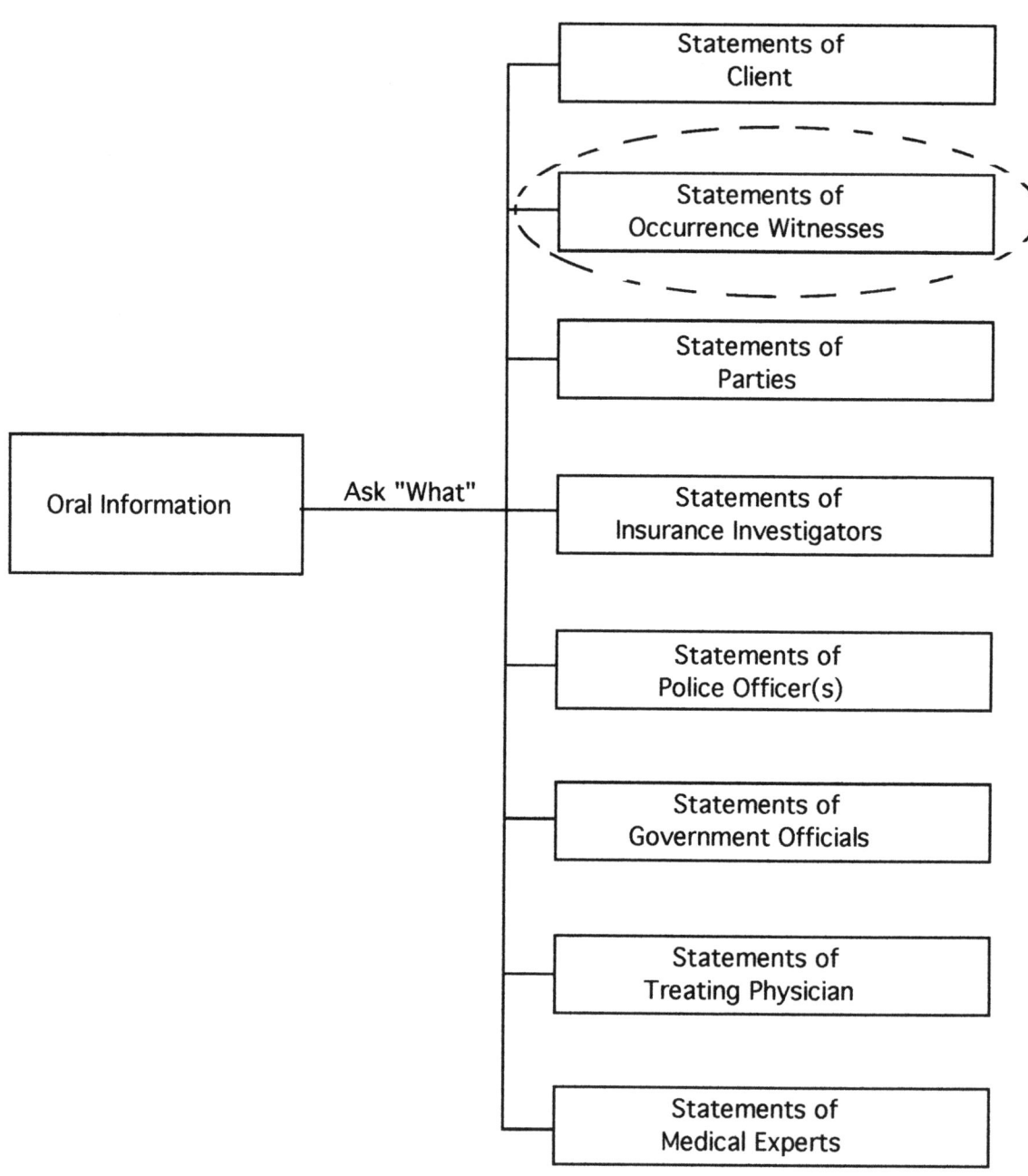

The "Statements of Occurrence Witnesses" branch is then further developed as follows:

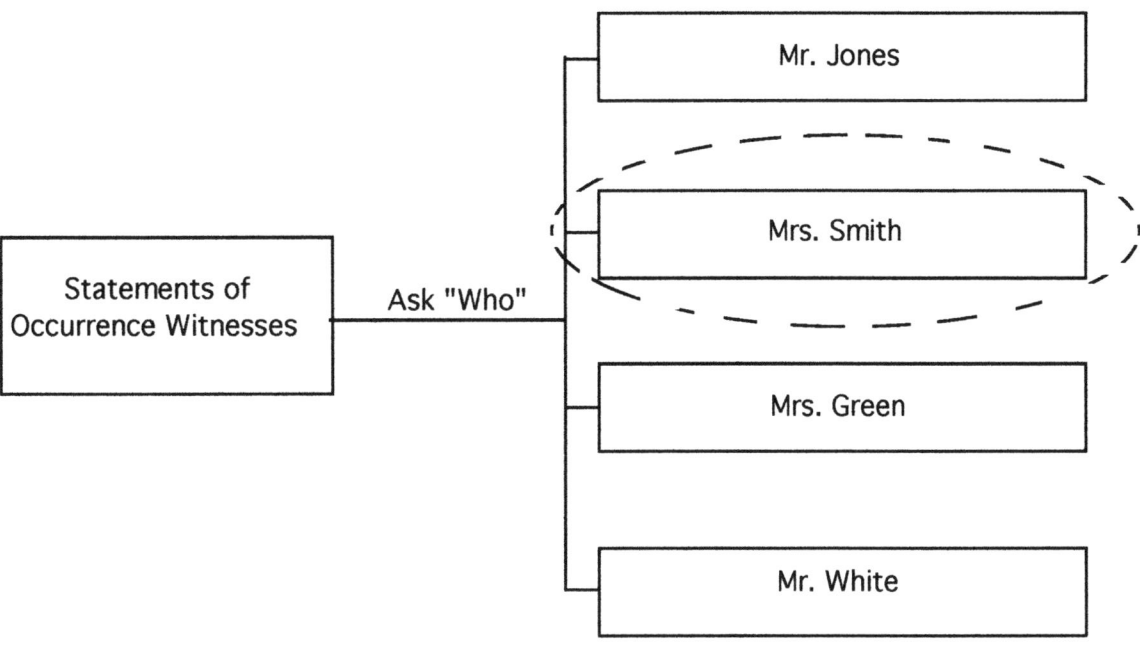

The "Mrs. Smith" branch is further developed as follows:

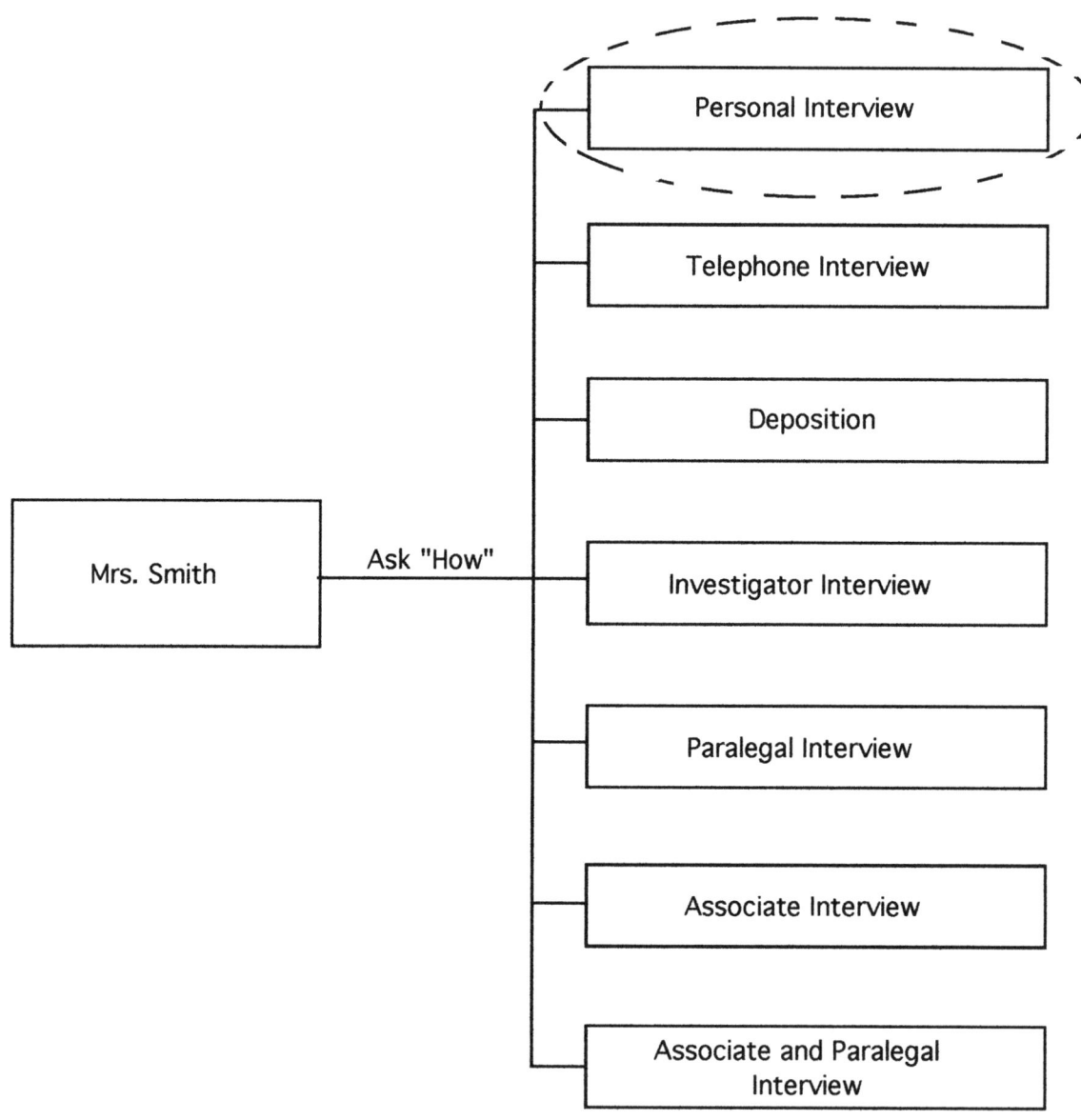

The "Personal Interview" branch can be further developed as follows:

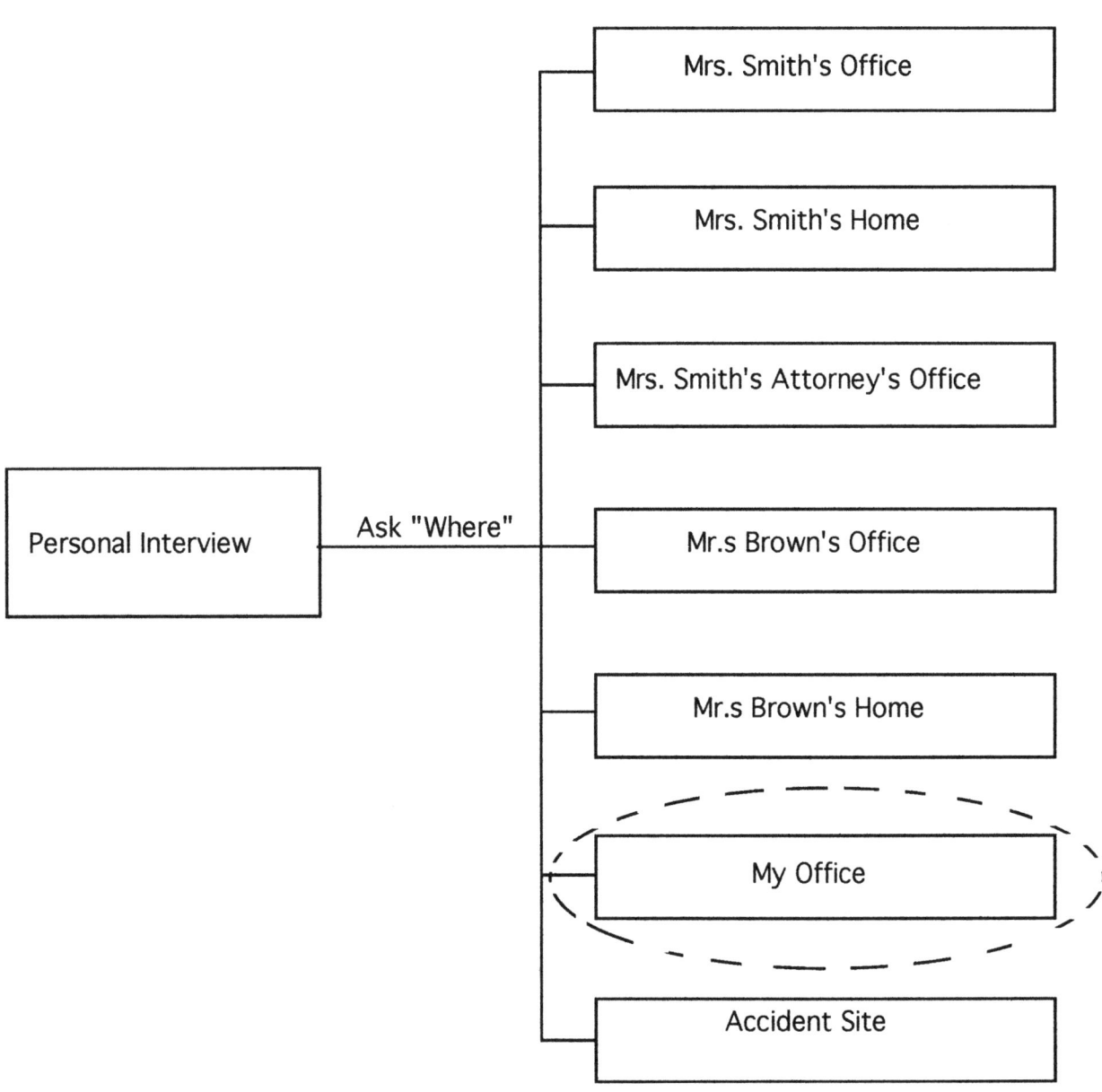

Similarly the "My Office" branch could be further developed by asking "When."

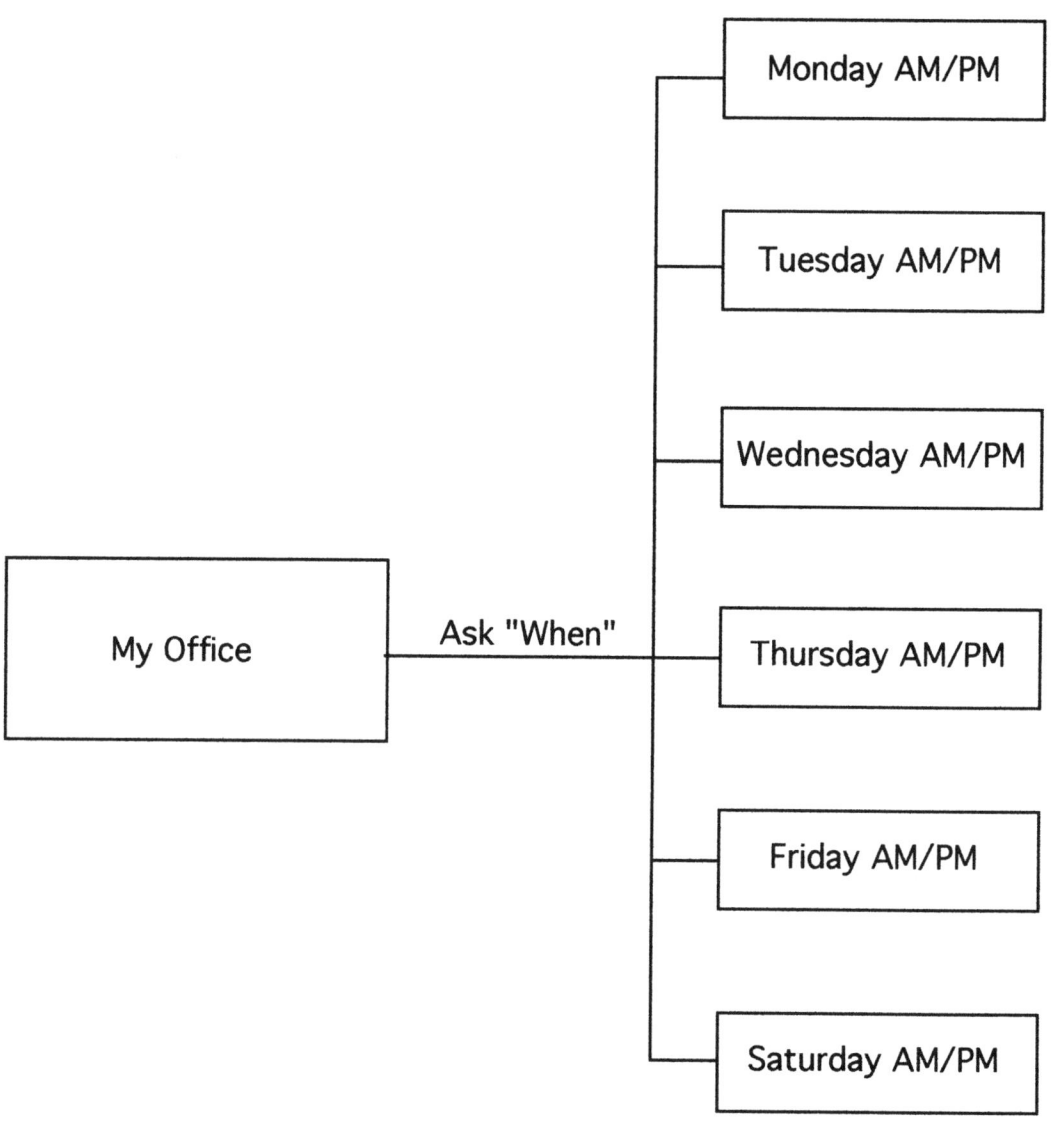

Three points should be noted about the development of Mrs. Brown's opportunitree: (1) only a partial development (a few branches) has been illustrated in this exercise; (2) an opportunitree does not have to be written down – it can be developed, in separate segments, mentally as you are walking to your next appointment, riding the train to work, or on a coffee break, etc.; and (3) you must actively engage your mind to the fullest extent in order to successfully generate useful alternatives. Now let's assume that the problem has been designed and we are ready to move on to developing an opportunitree for the process-design phase of Mrs. Brown's problem. We first ask the question "how," and that directs us to the process-design module. The process-design module provides this guidance in paragraphs A and B:

A. State Problem

B. Generate Alternative Processes (Methods and Approaches) to Solve Stated Problem.
   In doing so:
   1. Disturb Perceptions
   2. Reframe Perceptions

Then ask "how much," and for purposes of this exercise, we will assume there are no limiting factors. Let's further assume that the problem design analysis yielded this statement of Mrs. Brown's problem:

How can Mrs. Brown be compensated for $75,000 in economic and an estimated $100,000 in noneconomic (pain and suffering) damages for the injuries she received in the accident?

In process-design, the general rules for applying the heuristic tools are:

1. Ask yourself "how" at each fork of the opportunitree, when generating alternatives, until no more answers come to mind. (For those lawyers not familiar with available processes they will have to first educate themselves as to what processes are at their disposal in their jurisdictions).

2. *General Rule:* The root of the opportunitree should consist of the fewest and most general, and basic categories as possible.

Now let's apply these rules to generate alternative process designs, one of which may be ultimately applied to solve Mrs. Brown's problem.

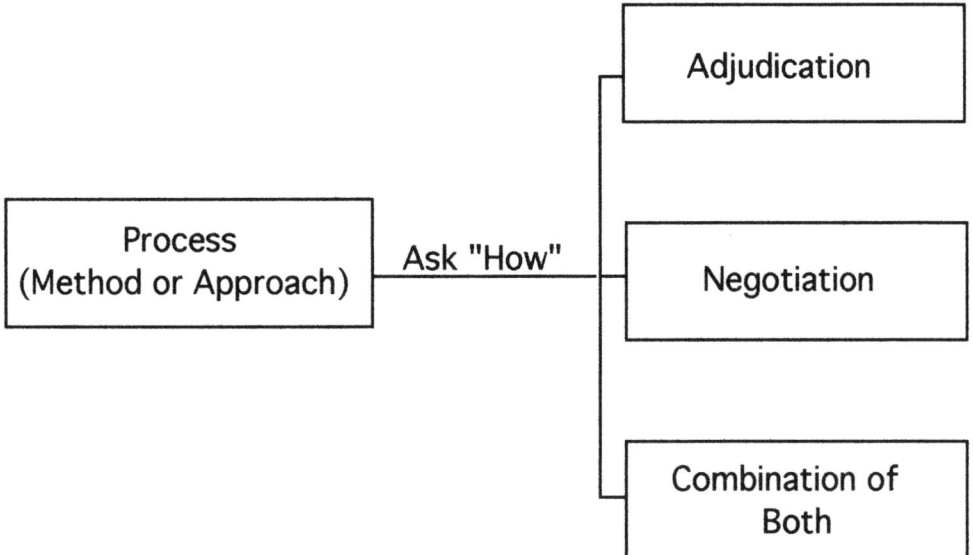

Creative Problem Solver's Handbook for Negotiators and Mediators

These three branches can be further developed as follows:

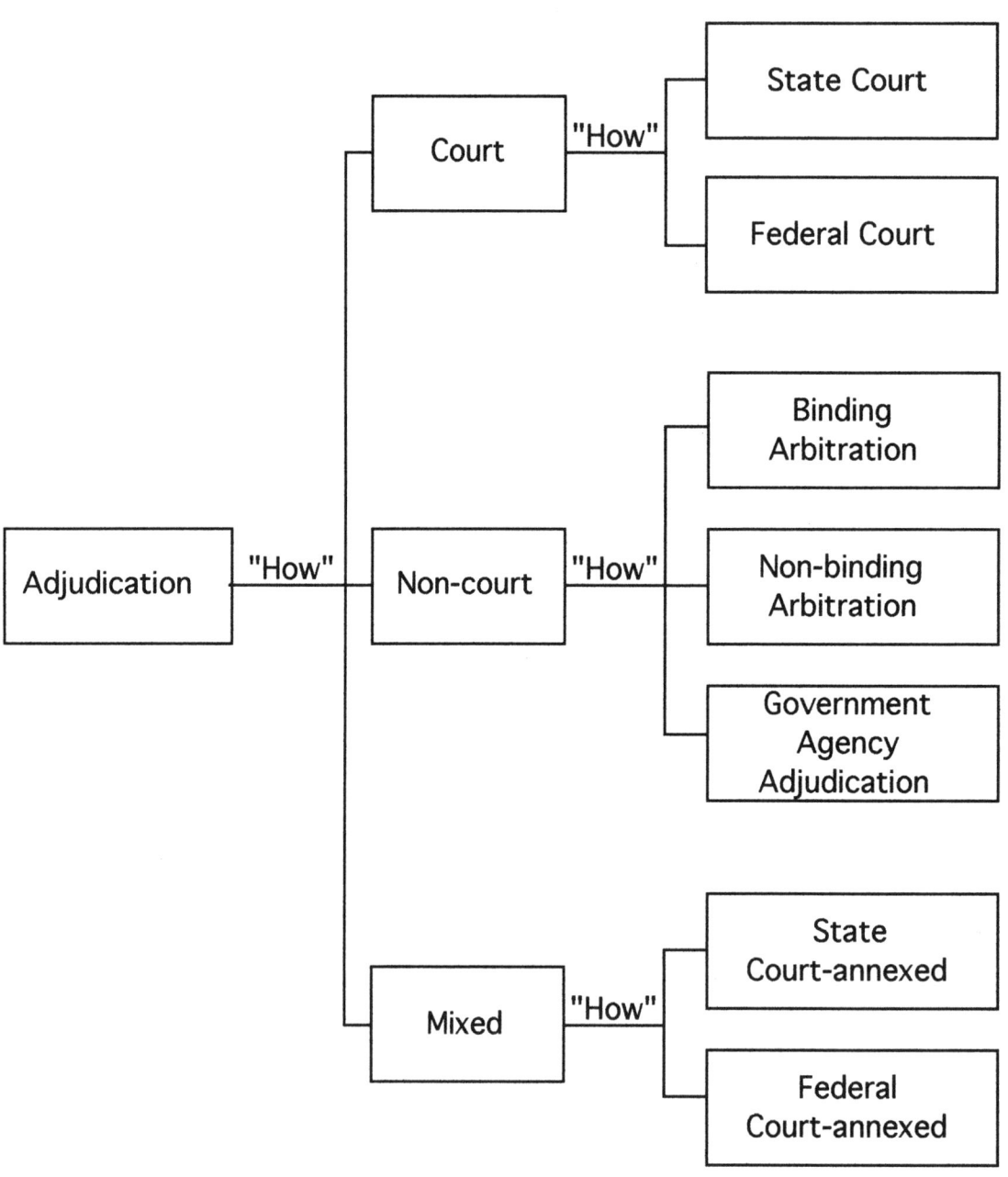

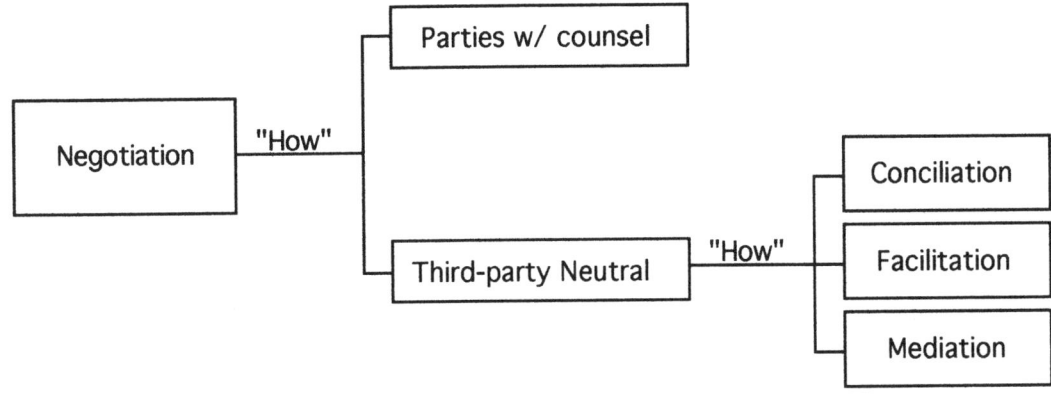

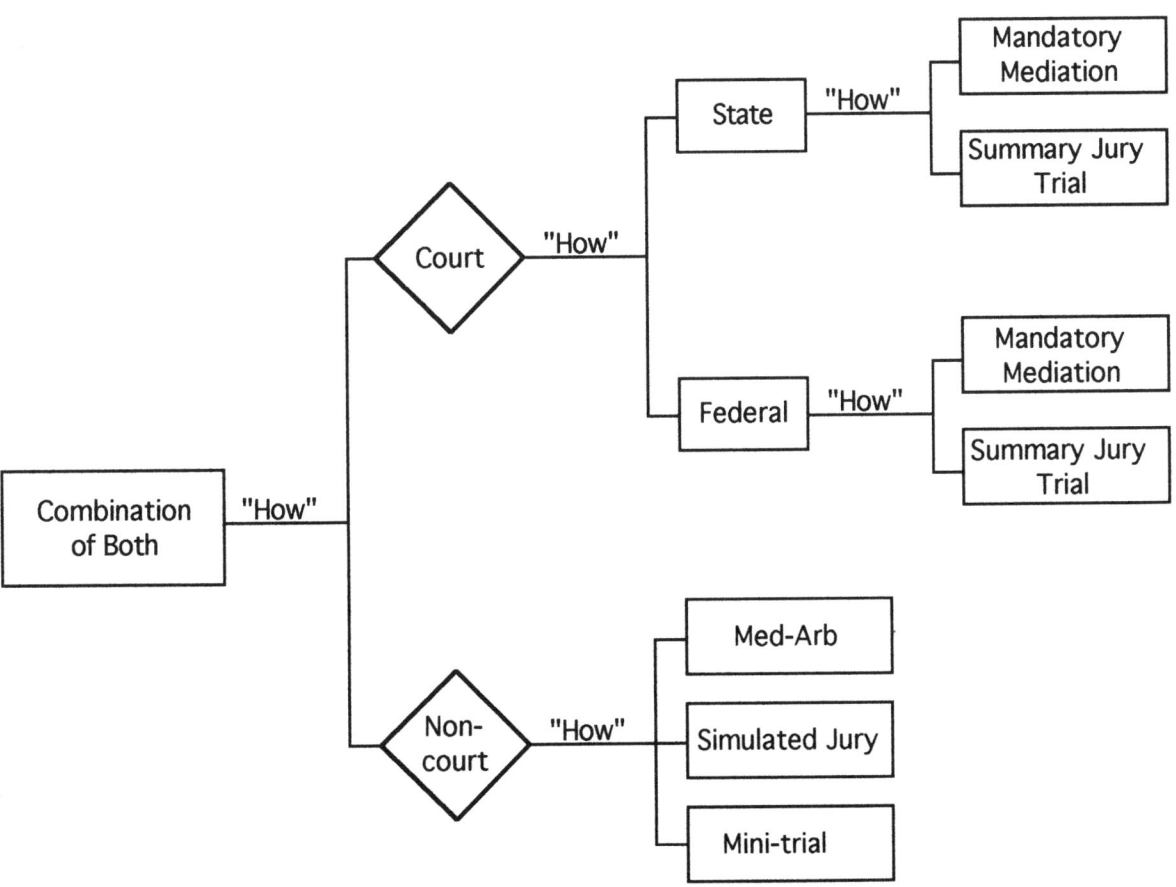

After applying the remainder of the analysis of the process-design module, a process would be selected, and then the analytical framework of the solution-design module would be applied. We must continually keep in mind in all our problem solving efforts that "generation of alternatives" is an important step to ensure quality of decision-making in the three-module approach to problem solving.

3.3.3 Probability trees

A probability tree has all the elements of a decision/event tree plus one: it enables one to analyze the entire tree and any of its branch from the viewpoint of probability. It also allows one to estimate which of several scenarios, and the events within those scenarios, is most likely and which is least likely to occur. An example of the application of the probability tree technique appears below. (Jones, 239-40; 334). As a reminder, "or" probabilities (mutually exclusive) are added together to obtain the combined probability. "And" probabilities (conditionally dependent) are multiplied together to obtain the combined probability.

Step 1: Identify the problem.

A small manufacturing company is a plaintiff in a commercial case in state court. It wants to go to market with a new product in six months, but it needs to obtain a settlement or a judgment after trial so that it has the necessary funds to give the new product adequate promotional support. A mediation of the case is scheduled for tomorrow. Three outcomes are possible as shown below with their related probabilities.

1. Case fails to settle (.2)

2. Main case settles, but a smaller related case which plaintiff won on summary judgment will require an evidentiary hearing on damages (.6)

3. Main case and small related case settles. (.2)

If the settlement is a total failure, the plaintiff only has a .1 probability to market the new product within six months. If the main case settles, but the evidentiary hearing on the smaller case must be held, there is a .4 probability of meeting the six month deadline. If both cases settle, there is a .9 probability of getting the new product to market in six months.

The problem is to design a probability tree that accurately portrays these events and answer this question: what is the probability that the plaintiff will meet its market deadline?

Step 2: Identify the major decisions and events to be analyzed. (See above in Step 1)

Step 3: Construct a decision/event tree portraying all important alternative scenarios.

Step 4: Assign a probability to each decision/event. Probabilities at each branch must equal 1.0.

Step 5: Calculate the conditional probability of each individual scenario.

Step 6: Calculate the answer to the probability question.

When these six steps are applied, the probability tree should appear as shown below:

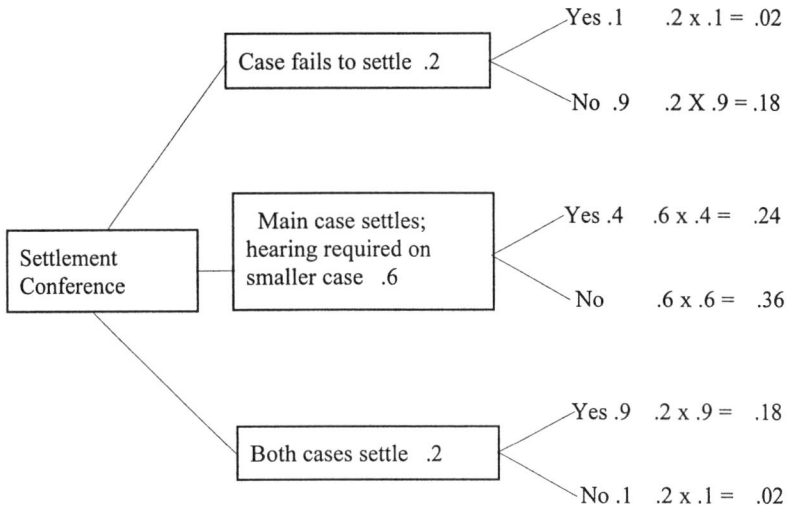

To determine the probability of meeting the six month deadline, add the three mutually exclusive probabilities opposite the "Yes" branches (.02 + .24 + .18 = .44).

3.3.4 Utility trees

The steps for creating a utility tree are practically identical to those for creating a utility matrix as described in Section 3.2.14, above. A utility tree based upon the fact scenario presented in that Section would appear as follows:

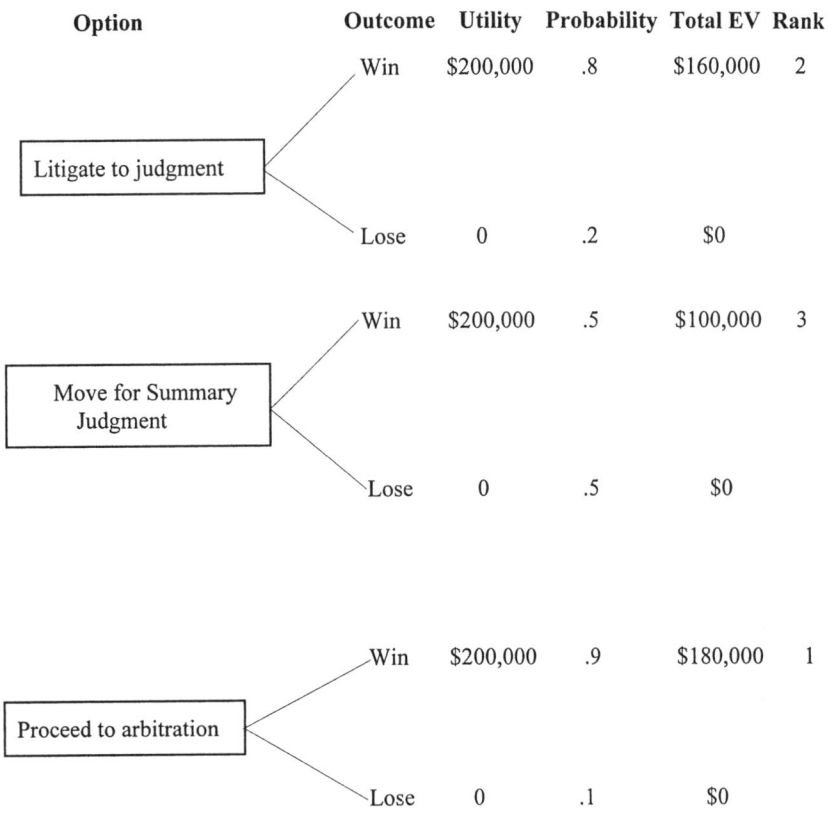

For more examples of how to apply the utility tree technique in various situations, see Jones, 246-71.

3.4 OFF-THE-SHELF SOLUTIONS FOR CREATIVE PROBLEM SOLVING

[**Editor's Note:** *These "stock" solutions for creative problem solving are adapted from Cooley(2), 226-28.*]

3.4.1 Structured settlement or payment in installments

In situations involving large money resolutions where plaintiffs are young and healthy enough to have a long life expectancy, structured settlements can provide a mutual gain solution. Through a structured settlement, the insurance company can deposit an agreed amount now, and a plaintiff can receive annuity payments over a period of time that total perhaps much more than the plaintiff could have received in a lump sum payment presently. Also, the settlement can be structured so that the amount of payments are tailored in size to the foreseeable needs of the plaintiff at various points in the future -- college, marriage, having children, etc. Aside from structured settlements, sometimes merely suggesting that an agreed settlement be paid in equal installments over a period of time or in a lump sum plus periodic installments can precipitate a resolution of a dispute.

3.4.2 Future business arrangement

In an inter-company dispute, often there are opportunities for the disputants to resolve their differences through future business transactions which allow the aggrieved party to recoup any present losses over time. These types of solutions are particularly attractive where there is an advantage, because of the specific market or of the status of industry competition, for both companies to continue to do business together.

3.4.3 Portion of the settlement to be paid to a mutually acceptable charity

Occasionally, there arises a situation where a defendant believes that it did nothing to injure the plaintiff and therefore rejects the idea of paying very much in settlement. But at the same time, the defendant desires very much to settle the dispute to avoid adverse publicity. This situation tends to arise in civil rights or discrimination cases. Suggesting that a portion of the settlement be paid to a mutually acceptable charity or civil rights organization can sometimes satisfy both parties' interests to ensuring that some future good can result from their joint solution.

3.4.4 Payment in kind instead of in dollars

In many types of disputes, resolution can be achieved through settlements permitting a transfer of goods or property, or a performance of services instead of a payment of money. You should always be on the alert for these closure-aiding opportunities.

3.4.5 Substitution of goods

In any dispute involving a purchase or lease of goods or of property that later proves unsatisfactory to the purchaser or lessee, a solution can often flow from a suggestion that the alleged unsatisfactory goods or property be substituted with goods or property of higher quality. A guarantee or warranty might also accompany the substituted goods or property.

3.4.6 Apology

A simple apology may be of great value to a complaining party. Indeed, in a defamation case for instance, an apology might be worth millions if coupled with a public retraction. Even in a small personal or business dispute, a sincere apology, particularly in written form, can provide an important element of a settlement package. Be vigilant for situations appropriate for its use.

3.4.7 Change in title, label, or description

For many people, a title or label has intrinsic value for self-identity, self-esteem, or other reasons. Thus, in an employment dispute, a change in an employee's title to reflect supervisory status may be as important to the employee as an increase in salary. Similarly, in a consumer class action against a manufacturer in a products liability case, an element of the settlement might reasonably include an agreed change in the label for the product, including a detailed description of the appropriate use of the product and a warning to the consumer of the consequences of inappropriate use. Other simple "label" changes might facilitate a settlement. For example, in a residential lease, changing the description of the living space to read "Penthouse Apartment" with a corresponding reference on the lobby directory, may, with other concessions, be a sufficient inducement for a celebrity tenant to drop a lawsuit for the landlord's failure to deliver timely possession of the premises.

3.4.8 Extra-dispute resources for satisfying a party's extra-dispute interests

In certain situations, resources for satisfying all or a part of a dispute lie outside the resources or power available to the actual parties in conflict. For example, in a sexual harassment case brought by a female lawyer against a male partner in a law firm and the law firm itself, part of a settlement could consist of satisfying the female partner's long held desire to become a member of a highly exclusive country club or to be appointed as an adjunct professor of law at a local law school. Senior partners in the firm could, through their network of well-placed contacts, perhaps see to it that those extra-dispute interests of the female lawyer were quickly satisfied.

3.4.9 Confidentiality agreement

A defendant's fear that the settlement in the present case will cause many other individuals to file claims and seek similar settlements often constitutes a formidable barrier to a settlement. This fear can sometimes be overcome and a settlement reached through the parties' entering into a confidentiality agreement as part of the settlement which imposes severe sanctions for violating confidentiality.

3.4.10 Propose a change in language or in the interpretation of language

In some contract or lease disputes, resolution can be achieved through an agreed change in language or an agreed interpretation of language as part of a settlement package. Thus, in a manufacturer-supplier contract, where a supplier is sued for failure to expressly comply with a contract term requiring the supplier to "ship the goods within ten days of the date of the purchase order," a settlement might, in part, consist of changing the contract to read "ship the goods on the tenth day following the date of the purchase order unless that day is a non-business day, in which case, the goods will be shipped on the next business day." The new language could then be interpreted to permit the supplier to ship goods on a Tuesday following a three-day holiday weekend, whereas a strict reading of the old language would have required goods to be shipped on a Saturday, one of the non-business days in a three non-business day weekend.

3.4.11 Split the difference

As a final gesture to avert a failed settlement attempt, mediators often suggest, where the final bargaining bracket is relatively narrow, that the parties split the difference. You must be careful not to make this suggestion until all efforts to close the bracket have been exhausted.

3.5 MISCELLANEOUS TOOLS AND TECHNIQUES

3.5.1 Neuro-linguistic Programming

Many negotiators and mediators are beginning to experiment with neuro-linguistic programming ("NLP") techniques in the resolution of disputes and in forming transactions. The concepts underlying NLP are simple. The "neuro" part of neuro-linguistic programming represents the idea that people's behavior results from the neurological processes of sight, hearing, smell, taste and touch. People experience the world through these senses, store the information they experience, and then they act on it. The "linguistic" component represents people's use of language to communicate with others, and the "programming" part refers to how people choose to convey ideas so as to get the optimal results. In short, NLP is the ability to respond effectively to others through a process of rapport-building and to understand the way people think based on their own model of the world (See Cooley (9), 53-59).

Mirroring and Matching

One-way negotiators and mediators achieve rapport is by "mirroring and matching" their communication partner. By taking this process of imitating movements and gestures into conscious thought, they usually are able to achieve rapport quickly and encourage free flow of information earlier than may have been achieved otherwise. Mirroring and matching is the way that two people subtly respond to each other's movements with similar movements and gestures of their own. Most people begin to mirror and match another person's activities unconsciously, but successful communicators can consciously create rapport, which will lead to trust and confidence. Mirroring and matching is innate and appears across cultures. Research has shown that in its first day of life a baby will move in synchronicity with its mother's voice, and later will synchronize with the voice of any person speaking any language. This research also indicates that human beings desire this type synchronicity or rapport. Simple examples of mirroring by a mediator include making the same amount of eye contact that a person makes with him, slowing down or speeding up the pace of his words so that he speaks more like the person, or using the same expressions as the person when dealing with emotional issues. Negotiators and mediators skilled in NLP also match hand and arm movements, posture, and even breathing rates, depending on the level of rapport that they have with another person.

Pacing and Leading

Pacing and leading in NLP is the way the negotiator checks her rapport level with whomever she is communicating. "Pacing" means establishing a common ground with a person that will lead to trust and respect. By pacing, the negotiator is making sure that her communications are understood by the receiver and that she has brought each new concept or idea down to common symbols. By "leading" she changes her behavior so that the other person follows. By leading, a negotiator strengthens rapport and establishes the non-verbal aspect of communication. Both negotiators and mediators use pacing and leading to give others a better understanding of the message they are trying to communicate, to lead people in a different direction than they originally considered, or to be sure someone is understanding the concepts they are explaining.

Representational Systems

People assess communication and assign personal meaning to it based on their internal "representational systems." This term encompasses the methods by which people take in, code, and store information in their memory. They record experiences through their sense of sight, sound, taste, touch and smell, and they store these experiences in their memory based on these sensory perceptions. People predominantly store visual pictures, auditory sounds and kinesthetic feelings. Everyone uses each of these three representational systems at various times and most people switch instinctively from one system to the next when it is beneficial to do so. When people recall information, their memory is usually dominated by a favored form of representation, and their memories and experiences reflect this sense more than the others. By age 11 or 12 most people have clear preferences in our representational systems and tend to use one internal sense habitually. They use their dominant representational system to encode and recall experiences in their memory and they are able to make finer distinctions in this system than in any others. NLP techniques teach that some people prefer to think in mental images or pictures, rather than sounds or feelings. These visual based people describe events and recall information through pictures that are triggered in their minds. Other people prefer to think in relation to sounds. These auditory based people will talk themselves through information, or will process information through words. Still other people will base their actions on their feel for a situation, or kinesthetics, rather than on what they see or hear. These people rely on gut reactions and emotion to describe and recall experiences. They convert external information into feelings and then convert their feelings into terms that can be related back in communication. Knowing how a person thinks, or what representational systems he or she is using helps the negotiator or mediator tailor his or her communication to achieve maximum effectiveness.

Language Cues for Representational Systems

To determine the representational system that other people rely on most, negotiators and mediators who use NLP begin by analyzing language and the specific words people use to communicate their thoughts. Then they try to "speak his or her language" or try to match his or her predominant system. To illustrate a representational system's link to language, the table below sets forth some common sensory based words and phrases that can help you to identify the system a person is using.

Language Identifying Representational Systems

Visual
Look, picture, clarify, insight, focus, perspective, shine, notice, outlook, reveal, see, show, colorful, hazy, bright, crystal clear, appear.

Visual Phrases
I see what you mean.
We see eye to eye.
You'll look back at this and laugh.
Beyond a shadow of a doubt.
Show me what you mean.

Auditory
Say, rhythm, tone, load, clear, tell, silence, speechless, vocal, harmonious, dumb, ring, listen, make music, tune in, deaf ears, be heard, question.

Auditory Phrases
On the same wavelength.
Its all Greek to me.
In a manner of speaking.
Loud and clear.
Hold your tongue.

Kinesthetic
Stress, tension, concrete, sensitive, heavy, smooth, scrape, hold, grasp, suffer, warm, cold, push, catch on, make contact, solid, hot.

Kinesthetic Phrases
I'll get in touch with you.
Hold on a second.
Heated argument.
Smooth Operator.
Scratch the surface.

Eye Accessing Cues

Another way NLP negotiators and mediators determine the representational systems people use is by observing the direction their eyes move during a conversation or when they talk about certain subjects. People's eye accessing cues give us information on the way a person chooses to store and access information mentally. People move their eyes in different directions and in systematic ways depending on how they are thinking. By understanding these cues NLP mediators determine which representational system a person relies on most, and then systematically tailors communication to that system so that it will be as effective as possible. The eye accessing cues appear in the chart below.

> **Visual Remembered** - Eyes move up and to the left visualizing something from the past in the way the person saw it before.
>
> **Visual Constructed** - Eyes move up and to the right, constructing a picture or image of something the person has never seen before.
>
> **Auditory Remembered** - Eyes move across and to the left, remembering sounds that the person has heard before.
>
> **Auditory Constructed** - Eyes move across and to the right, constructing sounds that the person has never heard before.
>
> **Auditory Digital** - Eyes move down and to the left, creating an internal dialogue or talking to oneself.
>
> **Kinesthetic** - Eyes move down and to the right, accessing feelings or emotions.

If the receiver of the communication is left-handed, the cues of the person will be opposite those illustrated in the above chart. Also, eye accessing cues are thought to be most useful if the information being solicited or the responses being analyzed are responses to open questions. For example, if the question asked is "What color was the car," the response is likely to be strictly visual. However, if the question is "What would you like to be the result of this mediation session today," the person can answer in any number of ways and will most likely answer based on their preferred representational system; with either visual, auditory or kinesthetic cues.

Other Accessing Cues

Although eye accessing cues are the easiest cues to notice, there are other forms of body language that can help to determine a person's preferred mode of communication. Voice cues, breathing patterns, gestures and posture can also indicate a preferred representational system.

- **Visual Cues:** According to NLP precepts, a person who relies on visual representations will often speak faster and in a higher pitch than someone who relies on auditory or kinesthetic representations. This is because the images relied on come into the brain quickly and people try to convey the content of the image before it is gone. Usually a visually oriented person will speak with her head up, will breathe shallowly, and will use short, pointed gestures.

- **Auditory Cues:** People that are thinking in sounds, or an auditory system, will breathe evenly and will speak in a clear, expressive tone. There will usually be minimal inflection in the voice and a very constant voice pattern. The head may be slightly angled as if they were actually listening to something, and their gestures will be very broad and sweeping.

- **Kinesthetic Cues:** If a person is thinking based on feelings, kinesthetic accessing can be recognized by deep breathing and relaxed muscles. This person will usually speak slowly and in a deep tone, with frequent pauses or words such as "ah" or "um" between sentences. Their gestures will be small and close to the body, and they will also keep their head down, as if deep in thought, when they are trying to access important information.

Thus, by paying close attention to the physical behavior of their audience, NLP negotiators and mediators believe they can develop rapport and move participants to agreement.

Creative Problem Solver's Handbook for Negotiators and Mediators

3.5.2 The Enneagram

The Enneagram (pronounced ANY-a-gram) is a study of the nine basic types of people, and it is beginning to be used by psychotherapists and mediators to help resolve interpersonal conflict (Baron and Wagele). Its exact origin is unknown, but it is believed to have been taught centuries ago in secret Sufi brotherhoods in the Middle East. The Russian teacher, Gurdjieff, introduced it to Europe in the 1920s, and it began being used in the United States in the 1960s.

In essence, the Enneagram system is symbolized by a circle containing a nine-pointed star-like shape. The name of the system is well chosen, as *ennea* is Greek for the number nine, and *gram* means "a drawing." As experts in the field have explained:

> The Enneagram teaches that early in life we learned to feel safe and to cope with our family situations and personal circumstances by developing a strategy based on our natural talents and abilities. By working with the Enneagram we develop a deeper understanding of others and learn alternatives to our own patterns of behavior... People of the same type have the same basic motivations and view the world in some fundamentally similar ways (Baron and Wagele, 2-3).

The nine types of people are configured in a circular shape as shown below:

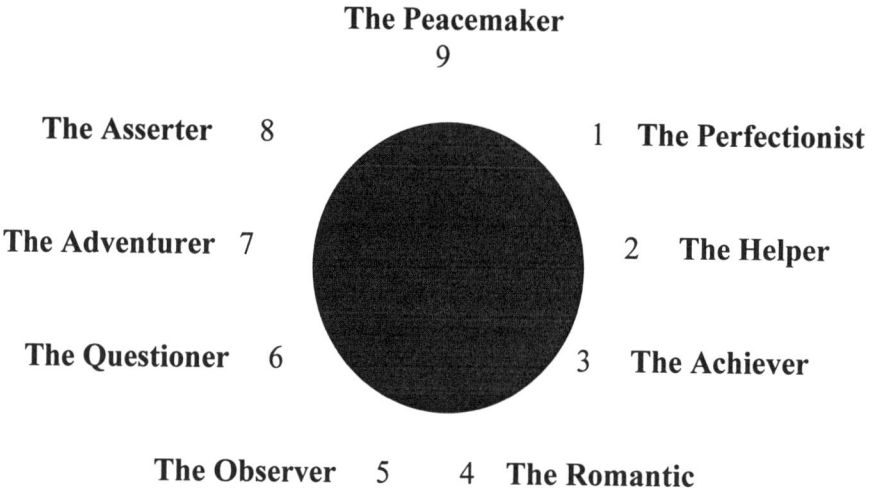

A brief description of the nine types is as follows:

1. *Perfectionists* are realistic, conscientious, and principled. They strive to live up to their high ideals.

2. *Helpers* are warm, concerned, nurturing, and sensitive to other people's needs.

3. *Achievers* are energetic, optimistic, self-assured, and goal oriented.

4. *Romantics* have sensitive feelings and are warm and perceptive.

5. *Observers* have a need for knowledge and are introverted, curious, analytical, and insightful.

6. *Questioners* are responsible, trustworthy, and value loyalty to family,

friends, groups, and causes. Their personalities range broadly from reserved and timid to outspoken and confrontative.

7. *Adventurers* are energetic, lively, and optimistic. They want to contribute to the world.

8. *Asserters* are direct, self-reliant, self-confident, and protective.

9. *Peacemakers* are receptive, good-natured, and supportive. They seek union with others and the world around them (Baron and Wagele, 2-6).

If you want to learn your own type by taking a personality inventory and much more about how you might use this tool in interpersonal problem solving, see Renee Baron and Elizabeth Wagele, *The Enneagram Made Easy* (HarperCollins, 1994); Helen Palmer, *The Enneagram: Understanding Yourself and the Others in Your Life* (Harper San Francisco, 1991); Kathleen V. Hurley and Theodore E. Dobson. *What's My Type?: Using the Enneagram System of Nine Personality Types to Discover Your Best Self* (Harper San Francisco, 1992). The final chapter of the Baron and Wagele book explains the Myers-Briggs inventory of Jungian types and compares it with the Enneagram system.

3.5.3 Whole-Brain thinking applied

While we have addressed the theory of whole-brain thinking in Section 1.3.3.3, above, in this section we will explore how you can apply whole-brain techniques in a negotiation or mediation setting (See Cooley (1), Ch. 2, 12-16).

3.5.3.1 Determining the brain preference of others

Proponents of whole-brain thinking would contend that, as a negotiator or mediator, you must not only be aware of your own lateral preference but, you must also be aware of the lateral preferences of other attorneys and participants in the negotiation or mediation so that you will be able to interact with and react to them effectively in your creative problem solving efforts.

If you are a logical person, you would probably think that determining someone else's brain preference would be rather easy. The logical person would reason that if our society is left-brained and 85 percent of the American population is right-handed, then there should be a direct correlation between the two. However, research has shown that right or left-handedness is not an accurate indication of lateral dominance. Left-handed people are generally left-hemisphere thinkers as much as right-handed people. Also, among people who show a much higher use of right-hemisphere faculties, there is no strong correlation with left-handedness. However, there are many ways quickly to gauge the lateral preference of persons with whom you interrelate. For example, by engaging in small talk with people, you can determine much about their preferred activities or behaviors. If the person engages frequently in swimming and bicycling, has a "passion" for fishing, speculates (takes risks) in the stock market, and pays little attention to time constraints or deadlines, that person is apt to be right-dominant. If he or she likes doing cross-word puzzles, plays chess daily, is highly organized personally, likes to design computer programs, he or she is probably left-dominant. If he or she prefers taking notes by printing them rather than by using long-hand style, it may indicate a right-brain or visual orientation. If you have the opportunity to ask another person for directions (say to the location of the place where settlement discussions are to be held), pay careful attention to the way he/she communicates the instructions. If he/she describes the proper route by giving precise details in street names (words) and number of blocks (numbers), he/she is probably left-brained. If he/she describes the proper route by referring mostly to landmarks (gasoline stations, restaurants, billboards, lake, horse farm, etc.) and/or includes colors in the description (red barn, green sign, big white house), it is probable that the person is visually-oriented and is apt to be right-brain dominant. Obviously, the more interaction you have with a person, the better you will be able to obtain a very reliable "picture" of that person's brain preferences.

However, you must be careful not to stereotype a person either as a left or right, based on one or two characteristics or on the basis of a brief encounter. An extremely verbal person (a classic left-brain type) may in fact be a right-brained dominant. This is possible because verbal dexterity is a skill which overlaps both hemispheres of the brain. In analyzing the laterality of such person, you might want to concentrate on the content rather than quantity of what he/she is saying. Content may give you a clue as to the degree of concreteness versus imagery in the communication. In short, when analyzing the brain preference of a person, carefully apply your own left-brain discretion and judgment.

3.5.3.2 Your dealings with co-counsel

Collaborating with co-counsel either in negotiation or mediation is not always an easy task. It often involves a great deal of negotiation ability to accomplish all the necessary coordination effectively and efficiently. A knowledge of or "feel" for your co-counsel's brain preference may facilitate the collaborative effort. As pointed out above, a left-brain oriented person processes information more efficiently and effectively by reading facts, figures, specifications, and details. Thus, in presenting to or identifying such person the problem jointly to be solved, you would want to do it in writing, using words and numbers, and in as detailed, organized, and logical a manner as possible. You would also want to present your suggested solutions to the problem in the same format to make them more appealing to the left-rained thinker. On the other hand, if you are dealing with a right-brain oriented person, you would want to present the problem and your suggested solutions in a graphic form to make them more understandable and appealing to that person. If possible, you might want to draw illustrations of the problem and the solutions on a chalkboard or on a flip-hart, using colored chalk or markers, and then invite the other person to draw other possible solutions. This will place your negotiating partner in a nonthreatening, comfortable, mode; stimulate his/her cooperation in the problem solving experience, and maximize the potential for a creative, mutually beneficial (win-in or better) solution.

3.5.3.3 Your dealings with senior or subordinate counsel on the case

Suggestions for using your knowledge of split-brain theory in dealing with co-counsel also apply to your dealings with senior counsel that you are working with on a case. If you are in a supervisory position on a case, you may be able to use your knowledge of split brain theory to your side's added advantage. For example, if you are in a position to select particular persons of your firm and assign them to particular tasks, you might want to seriously consider assigning a right-brain oriented person to the task of idea or issue generation and a left-brain oriented person to tasks requiring mechanical efficiency, detail, and organization. Ideally, if personnel resources and economics permit, you may want to "team up" a right-brain dominant with a left-brain dominant for the purpose of achieving a whole-brain approach to a particular problem or task.

3.5.3.4 Dealing with opposing counsel

Interacting with opposing counsel gives rise to many opportunities to apply whole-brain thinking skills. How successful you are in these negotiations will depend, to a large extent, on how well you employ your own thinking abilities and style, your success will also depend on how well you are able to anticipate your opposing counsel's thinking and behavior and to act effectively in response to it. For example in resolving a discovery dispute with opposing counsel, use a whole-brain approach to appeal to opposing counsel's dominant thinking style and enlist his/her involvement in a joint attempt to discover a win-win solution. This is just one example. Countless other similar situations arise during litigation.

3.5.3.5 Dealing with mediators, judges, or former judges

Judges are people too. Like the rest of us, they, or most of them, prefer to use one hemisphere of their brain over the other. Your ability to communicate with them and to persuade them to your viewpoint will be enhanced if you are able to accurately identify their brain preference and to present your argument or suggestion in a way which is most appealing to their dominant style of thinking. A left-brain dominant judge will probably be more easily persuaded by facts, figures, words, numbers, and a structured, logical approach. A right-brain dominant judge will be more easily persuaded by arguments that are accompanied by graphic aids and an appeal to emotions.

In summary, proponents of whole-brain thinking would contend that with a little effort you can use practical applications of split-brain theory to your decided advantage in negotiation and mediation. They would suggest that you seek to employ a whole-brain, balanced approach to litigation, negotiation, and mediation by developing and sharpening your skills in both vertical and lateral thinking.

CHAPTER FOUR

CREATIVE APPROACHES TO PROCESS DESIGN IN ALTERNATIVE DISPUTE RESOLUTION

*When you have a choice and don't
make it, that in itself is a choice.*

William James

In many situations, pure mediation or pure arbitration may not be the most appropriate alternative means for resolving a particular dispute. It is in these situations that people need to exercise creativity in selecting or designing an appropriate hybrid process to satisfy the specific needs of the parties. Mediators and negotiators must be knowledgeable of the various ADR hybrids in the event that they are asked to help design a process best suited to the resolution of a particular dispute. As the opening quote suggests, if parties or counsel have a choice and do not make it, that may be a choice which is not in their best interests. In this chapter we will explore ways to design ADR processes that best suit the needs of the parties and the dispute situation.

4.1 DESIGNING MULTIPLE-HYBRID PROCESSES FOR RESOLVING COMPLEX DISPUTES

As was mentioned in the Preface to this book, as an advocate, a negotiator, or a mediator, you will be increasingly called upon by clients or parties to design processes for resolving disputes. Some of the disputes requiring dispute resolution process ideas may be extremely complex. In this section we will walk through a design process yielding alternative process designs for a typical complex, multiparty dispute This Section is an adaptation of Cooley(3), 42-48.

Assume that a client has asked you to prepare alternative designs for a dispute resolution mechanism to resolve a complex litigation dispute involving at least two court cases. The dispute has multiple parties and primarily involves intellectual property ("IP" or "Liability") and insurance coverage ("Coverage") issues. You are told that the IP and Coverage issues overlap in the sense that some of the evidence and legal arguments relating to one may also be relevant to the other. The plaintiff in the case is an advertising company and the defendants are a major fast food chain, two of its parent companies ("Corporate Defendants") and three insurance companies ("Insurers"). The parties have already experienced an evaluative mediation that has been unsuccessful in resolving the dispute.

You should first be aware that cases involving Liability and Coverage issues are very complicated to litigate in the court system. In a typical tort suit of this kind, plaintiff files suit against an insured defendant. The insurer files a declaratory judgment action against the insured defendant alleging noncoverage of the claim. There are two possible judicial alternatives. The court can allow the declaratory judgment action to proceed, which may result in resolving the coverage issue before the conclusion of the underlying tort suit. Or, the court can stay the declaratory judgment action until the tort suit is resolved. The coverage question will thus linger unresolved during the pendency of the underlying lawsuit. Appeals taken in either of these proceedings can dash any hope of speedy resolution of the overall case. More importantly, there are usually major problems with allowing the Coverage case to proceed. Positions taken by an insurer in the Coverage case may seriously harm the insured defendant vis-a-vis the plaintiff in the tort case. For example, in the declaratory judgment proceeding, the insurer may try to prove that the insured caused the intentional injury. The insurer's evidence may seriously undermine the insured in the tort suit, even if the insured is being represented by independent counsel in the tort suit. If the insured were forced to argue in the Coverage proceeding that he acted only, or at most, "negligently", the insured may seriously weaken his position in the tort suit that he was not negligent at all. To resolve these problems caused predominantly by the highly-structured and public nature of court litigation, some experts have recommended the design and use of more flexible and dispute-tailored processes. Concurrent mediation is one such process. "Concurrent mediation" does not mean that all of the issues between and among all the parties are mediated simultaneously. Rather, the term means that the Liability and Coverage issues are privately mediated to resolution in a systematic and orderly fashion, without leaving one or the other issue for court adjudication (Pryor and Pryor).

Clients sometimes require lawyers to hastily suggest alternative process designs based upon extremely limited information about the parties and the configuration and substance of the respective claims and defenses. Since "form generally follows function," you might want to tell your client, in the present exercise, that you may need to modify some of your design proposals when you receive more specific information about the parties, claims, and defenses. Even on the sparse information provided above regarding the presented case, however, there are several potential process designs suitable for consideration. They include: (1) classic co-mediation; (2) classic mini-trial procedure; (3) modified mini-trial procedure; (4) any of these three mechanisms with a blind bidding enhancement. Before proceeding with this exercise, you may want to review Section 1.3.8, which describes these pertinent hybrid processes in considerable detail.

4.1.1 Classic co-mediation

As explained more thoroughly in Section 1.3.8.7, an ADR hybrid that has gained widened use over the past few years is co-mediation. Simply defined, co-mediation is a process in which more than one person serves as a mediator. It involves the concepts of team mediation and interdisciplinary problem solving and it can be tailored to the needs of a particular dispute. Multiple mediators are commonly used in complex disputes where there are multiple parties, sometimes on each side of the case, and an intricate configuration of claims, cross-claims, and counter-claims. Typically, one mediator is designated as the lead mediator. That mediator is the chief strategist, coordinating the mediation activities of the other mediators and serving as an advisor and clearinghouse of information for them. With respect to the presented case and configuration of parties and claims, the co-mediation process takes this format:

- Parties enter into a mediation agreement naming at least two neutrals as co-mediators;

- One mediator ("Coverage mediator") is assigned to Coverage parties; caucuses with each party privately; and then continues caucusing or brings Coverage parties together for a joint session. The Coverage mediator's goal is to help the insurers (and insured as appropriate) to reach a consensus on their percentage of contribution to a settlement, perhaps involving creative, mutual gain elements;

- Second mediator ("Liability mediator") is assigned to Liability Parties; caucuses with each party privately; and then continues caucusing or brings parties together for a joint session. The Liability mediator's goal is to help the parties reach a fair settlement value of the underlying IP and related claims, perhaps involving creative, mutual gain elements;

- The Coverage mediator and the Liability mediator will caucus at appropriate intervals and will control the sequence of the caucusing and joint sessions;

- This process is estimated to take three days, though, because of caucusing, the individual parties will not be engaged in it continuously.

4.1.2 Classic mini-trial procedure

As more thoroughly explained in Section 1.3.8.8, the mini-trial, as apparent from its name, is an abbreviated trial or hearing. This method of dispute resolution is a relatively new approach. Its principal advantage is that the mini-trial involves high-level corporate representatives in the dispute resolution process. It is best suited to large disputes and complex litigation. Cases involving breaches of complex contracts, particularly if there are complex technical issues; patents cases; antitrust cases; major construction cases; and products liability cases may be most appropriate for mini-trial resolution.

The mini-trial agreement specifies who will comprise the panel for the mini-trial. This panel normally consists of three people: a business executive from each side and a third party neutral. The third party neutral is instrumental in insuring that the resolution process stays on course. The business executives appointed to the panel must have the full authority to negotiate a settlement. Without that power, the hearing may be for naught. It is advisable that an executive deeply involved with the case not be designated as a panel member. No panel member should be asked to pass judgment on a superior or a person who reports directly to them in the ordinary course of the party's business.

Before the mini-trial hearing, the parties to the mini-trial exchange brief position summaries (and document and witness lists if evidence is to be presented at the hearing). After an abbreviated period (usually a few hours or a day) of argument and/or presentation of evidence (as the parties elect), negotiation commences. The success of the entire process rests on this period of negotiation. In order to insure its success, the mini-trial agreement sets up its parameters in a way most conducive to achieving settlement. The negotiation usually extends into several sessions. Normally, the two business executives meet by themselves or with the third party neutral. In the event that negotiations break down completely, the mini-trial agreement normally provides for a mandatory period of time to elapse before the decision is made to resume the original litigation. A "cool-down" period often allows the parties an opportunity to re-think their reasons for entering mini-trial negotiations in the first place and often generates new settlement ideas.

With respect to the presented case and configuration of parties and claims, the classic mini-trial alternative could involve a format comprised of two sequential mini-trials:

- Parties enter into a mini-trial agreement naming two neutrals - one neutral (Coverage neutral) for the Coverage mini-trial and one neutral (Liability neutral) for the Liability mini-trial.

- The Coverage neutral chairs the Coverage panel which is additionally comprised of high-level representatives of the insured and the insurers.

- Insured's and insurers' lawyers present abbreviated cases to Coverage panel.

- After conclusion of cases, Coverage neutral meets with other panel members and seeks to help them reach a consensus on their percentage of contribution to a settlement, perhaps involving creative, mutual gain elements.

- If parties are unable to negotiate percentages, they can preagree to accept the recommendation of the Coverage neutral as a last resort or can preagree to some other finally determinative method. In either event, the role of the Coverage neutral in the process ends. [It is estimated that this portion of the process will last one and one-half days.]

- The second or Liability phase of the process begins.

- The Coverage neutral agrees not to disclose anything that occurred in the Coverage mini-trial to the Liability neutral.

- The Liability neutral chairs the Liability panel which is additionally comprised of high-level representatives of the plaintiff and the insured defendant.

- Plaintiff's and insured's lawyers present abbreviated cases to liability panel

- After conclusion of cases, Liability neutral meets with other panel members and seeks to help them reach a consensus on the underlying IP and related claims, perhaps involving creative, mutual gain elements.

- If parties are unable to negotiate percentages, they can preagree to accept the recommendation of the Liability neutral as a last resort or can preagree to some other finally determinative method.

- It is estimated that this portion of the process will last one and one-half days.

4.1.3 Modified mini-trial procedure

The modified mini-trial procedure would provide for a technical advisor to each of the Coverage neutral and the Liability neutral described immediately above. The technical advisor for the Coverage neutral would be a lawyer skilled and experienced in insurance coverage law; the technical advisor for the Liability neutral would be a lawyer skilled and experienced in IP law. There would also be a third neutral called the Process neutral who would observe both the Coverage and the Liability mini-trial proceedings and intervene in them as explained below. The mini-trial procedure described immediately above would be modified as follows:

- After the conclusion of the Coverage mini-trial, the Coverage neutral and his/her technical advisor would confer with each other. The Coverage neutral alone would come to a decision as to the contribution percentages of the insurers (and the insured as the case may be), write it on a piece of paper, and place the paper in a sealed envelope. The roles of the Coverage neutral and his/her technical advisor would at that point end.

- The Process neutral (who does not know the decision of the Coverage neutral) meets with other panel members and seeks to help them reach a consensus on their percentage of contribution to a settlement, perhaps involving creative mutual gain elements.

- If parties are unable to negotiate percentages with the assistance of the Process neutral, they open the sealed envelope containing the decision of the Coverage neutral, and by preagreement, are bound by it. This hybrid ADR procedure is called Arb-med.

- This same procedure is replicated in the Liability mini-trial with the Process neutral intervening as mediator after the Liability neutral puts his/her decision in a sealed envelope.

- If parties are unable to reach a settlement with the assistance of the Process neutral, they open the sealed envelope containing the decision of the Liability neutral, and by preagreement, are bound by it.

4.1.4 Blind bidding enhancement

A blind bidding enhancement can be used in conjunction with any of the above alternative designs. This procedure is frequently used to help parties reach a settlement on the damage aspects of a case and has been successfully employed in the past to settle multi-million dollar claims. This procedure is most commonly used when the parties reach a bracket in negotiation or mediation but are unable to close the gap through the use of ordinary negotiation techniques. In this procedure, as a last resort, each party confidentially submits a bid to the mediator. For the plaintiff, the bid represents the lowest figure that the plaintiff will accept to settle the case; for the defendant, the bid represents the highest figure the defendant will pay to settle the case. Only the mediator knows both (or all) the figures submitted. By preagreement, the parties decide what they will do depending on the outcome. For example, they can preagree that if they are X dollars apart, the mediator will disclose the numbers and they will split the difference. They can also preagree that if they are only Y dollars apart, the mediator will not disclose the actual figures, but they will continue mediating (or negotiating). Finally they can also agree that if they are more than Z dollars apart, the mediator will not disclose the figures, and they will proceed to trial. This procedure encourages the parties to submit realistic bids in order to avoid the substantial risks and expense of proceeding to trial. Blind bidding is also discussed above in Section 3.2.11.

4.1.5 Location of settlement meetings

The place you suggest for holding the ADR proceeding may be as important as the ADR process you suggest. For complex multi-party cases, you should seriously consider recommending that a nontraditional, less-structured location than law firms be used for the final phase (or all) of the settlement meetings. The idea would be to choose a place that has an informal, comfortable, corporate retreat-like atmosphere. Research has shown that the choice of setting often can have a favorable influence on the success of dispute resolution discussions.

4.2 ROBERT A. CREO: OTHER CREATIVE APPROACHES TO PROCESS DESIGN IN COMPLEX CASES

Mediator and attorney Robert A. Creo has experimented with specially tailored ADR processes which have proven to be very successful in facilitating the resolution of complex, multiparty, multi-issue disputes. These processes are called the Creo Pie Chart Tool and the Creo Blind Trust Method. A detailed description of how these settlement techniques have been applied in actual cases may be found in CPR Institute for Dispute Resolution's Alternatives, Volume 18, No. 5, May 2000, page 1 (Creo Pie Chart Tool) and in Volume 17, No. 8, September 1999, page 1 (Creo Blind Trust Method). The text of the two articles are reproduced in Sub-sections 4.2.1 and 4.2.2 below with the permission of the CPR Institute for Dispute Resolution.

4.2.1 Creo Pie Chart Tool

As youngsters, we become familiar with the paradigm of two children sharing the final piece of cake or pie: one cuts it and the other chooses one of the two pieces. This model places a premium on accuracy because to miss the centerline by any discernible amount yields an advantage to the chooser; there is incentive to divide the pie fairly if not squarely. This negotiation is the ultimate in zero-sum bargaining since every crumb out of balance will be claimed by the other party to the detriment of the cutter.

Mediators and disputants often speak in terms of dividing or expanding pies when resolving economic conflict. A fundamental premise of interest-based bargaining and mediating is to avoid the assumption of a "fixed pie" and to create options for mutual gain. (See, Fisher, Ury and Patton, *Getting to Yes,* any edition, almost any page!)

As any experienced advocate or mediator knows, eventually every negotiation boils down to elements of distributive bargaining or apportionment of value, loss, or risk. Borrowing from the social and mental health professions, the pie charts adapted in this article are an aide to understanding issues and breaking impasse when mediating multiparty or multi-issue cases.

Mental health and social science professionals have long used pie charts to assist patients' expression of emotions, establishing priorities and as a communication tool. This tool is adapted to the mediation process for the same reasons it has proved successful in other fields. In disputes that are purely economic and there is little past or future relationship between the parties, the focus is on distributive bargaining. In tort claims, for example, the interests of the parties usually are to maximize economic gains while minimizing risk. This is often true in commercial transactions.

Although apology and empathy are powerful tools, there are, however, many disputes where noneconomic issues dominate the agenda. Pie charts are an excellent means to identify interests and sort out each participant's priorities.

In many cases, there are multiple defendants and it is acknowledged that the plaintiff has no or little liability. Often damages are liquidated or can be readily established within a reasonable range. The real fight is among the defendants on relative responsibility. One approach that has proved helpful involves each participant in the mediation drawing a pie chart delineating their perspective on the percentage liability of each responsible party. This is drafted individually and submitted to the mediator on a confidential basis. This technique is best illustrated by an actual construction defect case.

4.2.1.1 Case study

Facts: A hospital added a wing of new construction to house physician practices and ancillary services for its expanding acute care facility. The five-story structure was completed in July 1985 and comprises a structural steel frame with a reinforced pre-cast concrete exterior wall panel system.

In April 1993, the hospital's maintenance director reported that several panels had moved as much as 2.5 inches away from the building. In June 1993, while the matter was under investigation and before any affirmative action was taken, six of the pre-cast concrete wall panels on the third floor of this side of the building suddenly collapsed to the ground. Fortunately, no one was injured, although there was property damage, mostly to the HVAC units and sidewalks

Damages: The plaintiff hospital conducted an inspection of the remainder of the panels and identified widespread problems associated with their construction and installation. The hospital had to retrofit the anchorage system for the panels on two sides of the building and replace two sides with a synthetic panel system. The hospital also had to relocate the physician tenants during the remediation period. The hospital claimed relocation expenses and lost revenue of $50,000 and construction costs of more than $500,000. The hospital's insurance carrier honored the relocation expenses under its business interruption coverage but declined to fully reimburse the hospital while it pursued claims.

Defendants: The parties either named in the court action, or subject to claims via arbitration, cross-claims or indemnification, were:

- ABC General Contractor (Prime contractor) ("old" company)
- ABC/CDE General Contractor ("new" or "successor" company)
- FG Masonry (subcontractor who installed the pre-cast concrete panels)
- HIJ Cast Fabricators (fabricator of the pre-cast concrete wall panels)
- KLM Architects (project architect)
- NOP Design Engineers (wall panel system design consultant)

Between 1985 and 1995, the original prime contractor, ABC General Contractor, ceased doing business and exists solely as a shell company with no assets. Insurance coverage for the claim was denied by its former carrier. Some of its assets, including the right to its name, were sold to a newly formed company, the ABC/CDE General Contractor, which denied it was a successor-in-interest to "old" ABC General Contractor. This new company denied any responsibility for the wall panel system failure at the facility, but nevertheless lost a summary judgment motion on the successor liability issue.

Liability Theories and Claims: The plaintiff hospital and its experts asserted that:

1. The hospital has no responsibility regarding the wall failure.
2. The wall failure caused damage and created an unsafe condition.
3. The repairs by the hospital were necessary, reasonable and prudent.
4. FG Masonry primarily was responsible for the failures due to gross deficiencies in the methods by which it installed the panels.
5. HIJ Cast Fabricators, the panels fabricator was at fault since its representatives observed improper installation and documented it, but failed to act.
6. KLM Architects failed to notice and act upon the faulty workmanship and engineering; consultant NOP provided a defective design that forced the contractors to make inadequate modifications in the field.
7. As general contractors, both "old" and "new" ABC were accountable for all defects and faulty workmanship of its subcontractors.

Experts hired by the defendants investigated and filed detailed reports dispensing various degrees of blame upon the respective parties, while, not surprisingly, generally finding little or no fault with the party who retained them.

The Mediation: All parties, except for old ABC General Contractor, appeared with counsel, a representative with authority and an insurance adjuster present or participating via telephone. The counsel for old ABC was available via telephone but declined to participate in the mediation. He made it clear that there would be no economic contribution from that entity which had ceased doing business. As noted, a claim had been made under its prior carrier and coverage had been denied. There were fifteen participants in the mediation in attendance and three available via telephone.

All the defendants reached a global settlement, which involved paying $250,000 from the defendants and an assignment to the hospital of any claim old ABC General Contractor may have against its prior carrier for denial of coverage or bad faith. The hospital retained any proceeds received from its own carrier without offset or subrogation for the $250,000 paid by defendants. All actions were dismissed with prejudice. The mediator was appointed to arbitrate any disputes arising from the settlement agreement.

4.2.1.2 Dividing the pie

Pre-hearing submissions were received from most of the parties, so detailed opening statements were waived with only brief comment being made by the lawyers for some of the parties. With the consent of the parties, the author, acting as mediator, elected to caucus first with the defendants as a group. The group was advised that the mediation would proceed with each informing the mediator privately of what contribution they would make to marshal an offer sufficient to induce the plaintiff to settle.

All parties agreed to a key part of the pie chart method: that no party, including the plaintiff, would be advised of any individual party's own contribution. The slices of the pie of any offer would be added up by the mediator privately. The total amount would be presented to the defendants as a whole before being conveyed to the plaintiff. This avoids parties' jockeying for position and lowballing based upon relative liability concerns.

It also was made clear that if there was no global settlement, individual defendants could settle separately and obtain a joint tort release. If there was a settlement, only then would the defendants know others' contributions. It was critical for the parties to commit to their own offers and not be able to withdraw them once they learned what every one else is contributing.

[**Author Creo's note**: I decided against using a "Creo Blind Trust Method," in which parties indicate their contributions in a manner where no one, including the mediator, would know shares except their own. See Robert A. Creo, "How a 'Blind-Trust Method' resolves Multi-Defendant Cases," 17 Alternatives 145 (September 1999). My reasoning was that the damages were readily calculated, and my "gut handicap" from reading the submissions was that a proposal in the range of $250,000 to $350,000 would settle the case. Furthermore, I had worked with most of the lawyers successfully on numerous occasions so there was mutual respect and trust].

4.2.1.3 The pie chart method

Once these ground rules were agreed upon by all defendants, each was asked to draw a circle on a blank sheet of paper. At times pre-printed forms are used, but this mediation was freehand. Each participant was to write his or her organization's name on the bottom of the sheet of paper and then literally divide the pie into slices representing their view of liability based upon a percentage (not a dollar amount) for each party bearing legal liability. These were folded and handed to the mediator on a confidential basis.

Some defendants believed the plaintiff failed to mitigate damages or undertook repairs more extensive than necessary to remediate the problems.

4.2.1.4 What happened in mediation

At the conclusion of the first defense joint caucus, there was a consensus to raise $250,000. It was thought to be a reasonable goal because that it would be seriously considered by the plaintiff. Some defendants thought that $300,000 to $350,000 might be necessary but acknowledged that it might be impossible to obtain since there would be no general contractor contribution and the new company was vigorously opposing successor liability. From the charts and oral statements, it was clear that the consensus was that FG Masonry had the greatest liability; and the design professionals and the plaintiff the least.

Although the hospital bore little responsibility, it would have to steeply discount the claim to settle since it had the risk of any judgment against old ABC General Contractor being uncollectible.

The other four defendants placed FG Masonry at 85%, 75%, 50% and 50%, for an average of 65%.

There was consensus that HIJ Cast Fabricators had exposure, and it viewed its own risk, as did another defendant, at 20%. The order of exposure (and potential contributions) of the active participants at the mediation was developed as follows (most risk to least risk):

1) FG Masonry
2) HIJ Cast Fabricators
3) Plaintiff hospital
4) ABC/DEF General Contractor (new)
5) KLM Architect
6) NOP Design Engineers

In the first caucus round of individual defendants, the following contributions privately were authorized.

1) FG Masonry $50,000
2) HIJ Cast Fabricators   30,000
3) ABC/DEF General Contractor (new) 5,000
4) KLM Architect 5,000
5) NOP Design Engineers 5,000

A joint session was reconvened and the parties were advised that they had not made a credible offer because the total was less than $100,000. All agreed that this sum would be rejected immediately and making this offer would be counterproductive.

In a second caucus round, the following contributions were authorized:

1) FG Masonry $100,000
2) HIJ Cast Fabricators   40,000
3) ABC/DEF General Contractor (new) 10,000
4) KLM Architect 10,000
5) NOP Design Engineers 7,500

Once the joint defense caucus reconvened, the defendants were advised that $167,500 had been raised. The consensus was that this was insufficient, and that the mediator should meet again privately with each party and propose a specific contribution level to meet the $250,000 target. In the third round of individual defendant sessions, FG Masonry was advised that it could not expect to resolve the claim for less than a payment of $150,000. This was 60% of the liability of a $250,000 settlement and about 30% of the total claim. If FG Masonry met that number, the mediator was confident about raising the $250,000 with at least a 50% chance of it being accepted by the plaintiff. After a brief private discussion, FG Masonry agreed to add this sum to the pot but vowed no more additional funds would be contributed beyond the $150,000.

Next, private caucuses were held with each of KLM, new ABC/DEF General and NOP Design Engineers, who were advised that nothing less than $15,000 each would work. While they were in private meetings, the mediator suggested in a private caucus with HIJ Cast Fabricators that $55,000 was consistent with its own view of liability. The company's representatives agreed. Then, each of the other three were told that their commitment to $15,000 each would ensure the $250,000 would be met. They each agreed to this contribution still without knowledge of anyone else's payment.

The plaintiff hospital, in the course of several caucuses, already indicated that the "happy number" it sought was $300,000. The plaintiff had obtained a waiver of subrogation on a substantial sum already paid by its own carrier, but requested that this fact and the amount be kept confidential. It was clear that the plaintiff would not walk away from a defendants' proposal of at least $250,000.

This settlement was consistent with the pie charts if the self-portraits were considered with a jaundiced viewpoint. FG Masonry contributed 60% compared to the 65% average by the other defendants; HIJ Cast Fabricators paid 22% instead of the consensus and self-portrait of 20%. The three minor defendants contributed 6% and most participants placed them each at 5%.

4.2.1.5 12 Steps to settlement

Here is a 12-step approach that may be modified to fit the particular circumstances of any case or interpersonal dynamics:

Step 1. The mediator privately reviews all charts before starting the first round of caucus.

Step 2. Caucus with each party. Do not discuss the charts in the first caucus round.

Step 3. Convene a joint caucus of all defendants: Announce the total sum raised. Probe if there is a consensus on whether this sum should be offered now or another round of caucuses should occur next.

Step 4. Maintain or set a higher target for the defendants to hit on the next and each subsequent round. Determine if there is consensus and what may be acceptable to the plaintiff

Step 5. Without disclosing it, softly probe the defense's target figure with the plaintiff. Ascertain if it is within a range where settlement may be reached.

Step 6. If the target number appears feasible, return to a joint defense caucus and encourage the defendants to reach the target without committing the plaintiff to settlement. If the plaintiff does not seem likely to accept the target range, then go back to the defendants as a group and tell them that they should endeavor to move to the upper limits of their authority or start considering separate and individual releases. Advise them to think about it for the next round of private sessions. Do not discuss individual contributions in the joint sessions.

Step 7. The mediator privately develops a "pecking order" of liability based upon the submissions, the charts and the oral statements made in joint or private caucus. Compare individual contributions to the parties' own pie chart apportionments.

Step 8. Caucus with each party to obtain additional authority.

Step 9. The mediator evaluates which parties are not contributing sufficiently based upon the "pecking order" of liability, consensus of other parties and their own chart. Meet with these "slackers" and challenge them on their contribution by telling them your findings and reviewing their charts with them for any inconsistencies in their chart and economic contribution.

Step 10. Meet in joint defense caucus; advise the parties on new amount raised. Determine if it should be presented or how much of a gap exists.

Step 11. The mediator meets each defendant privately and asks for a specific dollar amount contribution from each party with the understanding that if any party declines, then the target will not be reached and the case may not settle. After these rounds with the defense, then the total is disclosed to all defendants with authorization to present it to the plaintiff without disclosing the respective contributions unless the offer is accepted.

Step 12. Present the offer to the plaintiff. If it is rejected, return to the defendants with a specific counteroffer and start another caucus round to determine if this demand can be met or countered. Continue the mediation using this approach until settlement or impasse.

4.2.1.6 Another case study: employment insurance claims

This case is an amalgamation of several actual employment cases the author has mediated over a number of years; pie charts were not used in most of these claims and information was obtained orally.

4.2.1.7 Facts

A young female assistant professor, Sue Knot, of a public university claims her male department head made unwelcome sexual advances to her over a two-year period. She decides that the situation was intolerable and that the tenured professor is too powerful and respected at the institution to challenge. She elects to accept a position in another university 1000 miles away. During her exit interview, she discloses to the human resources department the true reason for her departure.

At the start of the next academic year at her new school, she receives a personal letter from her former institution's president asking if she would cooperate in an investigation of allegations of improper sexual advances made by the department head to faculty, staff and students. Ultimately, in addition to Sue Knot, four female claimants-one professor, two staff and one student-hire the same lawyer and threaten suit against the institution.

A mediator is hired and the claimants, counsel for all parties and the institution's president participate in a mediation.

4.2.1.8 Methodology

In multiparty, multi-issue cases, the pie charts need not be done until a later stage of the mediation process, after parties have had an opportunity to vent and have had confidential dialogue with the mediator. The pie chart should be raised in private caucus; it should be done not only for themselves, but also on how they believe the other participants will prioritize interests.

These "perception charts" are invaluable for testing assumptions and correcting misconceptions about what is important to another party and what they might actually be willing to concede. All mediators have faced the disputant who is reluctant to state what he or she really wants because the party "knows" the other side won't give what he or she wants under "any" circumstances. The unarticulated interest is defeated at the outset.

The pie chart tests these positions and commits people in writing to their own interests. It is common for counsel to be widely off the mark on where the priorities of their own client lie. Lawyers are not accustomed to exploring and considering settlement options that are not remedies that can be obtained via a court verdict.

It also may be helpful in cases with pre-mediation submissions for the mediator to draft the first set of pie charts based upon his or her reading of the materials. Another set could be made by the mediator in mid-process before the participants make their own. This may serve as a check and balance to the mediator's perceptions and assist in managing the process.

4.2.1.9 Potential case-study settlement options

- Obtain consent to have claimants available as witnesses in any disciplinary action taken against the department head; offer a specialized rehabilitation program for offender if he accepts discipline and apologizes to each victim who wants him to do so;

- Confidentiality of any economic payments and other elements of settlement;

- Generous severance package for any staff or professor who elects to terminate employment;

- Award of significant attorney fees to counsel for claimant;

- Private apology by president to each claimant;

- Publication of sexual harassment policy;

- Establishment of internal complaint procedure;

- Required annual sensitivity and diversity training for faculty;

- Waiver of tuition for student;

- Reinstatement on tenure track for Sue Knot; minimal compensatory damages to her. Professor C chairs task force and committee on sexual harassment and training issues.

- Significant economic payments to Staff Member A who resigns.

- Economic compensation to Staff Member B, who is to participate in Professor C's task force.

The case study shows that there are infinite variations on the use of pie charts by mediators. Like any tool or technique, each mediator may adapt and evolve the method to suit the particular case, personal dynamics and individual style.

4.2.2 Creo Blind Trust Method

One of the barriers to resolution of multiparty claims is the apportionment of liability and contribution by each of the defendants. Often, defendants have formed a consensus on the appropriate evaluation of the plaintiff's case but are unable to resolve apportionment. Many defendants are rightfully concerned that a fair percentage of liability is attributed to all responsible parties.

Unfortunately, some parties don't focus on whether their own dollar contribution is the proper business decision, but instead fixate on not "paying for the other party" on a percentage basis. Parties may hold back their authority or decline to make a contribution within their reserves or conduct a risk analysis, solely based on their perception that another party is getting off cheaply. Despite admonitions from a mediator or settlement counsel to defendants that the dollars they are spending are real, while the percentages are abstract and secondary, the "relativity theory" of contributions has scuttled many settlement opportunities.

Early in my career as a mediator, I had a small personal injury case in which the plaintiff alleged that she had become ill eating a chicken sandwich at a fast food outlet. The vendor joined all its suppliers in the suit. The defendants were:

- a retail vendor;
- chicken supplier No. 1;
- chicken supplier No. 2;
- the mayonnaise supplier;
- the bread supplier, and
- a produce supplier.

Following the joint session, I had requested that the defendants explore an apportionment methodology while I met with the plaintiff. The defense reached an impasse, with some parties suggesting a pro rata approach and others firmly resisting any equality of fault.

Early in the mediation process it became clear that the case could be settled with the plaintiff for less than $50,000. After I returned with the plaintiff's final demand, which the defendants collectively agreed was reasonable and should be met, I caucused with each defendant. There seemed to be sufficient collective authority to settle the claim, but some parties would not commit their authority unless they paid less than other parties.

For example, the two chicken vendors agreed that they would march in lockstep - while "Bread" proclaimed he had to pay less than "Mayonnaise" since everyone "knew" that the condiment was the likely culprit! After many hours, an agreement ultimately was forged, despite the valiant defense of Bread and Produce against the onslaught of other food groups. The lawyers' strong emotions almost derailed a settlement.

Following this unpleasant experience, I developed a methodology that has been successful when faced with defendants who have a great deal of mistrust among themselves. I have dubbed this method the "Creo Blind Trust Method" and have shared it with my colleagues in the International Academy of Mediators. Below is the basic format without variations. It is most useful at the beginning of the mediation offer process, or to break an impasse. I often set the stage for introducing the method with the chicken sandwich story, as well as examples of the method's success in other cases.

4.2.2.1 Mission

The goal is to settle the case by raising a pot of money anonymously, without disclosing each defendant's specific amounts to the other defendants - or even, perhaps, to the mediator.

4.2.2.2 Charge to the defendants

The defendants need to commit privately and confidentially a specific dollar amount as a contribution to a settlement fund.

4.2.2.3 Tools

1) A large calculator without an adding tape.
2) A large manila envelope.
3) Small envelopes for each defendant.
4) Small slips of paper for each defendant.

4.2.2.4 Ground rules

Establish a consensus on the local rules in the caucus with all defendants. These rules govern disclosure, settlement issues and impasse. A fundamental premise is that no one can change their contribution after they learn later what other parties have contributed. Other rules govern what happens when the total is sufficient to settle the case and/or if it is disclosed - no matter how much is committed.

Parties must decide what happens to the excess. For example, should there be a pro rata reduction, or a reduction by percentages? Should there be another reduction formula? The parties also may agree that regardless of the amount raised, the mediator may elect to open the envelope to view the individual contributions of all or some of the defendants. The parties may agree that if a certain amount is not raised, the envelope will be destroyed without anyone viewing it. The defendants may agree that this is a last-ditch approach and that each must commit fully to this method. Another possibility is that if a global settlement is not feasible, the parties agree that the authority committed by them can be individually offered to the plaintiff by the mediator without anyone else knowing what sums are available from each separate party.

4.2.2.5 Step-by-step method

1. Ask each defendant to privately write a specific dollar amount they are willing to contribute to a settlement on a piece of paper, with their name on it, and seal that in a small envelope provided by the mediator. The name of each party should also be on the outside of the small envelopes.

2. After each party writes their amount privately, everyone places them in the large envelope and it is sealed. No one should look at any of the slips. Only each party knows their settlement contribution.

3. The mediator takes a calculator and privately enters a random number. The number should be one digit less than the settlement target number. For example, if the parties have agreed that the plaintiff's last position of $1 million is doable, then the mediator should enter a six-figure random digit – for example, 447,142 – since the target settlement is in the seven-figure range. If the target figure is in the six-figure range – say, $100,000 – then a five-figure number should be entered, such as 37,173. This is the "platform" number and should be random.

4. The mediator privately writes the platform number on a piece of paper and does not provide anyone else access to it.

5. The mediator presses the "Plus" key on the calculator.

6. The calculator is passed to the First defendant. This person privately enters their own settlement amount which was previously written on the piece of paper. They hit the 'Equal" key. A new number appears on the total screen.

7. The first defendant hits the "Plus" key and passes the calculator to the second defendant. Although the first defendant has seen the mediator's platform number, it is meaningless to the defendant and the case.

8. The second defendant enters its own "authority" amount and hits the "Equal" key. (The second defendant sees the new total on the calculator but has no ability to ascertain the contribution of the first defendant since the "platform" number is random and known only to the mediator and the first defendant). A new total shows on the calculator screen.

9. The second defendant hits the "Plus" key and passes it to the third defendant. (Again, the next defendant sees a total, but it is unable to compute the prior contributions of any of the prior defendants).

10. The third defendant enters its own authority amount and totals the calculator's figures before the next defendant enters its number.

11. Each defendant enters their authority amount. The calculator is returned to the mediator after all have entered their numbers confidentially.

12. The mediator subtracts the random platform number from the number shown on the calculator's screen. The mediator now has a total contribution available from all defendants without anyone having to reveal to anyone their own level of authority.

13. Important Step: Do not announce the result to anyone yet. Repeat the process by passing the calculator around again to double-check for any input errors by any of the defendants. If the numbers match again, then the parties proceed under the ground rules. If the parties have agreed to disclosure of the total sum, then it can be announced by the mediator.

This method also can be used to gauge obtainable ranges in preliminary negotiations or throughout the entire ADR process to convey each collective offer to the plaintiff. Making a collective offer without disclosing to the plaintiff the respective contributions of the defendants avoids the dynamic of plaintiff inflexibility based upon a perception that specific defendants are making an insufficient individual contribution.

This method also can be used without a mediator by having one of the parties act as moderator to enter the random number, and then that party enters their authority last.

The method lends itself to creative variations. I am certain that innovative advocates and mediators can build upon this method. Please keep me posted!

[Robert A. Creo, Arbitrator and Mediator
1807 Jancey Street, 1st Floor, Pittsburgh, PA 15206-1065
412-361-7893, robertacreo1@cs.com]

4.3 RODNEY A. MAX: DESIGNING THE MEDIATION

[**Editor's Note:** *This section consists of an article authored by Rodney A. Max and is reproduced and reformatted here with his permission.*]

4.3.1 Introduction

A mediation represents a unique opportunity to bring conflicting parties together to achieve a facilitated resolution. For many conflicts, "getting to the mediation" is simply a matter of agreeing to mediate, identifying a mediator, and meeting on the day of mediation. However, the great majority of disputes need a certain amount of preparation. That preparation includes choosing a mediator; exchanging information between parties; providing the mediator with the position statements; and preparing yourself and your client for the mediation. In the area of complex or multiparty mediations, even greater preparation is required in "getting to the mediation." This requires not only preparation of your side, but preparing with the mediator and your opposition.

Over the last several years I have had the opportunity of mediating hundreds of cases involving multiple plaintiffs, multiple defendants, and multiple claims. I have found that convening the parties in premediation caucuses, both jointly and separately, has been extraordinarily helpful in achieving the resolution. It is toward that end that I present "Designing the Mediation" for assistance to mediation advocates, their clients, and as mediators.

4.3.2 Identification of parties to conflict

In designing a mediation, it is vital that all persons intended to be included in mediation be identified and a commitment be obtained to participate in the mediation. Such communications can certainly be done by one or more of the parties. It can also be done by and through the mediator or his/her staff coordinator.

Is it necessary for all the plaintiffs and the defendants to participate? Are there interested third persons who may not be parties but may have an interest in the ultimate resolution? It is certainly preferable to have present all persons (whether parties or not) who will play a role in the ultimate resolution. This includes not only plaintiffs and defendants, but insurers, lienholders, interveners, as well as spouses and family members who may advise or support the decisions of the parties attending. If someone is going to criticize from afar, they may as well be present to be a part of the "give and take" of the mediation and be exposed both to the opposing side as well as the mediator.

In some mediations, if some of the parties or interested persons cannot attend, it is possible to achieve a level of resolution among those who are attending. Such interim resolution can be a stepping stone to a future mediation or negotiation with the remaining persons or parties. Bifurcating a mediation may be helpful if different parties need to be dealt with at different levels.

In designing the mediation, it may be helpful that the defendants be given an opportunity to caucus before the plaintiffs arrive. In a personal injury or wrongful death case involving multiple defendants, each defendant may have a different role relative to the injury or death. Such differences will affect the individual defendants' view of the overall value of the case as well as their participation therein. Conferring with all of the defendants at one time, prior to the plaintiffs' coming, can assist in expediting the mediation and avoiding unnecessary delay. At times I have advised that this premediation defendants' meeting occur a week or so before the mediation itself; at times I have advised that it should take place a couple of hours before the plaintiffs arrive; and at other times I have allowed the plaintiffs' attorneys to make an opening statement after which they adjourn for a day during which time the defendants confer among themselves. In this way the defendants can coordinate among themselves as to a reasonable verdict analysis, reasonable settlement analysis, a reasonable first offer, and their individual participations in the first counteroffer as well as future counteroffers.

Such premediation caucuses among plaintiffs are equally important. When a group of injured plaintiffs are having to deal with limited coverage among defendants, an agreement of participation among the plaintiffs can be most helpful. Some plaintiffs' attorneys have been able to obtain a premediation agreement among large groups of plaintiffs as to how they will participate in any offer. Such plaintiffs can agree that no one will negotiate separately and that any offer received at any time will be shared according to a prearranged formula. Other groups of plaintiffs may agree to pool and divide each offer according to what a majority of the plaintiffs will agree on. Others will agree to negotiate separately (see Section 4.3.6 below). Identifying all the plaintiffs who will participate will aid the defendants in being able to obtain complete resolution; therefore, bringing as many plaintiffs to the table as possible may be critical to obtaining full dollar value.

Absence of a lienholder can be fatal to a mediation. Therefore, whether that is a worker's compensation carrier, a medical insurer, a lending institution, or vendor's lienor, such persons' presence may be vital to the ability to achieve a negotiated settlement. Inclusion of such interested third persons must be well thought out, communicated to the other side, and invited (not as an afterthought, but as a forethought) to the mediation.

4.3.3 Nature of the conflict

In designing a mediation, separating material issues from nonissues helps expedite the negotiation process. Therefore, identifying whether or not the nature of this conflict is over only issues of liability, over issues of damages, over issues of both liability and damages, or over issues of counterclaims and cross-claims, will be helpful to the mediation process. Conferring with all sides on these issues is crucial. plaintiffs may believe that it is a clear liability case with only complex issues of damages. The defendants may assert that it involves crucial liability issues as well as counterclaims and cross-claims.

Accordingly, conferring separately with plaintiffs and defendants can assist in flushing out these issues prior to the mediation. Once I have met with each side, separately (and perhaps on more than one occasion), it is appropriate to bring them together through conference calls or premediation meetings to come up with an agreed upon strategy for dealing with liability, damages, as well as counterclaims and cross-claims. Such premediation communications assist in avoiding surprises at the mediation. They also help in working through these issues so that each set of parties can deal with the issues before getting to the mediation table. Finally, such premediation communications expedite the negotiation process once the day of mediation arrives.

4.3.4 Identifying mediation parameters

Mediation parameters include identification and agreement on place, date, time, and accommodations for the mediation. While this may seem fairly standard, in a complex mediation, it is crucial.

The place of the mediation must be able to accommodate all of the parties and their needs. You do not want to have multiple plaintiffs or defendants in crowded quarters or in rooms that are so close to one another so as to interfere with confidentiality. The place of the mediation must be able to accommodate any and all of the individual needs of all of the parties. Those who are physically challenged may have certain accommodations that must be taken into consideration. While in many mediations the location is at one of the parties' offices, neutrality may be an important factor that is not accomplished by such location. Accordingly, the mediator's region, state, city or office may be more appropriate than that of the parties. If it is an extended mediation over several days, the place of the mediation may need to include amenities such as recreation, restaurants, and areas in which the parties can "get away" over the course of several days.

The date and time of the mediation must be coordinated with an emphasis on effectively using each day without interference of travel, or absentee parties or third persons. The ability to work entirely through the process without one of the parties or representatives having to leave to catch a flight at 3:00 p.m. may be important to the process. The availability of a supervising or supporting individual in a different time zone than the location of the mediation may also be crucial. Likewise, providing multiple days allows for longer working sessions in the beginning and can accommodate airplane travel on a separate day. Mediations with multiple plaintiffs or defendants can take place over a number of days isolating certain plaintiffs or defendants on each day. Certainly, the earlier days may involve negotiations that continue into the night; whereas the last day of mediation should be able to conclude comfortably so that resolution occurs prior to the participant leaving for out of town travel.

Accommodations are equally important. If the site is in someone's office, hotels should be close by for easy access. Meals should be made available during the course of the day (nutritious morning amenities to include coffee, muffins, bagels and fruit); selections for lunch should be able to meet a variety of tastes; afternoon snacks should include chocolate chip cookies, pretzels, and peanut M&M's to assist all in making the day more "user friendly" and amenable to achieving resolution. Close access to airports is, likewise, an important issue. Not only must the parties reach a resolution, they must draft a document evidencing their agreement. An airport that is not within 15 to 30 minutes can be a hindrance to completion of the process.

All of these "mediation parameters" should be identified, agreed upon, and coordinated before the day of mediation.

4.3.5 Premediation exchange of information

To the extent that the discovery process is not complete, it is vital that an expedited exchange of information takes place prior to the mediation. I have always taken the position that qualified mediation advocates with reasonable clients can evaluate reasonable goals, and can achieve common ground, if they are looking at the same information. Thus, documents should be orderly exchanged to the extent this has not been done previously. To the extent that statements or depositions must be obtained, they too must be done before the mediation (the parties should be urged to take only those depositions that are vital to the evaluation of the case).

If certain preliminary motions must be heard before the case can be reasonably evaluated, they also should be presented for ruling. Certainly, dispositive motions may be a threat to one or more sides. However, if the result of such dispositive motion substantially impacts the values of the case, consideration should be given to what extent such dispositive motions should be filed, argued, or ruled on before the mediation process proceeds. The pendency of such dispositive motions, may, in and of itself, serve as an equalizer to the opportunity for reasonable resolution without obtaining a ruling.

The mediator should be prepared to involve himself/herself, as is necessary in the orderly exchange of documents, scheduling of depositions, and filing or tolling of necessary motions. The mediator's neutral position can facilitate not only a reasonable exchange of information, but also a process that will promote trustworthiness among the parties even before they get to the mediation table.

4.3.6 Opening statements and negotiations

Opening statements can be crucial to the mediation process. If the plaintiffs have one strategy and the defendants another, these strategies may contradict one another and raise obstacles to the negotiation process. In the design of the mediation, the parties can confer with regard to their separate strategies and attempt to work together on the manner in which the opening statement will be constructive. It may be necessary for the plaintiffs to be very factual; and, likewise, for the defendants to identify, in an empathetic but objective way, all of their defenses. On the other hand, it may be more appropriate for there to be a general conciliatory tone set among all those speaking on behalf of their clients. Still on other occasions it may be best for the parties to not say anything and only allow the mediator to introduce the process. Finally, it may be best that there be no opening statement or session. In a complex or multiparty mediation, these opening statement strategies should be designed by and among the parties with the assistance of the mediator before the mediation.

Among multiple parties, one issue will be whether or not the negotiation should be unified or diversified. That is, are the plaintiffs or defendants going to negotiate collectively or separately. Will there be diversified negotiations among different classes of plaintiffs or defendants? In some mediations, while the plaintiffs would like to negotiate collectively, the defendants may insist on individual negotiations. Through premediation design, counsel and their parties can come to an agreement on the appropriate way to negotiate before they get to the mediation day. In this way the mediation itself is not interrupted or obstructed by differences in the manner by which the parties will negotiate. Working this out prior to the mediation will allow the mediation day to be not only expedited, but more cooperative.

Many times there are nonmonetary remedies that need to be identified in addition to the traditional monetary remedies. Understanding how important such nonmonetary remedies are in dealing with them prior to the mediation may be crucial to the mediation itself. This can be accomplished both through premediation caucuses with counsel for the parties as well as with the parties themselves. These premediation caucuses will not only assist the mediator in identifying the nonmonetary interests of the parties, but will also help the mediator in achieving a higher level of rapport with parties before getting to the mediation day. This, too, is of great importance to the overall process.

In complex, multiparty cases, it is equally important to get all parties "on board" with how many moves it will take to get to their respective "goals" (reasonable expectation for resolution of the case). If one party believes they can get to their goal within two or three moves, but is not sure if the other side will get there in the same number of moves, such uncertainty interferes with the mediation strategies. On the other hand, if it is understood that each side will get to their goals in three to five moves, then an agreement on the designated number will allow each side to better prepare. Are the parties going to negotiate traditionally by offer or counteroffer, or is this negotiation going to be through simultaneous moves? Is this negotiation going to be through a double-blind method of negotiation, or are the multiple parties going to cooperate to combine their offers so as to present one unified number?

These negotiation strategies, which may traditionally be left confidential until mediation day, can be better dealt with before the mediation and allow the parties to come to the table with more confidence, trust, and cooperative attitude if designed prior to the mediation.

4.3.7 Conclusion

Designing the mediation helps not only the parties, but their representatives, mediation advocates, and the mediator. It enhances the trust among the parties (which is a vital element to the negotiation process). It allows for a more fluent communication between or among the parties, while at the same time facilitating a more cooperative effort even before the negotiations begin. The mediator has the principal responsibility for introducing, encouraging, and/or facilitating such premediation design. The parties and their counsel should consider its value and potential in ultimately achieving resolution. Said design has been a critical factor in the success of many complex mediations. It can and will be a factor in your mediation if effectively utilized.

[Rodney A. Max, Upchurch Watson White & Max
2000A South Bridge Parkway, Suite 400, Birmingham, AL 35209
205/933-1022, ramax@uww-adr.com]

4.4 RODNEY A. MAX: MULTIPARTY MEDIATION

[**Editor's Note:** *This section consists of an article authored by Rodney A. Max and is reproduced and reformatted here with his permission.*]

4.4.1 Introduction

Since 1981, I have had the honor of serving thousands of parties in mediations where resolutions have been achieved in approximately 95% of the cases. From simple two- party contract cases to complex sixty-five party products liability cases, the goal of resolution is always the same: allowing the parties to negotiate to a "reasonable ballpark" in which they, with the facilitation of the mediator, identify "homeplate" and create for themselves the opportunity of a mutual agreement. However, not all mediations are alike. Indeed, each has its own unique personality shaped by either the litigating parties, their counsel, the law of the case or the facts of the case. While simple mediations can implement the general procedures of opening statements, caucuses, and written mediation agreements; multiparty mediations provide many unique elements and procedures that must be identified, and when appropriate, implemented to achieve total success.

This article will identify those unique elements and procedures. It is divided into the following sections:

- The Mediator(s)
- The Facilities
- Mediation Parameters Identified – Pre-Mediation Attorneys' Caucus(es)
- The Position Statements
- The Opening (Joint) Session
- The Negotiations/Caucuses
- The Reasonable Ballpark
- Homeplate -- The Mediation Agreement

These elements and procedures will be discussed through anecdotal examples to illustrate their use and effectiveness. These anecdotes are real mediations which have been fictionalized so as to preserve their confidentiality. The anecdotal mediations are as follows:

A. 30,000 metal poles were allegedly defectively coated which caused premature aging and deterioration. The parties included the manufacturer and seller of the poles, the manufacturer of the chemical coating, the applicator, and the inspectors. In addition, each party was looking to their insurance carriers to assist them. The insurance carriers took the position that there was no coverage for such claims, in light of the absence of any death, injury or property damage having been incurred as of the mediation. These poles were manufactured over a six year period for which numerous insurance companies were involved. These poles were distributed throughout the United States. So long as these poles "fell in the woods" an anticipated breach of contract or breach of warranty action may result; however, if these poles should "fall on a school bus or land in a stadium," catastrophic injury, death and/or property damage would result. The manufacturer and seller of the poles sued all other parties who, likewise, filed numerous counterclaims and cross-claims. Declaratory judgment actions were also commenced by and between the parties and their numerous insurance companies over issues of coverage. (Hereinafter referred to as "30,000 pole mediation").

B. Seven women were admitted to a community clinic for a routine bladder surgery. A new nurse was instructed to deliver marked bottles of the anesthesia to the anesthesiologist who in turn administered the anesthesia. Unfortunately, the marked containers did not contain anesthesia, rather they contained detergicide. Each woman suffered varying degrees of burns and destruction of their bladders and other internal organs. The clinic, attending physicians, nursing staff and their superiors were sued. (Hereinafter referred to as "multiple medical malpractice mediation").

C. An insurance company was the subject of a class action for selling "vanishing premiums," "retirement plans," and "savings plans." Hundreds of policyholders opted out of the class action and filed individual suits in their respective state courts, joining not only the insurance company, but the local agents. While both economic damages and mental anguish were, for the most part, relatively small (less than $10,000), the potential for punitive damages in any one case was substantial. (Hereinafter referred to as the "multiple insurance policyholder mediation").

D. A teenager was killed while driving within the speed limit on the circumference road of a shopping mall. The deceased's father filed suit against the owner of the shopping center, general contractor, paving subcontractor, architect, landscape contractor, and retail store tenant in the vicinity of the accident. Plaintiff claimed liability, jointly and severally, against all of the party defendants for the wrongful death of his only daughter. Under state law there was no contribution among joint tort-feasors; however, there were contractual indemnification agreements among certain party defendants. (Hereinafter referred to as the "multiple party wrongful death mediation").

E. A residential development of garden homes suffered from allegedly improper drainage and allegedly defective workmanship in the construction of their garden home units. Twenty-eight property owners sued the owner of the development, as well as the two different general contractors who built the homes within the development. (Hereinafter referred to as the "multiple property owner mediation").

F. Five employees of three companies were killed or badly burned as a result of an oil fire. Sixty-six defendants included not only the operating companies, but also sixty-three working interest owners of the oil field. While each owner had an acknowledged percentage interest, each owner had different levels of liability insurance coverage. It was made clear from the beginning that each owner's contribution would be limited to their pro rata share (equivalent to their ownership interests). (Hereinafter referred to as the "multiple burn mediation").

4.4.2 The mediator(s)

The selection of a mediator is critical to a multiparty mediation. The mediator should not be overwhelmed by the multiplicity of parties, counsel, issues or negotiating strategies. The mediator must be able to get control of the process as opposed to trying to get control of the parties. An organized procedure that has been adopted by the parties and their counsel can achieve this end.

A team of mediators may be appropriate in certain multiparty settings. The first consideration should be the need to separately handle different groups of plaintiffs and/or defendants. In such case, a team of mediators may be able to better facilitate the separate groups.

In the multiple medical malpractice mediation, the seven injured plaintiffs were represented by different counsel. Each plaintiff needed to be separated from the other due to the fact that their injuries were different; and, accordingly, their settlements would not be uniform. It was necessary that each plaintiff be in a separate room and that the offers be separately communicated to each of them. At the same time, it was necessary that each party plaintiff and their family be kept apprised of the developments without too much time between each caucus. Accordingly, it was decided that there would be one lead mediator with two co-mediators. The head mediator would be principally responsible for the negotiations between the defendants and the plaintiffs' counsel, generally. However, the communication of specific offers to the party plaintiffs was done through the delegation of one co-mediator to every two or three plaintiffs. This kept the plaintiffs more fully informed on a more frequent basis and kept the process moving so as to enable the parties to accomplish full resolution of all cases within a twelve hour period.

A second consideration for a team of mediators is where a claim calls for a certain expertise, such as that of an engineer, an architect or a contractor. In the multiple property owners mediation, the mediator obtained the approval of the parties to hire an independent contractor to review the property damage claims of each homeowner. The mediator allowed the parties to agree on the identification of the contractor. The contractor was of vital help to the mediator, not only in verifying the specific items of damage alleged, but also in reaching compromises when conflicting degrees of damage or the costs of repair became a mediation issue.

It is imperative that mediation teams work together so that mediation strategies and communications are identical and in conformity with one another. This requires tight control and close coordination by and among the mediating team. It results in a more efficiently run mediation and one in which the parties are more meaningfully engaged in the process. Such an engagement is crucial to achieving resolution.

4.4.3 The facilities

It is imperative that the facilities for a multiparty mediation are accommodating to all parties and their counsel. There must be sufficient rooms for all parties collectively and individually as necessary. There must be a room sufficient to handle opening statements and other joint caucuses of all parties and counsel. There must be a room sufficient to house all defendants together so as to obtain unified or collective offers. For that matter, there must also be a room large enough for all plaintiffs to gather to the extent that such collective caucusing is appropriate among them.

At the same time, there should be a sufficient number of "break-out rooms" for defendants or plaintiffs to remove themselves from a joint caucus to meet privately over their individual positions. Finally, it is important to have an "attorney break-out room" so that the mediator can meet with attorneys or they can meet among themselves during different stages of the process.

During the 30,000 pole mediation, a separate room was established for the seller, the manufacturer of the chemical, for the applicator, and for the inspector. In addition, a room was established for all insurance carriers. There was also a joint caucus room where all parties, their insurance carriers and counsel met at various times during the course of this one week mediation. The climax of the mediation came in a joint session in which the mediator, having consulted with each party separately, identified a "mediator's interim proposal" that ultimately led to the resolution.

In the multiple medical malpractice mediation, each of the seven plaintiffs had a room to themselves. The defendants had a joint room in which they all met. The defendants had three break-out rooms available for their individual caucuses, and the plaintiffs' counsel had a break-out room separate and apart from their clients. The mediating team also had a room to facilitate their mediation strategies.

In the multiple party wrongful death mediation, the defendants were divided into group A and B defendants. In this case, unification of all defendants was not practicable, and, therefore, it was abandoned. Group A represented the major defendants while group B represented the minor defendants. Negotiations commenced with both groups. However, after several hours Group B was temporarily dismissed from the mediation while negotiations continued with Group A. Group A negotiations were successfully concluded, contingent on resolution of Group B. Thereafter, Group B returned to successfully conclude their negotiations. In addition to the facilities having sufficient rooms, the facilities should also have sufficient means of providing coffee, tea, cold drinks, as well as morning snacks, lunch, afternoon snacks and dinner. The mediation staff should be available to cater to these needs throughout the day and into the evening.

Mediation is a user friendly service, therefore the facilities and mediation staff are critical to providing friendly services in the midst of intense, complex negotiations.

4.4.4 Mediation parameters identified – pre-mediation attorneys' caucus(es)

Typically, the mediator, unilaterally or in conjunction with the parties, will define the parameters of the mediation. Usually this only requires the setting of a date, time, place and the request to all parties or their appropriate representatives to be present with full authority to settle the case. Further, the request for position statements is a constructive source of insight, not only for the mediator, but for the parties themselves.

In a multiparty mediation, the identification of mediation parameters is more significant. The parties and their counsel are going to be one of a number of people in attendance. The dynamics of interaction among multiple parties raises the level of the personal and professional anxieties and complicates the negotiation strategies. The last thing that is needed in a multiparty negotiation is for each party to enter the mediation with different ideas as to how the mediation will be conducted or how the negotiations will proceed.

Pre-mediation caucuses can address these issues in advance of the mediation. For instance, will the defendants be bringing an insurance claims representative or an officer of the company? Will the injured plaintiffs be coming alone or will family be accompanying them, and what is the relationship of these people with the plaintiffs? Inquiries as to whether persons present will assist or hinder negotiations are appropriate for discussion and for determining everything from the tone of the opening statements to the manner in which the negotiations will proceed.

Pre-mediation caucuses can also assist in getting opposing sides to agree on negotiation methodology. This is where the mediator can attempt to get some control over the process. By insisting that each party begin with an analysis of their case before they begin negotiating, the parties are urged not to establish offers or goals based on "what they want," but rather what is a reasonable settlement based upon a courtroom or other relevant analysis. This will be discussed in more detail in "The opening (joint) session" in Section 4.4.6 below. For purposes of this section, suffice it to say that if each side can agree on a general methodology of negotiation, then they can more effectively control their clients and maintain control of the process as they attempt to work towards resolution. The pre-mediation caucus can, likewise, assist the mediator in identifying the alignment of the plaintiffs or defendants and can determine if offers among multiple parties are going to be unified or presented separately.

Accordingly, a pre-mediation caucus or caucuses in multiparty mediations should be seriously considered. In its simplest form, the mediator can caucus with the attorneys and/or parties by a telephone conference. In its more complex form, the mediator may request a meeting with all counsel. Taken one step further, the mediator may unilaterally meet with each attorney and/or party representative to get their view of the mediation process and, thereafter, may call for a meeting or phone conference to outline the process based upon input from all.

This was, indeed, the methodology of the 30,000 pole mediation. The mediator met individually with each of the parties' counsel to hear not only their view of the process, but also their view of the facts.

The mediator accumulated the "common denominators" of the process and the facts and, thereafter, had a pre-mediation meeting with all counsel where he identified that to which they had separately agreed. One such concept of the agreement was the establishment of "a risk taker's pool" with certain terms and conditions. Issues such as who is to be the risk taker, who is going to contribute to the pool, and in what amounts or proportions, became the focus of the mediation for all parties.

In the multiple burn mediation, a pre-mediation caucus among all counsel devised the following strategy for the four day mediation: On the first day, all plaintiffs' counsel would make an opening statement, together with an opening demand. Thereafter, plaintiffs and their counsel recessed from the mediation while all defendants remained to caucus over their relationship to each other throughout the mediation and to devise an opening counteroffer. The second day would begin with the defendants making an opening statement to three of the five plaintiffs. Following these opening statements the defendants would communicate their first counteroffer to the mediator. The remainder of day two and three would be spent resolving these three cases. Day four would begin with an opening statement by the defendants to the remaining two plaintiffs. The remainder of day four would be spent negotiating with the two remaining plaintiffs.

In the multiple medical malpractice mediation, it was agreed in pre-mediation caucuses that both plaintiffs' and defendants' offers were to be presented in the aggregate. It was further agreed that plaintiffs' counsel would take that aggregate and divide it among their clients based on a formula to be agreed on. It was going to be up to the plaintiffs' counsel to consult with their clients as to the reasonableness of that division as the negotiations progressed. At the same time, the defendants had agreed in a pre-mediation caucus to present unified offers as long as they had the participation of all defendants.

In summary, the pre-mediation caucuses allow the mediation to proceed with everyone being on "the same wave length" of how the process will proceed as opposed to each party having their own vision as to how they want to proceed. As important as this is to the parties, it is equally important to the mediator(s) who is/are attempting to organize the means of achieving ultimate resolution.

4.4.5 The position statements

Generally, I am a strong advocate for the submission of position statements by the parties prior to the mediation. I believe it is even more important in multiparty mediations. Position statements have a dual purpose: first, they educate the mediator on the facts, issues and positions of the parties. Second, they allow each side to see those issues and positions of the other side which are critical to their individual evaluation and to their collective resolution. Some advocate that position statements should remain confidential between a party and the mediator. I take the view that the more shared, the healthier the negotiations. The more each side knows about the other's position, the more effectively they will be able to achieve resolution. Understanding full well that some things must be and remain confidential, this can certainly be dealt with in a confidential addendum to the mediator, or a "blind p.s." that does not go to the other parties.

The last thing the mediator and the parties want, is to go to the mediation looking at different facts, different issues, or different positions, and find they are in no way ready, willing, or able to negotiate. I am convinced that if counsel and parties know the strengths and weaknesses of their case and appreciate the venue they are in, they can identify reasonable verdict/settlement ranges (see, "The opening (joint) session" in Section 4.4.6 below, and "The negotiations/caucuses" in Section 4.4.7 below). With the help of an experienced mediator, they can achieve resolution. I call this knowledge "informed consent." Take away the information necessary to make an "informed" decision, and you have failure.

This is especially true in multiparty mediations where numerous parties are setting forth their independent positions on various issues. "Where do I fit within my own camp (of Plaintiffs or Defendants)" and "where does the opposition truly see its strengths?" Thorough position statements can answer these questions.

I suggest that position statements include the following:

- a brief recitation of the facts that gave rise to the litigation;

- the present posture of the case (any matters pending in court or in any related litigation);

- any recent developments that may impact on the resolution of the case (confidentiality optional);

- the history of any efforts to settle the case including any prior offers or demands;

- a summary of the parties' legal positions and a candid assessment of their respective strengths and weaknesses (confidentiality optional);

- identification of parties, representatives and counsel who will be directly involved in the mediation discussions; and a confirmation of their authority to settle the case;

- description of any sensitive issues that may influence any settlement negotiations (confidentiality optional);

- the nature and extent of any prior or future relationship between the parties that may affect the mediation (confidentiality optional);

- the negotiating strategy of the parties and counsel (confidentiality optional);

- any suggested approach you would like me, as your mediator, to take in an attempt to settle the case (confidentiality optional);

- any creative solutions (confidentiality optional).

4.4.6 The opening (joint) session

Mediation, itself, begins with the opening (joint) session. For the mediator as well as the parties, this is a critical stage of the negotiations. The tone for conciliation must be set (at least by the mediator) at the same time each comes in to identify their opposing positions. As a general rule, the opening session should not be avoided due to the frailty of the parties or their issues. I have seen numerous occasions where the parties insisted on not doing an opening statement, and half way through the negotiations they regretted that they did not have an opportunity to directly exchange positions.

In the multiple medical malpractice mediation, the attorneys believed that to bring the seven women and their families in to hear the positions of the clinic and personnel would alienate the parties. Despite the urging of the mediator to the contrary, the negotiations proceeded without opening statements. After three hours of negotiations, the parties were over eleven million dollars apart, the mediator requested a joint session to refocus on verdict/settlement range analysis. Within one hour following that joint session, the parties were two million dollars apart and proceeded toward resolution in a fluid manner.

At the very least, a joint session should allow the mediator to set the tone. Acknowledging the dignity of the parties and their positions, while acknowledging the issues between them, the mediator will stress that no one leaves the mediation "a loser." Both sides "win" by either agreeing to agree or agreeing to disagree. So it is really a day or a series of days during which the question must be asked "can we agree despite our differences?"

The mediator can also change the attitude of the negotiations from "what I want" (whether it is to get or to give) to "what is reasonable in the forum provided." To the extent that the setting is a courtroom analysis, it requires an analysis of a "reasonable verdict range," The mediator's monologue, in part, would be as follows:

The ability for all parties to understand how a jury comes to unanimity allows you to appreciate that your negotiations are not pure "compromise," but rather, are based upon the same compromising process that the "reasonable jury" will deal with in coming to a reasonable verdict. "What is reasonable verdict range?" A reasonable verdict range is a verdict which takes into consideration that among twelve jurors, four could absolutely agree with everything that plaintiffs say, while four can agree with everything the defendants' say (whether it is on the issue of liability or on the issue of lower damages), while four are confused over testimony after hearing the jury charges. These final four jurors, after two hours of deliberation, finally agree on a plaintiffs' verdict, but disagree with the amount proposed by the plaintiffs and insist on a "reasonable" level of damages. How do these three sets of jurors come to one unanimous decision (or other decision that results in a verdict)?

The "reasonable verdict range" is not the end of the analysis. Of course, it presumes a plaintiffs' verdict; and many defendants will come into a mediation saying that there is a better than a fifty-fifty chance that they will win the case outright (or at summary judgment). In addition, there is a cost to get to the finality of a trial and an appeal. Further, there is time and uncertainty in getting there and perhaps getting remanded on appeal for a new trial. Finally, there may be issues of collectability. In some cases, however, a reasonable verdict range will be the reasonable settlement range and in a few instances, it may even be less than a reasonable settlement range, where something can be attained in mediation that cannot otherwise be achieved in going through a jury process (the finality rather than the multiplicity of lawsuits; confidentiality; and the like).

Generally, however, the reasonable settlement range will have some diminished relationship to a reasonable verdict range. Thus, the parties must move from an evaluation of the reasonable verdict range to the reasonable settlement range. The reasonable settlement range will take into consideration all of the extraneous factors beyond achieving an actual verdict. A defendant may say "if I am going to pay the reasonable verdict range, I may as well go to the expense of a verdict with the chance of doing better." So, to what extent should the reasonable verdict range be discounted, if any, to achieve finality at mediation? Out of this analysis comes the reasonable settlement range and a reasonable goal within the settlement range.

As for a "reasonable goal", this is a level within the reasonable settlement range that a party decides to achieve. It must be realized that this is a unilateral decision and thus, each side is going to have a "reasonable goal." The chance that these goals are the same is small. It is more probable that these goals will be different. The question is not so much whether they are different, as whether or not they are in a reasonable range of one another. Of course, the plaintiffs want the defendants' reasonable goal to be on the high side of the reasonable settlement range, while the defendants want the plaintiffs' reasonable goal to be on the low side of the reasonable settlement range. Resolution requires that the respective goals be set at a reasonable level within the reasonable settlement range. The key to the negotiations will be whether the parties can make reasonable moves in relation to the goals they are striving to achieve.

The attainment of these goals will create the proverbial "reasonable ballpark:" One side creates left field, another side creates right field, and so on and so forth. If the parties can create a reasonable ballpark, the job of mediator is to assist the parties in identifying "homeplate."

The above monologue of the mediator sets the tone from which the parties' counsel make their own opening statements in a tone of advocacy with a touch of conciliation. This becomes the equation for healthy negotiations. A joint session may need to be reconvened during the course of the mediation to refocus on the process established by the mediator.

The opening statements in a multiparty mediation take on a number of different forms. However, the commonality of all such opening statements is that they must be personable to all opposition, cause all parties to rethink their positions and let all know they have a stake in the ultimate resolution by weighing the risks of proceeding to trial and the opportunities of a reasonable negotiation.

The plaintiffs' counsel has a unique role in the opening session of a multiparty mediation. Generally, this is the first time the defendants' representatives have met plaintiffs' counsel. The defendants may be represented by claims representatives or company representatives. This first impression is crucial to the mediation due to the fact that one of the elements of the defendants' evaluation will be the quality of the plaintiffs' legal representation. Thus, an articulate and well thought out presentation is very important to the success of the plaintiffs' case. I have heard many mediations where the opening statement, itself, added to or detracted from the value of the plaintiffs' case. The plaintiffs' statements must be personable with eye contact being made to the company or insurance representatives. The plaintiffs' statements must be thorough yet concise. Remembering that the defendants have reviewed all of the facts given to them by the defense counsel plaintiffs' counsel should deal with, the most controversial facts or issues as well as evaluation.

There are various aids that can be used by plaintiffs' counsel. They include videos, booklets/books, blowup charts, and enlarged deposition testimony. Recalling that mediations are not formal presentations of testimony, a video can be effectively used to view the plaintiffs in their own surroundings, can allow the plaintiffs to say what is on their mind and heart, and can show scenes that may otherwise be difficult to recreate in a courtroom. Videos can also be used to have expert witnesses or lay witnesses tell what they opine or otherwise know. These videos are presented in a "20/20" or "60 minute" magazine format.

In the multiple burn mediation, the enlargement of photos of the terrible injuries allowed for the re-creation of not only the pain and suffering of the plaintiffs, but also their families. The human dynamics of not only the plaintiffs' perspective, but those of the attending physicians, graphically depicted the agony experienced.

The defendants' counsel has an equally important challenge in a multiparty mediation. He/she must likewise be personable, but in a different way. In a personal injury, wrongful death case, his/her audience is typically neither a professional nor business person. It is the injured or aggrieved party sitting with a lot of emotion in an unfamiliar and thus uncomfortable setting. The goal is not to get the plaintiffs to see that they are wrong and should never have filed their action; rather, the message conveyed must be that of regret and apology for the accident, empathy for what the plaintiffs have gone through, while urging the plaintiffs to appreciate that there are reasonable defenses that may negate liability or minimize damages. While plaintiffs' counsel may have oversold expectations of the plaintiffs, it is up to the defense counsel to gently bring the plaintiffs back to reality. The key is reaching the plaintiffs, so that when the expectations of the plaintiffs are not achieved ("no, this is not a million dollar case") the idea of considering a lesser amount is neither unreasonable nor unacceptable.

Defense counsel, like plaintiffs' counsel, can effectively use aids such as videos, documents and charts. A defendants' reconstruction presentation can be very persuasive. The display of a clear and unambiguous contract term can cause the plaintiffs and plaintiffs' counsel to question the admissibility or credibility of contradictory oral testimony. The enlargement of the plaintiffs' deposition testimony or the deposition testimony of a key plaintiff's witness, can cause the plaintiff and his/her counsel to rethink the strength of their offense.

In the multiple party wrongful death mediation, an empathetic set of defendants' counsel was able to effectively reach the plaintiff in a way that ultimately made the difference in achieving resolution.

In the multiple insurance policyholder mediation, the policyholders were moved by the mediation admissions of the insurance company. In fact, the opening session established the "seed" by which an insurance relationship was revived and policy relief extended that, when coupled with limited monetary relief, made resolution possible.

In a multiparty context, the opening or joint session will also identify relationships among groups of plaintiffs or defendants. This may be accomplished in a separate joint or open session among all plaintiffs or all defendants. How does one plaintiff's liability and damages stack up against the other? How unified are the defendants, and will the multiplicity of comparable or contradictory positions be of disadvantage or advantage to the plaintiffs. And, as importantly for the mediator, how will that "reasonable jury" weigh the strengths and weaknesses identified at the joint session?

4.4.7 The negotiations/caucuses

In a multiparty mediation, the parties do not have time to arbitrarily throw out offers and counteroffers. The ability to "rationalize" and "legitimize" offers is critical to the success of such negotiations. As an example, when the multiple medical malpractice mediation was floundering with arbitrary offers and counteroffers, the ability to get the parties to identify the reasonable verdict ranges and settlement ranges brought their negotiations immediately to the "reasonable ballpark." Thus, it is imperative that the parties attempt to identify those ranges before numbers are arbitrarily thrown out.

Neither the reasonable verdict ranges nor the reasonable settlement ranges are necessarily communicated to the other side. In fact, they are generally kept confidential. There are times, however, when one side or the other will insist on the disclosure of their reasonable verdict range to let the other parties know where it stands. (Generally, if a reasonable verdict range of defendants is at one level, they are certainly not going to exceed that level).

The request of the mediator in the multiparty negotiation process is to stress that the parties make reasonable moves in relation to their reasonable goals and that reasonable goals should be contained within their reasonable settlement ranges (which should have a meaningful relationship to the reasonable verdict ranges). This is one way of establishing legitimacy.

It is also one way to focus the discussion on evaluation, as opposed to revisiting all of the factual issues previously raised in the opening statements. While this jousting will still go on to some extent in multiparty negotiations, the ability to work through the facts and the law and deal with evaluations can expedite the negotiations. This is another reason why more thorough disclosure in position statements can aid the multiparty negotiation process. By fully identifying the facts and the law in the position statements, the distinctions can be dealt with in opening statements and, thereafter, they can be set aside as the parties begin to negotiate.

Again, legitimacy is the key, and the sharing of one's verdict analysis can aid the legitimacy of a party's position or move. The verdict analysis may include other like or similar cases (whether plaintiffs' verdicts or defense verdicts). Likewise, settlements in like or similar cases can be of some persuasive authority. Prior verdicts and settlements are to mediation what mandatory and persuasive decisions are in the appellate arena.

Other areas of legitimacy include evaluations of the elements of the case: the ranking of the plaintiffs, defendants, plaintiffs' counsel, defense counsel, judge, and jury venire. Each of these will add to or detract from a plaintiffs'/defendants' verdict. More importantly, these elements will add to or detract from the reasonable verdict range analysis prompted by the mediator.

One unique aspect of multiparty negotiations is the ability for multiple defendants or multiple plaintiffs to mediate with and among each other. For instance, where six defendants are having to evaluate their respective positions, is it not inappropriate for them to consider, "what is the overall reasonable verdict range?" Thereafter, what is the reasonable settlement range and a reasonable goal for the group as a whole? The mediator can be a vital tool in facilitating that joint dialogue. The more dialogue jointly exchanged, the healthier the relationships will grow among the defendants. If necessary, the mediator can allow the defendants to caucus separately to make their evaluations. Once the defendants have collectively identified a reasonable goal, the question then becomes what is their respective relationships toward that goal. If that can be agreed on among all defendants, then the mediation process can begin to flow between the plaintiff(s) and the defendants without undue delay caused by infighting as to what contribution each defendant should make on any particular move. In the ideal situation, all defendants are moving toward one goal with a known and agreed upon relationship of contribution toward that goal.

Multiple plaintiffs have a similar yet different analysis to make. First, it is seldom that they are all aligned in the same litigation. Generally, they are before a different judge, in a different venue, and in separate cases. Thus, they are in need of defining different (or at least independent) reasonable verdict ranges for themselves and not collectively. This is not to say that plaintiffs' cases are not at times consolidated or that plaintiffs are not joined in the prosecution of their cases. When they are, their analyses will be similar to the defendants' analyses as set forth above.

What the plaintiffs must identify in a multi-plaintiff setting is the relationship of their injuries one to another such that as they are getting counteroffers from the defendants, they know among themselves how to divide and apportion an aggregate offer. A similar analysis unfolds: what is a reasonable verdict range, what is a reasonable settlement range, and thereby, what is a reasonable goal for the plaintiffs collectively? How does A's claim relate to B's, and how do A's and B's claims relate to C's? Whether they are different verdicts or the same, how do these collective verdicts relate to the policy limits and/or the collectability of a judgment against the defendants? Such restrictions will bring plaintiffs together to work for their common good, realizing that their individual interests are maximized by working together. The last thing that any plaintiff wants to see is the other plaintiff achieve all of the policy limits, leaving nothing for him/her. On the chance that he/she may get to trial first, why not work together so that all can achieve a reasonably successful result?

When dealing with multiple plaintiffs, some defendants will want to negotiate "in the aggregate." That is, "we will pay you the total sum for all of these cases and we will let you divide it up." This is certainly contingent on the plaintiffs being willing to deal in the aggregate (which assumes that the plaintiffs have an agreement among them as to how to apportion the aggregate offer).

When groups of plaintiffs or defendants are not amicable, or willing to negotiate together, it is sometimes necessary to work separately with different groups of plaintiffs and defendants. At times it requires one defendant to make an offer conditioned on the resolution of all claims. Similarly, plaintiffs may take the position that pro tanto (often limited to certain extent) is not possible and therefore acceptance of offers of one group of defendants is contingent upon the acceptance of offers with the remaining groups of defendants.

In the 30,000 pole mediation, no resolution could be achieved until a total aggregate sum was achieved. Thus, while some defendants were willing at an early stage to put up their proportionate shares, it was not until all parties acknowledged their proportional share that the "risk takers pool" was filled and resolution achieved.

In the multiple party wrongful death mediation, resolution with group A was conditioned upon resolution with group B. While group A represented the more substantial claims and resolution had been achieved at an acceptable level, this was not finally accepted until group B had achieved resolution. Had group B not achieved resolution, plaintiffs were not obligated to accept the resolution of group A.

In the multiple burn mediation, the plaintiffs had agreed on a formula whereby they would pool their medical expenses, pay their attorney fees and litigation costs and the balance would be equally divided among the three plaintiffs. At the same time, the defendants had operating interests and working owner interests relationships to be honored. Some of those defendants had certain policy limit restrictions. Once the primary defendants put up their policy limits, it became a question of whether the working interest could achieve an acceptable level among themselves and with the plaintiffs. Again, resolution was achieved.

In the multiple insurance policyholder mediation, the insurance company established a legitimate criteria for paying claimants: a grid was established in which claims were evaluated from "good" cases to "poor" cases. The company's attorney explained the grid to each party or his/her attorney. Each case was negotiated with the grid analysis. Over 300 cases were mediated and more than 275 were resolved.

In the multiple property owners mediation, the attorneys for all parties caucused after several hours of debate over liability, mental anguish and punitive damages. The mediator got them to identify a reasonable formula to apply to each property owner: each property owner would be entitled to the cost of repair, plus 35% attorney fee, plus $2,000 costs.

4.4.8 The reasonable ballpark

The above discussion assumes that each multiparty group is making reasonable moves in relation to their reasonable goals. In ninety-nine percent of these cases, the reasonable goal of the plaintiffs is not the same as the reasonable goal of the defendants. Then what? As suggested earlier, these reasonable goals create the proverbial "Reasonable Ballpark." If these goals are unreasonably evaluated, the ballpark may not be established. A wide settlement range among opposing parties will create a large "ballpark;" a small gap will create a smaller "ballpark." Assuming the identification of the ballpark – large or small – where is resolution? It is found at the proverbial "homeplate."

There are three ways to "slide" safely into "home":

1. The multiple parties may continue to negotiate beyond their goals. Where the prior negotiations have moved well, this is not difficult. Where there has been a struggle to find the ballpark, this may not be practical.

2. An attorneys' caucus may be helpful where further movement by the multiple parties is not likely. The attorneys can agree either to discuss further movement openly with other counsel, to discuss further movement confidentially with a mediator, or to simply agree to get back with their clients to continue the process. In either event, getting the attorneys together outside their respective rooms can be a "breath of fresh air" to the attempt to find homeplate. If the attorneys wish to discuss further movement openly with one another, that should be encouraged. To the extent that they do not, the idea of meeting confidentially with the mediator, either with or without their clients, may assist in finding where homeplate may be located. If the mediator sees a common homeplate being identified, he/she can let the negotiations proceed. However, if they are different, there is a third alternative to sliding home, the "mediator's proposal."

3. The mediator's proposal is a resolution concept that the mediator creates knowing (confidentially) where each party can be drawn. Certainly, if one side is at $1 million and the other side is at $750,000, it would not be appropriate for the mediator to propose either $751,000 or $999,000. Rather, the mediator must choose a level that represents common ground. Common ground may be mathematically equal distance between the parties, or it may be at some other level. It may include some other nonmonetary proposal that may have been confidentially shared and known to be of common interest and it may include some other components of resolution (such as tax advantages, confidentiality, or terms of payment).

How does the mediator achieve acceptance of a mediator's proposal? This is done by an exercise known as "all yeses or all nos." That is, the mediator will make his proposal to all parties, either collectively or separately. He/she will request responses be given to him/her confidentially. The mediator will get responses from all parties. The responses will not be known to anyone other than the mediator. Once the mediator receives all responses, he/she will identify either all yeses or all nos. A no from either side will result in all no's being disclosed. The only way resolution is achieved is if the mediator receives yeses from all parties.

Thus, it can be seen how critical it is for the mediator to identify a resolution that is perceived to be common ground for all parties. This is the test of the mediator's skill. What happens if the mediator gets one no? The question is better asked "What happens if the mediator truly gets all no's?" In the latter event, truly the mediation is over. In the former event, it may be possible for the mediator to keep the negotiations alive if the negating parties will identify how close to the mediator's proposal they will go. Thereafter, the mediator will need to see if the other parties will reconsider and accept. This exercise is not intended to have this secondary negotiation, but it is available to the mediator if it can achieve resolution.

Of course, in multiparty negotiations, obtaining acceptance of a mediator's proposal is all the more complicated. It requires multiple parties to move beyond their mutually agreed goals. Many times it requires realigning of percentages of participation, whether they are paying or receiving.

This process of getting to homeplate in multiparty negotiations requires the mediator and the parties to get a "second wind" and have the patience to work through new levels of resolution.

In reflection, it can be seen how important it is to move through the negotiation methodically and smoothly so when goals are reached that are not compatible with resolution, resolution can still be achieved. This can only be successful when the parties have not begrudged each other to move toward their goals, realizing that getting to those goals requires additional negotiations.

4.4.9 Homeplate – the mediation agreement

Just like in the two-party mediation, the mediation agreement in a multiparty negotiation is vital. The mediation agreement must memorialize each party's commitment and participation in the resolution. Details included should range from the identification of monetary sums and payment terms, to the identification of who is paying what should be addressed. At times, the parties (or their counsel) will insist on not disclosing who is getting what among the plaintiffs, or who is paying what among the defendants. While the opposing sides do not need to see this distribution, it is suggested that a written, supplemental mediation agreement be entered into among defendants or among plaintiffs to identify the distribution. To the extent that the payment is to be characterized as payment for personal injury as opposed to fraud and misrepresentations, this should be identified in the mediation agreement.

The terms of the release should be set forth as generally or as specifically as is required. Standard provisions in releases are well known in the local communities of attorneys. However, terms such as confidentiality, indemnification, and waiver of subrogation claims should be set forth. While one side may draft the release agreement, the other side should be given the opportunity to review and approve it. Thereafter, all parties participating in the release should be required to sign it and that requirement should be set forth in the mediation agreement.

Dismissal of the case with prejudice or such other judicial disposition should be set forth with the identification of the respective parties to pay their own or each other's court, litigation, and/or mediation costs.

The mediation agreement should be read by all parties and both the mediator and the attorneys should be available to answer any questions. Before the parties sign the agreement, they should be asked if they understand the terms and whether or not they are satisfied with the terms. So long as they answer affirmatively, all parties and their counsel should sign the mediation agreement. To the extent that any changes or modifications have been made in the drafting of the mediation agreement, those changes should be initialed by all parties and counsel.

The original mediation agreement should be left with the mediator, while copies of the mediation agreement should be distributed to all parties and their counsel. The court(s) will simply be advised that the mediation was successful to the extent that a mediation agreement is achieved. The court will be advised that the attorneys of record will be forwarding the appropriate dismissal documents in due course. The mediator should remain available to the parties should any conflicts occur in concluding the terms and conditions of the mediation agreement.

4.4.10 Conclusion

Multiparty negotiations are an art. The requirement of "met expectations" must be set in motion at the very beginning. Legitimacy and reasonableness must be a thread that ties the position statements to the opening sessions and the opening offers to the reasonable goals. The reasonable goals must be flexible enough to achieve homeplate and homeplate must be acceptable to all.

The very essence of multiparty negotiations is the totality of benefits to the parties, the attorneys and the courts. Consider: in one mediation multiple parties, allegations, defenses, and interests are being resolved in lieu of multiple motions, trials, and appeals, not to speak of the time and expense of those processes. In the same way that a ballplayer rounds third and heads for home with the determination to win, so do the mediator of a multiparty negotiation must have the drive and courage to persist and resolve.

4.5 RODNEY A. MAX: NEW AGE OF THE PARA-MEDIATOR

[**Editor's Note:** *This section consists of an article authored by Rodney A. Max and is reproduced and reformatted here with his permission.*]

The profession of mediation is alive and well and relatively new, as compared to the professions of lawyers, judges and arbitrators. Most people who are mediating are not doing it as a full-time profession. Rather, they are doing it as an adjunct to their other full-time professions - such as lawyers, psychologists, social workers, labor negotiators and the like. There are relatively few mediators who are mediating full-time. Among those full-time mediators, most are really doing it on their own or with organizations where they are listed as panel members. Such organizations can be non-profit, such as the CPR Institute or the American Arbitration Association or they can be for-profit organizations such as Mediation, Inc. or Upchurch Watson White & Max.

Individuals who are otherwise eligible to begin a mediation practice have an initial frustration over the absence of calls. The ability to get the first mediation that can spawn the second, third, and fourth is the key. In areas where there is an abundance of mediators, even a good performance does not necessarily mean that the new mediator will get a second call. This is due to the competitive nature of the marketplace. The excellent qualities of a mediator may never "bear fruit" in the absence of the opportunity to do so.

So where does this leave the new generation of mediators? As importantly, where does this leave a profession that is otherwise "gray around the ears" or on the verge of retirement? How do young, qualified, energetic, and creative mediators make their place into the profession?

The answer lies (in part) in the "New Age of the Para-Mediator." A para-mediator is one who works under the auspice of another mediator and who assists said other mediator in preparation, mediation, and post-mediation follow-up. This opportunity is available primarily with veteran mediators who have both a full docket of mediation and whose mediations are "high-end." Such high-end mediations include multiparty disputes, class actions, and other complex cases (whether in number of parties, number of claims, number of issues, or other such complexities).

The scope of work of a para-mediator includes the following:

- Contacting the attorney after the mediation has been confirmed.

- Soliciting information concerning the nature of the claims, relationship with the parties, and/or outstanding issues to be resolved.

- Identifying any particular or sensitive interests or needs of the parties or their counsel.

- Encouraging submission of position statements and/or pleadings to identify the various issues.

- Designing the mediation:

    o To what extent is an opening session appropriate.

    o To what extent have negotiations begun and can he or she assist in any pre-mediation negotiations.

    o To what extent can the mediation negotiations be coordinated prior to the mediation session.

    o To what extent do groups of plaintiffs or groups of defendants need pre-mediation caucus sessions.

    o What, if any, additional exchange of information is necessary between or among the parties prior to the mediation and what can be done to mediate any discovery or exchange disputes among or between the parties.

    o Identification of positive or negative relationships among or between the parties and/or their counsel to assist in conducting the mediation.

Each of the above actions can and will assist the veteran mediator in preparing for the mediation. As importantly, it will allow said mediator to more effectively handle the mediation. Of course, this requires good and effective communication between the veteran mediator and the para-mediator who accumulates this information. This communication can be done through written summaries, emails, or pre-mediation meetings between the veteran mediator and the para-mediator.

The above actions of the para-mediator can offer open additional opportunities for the para-mediator to participate in the mediation. In multiparty and other complex cases, the para-mediator's role prior to the mediation can create a need for the para-mediator to be present at the mediation. Especially, in a multiparty case, one mediator who is otherwise in charge of the entire mediation cannot efficiently and effectively keep all the parties engaged at the same time. The presence of the para-mediator who has had prior contact with the parties can assist in this regard. Further, there may be technical information that the para-mediator has learned prior to the mediation that can assist in the conduct of the mediation session. This does not interfere with the veteran mediator or make him or her subordinate to the para-mediator; rather, it simply helps make the veteran mediator's work more efficient and effective.

The para-mediator has additional opportunities where a mediation adjourns without resolution. Staying in touch with opposing counsel keeps, the process engaged, and keeps the veteran mediator engaged in that process. While the veteran mediator may be onto other mediations as a part of his or her active calendar, the para-mediator can stay focused on post-mediation efforts of the parties and their counsel. Said post-mediation work can include assistance or mediation of future discovery disputes; assistance in re-evaluating position statements; and even assistance in further negotiation efforts. A para-mediator role can also aid in completion of settlement agreements, especially where there are complex issues that are the subject of the resolution.

From a business perspective, the para-mediator provides the parties and their counsel with a reduced hourly rate while providing valuable services. The para-mediator's rates are usually a fraction of the veteran mediator. The para-mediator's charges are identified in the confirmation letter of the veteran mediator. The para-mediator is not imposed on the parties, but rather is an opportunity for the parties to engage his or her services. This is effectuated by a combination of the confirmation letter identification and an initial call by the para-mediator. Should any party or their counsel not wish to engage the services, they simply advise the para-mediator or a mediator of same. However, upon engaging his or her services, the para-mediator (or the coordinator for the veteran mediator) confirms same in writing. The fees for said services are accumulated until the mediation is conducted and the overall fee billed.

The pre-mediation billable charges can, at times, mature into billable co-mediation charges. A para-mediator will not bill for mediation time where it is not otherwise agreed. However, said environment of the mediation is an incredible marketing opportunity for the para-mediator. He or she will have an opportunity to be face to face with those individuals he or she contacted with prior to the mediation. The relationship-building at the mediation can have valuable consequences for the para-mediator. The requests of the parties or their counsel for the para-mediator's services in a billable context should be confirmed in writing prior to the mediation.

Certainly, the para-mediator's post-mediation activity (which can be suggested by the veteran mediator who confirms the adjournment of the mediation session) allows the para-mediator to continue in a billable fashion. While the para-mediator's time is billed at the conclusion of the mediation session, the post-mediation time can be accumulated and upon resolution ultimately billed as a supplement to the prior services rendered.

In summary, the para-mediator has a unique, professional and business opportunity. The experience, contacts, and involvement with high-end mediation, with experienced attorneys, and with sophisticated parties is a unique opportunity that can accelerate the initiation of a mediation practice. As importantly, it aids the parties, their counsel, and the mediator in achieving an efficient and effective resolution. The revenues to be generated (pre-mediation, conduct of mediation, and post-mediation activities) can, likewise, be meaningful. They certainly are a significant supplement to the beginning of a mediation practice while the para-mediator strives to build his or her own mediation clientele.

The logical development of the para-mediator is from para-mediator to Associate Mediator to partner or stockholder. The para-mediator certainly fits within the context of a mediation practice group. The utilization of para-mediation services should be seriously considered and encouraged for those who are developing a high-end mediation practice.

The utilization of para-mediators is, in fact, being utilized extensively at Upchurch Watson White & Max. We are finding extraordinary success for the parties, clients who serve them, and the para-mediators, themselves. I or my partners will be more than happy to address any questions or further explanations to those who may be interested in implementing such a practice.

CHAPTER FIVE

CREATIVE APPROACHES TO OVERCOMING IMPASSE IN NEGOTIATION AND MEDIATION

You cannot shake hands with a clenched fist.

Golda Meir

There are many examples from history in which innovators reached an impasse in attempting to find the appropriate solution to a problem. Guglielmo Marconi, the father of radio, for many years attempted to interest people in the idea that wireless communications could be transmitted over long distances. He proposed to send a wireless signal across the Atlantic Ocean. The "experts" scoffed at his idea based on the fact that the earth's curvature between two endpoints of the proposed wireless communication – Cornwall, England and Newfoundland – was so great that the straight-line path of the signal, they thought, would send the signal off into space. Despite the experts' lack of confidence, in 1901 Marconi succeeded in transmitting the Morse code letter "S" across the ocean between the two points of land. Later, scientists discovered the ionosphere, an electrically charged layer of the atmosphere which has the effect of bending low-frequency radio waves, causing them to follow the curvature of the earth. Marconi's persistence, his belief in trial and error, and his understanding of the value of experience allowed him to successfully solve a problem despite the ridicule of the elite who "knew" it would not work (Albrecht (1), 233).

In this chapter, we will review some techniques for overcoming impasse in mediation and negotiation, even where the potential for a successful resolution seems bleak and the parties and counsel "know" that no impasse-breaking technique will work. When you reach that point in a negotiation or mediation, be persistent, maintain your belief in trial and error, appreciate the value of experience, and re-read this chapter!

5.1 PETER S. ADLER: LEADERSHIP, MEDIATION, AND THE NAMING, FRAMING, AND TAMING OF TYPE-II AND TYPE-III PROBLEMS

[**Editor's Note:** *This article is printed and reformatted here with the permission of its author, Peter S. Adler, Ph.D.*]

5.1.1 The challenge

For every complex problem there is a simple solution. And it's wrong.
Anonymous

Under normal circumstances, conflicts over social, political, economic, and environmental policies present strenuous challenges to negotiators, mediators, and problem solvers. The resolution of multi party disputes that also involve ambient patterns of threats, fears, power plays, political intrigue, and chronic failures to make progress are especially hard and require extraordinary diplomacy and leadership. These conflicts seem to offer few clear adhesion points for problem solving. They obdurately resist closure, and on their face, often appear non-negotiable (Heidi and Guy Burgess).

"The human side of complex public policy problems," writes Susan Podziba, "reflects a chaotic mix of passions, values, interests, emotions, self interest, and altruism" (Podziba, 285-290). As disputes, they are protracted, entrenched, and unpredictable. Battles over abortion, same-sex marriage, genetically modified foods, spotted owls, arsenic levels in water, cloning, salmon recovery, dam deconstruction, and climate change policies come to mind, no less than the oft cited disputes between Israelis and Palestinians and Indians and Pakistanis. Many private disputes also have deep emotions and long memories and mirror the dynamics of public controversies. Divisional fights in manufacturing companies, multi-generational probate conflicts, and entrenched divorces over children and property sometimes have Bosnia-like qualities to them.

Public policy problems have additional complexities. They deal with competing ideologies of how public "goods" and "bads" should be allocated. They impact future generations, and create long running, if not irreversible decisions in the form of altered landscapes or chemical body burdens whose long-term impacts are uncertain. And under constitutional and parliamentary forms of government, they sprawl across and play out in different jurisdictions, often simultaneously (Table 1). "In the United States," say Lawrence Susskind and Jeffrey Cruikshank, "we are at an impasse. Public officials are unable to take action, even when everyone agrees that something needs to be done" (Susskind and Cruikshank). The power to stop, delay, or checkmate others rests in many hands.

Table 1

The Jurisdictions in Which Public Policy Conflicts Play Out
Legislative
Executive
Judicial
Federal
Congress
President
Federal Courts
State
Legislature
Governors
State Courts
Local
Mayors
Councils
Municipal Courts

Public policy conflicts have other unique dynamics. Much of their political intensity arises from the real or symbolic decisions that will seemingly determine how public purposes are conceptualized, honored, or made subsidiary, whose values from the political left, right, or center will prevail on a given issue, and who will take what specific political gains or losses in the social, environmental, and economic arenas. Procedurally, these disputes (like other disputes) rely on authority, competition, or cooperation strategies to mobilize constituencies and either escalate or de-escalate conflict as may be desired by political actors. As shown in Table 2, authority, competition, and cooperation strategies each have certain advantages and disadvantages for problem solving (Roberts (1)).

Table 2

	Authority Strategies	**Competition Strategies**	**Cooperation Strategies**
Advantages	Make use of professionals who are trained to delimit the problem. Fewer people are involved reducing complexity. Problem solving is quicker because it relies on "logic."	Encourage (and often turbo-charge) the search for new ideas. Keeps the power to define and solve problems circulating. Prevents monopolization of ideas. Weeds out weak solutions that might otherwise survive.	Alliances, partnerships, and coalitions create multipliers, synergies, and strength in numbers. Helps eliminate redundancies. Builds relationships that can potentially be applied to other issues, problems, or projects.
Disadvantages	People who actually have the problem often feel excluded or disenfranchised. Experts are often wrong. For many problems, there is no single definitive forum or jurisdiction.	Consumes time and resources that could be applied to solutions. May result in impasse or gridlock. When it becomes extreme, can become manipulative, deceptive, or violent.	Increases complexity (more meetings, more people, more time). Requires practice and skills that many people do not have. Takes time with no guarantee of success.

Regardless of which strategy seems to be employed, intractable problems are very rarely "solved." More often, they are slowly "tamed" during the interludes that seem to occur between more furious periods of conflict. In our work at The Keystone Center on issues ranging from federal facility siting practices to the cleanup of polluted rivers, we find that intractable problems also typically involve contested technical information and scientific uncertainty, both of which are often linked to divergent values and competing ideologies. We have further learned that the search for mutually usable information in the context of intractability seems to unfold as a succession of small windows of opportunity that open and close, that are usually beyond any single actor's control, and during which parties can potentially *re-name, re-frame,* and try to *re-tame* long-running problems for which short-term comprehensive solutions seem impossible.

To that end, it is also helpful to distinguish at least three broad categories of problems that have been variously alluded to or described by thinkers in different fields (Adams (1); de Bono (1); Schumacher; Tenner; Roberts). As illustrated in Table 3, these categories or "types" are defined by two factors: the degree to which there seems to be a common definition for a problem and the degree to which there is agreement on a list of possible solutions.

Table 3

	TYPE-1 (Technical/ Convergent)	**TYPE-2 (Value/ Divergent)**	**TYPE-3 (Wicked/ Intractable)**
Agreement on Problem Definition	Yes	Yes	No
Agreement on Possible Solutions	Yes	No	No

Issues with any degree of depth, breadth, or complexity rarely fit these kinds of neat categorizations. Our use of this typology at The Keystone Center (and our suggested use for others who take interest in public policy conflicts) is therefore diagnostic rather than formulaic or prescriptive. Stated differently, conflict resolution practitioners as well as researchers will do well to examine stubborn issues and problems with an eye towards (a) identifying their Type-I, II, or III characteristics; (b) identifying different potential leadership strategies and interventions (including the option of waiting and doing nothing) that are suggested by this problem diagnostic; (c) designing an appropriate choreography for bringing people, process, and data together when and if "doing something" is appropriate; and (d) approaching implementation as an improvisation, as if one were playing jazz (Bellman, 205-210).

5.1.2 Type-I Problems and the myth of conventional problem solving

Each situation changes the situation.
John Madden

"Type-I" problems are fundamentally "how to" questions. They are technical or, to use E.F. Schumacher's term, "convergent" in nature, meaning, they can be intellectually bounded and there are high levels of agreement on both the definition of the problem and a short list of possible fixes. The more that people of reasonable intelligence and reasonable good will study these problems, the more likely that possible solutions congregate into a narrow range of choices.

Generally, Type-I problems are amenable to expert-generated solutions. Intrinsically, these problems tend not to require much consideration of values and beliefs and may not even always require high levels of participation and involvement by those who have the problem. Hypothetical examples of Type-I problems might include retrofitting an older water system for conservation ("how do we best fix up old pipes"), finding the fastest route to Mexico City ("how can we get to Mexico City as quickly and comfortably as we can"), setting a broken arm ("how do we reduce the fracture so it heals the quickest and with the least amount of discomfort"), or eradicating a termite infestation ("how do we get rid of the termites without poisoning the people inside.")

To say that Type-I problems are technical in nature is not to say that they are simple. Think, for example, of the Apollo 13 mission during which astronauts Lovell, Haise, and Swigert were stranded 205,000 miles from Earth in a broken spaceship and with most of their life-support systems at or near failure. Or consider the challenges of designing, testing, and commercializing a new generation of hydrogen-fuel cell vehicles and the roadside service stations that will be needed to support them. Or building a new kind of airplane, searching for survivors in the aftermath of a 7.5 earthquake, or even the more day-to-day professional tasks performed by traffic engineers, tree trimmers, dentists, architects, forklift operators, plumbers, or social workers.

Most professions and trades – truck drivers, lawyers, printers, and doctors, to name a few more – are taught one or another version of a basic planning and problem solving model that has many variations. While steps and phases will differ from author to author, the usual fundamentals are described in Table 4:

Table 4

Conventional Type – I Problem Solving Model
(1) Problem identification.
(2) Analysis and information gathering.
(3) Formulation of alternative solutions.
(4) Formulation of criteria for weighing alternatives.
(5) Scaling and weighing choices.
(6) Choosing the most optimum solution.
(7) Implementing the solution.
(8) Evaluating the solution and making appropriate changes as needed.

This problem-solving model has many variations and uses (Fisher and Ury, 70; Goodpaster, 92).

Interestingly, an experimental simulation done at the Microelectronics and Computer Technology Corporation (MCC) suggests that few professionals actually use it. MCC asked a number of engineers to design an elevator control system for a new office building. All of the participants in the experiment were experienced systems designers though none had actually worked on elevator systems. The designers were asked to think out loud while they worked on the problem. Their sessions were videotaped and then analyzed to try and detect the actual individual and collective problem solving moves that were used as they attacked the problem (Guindon, 305-344; Conklin and Weil).

The observers noted two things. First, the engineers persistently worked to understand the requirements for the system. Second, they performed mental modeling efforts to try different solutions. For example, one of them would say: "Let's see, I'm on the second floor and the elevator is on the fifth floor and if I push the button, its going to go down when I want to go up...."). None of the engineers actually used anything similar to the formal sequence of the steps described in Table 4. Instead, the logic pattern seemed to be (1) here's what I'm trying to do; (2) here's the problem (i.e., "I have to get the elevator to the top floor;" (3) here's the solution (i.e., "send the elevator up"); (4) here's what is wrong with that solution (i.e., "all the elevators will go up at the same time, or they won't stop for others going up also;" and (5) here's the new solution (i.e., "stagger the cars in the elevator bank and program them to make stops going in only in one direction.")

Generalizing from the MCC experiment, normal problem solving behavior, despite professional training to the contrary, appears to be to first formulate a problem, then leap to a possible fix, then find the flaw with the fix, then find a new fix, and so on. What happened in the elevator experiment is instructive for groups working on Type-I problems. With single designers, the "problem-fix" sequence remained stable, though not necessarily effective. With multiple designers at work, the "problem-fix" sequence became chaotic, that is, different designers worked simultaneously on different problems and different fixes with no reference to what others were working on. This introduced additional psychological and social complexities.

Several conclusions emerge from the MCC game. First, the use of conventional problem solving procedures by experts is probably mythical. Left to our own devices, most of us will use a more intuitive approach that probably works most of the time. In many situations – perhaps most – this sequence suffices. It gets us by. Second, problem solving groups become vulnerable to breakdown for reasons that have little to do with the nature of the problem or the nature of the fix but more because of interaction issues: competing egos, differing agendas, divergent paces, dissimilar mental roadmaps (deductive vs. inductive reasoning, big picture vs. detail orientated, etc.), and the perennial tension that emerges in groups between "good" and "perfect" solutions.

Third, the disciplined, sequential, and bounded problem solving processes learned by most professionals turn out to be quite useful when problem solving requires people to work together on issues that are dominated by Type-I characteristics. Bringing leadership to more challenging Type-I problems seems to require a more disciplined version of the steps outlined in Table 4 when experts need to work together, when other conflicts are present, or when a problem appears to be extraordinarily complex. The conventional model doesn't need to be used all the time but it will have salutary effects when chaos threatens to overwhelm the usual "problem-fix" intuition. In this kind of situation, mediators can potentially do a great service by holding people's feet to the fire and keeping them working in a disciplined manner.

5.1.3 Type-II Problems and the misapplication of Type-I problem solving strategies

People, things, unseen forces, sort of come together from time to time.
Michael Connelly

If Type-I problems are characteristically "Technical/Convergent" in nature, Type II problems are best thought of as "Value/Divergent." The more that people of reasonable integrity, reasonable good will, and reasonably good working relationships study such matters, the more likely it is that ideas about "the reasonable solution" seem to swerve away from each other. Even though there may be general agreement on the definition of the problem, there is little or no agreement on potential solutions. In fact, solution-seeking discussions cause people to confront painful choices that they will either try to avoid or dominate.

Consider that particular scene in Kevin Costner's film *Dances With Wolves* when the Lakota Sioux chiefs are sitting in council pondering what to do about Lt. John Dunbar who is stationed alone at a remote cavalry outpost nearby. There is general agreement among the chiefs on the problem: the whites are overrunning the traditional lands of the Sioux. However, one faction favors sending warriors over to Dunbar's encampment and shooting a few arrows into him to see if he really has "medicine." Another faction believes they should try to talk with him and see if agreements can be made. A third chief says: "No man can tell another what to do but killing a white man is a delicate matter. If you kill one, more are sure to come." He urges the group to talk further before deciding what to do, in effect, to not act precipitously and to continue exploring the different value premises that are at play.

Unlike Type-I problems that lend themselves to the diagnostics and interventions of experts, Type-II matters require a serious consideration of values, not just by the experts, but by those who in some way must implement the solutions or live with the outcomes. In these circumstances, information alone won't fully inform decision-making because the problems involve matters of the heart. Not only can the full contours of the problem not be well described intellectually, the consequences of any one proposed course of action cannot be fully predicted or relied upon. Type-II problems are therefore more visceral. They evoke the emotions and stubborn responses associated with worldviews, ideologies, and belief systems.

Technical experts can help inform possible solutions to Type-II problems but without the participation of those who actually bear the full brunt of the problem (stakeholders), progress remains elusive. In day-to-day life, examples might include determining how we will expand a water supply once existing sources have been tapped out ("Gray-water recycling? Desalinization? Importing from elsewhere?"), deciding "why" we want to go to Mexico City and what we are going to do once we get there ("See the cultural sites? Take in the nightlife? Go to language school and learn Spanish?"), or determining how we will effectively educate our children ("Charter schools? Year-round school? National standards? Voucher system?").

Bringing leadership to Type-II problems requires skills and strategies very different from those needed for Type-I problems. Faced with more emotion-laden and value-driven problems, the inclination of many professionals is to apply one or another version of the conventional problem- solving model outlined in Table 4, i.e. systematic problem identification, analysis and information gathering, formulation of alternative solutions, etc. The elements of this model may be useful, but only after some of the following other tasks may have been set in motion, if not accomplished:

- Gathering together a strong but representative cross-section of voices and perspectives.

- Establishing the goals and protocols needed for sustained and disciplined Discussions.

- Collecting multiple narratives that help illuminate different descriptions of the problem as seen through different eyes.

- Naming the fears and risks associated with different problem definitions.

- Reframing narratives into mutual questions.

- Managing the pace of problem solving.

- De-positioning and/or preventing premature negotiation.

- Helping everyone to avoid the wishful thinking that one value set will ultimately prevail.

- Helping everyone understand the trade-offs involved in tough choices.

5.1.4 Type-III Problems and the challenge of bringing leadership to "wicked" problems

Dance with your demons and they become angels.
Anonymous

In the various literatures on problem-solving, Type-III problems are often referred to as "wicked" or "intractable" because they seem to be diabolically complicated by multiple stakeholders, overlapping jurisdictions, powerful moral dimensions, and deep, nasty, and much remembered histories. Simon Shum says these problems cannot be easily defined so that all stakeholders actually agree on the problem to solve. They require complex judgments about the level of abstraction at which to define the problem, have no clear starting or stopping rules for defining the problem, and have no objective measure of success (Shum). Similarly, the concept of "intractability" carries a variety of connotations and denotations, not the least of which is the inability to find or create a traction point from which to try to tame or resolve the problem (Burgess).

Type-III problems preoccupy us because of their volatility, drama, high public consequences, and difficulty to tame. One key indication of a Type-III problem is that communication channels have been clogged, if not actually severed. Stakeholders are unable to talk with each other without inflaming the situation. If there is communication, it takes place through lawyers, press releases, symbolic acts (violent or non-violent) that "send a message," and through escalatory or retaliatory behaviors. This does not mean that simply restoring communication is the answer. Communication failures are a symptom and must be part of a solution-finding process. By itself, good communication is insufficient.

In Type-III problems there is inevitably broad disagreement on what "the problem" actually is and competing solutions that create on going discord among stakeholders when they try to discuss "it." Further, there is a diffusion of power that makes any one party incapable of both defining the problem in a way that sticks or imposing a solution. Because integrity, goodwill, trust, and working relationships are perceived to be missing, people often actively seek to defeat each other. The conflict seems to have a life unto itself. In the most extreme stages, writes Friedrich Glasl, disputants give up their deepest instincts for self-preservation and charge headlong and together into the abyss (Glasl).

Like Type-II problems, Type-III problems are driven by deeply conflicting values. Unlike Type-II challenges, proposed solutions are suspect simply because they are brought forward by someone who is typically defined as an essential part of the problem. For example, a proposal from Ariel Sharon or Yasser Arafat is distrusted simply because it comes from either Ariel Sharon or Yasser Arafat. Intentional and unintentional signals create complexity. Offers are confused with bribes and demands are considered extortion.

Bringing leadership to Type-III problems requires both the right political timing (the "window" opens) and a suite of different strategies, tools, and formats that can be used to organize and sustain disciplined naming, framing, and taming efforts. Most writers believe that these kinds of problems can only be solved by groups of disputants made up of people with knowledge pertinent to all aspects of the problem, artfully organized into sub-groups that correspond to the elements and structure of the problem. Further, the process must be choreographed as a series of events or meetings with time-breaks between events. The team must be unconstrained in applying knowledge tools, creative intuition, and common sense. Finally, the group must be unshackled when it comes to finding unconventional solutions (Hutchinson, English, and Mughal, 257-279).

At The Keystone Center for Science & Public Policy, we are often asked to help parties try to resolve frictions associated with energy, environment, and public health problems. This brings us into the political eye of the storm on disputes ranging from prescription drug labeling to the use of military live-fire training on environmentally and culturally sensitive lands. Our projects typically have non-governmental organizations (NGOs), industry, and government at the table questing for solutions. Most of these conflicts have characteristics that span all three problem types: they are scientifically and technically complex; they are riddled with value dilemmas; and there are difficult failures in the past that color how stakeholders from all three sectors think about the present and the future.

In our work on politically sensitive and science-intensive problems, we use a generic template of interventions for both Type-II and Type-III problems that probably represents most of the core moves that public policy mediators and negotiators use in other settings. The focus is on achieving both a politically actionable plan as well as the highest possible level of consensus. In effect, we set out to create a new political "center" that improbable partners can rally around and defeat actors on the extreme who will never accept anything less than their own dictated solution. Some of the core moves are described in Table 5 below.

Table 5

Core Moves For Building a New Political Center   For Type-II and Type-III Problems

(1) Appraising and diagnosing the problem to understand its Type-I, II, or III characteristics and whether a "window" of opportunity can be opened.

(2) Organizing leadership, sponsorship, and permission to convene a diverse group of voices and viewpoints.

(3) Gaining the participation of a critical mass of affected stakeholders.

(4) Designing a forum, venue, and choreography.

(5) Establishing protocols and forging working agreements on the definition of the issues and memorializing these in a charter, a convening document, or terms of reference.

(6) Organizing productive and respectful exchanges of relevant information, including scientific, legal, economic, social, and political "data," and further confronting the problems associated with contested information or information with high levels of uncertainty.

5.1.5 The ACWA Case

> *Whenever I'm confronted by a choice between two,*
> *evils, I always choose the one I haven't tried before.*
> Mae West

The decommissioning and destruction of aging chemical weapons presents extreme technical, social, and political challenges. Old munitions (bombs, artillery shells, canisters of gas) are dangerous to handle and must be destroyed in a manner that complies with environmental laws and the standards of best practice for dealing with unexploded ordnance. Military experts find chemical weapons destruction challenging. Lay people find it confusing. Cities and townships don't want these materials in their neighborhoods; lives are at stake if anything goes wrong.

The Keystone Center's "Dialogue on Assembled Chemical Weapon Assessment" ("ACWA") was set up in response to mounting controversy and increasing public and congressional concerns regarding the U.S. Army's plans to destroy antiquated and dangerous stockpiled weapons. The Army's plans to incinerate aged weapons, some dating back to before World War I, was met with strong social and environmental opposition in the communities targeted to host the destruction processes. The group of approximately thirty-two members met thirteen times over five years and included community members from nine sites; federal and state regulators; representatives from tribal nations; national activists regarding chemical weapons destruction; and national and local military staff. Most of the participants had been involved in long-term legal battles and had often testified against each other in Congressional hearings.

Despite a bitter history on this issue, the Dialogue moved through the stages described in Table 5 and accomplished three major goals. First, the group achieved a full consensus on a highly technical, 120-

page Request for Proposal (RFP) for identifying and evaluating alternative technologies to incineration. The consensus was forged during a three-month period and the government committee conducting the official evaluation later adopted the exact evaluation criteria developed by the group.

Second, a full consensus was achieved regarding which alternative technologies should be demonstrated and how they should be evaluated. For the first time to anyone's recollection, several citizen members participated directly in the government procurement process along side the federal officials. Finally, a series of annual consensus reports to Congress were developed regarding the Department of Defense's (DOD) chemical weapons destruction programs.

Since the Dialogue ended in 2002, the DOD has announced that the alternative technologies identified through this Dialogue process will be implemented at sites in Colorado and Kentucky. These two billion dollar facilities mark the first chemical weapons sites where DOD has not encountered lawsuits and extensive delays. In fact, the communities have come out in full support of the projects and are working cooperatively with the DOD and regulating agencies to expedite permitting and the actual destruction of chemical weapons.

Other less tangible accomplishments also emerged: an increased understanding by all parties of the complicated decision-making processes required and their inherent trade-offs as well as more realistic expectations and the ability to creatively compromise, when appropriate. In the ACWA proceedings, community representatives were forced to struggle with budget limitations and the uncertainties of the science. Military officials no longer could view the potentially affected citizens as uneducated and nameless masses.

ACWA did not resolve or smooth over the ideological differences between people with distinctly different philosophies about the environment, the military, and the use of public lands. However, increased trust among all parties developed in the specific instance of grappling with a dynamic problem that had many Type-I, II, and III characteristics. Political momentum to find solutions emerged simultaneously with strong leadership from the military, environmental, and community stakeholders. One small example is instructive. Many community members opposed the appointment of the lead DOD official for this effort. By the end of the effort, this same leader was promoted to be in charge of all chemical weapons storage and disposal issues for the country - partly based on community members going to Congress and requesting his advancement. As one Dialogue participant noted at the end of the process: *"Distrust and suspicion gave way to trust and a sense of possibility which gave way to political reality and frustration which evolved into acceptance, perseverance, and a sense of accomplishment."*

5.1.6 Mediation and leadership

There is no trick to being captain so long as the sea is quiet.
Anonymous

Though rarely called such, mediation is a form of political leadership. Conflict is the crucible of change and change is the business of both political leaders and mediators. Mediation not only requires a certain manner of guidance amidst fields of fiercely contending forces, it is also predicated on bringing out the highest and best leadership qualities in those others who bear direct responsibility for solutions and failures, and whose professional and political reputations are on the line as a result. Like mediation, leadership is intimately linked to the naming, framing, and taming of problems and to the direct application of the authority, competition, and cooperation strategies detailed in Table 2. Mediation is a crossroads where the currents of power converge and potentially transform.

In the voluminous literature on leadership, both popular and scholarly books (including the inevitable airport books on "Leadership Secrets of ..."), many writers touch on this. Robert Greenleaf describes a certain practical manner of leading that relies on collaboration, trust, foresight, listening, the ethical use of power, and the empowerment of others (Greenleaf).

Barry Johnson talks about the need to manage paradoxes and work with the naturally occurring and reoccurring polarities that humans working in groups face. Examples include the challenge of stabilizing what we have while working towards change, working in teams while fostering individual creativity, and forging clear directions while simultaneously staying reflexive to new circumstances (Johnson).

Similarly, Jim Collins and his colleagues have written about "Level 5 Leadership" and the paradoxical abilities needed to create sustained performance. Level 5 leaders form a small universe of unique people who Collins identified by screening down to a small number of companies with persistently good results. These leaders, Collins discovered, not only helped shape financially successful enterprises, they helped develop sustainable enterprises over many years. "Good-to-great leaders," as he calls them, turn out to be self-effacing, smart, quiet, and reserved. They build and maintain cultures of discipline but ironically turn out not to be tyrants or disciplinarians themselves.

These leaders of highly successful businesses adhere to what Collins calls the Hedgehog Strategy in which they brutally and realistically determine what the company can be the best in the world at, decide the most effective way of generating sustained cash flow and profitability, and then determine the single metric that most tracks their success or failure. These leaders have an unwavering resolve to produce long-term results without hype, spin, rationalizations, or excuses for less than successful achievements (Collins).

Charles Farkas and Suzy Wetlaufer, in a different study of highly successful CEOs, found five distinct leadership patterns. Some focused on broad strategy and spent most of their time on horizon issues. Others embodied a "Human Assets Approach" in which strategy is left to the business units with the CEO concentrating on cultivating (or getting rid of) key leaders. Some focused on technical expertise and on the cutting edge of the business. Others seemed to focus on managing the "four-corners" of the organization. A few were change artists, specialists in turn-arounds and major business transitions (Farkas and Wetlaufer, 115-147). All of these mirror the different, smaller scale choreographies that take place in mediation.

Look carefully at the best mediation processes, and the traits, qualities, characteristics, and behaviors described in the best leadership literatures. There is a powerful and intimate connection between leadership, problem solving, and mediation. While much is often made of the vision and inspiration we look for our leaders to fulfill, fundamentally we also want our leaders to solve the smaller and larger problems that touch our lives. That they can't always do this is a reminder that the solutions to our toughest problems, those that have strong Type-II and Type-III characteristics, require the participation of those who must live with the trade-offs the solutions create. The job of leaders, like the job of the mediator, is to bring that participation out, to get as many people into the action as possible, and still get action.

Mediation is ultimately about the adaptive political management of human conflict and the recognition that humans do not know everything that is required to solve complex Type-I, II, and III problems. Conflict, conflict resolution, problem formulation, and problem taming are protean and sometimes venal crucibles of human affairs. Sometimes they involve big theater and lots of drama. Just as often, they take place in the soft light of little windows that have opened for a moment. The result? Long stretches of steady, hard work done by people who have parked their fury to the side long enough to explore the possibilities of change. That is what leaders, mediators, and problem solvers of all stripes aspire to do.

[Peter S. Adler, Ph.D., President, The Keystone Center
1628 Saint John Road, Keystone, Colorado 80435
970-513-5841, padler@keystone.org]

5.2 STEVEN J. BRAMS AND ALAN D. TAYLOR: USE OF FAIR-DIVISION PROCEDURES IN RESOLVING DISPUTES

In their book, *The Win-Win Solution: Guaranteeing Fair Shares to Everybody* (W.W. Norton & Co, 1999), Steven J. Brams and Alan D. Taylor describe three fair division procedures that can be used in two-party disputes from the inception of a mediation or at a point of impasse. The authors note that these procedures leave to the disputants what choices they will make, as allowed by the rules of the particular procedure. The mediator's role in using these procedures is to serve as clarifiers and facilitators without dictating what the settlement or its terms should be. Mediators may help to define what the issues are, but they may not decide what the division will be. Fairness is guaranteed by the procedure as appropriately used, not by the wisdom or benevolence of the mediator. The three procedures - strict and balanced alternation, divide-and-choose, and adjusted winner are briefly described in this section and readers are encouraged to learn more about the applications of them by referring to the book cited above. Additionally, the four criteria by which to judge the fairness of settlements and a few observations about rules and strategies used in settlement procedures are also briefly addressed below.

5.2.1 Strict and balanced alternation

Strict alternation is simply taking turns: you pick an item; then I pick one; you choose again; and so on. Of course, going first can be a huge advantage, and much of what is done later, including giving extra choices to compensate for going second, involves finding a reasonable way to reduce, if not eliminate, this advantage. That is, a specific way of balancing choices leads to a procedure called balanced alternation (Brams and Taylor, 10-11).

5.2.2 Divide-and-choose

This is the familiar "I cut, you choose" method, with which almost everybody has had some experience. What most people probably do not know is whether it is better to be the divider or chooser ... [I]t all depends on what the parties know about each other's preferences, as well as whether they wish to spite their opponents or think they might be spited themselves.

The trimming procedure extends divide-and-choose to more than two parties by requiring that, at different stages, they create equal shares for themselves. They do so by trimming what they consider to be the largest pieces to tie with smaller pieces, repeating the same procedure on the trimmings, the trimmings of the trimmings, and so on. Of course, this procedure can become very complicated, especially when there are many participants (Brams and Taylor, 11).

5.2.3 Adjusted winner

Under this procedure, the two parties begin by independently (that is, secretly) distributing a total of 100 points across all the items to be divided, depending on the relative value they attach to them. Thus, if you consider a certain item to be worth one-fourth of the total value of everything to be divided, then you would place 25 points on it.

The term winner in adjusted winner comes from the next step: Each party is (temporarily) given the items on which he or she placed more points than his or her opponent. Thus, if I place 24 points on the apartment and you place 25 points on it, you will get it at least for the moment. Now the adjusted part comes in: Suppose, initially, I win items totaling 55 of my points, and you win items totaling 65 of your points. Then we start transferring items from you to me, in a certain order, until the point totals are equalized (at, say, 60 points each). This order of transfer, which usually requires splitting one item, guarantees that the final allocation will satisfy some important properties of fairness (Brams and Taylor, 11).

5.2.4 Criteria of satisfaction

Brams and Taylor identify four criteria by which to judge the fairness of settlements: proportionality; envy-freeness; equitability; and efficiency. Proportionality, they point out, is just a weaker version of the second, and therefore, practically speaking, can be eliminated. A procedure is fair to the degree that it satisfies the following criteria.

Proportionality. Satisfaction is linked, presumably, to receiving a "fair share ..." [P]roportionality will arise only when contributions are equal. If there are two parties, proportionality will mean that each party thinks that it is getting at least one-half of the total value. If there are three parties, each thinks that it is getting at least one-third of the total value. And so on.

Envy-freeness. What more than proportionality can one ask for? The answer is something called envy-freeness, which says that no party is willing to give up the portion it receives in exchange for the portion someone else receives. Hence, no party envies any other party. In two-party disputes, there is no difference between a proportional and an envy-free settlement ... In the case of three parties, however, envy-freeness is stronger than proportionality. For example, I may think I'm getting one-third, but if I think you're getting one-half (because the third party, in my eyes, is getting only one-sixth), then I'll envy you. On the other hand, if an allocation among three parties is envy-free, then I must think I received at least one third ... Hence an envy-free allocation is always proportional, even if there are more than two parties, but a proportional allocation is not necessarily envy-free.

Equitability. There is an aspect of satisfaction, related to envy-freeness, that is more subtle than envy-freeness. Think about a divorce settlement, in which you think you got 51% of the total value of the joint holdings but in which your spouse thinks he or she got 90% of the total value, because your spouse had little interest in what you got. Do you envy your spouse? The answer is no ... Equitability is used here to mean that both parties think they received the same fraction of the total, as each of them values the different items. ...

Efficiency. A settlement is efficient if there is no other allocation that is better for some party without being worse for another party. Efficiency by itself ... [when not linked with the other three criteria] is no guarantee that an allocation will be fair. For example, an allocation that gives everything to me and nothing to you is efficient: Any other allocation will make me worse off when it makes you better off. It is the other properties of fairness, combined with efficiency, that ensure that the total value is distributed to everyone's satisfaction (Brams and Taylor, 13-15).

5.2.5 Rules and strategies

Brams and Taylor also describe how rules and strategies affect the application of the fair-division procedures as explained below.

Impartial procedures which do not favor a particular party, are key to finding a fair settlement of a dispute. A procedure is described by its rules ...

Rules are legal choices that can be enforced by a referee, without knowledge of any party's preferences. Thus, a rule might say, "Divide the collection of items into two separate piles." By counting piles, a referee can tell whether this statement has been followed. But a rule cannot say, "Divide the collection of items into two separate piles that you consider to be equal in value" because a referee would have no way of knowing if the latter part of this statement were being followed.

Parties base their strategies or courses of action, not only on the rules but also on their own private knowledge (for example, of the values of different items). Once the rules have been laid down, there are many possible strategies that parties can select. For example, if you are the divider in divide-and-choose, then one rule says that you must divide the items into two piles. The added phrase "that you consider to be of equal value" is a strategy that provides a certain kind of guarantee ... Nothing says that you must use the prescribed strategy. In fact, ... there ... [may be] situations in which you might want to deviate from such a strategy, based on information you have about how your opponent values the different items... Our goal is to find procedures, governed by rules, that the disputants themselves can implement. Associated with these rules will be strategies that the disputants can use to guarantee themselves a certain degree of satisfaction (Brams and Taylor, 16-18).

5.3 ROBERT A. CREO: BREAKING IMPASSE

[**Editor's Note**: *This section consists of an article authored by attorney and mediator Robert A. Creo and is reproduced and reformatted here with his permission.*]

5.3.1 The mediation process framework

The following dynamics, concepts, themes, core values, orientations, philosophy, style, approaches or paradigms create the framework for breaking impasse. Most of these points assume a traditional two party or multi-defendant case which would be resolved in a civil court of law by payment of monetary damages.

1. Mediation is an ALTERNATIVE process. It is an alternative to direct negotiation, third-party adjudication, avoidance or self-help. It should look and feel different than those processes and provide other or extra options not present in any of those methods of resolving disputes. Bilateral negotiation must be reactive and direct between principals and/or their agents. There are inherent tensions in direct communication models and/or agency relationships. (Mnookin et. al.) Mediation can be pro-active and involve different bargaining models (Creo, CPR Alternatives article)

2. Mediation involves party self-determination, recognition, voice and empowerment sometimes absent in negotiation, adjudication, avoidance or self-help. The prime goal of mediation of civil claims or trial litigation is settlement. Transformation may or may not occur in the process as a platform for, or as a direct by-product, of settlement.

3. A large percentage of cases involve the mediator uncovering a pre-existing zone of settlement or a "near-zone" which, once it is uncovered and communicated, the parties can bridge. A facilitative approach to removing "strategic barriers" with mediator impartiality and relative passivity will generally succeed in these cases (Robert Mnookin et. al.).

4. A significant number of cases involve a true, good faith disagreement, and gap, based upon a recipe of intersecting factors such as different perceptions as to the facts, credibility, law, skill of counsel, venue, risk tolerance, party values/principles, precedents, historical and personal narratives, strategic goals and priorities. Breaking impasse involves an actual transformation of the choices, and/or perspectives, of at least one of the stakeholders of the dispute.

5. An approach involving more challenges of party autonomy and self-determination is required for the intervention to be successful. This may involve tension between traditional concepts of neutrality and impartiality and a more proactive, directive or evaluative approach.

6. Mediation is a trilateral negotiation process. The mediator is a participant negotiating both process (procedural fairness or due process) and substantive outcome.

7. Parties care deeply about both process and outcome. Procedural fairness provides voice and participant recognition. Substantive outcome involves empowerment to make informed choices within the risk tolerance of each participant.

8. Mediation may often be an asymmetrical process based upon a number of factors. Excessive attention to concepts of neutrality or balance may prove to be ineffective in providing choice points and/or transforming the participants' views of each other or the dispute. Asymmetrical dynamics or paradigms may include, among other elements:

a) One party, usually defendants, are repeat players in the legal system or manage a book of business risks or disputes.

b) The case for plaintiffs, especially tort and employment claimants, is often 100% of their court docket and/or experience with the legal system.

c) Repeat players, including plaintiff counsel, benchmark against other cases; consistency, predictability and uniformity are often core values of repeat players.

d) Participants may have different perspectives and expectations of the processing of legal claims via the courts.

e) Defendants' proposals involve real dollars; demands involve abstract sums, goals or "aspires" and not relief in present, real time. The language itself recognizes this by nomenclature of "demand" and "offer."

f) One of the parties, usually claimants, may have suffered "personal trauma" which forms the basis of the claim; this may involve a personal injury, business or economic disruption or a perceived grievance involving their personal self-esteem or public reputation. The other participants' key interests may be "impersonal" and involve primarily economic impact. In short, one party may be making a personal decision with profound consequences while others are involved in a business transaction.

g) There may be a real or perceived power imbalance among participants.

h) Preparation for the negotiation may differ.

i) Participant preparation for the mediation, or experience, expectations and attitudes about the process differs.

j) Participants process information and make decisions with different cognitive preferences, e.g., Meyers-Briggs theory (See, e.g., *Harvard Negotiation Law Review*, Vol. 9, Spring 2004, R.Lisle Baker, Pages 115 to 186).

9. Mediation does, or should, fit a classical definition of "argumentation" such as: Argumentation is an interaction in which participants maintain what they think are mutually exclusive positions and that they seek to resolve their disagreement (Northwestern Professor David Zarefsky).

This differs from adjudication and adversary at-law processes in function, approach and goals. Adjudicatory paradigms and/or legal values should not be grafted onto an argumentation process.

10. Mediation is a complex, non-linear system. It is reactive and adaptive. (Sometimes framed as "complexity theory" and/or "chaos" theory). Attempts to build a consensus definition of mediation or portray it by grids, schemes or other integrated methods may not be helpful and may in fact be counterproductive if it empowers an orthodoxy of mediation practice.

5.3.2 Process and personal preferences of participants

In general, Robert A. Creo believes the majority of people will act in accordance with the following heuristics or principles.

1. People want closure. Yet, people tend to procrastinate and wait until the last available moment to make a final decision. People not present or outside the process may influence choice.

2. People are motivated by self-esteem and seek or expect personal dignity. The legal system generally works against personal and human dignity by applying broad concepts and converting people into claims and precedents.

3. People make choices in a holistic manner. This involves traditional concepts of rationality (Enlightenment, Age of Reason and Descartes), but also involves a complex mix of emotion, intuition, memory, risk tolerance, values, faith interacting within their personal narratives and perceptions/reactions to power/leverage. In classical negotiation and mediation theory, this involves positions, interests and needs. Professor Abraham Maslow framed it as the "Hierarchy of Needs" and depicted it as a pyramid. Holistic decision-making, (i.e, problem-solving) thrives when given value-creating, and not just value-claiming, tools and options.

4. People process information in more than one way. Some are visual, some auditory and some kinetic. Some are "macros" (focused on big picture and bottom line) while some are "micros" wanting detail and piece-by-piece building blocks. People perceive and remember differently. People give different meanings to the same words, especially subjective words, such as fair or reasonable, and also to "objective" words (often, sometimes, seldom, frequently) which are intended to connote quantitative distinctions.

5. Cognitive bias exists. This affects decision-making and choice, especially under conditions of uncertainty. These have been studied (behavior economics) and documented over many years (See, Amos Tversky and Daniel Kahneman, Max Bazerman et al). There are "irrational" heuristics and behavior which are somewhat predictable over a large population base. Some of these cognitive prejudices involve:

a) Irrational escalation of commitment
b) Framing
c) Familiarity
d) Anchoring and Adjustment
e) Loss Aversion; especially sunk costs
f) Status Quo Confirmation

Some of these are involved in every mediation. Some of the most common "translations" to the mediator involved how claimants and defendants view risk. For example, people prefer certainty over uncertainty. A bird in the hand is worth at least two in the bush. Yet, people have different risk tolerances.

6. There is a strong "inequity aversion" either hard-wired and/or acquired culturally (See, *Nature,* Vol. 425, p. 297, 18 Sept. 2003). The legal system core values support the "inequity aversion" and this may result in a focus on uniformity, consistency and predictability. Participants will attempt to benchmark against whatever prior experience, objective or subjective, may exist for similar claims.

7. People appreciate and respect candor and authenticity. Empirical research and mediator experience shows that disputants connect with "stories" and narratives, especially those involving the mediator's experience. People respect sympathy but react positively to an "engaging empathy" from the other side and/or the mediator.

8. Reciprocity is a powerful dynamic, especially for risk professionals (lawyers, adjustors, managers) (See, e.g., Robert Axelrod, *The Evolution of Cooperation*). The bargaining model must pay at least nominal respect to a traditional concession pattern bargaining.

9. Lawyers are the gate-keepers to the decision-makers and must be respected. Gates must be unlocked with the consent of the lawyer and not rammed down by the mediator. Legal ethics are one tool the mediator utilizes to obtain consent from the lawyer to access the client's decision facilities. Risk is another tool since there is a risk tolerance disconnect between agent and principal.

10. Interpersonal relationships and dynamics among the principals and agents have significant impact upon the negotiation which occurs within the mediation. The historical narratives between "pairs," "triplets" or "quads" of the professional negotiators, especially counsel, is part of what the process, and the mediator, adapts to as mediation session unfolds.

5.3.3 Process preferences and heuristics of Robert A. Creo

1. The most efficient, and common, symbol or analogy for the mediation process is a funnel. The first stage, the wide-end of the funnel involves information gathering and exchange. The next phase is a risk analysis which narrows to bargaining or choices. Throughout the process the mediator is building rapport, credibility and trust. An efficient mediation process should be fluid and flow in only one direction and not repeat or flow upstream. There can be funnels within funnels as parties and mediators resolve intra-party tension or conflict.

2. Transparency, especially on procedural issues, is effective (See articles by Professor Michael Moffit).

3. Engagement, between mediator and participants, and either directly between disputants or "virtually" via mediator as a conduit or translator, is essential. A mediator builds connection via

authentic engagement with the participants. This requires validating and legitimatizing the narratives of the participants.

4. Progress often involves reframing or transforming "qualitative" positions, interests and values into "quantitative" frames or choices. This is what courts of law do, so mediators may often be successful by resolving non-economic issues in an integrative manner while addressing other issues in a distributive manner. Once the final issues are about how much money passes hands, i.e, solely distributive bargaining, proven techniques can be applied to narrow gaps. Building bridges or common grounds in cases where a true, good faith impasse exists, often involves transformation of qualitative issues into quantitative options. This leads to the following Creo Paradox:

The more qualitative the dispute, the more resolution options available but the more likely the mediator must resort to higher risk, activist strategies involving mediator direction and evaluation to a resting point of settlement.

This sometimes involves the difference between what has often been framed as Retributive and Restorative Justice. Participants focused on retribution usually are unable to achieve concrete results in mediation to satisfy these needs; successful mediation often involves transforming retribution into restorative channels. It is easier to translate restoration into civil damages than retribution. Restoration is usually quantitative while retribution is qualitative.

5. "A foolish consistency is the hobgoblin of little minds." Ralph Waldo Emerson. Mediators must treat each case uniquely and freshly, calling upon a wide-variety of tools. Mediators must make deliberate choices. Mediation involves a series of strategic macro and micro choices by the mediator. Macro choices involve the next "goal" or "choice point" while micro choices involve the moves or steps (tools) necessary to reach the goal.

6. Aristotle said "The ethos of the speaker is more important than the content of the message." The process provides the mediator as an alternate or surrogate speaker for a participant. Adverse messages and realities can be conveyed or affirmed by the mediator. This should be a deliberate choice implemented in as transparent a manner as feasible.

7. Mediators must be guided in their choice of macros and micros by the past, present and future relationship between the participants. Many relationships, such as arising from personal injury claims, are random and temporal; they involve only the dispute and are terminated once the legal case is over. Availability of non-economic solutions may be affected by the relationship dynamics.

8. Mediators strategic choices involve the form of communication which is chosen because it "feels" right at that moment. This involves the mediator's awareness of all elements of the process, the participants and meta-mediator (self). This is often referred to as the "gestalt" of the mediation. The mediator makes these choices or "moves" based upon an interaction of rationality, intuition, emotions, values, etc. based upon the mediator's own experience. The form of communication may be narrative, questioning, silence, physical, illustrative or some other manner. One Creo frame is to determine if it is time for a "unilogue" or a "dialogue" or a "trilogue" of communication by the participants.

9. Mediation can be a forum for equitable remedies not available in law courts. These remedies/solutions may involve, or result from, implementation of recognition and empowerment paradigms. Some non-economic remedies may be accomplished at the session as a platform for settlement and others as a byproduct. Some may mature in the future as a consequence of mediation. For example, acknowledgment, explanation and apology are events while forgiveness is a process which may not be concluded contemporaneously with settlement (See commentators such as Jennifer Gerarda Brown, Kenneth Cloke, Jonathan Cohen, Donna Pavlick, Wescoat Sandlin and Donna Tait Sandlin).

10. Professor Randolph Lowry of Pepperdine reminds us that we are often an invitee into the gravitas of human tragedy or conflict. There may be a profound impact upon the mediator in these cases. Many mediators acknowledge the personal and/or spiritual benefits which inure to the mediator following successful conclusion of cases. This "mediator high" is not only common but perhaps a prerequisite for the mediator as artist.

5.3.4 Some common paradigms

5.3.4.1 Paradigm No. 1: Creo hierarchy of case values

My experience in tort claims, which may also apply to employment, securities and other lay-claimants, is that there is a general predictability to the "pecking order" of case evaluation. This follows the general ascending order:

Additional Defendants (clients)
Original Defendant (target tortfeasor)
Insurance Adjusters for Additional Defendants
Insurance Adjuster for Original Defendant
In-House Counsel or Risk Manager for Original Defendant
Outside Counsel for Additional Defendants
Outside Counsel for Original Defendants
Lead Trial Counsel for Defense
Lead Trial Counsel for Plaintiff
Referring Counsel of Plaintiff
Plaintiff
Plaintiff's spouse or parents
Plaintiff's children or other family members
Plaintiff's formal advisors (e.g., spiritual or financial)
Plaintiff's informal advisors (e.g., "kitchen cabinet")
Plaintiff's neighbor's second-cousin, twice-removed, who had a similar case worth millions.

My experience is that settlements tend to cluster, or bell-curve, around the values set by trial counsel.

5.3.4.2 Paradigm No. 2: Phantom negotiators

Many claimants and "participants with full authority" are engaged in continual communication via telephone with individuals on the Creo Hierarchy of Value not actually present at the negotiation. Nevertheless, their presence may be profound. One of my macro goals in every mediation is to identify early in the process who these ghosts are and the medium of communication. I do this in a transparent manner by asking and explaining why I need to know this information. If the people are critical to decision-making, I ask the participants if they want to invite them to attend or have them on a speaker telephone.

5.3.4.3 Paradigm No. 3: Settler's remorse

Most people question any major decision in hindsight. There is always going to be some lingering doubt about whether or not the participant made the correct decision. I anticipate this dynamic at the final choice-point and address it in a transparent manner. I usually note that the next few days or until final papers are signed and money exchanged, there may be a tension between the good "feel" of closure and certainty and doubt if the right choice was made. I tell them my experience, and this is usually echoed by their own lawyer, is that over a relatively short time period, closure generally prevails. It may be as soon as tomorrow but it almost always arrives.

5.3.4.4 Paradigm No. 4: Trading body parts?

Usually in tort cases, sometimes in joint session or in an early caucus, I discuss the concept of good health versus economic damages. We discuss how we cannot restore good health and that money damages are a poor substitute for any injury. We discuss how if someone came into the room with a large sum of money and offered it in exchange for removing a healthy body part, few would make that deal. This is one of the many asymmetrical elements of tort cases.

5.3.4.5 Paradigm No. 5: Time is not on your side

Usually, unless the case is literally on the courthouse steps, one party's case is as good as it will ever get. I discuss this with that party in caucus. I explain that time is not on your side and that the intersection of time and settlement is fluid and catch-as-catch can. Many times, more than one party perceives that time is against them.

5.3.4.6 Paradigm No. 6: Look ahead, not backward

You live in the present and for the future. Living in the past may be detrimental for your health. Therefore, I explore what positive events can happen as a result of settling the claim today. I explain that mediation is a process about future while litigation is about assessing blame or fault for a past action or event.

5.3.4.7 Paradigm No. 7: Jury justice?

I always explore people's goals in a lawsuit. I ask what they expect from a jury verdict. I ask what they have to risk from an adverse verdict beyond economics. I often frame this as a question about what they believe in their heart of hearts, and if a jury finds against them, will that be a transformative event. In other words, will that change the belief in their hearts. This is a no-lose line of questioning for the mediator.

If they answer negatively, i.e., their personal or historical narratives will not change and they will continue to believe that they are right and the other side is wrong. I explore with them what, if anything, is the point of a jury determination then. On a normative basis then, isn't it just as "fair" or "legitimate" to flip a coin? Isn't the effect of what they are saying is that "heads I win, tails you lose" since the verdict will have no impact on their views of the claim, accountability or right or wrong variables?

If they respond affirmatively, i.e, that the verdict will equate to repudiation or transformation of their views and a rewrite of their historical narratives, then the focus shifts to what personal risk this may entail to them and their self-esteem. Can they live with an outcome that may involve a finding of contributory or comparative negligence or causation attributable back to themselves?

Here is one example among many applications of this approach: a medical malpractice claim involved a baby who was deprived of oxygen which caused a permanent vegetative condition. There was a legitimate causation defense alleging that the mother accidentally suffocated the baby while sleeping in the same bed. This defense had significant merit. Nevertheless, a multi-million dollar proposal was made to settle the case; this provided lifetime financial security for the child and the single mother. Plaintiff counsel expected a significantly higher verdict if the case was won at trial. In plaintiff caucus we discussed the fact that a defense verdict could only result if the jury concluded that the mother was solely at fault. The mother concluded this was an unacceptable personal risk to her beyond the economic devastation of an adverse verdict. Confidential information I had from counsel for each party led me to formulate my own conclusion that this was more likely than not the actual cause of the event.

5.3.4.8 Paradigm No. 8: All lawyers are created equal

I am uncomfortable with participants who evaluate claims and assign settlement value based upon the superiority of their own trial counsel over the opposing counsel. I explain how I think that is risky to rely upon the other side making "mistakes" and that I think a better analysis is to assume that each side will present their most effective case by the time of trial.

5.4 ROBERT A. CREO: FROM NO MAN'S LAND TO COMMON GROUND: ESTABLISHING THE BARGAINING MODEL

[**Editor's Note**: *This section consists of an article authored by attorney and mediator Robert A. Creo is reproduced and reformatted here with his permission.*]

Often there is a "zone of settlement" where parties' true final positions meet or overlap. This occurs when each party meets its individual goals by satisfying an undisclosed "reservation price" via bargaining. Harvard Law School Professor Robert H. Mnookin and other commentators have postulated that a number of cultural, cognitive and other strategic barriers exist that often preclude settlement despite the existence of a zone of settlement or common ground.

There are, however, many disputes and negotiations where there is no pre-existing zone of settlement that can be traveled to, by negotiating either directly or via mediation. Borrowing from the military, the parties have a gap in their final positions - a negotiator's No Man's Land fraught with peril and danger. In most cases, parties are reluctant to publicly approach their final position since they correctly assume this will place them at the edge of No Man's Land with nowhere to go since retreat is impossible once ground is yielded publicly. The negotiator does not want to be exposed to their adversary who is safely on their own turf. To avoid this, bargainers stall within their own boundaries, far from the edge of No Man's Land.

In cases where there is a true zone of settlement, the mediator's intervention assists the parties in identifying this zone and removing the strategic barriers inherent in the creation and claiming of value in traditional negotiation models.

A pure facilitative approach by the mediator in the context of a traditional bargaining model is efficient and perhaps the model preferred by the parties; the mediator is a passive player in this trilateral negotiation. Facilitative approaches and tools should always make apparent the pre-existing zone of settlement while allowing the mediator to avoid placing the parties at a specific place in the zone. The parties must be free to negotiate to their own final resting ground in cases of unidentified overlap.

When a No Man's Land is real, the mediator should assume a more aggressive posture, since the mediator is actively–not passively--assisting the parties to create and claim value. The mediator is an integral part of converting No Man's Land into common ground since it is highly unlikely the parties will succeed without the intervention of a third negotiator.

5.4.1 The traditional demand-and-offer model

The traditional model of two-party bargaining, including cases involving multiple defendants, consists of one party making an initial proposal (referred to here as the "demand") and the other responding with a counterproposal. If the initial demand is deemed to be too high, there may be no counterproposal and bargaining often ceases for a long hiatus since the "demander" does not want to bid against itself and usually declines to modify the initial demand.

Negotiation theory commentators recognize this phenomenon and have written about initial positions and cognitive behavior of choice and decision-making. For example, Harvard University Prof. Howard Raiffa noted:

> If you open first, and if your opponents are ill prepared, you might influence their perception of their own reservation price by your opening offer; your opening offer anchors their thinking about the value to themselves. Be aware of this anchoring phenomenon if the situation is reversed.

> Don't get locked in by talking about your opponents extreme offer; don't let their offer be the vantage point for subsequent modifications. The best strategy in this case is to either break off negotiations until they modify their offer, or quickly counter with an offer of your own. When two offers are on the table, the midpoint is a natural focal point, so think about this when you make an initial counteroffer "The Art and Science of Negotiation," Harvard University Press (1982).

In a face-to-face bargaining session, what is perceived to be an extreme or unreasonable opening demand often produces "The Walk Away," or, as this author prefers to call it, the beau geste. A dramatic action which symbolizes a person's triumph, boldness or resolve is called a beau geste. Just like in direct bargaining, every mediation is subject to termination by the beau geste. This is when parties break off negotiations in a dramatic manner by actually walking away from the bargaining table, often with stinging accusations directed against all within a long earshot, about bad faith or wasting time.

5.4.2 How to avoid the beau geste

Parties retain a mediator because of a past beau geste or the real fear of bargaining going into a downward spiral because of unworkable proposals and counterproposals. The parties elect mediation to avoid the beau geste, and if it happens anyway despite the mediator's best efforts, it ultimately is perceived to be the mediator's fault by all or some of the participants. The beau geste is bad for the process and especially bad for the mediator's reputation and future business. Care in establishing the bargaining model minimizes the mediator being caught in the beau geste trap.

Mediation is a trilateral negotiation. It is naive to believe that the intervention of mediation and the mediator has no impact on the relationship between the parties. This is why many experienced mediators believe that the concept of a pure facilitative model, and traditional views of impartiality and neutrality of the legal system, are inappropriate paradigms (See, e.g., Daniel Bowling and David Hoffman, "Bringing Peace into the Room: The Personal Qualities of the Mediator and Their Impact on the Mediation," 16 Negotiation Journal 5, pp. 5-28, (January 2000)).

Physicist Werner Heisenberg in the 1920s postulated the "Uncertainty Principle" which states that any observation, even if passive, influences the behavior of particles. In the social sciences, this is called the "Hawthorne Effect," which describes changes people make in their behavior when they realize they are being observed. The Bowling and Hoffman article notes that some mediators have observed what they describe as "negative Hawthorne effects" when parties seem to negotiate less productively when a third party is present.

Mediators influence and are influenced by the process they are not separate or aloof from conflict systems. The degree of activism, and the mediator's level of transparency, are choices which must be made on a deliberate basis and communicated, expressly or impliedly, to the parties at appropriate times. The mediator style, approaches, personal values, and qualities will create dynamics that ultimately control the bargaining interaction between the parties.

Mediation is complex and dynamic. It is not linear nor static. Mediators must be cognizant of many aspects of conflict, decision-making in the context or "shadow" of the law, and principles common to social sciences, such as linguistics, communication modalities, cognitive behavior and the impact of culture and values of the participants, including the mediator. Lawyers tend to pigeonhole behavior into rational constructs even though cognitive behaviorists have identified numerous "irrational" choices or bias in objective thought processes.

Detailed consideration of these subjective areas and their interplay with mediation are the subjects for other professionals or for other days (See Richard Birke, "Settlement Psychology: When Decision-Making Processes Fail," 18 *Alternatives* 203 (December 2000)). The experienced mediator, however, ignores an interdisciplinary approach not only at his or her own risk, but at the peril of the parties.

The following basic tenets of practice should be considered by the mediator of bilateral negotiations that have been converted into trilateral negotiations by the process's entry into mediation. These heuristics apply to cases that are primarily of an economic nature, as opposed to interpersonal conflict such as public policy, community and domestic relations conflict.

5.4.3 Common sense rules for mediators

1. The Mediator Presents Proposals in Caucus. There is great risk in the parties exchanging proposals in a joint session. Caucus is the heart of mediation, and what many parties view as the key role of the mediator.

2. Sometimes It Makes Sense to Deviate from No. 1 to Let an Advocate Articulate a Proposal Directly to the Other Advocate and/or Their Side. At times parties want to make a proposal that the mediator believes will be counterproductive. The mediator should strive to create distance between the mediator and the proposal itself by avoiding the risk that the party will irrationally slay the mediator as messenger. This allows the mediator to step back in with minimal harm to the mediator's credibility and rapport, and minimal risk to the mediation process itself. If the party responds with a beau geste, it is easier for the mediator to excuse the other side and work in caucus to attempt to avoid impasse.

3. Present Proposals in the Clients' Presence, Not Just to the Advocate for Presentation to the Client Outside the Mediator's Presence. But if the mediator has a good relationship with the advocates, her or she may tell them privately what the proposal will be to avoid surprise and allow the advocates to prepare for a reaction. A preview to the advocate may be helpful if there is an indication or belief that their own recommendation or expectations are lower than their client's or they have client control issues.

4. Convey Self-Confidence, Control and Optimism. Unless the parties have expressly elected a pure facilitative or transformative model, the mediator was retained for this purpose. Death of hope results in impasse. Look people in the eyes with an appropriate facial expression when making presentations of proposals. Do not look at notes or away from participants since this may lessen the mediator's credibility and role in the process. The Bowling and Hoffman article contends that "the effectiveness of our interventions often arises not from their forcefulness but instead their authenticity."

5. Use Preambles and Foundations. Without being dramatic, condition the parties for what is coming with appropriate introductory comments or questions. Advise them what stage they are in of the bargaining model being used. One mediator in his own folksy manner tells people that the offer may be a "smelly fish" but it is a fish nevertheless and to focus on the fish itself and not the smell.

6. Present Proposals Orally Without Writing, Except for True Drop Dead Positions. It avoids the "etched in stone" mentality until true final positions are revealed or exposed.

7. Establish Any Preconditions or Unusual Terms and Boilerplate Prior to Making Substantive Proposals. In opening remarks, state that the confidentiality of any settlement obtained will be presumed unless the parties expressly bargain for it by raising it in the first proposal. Depending on the subject claim's area, other boilerplate assumptions are listed at the outset and the parties are advised to raise deviations at the start of the bargaining stage.

8. Be Observant. It is critical to observe body language, who reacts, and in what manner, while not unintentionally giving anything back to the advocates and the parties.

9. Assume Ownership of Proposals When Appropriate. There are no pure facilitative mediators. Despite the mediator's best efforts, his or her hand will be tipped unintentionally, or the parties will create perceptions or misperceptions of what the mediator really thinks. Jump in with opinions and evaluations in an appropriate manner, consistent with the tone of the opening statement, mediation philosophy, expectations of the ADR vendor/advocates/parties and "temperature" of the room.

10. Excuse Yourself to Let the Parties Discuss the Proposal in Private. This recognizes the principle of party self-determination and empowerment. If the mediator pushes too hard, it will backfire or result in a settlement that is not durable.

11. Use Joint Sessions, Caucus, Sub-caucus or One-on-One Sessions as Appropriate. Do not get mechanical or linear in approach. Mediation is an art and not a science. Be flexible and creative to respond to the environment as it exists, not as someone intended it to exist.

12. Write Your Own Rules Reflecting Your "Personal Power" or "Force of Personality." Jeffrey Kottler is quoted in the Bowling and Hoffman article in a discussion of great therapists, noting that they commonly "radiate positive energy. They are upbeat, enthusiastic, witty, and quick on their feet. They have good voices and are highly expressive in using them ... They are being themselves in allowing the force and power of their personalities to guide what they do. All the theorists invented styles that made it possible to play on their strengths."

5.4.4 Specific bargaining models – standard approaches

The mediator must choose a specific approach, tool or technique when it is time to play the main act and climatic scenes of the mediation drama. Here are some of the bargaining models to consider and modify for a particular case or circumstance.

5.4.4.1 The auction dossier

This is a bilateral symmetrical process to establish fair-market value. It is a traditional approach of demand, counterproposal and trade-off, or a pattern of concessions. There is an expectation that parties will gravitate to the midpoint; some negotiators consciously respond with a target midpoint as a goal or bottom line. The midpoint phenomenon is only valid as both parties approach the "zone of settlement" from the same ranges or if they have started from the exact same distance as the hypothetical midpoint in their opening positions.

Strengths

- Meets the reasonable expectations of traditional bargaining.

- Integrates well into a facilitative mediator approach.

- Predictable, and should be easy to implement even by those who are challenged by math.

- Based in the cultural norm of "reciprocity" and therefore has reason, justice, mom and apple pie and the American way in its favor.

- Allows parties to save face.

Weaknesses

- Does not work well in mediation since it is designed for bilateral communications outside the presence of a third party. If this would work, they would not have hired a mediator.

- No role for non-economic and relationship value, apology, and other interests that are difficult to translate into dollars.

- Subject to manipulation by the parties and their advocates who can hide their true "reservation price" under the guise of a "splitting-the-difference" principle of reciprocity.

- If the "demand" is high or otherwise made for "anchoring" purposes, a huge concession must be made before the auction can begin. This may not be a problem for the advocate, but is problematic for the client. Despite the advocate's best efforts, the "unreasonable" opening position has in fact anchored the client to an elevated aspiration level.

The mediator's choices are straightforward: play the auction game or have the parties consent to a different bargaining model.

5.4.4.2 Take it or leave it dossier

George Boulware was the labor representative responsible for collective bargaining for General Electric in the 1950s and 1960s. He developed a system of making one reasonable and fair offer to the union on a "take it or leave it" basis. When challenged by the union, the U.S. Supreme Court held that this was an unfair labor practice and not an appropriate manner of bargaining even if in fact the initial offer ultimately would have been reached via give-and-take bargaining. The Court made any approach other than the "auction" mode illegal in the context of collective bargaining.

Strengths

- Clarity.
- Predictability.
- Credibility … if credible.
- Works if backed by sufficient leverage.

Weaknesses

- Runs against the cultural expectations of reciprocity and bargaining.

- Makes future bargaining unlikely since issue now becomes the credibility of the negotiator, and it makes people the problem.

- Invites an opposing harsh response since the opposite bargainer is unempowered and can only save self-esteem by saying no.

- Works only if backed by the perception of sufficient leverage of the offeror.

- Deflects focus away from interests to positions and competitive, rather than cooperative, modes of resolution.

Just because it doesn't work as a labor bargaining model doesn't mean that you won't be faced with it. If as a mediator you encounter one party who discloses an apparently immovable number as its "best reservation price" in an unequivocal or credible manner, the following options exist:

- Explore with the other side in caucus the possibility of the offer, or one close to it, being accepted, and

- If there is no reasonable probability of it settling the case, then

- Resolve to resolve another day - adjourn the mediation without any new proposal by either party. This avoids the beau geste and leaves open the possibility of future dialogue if one or both parties revisit their positions. It also calls any bluffs by one or both of the parties.

- Disclaim any ownership in the immovable number - have the inflexible advocate present their best number in person, with its rationale, to the opposing advocate - and expect an impasse. This avoids ownership by the mediator and maintains your credibility with both parties for future cases.

- Ten percent challenge - move the number at least ten percent in the direction of the opposing party and ask if they would walk away from that number if it would close the case. Again, do this in front of everybody on their side of the table.

- Evaluate--If you have an evaluation that differs from the immovable number, lay it out to the inflexible party in caucus to both advocate and clients. Leave the room and sit alone until they come to get you.

If, however, the number is close enough to be viable, then, in no particular order:

- Play the reciprocity auction dynamic: advise the party with the immovable number that it will be more productive not to race to the reservation price but to engage in a traditional auction. Or advise the party to hold an amount or percentage in reserve, and to make a firm offer with the preamble that it is intended to settle the case without a counteroffer but it is not being framed in an insulting take-it-or-leave-it manner.

- Settle it in your pocket first: Structure the communications in such a manner that you have obtained private acceptance on a confidential basis of each party's immovable number. Keep the two acceptances in separate mental pockets and then bring them together in a public manner by obtaining requisite authority to commit publicly to the number.

- Advice and consent: create a sham pattern of bargaining with the parties' tacit or express consent. Advise the parties each step of the way what to publicly put forth to the other side, with the offers and counters predetermined and calculated by you to lead to the immovable number that you know will settle the case.

- Mediator proposal: If you have two immovable numbers within a small percentage or amount of each other, then choose a number somewhere between the two--not necessarily the midpoint - and make it a mediator's proposal. Often parties can save face by accepting your proposal since it avoids reactive devaluation and the idea that one party weakened or caved in.

5.4.5 Specific bargaining models - soft approaches

5.4.5.1 Roaming the range of the "zeros dossier"

People are fascinated with numbers that end in zero. Marketing has long recognized this by pricing and advertising consumer products and services with the numbers ending in nine.

This message seems to have been lost on mediators since hourly and per diem fees always end in a zero or a five. There also are breakpoints that are common psychological barriers and resting points. Many times, especially in personal injury and other claims handled on a contingent basis, these are divisible by three to end in a zero. These numbers obtain even greater significance. Key monetary amounts are:

$50,000; $75,000; $100,000; $150,000; $200,000; $250,000; $300,000; $450,000; $500,000; $600,000; $750,000; $900,000; $1 million; $1.2 million; $1.5 million; $2 million; $2.5 million; $3 million $5 million and $10 million.

People also like to frame outcomes in terms of "quarter million" or "half million" dollar target goals. Regis Philbin does not focus on who wants to be a "third of a millionaire," but talks about the quarter or half-million levels. Negotiators are drawn to these numbers like iron filings to magnets.

The mediator can explore in a soft manner, in caucus, numbers that may work for a party without pushing them to disclose their bottom line. This is useful when you believe the advocate is "gaming" you and not being forthcoming when expressing his or her position.

Mediator Peter Contruzzi of Massachusetts, in the Spring 2000 ABA Dispute Resolution Section publication, Dispute Resolution Magazine, recounts a statement made by an advocate at the 1999 Dispute Resolution meeting in Boston that advocates should not be candid with the mediator in disclosing true positions. "Don't do it! I tried it once and got burned by the mediator. All he used it for was to try to leverage me further. Never again."

When in this situation, the mediator can talk about ranges in five, six or seven figures or set other parameters. For example, if parties are far apart, with, say, seven-figure demands and five-figure offers, attempt to move them both publicly to vague "six figures" settlement commitments.

For example, a plaintiff has demanded $1.5 million and the offer in response was $25,000. By a series of simple questions, the mediator can have both parties acknowledge that there is no reasonable expectation of either party that the case will settle in either five figures or seven figures. The mediator has now moved them publicly to $999,000 and $101,000.

This has begun a "mutual decompression and inflation" process. The next step is to explore in confidence if the parties are each thinking "low, mid or high" six figures, without initially defining these three terms. Real movement often can be obtained without committing parties to specific concessions or a specific new immovable number of a public nature.

A variation of this "soft number" approach is to create the first number that establishes a range within a "Block of Zeros." For example: the parties in one case were publicly stuck hundreds of thousands of dollars apart but privately each indicated there was "a little" movement left. The plaintiff was asked to make public the following commitment: "No number starting with a two will be considered - but a number starting with a three will settle the case."

The defense indicated that no number starting with a four or higher would be considered. The dispute was narrowed from one of a $950,000 public demand and a counteroffer by the defense of $150,000 to much less of a public gap, based upon the fact that both parties were willing to continue negotiations once a possible zone of settlement between $300,000 and $400,000 was established as a "possibility to be considered" by each party.

After additional probing in private caucus, the true gap of only $50,000 became known to the mediator based upon confidential communications. Higher and lower numbers were discussed as possibilities in caucus. After more give and take, the plaintiff publicly committed to $350,000 in response to a new offer of $250,000 made by defendants.

This was the true preexisting reservation price of both sides; no zone of settlement existed without strong intervention by the mediator to create common ground from No Man's Land. The case ultimately settled at a number between these two final public positions. The parties were moved closer by discarding numbers that were unacceptable to one or the other, yet keeping hope alive by discussing ranges and soft numbers as a "possibility" in private caucus.

5.4.5.2 The "what if?"

In conjunction with attempting to establish a range, a common mediator approach is to explore hypothetical numbers that are floated by the mediator in caucus. This can be done with one or both parties, and in a serial or parallel manner. It can be the direct approach of stating "Will $X settle the case?" Or "How would you respond to a proposal of $X?" Follow with "May I disclose that to the other side?" if you think that will be productive by increasing hope and not dashing it.

5.4.5.3 Anticipation

A variation of "What If?" is "Anticipation," which involves the concept of testing the perceptions of the parties against each other in caucus. The mediator asks the parties what they anticipate the opposition is looking for and what concession pattern the parties plan to use. This often involves speculation on two or three numbers: their "painful" number, a "comfortable" number and their "joyous" number. Often the parties have a misperception about these soft numbers that can be used by the mediator to gain momentum when the time is right.

5.4.5.4 Handicapping

This is a technique popularized in the early 1990s by mediators when faced with parties who take a quantitative and risk analysis approach to dispute resolution. It creates a range of expectations with the mediator placing a percentage chance of success to each number based upon the situation at the mediation. For example, the mediator may say to a defendant in caucus, "the number $100,000 has a zero percent chance of success while $125,000 has a twenty-five percent handicap, $150,000 has a fifty percent chance of success and $175,000 a ninety percent chance of being accepted." In the plaintiff caucus, the mediator may express the odds similarly, but differently: "the amount of money which you may obtain today is a ninety-five percent chance of $100,000, a seventy-five percent chance of $125,000, a fifty percent chance of $150,000 and a zero percent chance of a figure of $190,000 or above. This has both parties thinking a zone of settlement of $125,000 to $175,000 is feasible.

Obviously, both parties are thinking of numbers closer to their side of the zone, but that is okay for the mediator, because it has moved them to a point where the amount of money necessary to split the difference is a less painful leap.

5.4.5.5 The corkscrew

In limited circumstances, where the parties have trust and previous good experience with the mediator, one approach is to have them engage in blind bidding without disclosing the current bid of either party to the other one. This effect is similar to a corkscrew, which goes in slowly, and blindly, until it is time to pull it out, suddenly, and smell the sweet aroma of success!

The situation is where the parties have stated public positions which are apart, but neither one has closed the door on further movement. In fact, both have indicated they would move substantially but do not believe in the good faith of the other party to reciprocate in an appropriate manner. They believe they will be "gamed" if they act in good faith.

The mediator approaches each party in a serial and parallel manner to solicit their successive bids and only discloses that the other party is still actively bidding and there is movement toward each other. When the parties are almost on top of each other, the mediator either discloses the gap and suggests splitting the difference or suggests an obvious number to each in caucus to obtain settlement consent.

For example:

	Plaintiff	Defense
Public Positions	$325,000	$175,000
Mediator Corkscrew:	295,000	200,000
	265,000	225,000
	250,000	235,000
	245,000	240,000

This case could settle for $242,500 to avoid overlap risk.

5.4.5.6 Double blind mediator proposal

Mediators have used a double blind approach, which was invented by a mediator unknown to this author years ago. In its simplest form, the mediator proposes a number orally to both parties and asks them to give only a yes or no response. It is not proper to respond with a counterproposal or different number. If the mediator receives two yes responses, the case settles. Anyone giving a no response, is not entitled to know the response of the other side.

This approach is often varied by the mediator picking a number that he or she is confident at least one side will agree to if it settles the case. That is a comparatively easy "yes," and it is followed by a request for permission to disclose it to the undecided party. Often, the certainty of closure works and at a minimum, it shifts the responsibility, and risk, to the undecided party. Do not give up because there is one "no." Opinions change, and deals shift, often slightly, but enough to reach a face-saving resolution.

5.4.5.7 Contuzzi safety deposit box

Massachusetts mediator Peter Contuzzi uses a technique as a prelude to the double blind mediator proposal used by many mediators. Contuzzi creates a deadline by allotting a specific amount of time to the mediation and as time expires on the resolution game clock, he advises them:

> I will separate you one last time in a few minutes and ask you to put your final bottom line number into the Safety Deposit Box. Please give careful thought to your number, because it will be used by me in several ways. These numbers will not be disclosed unless, as happens occasionally, they are the same (Peter Contuzzi, "Should Parties tell Mediators Their Bottom Line?" 6 Dispute Resolution Magazine 3 at pp. 30-32 (American Bar Association Section of Dispute Resolution, Spring 2000)).

If the numbers overlap, writes Contuzzi, the midpoint becomes the settlement amount. If there is any significant gap, the parties are told that the gap exists without learning of the other side's number or the gap size. Then, the parties are told that they may 1) keep their number confidential; 2) disclose their number; or 3) agree to disclose only if the other side agrees.

If the parties are close, the mediator doesn't mutually disclose the Safety Deposit Box numbers but instead adopts a number which is usually not the midpoint between the two bottom lines to recommend to the parties. The mediator is transparent about this intent and tells the parties, as Contuzzi writes:

> Sometimes, I believe the final number of one party is significantly more fair than the other. Then I adopt that same number as my own number in my proposal. In fact, my preference is to do this in order to provide an extra incentive for you to be as candid as possible when putting your number in the Safety Deposit Box ... Sometimes, however, I develop my own number.

He then uses the double blind approach.

5.4.5.8. Blind trust method for multiparty claims

This is a complicated method devised by the author of this article to obtain positions and reservation prices of defendants without the necessity of disclosure to the mediator (See 17 Alternatives 145 (September 1999)). See Section 4.2.2, *supra*.

These bargaining models aren't exhaustive. Many experienced mediators have invented or modified approaches to bargaining models or specific impasse-breaking techniques, it has happened with a great deal of advanced planning and on the spur of the moment. There is substantial opportunity for creativity, flexibility and growth in mediation approaches.

5.5 HON. MORTON DENLOW: BREAKING IMPASSES IN SETTLEMENT CONFERENCES – FIVE TECHNIQUES FOR RESOLUTION

[**Editor's Note:** *This section consists of an article authored by the Honorable Morton Denlow, United States Magistrate Judge and published in the Fall 2000 issue of The American Bar Association's Judges' Journal. It is reproduced and reformatted here with the permission of the author and the publisher.*]

Being able to break impasses between parties is often the true test of a judge during settlement conferences. First, a judge must evaluate the situation to determine whether the deadlock can indeed be overcome or whether it should be permitted to remain. If the stalemate exists because information is lacking or settlement authority has not been extended to the parties present, the judge will want to allow additional time to achieve a successful resolution. If the impasse is a result of honest differences between the parties or a matter of negotiation strategy, a judge can use a number of techniques to affect the standstill and ensure speedy and satisfactory progress for the parties.

To achieve settlement, a judge should not be afraid to adopt an active role. He or she may need to shift from the position of a neutral facilitator who serves as a catalyst to help the two sides communicate to the position of an active participant who suggests possible settlement terms and voices an opinion about the feasibility of settlement. This involves discussions of monetary considerations including the overall costs of litigation and the relative risks to the parties. Granted, before taking this step, the judge must clear it with all parties involved. Usually, however, if the parties truly desire to settle, they will appreciate this proactive stance, welcoming one of the five approaches that are discussed below. Each technique is considered distinctly, but the judge can combine and/or tailor them to achieve settlement in the individual scenario at hand.

5.5.1 Creating a range

Parties typically are not in the same ballpark when they initially exchange settlement proposals. This is sometimes due to legitimate differences in their evaluations of the case's merits. These differences result in a desire to negotiate aggressively, with the lawyers hoping to achieve better results for their clients and fearing the relinquishment of too much too soon. A judge, having listened closely to parties who have expressed a sincere desire to settle but who, despite extensive negotiation, still find themselves in two different ballparks, can employ a "creating a range" technique to determine whether settlement is possible. The following case study demonstrates how this can be applied.

Case Study 1: The Leaky Building. The plaintiff's condominium association filed suit against the defendant contractor, alleging the contractor improperly applied an exterior waterproof coating to the concrete building, resulting in water damage. In the complaint, the plaintiff sought two million dollars in damages. Pursuant to my standing order requiring parties to exchange written demands and offers before the settlement conference (see page 8), the plaintiff had demanded $1,700,000 and the defendant had offered $50,000.

The initial settlement conference, in which I played a strictly facilitative role, resulted in slight progress. By the end of the session, the plaintiff had reduced its settlement demand to $1,125,000 and the defendant had increased its offer to $350,000. The parties then agreed that an additional exchange of information and discovery would be useful before engaging in a second settlement conference. We convened a second settlement conference several months later, again with little progress after several hours. The defendant authorized me to communicate a new offer of $500,000, to which the plaintiff responded with a reduced demand of $1,100,000. In separate caucuses, each party stated it was approaching its limit.

In a joint session, I informed the parties of the apparent impasse created by the $1,100,000 demand and the $500,000 offer. I asked them if they would permit me to suggest a settlement range to determine whether it made sense to continue negotiations. I insisted that this process would be governed by the following ground rules: (1) the settlement range would be explained to the parties in a joint session; (2) each party would then meet separately outside of my presence to discuss whether it would be willing to continue discussions in the suggested range; (3) each party would respond to me separately on a piece of paper indicating "yes" or "no"; (4) if either party responded "no," the conference would immediately terminate; (5) if both sides answered "yes," negotiations would continue; and (6) it would not be disclosed that one party responded "yes" unless both sides responded in the affirmative.

After both parties agreed to this approach, I recommended a $200,000 range of $650,000 to $850,000, large enough, I hoped, to attract both sides, but small enough to make settlement feasible. I explained to the parties why this range made sense for business and financial reasons, summarizing many of the points we had discussed in the separate caucuses.

The range took into account information learned from the parties that could be justified to both sides. The $200,000 range made settlement feasible if both sides responded "yes." It would not have advanced the process significantly if too large a range was suggested, say $550,000 to $1,050,000. Similarly, it was premature to offer the parties a single number because they were too far apart, and neither side had expressed a desire to make a substantial move. A specific figure would have likely led to a rejection by at least one side and could have prematurely terminated discussions. The proposed range of $650,000 to $850,000 tested whether the plaintiff was prepared to settle for less than $1,000,000 and whether the defendant would move significantly toward $750,000. This would determine whether the parties had the flexibility that could lead to a settlement that day.

The parties went to separate rooms to discuss the range. After approximately ten minutes, each delivered a "yes" on paper. I then brought the parties together and informed them of the positive responses. We continued to negotiate and settled at $725,000 within forty-five minutes, complete with a payment schedule and security. In the event that one or both sides had responded "no," I would have explained that because both sides had not agreed to proceed, the talks would terminate for that day. At no time would the fact that one party said "yes" be disclosed.

This procedure creates a no-risk environment for both sides. If the parties are truly firm at their prior figures, the settlement conference terminates without wasting any more time. If only one party is prepared to negotiate within the range, it is not prejudiced in its negotiating position. Given the no-risk nature of the process, parties are quite receptive, particularly where a substantial chasm exists.

This method of breaking an impasse provides the following advantages: (1) it saves time; (2) it preserves the parties' settlement postures in the event the range is not agreed upon; (3) it does not commit the judge to a specific number; (4) it leaves the parties in control of the settlement process; and (5) it requires the parties to seriously consider whether to proceed or terminate the settlement process. This approach is recommended primarily in cases with large dollar amounts where significant gaps still exist after lengthy negotiations.

One disadvantage is that this technique can lead to termination of settlement discussions and therefore should not be used until a clear impasse exists. As long as the parties are making substantial movement, setting a range is not needed. Also, creating a range that appears weighted heavily toward one side may anger the other. Finally, because both parties must agree to the process before it is implemented, either side can veto the process and prevent its use, which may be viewed as either an advantage or disadvantage.

5.5.2 Recommending a specific number

Although my settlement conferences are always begun as a facilitative mediation, I am not reluctant to suggest a single settlement number when an impasse arises and both parties desire my input. The following case study demonstrates this technique.

Case Study 2: An Employment Discrimination Claim. The plaintiff filed an action alleging a violation of the Americans with Disabilities Act for wrongful termination and retaliatory discharge. Although the plaintiff had been employed by the defendant for thirteen years with a fairly good work history, since her termination she had been out of work for two years and was unable to find a comparable job. Based on itemized damages of $60,000 in back pay and $15,000 in front pay, plus attorneys' fees, the plaintiff had made a written settlement demand before the settlement conference of $75,000 and reinstatement. The defendant had responded with a $5,000 settlement offer. The case was in the early stages of discovery when we held the settlement conference.

Limited progress was made during the several hours of joint meetings and separate caucuses. The defendant evinced no interest in reinstating the plaintiff, and the parties were left with a discussion of money. The case did not appear suitable for summary judgment because a clear factual dispute existed regarding what was said at the time the plaintiff was terminated and the reasons for her termination. We reached an impasse after the plaintiff reduced her demand to $65,000 and the defendant increased its offer to $20,000. In separate caucuses, the parties clearly stated they would not budge.

In a joint session, I explained that neither party seemed interested in continuing negotiations but that I would recommend a settlement figure if they wished. As with the "creating a range" case, I had specific conditions: (1) the suggested amount would be explained to the parties in a joint session along with the rationale for why the number should be considered reasonable by both sides; (2) the parties would have three business days to consider the recommendation; (3) by the close of business on the third day, they would each send me a fax with a one-sentence acceptance or rejection of the recommendation; (4) if only one side accepted, the other would not be advised of this; (5) we would discuss all other settlement terms (e.g., releases, dismissal of litigation, confidentiality, etc.) before the number would be disclosed; and (6) both parties must consent to the process before proceeding. After several minutes of private conferences, both parties agreed to proceed. We then promptly resolved the standard settlement issues, leaving only the dollar amount for resolution.

I recommended that the parties settle the case for $45,000, explaining that my reasoning was based on issues such as litigation risks, litigation costs, and other factors that had been discussed in separate party caucuses. After presenting a balanced explanation, I instructed the parties that, while neither was happy with the number, they should take several days to consider it and advise me of their decision. Three days later, both parties faxed acceptance of the recommendation and the case was settled.

When monetary differences are small, it may be useful to take advantage of the momentum created and require immediate responses from the parties at the conference. However, where the differences are substantial, an additional three days to reflect on the court's recommendation helps facilitate agreement in many cases.

This method also gives the parties a no-risk opportunity to settle. Because they are not required to accept the number, they can reap the benefit of a judge's recommendation without compromising their settlement positions. In this example, if the plaintiff had accepted the recommendation and the defendant had rejected it, the plaintiff's bargaining position would have been protected. The defendant would not have discovered that the plaintiff was willing to accept $45,000, and would only have known that the plaintiff's last demand was $65,000.

This technique is particularly useful when one side does not wish to exercise its settlement authority at the settlement conference and would prefer to discuss the judge's recommendation with the powers "back home" before making a final decision. Although my standing settlement order requires parties present at the conference to have full settlement authority, and although I confirm this during opening comments, designated representatives are sometimes reluctant to exercise that authority for fear of how they will be perceived at their offices. Parties often appreciate the judge making a recommendation, which can carry considerable weight in the deliberations. The procedure is optional; therefore, it should be made clear to the parties that the judge will not suggest a number if they do not both want to hear it.

This method is not without disadvantages. If the court does not make a clear presentation explaining why the suggested dollar amount should be considered by both sides, a party may perceive the judge as arbitrary or biased. A recommendation that focuses on the costs of litigation and the risks involved enables the judge to make a recommendation while avoiding any specific prediction as to the outcome.

My experience tells me that this process is effective in breaking impasses approximately fifty percent of the time. Even though the parties are deadlocked at the conference itself, the additional time to reflect and the court's input assist the parties in taking a second, perhaps more sober, look at their case.

5.5.3 Splitting the difference

Parties frequently reach a stalemate while relatively close to a settlement figure. Under these circumstances, where no objective basis exists for recommending a specific number, splitting the difference may overcome the deadlock. The questions of when, who, and how to raise the topic of splitting the difference creates a number of possibilities. The following two examples illustrate the "splitting the difference" technique to achieve a settlement, the first by means of separate caucuses and the second in a joint session.

Case Study 3a: A Civil Rights Case. The plaintiff, an attorney, filed a civil rights action for false arrest and malicious prosecution, claiming that police officers had planted narcotics on him while he was in the lockup on an unrelated charge. The drug charge was ultimately dismissed, and the plaintiff sued the officers.

The plaintiff's initial settlement demand of $75,000 had been countered by the defendants' initial offer of $20,000. In the course of conference shuttle diplomacy, the plaintiff subsequently reduced his demand to $50,000 while the defendants increased their offer to $30,000. At that point, both sides stood firm.

When I evaluated the position of each party, I assumed that the plaintiff might be willing to move further, having come down from $75,000 to $50,000. In a separate caucus, the defendants had shown only a slight willingness to move upward from $30,000. Based on this, $40,000 appeared to be a number that should seriously be considered by both sides. In a separate meeting with the plaintiff's side, I asked them to consider splitting the difference at $40,000, to which the plaintiff agreed. The attorney did not want this fact revealed to the defendants unless the defendants were also willing to pay $40,000.

In a separate meeting with the defendants' side, they were advised that I had requested the plaintiff to seriously consider $40,000 and was now asking them to do the same. The defendants also agreed to pay $40,000 but did not want this fact revealed unless the plaintiff would accept it. The defendants authorized me to advise the plaintiff that they would pay $40,000, but only after the plaintiff confirmed he would accept the $40,000. After I returned to the plaintiff's camp, he once again confirmed his willingness to accept $40,000. At that point, the plaintiff was informed that we had a deal, and the defendants were brought back in to summarize the settlement terms.

The principal advantages of discussing the concept of splitting the difference in separate caucuses are: (1) it avoids one party revealing to the other that it is willing to split the difference unless both parties have agreed, thus preserving the parties' settlement positions in the event no agreement is reached; (2) it reflects an attempt at compromise raised by the judge by which both parties can save face; and (3) if one party makes it clear that it will not split the difference, the court is free to shift gears to adopt a different strategy.

However, splitting the difference has the danger of placing the judge in the position of recommending a number that may alienate one of the parties. Therefore, when raising the possibility of this approach, it is generally helpful to frame the discussion to each side separately as, "What would your reaction be if the other side would agree to split the difference?" In this way, the number does not represent a recommendation by the court; rather, it is a testing of each side's readiness to compromise.

Case Study 3b: An Employment Discrimination Case. In this case, the plaintiff brought an action alleging wrongful termination due to racial discrimination, seeking back pay of $50,000, compensatory damages of $25,000, and attorneys' fees of $20,000. Before the settlement conference, the plaintiff had made a settlement demand of $70,000, to which the defendant had offered $22,000.

During the settlement conference, substantial progress toward settlement was made. The plaintiff's demand was gradually reduced to $40,000 while the defendant's offer increased to $30,000. At that point, both sides were able to agree on nonmonetary issues, converting the termination to a resignation and reinstatement, and cleansing the plaintiff's personnel files. However, there was no further movement on money. In a separate caucus with the defendant, the defendant's representative revealed that he did not have authority to move beyond $30,000, despite my standing order requiring full authority. Both parties desired to settle, but neither side would, or could, budge.

The parties were brought together in a joint session to review the progress we had made on both the financial and nonfinancial issues. After asking the parties if they would like my recommendation on the financial issues, both consented. I recommended they split the difference, to which both sides promptly agreed, with a commitment by the defendant's counsel to recommend the amount to his superior and an expectation of final approval by the next day. Approval was received and the case settled for $35,000.

When a relatively small amount is involved and one of the parties appears not to have full authority to settle, splitting the difference based on the court's recommendation in a joint session enables the party to go back and assure the decision maker that the case will settle if the party goes along with the court's recommendation. The judge has persuasive powers in urging a compromise over small differences. By suggesting the parties split the difference, both sides save face.

If one party agrees and the other does not, the party who agreed may feel taken advantage of. Therefore, this method should be used only where the differences that separate the parties are quite small. It is one thing to let the other side know you are willing to split the difference between $30,000 and $40,000 but something else to agree to split the difference between $1 million and $3 million when the other side fails to reciprocate.

5.5.4 Clarifying objective facts

Many times differences in settlement demands and offers reflect distinctions in the respective parties' versions of the facts. To the extent that the issues involved are subjective - for example, parties' disagreement as to what was said in a particular conversation - it is difficult to bridge the gap. In these instances, focusing the parties on how a jury would perceive the issue is very helpful, allowing them to factor this into their litigation risk rather than trying to persuade them to agree on who is right and who is wrong.

Sometimes differences exist because of a misperception of an objective fact by one side. The following example shows how clarifying an objective fact can break an impasse.

Case Study 4: A Pregnancy Discrimination Claim. The plaintiff claimed that she had been wrongfully terminated because she was pregnant. The defendant contended that the plaintiff was terminated because of substandard performance on the job and excessive absenteeism. Based on monetary damages of approximately $6,500, the plaintiff had made a demand for $10,000 before the settlement conference, which was countered by the defendant's offer of $3,000. During the settlement conference, the parties reached an impasse when the plaintiff's demand was reduced to $6,500 and the defendant's offer stood firm at $5,000. In separate meetings, a dispute arose regarding whether the plaintiff had received $500 in unemployment compensation. The parties came together to discuss whether the plaintiff had in fact received $500 in unemployment compensation. Once the plaintiff acknowledged that she had previously received the $500, she reduced her demand to $6,000 and the defendant promptly agreed to settle.

Where differences between the parties depend upon a determination of an objective fact, bringing the parties together to focus on the disputed issue makes sense and frequently leads to resolution. I can think of no disadvantages to focusing on objective facts as a means of limiting differences and breaking impasses.

5.5.5 Setting firm deadlines

Negotiations have a way of accelerating as parties near an imposed deadline. In the initial explanation of the settlement conference process, I generally inform the parties of any time constraints. Settlement conferences are normally scheduled for no longer than two or three hours, and parties are told at the start what time I will end the meeting. In some cases, knowledge of a deadline causes the parties to move more expeditiously toward settlement. The following scenario illustrates this point.

Case Study 5: A Breach of Contract Action. The plaintiff filed a breach of contract action arising out of a management agreement to operate five separate golf courses, to which the defendant filed a counterclaim alleging fraud and breach of contract. The parties had a total dislike for one another and had engaged in extensive discovery.

The settlement conference commenced at 2:30 p.m., and I informed the parties that I would leave no later than 5:15 p.m. to meet a family commitment. During the afternoon, little progress was made even though both sides expressed a strong desire to settle. Seven issues required resolution, and by 4:30 p.m. we had resolved exactly one.

At that point, I once again emphasized my intention to leave at 5:15 p.m. In the next forty-five minutes, we resolved all but one issue, on which both sides refused to budge. It seemed unlikely the parties would let a settlement fall apart over this one issue. I brought the parties together and told them that they were both being unreasonable regarding the final point. As I left, I explained that they were free to use my courtroom to continue their discussions and that they should leave a note regarding the outcome. The next morning I found a note indicating the case was settled.

Judges almost always have the pressure of a backlog of other cases and rarely have the luxury of setting aside days or weeks to devote to the settlement of one case. Therefore, setting a deadline becomes necessary to control one's docket and to schedule other matters. In addition, setting a firm deadline causes parties to become more serious in their discussions, similar to the way setting a firm trial date accelerates settlement talks. Applying a deadline is most effective when many major issues have been resolved and only minor ones remain, as parties are reluctant to see a settlement fall apart on minor matters.

On the other hand, parties may feel undue pressure when facing a deadline. This can lead to buyer's remorse and difficulty in consummating the settlement. In addition, a deadline may result in a failure to settle cases that could otherwise be settled if additional time were available. In these situations, a converse approach may be effective. If the judge informs the parties that he or she is willing to work late through dinner, things can start to progress quickly as dinner time approaches.

5.5.6 Conclusion

The vast majority of civil cases settle, and judges are becoming increasingly involved in that process. Judges must be aware of techniques to work through stalemates to assist parties in achieving settlements. Giving up hope simply because the parties appear to be at a standstill is usually not the proper course. Judiciously taking advantage of impasse-breaking techniques can only help result in mutually satisfactory settlements for all parties.

[The Honorable Morton Denlow, United States Magistrate Judge
219 South Dearborn St., Chicago, Illinois 60604]

5.6 ROBERT H. MNOOKIN, SCOTT R. PEPPET, AND ANDREW TULUMELLO: CREATING VALUE IN NEGOTIATION AND MEDIATION

In their excellent book, *Beyond Winning: Negotiating to Create Value in Deals and Disputes,* Robert H. Mnookin, Scott R. Peppet, and Andrew S. Tulumello of the Harvard Negotiation Research Project, suggest not only techniques for breaking impasses, but also an approach to negotiation that serves to help prevent impasses from occurring at all. The book uses an interdisciplinary approach to the topic of negotiation by weaving together insights from economics, game theory, psychology, and law. It proceeds from the central premise that for the most success in negotiation, each party, agent, or lawyer should have a mindset of a "realistic optimist." This mindset, the authors define, is one where you adopt the basic belief that there is almost always the potential to create value in a negotiation - but you don't fool yourself into assuming that distributive exploitation isn't also a possibility. They further suggest that a lawyer with an optimistic realistic frame of mind is less likely to be knocked off balance by the other side's tactics. In this regard, and in contrast to other experts' advice to be reactive initially in a negotiation, the authors here encourage a proactive, "take charge" approach to engage negotiators across the table in problem solving. This approach is not initially directed to the substance of the dispute or transaction, but rather to the nature and structure of the negotiation process which the parties might together design.

To some negotiators who like to jump headlong into the subject matter of a negotiation, the authors' advice might seem foreign. However, the authors' thesis is simple and persuasive: negotiation is a game and the rules of the game are, in their words, "up for grabs" at the outset. Indeed, much of the book is about how to change the rules of the traditionally competitive game. In a very real way, the authors' advice captures a technique of mediation. It would be a rare instance indeed where a mediator would give an opening statement without describing the mediation process and the ground rules for participation in it. Similarly, a negotiator's proactive approach in addressing how the negotiators should conduct themselves can have, the authors suggest, several benefits. Among them are diffusion of competitive attitudes, an increased awareness of the potential of problem solving, and process efficiency. The book provides an excellent example of how a negotiator's opening statement regarding process might be worded. The key to effective process orientation, they suggest, is a negotiator's proposing rather than imposing a collaborative way of proceeding.

One of the principal strengths of the book is its bifurcated approach to discussing negotiation in legal dispute and transaction contexts. Chapters nine and ten address these separate topics in the context of providing sage advice and proposing techniques for use in creating value in each context. By using a "two table" metaphor - the net-expected-outcome table and the interest-based table - the authors offer detailed guidance on how to keep potential distributive (litigation) solutions in sight while mining for interest-based settlement opportunities. Applying this dual frame of reference, they explain with uncommon clarity how a negotiator can do what a skilled mediator does in many commercial disputes - convert the legal dispute into a new business transaction having many opportunities for integrative solutions. Their value creation techniques proposed for use in this dual frame of reference (dispute and transaction) are briefly described below (Mnookin, 224-71). For more in depth discussion, the reader is invited to explore Chapters nine and ten of the book.

5.6.1 Ask three important questions up front

Mnookin et al suggest that where appropriate, negotiators should try to settle legal disputes early rather than late, and additionally, to initially make efforts to design a bargaining process that permits early exploration of deal-like trades. Negotiators should try to tailor a negotiation strategy to a client's situation. They can do this by asking three questions. The first question is: "Is this the rare case where settlement may not make sense even if the other side is willing to settle?" Maybe the client needs case precedent to stave off substantial additional litigation; or maybe the client does not want to bargain away certain of its intellectual property. In such situations, pursuing settlement early may not be in the client's best interest.

The second question is: "How can I create value by minimizing transaction costs and exploring trades based on differences in time or risk preferences?" This type of creation of value might be achieved even before a lawsuit is filed. If there is sufficient information available, the lawyer and client may jointly construct a decision tree to evaluate the risk of going forward in litigation.

The third question is: "Could the parties to this dispute conceivably create value by exploiting opportunities for a broader range of trades?" Many disputes arise between individuals or companies who regularly do business together. Lawyers and their clients should search for ways to turn the dispute into some kind of deal or new transaction.

5.6.2 Change the rules of the game

In a dispute situation, consider doing something innovative in designing the negotiation process and in conducting negotiation. For instance, a client might consider using a settlement counsel, in addition to the litigation counsel. The settlement counsel has no authority to conduct litigation. The settlement counsel's main task is to represent the client in negotiations when the time for negotiating is ripe. Litigation counsel may attend the negotiation sessions, or not, depending on what an optimal settlement strategy may be. Another innovative way to change the rules of the game might be to work out an informal discovery process with the party on the opposite side of the case. Formal discovery is often time consuming and very expensive. An agreed method of sharing relevant information according to a pre-agreed time table may be very helpful to the negotiation process. Or, the parties could decide to share information informally and conduct some formal discovery.

5.6.3 Identify interests and search for trades

Take time to sit down with the opposing side and sincerely conduct an inventory of interests and then from those interests, jointly search for possible trades, or trade-offs. Look beyond the subject matter of the litigation. There may be compatible interests and resources for satisfying those interests that can result in a win-win solution. These other interests or resources could be real property, personal property, investments, any number of services, manufacturing opportunities or distributorship opportunities that are not in issue in the litigation. Integrating such interests and resources can create value in the deal or settlement that far exceeds the money value in dispute.

5.6.4 In transactions, consider creating the first draft of the agreement

If you want to create a problem solving atmosphere in negotiating a deal, you may be wise to consider volunteering to create the first draft of the agreement. Before you prepare the first draft, however, it is very helpful to know not only what your own client's interests are, you should also through discussion with the opposing side, determine what their interests are too. You should also understand how your client and the other side prioritize their interests.

5.6.5 In deal-making, consider changing players to break an impasse

It is not uncommon in transaction negotiation for the lawyers to change players in order to break a distributive impasse. For example, if the lawyers are having difficulty working out some provision of an agreement, involving clients who are friendly with each other may assist the lawyers overcome that hurdle. It might also be appropriate in some situations to suggest involving a mutually agreed-upon expert (economist, certified public accountant, scientist) where contract provisions are very technical and complex.

5.6.6 In deal-making, look to the future and reality check all the contract provisions

Meticulously reality check all contract provisions to determine what disputes might arise out of them in the future. Then redraft provisions to accommodate the avoidance, prevention, or minimization of those disputes. Include a specific contract provision requiring the use of alternative dispute resolution (mediation and/or arbitration) in the event that a dispute arises.

5.7 RODNEY A. MAX: BREAKING THE IMPASSE: THE UNIQUE MEDIATION OPPORTUNITY

[**Editor's Note:** *This section consists of an article authored by Rodney A. Max and it is reproduced and reformatted here with his permission.*]

Mediation provides a unique opportunity for the parties as it relates to the opportunity of a negotiated resolution of their case. Typically, in a negotiation, one party gets to his/her/its goal, the other party gets to his/her/its goal, and rarely are those goals the same. If impasse occurs, litigation will commence, continue, or be completed. Absent facilitation, no one is encouraging getting back to re-evaluation or re-negotiation. Certainly someone can suggest continuing negotiation, but typically neither side wants to show the other such interest (it being perceived as a weakness in the negotiation process).

Mediation, on the other hand, brings to the table the facilitatve element that is otherwise missing in a pure negotiation context. The neutral, while there to facilitate the negotiations, is also there as an advocate for the process. The mediator represents resolution similar to the responsibility of an attorney to represent his/her client. The mediator is going to work as hard for the process as the attorneys are going to work for their respective parties.

In this regard, the mediator serves as both the vehicle and the opportunity for breaking impasse. The sooner the mediator is brought into the process, the better and more able the mediator is to assist the parties in getting to "yes." The mediator can assist with the exchange of information and the exchange of communications, and the exchange of offers. The mediator can expedite information gathered, and filter communications. Therefore, "breaking impasse" becomes the mediator's responsibility from beginning to end.

In the beginning, the mediator can assist parties in getting to the table through the design of the mediation process. This can include not only exchanges of information, but also the establishment of pre-mediation caucuses with one or more parties. Especially in multi-party, mass tort, and class action cases, design of the mediation is vital to the ultimate resolution. It also stabilizes the relationship of the parties in getting to the table.

In a previous article entitled "Designing The Mediation" (see Section 4.3), I elaborated on the various design techniques that facilitate the parties in getting to the table. In this article, I am going to focus on "breaking impasse" as it relates to closing the deal. In complex cases (including mass torts and class actions), there are four aspects to the opportunity of breaking impasse in closing the deal.

5.7.1 Calling on the leadership

It is not unusual in complex cases for each room to have a number of participants - both lawyers and non-lawyers. Among the lawyers there may be in-house counsel, as well as outside counsel; there may be referral attorneys, as well as litigating attorneys. As for the parties there may be the plaintiff, as well as, plaintiff's family (sometimes to include extended family). On the defendant's side there may be corporate representatives, as well as, insurance coverage representatives. Among insurance representatives there may be primary carriers, as well as excess carriers. Speaking to a particular side involves a multitude of personalities, interests, and perhaps negotiating strategies.

The ability to call on the leadership of each room is a matter of timing, and identification. Who is the right person to call on at that right time to meet with the right representative from the other side? Sometimes this requires more than one person from each side.

In a case where two companies were suing one another (one on a promissory note and the other on fraud) each room had a combination of corporate representatives, in-house counsel, and outside counsel. It was clear that the formal position of the parties would not and could not achieve resolution (Each side was insisting on the flow of money going to them, not from them). The ability to break impasse was the ability to bring the corporate representatives together to make a business decision as opposed to a litigation decision. This could not occur first thing in the morning nor after the opening session. In fact, it could not occur until both sides had frustrated their formal negotiating positions and reached a point where their negotiating strategy had, in essence, failed with neither party willing to cross the demarcation line of zero. The opportunity of bringing the corporate representatives into a room (with the agreement of their counsel, both in-house and outside) was the key to the ultimate resolution. In a private session, the parties agreed to enter into a buy-sell arrangement of the outstanding minority shares which one party had of the other parties' company. The note was forgiven and the claim for fraud was dismissed. The case was resolved.

In a case where sixty-three property owners were being sued for wrongful death and personal injury of several workers, each room had a multitude of parties, party representatives, and/or attorneys. Prior to the mediation, leaders from both rooms emerged among counsel so as to be able to look for direction from that counsel during various stages of the negotiation. By establishing this leadership prior to the mediation, the parties knew who the leadership was and the mediator knew who the "go to" persons were so that after a multiple-day mediation, all claims of all parties were resolved against all defendants.

There are circumstances where insurance representatives may have conflicting interests with corporate representatives, or where insurance representatives have conflicting interests among themselves (especially where primary and excess carriers have different interests to protect). So too in a plaintiff's room, there may be differing interests between the plaintiff's referral attorney, the litigating attorney, and a guardian ad litem. In each case, calling on leadership at the right time avoids divisiveness and gets direction where impasse may otherwise occur.

Once that leadership is identified and can be brought together from the respective sides, separate or joint dialogue can occur to (1) rebuild trust, (2) define goals, and (3) find a new direction to the negotiation that is mutually acceptable.

5.7.2 Court decision

Court direction can be a vital tool whether suggested or actually implemented. Where parties have varying views as to what a judge, jury, or appellate court will do, the opportunity of "testing it" can be a means of breaking impasse. Such court opportunities exist with pre-trial conferences, summary judgments, and settlement conferences. They also exist in mock juries, focus groups or settlement juries.

Where a court can give some direction without the parties disclosing the status of their actual negotiations, such direction can be very helpful. A summary judgment motion as it may relate to one or more issues may, likewise, be of great help. It is usually best to keep the judge away from the actual settlement between the parties; however, there may be times that the judge can assist in requiring all parties or persons with full settlement authority to be present, whether in subsequent settlement conference or in a court ordered re-mediation.

While pre-trial conferences, summary judgments, and settlement conferences are well-known, mock juries or focus groups and settlement juries may not. Mock juries and focus groups give the parties an opportunity to test the receptiveness of their position before jurors of similar backgrounds to that of the venue at issue. When such mock juries or focus groups produce conflicting results (plaintiffs' focus group shows results contrary to what the defendants' focus group may show, resulting in impasse), a mediation focus group may be in order. Such a mediation focus group allows the mediator to facilitate assembling a group of jurors and allows each party to make their own private presentation to said jury. Thereafter, the jury can render a decision and confidentially answer questions posed by each side. Neither side will know the other's questions or the jury's answer to those questions. To the extent that a verdict is requested, it will be forthcoming and made known as agreed upon by the parties. Obviously, any such result is non-binding and remains confidential as to the participants.

The implementation of a court order or focus group may not be necessary. Merely the suggestion of the utilization of such direction may allow the parties to re-think their positions and provoke further dialogue and re-evaluation.

5.7.3 Conditional offers

Where negotiations are stalled either because the plaintiffs are too high or the defendants are too low, conditional offers can be a means of breaking impasse. Where plaintiffs will not move below ten million dollars and the defendants suggest the opportunity of negotiating is in six digits, conditional offers can free the parties from the "cancer" of relationship bargaining. Many times higher offers from plaintiffs and lower counter-offers from defendants are provoked because each side is looking at the relationship of their offer to that of the other side. Such relationship bargaining is not helpful to the mediation process.

While the mediator will typically urge the parties to make negotiating moves, not in relationship to the other side's numbers, but in relationship to their own goals, often times the parties do not abide by such worthy suggestion, or cannot do so. It is in this circumstance that conditional offers play a role. Many times such conditional offers must await several rounds of negotiation. However, when the parties remain very far apart after two or three moves, sometimes conditional offers are called for at an earlier stage.

Conditional offers are also known as bracketing or framing of the negotiation. The beauty of the conditional offer is that where a plaintiff will not go below ten million dollars because a defendant has not gotten to a million dollars (or vice versa), a conditional offer can suggest that the plaintiff will come below ten million dollars, if the defendant will come to a certain level. Alternatively, a defendant can indicate that it is willing to go to a certain level if, and only if, the plaintiff comes below a certain level.

While it is each side's intention to get the other side to accept the conditional offer or bracketing, the failure of such acceptance is not fatal. In fact, it can assist in "jump starting" the negotiations. That is to say that where the parties have been above ten million dollars and below one million dollars, a conditional offer from the plaintiff can suggest some seven digit area that the defendant may be able to accept or be willing to negotiate at a different or competing bracket. Once the brackets are identified, there is a means of negotiating between the brackets, typically called "negotiating" or "narrowing" the brackets. A number of offers or counteroffers involving bracketing can get the parties to "yes" in an expedited fashion. Bracketing opportunities can reinvigorate the process.

5.7.4 Mediator's proposal

Where the parties have gotten to the point that neither side will make any further movement, impasse occurs. In a negotiation, "it's over." In a mediation, "it's just begun."

The mediator and the parties need to realize that the Mediator's Proposal may be the mediator's one "silver bullet" to assist the parties in resolving their case. Therefore, it must be used with a high level of discretion and at the end of the negotiating process in order to break the impasse.

This proposal can not be a proposal of any one party. Rather, it must be that of the mediator. The Mediator's Proposal is not a suggestion of what the judge, arbitrator or jury will do; rather it must be understood to be in the context of the mediation. That is to say, the Mediator's Proposal is an effort to "stretch" both parties beyond where they would otherwise move in a negotiated fashion, but not so far as to lose the opportunity of obtaining a resolution.

The mediator must first determine that the parties are willing to accept the concept of a Mediator's Proposal. That concept works as follows: if the concept is accepted, the mediator will determine that number above and below which he/she thinks the parties will be willing to go. The number is published to both sides either separately or jointly (typically, it is done separately). The mediator then solicits two yeses or otherwise publishes two no's. The responses will be and will remain strictly confidential.

The mediator will never disclose what a party individually says. The mediator will simply disclose two yeses or two no's. If the mediator confidentially hears a yes and a no, he/she will only publish two no's. The mediator will never disclose if any one party said yes. Sometimes the parties can make their response at the mediation itself. Sometimes the mediation must adjourn to give the parties an opportunity to reevaluate their position in light of the proposal made.

While sometimes the only issue is "the number", there are occasions - especially in complex cases - where other terms and conditions must be a part of this proposal. Accordingly, the mediator should include all material terms as a part of the Mediator's Proposal. Such terms include non-monetary remedies, as well as monetary remedies. They include payment terms, releases, and dismissals. Some proposals can be quite brief; others may be quite elaborate. Some proposals may need to take stages, i.e. preliminary framework approval and thereafter more specific details, terms and conditions. Once the Mediator's Proposal is established and communicated, the parties should be given a reasonable period of time for determining its acceptability and delivering their confidential response to the mediator. Considerations in this regard are as follows: (1) Should you allow the parties to leave the mediation session and have the opportunity to consult with other people? (Sometimes this can be very helpful; sometimes it can be very harmful). (2) Do the parties need to seek advice of persons of higher authority whether individually, committees or boards? (3) Is it helpful to "get away" from the table, take a "breather," and "sleep on it." (Again, this can be both helpful and harmful depending on the circumstances and the people involved). Such reasonable time period, therefore, must be determined under the particular circumstances of the mediation.

The Mediator's Proposal is the most unique aspect of a mediation that clearly separates the value of the mediation process from that of the negotiation process. The successfully executed Mediator's Proposal makes the difference in breaking impasse.

5.7.5 Conclusion

Parties call on the mediation process anticipating that a third person is necessary to help the parties do what they cannot otherwise do. Mediation concepts such as convening or designing the mediation, conducting opening sessions, and facilitating negotiations all have their own unique values. Breaking impasse is the most vital role a mediator can be called on to achieve. The parties must be patient with both the mediator and the process so as to be able to look for such opportunities at the right time in the right way. Premature efforts to break impasse will result in failure. Allowing the parties to define their own impasse and then be prepared to do something about it is vital. Remember to establish the distinction between breaking impasse of the process and breaking impasse of the negotiations. The former should be considered at an earlier stage, the latter should be considered at a later stage. Each case has its own timeline; and other than a general statement, no one rule can apply to all mediation circumstances. The mediator's ability to break impasse of process or negotiations at the right time in the right way is the key to a successful mediation.

5.8 V. MICHELLE OBRADOVIC: PREVENTING DEADLOCK, STALEMATE AND IMPASSE IN MEDIATION

[**Editor's Note:** *This section consists of an article authored by V. Michelle Obradovic, Esq. and is reproduced and reformatted here with her permission.*]

In a mediation where the parties have developed a functional working relationship and where potentially acceptable solutions are relatively identifiable, standard mediation techniques are usually effective. In less resolution-friendly circumstances however, negotiations may stall, and the mediator must take appropriate steps to prevent deadlock. I define deadlock as a state of inaction resulting from the opposition of equally powerful uncompromising decision-makers. The terms stalemate and impasse, among others, are often used synonymously with deadlock.

For purposes of this article, assume that the mediator is an independent third party, who is both neutral and impartial and who has been invited to the dispute to provide extensive procedural assistance.

Further assume, as a baseline, that the mediator has thoroughly prepared for the mediation day and is focused on the case at hand. Additionally, assume that a pleasing atmosphere has been created in an adequate facility, that the mediator is viewed as credible and that an appropriate approach to the mediation day has emerged through consensus. Finally, assume that the parties have been encouraged to trust the process and that some rapport has been established. With this being the setting of the mediation, the essential question to be addressed in this article is: what steps can the mediator take to exert an appropriate level of process influence and prevent deadlock?

It is common knowledge that negotiators sometimes attempt to gain bargaining power over an opponent by threatening impasse. To work, the threat must be perceived as credible and the recipient of the maneuver must view settlement as the preferred method of resolving the case. Credibility usually rests on one party convincing another of a preference for a method of resolving the case, other than the current proposed settlement. A preference for settlement usually rests on a risk analysis and particular risk tolerances.

From the mediator's perspective, this tactic creates more of a temporary state of deadlock, stalemate or impasse. The mediator is well aware that the usual formula for genuine (as opposed to tactical) deadlock is a gap between the parties' "best" offers which they define as a significant gap, in combination with exhausted, emotionally spent decision-makers who are unwilling or unable to continue efforts to achieve settlement. This is a crisis in the mediation process. The only person who may believe resolution is still possible at this point is most likely the mediator. How did this happen? What is the mediator to do?

Starting at the beginning, the procedural aspects of the mediation process should first be examined. Empirical and anecdotal evidence tells us that in order to reach agreement, parties engaged in mediation activities progress through various stages. Further, the mediator moves parties through these stages at a quickened pace. Although identified differently by different texts, the stages are generally described as: (1) information gathering; (2) identification key of interests and tensions; (3) generating options for settlement; (4) assessing those options; (5) achieving agreement, and (6) closure. The stages often blend into each other or are revisited during the course of the mediation day.

Next is to gain an appreciation of negotiation styles, negotiation strategies, and the theoretical underpinnings of negotiation in the context of mediation. A negotiation *style* is the overall negotiation behavior engaged in by the negotiator, such as: (1) adversarial; (2) competitive; (3) collaborative, or (4) problem solving. A negotiation *strategy* is a negotiation behavior demonstrated in a given circumstance. One negotiation strategy is the start high, stay high approach. Under this approach, a party usually begins with a demand that is somewhat high relative to objective criteria, such as established verdict and appellate awards. That party does not move significantly on the monetary demand until an entire settlement package has been outlined, at which point, the demand drops dramatically. A second negotiation strategy is the agreement in principle approach. Under this approach, parties have usually had significant substantive discussions prior to mediation and seek the assistance of the mediator to move the parties towards a more specific one and to bring the final decision-makers into the conversation. A third negotiation strategy is the search for the bargaining zone approach. Under this approach, parties proceed through a series of offers and counteroffers until a settlement range becomes apparent. This is often described as "getting to the ballpark." The activities in the mediation are viewed as tactical maneuvers designed to identify if such a zone exists and if so, to define and redefine its boundaries. Tradeoffs or concessions are usually the method by which this is achieved and the mediator's main tasks are to coax new information from the parties and to tentatively explore boundaries with each party. Finally, in broadest terms, negotiation *theory* tells us that negotiations can occupy a place either on the continuum between positional and principled; or alternatively on the continuum between distributive and integrative theories. Although often broken down for purposes of analysis; theory, style, and strategy are, in practice, highly interrelated and dynamic. These terms of negotiation theory are explained in more detail immediately below.

Positional negotiation. The parties take up a position and spend the mediation defending it against attack. Underlying interests are not considered. Hard or soft negotiation styles are usually chosen by the parties, ranging from confrontational behavior to yielding behavior - a.k.a. rights-based negotiation. The settlement is usually anticipated to be a win-lose result.

Principled negotiation. The parties focus their efforts on discovering underlying interests and developing viable alternatives to achieve maximum satisfaction for all parties - a.k.a. interest based negotiation. Opportunities for mutual gain are considered. The settlement is usually anticipated to be a win-win result.

Distributive negotiation model. In this negotiation situation, limited resources are available to be distributed between claimants. One party's gain is another's loss. Adversarial or competitive styles are often chosen by parties. Rights or entitlements are usually the focus of discussions. The settlement is usually anticipated to be a win-lose result. "Defining the bargaining zone" is an example of distributive bargaining where the activities in the mediation are viewed as tactical maneuvers designed to identify if such a zone exists and if so, to define and redefine its boundaries. Negotiators need to be convinced that they are not leaving dollars "on the table." As noted above, this is often described as "getting to the ballpark."

Integrative negotiation model. In this negotiation situation, options are explored, some of which may not be an area of disagreement between the parties, thereby creating opportunities for mutual gain. A collaborative or problem solving negotiation style is usually chosen by the parties and creativity in the search for added value is encouraged. The settlement is usually anticipated to be a win-win result.

Many texts have been written on these subjects and are readily available for further study. Mediators must be aware that negotiators often change styles and adopt new strategies during the mediation. The mediator must determine whether negotiators are unaware of their shifts or if they are intentional and project what impact these shifts will likely have on the process. It may be necessary for the mediator to offer process feedback or to begin preconditioning other parties for what they are about to hear. The mediator must also watch for particularly precarious negotiation behaviors which include: (1) preconditions to negotiation; (2) extreme demands and offers; (3) changing negotiators in the middle of the mediation; (4) relationship moves; (5) feigned lack of authority; (6) reopening settled issues; (7) the bottom line, and (8) take it or leave it. The mediator must also be on the look out for special situations, which if not addressed, could send the mediation into a slow spiral toward deadlock. An example of a special situation would be sabotage. Occasionally, a particular faction attempting to advance a personal agenda emerges as a saboteur to the negotiations by either polarizing negotiation counterparts or by attempting to undermine internal leadership, or both. The mediator must take steps to gain support for continuing the process from influential people within the room and must attempt to de-escalate the conflict created between counterparts. Saboteurs can be parties and/or corporate or litigation counsel.

One of the primary roles of the mediator is to discover what barriers separate the parties conceptually, and then design a specific process to allow the parties to attempt removal of these barriers. For example: (1) the mediator may determine that poor communication is a barrier, either in quantity, quality or form. In this circumstance, the mediator may keep the parties separate and carry messages between groups, thus serving as an adapter; (2) the mediator may determine that lack of information, unverifiable information or lack of agreed upon criteria to evaluate information is a barrier. In this circumstance, the mediator may focus on organizing, categorizing, summarizing, examining the underlying assumptions and articulating the available information. Further, the mediator may assist the parties in developing a schedule for collecting and sharing additional information in the future; (3) the mediator may determine that misperceptions, bias or overwhelming emotion is a barrier. In this circumstance the mediator may allow the party to express their feelings in private session; may attempt to de-escalate the behavior; may try to remove or resolve the identified trigger, or may attempt to elegantly reframe the circumstance to bring about a change in the emotion; (4) the mediator may determine that risk evaluations or assessments of what will happen if settlement is not achieved differ so greatly that it is a barrier. In this circumstance, the mediator may guide the conversations toward objective criteria and urge the parties to go through different kinds of analytical exercises.

Other techniques the mediator might use for breaking deadlock, stalemate or impasse are: (1) reframing the gap in different language; (2) exploring the assumptions underlying the way each party has defined the gap; (3) retooling existing relationships to create value if possible; (4) breaking down the gap into smaller issues and attempting to narrow the gap; (5) taking a bird's eye view of what the outline of a global resolution might look like, leaving off the discussion of details for the moment; (6) orchestrating blind moves; (7) orchestrating conditional moves; (8) using straw models; (9) handicapping; (10) bringing attorneys together; (11) bringing decision-makers together; (12) looking for the counterintuitive approach; (13) achieving a settlement with High/Low provision; (14) splitting the difference; (15) adjourning and reconvening at a later date; (16) achieving a partial settlement and considering reconvening non-settling parties at a later date; (17) creating a mediator's proposal (if asked, and there is no other option); and (18) suggesting that the parties change mediators.

In conclusion, mediators are the experts in process; a process that when properly done, makes the wise resolution self-evident to parties committed to the concept of self-determination. Prevention of deadlock therefore rests in the mediator's developing of a knowledge base and using it to recognize recurring patterns in mediation. Further, the mediator should use the insight gained from such recognition to make appropriate process decisions.

The fusion of the elements knowledge, recognition, and decision-making, empowers the mediator to be an extraordinary advocate for resolution and to remain true to the commitment to serve others through the mediation process.

[V. Michelle Obradovic, Esq. lives in Birmingham, Alabama and may be contacted at Michelle@WiseResolution.com. She is a former litigator and trial attorney and is Mediation Counsel to Upchurch Watson White & Max. Her mediation practice includes complex litigation, torts and class actions. She is an Associate Professor at Cumberland School of Law at Samford University.]

5.9 JOHN W. COOLEY: FORMULA FOR ESTIMATING FAIR SETTLEMENT VALUE

In personal injury cases, there are crude "rules of thumb" for determining the settlement values of cases, which insurance claims adjustors customarily eschew. Nonetheless, whether or not these "rules of thumb" are actually verbalized in any particular negotiation or mediation, they are often applied tacitly when a party or the mediator suggests a settlement figure. In a case not involving permanent injury, the most common rule of thumb is three times the alleged special damages. Special damages normally consist of hospital bills, doctor bills, other medical bills, lost wages, and the like. Thus, in a personal injury case where the plaintiff has nonpermanent injuries and special damages totaling $5,000, applying a factor of three would yield a settlement figure of $15,000. Practically, speaking this would break down into $5,000 to reimburse the client for medical expenses and lost wages, $5,000 to the plaintiff for pain, suffering, and inconvenience, and $5,000 as the lawyer's fee. In cases involving permanent but not incapacitating pain or disability, the factor may increase to five, and for permanent disability interfering or precluding gainful employment of the plaintiff, the factor may increase to ten or more. Some situations would dictate that the "rule of thumb" factor would be less than three, particularly where, for example, the issue of liability is a close one or where the plaintiff would not be a very good witness. This section is an adaptation of Cooley(2), 229-32.

Another method of case evaluation, more accurate than the rule of thumb technique, involves the use of a fair settlement value ("FSV") formula. The FSV formula is also adaptable to cases other than those involving personal injury. Determining the fair settlement value is a prerequisite to determining the reasonable settlement range and the opening positions and bottom lines. The FSV formula was originally developed by Robert L. Simmons and published in *Winning Before Trial: How to Prepare Cases for the Best Settlement or Trial Result* 708-15 (Executive Reports Corporation, 1974).

The elements of the formula are as follows:

PAV	-The probable average verdict.
PPV	-The probability of a plaintiff's verdict.
UV	-The uncollectible portion of the verdict.
PC	-The plaintiff's cost in obtaining the verdict.
DC	-The defendant's estimated cost of defense.
I	-The value of other intangible factors.
FSV	-The fair settlement value.

Algebraically, the formula may be expressed:

$FSV = (PAV \times PPV) - UV - PC + DC \pm I$

The mediator develops information to insert in this formula through caucusing and joint sessions with counsel. The way in which a mediator may typically determine a value for the individual elements of the formula is as follows:

- **PAV** assumes a situation where liability can be proved, and its value can be determined by reviewing the jury verdict reports in plaintiff's jurisdiction for the type of injury the plaintiff sustained. In some jurisdictions this information is available by periodical publications, subscription computer disks, or is available through a computer online service. If it is not available, after a discussion with counsel on both sides, you will have to insert amounts for incurred special damages, estimates of expenses for future medical care, including surgery and rehabilitation, property damage, and realistic estimates for related intangible damages (pain and suffering, disfigurement, loss of consortium, etc.).

- **PPV** takes into account the strengths and weaknesses of plaintiff's case both on law and facts, considered independently. For example, if, after consulting with counsel for plaintiff and defendant, you believe that all the legal instructions the judge will give to the jury will be favorable to plaintiff's case, plaintiff's probability of winning a verdict on the law is 100 percent or 1.0. If he estimates that only ninety percent of the instructions will be favorable, then the probability is .90 and so on. This analysis would also take into account the risk of modification of any pertinent case law prior to final judgment.

  As to the facts, if you believe that a jury will find for plaintiff on 85 percent of the critical facts, then the probability of winning a verdict on the facts is .85. This determination includes an evaluation of the relative credibility of witnesses, of whether critical items of evidence (his and/or the other side's) will be admitted into evidence at trial, and of the relative reliability of both sides' documentary and other evidence. The combined probability for these two independent events - the judge determining the instructions and the jury determining the facts and applying the law as the judge instructs - is the product of the two probabilities. Thus, if plaintiff's probability on the law is .90 and his probability on the facts is .85, the combined probability of a plaintiff's verdict is .90 x .85, or 76 percent.

- **UV** is present in some cases where some parties are uninsured, underinsured, or, for some other reason, are partially or fully judgment-proof.

- **PC** costs include court costs, discovery expenses, fees for expert witnesses, model construction costs, etc. (Include attorney fees and expenses if plaintiff's attorney is not on a contingent fee).

- **DC** costs include those of the type described immediately above with the addition of attorney's fees.

- **I** is intangible factors which might be considered by the jury in a particular case in determining a higher or lower award of damages including skill or experience of counsel, reputation of corporation(s), ability of parties to elicit the jury's sympathy, the nature of the illegal conduct, etc.

Let's now consider a hypothetical example and apply the formula to determine a fair settlement value. Assume that the plaintiff has sued a small construction company and the driver of one of its pick-up trucks. The driver of the pick-up truck struck plaintiff while she was crossing the street late one afternoon and caused her serious injuries. The plaintiff sustained a compound fracture of her right leg, which left a lengthy scar, a serious knee injury requiring surgery, and bruises and contusions over much of her body. The accident left her toes without feeling. This has precluded her from engaging in many of her favorite recreational activities, including dancing, ice skating, and skiing. She also frequently experiences severe pain in her knees, especially if she stands for long periods of time. This has caused some problems for her in her job as a customer service representative for a local bank. The plaintiff's expert testified in his deposition that the feeling would never come back to her toes and that she would experience pain in her knee probably for the rest of her life. Defendants' expert testified that the feeling in her toes would return and the knee pain would all but vanish in five years with the appropriate exercise and rehabilitative treatment.

In deposition, plaintiff testified that she was crossing the street at the intersection, with a "walk" signal, and within the lines of the cross-walk when she was struck by the defendant driver. The driver testified that she stepped off the curb and ran in front of his truck fifty feet in front of the intersection while he had a green light. Witness testimony was mixed. One witness supported plaintiff's version of what occurred, but two witnesses placed her outside of the crosswalk and testified in deposition that the truck had a red light. There are a few depositions left to be taken in the case. One witness to be deposed is a bartender who was with the defendant driver a few minutes before the accident occurred. He apparently will testify that the driver had a couple beers, but was not drunk when he left the bar. Another complicating factor is the issue of whether the driver was acting in the course of his employer's business at the time of the accident. Because of the lateness of the day, and the driver's activities immediately before the accident, it is possible that the jury could find that the driver was off-duty when the accident occurred. This could pose a potential problem for your case since the driver's personal insurance policy has limits of $150,000.

The values for the individual terms of the FSV formula might be computed as follows:

PAV = $550,000. A review of online jury verdict information for cases in which plaintiffs sustained similar injuries yielded an average jury verdict of $350,000.

PPV = .64. You estimate that the probability is eight-five percent that the trial judge will give the jury instructions on the law favorable to plaintiff's case. This includes the consideration that theseventy-five probability that the jury will find in favor of plaintiff's version of the facts. Thus, the combined probability of a verdict in plaintiff's favor on the law and the facts is .85 x .75, or .64 (rounded).

UV = 0. You have reviewed the pertinent case law cited by counsel, and you are convinced that the driver will be found to have been acting within the scope of his employment. Thus, in your opinion, the defendant company can be held responsible for a portion of the judgment, and there will be no uncollectible portion.

PC = $80,000. Plaintiff's case preparation has already cost $40,000, largely because of the several experts hired to review the case. At least three experts will testify at trial. Plainitff's counsel believes that to take the case through the remainder of discovery and trial will cause the expenses to double.

DC = $70,000. Defense counsel believes that a reasonable estimate for the total defense expense would be $70,000.

I = $25,000 in favor of defendants. As for the intangible considerations, the driver came across rather brash and indignant at his deposition. The jury is probably not going to like the fact that the driver was drinking before the accident. You believe that this will potentially boost a jury verdict $25,000 in plaintiff's favor. Other considerations may tend to reduce the jury verdict. Plaintiff's yuppie attitude tends to make her testimony seem condescending. Her starchy, stiff-upper-lip style may put off some jurors and make her complaints about frequent severe pain less believable. The defendant company has a very favorable reputation in the community. It annually spends tens of thousands of dollars sponsoring programs for handicapped children, a TV telethon, and the Special Olympics. You estimate that these considerations may have the effect of reducing the potential jury verdict by $50,000. The combination of the favorable and unfavorable intangible considerations may be estimated to have a $25,000 negative effect on the jury verdict.

If you substitute these figures into the FSV equation, you arrive at the following estimate of a fair settlement value for the case:

FSV = (PAV x PPV) - UV - PC + DC ± I
FSV = ($550,000 x .64) - 0 - 80,000 + 70,000 - $25,000
FSV = $352,000 - $10,000 - $25,000
FSV = $352,000 - $35,000
FSV = $317,000

It must be emphasized that no one figure represents the number at which a case must settle. If your estimates have been accurate, $317,000 figure should fall within a "reasonable settlement range." That range is determined by establishing a bracket whose endpoints are 10% on either side of an objectively estimated fair settlement value. Thus, in the example presented above, the reasonable settlement range would be roughly between $350,000 and $285,000. If your analysis is correct, theoretically the plaintiff would not be expected to accept less than $285,000 and the defendant would not be expected to pay more than $350,000 to settle this case. These bottom lines, of course, might be modified as information is developed during the course of the mediation.

Whether or not one finds the FSV formula helpful in determining a fair settlement value for a case, the important point to be derived from this exercise is that, in a damages-only case, counsel for the parties and the mediator should consider using some type of objective, systematic method of valuing a case that has a solely monetary solution.

[John W. Cooley, JAMS, 222 S. Riverside Plaza, Suite 1850, Chicago, IL 60606.
847-328-7285, jackwcool@aol.com]

CHAPTER SIX

ADVANCED PRACADEMIC STRATEGIES FOR CREATIVE PROBLEM SOLVING IN NEGOTIATION AND MEDIATION

The world is a tragedy to those who feel, and a comedy to those who think.

William Shakespeare

As pointed out in Sub-section 1.2.1, Pracademics is a term that I use to describe the art and science of translating the theory of creative problem solving into practice, and conversely, converting the practice of creative problem solving into theory. It envisions practitioners and academics collaborating to create new and better ways to solve problems by sharing insights and experience from laboratory and field settings. A pracademic knows and understands that, as an architectural designer of problems, processes, and solutions, he or she must have a keen interest in and respect for use of metaphor. This chapter contains several articles and excerpts providing examples of practitioners and academics using a number of metaphors to describe the essence of mediation. The metaphors used here include: humor, music, magic, mathematics, physics, war, and art. It is hoped that these metaphorical essays and articles will inspire practitioners and academics to find other useful metaphors for explaining mediation and negotiation.

6.1 JOKE THINK

[**Editor's note:** *This section is an adaptation of an article appearing in Cooley(10), with footnotes omitted Copyright © 1998 by the University of San Francisco Law Review. Reprinted by permission of the USF Law Review.*]

6.1.1 Joke model of creative thinking

The joke model of creative thinking is applicable to problem solving in negotiation and mediation. The two basic principles of achieving creative results are: (1) conflict or incongruity of some type precedes all creative results; and (2) conflict or incongruity resolution, involving the application of creativity, is the process which produces creative results. The structure of a standard joke offers a clear illustration of these principles. The standard joke structure has two stages - incongruity and resolution. The first stage consists of two parts: a fact statement, or text, and a punchline. The text generates in the perceiver certain logical expectations that are disconfirmed by new information - or punchline - yielding an incongruous, surprise result.

The second stage consists of a problem solving process. In that stage, the perceiver mentally searches for a cognitive rule to reconcile the incongruity or tension existing between the text and the punch line. If a cognitive rule is found to reconcile the joke parts, the perceiver deems the punch line to make sense, he "gets" the joke, and laughs. If a relevant cognitive rule cannot be found, the joke parts are not reconciled, the punch line does not make sense, and the perceiver neither "gets" the joke nor laughs. Consider this example:

A friend recently asked me: "Are you going to be cremated after you die?"

To which I responded: "I certainly wouldn't want to do it any sooner than that."

Here, in the first stage of the joke, the text generates the logical expectation that the response will be either that I will be cremated or that I prefer burial under ground or in an above-ground vault. The punch line disconfirms that logical expectation and produces incongruity and surprise. In the second stage of the joke, the perceiver - here, my friend - searches for a cognitive rule to reconcile the incongruity between the issues of whether or when I wish to be cremated. The discovery of the cognitive rule that "I don't mind being cremated, but not before I die" reconciles the joke parts, causing him to get the joke and laugh.

Actually, as the chart below reveals, the stages of the joke process and the conventional mediation process correlate quite closely.

Joke Model	**Mediation**
Introduction (read or heard)	Initiation
Setting and Context Stored	Preparation
	Introduction
Narrative Schema Formulated	Problem Statement
Forthcoming Text Predicted	Problem Clarification
Punchline Communicated Prediction Match Tested No Match Surprise	Generation and Evaluation of Alternatives
Cognitive (Reconciling) Rule Found (Reframing Occurs)	Selection of Alternatives
Laughter	Agreement

In each process there is a fact statement stage and a resolution stage. The primary difference between the two processes is that in the joke process, a stimulus in the form of new information - the punchline - is intentionally and suddenly injected into the process which causes or allows the initial information to be perceived in a very different way, thus yielding an unexpected, satisfactory resolution or interpretation. It is the quality and the timing of the punchline that comprise the creative act and speeds the joke to a satisfying resolution. It is this same kind of punchline - specially selected new information - that must be injected into the mediation process at the appropriate time in order to yield highly satisfactory, optimal, or even super-optimal, solutions. A point deserving special emphasis, which may indeed serve as the punchline of this article, is as follows:

It is the mental process which occurs in joke processing in a microsecond - at the time of and just before surprise - that must be replicated in the mediation setting in order to achieve super-optimum solutions; it is as if that mental process of reframing be viewed under a microscope and in slow-motion to be effectively discerned and applied.

The substantive steps of reframing in the joke process may be replicated in mediation on a gross scale and at a cosmically decelerated rate of speed. Two questions present themselves: first, what are punchlines in mediation? And second, at what stage of the mediation process should they be introduced? The second question quickly finds its answer by simply reviewing the above chart that correlates the information processing stages in jokes to those of conventional mediation. The specially selected new information (punchline) in the joke process appears in the stage corresponding to the generation and evaluation stage of mediation. Thus, a reasonable hypothesis would be that the mediation punchline should occur in the "generation and evaluation of alternatives" stage in order to convert a conventional mediation into a super-optimum one. Usually, the punchline is delivered by the mediator, although in some situations, the punchline has been delivered party to party, or counsel to counsel, both in the mediator's presence. The answer to the first question – What are punchlines in mediation? – is decidedly more involved.

6.1.2 Mediation punchlines

Mediation punchlines consist of information of two types: the respective interests of the disputing parties and the available resources for satisfying those interests. Sometimes these interests and satisfaction resources are not even consciously perceived by particular disputants. It is the mediator's challenge to discover these interests and resources, to match compatible ones, and to communicate or to have these possible matchings communicated to the other disputants.

Below appears a list of basic mediation punchlines that may have potential use in any mediation. These are the same interest/resource possibilities described in Section 3.1.18. With a little creative thinking, you could add more basic punchlines to the list.

BASIC PUNCHLINES FOR MEDIATION

Time	Words	Secrecy
Place	Apology	Release
Quantity	Control	Reinstatement
Quality	Persons	Assurances
Size	Nature	Procedure
Context	Structure	Opportunity
Distance	Types	Guarantee
Responsibility	Volume	Publicity
Rate	Proportion	Security
Space	Exchange	Share

This is just a list of words - basic punchlines that can be used to trigger others through use of imagination. There are thousands of potential punchlines – interests and satisfaction resources – that can be generated from this list.

6.1.3 Six standard joke formulas

These basic punchlines can be enhanced even further by applying techniques derived from the six standard joke formulas: (1) play on words; (2) reversal; (3) exaggeration; (4) visualization; (5) pairs and triples; and (6) routining. To be effective, mediators need to fully understand how these six formulas can be used to construct and communicate punchlines and appreciate how these formulas inter-relate with the standard joke structure. For examples of how these formulas can be applied to an actual dispute situation, see Cooley (3), 201-210 and Cooley (10).

6.1.3.1 Play on words

Let us walk through some examples. Take the formula, play on words, for instance. This formula type includes puns, limericks, and other clever witticisms of which the cliche usually provides the operative mechanism. There are five basic techniques for using cliches. The most common play on words, however, involves manipulating words that sound the same, but which have more than one meaning. Here are a couple of well-known examples:

An actor is the only ham that can't be cured.

Did your watch stop when it hit the floor?

Of course! Did you expect it to go straight through?

Actually, the "play on words" technique can be used to come up with additional meanings for the words in the chart *supra* in Section 6.1.2. The metaphor and the play on words techniques are quite similar. Both rely on the "play" idea -- because that is, in effect, what one does with the words on the basic punchline list.

6.1.3.2 Reversal

Applying the reversal formula, you turn things around. You lead people to believe that you mean one thing, but in fact you mean the opposite. For example, typical jokes using the reversal formula would include:

For twenty five years my husband and I were deliriously happy.
Then we met.

I'd like to introduce a man with a lot of charm, talent, and wit.
Unfortunately, he couldn't be here today.

The punchline is the antithesis of what is expected. As a mediator developing possible mediation punchlines, you would experiment with some antonyms from your Basic List.

6.1.3.3 Exaggeration

The exaggeration joke formula employs either overstatements or understatements of real situations as illustrated in the following examples:

Overstatement: My mother always believed that cleanliness was next to Godliness. She starched everything. It got so bad that my brother fell out of bed one night and broke his pajamas.

Understatement: I had heart surgery recently. In fact, my surgeon is here at

this banquet tonight. I was pleased to see him until
I overheard the surgeon ask his wife to cut his meat for him.

6.1.3.4 Visualization

When the creative comic uses visualization, he or she designs a punchline which generates a vivid picture in the mind of the audience. Consider this joke:

My father taught me how to drive years ago ... when I mentioned I was thinking of leaving home. He skipped all the technical parts. When we came to our first steep hill, he said "Write to Momma," and jumped out.

6.1.3.5 Pairs and triples

Using the pairs and triples technique, the creative comic puts two or three ideas together and then designs a punch line to achieve irony or to maximize reversal. In the following joke examples, the "pair" joke example demonstrates a reversal effect.

Pair: Boy to friend: If I'm too noisy, my mother gives me a spanking.
        If I'm too quiet, she takes my temperature.

Triple: Young child: Why are you putting on so much face cream, Mommy?
        Mother: Because it will make me young, healthy, and beautiful.
        Young child: (long pause) Well, when-zit gonna work?

6.1.3.6 Routining

The last formula, routining, is the most time consuming to employ, but if used properly, audience satisfaction can be maximized. Routining combines many of the joke-design techniques discussed above. Consider this slightly edited routine which Gene Perret (one of Bob Hope's joke writers) designed around the simple idea of a crowded expressway that is very dangerous and that people hate to drive on. He uses Pennsylvania as the setting for the routine, but if he were writing the joke for a New York, Chicago, or Los Angeles audience, he would have used those cities' names in his design. As you read through this routine, visualize Bob Hope delivering it:

I had a very pleasant trip over here on the Schuylkill Expressway. A pleasant trip on the Schuylkill Expressway . . . that means you finish in the same car you started with.

That road takes you from South Philadelphia to Valley Forge in twenty-five minutes flat ... whether you want to go or not.

I can always tell when I'm approaching the Schuylkill Expressway. My St. Christopher statue gets down from the dashboard and climbs into the glove compartment.

It's the only road in the world that you can travel on from one end to the other without once leaving the scene of the accident.

Actually, our Schuylkill Expressway is a famous road. It has been cited by religious leaders all over the world. It ranks second to World War II as a cure for atheism.

The Pope blessed it, but he won't ride on it.

Application of the routining formula in mediation is quite easy if you have designed good jokes - or settlement elements - all along during the course of the mediation. Routining merely consists of stringing the settlement elements together in a format that achieves the highest degree of satisfaction for the parties.

6.1.4 Example of application of joke formulas in the mediation of a dispute

Before concluding this section, let us consider a very simple example of how these joke formulas could be used to generate ideas for resolving a problem involving two neighbors (See Fobes, 68-78). Let's assume that Neighbor A likes to grow vegetables in a backyard garden. And let's suppose that Neighbor B has chickens that wander freely and eat the vegetables in the first neighbor's garden. A dispute erupted and the neighbors are not talking to one another and Neighbor A with the garden is threatening to sue Neighbor B with the chickens. How could you use the joke model of mediation to help them resolve their dispute? You might try the reversal formula of the joke model. In the reversal formula, the punch line is the antithesis of what is expected. As a mediator developing possible mediation punch lines, you would experiment with some antonyms from your Basic List. Here is an example of how you might apply the reversal and exaggeration formulas.

Reversal Formula

Basic Punchline	(Near) Opposite Meaning	Enhanced Punch Line
Words	Actions	Call animal control; scare chickens using intermittent water sprays or noises; place moving, mechanical fox near garden
Space	Restrictions	Neighbor A builds fence; (or neighbors do it together); dig a moat; plant dense bushes; build fence only around garden
Persons	Animals	Get a cat or dog; use rubber snakes

Exaggeration Formula

Basic Punchline	Over/Understated Form	Enhanced Punch Line
Types	Expand varieties of vegetables	Grow vegetables that chickens don't like; grow vegetables that chickens like – but at a distance from main garden

Exchange	Consider unusual reciprocities	Exchange vegetables for chickens (or eggs) as a good will move: Neighbor A offers to show Neighbor B how to plant and care for a garden in Neighbor B's backyard
Share	Consider sharing expenses	Neighbor A offers to pay part of Neighbor B's cost to build chicken coop or to pay for additional chicken food so chickens will stay on Neighbor B's property

Now that you have seen how the reversal and exaggeration formulas can be applied to solve problems, you may want to experiment with the other four joke formulas to come up with more possible solutions to this neighborly dispute.

6.2 MAGIC THINK

[**Editor's Note:** *This section contains edited excerpts from Cooley (9) and Cooley (14), with footnotes omitted.*]

6.2.1 General

This Section is about only one thing – deception. More specifically it discusses types of deception and addresses whether they are acceptable or unacceptable forms of persuasion in mediation. Further, it analyzes how to recognize types of deception, how to deal with them, and how to use acceptable types of deception considered from both the perspectives of an advocate in mediation and of a mediator.

Robert Benjamin, a nationally recognized mediator and teacher of mediation, negotiation, and conflict management theory and skills has written:

> Mediators, like trickster figures, are in some measure illusionists ... Their use of deception and strategic intervention is calculated not for self-gain at the expense of conflicting parties but rather for the parties' benefit. As a result, ideally, the parties learn, but at the very least they survive the conflict. All human beings, and especially mediators, deceive, manipulate, and even sometimes lie. That is a given. It is the purpose of the deceit that must be examined ... If ... the deception is designed to shift and reconfigure the thinking of disputing parties, especially in the midst of conflict and confusion, and to foster their cooperation,
> tolerance, and survival, then the deception may well be a "noble lie" (Benjamin, 17).

Consensual deception is the essence of caucused mediation. It is rare that caucused mediation, a type of informational game, occurs without the use of deception by the parties, by their lawyers, and/or by the mediator in some form. This is so for several reasons.

First, a basic groundrule of the information system operating in any mediated case in which there is caucusing is that confidential information conveyed to the mediator by any party cannot be disclosed by the mediator to anyone (with narrowly limited exceptions). This means that: (1) each party in mediation rarely if ever knows whether another party has disclosed confidential information to the mediator; and (2) if confidential information has been disclosed, the nondisclosing party never knows the specific content of that confidential information and whether and/or to what extent that confidential information has colored or otherwise affected communications coming to the nondisclosing party from the mediator. In this respect, each party in a mediation is an actual or potential victim of constant deception regarding confidential information – granted, agreed deception – but nonetheless deception.

A second reason that caucused mediation necessarily includes deception is that the parties and their counsel are normally engaged in the strategies and tactics of competitive bargaining during all or part of the mediation conference. That is, the goal of each party is to get the best deal for himself or herself. These competitive bargaining strategies and tactics are layered and interlaced with the mediator's own strategies and tactics to get the best resolution possible for the parties – or at least a resolution that they can accept. The confluence of these initially unaligned strategies, tactics, and goals creates an environment rich in gamesmanship and intrigue. Such an environment is naturally conducive to the use of deceptive behaviors by the parties and their counsel, and even the mediators. Actually, mediators are more likely to use deceptive behaviors because they are the conductors – the orchestrators - of an information system specially designed for each dispute, a system with ambiguously defined or, in some situations, undefined disclosure rules in which the mediators are the Chief Information Officers with near-absolute control over what nonconfidential information, critical or otherwise, is *developed*, is *withheld*, is *disclosed,* and when disclosure occurs.

The third reason for the presence of deception in mediation is that the information manipulated by the mediator in any dispute context is itself imperfect. Parties, rarely, if ever, share with the mediator all the information relevant, or even necessary, to the achievement of the mediator's goal – an agreed resolution of conflict. The parties' deceptive behavior in this regard – jointly understood by the parties and the mediator in any mediation to fall within the agreed "rules of the game"- sometimes causes mediations to fail or prevents optimal solutions from being achieved.

6.2.2 Truth, deception, and magic

Deceptions of various types are generally accepted as integral to our way of life. "White lies" permeate all aspects of social interaction: "How nice to see you!" – when it is not: We give false excuses in response to invitations or requests in order to avoid hurting feelings. We flatter the ordinary; bestow a cheerful interpretation on depressing circumstances; and show gratitude for unwanted gifts: Modern society tolerates outright lying in a variety of circumstances. In some circles, lying is justified when it avoids harm, produces an overriding benefit, maintains fairness, or preserves confidence or reputation. Some examples include the following: lying to protect oneself or someone else from physical harm, the government using undercover agents, physicians withholding information from dying patients to spare them fear and anxiety, parents concealing from children for years that there really isn't a Santa Claus or an Easter Bunny. Some commentators make a distinction between lies – intentionally deceptive statements – and all other forms of deception that might be described as less direct ways to "manage information." Viewed in this manner, deceiving is "the business of persuasion aided by the art of selective display," and it is effected by two principal behaviors: hiding the real and showing the false. This is exactly the business of magicians.

6.2.3 The magician's tools

Unique among all deceivers is the magician (and by analogy the mediator and mediation advocates). He proclaims before all whom he is about to deceive that he is going to do so. Members of the audience actually know in advance that he will be trying to trick them. Despite this knowledge on the part of the audiences and their ardent efforts to detect the magicians' methods, magicians are consistently effective in deceiving them. Magicians employ five primary tools to keep their methods secret: (1) encouraging the public to accept myths of how magic is done (e.g. audience will miss the slow moves if they are looking for fast ones); (2) distracting and confusing the audience with irrelevancies or "noise"; (3) never telling the audience exactly what he or she is about to do (if the audience doesn't know what the trick is to be, the audience won't know what to look for); (4) using the one-ahead technique (if the audience cannot perceive the beginning of a trick, it will not discern the significance of certain key moves being made in plain view); (5) using the principle of multiple causation (i.e., the magician simulates an alternative method or dissimulates the one actually used, and diverts the audience from settling on the correct hypothesis).

6.2.4 Magicians as problem solvers

Magicians are problem solvers. The problems that they solve are of two principal types: presented problems and discovered problems. Performing tricks and illusions largely entails solving presented problems, while designing new tricks and illusions primarily involves solving discovered problems. Tricks are usually too brief to have complex structures. Illusions are different. All illusions have five basic elements: the phenomenon, the effect, the device(s), the prop(s), and the magician's characterization. They also follow a standard pattern: interest catcher, introduction, statement of theme, kickoff point, preliminaries, instructions, action, presenting the effect, and ending. How effective the magician is at solving either type of problem depends upon how completely he or she understands the psychology of magic.

6.2.5 Effects of magic

To perform magic, magicians need to know both the effects and the methods of magic. There are six principal types of magic effects: appearance (or production), disappearance (or vanishing), transformation, transposition, defiance of natural laws, and mental phenomena. These six basic effects and their counterparts in mediation will be discussed briefly below. In the discussions which follow, in the analogies to caucused mediation, the term "advocate" refers both to parties and their counsel; and "magician mediator" refers to a mediator. Because it is difficult, if not impossible, to explain the effects of magic without collaterally illustrating the methods, which produce them, the discussion which follows in this Section necessarily discusses some of the methods used by magicians to produce the six effects. To learn about magic effects in more detail, consult the Cooley (9).

Appearance. Magicians in mediation sometimes use statistical data and graphs to lure other mediation participants (audience) into believing that certain conclusions should be drawn from a given set of data. Magicians create a materialization of something - an appearance - that is often not fully supported by the data or is not the most relevant portion of several possible aspects of the data. They can accomplish this by selective use of data; the silent majority ruse (the "more people" statement to achieve the appearance of the majority); expansibility (using big numbers instead of percentages); and the selective use of frame of reference.

Disappearance. Magicians cause conclusions drawn from statistics to disappear by deceptive refutation. Types of such refutation include alleging the sample is not random; using the statistics deceptively for creating an appearance, and by using counterstatistics and graphs. Even if they are unsure of the truth of their declaration, magicians declare that presented statistics are not based on a random sample. They can declare, for example, that a sample is not representative in time, space, economically, geographically, or on the basis of sex or age, regardless of whether the particular is even important. Such declaration, whether or not true, can sometimes totally undermine the validity of statistics and make their significance or relevance disappear. Also, if the presenter of statistics uses a frame of reference that is unfavorable to the magician, the magician can shift the frame of reference to a favorable one - without disclosing several other frames of reference unfavorable to the magician. Finally, to achieve disappearance magicians not only use counterstatistics which contradict the originally presented statistics, but they also use those which supplement the original set in such a way that a different conclusion must be drawn.

Transposition. Magician mediators effect simple transposition through the device of postponement. In some situations, when problems seem to the mediator to be unresolvable, the mediator makes them disappear temporarily by tacitly postponing consideration or discussion of them. The mediator then causes the issues to reappear later in his routine when it is more convenient or when it better suits his purposes. All the while, the mediator allows the parties to assume that they have no say in controlling the direction of the discussion. In other situations, the mediator allows the parties to believe that a particular issue relates to one aspect of a problem (is under a particular shell), but later the mediator raises the issue unexpectedly in connection with another aspect of the problem (under another shell) in terms of a trade-off. The mediator then uses the audience's surprise to help reframe its perception of the relative status or substance of the issue.

In mediation, magicians effect compound transpositions by asserting that two things similar in one or more respects will be similar in another or future respect. Magicians know that similarity is not identity and that any analogy is deceptive in that in some respect -- and perhaps a very important respect -- it does not hold true. There are essentially two kinds of analogies used by magicians: literal and figurative. Literal analogies are used to show that two things are similar in structure and/or function. The magician may show the similarities of two things while hiding a serious incompatibility between the two in their structure or function.

Transformation. Magicians can transform the meaning of data by manipulating the dimensions of the data, the medium of it, or both. Furthermore, mediators consider their primary task is to do their best to help parties achieve an agreed solution. In order to do this effectively, they must transform their appearance into a less threatening, camouflaged form. They must assume the construction of reality of each party, gain the trust and respect of each party, and get "in sync" with the hopes, desires, fears, and needs, of each party. Once the intervenor-mediator manages and manipulates verbal and non-verbal cues and language to get in sync, he or she can then move to alter the party's construction of reality by modifying the language and metaphors in use. But the mediator's transformation of self must come first.

Defiance of Natural Laws. Often parties on one side in a mediation marvel at how the mediator is able to penetrate the other side's resistance to settlement. The truth is that the mediator normally does not penetrate the resistance at all; rather, he or she goes around it or causes part or all of the resistant behavior to collapse voluntarily. In certain cases, the mediator physically "goes around" the resistant party representative - usually with, but sometimes without, the representative's permission - and communicates with someone in a higher position of authority. This can serve to destabilize the representative's position of power, particularly if the representative is already insecure in the bureaucracy and if the mediator shares little or no information with the representative that was obtained in the discussion with the superior. Sometimes the representative will become less resistant as soon as he or she has been informed that the mediator intends to converse with the representative's superior or has had a conversation with the superior. If the mediator plays his cards right, and the superior favors compromise to obtain resolution, the representative may become quite flexible and a solution to the conflict may be quickly achieved. The other side may have no knowledge of the method by which the mediator achieved the apparent penetration of the representative's resistance.

Mental Phenomena. The body has a language all its own. A person's posture, gestures, the way they hold their arms, and their facial expressions can communicate messages along with the words they are uttering. Sometimes the nonverbal message is opposite to the verbal message. Magicians are aware of this phenomenon and some of them carefully watch a party's or advocate's body movements and facial gestures to gain insight into what they are actually thinking.

Furthermore, without disclosing what they are doing, some magicians in mediation routinely use neurolinguistic programming techniques to enter another person's construction of reality with a goal of altering that reality. They accomplish this by analyzing, imitating, and approximating another party's speech and language patterns. By pacing or gently mirroring a person's style, gestures, body language, voice tone, timbre, and volume, and use of similar words and metaphors, the magician can build rapport and begin to influence and modify that person's thinking and decision making.

Finally, it is common for magician mediators conducting evaluative mediations to predict the outcome of a case based on their own court experience, jury verdicts, or decisions in similar cases. In fact, such magician mediators, if they were honest with themselves, would have to admit that their predictions are highly speculative. Juries are highly unpredictable in their decision making and the decisions of many appellate courts with judges of diverse political and philosophical orientations are equally unpredictable. The appellate court decision one receives in a case is often dependent on the composition of particular panel of judges randomly assigned to hear and decide the case. Judges may rely on insignificant and even inconspicuous differences to distinguish a case from legal precedent. Thus, in many cases, the magician mediator's prediction is a "best guess" that is accepted by the parties as valid. If the case settles, the truth of the prediction is never tested and the mediator's prediction is deemed by the parties to be truth for that particular dispute.

6.2.6 Methods of magic

In the broadest sense, magicians achieve magical effects by two actions: hiding and showing, magicians hide the real and show the false. There are two principal means by which magicians hide and show to achieve an effect through deception. One relates to the physical, the other to the psychological. Standard deceptive techniques (tricks) using the hands or other physical objects are called devices. The rest of the deceptive techniques are psychological. Any effective method or sequence of steps (a routine) yielding a magic effect usually combines both devices and psychological techniques.

Devices. Magicians use four basic types of devices for deception: sleights, prearrangement, secret apparatus, and arcana. The mediators' "sleights" consist of both noncontingent moves and contingent moves. Noncontingent moves consist of general interventions that mediators initiate in all disputes. Noncontingent moves include identifying important issues, building an agenda, and identifying interests. Contingent moves consist of responses to special or idiosyncratic problems that occur in some mediations. Such moves include mediators' management of the parties' intense anger, bluffing, bargaining in bad faith, mistrust, and miscommunication. Caucuses are contingent strategies which "provide mediators with the greatest opportunity to manipulate parties into an agreement because disputants do not have the advantage of face-to-face communication to test the accuracy of information exchanged."

Mediators use the device of prearrangement to structure the settlement building process so that it has the optimum chance for success. From the time of appointment or selection by the parties, mediators characteristically look for ways to "stack the deck" in favor of settlement in terms of the timing and location of the conference, the parties to be in attendance, the number and types of premediation conferences, and the sequence of premediation caucuses. Normally, for strategic reasons, mediators want control of these premediation decisions. Once the mediation conference begins, the mediator normally establishes himself or herself firmly as the controller of the process and manager of the information exchange, the structure of which the mediator often prearranges instantaneously as the meeting proceeds.

Secret apparatuses used by mediators include pre-planning the physical set-up of the meeting room, regulating the lighting, color, and/or temperature environment of caucus rooms, and specialized gimmicks, such as the availability of meditational music, creative thinking reading material, selected video or audiotapes, puzzles, rubic cubes and the like in caucus rooms. Arcana devices, which work because of mediators' secret knowledge, include effective listening, effective questioning, use of intended and unintended mistakes, instilling fear, inciting anger, and manipulation of mediator and disputant power.

Psychological Methods. Disguise and misdirection or "controlling the spectator's attention," are the two basic psychological methods for achieving magic effects. Mediators use physical disguise in the sense that they assume various roles and change their behavior to meet the needs of the changing situation during the course of a mediation. To elicit certain types of information, a mediator might appear naïve. To "sell" a particular proposal, she might appear compassionate and appeal to the potential "buyer's" emotions. To gain leverage after a party has been caught providing misleading information, she might appear indignant or angry momentarily. To spare a party embarrassment for a mistake or misstatement, she might accept responsibility and serve as a scapegoat. To obtain closure in the final stages of bargaining, she might channel her persuasive power and actively advocate one side's position in a caucus.

Apart from physical disguise, magicians in mediation also use psychological disguise. There are several types of psychological disguise, including simulation, dissimulation, maneuver, and ruse. An explanation of those concepts is beyond the scope of this work. Readers who wish to learn more about them should consult Cooley (9), pp. 60-69.

Misdirection in magic may be defined as "the act of deliberately misguiding from cause to an erroneous effect, to serve an ulterior purpose." There are seven types of misdirection: anticipation; premature consummation; monotony; confusion; diversion; distraction; specific direction. Anticipation, distraction and specific direction are explained immediately below.

A mediator employs the psychological method of anticipation both before and during a mediation. When employing it before the conference, the mediator may "load" the mediation by doing intensive investigation and research. For example, he might do preparatory statistical, survey, or legal research beyond that provided by counsel for the parties. He may also make inquiries to understand the nature and history of the parties' relationships and the history and results of any prior disputes between them. Through this process he may form initial impressions as to what the parties' true needs and interests are and what resources are available to satisfy them.

Mediators employ the misdirection stratagem of distraction when they use the paradox, an effective technique which can change the context of a dispute. The paradox uses the force of a party's resistance to cause shifts in his or her thinking. Thus a mediator who wants parties to consider their needs and interests may not go to that topic directly at the outset of the mediation. Instead the mediator may use the paradox to distract the parties' attention from his true goal. It is well known that an entrenched party thwarts any perceived challenge to his or her position. Armed with this knowledge, the experienced mediator, instead of challenging the party's position, initially encourages the party to pursue the course of action compelled by her position and to do everything necessary to obtain the result on which she is fixed. Thus the paradox – intensifying her commitment to a stated course of action – actually results in the lessening of that commitment. Thus, the mediator might initially distract the entrenched party, skeptical of mediation, as follows: "You certainly have every opportunity and right to go to court. Far be it from me to try to keep you here in mediation and convince you of something against your will."

The most common specific direction stratagem used by mediators is issue selection. After uncovering a broad range of issues through discussions in the initial joint sessions and through caucusing separately with the parties, mediators consciously select the issues most likely to be settled, to the exclusion of others, even though one or more of the parties wish to focus on other issues.

It is hoped that this discussion assists mediators: (1) in identifying and classifying deceptive strategies and tactics in the layered processes of negotiation and mediation; and (2) by generating interest among scholars and practitioners to begin exploring and identifying the ethical limits of acceptable deception as practiced by mediators and mediation advocates.

6.3 MATH THINK

[**Editor's Note:** *This section contains edited excerpts from Cooley (7), pp. 97-129, and Cooley (8), pp. 32-39, with footnotes omitted.*]

6.3.1 Descartes' Rules for the Direction of the Mind

René Descartes, widely regarded as the "father of modern philosophy" and the discoverer of the foundations of analytic or co-ordinate geometry, was from a family of lawyers and judges. Although

Descartes shunned a career in law and instead chose a life path in mathematics and philosophy, his intellectual achievements as a problem solver in mathematics are, paradoxically, more relevant to law practitioners now, nearly four hundred years after he received his law degree, than they ever have been in the past. With the advent of alternative dispute resolution and its principal problem solving processes of collaborative negotiation and mediation, Descartes' lifetime quest to invent a universal method for solving problems takes on an aura of special significance for practicing lawyers.

When Descartes set out to write his Rules for the Direction of the Mind, which is essentially a paradigm of analytic method in problem solving, his goal was to draft 36 Rules, contained in three separate books. The first book (Rules 1-12) was to deal with what he called the "simple natures" of problems; the second book (Rules 13-24) was to deal with natures deduced from the natures which are most simple and self-evident; the third book (Rules 25-36), from "those natures that presuppose others which experience shows us to be composite in reality." Distracted by other work, Descartes completed only Rules 1through 21 in his lifetime. As actually drafted, Rules 1 through 11 provided general guidance for problem solvers, and Rule 12 and those which followed described this analytic method in more detail. This Section will explore the first eleven of Descartes' twenty-one Rules for the Direction of the Mind and their application in the mediation and collaborative negotiation settings (referred to collectively as "mediational problem solving").

> Rule 1: Your goal in problem solving should be to direct your mind with a view to forming true and sound judgments

In explanation of this rule, Descartes notes that when people see similarity between two things, they have the habit of ascribing to one what they find true of the other, even when the two are not in that respect similar. From this premise he finds a basis to draw what he believes to be clear distinctions between art and science. He does this to make the point that a properly "scientific" approach to finding truth can be compromised inappropriately by artistic interference. He sees the separate sciences as interconnected and, together, constituting human wisdom. For him, what makes us stray from the correct way of seeking the truth is chiefly our ignoring the general end of universal wisdom and directing our studies towards some particular ends. Rule One suggests a very useful problem solving mindset for mediators and negotiators. In essence, as the key to achieving sound solutions, Descartes is advocating a study of problem solving process as opposed to the particular substance of particular problems. The process should be applicable to the entire universe of problems confronting the problem solver, regardless of topic. The mediator or negotiator should be conditioned to see the whole, to see connections and patterns, and to avoid concentrating unnecessarily on details. In some ways, Descartes' Rule One finds a reflection in Edward de Bono's discussion of "attention areas" in his book Lateral Thinking: Creativity Step by Step.

> Rule 2: Attend only to those objects which your mind seems capable of having certain and indubitable cognition.

In explanation of Rule Two, Descartes defines knowledge as "certain and evident cognition." At the same time, he recognizes that knowledge, so defined, is difficult to obtain. He notes that whenever two persons make opposite judgments about the same thing, the only thing certain is that at least one of them is mistaken, and it is unlikely that one of them has knowledge. It is likely that neither has knowledge because if the reasoning of one of the two were compelling, the other should be convinced of the certainty of the asserted conclusion. He further contends that it is better never to study at all than to study objects which are so difficult that it is impossible to distinguish what is true from what is false, because in such case, we are forced to accept the doubtful as certain.

He further asserts that the two ways of arriving at a knowledge of things is through experience and through deduction. According to Descartes, errors in finding truth rarely arise from faulty reasoning, rather such errors occur because problem solvers take for granted certain poorly understood observations or rely on rash or groundless judgments. Many people, he points out, feel free to make more confident guesses about matters which are obscure than about matters which are clear.

The message of Rule Two for mediators and negotiators is that when solving a problem, it is advisable to suspend judgment about any perceived set of facts and to challenge, at least mentally, any and all assumptions about what is evidence, what is appropriate inference, what is fact, and what is an appropriate conclusion. The parties' perceptions, derived through their experience or observation of an event, are not necessarily fact regardless of how honest their beliefs are that their perceptions are accurate. It may be an illusion, much in the way a person's perception is "tricked" by an optical illusion. It is a wise strategy for the mediator or negotiator to assume certain information as true for the purpose of proposing a solution or an avenue for solution rather than to come to any firm conclusion in his or her own mind as to the actual truth or certainty of the information. Keep the problem solving process, pure, simple, and untainted by the substance of the problem, or by your conclusions concerning that substance. Have faith in the inevitability of the process and let the appropriately applied and gently guided process solve the problem. In many situations, the solution will find itself.

> Rule 3: Investigate objects that you can clearly and evidently intuit or deduce with certainty, without regard to the views of others or your own conjecture.

The advice offered by Descartes in explanation of Rule Three is critical to mediators and negotiators. In essence, he communicates that while knowledge gained by reading the writings of experts may be of some benefit to problem solvers, it cannot substitute for developing one's own mental ability in problem solving. It is not sufficient, Descartes implies, for problem solvers merely to copy or mimic another problem solver's successful technique in solving a specific problem, or to have a "toolbox" of techniques from which to select and to use, mechanically, for trouble-shooting purposes. These things are helpful, but not sufficient. The effective problem solver must first understand how his or her mind works, must know the difference between intuition and deduction, and must know when and how to use each. The effective problem solver needs to be comfortable thinking about thinking and in applying the appropriate thinking process or processes to the problem presented.

> Rule 4: You need a method if you are going to investigate the truth of things.

Descartes urges problem solvers not to leave investigation for solutions to chance. He believes that "It is far better never to contemplate investigating the truth about any matter than to do so without method." He defines method to be "reliable rules which are easy to apply, and such that if one follows them exactly, one will never take what is false to be true or fruitlessly expend one's mental efforts ..."

Rule Four is instructive for mediators and negotiators in that it suggests that mental capacity or thinking ability is not, in itself, sufficient in problem solving but rather the problem solver must employ a method to guide and direct the thinking function.

> Rule 5: The method consists in ordering and arranging objects on which you must concentrate your mind's eye in order to discover some truth.

> Rule 6: Attend to what is most simple in each series of things in which you have directly deduced some truths and observe how all the remaining things are more or less removed from or equal to the simplest.

> Rule 7: Survey every single thing relating to your undertaking in a continuous and wholly uninterrupted sweep of thought, and include them in a sufficient and well-ordered enumeration

A modern interpretation of Rules Five, Six, and Seven, as they relate to problem solving in mediation and negotiation, might be as follows. When approaching a negotiation problem, be prepared.

Have in mind some type of overall ordered arrangement or method by which to proceed. This, of course, can be modified as you go along, but initially you should be prepared to give the problem solving process structure and direction. Be mindful that in most problem solving experiences in collaborative negotiation, there are few absolutes -- i.e. unchangeable positions, unmodifiable interests, uncompromisable objectives. Consider most things to be relative, not absolute, in negotiation, while recognizing that some things might appear more absolute than others from one point of view, yet more relative from a different point of view. Start with easy, rather than difficult, matters in the problem solving process. The problem solver should first look for basic characteristics of both the relationship of the parties and the substance of the dispute. From these basic characteristics, other characteristics might be able to be deduced which might suggest problem solving routes. Do not, however, get so carried away with isolated matters, or details related to them, that you cannot see the forest for the trees. Step back, mentally, at various intervals throughout the problem solving process and take a look at the big picture. From time to time, reflect attentively on previous negotiation and mediation experiences to discover common basic characteristics of relationships or of disputes and consider why it was possible to discover some of these basic characteristics sooner and more easily than others. This procedure may enable the problem solver to determine, when approaching any specific problem in negotiation or mediation, which points or topics he or she may usefully concentrate on discovering first.

> Rule 8: If in your examination of a series of things you encounter something which your intellect is unable to intuit sufficiently well, stop at that point.

In explanation of Rule Eight, Descartes states that the knowledge required in problem solving is divided into two types: knowledge of the faculties of the problem solver available to that problem solver and knowledge of the things it is possible to know to solve the problem. As to the first type, Descartes says that while the intellect is capable of knowledge, it can be assisted or impeded by the faculties of imagination, sense-perception, and memory. These three faculties, he urges, should be examined carefully in each situation to see which would be a hindrance and which would be an asset in the problem solving process. As to the second type of knowledge, Descartes recommends that problem solvers should deal with things it is possible to know in solving a problem only insofar as they are in reach of the intellect. He divides these things into two parts: absolutely simple natures and complex or composite natures. Finally, he observes that in problem solving, a problem solver should realize that success depends upon some observation which is not within his power to make, and therefore he/she should not blame his/her intelligence.

Descartes' advice in Rule Eight holds great significance for mediators and negotiators. Essentially, he is saying that in problem solving, mediators and negotiators must be consciously aware of their own mental faculties and understand which of their mental faculties are helpful or unhelpful in the various phases of problem solving. He also puts mediators and negotiators on notice that there may be problems incapable of solution because of obstacles presented by the nature of the problem itself or by the human condition. Mediators and negotiators who have ably employed their mental faculties should not blame themselves when they are unable to produce a mutually acceptable solution. The discovery that a problem cannot be negotiated or mediated to a solution is knowledge in itself, and may suggest that a solution can be achievable only through the parties' relinquishing their joint decision making (problem solving) function to another decision-making person or entity, perhaps an arbitrator, who will make the decision and solve the problem for them.

> Rule 9: Concentrate your mind's eye upon the most insignificant and easiest of matters, and dwell on them long enough to acquire the habit of intuiting the truth distinctly and clearly.

After first reminding the reader that intuition and deduction are the actions or operations of intellect on which problem solvers exclusively rely in the acquisition of knowledge, Descartes states that the purpose of Rule Nine is to explain how the problem solver can make the employment of intuition and deduction more skillful and how the problem solver can cultivate two special mental faculties:

perspicacity in the distinct intuition of particular things and discernment in the methodical deduction of one thing from another. His explanation of Rule Nine largely relates to perspicacity; his explanation of Rule Ten (see below) mostly concerns discernment in the methodical deduction of one thing from another.

For mediators and negotiators, Descartes continues to emphasize the importance of focusing on the easiest and the simplest aspects of the problem first. The ability to focus on and analyze one object (each tree in the forest) at a time – perspicacity - is as important to the problem solver, as being able to step back mentally from time to time to see the "big picture" (the entire forest) as described in Rule Seven. Indirectly, Descartes is also suggesting that using simple analogies is a helpful method in initiating the problem solving process or in finding new avenues to solutions.

> Rule 10: Investigate what others have already discovered and methodically survey even the most insignificant products of human skill, especially those which display or predispose order.

In explanation of this Rule, Descartes exhorts problem solvers to recognize the limits of classical dialectic, syllogism, and rhetoric in producing truth. He further urges problem solvers not to take the ancient Greek reasoning tools at face value without questioning their utility and valid application in the particular problem solving task at hand.

The message here for mediators and negotiators is that, in problem solving, one should always be on guard to test the validity of all reasoning being used. Not only can the truth of premises be flawed, but also inferences drawn from premises can be defective.

> Rule 11: If you deduce something from a number of simple propositions, run through them mentally, reflect on their relations to one another, and form a simultaneous conception of several of them.

In explaining Rule Eleven, Descartes describes the ways in which intuition and enumeration aid and complement one another. He asserts that they actually seem to coalesce into a single operation, through a movement of thought, which involves carefully intuiting one thing and passing on at once to the others. It is suggested that mediators and negotiators apply this Rule in connection with Rules Three, Seven, Nine, and Ten. Readers who wish to learn more about Descartes' Rules for the Direction of the Mind and about the art of geometric imagineering should consult Cooley (7).

6.3.2 Leibniz's Geometry of Situation

Gottfried Wilhelm von Leibniz (pronounced Libe - nits), most well known as the inventor of the infinitesimal calculus (differential and integral calculus), exemplified the Renaissance ideal of the universal man with his multi-faceted interests and accomplishments. He was a lawyer, scientist, inventor, diplomat, poet, philologist, logician, moralist, theologian, historian, and philosopher. But above all, he was a problem solver, intent on identifying a universal method for interpersonal communication and for solving problems, which he referred to as the "universal characteristic", an essential ingredient for his dream of human progress and social harmony.

Leibniz conceived what he called his "geometry of situation," a new form of graphic representation that he viewed as entirely different from algebra and that would have great advantages in representing to the mind, exactly and in a way faithful to its nature, even without numbers, everything which depends on sense perception. This new technique, according to Leibniz, followed visual figures, could not fail to give the solution, the construction, and the geometric demonstration all at the same time, and in a natural way and in one analysis, through determined procedure.

Leibniz's "geometry of situation" had ten propositions, the first four of which are as follows:

GEOMETRY OF SITUATION

1. All points in the world are congruent to each other, that is, one can always be put in place of another.

2. The situation of one point in relation to another can be thought of without expressing the straight line joining them, provided they are thought of as joined by some line, whatever it may be; and, if this line is assumed to be rigid, the situation of the two points in relation to each other will be immutable.

3. Two points can be thought of as having the same situation in relation to each other as two other points have, if the one pair can be joined by a line which is congruent with the line joining the other pair.

4. There is a difference between the endpoints of a line and the situation of the endpoints in relation to each other, and the line itself.

In his advanced thinking on geometry of situation, Leibniz (through his theory of analysis of situation) distinguished between mathematical analysis and situation analysis. Mathematical analysis, in Leibniz's thinking, deals with magnitude not situation. Situation, on the other hand, deals with data and with the positions of the unknown entities or their loci. In Leibniz's mind, analysis must be carried through to first principles and elements of situation -- what he called the "perfect analysis."

Geometry of situation was, for Leibniz, part of his larger theory of relations. Leibniz believed:

LEIBNIZ'S THEORY OF RELATIONS

1. Society ascribes labels to many types of human relations: parent-child; employer-employee; family; husband-wife; partner-to-partner; master-servant; business-to-business or corporate; government-citizen, etc. These are the paradigm structures – the ideal structures of relations. This is the first aspect of relation.

2. The second aspect of relation consists of:

    (a) the actual structure of the relation and

    (b) the actual substance of the relation - the emotional and communicational foundation, which includes adaptability to change.

3. Change can occur in the actual structure of the relation only when, over time, there is change in the substance - or emotional and communicational foundation – of the relation.

Using Leibniz's geometry of situation and theory of relations, an analysis of a particular interpersonal relationship can be geometrically engineered as described below.

For simplicity, the vehicle we will use for analysis is the typical parent-child relationships existing within the family setting. Assume that the particular family under consideration consists of a Father (F), Mother (M), and a Daughter (D). The particular issue causing the present conflict is the Father's requirement that the Daughter, who is a junior in high school, be home by midnight on Friday and Saturday evenings. Assume further that through extensive discussion with all three family members, you, a neutral third party, have discovered much about the conflict behavior of each of them and the family's rule-creating and rule-enforcing processes. From what you can presently decipher, the family is hierarchical in structure, though the individual perceptions of the family members vary somewhat on this matter. You are aware of the five types of conflict behavior (avoiding, accommodating, competing, compromising, and collaborating), and have ascribed geometrical symbols to each of them as shown in the chart below.

CONFLICT BEHAVIOR	DESCRIPTIVE WORD	GEOMETRIC SYMBOL
Avoiding	Obtuse	▽
Accommodating	Form-fitting	C
Competing	Squared-off	□
Compromising	Half-a-slice	◺
Collaborating	Roundly satisfying	○

Through your discussions, you have determined that the Father is predominantly competitive, the Daughter is compromising, and the Mother is collaborative. But as we shall see in the analysis infra, the individual family members may perceive that the members have conflict behavior styles different from these. You are now ready to geometrically imagineer some ideas about the structure (as opposed to substance) of the parent-child relationships existing within this family and about the family relationship overall.

Keeping in mind, Leibniz's propositions 1 through 4 of his geometry of situation, the above-described family situation is perceived from the perspective of each endpoint (family member). However, instead of using points to identify the family members, you can use the geometrical symbols described in the chart immediately above. Thus, in graphically illustrating the structure of the relationship, the father could be represented by a square, the daughter by a right triangle, and the mother by a circle. The size of these symbols may vary in relation to the perspective of each individual family member, depending on the amount of power or authority each member perceives himself or herself and the other two members to possess. The family authority structure, as perceived by each individual family member, appears in the chart below along with the authority structure each family member believes would improve the current rule-creating (C) and rule-enforcing (E) process. The arrows indicate the source of responsibility for rule-creating and rule-enforcing as directed toward the member who is expected to conform. The letters dC and dE stand for participation in the decision making processes for creating rules and enforcing rules, respectively.

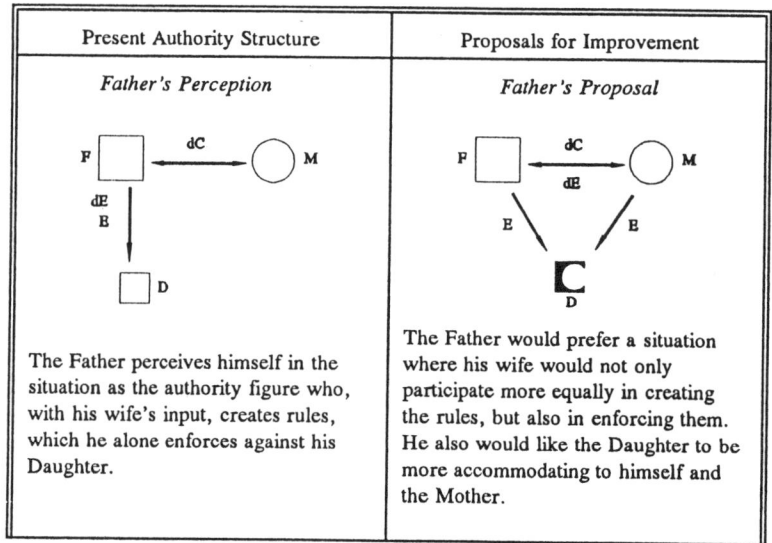

Creative Problem Solver's Handbook for Negotiators and Mediators

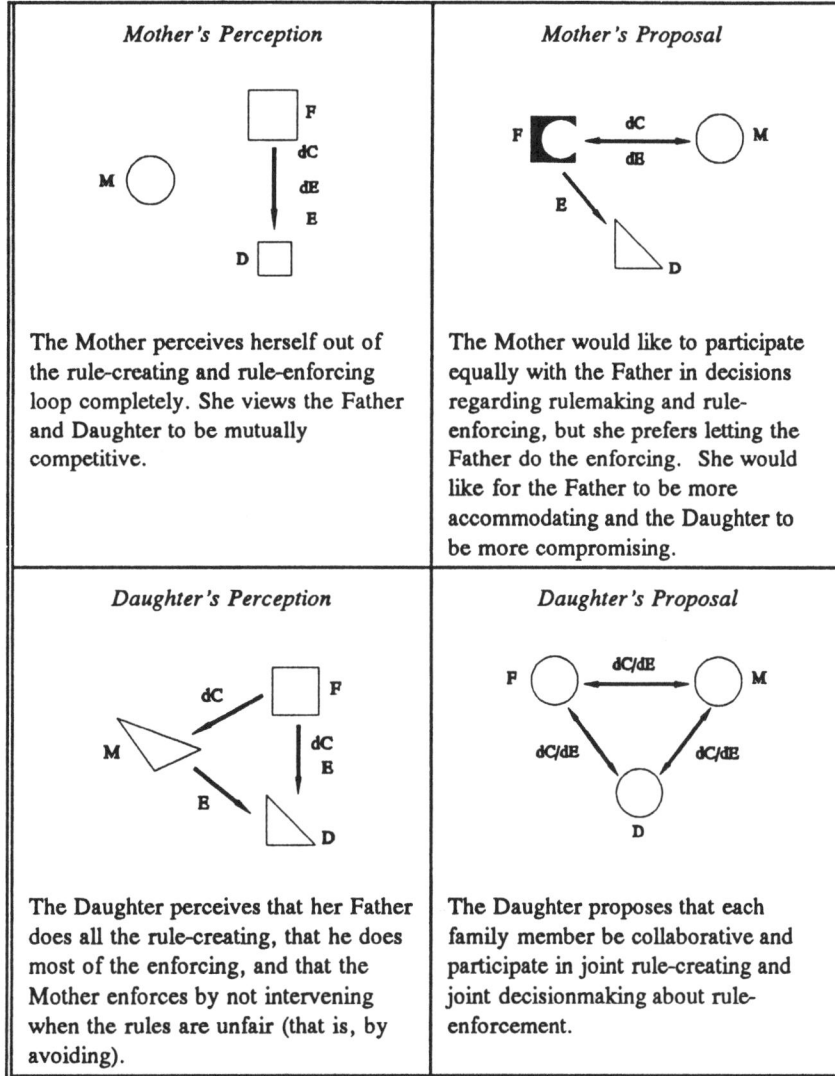

Readers who wish to learn more about geometric imagineering the substance of relationships and about the calculus of change in negotiation and mediation should consult Cooley (8).

6.4 MUSIC THINK

[**Editor's Note**: *This section contains edited excerpts from Cooley (12), with footnotes omitted.*]

6.4.1 The music metaphor for mediation

Whether or not you agree with my thesis that mediation is music, perhaps you will be able to accept, at least, that music serves as a useful metaphor to describe mediation and to acquire insight into the mediation process and the role of the mediator.

To some, music (including both composition and performance) and mediation may be seen as a conflict of two separate mental representations. But on closer scrutiny, this initial conflict of mental representations can be resolved by identifying and examining the essences of each. The nature and shared essence of these two phenomena are not seriously disputable. Each is an art form and the essence of each is art. If we accept this statement as axiomatic, the next step is to compare their essential art to determine similarities or differences.

Descriptions of "art" evoke the question of the relationship between different art forms, e.g. literature, poetry, drama, sculpture, painting, music, etc. Is the meaning of the word "art" the same as applied to all art forms? Is there a "hierarchy of arts," depending on the art form, or is there truly a "commonwealth of arts?"

Most art experts would agree that all of the arts are, in essence, one, but that they separately have discrete differences which make them unique. Essentially, all arts create forms to express the life of feeling (not necessarily the feeling the artist happens to have); and they all do it by the same basic principles. But there the simple comparison ends. Each art form creates a different kind of experience altogether; each makes its own peculiar primary creative end product. Sculpture creates a real three-dimensional visual space; painting, a virtual two or three-dimensional space; dance, a realm of interacting powers.

Music is an unusual art form in that it has three discrete types of creative products: a visual space (written symbols - composition); audible tones (performed composition); and virtual time. The art form of mediation also shares these discrete end products. Mediation has a visual aspect that consists of written and nonwritten symbols (i.e. compositional - agreement to mediate, settlement agreement - and nonverbal (body) language), an audible aspect that is in the nature of performance, and a virtual time aspect (which permits the mediator to expand or contract time to meet the needs of the performance). This correlation of creative aspects between music and mediation preliminarily indicates that music may serve as a useful metaphor to describe mediation and to acquire insight into the mediation process and the role of the mediator.

The five basic elements, then, of sensed music include sound, tone, melody, harmony, and rhythm. High order applications of the human sensory system to these basic elements include: composition, performance, listening, and understanding. Since the effective mediator must perceive and comprehend the basic elements and their sensory applications, it is to these topics we now turn. Addressed in the next subsections are sound and tone, two of the five basic elements of sensed music and their sensory applications in mediation.

6.4.2 Sound in music

The most basic element of music is sound. But sound has different definitions depending on the perspective of the living organism that senses it. To the physicist, sound is nothing more than vibrations - of or in matter, including air molecules. A physicist can precisely measure quantities and qualities of sound. In contrast, to the psychologist, sound is a kind of experience, a sensation that the brain extracts from the environment. Sound registers as vibrating air molecules on human ear drums. Not all living creatures sense sound, as vibrations, identically. To the cricket, the "sound" of certain frequencies of its colleagues' rasping legs registers as vibrations on thinnings of its front knees. Thus, a cricket's experience of sound is "soundless" by human standards. To a bird, the sounds of its colleagues' noises consist of many frequencies. Birds search for patterns of repetition of frequencies and are able to recognize each other's individual voices, even regional dialects. Whales, similarly, engage in half-hour-long chants of monotonous repetition. But crickets, birds, and whales have no experience of music. Only human beings experience music. It is our brains, not theirs, that can relate their sounds to the concept of music. Music is much more than mere sound.

6.4.3 Sound in mediation

In mediation, sound is information, both auditory and visual, from any source. Mediation sound includes both relevant and irrelevant information, and it has different definitions depending on the perspective of the person who senses it. To the disinterested observer unfamiliar with the subject matter or context of a particular mediated dispute, mediation sound, initially at least, often seems to be nothing more than an oscillation of contentions based on contradictory facts and/or conflicting prescribed norms. This disinterested observer can objectively measure quantities and qualities of this informational sound, and if asked, could evaluate and categorize it in relation to some prescribed norm. This, in essence, is what the judge or arbitrator does in relation to informational sound. In contrast, to the experienced mediator, mediation sound, which initially registers as oscillating contentions, is a kind of experience. It is a sensation triggering recalled similar situations that the mediator's brain extracts from the environment of memory.

Not all mediators sense informational sound identically. To the purely evaluative mediator, the oscillations of the parties' contentions register as a request for an opinion. On the other hand, this purely evaluative mediator's experience of mediation sound is "soundless" by the standards of a purely facilitative or purely transformative mediator. The latter two types of mediators know that the initial mediation "noises" actually consist of many frequencies, most of which are totally obscured by the predominant informational oscillations. These two types of mediators search for patterns of similar frequencies and are able to recognize individual voices and even aligned voices. Mediation, however, is much more than the mediator recognizing mere informational sound.

6.4.4 Tone in music

Tone, as an element of music, is formed from a particular pattern of sound "produced only by the vibration of certain simple shapes." Though wind may occasionally "whistle" and brooks may "babble," these sounds are generally thought to be noise. The vibrating shapes that produce tone rarely occur naturally. Simple man-made shapes of matter often make beautiful sounds because they vibrate in simple ways.

Thus, shorter string lengths produce higher frequencies. However, even when a guitar string is divided and plucked, its top and bottom halves vibrate independently at double the fundamental frequency – the frequency at which the undivided whole string vibrates. These independent vibrations are called overtones (or harmonics, or partials). A perfect or ideal string would produce an infinite number of overtones, but most sounds deemed musical produce twenty or fewer overtones. A tone, as an element of music, results when sounds are arranged in an orderly pattern of overtones. Pleasing tones in music have a mathematical basis.

Besides the frequencies of tones and overtones, the resonance of originating frequencies plays a key role in producing music. Every object has resonant frequencies. Some objects are massive and stiff, which causes them to repel sound; other objects are more flexible. Massive objects resist rapid vibration and tend to resonate at low frequencies; smaller objects tend to resonate at high frequency. When sound approaches an object, the sound consists of many frequencies. The object's resonant frequencies tend to be sustained, while other frequencies tend to be damped.

6.4.5 Tone in mediation

In mediation, parties and their lawyers are the musical instruments that produce mediation sound. Particular patterns of mediation sound are called tones. Mediation tones are of three types: high frequency – tones are legal positions (and/or high emotions); mid-frequency – tones are bargaining positions (and/ or moderate emotions); and low or fundamental frequency – tones are the basic needs of the parties (low emotion). There are seven categories of basic needs or fundamental mediation tones: physiological, safety and security, love and belonging, esteem, self-actualization, to know and understand, and aesthetic. All mediation tones are constructed by orderly, though often indiscernible, sequences of overtones - the parties' underlying interests. These interests can range across the bargaining and legal positions of the parties, but commonly are not separately identifiable in those ranges because they energize and buttress the seven fundamental mediation tones. A perfect dispute situation could produce an infinite number of interests (overtones), but most mediation sounds deemed overtonal that recur in dispute contexts number in the range of thirty or fewer. These recurring interests (overtones) are identified in the table of interests/resources appearing in Section 3.1.18 above. But, of course, many of these interests (overtones) shown in the table can manifest themselves differently, depending on the dispute context and on the nature of the fundamental need (tone) to which they are related. For example, consider the items in the table metaphorically -- that is, in the broadest sense possible. Thus, in the mediation of a business dispute, "volume" could refer to tripling a marketing effort (i.e. turning up the volume of the corporate message), or decreasing the amount of production output, or increasing the amount of storage space in a warehouse. "Rate" could refer to frequency of occurrence, or a commission or discount, or an evaluation of products, services, or performance, and so on.

Resonance of the above-described tones and overtones in mediation plays a key role in producing the music of mediation. Every participant in a mediation has resonant properties. Some participants (e.g. multi-national corporations) are massive and stiff, which may cause them to repel mediation sound of other participants; still other mediation participants may be flexible. When mediation sound approaches a participant, the sound often consists of many mixed frequencies in terms of substantive and emotional issues. Massive and/or powerful participants tend to resist rapid vibration (others' legal positions) and are more likely to resonate with other participants in lower frequencies, where their and other participants' basic needs (including the need for a bargained result) are at stake. Mediation participants with little power tend to resonate at high frequency when matters of emotion are involved. When mediation participants interact, their dominant, separate resonant frequencies (e.g. process preferences and issue priorities) are identified and tend to be sustained through the help of the mediator, while other less dominant or inconsequential frequencies tend to be dampened.

6.5 ROBERT D. BENJAMIN: THE PHYSICS OF MEDIATION: REFLECTIONS OF SCIENTIFIC THEORY IN PROFESSIONAL MEDIATION PRACTICE

[**Editor's Note:** *This section consists of edited excerpts from an article by the same title and by the same author published in* Mediation Quarterly, *Vol. 8, no. 2, Winter, 1990. Copyright © 1990 by John Wiley & Sons, Inc. Reprinted with permission of John Wiley & Sons, Inc..*]

6.5.1 Mediation practice and scientific inquiry: science and scientism

Developments in scientific thought and theory provide a helpful analogue for understanding the emergence of mediation practice. Using science as a model, however, requires that a distinction be drawn between scientific thought and "scientism." Scientific thought is too often misapplied in non-scientific realms to postulate that human behavior can be accounted for by scientific principles. Such efforts are susceptible to reductionist notions, which arise from a fundamental misconception of what science is about....

Law and mental health, as they have traditionally been practiced are the flat worlds of the metaphor; mediation, by comparison, is a round world. Mediation practice is far more than a compilation of skills, strategies, and techniques to settle conflicts; it offers a significantly different model for professional practice in general. Mediation works from a conceptual framework and epistemology [thinking processes and belief systems] that differ from notions of traditional practice....

Chaos theory, much like mediation in its own context, is proceeding to change the thinking frame within science. Like mediation, chaos theory emerged out of necessity, not as a predictable point on a straight line of scientific discovery. The theorists who developed chaos theory broke across the established lines of scientific and technological disciplines: physicists, biologists, mathematicians, meteorologists, and engineers al contributed to a systemic vision that all the theory to clarify. Each contributor had to fight the trend in his or her own discipline toward specialization and reductionism. Each had to stray outside the normal bounds of the special to pursue an idea that to some extent still is not recognized as a legitimate line of inquiry.

The origins of mediation practice are very similar. Mediation requires a different thinking frame that cuts across the lines of the traditional established disciplines. Psychologists, social workers, sociologists, social policy analysts, lawyers, court administrators, and political scientists all came to the realization that the traditional practice models of their separate disciplines were inadequate to effectively understand, accommodate, and resolve conflict. That inadequacy was especially clear when families were concerned. Divorce and separation are, after all, simultaneously legal, interpersonal, and economic events. Treating divorce solely as a legal matter is dysfunctional at best and in some cases downright harmful to clients....

6.5.2 Professions and professionals from a systems theory perspective

To understand how paradigm shifts [see Kuhn's *Structure of Scientific Revolutions*] occur across professions, it is necessary to understand systems theory ... Systems theory is premised on the synergistic notion that the whole is greater than the sum of its parts. A profession, as an organization, is more than a collection of people with the same vocational interest. The system is an organism in a real sense. It functions and responds to stimuli, external and internal, first to preserve and maintain itself and then to advance toward shared goals. Systems are characterized by set boundaries (or jurisdictions), internal hierarchies, developed interactional and communication patterns with the system, and transgenerational patterns (history). Within the system, subsystems of members or parts of the organization emerge. The prevailing paradigm of a discipline is susceptible to all these forces and dynamics.

The paradigms that define how a professional (doctor, lawyer, or therapist) is supposed to practice are in a real sense a reflection of the purpose, history, and politics of the professional organization. When the boundaries or jurisdiction of the organization or discipline is too open, then the body's [reason for being] will be diffused and lost. If anyone can claim to be a professional the validity of the profession is destroyed. If, on the other hand, the boundaries of the organization are too rigid, and the entrance requirements cannot reasonably be met, then the system will wither and cease to function .... Similarly, within the system, if the professionalization of the discipline becomes wed to an unyielding practice paradigm that restricts the practitioner's vision, then no new growth can emerge. Paradoxically, it is only against a firm established paradigm of practice that a practitioner may recognize that something has gone sufficiently wrong to require a paradigm shift .... For professional systems, as for all systems, there is no right balance or stasis, but rather an ongoing dynamic to maintain balance in the face of change.

6.5.3 Toward a theory of mediation practice

Mediation practice is to traditional and mental health disciplines what quantum mechanics and the theory of relativity are to classical Newtonian physics. Thinking and explaining events in linear terms is appealing, but nature is in reality a complex network and not a chain of events. The family system, an organism with its own internal chemistry, functions systemically, not mechanistically. As a nonlinear dynamic system, it is synergistic: the whole is greater than the sum of its parts. A family system, like subatomic particles, responds to forces in the macro systems of the society at large – social, legal, and economic. Just as scientists are compelled to understand multivariate biochemical factors in order to deal with complex phenomena, so must mediators understand multivariate psychosocial and legal factors in problem solving.

6.5.4 Mediation as a paradigm for professional practice: the reflective practice paradigm

As mediation practice continues to develop, it provides a paradigm for professional practice outside mediation. Much of a mediator's job requires what Donald Schön terms "reflection in action." Reflective practice, like quantum mechanics, addresses the uncertainty and complexity of the issues that face present-day professionals. Its emphasis is not on knowing the right answer but on having a sense of how to proceed, how to approach problem solving. The professional must improvise, [as Schön says] "combining and recombining a set of figures within the scheme which bounds and gives coherence to the performance." In fact, the imagery of quantum theory is slowly insinuating a whole new metaphor and worldview into society in general and especially into mediation practice ... Mediation requires "the systematic use of intuition," an oxymoron that connotes an approach to problem solving that uses both analytical and intuitive skills and strategies....

Four assumptions of mediation practice that most clearly demonstrate the paradigmatic shift from a technical-rational to a reflective epistemology are implicit in most primers on the mediation process ...

1. Conflict and change are constants in human relationships. There is no final resolution ... Conflict can be constructive, offering opportunity as well as risk. Change is accepted as part of the life cycle that can be effectively managed by not stopped ... Thus, a dynamic conceptualization is substituted for a static notion of change.

2. Parties can be empowered and take responsibility for the resolution of conflict within their family systems, obtaining outcomes that suit their purposes.

3. The mediator (or professional) is responsible for the process, not the outcome ...

4. The circumstances of each case are situational, not deterministic. The mediator must tailor strategies and apply knowledge in the particular case rather than impose formulaic solutions ... .

... [R]ather than pretending to play the static role of a neutral party, the mediator's task is to assume a balanced position between the parties in the dynamic and ever-shifting conflict. Equilibrium is not viable; the system is never at rest. Conflict and change are likely to continue even after the present issues are ostensibly resolved. The mediator's purpose is to help the parties adopt a process for future conflict management ....

6.5.5 Application of the reflective (mediative) paradigm

Those who view mediation practice as merely a bundle of skills, strategies, and techniques to be used in lieu of litigators unnecessarily limit the importance and significance of the underlying thinking frame of the mediation process. The development of mediation is helping to change the nature of professional practice. As more lawyers and mental health professionals engage in learning and understanding the mediation process, they are beginning to adopt, intentionally or unintentionally, that underlying reflective thinking frame. As that happens, the epistemological premises of mediation and the reflective paradigm will continue to infiltrate the professional culture of the practitioner's profession of origin.

That the reflective practice paradigm is becoming more evident in many disciplines should not be surprising, since professional disciplines are interdependent .... Scientific research and development in physics, biology, and engineering have been significantly affected. Medical practice is being reviewed in light of the underlying principles of systems theory and by extension, the reflective paradigm .... Architecture, urban planning and environmental engineers have all begun to adopt a systemic approach to practice simply to cope with the complexity of problem solving in that context. Even in organizational management and business, there is a growing recognition that the manager cannot just impose directions but must be an effective problem solver .... In the mental health professions, while systemic thinking has been applied in family therapy, many recognize the importance of applying that thinking frame to the societal macro systems that have a direct effect on their clients ....

6.5.6 Significance of the paradigm shift to the practice of mediation

. . . Professionalization of mediation in the traditional sense, could contribute to the disempowerment of parties .... Too often, the discussion of professionalization becomes confused with professionalism .... Professionalization looks back to the technical rational epistemology of the professional as expert and a profession characterized by a body of knowledge and transmissible skills. Regulation of a profession is inherently dependent on logical positivist notions and forced to focus on linear criteria such as credentials and degrees.

Although traditional regulatory schemes pose a troublesome dilemma for the development of mediation, they need not impede that development. Without focusing on who should be permitted to mediate, legislative provisions can protect the integrity of the mediation process and foster the availability of mediation and can encourage the development of the profession. The emphasis should be on defining and enhancing the competency of mediator practice rather than merely on professionalizing practice....

[Robert D. Benjamin, M.S.W., J.D., has been a practicing mediator for over 25 years in most dispute contexts, including business, civil/commercial, family/divorce, employment, health care, and organizational matters. He presents negotiation, mediation and conflict management workshops, seminars, and training courses nationally and internationally. He is a Fellow at the Straus Institute for Dispute Resolution and an Adjunct Professor at the Pepperdine University School of Law, and an Adjunct Professor in several graduate programs, including Southern Methodist University, Conflict Resolution Program and Washington University in St. Louis. He is a past president of the Academy of Family Mediators and an Advanced Practitioner Member of the Association for Conflict Resolution. He can be reached at: rbenjamin@mediate.com.]

6.6 ROBERT D. BENJAMIN: GUERILLA MEDIATION: THE USE OF WARFARE STRATEGIES IN THE MANAGEMENT OF CONFLICT AND PURSUIT OF PEACE

[**Editor's Note:** *This article was originally posted at Mediate.com in October, 1998, and is reprinted here with the permission of its author, Robert D. Benjamin, and Mediate.com.*]

6.6.1 Introduction – conflict mediation as a fanciful idea or realistic option

The real test of the acceptance of professional mediation in our society will be the sustained and regular use of those services by a substantial number of people to manage conflicts that arise in their personal and business lives in the private market.

The use of mediation in the public sector, exemplified by the rapid proliferation of court programs and legislation that encourage and legitimate mediation is helpful but cannot be taken as competent evidence that people in general have accepted negotiation as a viable means of conflict management. Even so, many mediators are waiting for, or actively lobbying legislatures or courts to create, enact or implement mediation programs in the belief that they will deliver mediation work to their doorstep. However, the steady stream of mediation business has not materialized for many mediators. In fact, ironically, some court sponsored mediation programs have engendered an unintended consequence - the increased resistance to mediation, especially from those people who have felt coerced to participate. Anecdotal reports hint that an increasing number of people are voicing resentment at being forced to mediate (Benjamin (2)). In any event, the private demand for mediation services remains underwhelming in most of the country with only a few areas and contexts being of modest exception. For the most part, it appears that most people in our culture remain leery of negotiation as a means of settling disputes.

Some suggest the reason mediation is under-utilized is because the marketing of those services has been minimal. While that may hold some truth, it could also be that the marketing message of many mediators is ineffectual. Mediation is often portrayed as the "kinder-gentler" alternative. The common operating assumption is that if people knew about the mediation process and how it could save them time and expense and give them greater control over their lives, that consumers, as thoughtful and rational people, would prefer mediation over the more traditional process - reliance on lawyers, judges, and other experts - for the settlement of disputes. The presumption is that consumers, faced with conflicts, will apply a cost/benefit analysis and act out of their self-interest to choose the most efficient means of dispute resolution. Some do, many do not.

It should come as no surprise that logic alone does not necessarily sell even the best product. If people were to act based purely on objective data, none would smoke, all would wear seatbelts in their cars, none would be entrepreneurs, many would not marry, and not many would have children. Few purchases, whether it is a car, a house, or a doctor's, lawyer's or mediator's services are made solely on a rational basis. A strictly rational marketing approach often fails to effectively reach many prospective consumers.

Marketing experts have long appreciated the importance of taking into account human nature and emotion in sales and advertisement. A significant part of any promotional strategy is deciphering how the service/product enhances consumer self image or alleviates fears and insecurities. Choosing to mediate a dispute remains for many, a non-traditional, untested and risky business. When faced with conflict, the emotion many experience is fear, specifically their fear of being taken advantage of or being played for a fool if they negotiate for themselves. The rational reasons to mediate do not easily overcome that overriding fear and an effective marketing message must address that underlying emotion directly.

Beyond just selling a product, however, marketing strategy reflects how mediation is professionally understood and practiced. Currently, many mediators view their work as a thoughtful, humanistic enterprise intended to help others resolve conflict; their process relies on trust and goodwill. Some well-intentioned practitioners even find marketing distasteful or unseemly. However, while human beings have the capacity to act rationally and collaboratively, they don't necessarily start there when faced with a conflict. The resistance to negotiation and mediation are long standing and deeply seated in our culture.

There are two significant sources of resistance to mediation. First, the idea of mediation or negotiation of a conflict is a difficult one for many people to accept, especially in our culture where there is a strongly ingrained sense of being right and a belief that the truth will prevail. Case in point: John Wayne, a cultural icon, never negotiated in any of his many and varied movie roles. He remains a hero for many people and professionals alike, who have taken from his modeling the belief that to negotiate is to compromise, "give-in," or even sell-out your principles. Note that the resistance to mediation follows directly from the resistance to negotiation; mediation is merely a negotiation between three (or more) people. The mediator essentially negotiates his or her authority with each of the participants. For all intents and purposes, the terms negotiation and mediation are interchangeable, mediation being only a more formalized, third-party facilitated negotiation process.

To consider mediation requires a break with traditional thinking patterns as a means of managing conflict. Mediation, like negotiation, requires that people take responsibility for their own decisions. Many people are afraid, or simply do not want that responsibility. They prefer to believe, or are conditioned to think that professionals – lawyers, judges, doctors, therapists, etc.– know more and are better able to make decisions for them   (Benjamin (5)).

There has, however, been some breakdown of this resistance, albeit slowly. People are becoming more aware that conflicts are complex and that there are not simple, formulaic right answers. As well, people are increasingly cautious, skeptical and critical of professional services, advice and directives. (Benjamin (6)). This is reflected in the increased use and availability of alternative sources of information, products and services in both health care and law. The internet is, no doubt, a significant contributor to this dynamic.

The second source of resistance is more troublesome because mediators themselves bear the blame. Mediation is often presented in an overly simplistic manner that makes it all the more difficult for prospective consumers to take seriously. Mediation is described in misleading and Pollyannaish terms, such as: "a win/win process," or as "a collaborative problem solving process." The implicit suggestion is that all parties will be satisfied with the outcome, respect each other or even be friends. Many mediators see themselves as peacemakers and mediation as a healing or "transformative" process (Bloom). While that might occur on occasion, it is by no means the rule, and in any case not the purpose of mediation.

There is a still greater risk: the expectations of the mediation process are, by those simplistic descriptions, set unrealistically high and in many cases unobtainable. The terms believe a quasi-utopian vision that conflicts can be, not just managed, but finally and completely resolved. The result may be the increased likelihood of failure, which in turn can generate even greater resistance to mediation. Many parties already do not consider mediation because they believe the process requires a level of trust, reasonableness and goodwill that they have predetermined the opposing party lacks. Common refrains heard from consumers in ruling out mediation are: "(s)he is not trustworthy" or "I'm reasonable, but (s)he is not." The risk is exacerbated by the presentation of the mediation process in fanciful and idyllic terms.

Countering this resistance will require a shift in the thinking of mediators from a soft, idealized approach to conflict management to a more rigorous, strategic approach. To encourage the acceptance of mediation in the real world, it must pass the test of being cost effective, efficient and, most important of all, be safe. Mediation cannot be limited to those rarefied situations that rely and depend on all parties being reasonable, rational, acting in good faith, trusting or even trustworthy. If mediation services come to be viewed as applicable only to those matters where all parties concerned exhibit a collaborative, cooperative and humanistic demeanor at the same time, then mediation might as well await the simultaneous alignment of the stars and planets. The number of available cases susceptible to mediation will be reduced to a fraction of one percent. To flourish, the mediation process must be recast as good business that need not rely on trust or goodwill. Mediators must work in the real world, not in an idealized world of their own concoction.

6.6.2 The sources and rationale for Guerilla Mediation

For mediation to work in the real conflicts of everyday life and be accepted as a viable mode of conflict management, then the approach taken must be active, strategic and calculated to constructively redirect the energy of the conflict. Human nature must be confronted directly. Instead of hoping for, or expecting people to be reasonable and thoughtful in the face of conflict, mediators must non-judgmentally accept their more base motivations for power and control as well. While messengers (Machiavelli, Kissinger, et. al.) and methods might be criticized, the primary postulate of "realpolitik" is as applicable today as it has been throughout human history: "Those who desire peace, should prepare for war." For mediators, the corollary axiom is: "Those who pursue settlement, should be prepared for conflict" (Kagan). Perhaps ironic, but not surprisingly, warfare strategies and tactics offer parallels in thinking and approach that are useful to a mediator. If conflict is understood as a lesser form of warfare that left unchecked can quickly escalate into open warfare, then the strategies and techniques effective in war may also be applicable in the negotiation of conflict. Only the purposes remain fundamentally different. Parties in conflict are not an enemy to be subdued or defeated; for the mediator, the purpose will be to carefully hone their thinking and skills to effectively manage the jungle of fears that seize many parties in conflict. The purpose of scrutinizing warfare practices is to strip out from that higher intensity conflict circumstance the thinking and strategies that are useful in order to apply them preemptively to avoid the escalation of conflict. What is common to both war and negotiation, and essential for success in either field of engagement is the recognition of the basic nature and behavior of the opponent or parties. In short, not to underestimate your opponent and to accept him on his own terms

The term and concept of guerilla mediation is derived in some measure from the writing of Sun Tzu in The Art of War. He was a Chinese general who, by varying accounts, recorded his approach to warfare sometime between 500 and 300 B.C., and has been studied throughout the centuries up to and including the present. The principles he enunciated for the preparation for war, apply to the management of conflict by other means, including negotiation and mediation. In fact, early on and often, Sun Tzu emphasizes that to fight and conquer is not "supreme excellence;" that excellence is reserved for breaking the enemy's resistance without fighting.

While there could be some quibbling over the exact meaning intended in the phrase "breaking the enemy's resistance," the writing provides good instruction for the practicing mediator. It is neither cynical nor utopian, but instead is soberly realistic. He reflects an appreciation for the human rhythms of conflict: "in peace prepare for war, and in war prepare for peace." Not unlike the warrior, the mediator necessarily relies on strategic planning, tactics and maneuvering, observing the terrain of the conflict and the use of deception. Specifically, the analogy of mediation to guerilla warfare, as distinguished from more formalistic approaches to warfare, highlights the parallels between mediation and the nontraditional, more fluid and mobile form of combat that guerilla tactics conjure. (Kagan). The mediator, as does the guerilla fighter, must creatively use the resources immediately at hand and cannot depend on outside reinforcements or the traditional sources of authority (e.g., a court) to impose an outcome on conflicting parties.

The risk of using guerilla warfare as a metaphor for mediation is for some perilously close to encouraging the combative and argumentative nature of many disputes that most mediators want to disavow and distance themselves from. In fact, Deborah Tannen gives a searing critique of the language of our culture that encourages argument instead of dialogue in The Argument Culture (Tannen). Yet, while her observations are valid and useful, they fail to sufficiently take into account the reality of our human circumstance. While human cooperation occurs and is evident to greater or lesser extent in many circumstances, war, violence and conflict are not unlikely to be extinguished any time soon by social engineering. The proof is in our history, biology and psychology (Bloom; Kagan; Keegan; Lakoff and Johnson). The extent to which conflict and warfare can be mitigated or averted, may be a function of looking directly at what war and conflict are about, not merely pretending it could be otherwise.

George Lakoff and Mark Johnson, in *Metaphors We Live By*, observe that our ordinary conceptual system is metaphorical in nature; linguistics – our words and metaphors – are how we experience one thing in terms of another (Lakoff and Johnson). In short, in disputes where argument is the preferred tactic, argument is a subspecies of war and while argument is not war, it is partially structured, understood, and performed in terms of war. A dispute is metaphorically structured as a battle; our language reflects this reality: one party "attacks" another's position, a claim is considered "indefensible," or the comments are "on target." With the war metaphor so deeply ingrained, to pretend mediation is about peace and good will, when people are thinking in terms of war and distrust, disregards reality and is blatantly naive. The way to shift a dispute away from open warfare toward settlement is not to deny this reality and pray for peace but to strategically re-deploy and re-align our argument metaphors in ways that encourage constructive dialogue. The first step however, is for the mediator to relinquish the notion that parties in conflict can be expected to be reasonable and trusting. Managing conflict in a hostile terrain requires all of the wit and wile a mediator can muster (Benjamin (7)).

For most people faced with conflict, mediation is not their first thought or a term on the tip of their tongue; in fact, even settlement is a remote idea, especially at first. More likely than not, they are thinking "lawyer" and "fight." At the outset of a conflict, whether it is a personal or business dispute, the idea of settlement is an anathema, the mere suggestion of which is taken by them to be indicative of a lack of resolve in their position or a moral sellout of their principles (Benjamin (5)). Most people faced with a dispute of almost any kind or level of seriousness, take it personally; while negotiation may make perfect sense and be in their self interest, they have an abiding fear of being played for a fool that trumps rational thinking. Parties in conflict can move to a place where they can consider more thoughtfully what decisions make sense and how they want to handle difficult situations, but not until they feel safe. That safety is not gained by merely being told to trust the mediation process, or the mediator, and certainly not the opposing party; the process is, at least at the outset, an abstraction, and trusting the other party is simply too far a reach. The first task of the mediator, then, is to manipulate the situation in such a way that the parties need not be required to trust, but to believe they will not be left at a disadvantage.

Notwithstanding this reality, many mediators insist on presenting and approaching disputes out of preset principles and belief in reasoned discussion and collaborative values. They proceed to carefully and methodically analyze the interests and needs of the parties and try to explain to the warring participants why their positions are not sensible or in their self-interest (Fisher and Ury). To read the literature in the field and listen to mediators discuss their craft, it is quickly apparent that many encourage and some even insist that the participants in mediation be reasonable, calm and collaborative if they are to negotiate successfully. Mediators often disregard that many people in conflict, when they are facing the loss of their dreams and life as they know it is disintegrating before their eyes, are not able to be calm and trusting on command. For a mediator to presume parties can or should be so is patronizing at best, and may be down right insulting. Few of us, mediators included, could maintain the equanimity seemingly required, when directly faced with a personal conflict.

The irony is that guerilla mediation, though the term may sound antagonistic and harsh, may well be more respectful of parties in conflict than the more conventional approaches to mediation. If there is an assertive sensibility to this approach, it is because the force and energy that most conflicting parties bring to a dispute must be met by a sufficient counter force if the energy is to be redirected constructively.

6.6.3 The basic tenets of Guerilla Mediation

There are three basic tenets of guerilla mediation: (1) respect for human nature as it is, not as we would like to believe it could be; (2) a realistic understanding and acceptance of conflict; and, (3) the effective use of strategic planning. Assuming the acceptance of these basic tenets, the techniques for implementation and the requisite skills necessary to accomplish the purpose of mediation, can be more readily clarified and applied. Notwithstanding the use of a warfare metaphor, the purpose of mediation and the role of the mediator remains to facilitate the substantially informed and consensual management of issues or conflicts by disputing parties.

6.6.3.1 Respect for human nature as it is, not as we would like to believe in could be

Borrowing from the principles of evolutionary biology and psychology, the human animal has ingrained multiple kinds of behavior patterns that are sometimes contradictory. Generally, humans can be (1) altruistic, good natured, and trusting (de Waal); (2) rational, analytical, and objective, acting more or less predictably out of self-interest (Axelrod); and, (3) fearful, spiteful, deceptive and manipulative, acting in ways that appear to be anchored in pure emotion and seemingly irrational (Niehoff).

The most prevalent approaches to the mediation of conflict, the rationalistic and humanistic, are premised on the belief that parties in conflict are capable of being collaborative in the reasoned pursuit of an outcome that meets the needs of all parties. Humanists believe people are basically good at heart, rationalists believe they essentially operate out of predictable patterns of self interest. Short shrift is given to that part of our human nature that is deceptive or manipulative and there is often attached an implicit negative moral judgment of that behavior. There is nothing wrong with the conventional approaches, they just do not systematically and holistically account for the whole repertoire of human behaviors that are commonly displayed in human interactions and especially in conflict.

To round out the field, there is the competitive/opportunistic approach to negotiation and mediation that most people popularly tend to associate with negotiation. This style is typified by the used car dealer; it is essentially Machiavellian, and operates from the belief that humans are basically evil, self-interested, deceitful and manipulative, and bent on the accumulation of power and control. Once again, it is not so much that this approach is inaccurate as it is incomplete; it fails to account for the prospect that humans are able to cooperate and might be able to negotiate collaboratively. In short, none of the prevailing negotiation approaches take into account the whole range of the human behaviors, and to the extent they do not, the approach will be found lacking.

The naturalistic/pragmatic approach to negotiation is premised on the belief that humans operate out of the full range of ingrained human behavior patterns. The approach is not intended to dismiss or denigrate the prevailing approaches, but rather to provide an integrative framework that includes them all and offers a more comprehensive view of humans' behavior in the negotiation of conflict. It is premised on the belief that to effectively negotiate issues or disputes, parties must be accorded the respect that they will be simultaneously desirous of reasoned communication and at the same time likely to be fearful, deceptive and manipulative. Deception is a natural behavior common to all animal species, including humans, which has evolved over time to foster procreation and survival. It cannot be dismissed and should not be morally judged (Niehoff). The naturalistic approach does not presume to dictate how people should behave for negotiation to proceed and takes full account of all human behaviors.

The naturalistic approach to negotiation is well suited to guerilla mediation, reflecting the same views of human nature and conflict. Thus, while communication and empathy between parties are necessary and important, and the reasoned analytical discussion of issues and options are helpful, both approaches are incomplete in themselves. The guerilla mediator, in sizing up the conflict terrain, does not rely upon reason, trust and goodwill to manage a dispute; he or she may well have to employ constructive forms of deception to accommodate and counter the anticipated fears and resulting manipulations of the parties. The mediator is obligated to accept the parties as they are, not how he or she would like for them to be.

6.6.3.2 A realistic understanding and acceptance of conflict

Conflict is part of the natural terrain, and unless one subscribes to the millennial belief that with the coming of the messiah, where "the lion will lay down with the lamb," is likely to continue to be so. Too often, however, conflict mediation is confused with peacemaking. Many mediators accept conflict only grudgingly in theory and are even less tolerant of its open expression in practice.

Conflict is a basic ingredient in our evolutionary biology and psychology; it is part of our human makeup and chemistry. Analogically, conflict is to the body politic what cholesterol is to body physiology; some cholesterol, the LDL, constricts the arteries, immobilizes the body and can ultimately kill. Other forms of cholesterol, the HDL, help the body metabolize and cannot function without it. Likewise, some forms of social conflict are peripheral, unnecessary and destroy the body politic, while other conflict is substantive, that is, necessary and useful, encouraging the growth and development of society.

In our Western, techno-rational culture, there is a strong tendency to suppress and dismiss emotion in general and conflict in particular. The mind-reason/body-emotion dichotomy, postulated originally by Plato and articulated by Descartes, reflects the traditional pejorative notion of conflict. The conventional wisdom posits that conflict results from the absence of reason and from being overrun by emotion. Many mediators of the rationalist persuasion use techniques derived from that view. For instance, establishing communication ground rules in mediation are ostensibly calculated to preclude or limit unhelpful emotional outbursts by a party which are thought to impede the calm discussion of substantive issues. The reigning conventional wisdom is that emotion unchecked will likely or even predictably lead to physical aggression. The technique may have the reverse effect: suppressing the expression of emotion may lead to an escalation of the conflict.

By contrast, the guerilla mediator accepts the expression of emotion as a natural and necessary part of the conflict, not to be suppressed but constructively managed. Ironically, current studies in neuro-biology suggest that reason and emotion stem from the same area of the brain and it is difficult, if not impossible, to separate the two; reason cannot be accessed without emotion (Damasio). In the same way physical pain or discomfort is symptomatic of an underlying body dysfunction or illness, emotion is the expression of underlying personal or interpersonal stressors. As health care providers are coming to understand, treating the pain without assessing the underlying circumstance makes no sense, nor does managing the illness without addressing the pain. Likewise, quashing the emotion in a dispute may serve to cosmetically cover up the underlying stressors without effective management of the conflict.

The guerilla mediator redirects and uses the energy the conflict generates constructively. Conflict contains within it considerable natural force and energy. To liken some conflicts to a "class 5" river (serious white water), the force of the water flow can easily sweep away the unprepared. In rafting that river, and negotiating the rapids, the pilot understands the necessity of bringing his or her own energy to bear on the river; if he puts the paddle down, he will be swept away. There is no quiet, calm way to face a wild river; the pilot will never control the river and there is no suppressing or containing the river's energy. The only hope will be to deal with the river on its terms, which means to paddle hard and fast enough to approximate the river's speed, thereby allowing the pilot to position him or herself to use the river's energy. The trick is to stay centered, off the rocks and out of the sinkholes. A good pilot reads the river and sometimes must calculate bouncing off of one rock to avoid a more perilous one or a worse situation. Similarly, a good mediator reads the conflict between the parties and devises a strategy that effectively uses the parties' force and energy to negotiate the conflict.

6.6.3.3 The effective use of strategic planning

Strategic planning is the key to both winning wars and the effective negotiation or mediation of conflict. Curiously, the etymology of the word strategy is from the Greek, "strategama," translated as a trick or ruse, and still commonly defined as a military maneuver to deceive or surprise an enemy (van Creveld). The notion of being strategic has also long been associated with business and negotiation and carries with it a pejorative connotation. This is so, especially in the Western cultural tradition where humanism and rationalism are highly valued. From the rationalist and humanist perspective, strategy is unnecessary if the argument is rational and the motives genuine; the use of logical reasoning, communication and empathy should theoretically, at least, obviate the need for tactical presentation (Benjamin (5)). Unsavory strategic devices are associated with "spinning the story" in politics, or being disingenuous, inauthentic, or outright deceitful in personal relationships.

Ironically, despite the disinclination to accept the human necessity of being strategic, there is little doubt that most people, successful in managing their public and private affairs, are careful to consider how and when to most effectively present themselves and their ideas in pursuit of their goals and to obtain a desired result. Most mediators, as well, even those of the rationalist and humanist persuasion, as a practical matter, are forced to be strategic at some point. Therein lies the gap or incongruence between what they say is their approach to mediation and how they are observed in their actual practice (Keeley).

The naturalist/pragmatic mediator understands from the outset that he or she will not be likely to overpower the parties by the strength of argument, overwhelm them with a brilliant solution previously unconsidered, or that talking alone will resolve difficult conflicts. Drawing from that understanding, the guerilla mediator must rely on finesse and other stratagems to redirect the conflict energy constructively toward settlement. There are countless examples of techniques that effectuate strategy in the negotiation/mediation of conflict. The three most basic: are the use of confusion, structuring of the process, and the use of time.

Far from being calm, rational and patient, the mediator must use "hit and run" tactics to confuse entrenched parties and undermine their belief that their cause is just and they are right (Benjamin (4)). If they are allowed to remain sanguine in their original entrenched positions, there will be little motivation to negotiate. People function less by rational calculation than by ritual and operative myths - stories they tell themselves to make sense of the world around them. Their myths of Justice, Truth, Rationality, Finality and Objectivity, disincline them to consider other alternatives to managing conflict. Most parties in conflict want to be vindicated in the belief that they are right and that any fair-minded, impartial and neutral review of the matter at hand will so determine their cause to be just. The quest for the truth of the matter, however, is of little relevance in the mediation of conflict (Benjamin (6)).

A mediator must pierce that operative mythology. Sometimes reflective questions can do the trick, confusing and unsettling one or both party's certainty that justice will prevail. For example, the reflective question, "Are you sure that your position can be proven and that the court will agree with you?" insinuates into the discussion a measure of doubt. The purpose is to throw them off guard and dislocate their thinking, to make just enough space for the consideration of other options that can possibly open the door for agreement (Benjamin (2)). By contrast, a frontal, straightforward logical statement, such as, "I don't think the court will agree with you," is likely to be viewed as confrontation or attack which summons argument and rebuttal, "Yes, they will, it's the law, and I'll win." Logic, of course, is the least effective means of convincing anyone of anything. The mediator does not want to be caught in an argument, which are, by definition, unwinnable. Even if you win, you lose. Thus, he or she merely plants the seeds of doubt and moves on: the hit and run.

In structuring the process, the mediator may strategically use deception to delay and avoid direct discussion of the key issues until the parties are ready. Many negotiations break down because people begin to discuss the ultimate issues too soon and negotiate out of fear, without sufficient or accurate information. They want to begin by discussing the hardest issues first, which may be self-defeating. Without a negotiation strategy, or game plan, it is common to "cut to the chase" and ask "what do you want/what will you give." Conventional wisdom and the logical approach often encourages direct discussion of the issues in the belief that the shortest distance between the problem and a solution in a dispute is a straight line. Few conflicts are that simple or linear.

In contrast to the conventional wisdom, a surreptitious, surprise approach may be more effective. Strategically, using paradoxical logic, the shortest distance in a dispute between the stated problem and possible outcomes is not a straight line. A more circuitous route allows time for the parties to reflect on their perspectives, communicate with each other, and assure all parties are working with sufficient and accurate information in preparation for the ultimate negotiation (van Creveld; Benjamin (1)). The more complex and difficult the issues, the more important the structuring of the process will be in the management of the conflict. The mediator must build a solid foundation, first slowly gaining commitment to the process, next gleaning the story, then clarifying the issues, and finally assuring all options are available and considered. The mediator uses techniques that are calculated to delay and avoid the actual discussion of key issues until the parties are ready - "no conflict before it's time." By initially sidestepping the hardest issues in a dispute, the mediator defeats what conflicted parties think they want to do, in favor of a more productive approach that allows him to effectively sneak up on the hardest issues.

Finally, as in warfare, in mediation time is of critical strategic value. For most disputing parties the conflict did not arise overnight and is not likely to be resolved quickly. Notwithstanding that reality, most expect the matter to be resolved immediately, and if not, to presume it cannot be resolved at all, let alone in mediation. With that thinking, it is easy to see how so many people slip-slide into the more traditional, formalized and extreme modes of conflict management such as litigation. Time allows for the parties to shift in their perspective and consider alternatives. Therefore, the mediator often stalls for time: parties cannot shift in their perspective faster than it takes for them to assimilate that change. Thus, sometimes it is what the mediator does not do that is more important than what he or she does do. Setting the pace of the negotiation process and knowing when to stop a session after there has been some progress, but before the parties become too tired, are critical timing skills. The mediator must sense the point of diminishing returns; moving too quickly to "close the deal" can unduly risk any progress that has occurred, bring on "buyers remorse," or even place the whole negotiation process in jeopardy. Contrary to conventional wisdom, "holding peoples' feet to the fire" to obtain an agreement is likely to be counterproductive. There is a Zen aspect to negotiation: the less parties feel pushed to agree, the faster they may decide to settle in their own time.

A guerilla fighter does not seek to win the war in one skirmish, likewise a mediator does not expect to reach agreement in one fell swoop. In fact, for the mediator, the purpose may not be for the parties to come to agreement at all - that is for them to decide. The purpose of the mediator is merely to give them every opportunity to reach an understanding and not defeat themselves. The process, especially in difficult matters, must be drawn out to allow the parties sufficient time to re-appraise their negotiation perspectives. Time allows for them to save face and accept some measure of the reality that one does not necessarily win because they are right or lose because they are wrong. Settlements in hard cases are not so much forged as they are allowed to emerge in due course. Just as in guerilla warfare, there are no clear victories. In mediation parties don't win or lose, they merely find a means to survive.

6.6.4 Conclusion – The promise and future of mediation

In the last quarter of this century, conflict mediation has gained a small foothold in the cultural and legal landscape of the United States and numerous other countries around the world as a means of managing conflict. At core, the promise of the mediation process is the opportunity it gives people to settle their own disputes without the undue interference of government authorities or others. In this age, people often feel they are losing control over their lives, face an ever increasing onslaught of rules and regulations, and confront countless professionals who presume to know better about how they should live their lives. Mediation is one way people can re-assert themselves and seize back some measure of control in the decisions that most affect their personal relationships and business dealings.

But the footing of mediation is precarious at best. If the success and acceptance of the mediation process is left to the courts and other public authorities, and mediators wait for it to be legislated into existence, then it risks becoming just one more cog in the institutional machine and the heart of the process may be fundamentally compromised. For mediation to flourish, it must make sense to consumers and work, not just a good or worthy idea.

To that end, guerilla mediation is not a regression to a primitive, "win at all costs" approach to negotiation; nor is it in anyway intended to suggest that the mediator should design the outcome of a dispute. It does however, pointedly intend to suggest that for mediation to survive as a viable form of conflict management, then mediators must look directly into the heart of conflicts in the real world and manage them. Force-fitting hard issues and stressed parties into mediation approaches that are based on wishful thinking about what human beings could become does not sufficiently take account of the power and energy of human emotion. This limits and impairs the effectiveness and validity the mediation process could have in our culture.

Ultimately, if mediation cannot be demonstrated to work outside of hothouse conditions, where parties meet preset standards of reasonableness and cooperative demeanor, then the process will remain a marginal mode of conflict management, or worse, be relegated to history's trash heap of good ideas and good intentions that did not work or were not accepted. If mediation is to effectively become part of our cultural pattern of managing conflict, then mediators must adopt a rigorous, reality-based approach that can manage conflicts as they present themselves, not as we might hope for them to be.

6.7 ROBERT D. BENJAMIN: THE STRATEGIC USE OF COGNITIVE ART IN PROBLEM SOLVING

Natura in reticulum sua genera connexit,
Non in catenam: hominess non possunt nisi
Catenam sequi, cum non plura simul
Possint sermone exponere.

Nature knits up her kinds in a network, not
in a chain; but men can follow only by
chains because their language can't handle
several things at once

Albrecht von Haller (Nemerov (1), 471).

6.7.1 Escaping flatland

"Cognitive art" includes images as basic as graphs, tables, guides, instructions, lists, and directories and as complex as maps, diagrams and even abstract representations. Largely taken for granted, the utility and sometimes downright beauty of these display, often provide a visceral level of understanding and clarity that is otherwise unobtainable through mere verbal communication. Nowhere is that is more apparent than in the field of conflict management where issues are often complex and unwieldy and resist easy description. Edward Tufte, an early and important proponent of cognitive art, commented in the introduction to his book, *Envisioning Information*: "Even though we navigate daily through a perceptual world of three spatial dimensions...the world portrayed on our information displays is caught up in the two-dimensionality of the endless flatlands of paper.... Escaping this flatland is the essential task of envisioning information. All the interesting worlds (physical, biological, imaginary, human) that we seek to understand are inevitably and happily multivariate in nature. Not flatlands (Tufte, p.12, 1990)

Tufte quotes Paul Klee, a renowned modern artist, who addressed a critical issue directly relevant to mediators when he observed how our language (spoken words) lacks the capacity to communicate a sense of dimensional complexity. "It is not easy to arrive at a conception of a whole which is constructed from parts belonging to different dimensions ... It is difficult enough, oneself, to survey this whole, whether nature or art, but still more difficult to help another to such a comprehensive view (Tufte, at p.15, 1990; Klee, P., p.15, 1948)

While technically still two-dimensional, the graphic display (drawing a picture of the conflict or issues) by the mediator or the parties themselves, allows for the contours, ridges and ruts to emerge off the page. Visual display gives a depth of field perspective so that the complexities and connections of the parties or groups involved (the background politics) can be fully appreciated. A graphic illustration, done by the mediator and participants, allows each party to see herself with proximity to the others, and a more realistic sense of the boundaries, blocks, resistances, and alliances in play, as well as the direct and indirect resources available. As a direct result, subsequent discussions and consideration of options, are more likely to be better informed, focused, and efficient. In short, the whole picture of the situation can be taken in at once in a way that mere verbal description and exchange alone cannot provide. The visual display of the conflict can be the single most effective means of breaking-down the entrenched patterns of thinking that often choke off the opportunity to see matters from a different and fresh perspective, literally and metaphorically. As the photographer Gary Winogrand has said, "There is nothing as mysterious as a fact clearly described."

While unfortunately under-utilized, this art form should be at the core and the beginning point of almost every strategic approach to problem solving. If the issues involved are of the Type-I variety ("technical/convergent"), with "high levels of agreement on both the definition of the problem and the range of possible fixes," graphics are, at the very least, a helpful organizing tool. For more complex issues of the problem Type-II ("value/divergent") or Type-III ("wicked/intractable") forms, where there is less clarity or agreement on the problem definition or on possible solutions, graphics are essential and indispensable as a point of departure to chart the difficulties. (Adler, P., 2004; see also, Heifetz, R., 1994) It should come as no surprise, that in our 'techno-rational' Western culture, the more linear "problem-fix" approach, effective with Type-I problems, is all too often foisted upon Type-II and III issues. The results are sometimes disastrous; simplistic solves may do little more than encourage the onset of unintended consequences. Edward Tenner has catalogued many such circumstances. One recent example gaining attention is the overuse of antibiotics which has resulted in more resistant and virulent strains of viral infections (Tenner, 1997).

"A problem...", says Edward de Bono, "...is simply the difference between what one has and what one wants. It may be a matter of avoiding something, of getting something, of getting rid of something, (or) of getting to know what one wants" (de Bono, p. 58, 1970). The enigma and difficulty of problem solving in many disputes lies in that last phrase, "getting to know what one wants." The faulty assumption, too often made by mediators and other conflict management practitioners, is that people in fact know what they want, can articulate it clearly, and what they say they want is what they want. Jennie Holzer, a post-modern conceptual artist, poignantly shouts out the point in an installation series of large scale neon signs placed strategically in prominent locations, such as, Times Square in New York City and on the front of Caesars Palace in Las Vegas, one of which read: "Protect Me From What I Want" (Survival Series, 1986).

The most critical part of problem solving is in gaining some sense of the real issues, concerns and fears of the parties, that may or may not be the same as the stated interests and needs. The trick is to set up the issue(s) in a manner that is susceptible to considering options that are outside the natural patterning behavior of their minds. To do that first requires the mediator to disrupt the thinking frame of parties sufficiently so that they are willing to allow consideration of different constructions of the problem and admit other options. For example, experienced mediators realize that many parenting disputes are money disputes in disguise. Health treatment disputes are frequently as much about the absence of doctor-patient communication as they are about the outcome. Similarly, employment grievances and discrimination cases are often the outgrowth of feeling treated like little more than a machine part. Bringing those confusions to the surface can often be more effectively done with graphic displays than with verbal statements. On a most basic level, pictures allow the parties to "see" and recognize for themselves what the dispute may really be about as opposed to being told. That kind of learning is invaluable

6.7.2 Cognitive art allows and encourages the lateral thinking essential for problem solving.

A core operating premise of our cultural heritage, drawn from Descartes' cogito ergo sum and the Enlightenment, is a near fanatical faith in the power of reason and rational thinking. Not entirely without good reason, in many respects it has served us well and allowed for great strides in science and technology. Yet, that belief has lapsed over into our approach to mediation and conflict management, where strict notions of reason can be problematic, especially when dealing with complex issues or problems embedded in emotional tissue and political muscle. Nonetheless, the predominant approach to problem solving remains a linear, rational, or as Edward de Bono terms it, 'vertical' thinking frame (de Bono, p. 57, 1970).

We rely on the power of logic and persuasion as a primary means of conflict management. The unwarranted assumption that follows, often undermining the negotiation process, is that people who are stuck in "unreasonable" positions in a dispute are merely lacking in sufficient information, misguided or stubborn. We need to believe that with enough logic, they (the other person) will see reason and be persuaded to change their minds (Ross, Lee and Ward, 2001). Of course, if they continue to refuse, that is proof positive of either stupidity or a blinding fanaticism. Ironically, our belief in rational discourse is almost irrational. Most experienced mediators recognize that the least effective means to convince anyone of anything, let alone people in the middle of an emotional dispute (and all disputes are emotional), is logic. Sometimes the mediator contributes to the problem by trying too hard to be rational and logical in their approach (Benjamin, R., 2004).

De Bono does not dispute the value and importance of vertical, rational and analytical thinking. He simply insists that vertical thinking must be complemented by "lateral thinking," an intuitive, creative thinking frame. Allowing vertical thinking to take hold too soon squeezes out the opportunity to see the situation in a different way. The risk is that the problem solving process will be caught in the strong cultural gravitational pull of pursuing the right answer and pressured to "cut to the chase." The "lateral thinking" frame encourages a restructuring of the thinking patterns that are often a source the conflict. However, to those heavily invested in being rational and practical, engaging in lateral thinking can initially appear to be little more than a digression or distraction from the "real" work of finding an answer to the problem.

Drawing a picture of the conflict terrain can be a very useful form of constructive deception. While appearing to be directly relevant to the task at hand, it allows for the onset of lateral thinking to take hold - thinking about the situation differently. Lateral thinking in general, and especially the use of cognitive art techniques, carry with them a piece of "crazy wisdom" (Nisker,W., 1990). The former Poet Laureate of the United States, Howard Nemerov, captured the essence of lateral thinking in his essay, "On Metaphor:"

> It is like being told: If you really want to see something, look at something else.
> If you want to say what something is, inspect something that it isn't.
> It might go further, and worse, than that:
> if you want to see the invisible world, look at the visible one.
> If you want to know what East really is, look North.
> If you have a question concerning the sea, look at the mountains.
> And so on (Nemerov, p. 223, 1991).

6.7.3 Techniques and Applications

Cognitive art is at once a strategic approach that emphasizes the importance of accessing intuitive, lateral thinking, and an applied technique requiring practice and skill. Visual display and other techniques that allow for the experiential or kinesthetic integration of information are central to the strategy.

The applications are endless. They can include storyboards of the "facts" at issue, chartings of options with comments about the attendant risks and advantages of each, or drawings of the biggest "monsters" in the field and ways to circumvent or confront them. The most basic, however, begin with an in-session diagram, with the participation of all parties, of the conflict system. This involves initially noting the boundaries, all necessary groups and individual parties, consultants, connections, and their place in the organization or family structure, and brief histories of significant relationships. This allows all concerned, including the mediator, to follow along as the story unfolds, and for everyone to maintain a common focus on the same graphic. At the next level, brief notes can be made next to particular players in the system about their relative degree of resistance, available resources, or other considerations of relevance. In the end, the diagram should reflect the politics of the situation.

Graphics allow for visual learning, provide tangible "anchors" to reference back to important concepts, and focus the parties on a common problem (Benjamin, 2002). Graphics are helpful in the following ways:

1. Graphics compel the mediator to be organized, and help to stay focused on the task.

2. The appearance of structure and organization gives parties a sense of movement and progress toward an end. The illusion of progress leads to the reality of progress.

3. With a visual picture, the mediator can better identify, clarify, and frame the issues.

4. Graphics minimize the risk of misinformation and the peripheral conflict that results from that confusion is minimized by the use of a common document.

5. The use of graphics residually provides an effective conflict management technique because it is a constant reminder of the task at hand and the mediator controlling the graphic is visually "in charge." The mediators control is thus established without being controlling.

This graphic mapping of the conflict system is essentially no different from the "war room" relief maps a general might survey in a military campaign, or for that matter, the site plans an architect requires for competent building construction, or a doctor's review of x-rays and MRI pictures in preparation for surgery.

Just as a general will be looking at the topography of the battlefield terrain, including the intelligence about the enemy's strongest and weakest points and logistical requirements to support his forces in a successful attack, a mediator should assess the topography of the dispute. This includes the history, sources of resistance and antagonism, and alliances and support for the negotiation process. While the general and mediator are pursuing different ends – winning the war versus obtaining a resilient agreement – the strategies and techniques are largely the same. Both, for instance, must always be aware of the necessary logistical support required to maintain the negotiation process or the prosecution of an offensive (Benjamin, R. 1998). Both the mediator and the general draw from "field" and "systems" theory to establish the basic parameters and markers for the mapping their respective conflicts. Both must be able to visualize the conflict terrain in which they are operating (Benjamin, R, 2004).

The figures below illustrate the generic elements of virtually every human organization, business, family, agency, or profession:

- *Boundaries of the conflict system.* Who is in or out of the dispute is shown graphically. In a family or divorce dispute, the parents are in the core circle defining the immediate boundary of the family, while grandparents or new spouses or significant others are outside the boundary.

- *Hierarchy of the system.* Who makes decisions in the family or is the identified head of the organization or family.

- *Interactional patterns.* How do participants, departments, or individuals communicate with each other in the family or organization? By memo in triplicate or in face-to-face conversation?

- *Tran-generational patterns*, the folklore of the family or organization. Every organization has a unique culture. "There is a right way and a wrong way, and the way we do things around here." Brief discussion noted on the graphic anchors the awareness of that culture.

- *Subsystems within the organization or family.* These associations, generally based on gender, interest, or purpose can be highlighted. The research and marketing departments, for example, are each a subsystem of a corporation and, depending on the theory of management, encouraged to compete or cooperate with each other. Likewise, in a divorce, the children, parents, grandparents, and sometimes lawyers, are each subsystems of the family system in conflict and should be noted.

- *Developmental pattern.* A family or organization is an organism in its own right, which is different from the sum of its parts. As such, it has a life span where the focus is different depending on the stage of development, just as an individual progresses through life. In early stages, there is a greater tendency for the organization to take risks, and as it ages to become more conservative. This can be reflected graphically with age notes and comments.

An example from each of three different dispute contexts, illustrates how cognitive art (pictures of the conflict) add essential depth and perspective and allow the mediator to more effectively problem solve.

THE FAMILY SYSTEM: graphic drawn in session

Example Matter: Family or Divorce Conflict

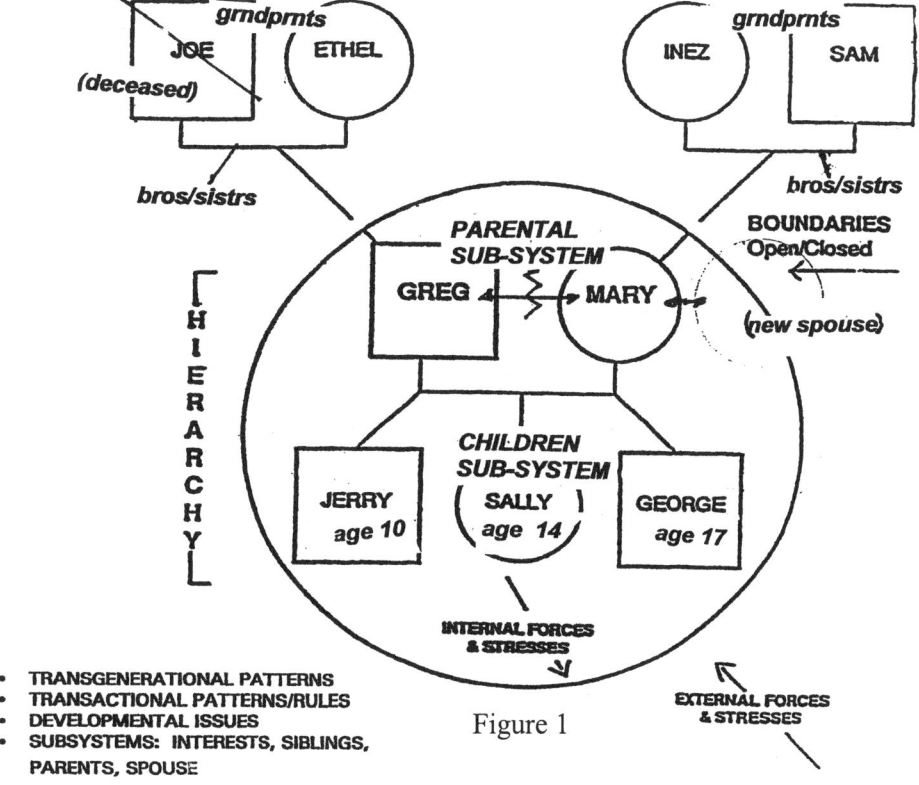

Figure 1

In the family system figure (Figure 1), used in divorce and family mediations, note the place for each spouse's parents and family to be drawn. This offers two immediate advantages germane to problem solving. First, in setting other family members outside the circle, boundary issues are clarified with regard to whom the primary parties (and decision makers) are and need to remain. Having this graphically displayed and remaining in view carries more weight than a mere comment to that effect.

In addition, in more than a few cases, both parties will remember as a result of the graphic, that there may be resources in one or both of their extended families that can ease the tension. Her brother, who is an accountant and not a threat to her husband, can be helpful with regard to financial issues.

In an employment or workplace dispute, a "sexual harassment" matter, (which is preferably termed an appropriate conduct dispute), a factor frequently overlooked by the parties and the mediator is the potential for there to be a structural imbalance between the parties. If one is in a supervisory position and the other person lower in the organizational hierarchy, then it may be naïve to presume that open and direct negotiations can happen without at the very least, some overt discussion about their respective status in the organization. Specifically, assuming both desire to continue working in the same business, the first question that will come to mind is by whom and how future work performance evaluations will be conducted. This is no mere academic issue; it goes to the heart of the integrity of the mediation process. A graphic illustration, as shown immediately below, where each can observe the structural imbalance, effectively brings this issue into the foreground, and offers hints as to available options and resources to manage the situation and allow the mediation to continue.

THE BUSINESS/AGENCY ORGANIZATION: graphic drawn in session

Example Matter: Employment/Organizational Dispute

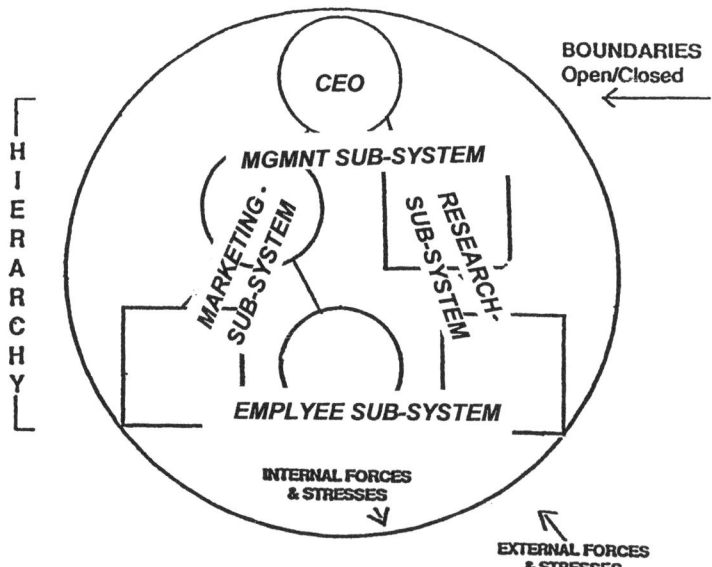

- TRANSGENERATIONAL PATTERNS (Folklore, Corporate Ethos)
- TRANSACTIONAL PATTERNS/RULES (Employee handbooks: written vs. Oral tradition)
- DEVELOPMENTAL ISSUES (Ages and career status: retirement level, entry level/climbers)
- SUBSYSTEMS: INTERESTS, departments, divisions, top management/middle management/line workers

Figure 2

Finally, on the most basic level, a graphic allows for the most effective review possible of the necessary parties to a dispute. Specifically, who may be missing and needs to be included in the mediation process if it is to be a competent process. As experienced mediators know, the failure to include a key player - one who upon being left out can and likely will sabotage the agreement - is risky business and a waste of time and money. In fact, leaving out a necessary party not only places in jeopardy the immediate mediation process, but any future process. The left out party always remembers the slight. In a land use dispute, for instance, where the issue was an application for a zoning variance to allow a home for the developmentally disabled to be established in a a "single family" use area, the graphics helped to identify a group of residents opposed to the variance and conveniently disregarded by the other participants (the agency, the city planning department, the state department of mental health underwriting the group home, and some supportive neighbors), because they were so difficult to work with. Experience teaches that any agreement that is allowed to go forward on that basis is likely to be suspect. The graphic display, as shown below, anchored the necessary discussion and allowed the gathered parties to more fully appreciate the risk.

MULTIPLE SYSTEMS: 'PICTURE' OF THE CONFLICT:
Graphic drawn in session

Example Matter: *Medical Treatment/ Elderly/Special Educ./Land Use/ Public Policy*

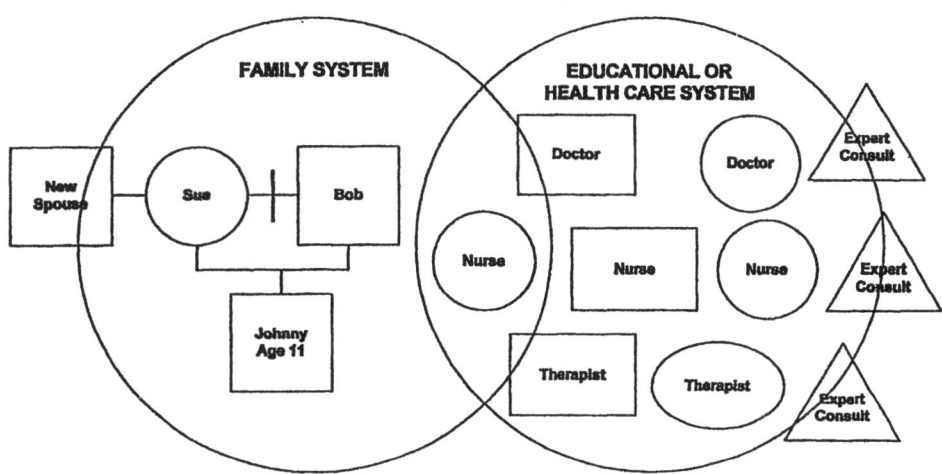

Each of the system may be internally in conflict concerning the nature of treatment and the systems may also be in conflict with each other (the family vs. the health care system). The use of graphics can offer aid to assure a necessary party is not missing or that an available resource is not overlooked.

Figure 3

Creative Problem Solver's Handbook for Negotiators and Mediators

6.7.4 Commotion and order

Managing the natural energy of conflict is similar to running the rapids of a wild river. While naïve and perhaps even pretentious to think one can control the river, there are available strategies to navigate the turbulence and maintain a measure of control. One of the most important of these is the site mapping of the conflict, to check the primary obstacles and best channels of flow. Sometimes, the rafter, like the mediator, must choose to intentionally engage one obstacle - a boulder, for example - in order to avoid a more perilous risk - a sinkhole that can flip your boat in an instant. The use of cognitive art in mediating conflict is akin to site mapping a wild river. It will never be a perfect representation, and the river will change course and circumstance from season to season, year to year, and sometimes, day to day. But like any good artist, the mediator must constantly revise his picture.

There are countless applications for cognitive art in mediation practice. Graphical timetables allow parties to estimate and gauge where they are in the process and initially create an illusion of progress that can become a reality. Charted agendas and assignments prepared in session, copied and given to each party, likewise offer a solid feeling of movement toward a goal all of which is critical for problem solving to take place.

Cognitive art offers a system of notation that translates and communicates the actions, intensity, and responses of parties in conflict and transcribes them onto flatland, permanently preserving the visual instant (Tufte, p. 114). Visual displays in mediation allow for some order to be brought to bear on the commotion and chaos of conflict without unduly constraining the natural energy of the conflict.

6.8 ROBERT A CREO: MEDIATOR 2004: THE ART AND THE ARTIST

[**Editor's note:** *This section is based on Parts I and II of an article by the same title authored by Robert A. Creo and is reprinted and reformatted here with his permission.*]

6.8.1 Introduction

6.8.1.1 Experience

This Article is a reflection of my views on the state of the art of mediation and the commercial mediator. The focus of my practice, and the audience for my thoughts, is the mediator who works his or her own craft to resolve economic disputes. These disputes almost always involve claims or cases in the civil litigation system. Disputants are almost always represented by counsel in processing their claim in court or in mediation. Many of my perspectives and experience, however, are applicable or adaptable to other mediation forums.

By way of background, my experience as a neutral began in 1979 as a labor arbitrator. This is a profession that still constitutes a significant amount of my practice. My formal classroom training as a mediator was primarily in the late 1980s, first with Professor Len Riskin, then with United States Arbitration and Mediation, and then a few days with Linda Singer and Michael Lewis for the Johns Manville Trust project. My mediation practice consists almost exclusively of commercial, construction, employment, and tort claims where all parties are represented by counsel. I have done very little family, community, and/or public policy matters in my caseload (over 2500). I have trained commercial mediators at the basic and advanced level for many years.

The key prompt for this article and its format is a 2003 publication of the Pennsylvania State Law Review, which published articles by participants in an April 2003 Symposium at the Dickinson School of Law of the Pennsylvania State University. I attended portions of the symposium, which was entitled "Dispute Resolution and Capitulation to the Routine: Is There a Way Out?" It was an excellent event calling upon luminaries in disciplines other than law and mediation. I strongly urge every mediator to read the published articles. Although there were many excellent presentations and subsequent articles, for purposes of this piece I will focus mostly on the perspectives articulated by Louise Phipps Senft and Cynthia A. Savage, Deborah R. Hensler, and David Sally. Although many of these ideas have been floating around the dispute resolution community for years, these articles contain some new perspectives, insights, and/or articulations.

The second prompt is the excellent book *Bringing Peace into the Room*, edited by Daniel Bowling and David A. Hoffman. Another prompt is the upcoming 2004 joint conference of the American College of Civil Trial Mediators and the International Academy of Mediators. The unifying theme addresses the issues facing the professional commercial mediator. A Symposium on Issues Affecting the Professional Mediator was held in the spring of 2004 in New Orleans, Louisiana.

Like most experienced mediators, I have been active in numerous professional organizations and presented at conferences hundreds of times over the last twenty-five years. There are many others, including colleagues and friends of mine, who have presented or written on many of these same themes. I want to thank my International Academy of Mediators Colleagues, especially Tracy Allen, Robert Jenks, and Keith Seat, for helpful review and comment on the first draft of this article. For purposes of my article, the April 2003 Dickinson Symposium provides a framework to consider the state of the art and the artist.

6.8.1.2 Abstract and conclusion

Creeping, if not galloping, legalism and institutionalism is inevitable. Free market principles, however, not external regulation or mediation orthodoxy, should be the guiding force in any movement toward formal professionalism. There are many challenges facing professional mediators generated by uniform standards of conduct, mediator liability, the relationship with the legal profession, globalization, and transnational political, legal, and economic trends. Mediators should resist trends toward consistency and uniformity of rules or practice. There are many illustrations of regulatory intrusion into the conduct of the mediation session. Restricting mediation to narrow channels of styles or tactics inhibits self-determination by disputants. Mandating a facilitative model (by definition or through ethical standards), which forces mediators into indirect communication modalities, clashes with transparency and other dynamics that are utilized to build credibility and trust in the process. Best practice guidelines, when postulated as ethical codes or standards of conduct, inhibit mediator discretion and flexibility. Tolerance and diversity of practice is a core value of the mediation community.

Functioning as the agent of the Rule of Law, court litigation serves different purposes than mediation. Mediated settlements of what essentially are private, economic disputes of commercial litigation provide benefits to the litigants and society without undermining the ability of the courts to serve the Rule of Law. If mediation reduces the court docket or makes case management more efficient, this enhances, not diminishes, access to justice. To the extent that judges have become discovery masters and referees for courthouse-step settlements, transformation of the courts back to the traditional functions as forums for trials is a healthy symbiotic relationship between courts and mediators. Mediation should be integrated into the Rule of Law in such a manner that any clashes between core values of courts/litigation versus mediators/mediation are accommodated. The legal professional and/or courts should not co-opt mediation by annexation or regulation. Regulation of lawyer representational and other activities should be within existing attorney disciplinary systems and not addressed by standards or codes of conduct for mediators. Courts should be true to their core adjudicatory values by focusing on the key tasks of marshaling evidence for fact finding, defining due process in litigation, and providing the interpretations central to the Rule of Law. Many "equitable" and other non-economic remedies are given a voice in mediation that has been lost in the civil justice system. Disputants can choose court adjudication for many reasons, including the need for a public answer on truth and justice; other disputants may self-determine that acceptability of outcome, privacy, avoidance of risk, healing, and closure are more likely to happen in mediation than adjudication. The legal system can accommodate both by offering choice and promoting voluntary contracts on mediator selection, models, and procedures. This is the heart of the original concept of the multi-door courthouse; having mediation as a preliminary requirement to access trials is consistent with this model provided that it is a distinct and separate process involving minimal regulation by legislation, rule, or common law and that respect for party self-determination is implemented contractually.

Processes are looking more and more akin. The blurring of the two separate and distinct processes of mediation and arbitration is harmful; mediation is negotiation, and arbitration is adjudication. There should not be transient standards applicable to both arbitrators and mediators. The more mandatory and rigid mediation becomes, the more restrictive it becomes for practitioners and the participants. Institutionalization of mediation stifles the voice of the mediator.

Mediation is an art and not a science. Despite the trend towards formalism and legalism in mediation, the mediation community has been adept at accommodating tension between core values. We must encourage creative juices while avoiding any capitulation to the routine. Mediators should continue to talk our own talk in a range of voices. We walk our walk by providing effective value-added services in a multitude of ways and means. A voluntary certification or mediator credential coming from an organization representative of the diversity of the mediation and legal communities is both timely and appropriate. Civil claims mediators must continue to seek additional process and professional gains, both within and without the court system, by promoting mediation as both an alternative and complementary process, which supports the Rule of Law. Mediators have adapted and evolved while furthering the best ethical and business practices that respect core values of mediation. Mediators have successfully consolidated gains while avoiding major loss to autonomy and capitulation to the routine. Nevertheless, conformity of mediation theory, rule, or practice still must be vigorously challenged to avoid the angst of mediation orthodoxy.

6.8.2 State of the artist

6.8.2.1 Two types of civil litigation impasse

My experience as a mediator of civil claims is that there are two types of cases that come voluntarily to the mediator. The first group of cases is where the impasse is dominated by communication failure, tension between agent and principal, lack of creativity, and other process issues. Professor Robert Mnookin and others have generally referred to these issues as strategic barriers. The other group of cases may involve many of these same dynamics, but ultimately the impasse is a result of a good faith difference in evaluation, risk analysis, principles, or goals of the disputants. In a simple view, in one type of impasse successful mediators uncover existing value, while in the other types of cases successful mediators break impasse by helping the parties create value. One legitimate perspective may be that for the latter cases to be resolved some transformation of at least one, if not both, of the parties must occur.

Mediators uncover value by removing strategic barriers, mostly involving trust and communication, and by reconciling interests in an environment supportive of cooperation. A facilitative, minimalist approach can be very effective for these impasses. These are the easier disputes. In other conflicts, mediators create new value by resolving good faith impasse on fair market value of a claim or by having parties reassess goals, values, standards, risks, options, or consequences. Both mediators are value-added for the parties.

Traditional mediation methodologies have focused on the former to the detriment of the mediator's role in creating new value. Initial mediation training teaches a facilitative approach; this is excellent in uncovering value but is more problematic in breaking good faith impasse. As an acknowledgment to Professor Hensler and other commentators, the uncovering value cases do generally involve educating lawyers how to become better partners in negotiation with their adversaries. The other cases may not, and there mediators serve an invaluable role in resolving intractable conflict.

6.8.2.2 The state of my mediation art

Over the last fifteen years, I have seen a significant amount of growth and development in both the use and practice of mediation. Yet significant issues that were raised in my initial mediator training are still being addressed and debated. No definition of mediation or the role of the mediator has been universally accepted. Mediation models and styles have evolved and been implemented by institutions and practitioners with varying degrees of success. A mediation business prospers for some and languishes for others. Mediators are struggling to develop or transition into a recognized profession. Dispute resolution organizations proliferate in an incomprehensible alphabetical mish-mash barely digestible by the marketplace. For some, mediation has become routine, and there are commentators who wonder if this is a form of capitulation.

6.8.2.3 My common mediation modalities view

I view mediation as a trilateral negotiation process. Although the mediator may default to certain approaches, or insist on specific actions, all mediators negotiate process with the parties at some level. As a mediator, I am an activist in managing the process, while respecting participant self-determination. I attempt to assess the expectations of all the participants, including counsel and stakeholders like insurance carriers. I do this often in advance of the mediation but more often at the mediation session itself. I customarily start out with a long orientation statement and foreshadowing of the approaches that will most likely be utilized that day.

I am also attentive to building rapport and credibility at every step of the process. Deborah Kolb and Judith Williams talk in terms of creating "spaces for mutual engagement and connection" in the context of what they call a "shadow negotiation." They state:

> Negotiations, it turns out are not purely rational exercises in the pursuit of self-interest or the development of creative trades. They are more akin to conversations that are carried out simultaneously on two levels. First there is the discussion of substance – what the bargainers have to say about the issues. But then there is the interpersonal communication that takes place – what the talk encodes about their relationship. Yes, people bargain over issues; but they also negotiate how they are going to negotiate. All the time they are bargaining over issues, they are conducting a parallel negotiation in which they work out the terms of their relationship and their expectations.

I agree with the formulation that negotiation occurs simultaneously on multiple levels. I am not sure it should be compartmentalized into only two levels, i.e, substance and relationship. This may be likely in bilateral negotiations where each principal is bargaining in their own self-interest. It may hold truer in transactional bargaining than in dispute resolution. There is the issue of agency (surrogates, representatives) and the natural tensions that exist between advocate and principal(s). There may also be other stakeholders or a public interest in the matter or outcome.

My approach is to acknowledge the shadow negotiation with the participants. I am as transparent as possible without risking offending participants. I move slowly, especially at the beginning of the process. I attempt to note the human elements. If people have suffered personal injury or loss, I express appropriate empathy, usually during the opening statement and at other critical times. I do this in a manner that recognizes the adversarial nature of the dispute.

After my opening statement, I am passive in the joint session. I allow the participants free reign to make any presentations or monologues they deem appropriate. I add consensus of recognition and empowerment. I ask few questions and seldom make a narrative statement about the substance of the dispute in any joint session. When faced with human tragedy, I am authentic. Although I attempt to be stoic, if I am affected emotionally, I acknowledge it. Tort claims involve serious injury or death. Parents have described holding their child or spouse while they died or otherwise watching a horrendous accident. That fact that I cry or want to cry does not mean I lose my impartiality. I have seen hardened defense counsel well-up in joint sessions. I weave any of my reactions into the risk analysis ("reality testing") phase of the mediation. My own humanity is often challenged, and ultimately expanded, by the substance and dynamics of disputes. If that happens in the joint session, then I deal with it in a transparent manner. Following conclusion of the joint session, I usually caucus with the party bringing the claim unless otherwise negotiated by all participants.

I do not get bogged down in mediation considerations of a "philosophical" or "religious" nature. I believe that any duality between facilitative and evaluative mediation models is artificial and false. I actively engage in approaches across any facilitative-directive-evaluative spectrum. It varies from context to context and especially from case-to-case. For example, I have mediated numerous medical malpractice claims in Pennsylvania this past year. In some of those cases my dominant approach has been facilitative, while in others evaluative, and multiple styles are utilized for some aspect of almost every case. I do not decide the night before what I am going to do by a review of Professor Riskin's grid or any of the other literature. During the mediation, I assess and re-assess the expectations of the parties and my own belief about what will be appropriate and effective in the unfolding dynamics of the mediation process. Michael D. Lang and Allison Taylor note the following:

> As mediators reflect on and examine the inner logic of the ideas and models they embrace and become aware of inconsistencies between and among them, they identify gaps in their constellations. Mediators often have (but may not be aware of) conflicting or disparate beliefs; they may believe that disputants know best how to resolve the conflict, yet they may use an evaluative mediation approach that implies that the mediator rather than the disputants is the expert. Mediators may not have complete consistency among all of the rings of their constellation, and when they experience internal conflicts they should examine those conflicts and determine which theory or belief will govern in the given situation. Such choice is a sign of ethical, reflective mediation practice and leads to artistry.

I believe current practice and the better frame of this issue is as noted above. Diversity of practice requires art and not science. Mediation is neither linear nor monolithic.

6.8.2.4 My mediation day funnel

When I train mediators, I describe the party participatory portion of the mediation process as a funnel. My funnel is usually viewed in stages, or phases, as follows:

1. The Lip: Pre-mediation communications; written submissions; determining participants; mediator opening statement.

2. Wide Upper Portion: information gathering; initial trust, credibility and rapport building.

3. Narrow Middle Portion: risk analysis; case review or evaluation.

4. Bottom Tip: bargaining; exchange of proposals; impasse breaking techniques.

I teach people that it is a funnel, which should flow in only one direction. The mediator should manage the flow in the above steps and avoid a counter-productive back-flow. Although mediation is a forgiving process, following the funnel's natural flow will rarely get a mediator into a posture where recovery is not possible.

Each step, joint session, or caucus may also be viewed as a funnel. Independent of my own views, my colleagues at Mediation and Professional Systems, Inc. ("MAPS") in Louisiana developed for their own basic training the concept that mediation is a series of funnels within funnels. Each caucus may start out broadly, but the mediator should continuously be narrowing the focus of the interaction and should stop at an appropriate time to move onto the next step or aspect of the case.

Likewise, issues can be treated in a "funnel" approach. Analogies, especially non-linear and multi-dimensional ones, are useful heuristics for mediation education. Questioning, narratives, and storytelling are all appropriate communication methods.

6.8.2.5 My mediator values and tools

Mediators must consider the following at all times in the process.

1. Engagement;
2. Expectation of participants, especially procedural due process;
3. Initial validation of positions and participant values;
4. Participant voice and values, recognition, empowerment;
5. Construction, de-construction, and re-construction of narratives and alternative perspectives;
6. Transparency, translucency, explanation of process imbalances or asymmetry;
7. Risk tolerances;
8. Cognitive and emotive processes, decision-making and choice;
9. Building and maintaining trust and credibility;
10. Macro strategies and micro implementation moves;
11. Validation of outcome or impasse; and
12. Respect for mediation process.

This is not an exhaustive list, but is illustrative of many core values, competencies, or approaches. A mediator must remain aware and mindful of what is happening in the process. Most of the above must not only be considered from the mediator's perspective but also from that of each participant.

In some ways, a mediator is an arbitrager. Arbitraging involves taking disparate pieces of information, usually known only to one party, and using that to effect a simultaneous transaction at a profit to the broker. It is buying one market to sell in another. Mediators who rely primarily upon a caucus model often use the cat bird's seat of superior information to educate, and then transform, the perceptions and choices of the parties. Mediators may arbitrage information.

The Basque people of Spain use the following folklore as a guide:

1. Show-up.
2. Pay attention.
3. Tell the truth.
4. Be open, but not attached, to outcome.

My experience leads me to this same heuristic for mediators.

6.8.2.6 The integration of mediation and the expanded role of mediators

ADR in education. Since I began mediating, I have been pleased with the expansion of dispute resolution and conflict management offerings in law school, graduate, and undergraduate curriculums. About fifteen years ago, I proposed adding an ADR course to the offerings of the two law schools here in Pittsburgh. I was pleased when both accepted the proposals, and I was retained as an adjunct to teach the course at Duquesne Law School. Recently, I added a course on international ADR to the University of Pittsburgh School of Law curriculum. I am pleased to be a part of the early crowd of practitioners and academicians teaching mediation to law students.

The growth of mediation courses in law schools has been phenomenal over the last ten years. There are numerous graduate offerings for those seeking an advanced degree at the Master's level in mediation and conflict resolution. There are numerous mediator training programs for lawyers and judges. There are seminars and CLE programs conducted on mediation on an almost daily basis. The concept of mediation as an integral aspect of a legal education has been accepted and institutionalized.

My view is that this is good. In contrast to some commentators, I believe this has been more than just teaching law students and lawyers to become better negotiators. I do believe it has resulted in a paradigm shift among younger lawyers. I speculate that this has been one of the factors in the decline of the number of civil trials over the last decade. As Professor Carrie Menkel-Meadow has noted in many of her numerous publications on this subject, there has been a shift in attitude that litigation is the prime, if not only tool, of lawyers. She notes:

> Seeking to define a universal human propensity for procedural fairness, Hampshire reduces conflict resolution to the single principle, audi alteram partem, ("hear the other side"), a universal principle of "the adversary argument" in which thinking is identified with the use of reason to weigh alternatives . . . . Furthermore, despite what law professors teach in civil procedure or constitutional law, "due" or "just" process does not necessarily require litigation, a "day in court," or a lawsuit.

Transactional application and integration. Mediators have applied their process skills to the creation or improvement of relationships. Mediators act as facilitators to identify potential areas of conflict and to build ADR into the relationship as a fundamental core value. This type of intervention may occur at any stage of the acquisition, merger, or creation of a strategic alliance or other business relationship. In the public policy context, there has been fruitful utilization of "neg-reg" (regulatory negotiation) and other participatory processes guided by a neutral intervention at an early stage in the process. The construction industry has integrated mediation by mandating "partnering" and other collaborative methods in the design stages of projects. For many years, win-win bargaining concepts have been the platform for "early-bird" and other interventions into collective bargaining relationships in the public sector, especially between school districts and their unions. The core focus of mediation as a communication process has been successfully integrated into a range of applications to avoid or manage conflict.

Settlement counsel: collaborative law. About five years ago, I was approached by a small law firm to be their negotiator on two complex cases arising from death claims. One involved bad faith against a carrier and the other a medical malpractice claim. The firm became aware of me via advertisements for negotiation and mediation CLE programs. Research found a number of articles advocating the concept of settlement or resolution counsel. It was clear that my experience as a mediator fit this role. I accepted the assignment and contacted the defense firms to advise them of my special role. I described it to them as acting in a formal, representative capacity but that they should consider me as a "partisan mediator" whose goal was to resolve the case. Although hesitant at first, in the bad faith case, the defense ultimately embraced my involvement and the matter was resolved on terms deemed favorable by all parties. One of the interesting practice issues that arose was that while I was serving as settlement counsel, I was active as a mediator in a number of other cases where defense counsel represented clients. After full disclosures, no one had any issues with my dual roles and all claims settled. I also served as settlement counsel in a number of complex claims, often negotiating with a counterpart whose function was resolution counsel. Mediation skills made it possible for me to easily integrate this into my practice.

A welcome recent trend is lawyers devoting their practice to what has become known as collaborative law. Stuart G. Webb, a Minnesota family law attorney, is credited with originating the model in the early 1990s. Collaborative lawyers decline to litigate and advance a system of negotiation first and foremost for their clients. Each side is represented by a collaborative lawyer and if an impasse is reached, then different sets of lawyers are retained to represent the parties in litigation. One non-profit organization, which trains lawyers in collaborative law, explains this approach on its website:

> Collaborative Law provides clients and their lawyers with a new, formal and strictly non-adversarial approach to resolving legal disputes. It encourages mature, cooperative and non-combative behavior, as the parties contract to eliminate litigation as an option. . . . Also, if one party changes its mind and chooses to initiate court action, the collaborative lawyers all must withdraw from the case and the clients will have to start over with new litigation lawyers.

Collaborative law should appropriately be viewed as an evolutionary branch of mediation.

Special master; expert witness. Especially during the implementation phase of class action settlements, many of my colleagues often serve as a Special Master. Class actions involve specialized rules and a complex body of law that has developed in this area. Fairness hearings are mandatory; the judge has broad discretion in approving settlements, relief to the named plaintiffs, and attorney fees. Recently I was retained to mediate a Fair Labor Standards Act case where the final result was a settlement where 99% of the claimants opted-in, and the oral recommendation I made to the court on individual relief and attorney fees was accepted. These two points were a challenging part of the mediation because defendants would not agree to settlement without an exact calculation of all liabilities, including plaintiff's counsel's fee, and the other side was equally reluctant to settle without knowing the relief and attorney fee amounts. After months of mediation, the parties agreed upon a fixed amount for the Common Fund and a maximum sum for individual relief and attorney fees. The court was petitioned in a joint motion to appoint me as Special Master with specific, limited duties. At the Fairness Hearing, where there were no objectors and a 99% opt-in participation, the federal judge praised the parties for cooperation and professionalism.

From time to time, I am asked to serve as an expert witness in a federal or state court action. Usually this involves some aspect of negotiation or ADR processes. It seems like the lawyers are attracted to my practice as a neutral and my teaching experience. They like the blend of theory and everyday practice. If after review of the file I am comfortable with the scope of my involvement, then I accept the assignment. Although I have written reports, so far I have not testified in a deposition or at trial. Again, my ADR experience makes this a natural extension of my traditional practice.

Jury focus groups. Occasionally I am asked to facilitate a jury focus group by one or more parties involved in litigation. Colleagues of mine have engaged in similar functions. It is a natural annex to the practice of a neutral. Experiences as a neutral, especially by those who have been judges, are valuable in this context. Mediators should feel free to accept assignments of this nature if they believe they add value to the parties and are comfortable there are no conflicts of interest.

CHAPTER SEVEN

TEACHING CREATIVE PROBLEM SOLVING TO NEGOTIATORS AND MEDIATORS

There is one thing stronger than all the armies in the world; and that is an idea whose time has come.

Victor Hugo

Interest in teaching thinking and problem solving in a classroom setting is not new. John Dewey (1910-1991) devoted considerable energy in the 1920s and 1930s to making the development of reasoning ability a fundamental goal of education. Since that time there has been a growing interest in teaching both thinking skills and problem solving at all levels of education. In the 1960s and 1970s and up to and including the present, psychologists and educators (Torrance, Osborn, Parnes, Treffinger, Noll, etc.) have formulated creative problem solving models and have experimented with teaching techniques and methods. Today, there is an abundance of literature on suggested techniques and methods to teach creative problem solving. Many of these techniques and methods are generic in the sense that they can be used to teach creative problem solving in any setting or in any discipline. In this chapter, we will explore techniques and methods that may be useful for teaching creative problem solving specifically to negotiators and mediators.

7.1 INTRODUCTION

One researcher has described the process of creativity as a "system involving a person who shapes or designs his environment by transforming basic problems into fruitful outcomes facilitated by a stimulating climate" (Taylor, 4). A "creative climate" has been defined as the conditions that *facilitate* and *stimulate* creativity (Taylor, 19). Those who wish to teach creative problem solving should be aware of some of the facilitating and stimulating conditions that serve to generate a classroom climate conducive to creativity.

7.1.1 Facilitating conditions

As pointed out in sub-section 1.3.15.2, research has disclosed that the following management attitudes facilitate and promote creativity in an organization: (1) trusting; (2) open; (3) allowing; and (4) interdependent actions. The more the manager creates conditions in which persons initiate, feel responsible for achieving goals, and feel free to create their own goals, the more the persons create the internal conditions that maximize the creativity potential (Gibb, 23, 29-30).

Research conducted in an educational setting has suggested the following specific behaviors as facilitating creativity:

- Rewarding diverse contributions;
- Helping creative persons recognize the importance of their own talents;

- Making use of opportunities;
- Holding to purposes;
- Avoiding equating divergence with delinquency;
- Reducing or eliminating emphasis on sex roles;
- Respecting unusual questions;
- Respecting unusual ideas;
- Showing that ideas have value; and allowing performance to occur without constant threat of evaluation (Taylor, 19, 26).

Now that we have surveyed some of the conditions found to facilitate creativity in group situations, let us examine some of the specific techniques found useful to stimulate creativity.

7.1.2 Stimulating conditions

Studies of what specific techniques can stimulate creativity in the classroom have yielded results helpful to our exploration here. Research conducted with both adults and children as subjects has shown that: (1) an instructional procedure which combines instruction, reinforcement, and practice can be successful in changing human behavior; (2) group interaction has the tendency to enhance the production of new ideas; (3) control-orientation or freedom-orientation of participants in a group problem solving activity affects how much structure or clarification the instructor will be required to provide; (4) control-oriented participants require significantly more structure than freedom-oriented participants; (5) evaluative feedback usually improves the performance of control-oriented problem solvers; and (6) creative feedback usually improves the performance of freedom-oriented problem solvers (Glover & Gary, 79-84; Torrance, 75, 87).

Feldhusen and Treffinger offer six general guidelines to assist in planning, conducting, and evaluating a classroom project on creative problem solving. They are:

1. Know how to define creative thinking and problem solving processes and abilities.
2. Be explicit in specifying the processes, skills, and content you will help the students in your class to learn and develop.
3. Try out your plans and new ideas before you begin to use them with your class.
4. Create an atmosphere in your class in which creative learning can occur.
5. Utilize learning procedures involving many activities and products.
6. Conduct a careful review and evaluation, not only of the students' learning, but of your own project and efforts, and plan revisions accordingly (Feldhusen and Treffinger, 75).

We will now turn to descriptions of teaching techniques used by several teachers of creative problem solving across the country.

7.2 PROFESSOR LINDA MORTON: TEACHING CREATIVE PROBLEM SOLVING

[**Editor's Note:** *This section is based on an article authored by Professor Linda Morton, California Western School of Law (*Teaching Creative Problem Solving: A Paradigmatic Approach*, 34 Cal. W. L. Rev. 375 (1998)) and is reprinted and reformatted here with permission.*]

7.2.1 General

I find that law students are often frustrated by the lack of structure to the somewhat amorphous skill of problem solving. Following is an exercise I use in all my clinical courses (externship, in-house, and simulation) to teach creative problem solving. The exercise can be used in doctrinal courses, as well. (For descriptions of how faculty may use this exercise in a Property or Constitutional Law course, see Morton, 386-38).

I begin with a scenario from my own law practice, with the students playing the role of the new lawyer. If there is time in class, I have an outsider role play the client; otherwise I play her myself or simply narrate. One scenario I use goes as follows:

> *You just started your own practice. A client walks into your office with a broken shoe. Apparently, the shank broke the first time she wore the pair. They were moderately expensive, and a shoe repair person told her this should never have happened. She took the shoes back to the store, expecting a new pair, or at a minimum, a store credit. Instead, the manager refused to do anything for her. When she began to complain more loudly, the manager placed his hand on her back, physically ushered her out the door, and shut the door behind her. As she talks to you of her experience, the woman is visibly upset, with emotions running from outrage to tears.*

In an initial brainstorming session, I ask the students what they should do in terms of this potential client. Generally, some speak of causes of action; others talk of letters demanding apologies. Students are unsure of what "category" of law the matter falls under and are uncomfortable with the potential client's emotional state. They clearly want to help, and have some excitement over having an actual case. Nonetheless, when I ask them specifically what the problem is and how to solve it, they have difficulty articulating it, much less knowing where to begin solving it.

I explain that this, like the majority of legal problems, does not arrive at our office doorstep in a neatly wrapped package. I state that the first course of action is to attempt to comfort the client, as we try to get a handle on what the problem is. I then offer a variety of visual models for diagnosing and solving problems. I offer my own model in visual and in outline form. Once we have talked through the model (eliciting from the students, if time, the steps and relevant questions to ask at each phase), I have the students, in groups, use it to analyze the shoe case and come up with an action plan. At this point, I do not discuss creative thinking but allow the students to focus on a more linear, legal analysis, with which the vast majority is more comfortable.

The group's action plans generally reach the same types of conclusions we reached in our initial brainstorm session, only they are better thought through, with a greater awareness of client needs, parties' values, problem prevention, and information required. As a result, the students are far more confident in their proposed action steps.

Once their confidence has accelerated, I take them to the next step (possibly in the following class): If our client decides she does not want to sue the store, what do we do? How can we approach this client's dilemma creatively? Referring back to my own model, I tell students the process of creative thinking most frequently arises when considering general approaches to the client's problem, as illustrated in the visual model.

To legitimize creative thinking's place in lawyering, I tell the students my belief that creativity in problem solving is one skill that separates great lawyers from good ones. To further ground the concept for the disbelievers, I briefly explain to the students, in simplistic neurological terms, how our brains become "stuck in a rut" and what we can do to have them leap to new neurological pathways. (For a more detailed description of the brain's neurological processes and potential exercises for jumping these neurological ruts, see Janet Weinstein and Linda Morton, Stuck in A Rut: The Role of Creativity in Problem Solving and Legal Education (draft available from the authors)). Then, I explain a series of creative thinking methodologies, and relate how I have used each one in the practice of law.

I divide up the class into six groups, assigning a different creative thinking technique to each group. After we try the exercises in our groups, students produce another series of action steps for our shoe case, some humorous, as well as creative. For example, students have suggested the following:

going back to the shoe repairperson to further discuss the matter of possible repair; taking a picture of the client with the broken shoe to perhaps reveal additional issues (a faulty ankle, perhaps?); and even breaking the other shoe to start a new footwear trend. Although they seem to enjoy the process, the main purpose is to have them think about the problem in a different way than they did previously. Despite the occasional skeptic, students have reacted to the exercise quite favorably. Comments from an anonymous survey were as follows: "I like the concept of thinking from a different angle;" "I want to learn more"; "good-different ways of looking at problems and creating solutions;" "the topic was beneficial and applicable not only to the internship, but to life in general." Two students expressed that they would like to spend more time on the topic.

I conclude the class by having students apply the entire problem solving model, including the creative exercises, to one of their own problems, either personal or legal. If we have run out of time, I have them do it as a journal assignment for the following week. Throughout the remainder of the semester, I make an effort to have students identify instances of creative problem solving and discuss them with the class in order to reinforce this important skill.

7.2.2 A process for creative problem solving

Below is a description of a problem solving model. Each phase incorporates potential inquiries to better understand and solve the problem.

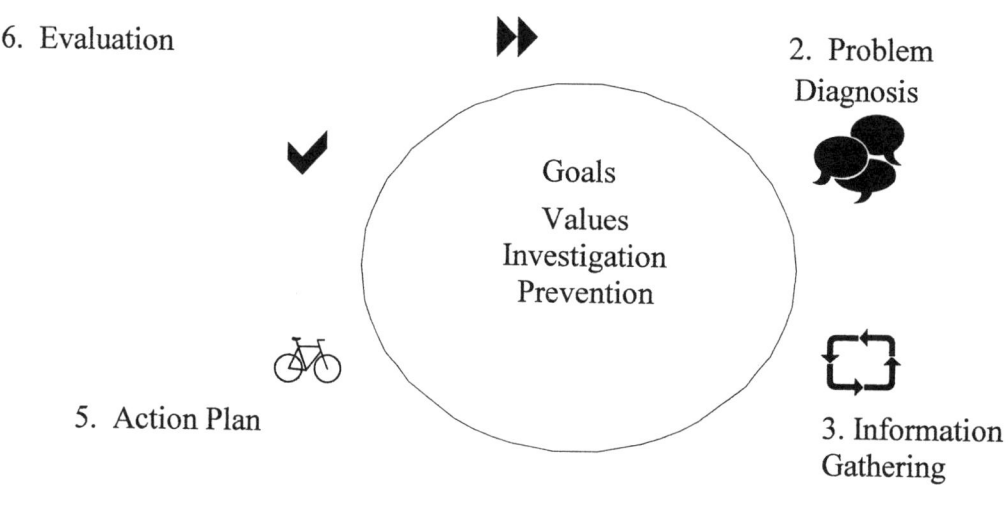

The model must be viewed as fluid and flexible: neither phases nor questions proceed in lockstep order. Problem solving frequently requires returning to earlier phases, or may even skip a phase. Some questions may be redundant or inapplicable. Throughout each phase, the client's and lawyer's values and objectives, as well as the concepts of further investigation and problem prevention, should be considered.

I. Situational Analysis
What is happening right now?
What is wrong with the client's/lawyer's current situation?
What are the symptoms?
What is the client's/lawyer's preferred situation?

II. Problem Analysis
What is the client's problem?
Do we need anyone else's help in identifying the problem?
Whom/what does the problem affect?
Who/what is responsible for the problem?
Is it part of a larger problem? If so, which should we address first?
Could it have been prevented?
What are the client's/ lawyer's objectives?
What are the client's/lawyer's underlying interests?

III. Information Gathering
What else do we need to know? (facts? feelings? legal issues?)
Who/what can help us?
Are we the appropriate person/entity to fix this problem?
How could this problem have been prevented?

IV. General Approaches
What would the client like us to do?
What approaches does the law allow us to do?
What other approaches might there be? (creative thinking)
What are the costs and benefits of each approach?
What new problems might each approach create?
Can any potential new problems be prevented?
Which approaches might be most effective?
Whose values and objectives does each approach reflect?

V. Action Plan
What is our course of action to solve this problem?
Who should be involved?
Who is responsible for its implementation?
How should decisions be made?
What specific steps should we take now?
What effects will these steps have?
What steps should we take to prevent further problems?

VI. Evaluation
Are we on the best path?
What new problems have been created?
Do we need to re-evaluate?

7.2.3 Six ways to jump out of a rut

7.2.3.1 Theoretical overlay

Take a theory from one discipline and use it in another. For example, many lawyers now use a psychological theory of client-centered counseling in their law practice.

7.2.3.2 De Bono's Six Hats (Edward De Bono, *Six Thinking Hats* (1985))

Isolate aspects of a problem (factual, emotional, positive, negative) and examine them separately. What are the positive aspects of the problem? How do you feel about it?

7.2.3.3 Synectics

Apply words from a different context or comparative adjectives (smaller, bigger, tighter) to the problem.

For example, apply the word "toast" to the problem of an underfunded organization, and we might come up with the idea of inviting potential donors to breakfast. Or, if we make the underfunded organization "wider," we might develop branch offices to attract local donors.

7.2.3.4 Mind Mapping

Write the problem in the center of a piece of paper and delineate your trains of thought in different directions from the center.

For example, if you are trying to think of a title for an article or a more specific topic, write down the general subject in the center of a blank sheet of paper and record your trains of thought in lines radiating outward from the center.

7.2.3.5 Visualization

View the issue from a photograph or visual model or imagine the issue from a different view (aerial, underneath, future, etc.).

For example: What will the problem look like one year from now? If the problem were sculpted, how would it appear?

7.2.3.6 Incubation

Once you've given the problem some thought, interrupt the process by doing something completely different, then go back to it. (This can be done over two classes, by "shelving" the analysis and returning to it the next class).

7.2.4 Creative thinking instructions

7.2.4.1 Theoretical overlay

Write your problem down, and think through how someone other than a lawyer (e.g., a doctor, artist, businessperson, psychologist, child, and/or teacher) might approach it.

7.2.4.2 Six Hats

Before you begin, assign someone the Blue Hat. That person's role is to run the process. Then, analyze your issue as follows, giving about one minute to each "hat":

1. Put on the White Hat and discuss only the facts pertaining to the issue.
2. Put on the Red Hat and discuss only how you feel about the issue.
3. Put on the Yellow Hat and discuss only what is actually positive about the issue.
4. Put on the Green Hat and discuss any and all possible solutions to the issue.
5. Put on the Black Hat and discuss the flaws of the potential solutions.
6. Write down your results.

7.2.4.3 Random Word Analysis

Pick any word, unrelated to your problem, and apply it. Or, try an adjective to make your problem "larger," "more narrow," "less expensive," etc.

7.2.4.4 Mind Mapping

Write your issue in the middle of a blank sheet of paper. Draw a circle around it. Write out your trains of thought from the center and see where this takes you.

7.2.4.5 Visualization

Imagine what your issue looks like. Imagine the people, place, objects involved. Try looking at it from another view, such as an aerial view, futuristic, or underground view. Describe, or draw a picture of it for others.

7.2.4.6 Incubation

Think about the problem, go for a walk, or check your "to do" list, then go back to the problem.

Teachers are free to copy this exercise for use in law and graduate school courses, provided that appropriate acknowledgment of the author is made. For permission to use this exercise for any other purpose, contact the author: Linda Morton, California Western School of Law, lm@cwsl.edu

7.3 PROFESSOR LYNN COHN: NORTHWESTERN UNIVERSITY SCHOOL OF LAW; "LAWYER AS PROBLEM SOLVER" PROGRAM

[**Editor's Note:** *This article is published here with the permission of its author, Professor Lynn Cohn.*]

7.3.1 Purpose

The Northwestern University School of Law "Lawyer as Problem Solver" Program is an innovative interdisciplinary program focused on introducing first year law students to the problem solving role lawyers fulfill and the skills necessary to accomplish that task.

7.3.2 Overview

What does it mean to "think like a lawyer" in the 21st Century? Increasingly today, lawyers facilitate problem solving for clients in settings outside of the courtroom or boardroom. In addition to knowledge of a range of substantive areas of law and skills in legal analysis, lawyers need skills in communication, negotiation, decision-making, creativity, interviewing, effective presentations, relationship-building and quantitative analysis all the while performing these tasks in a professional and civil manner. These functions cut across all areas of practice and apply to lawyers practicing in law firms, public-interest settings, corporations and government agencies.

Northwestern Law School has been a leader in encouraging student exploration of these roles and skills during the second and third year educational experience. The first year curriculum, however, appropriately focuses on building students' reasoning skills predominantly relying on the case study methodology. The Lawyer as Problem Solver Program serves to bridge the traditional first year curriculum to the broader roles lawyers serve as problem solvers.

7.3.3 History

The Lawyer as Problem Solver Program began as a mandatory one-day Conference held at the Westin Hotel in January 2002 for the class of 2004. In preparation for that conference, during 2001, a committee developed a curriculum addressing conflict management, negotiation, creativity, team-building, interviewing and counseling. Teams of faculty members and practicing lawyers led inter active sessions with small groups of students. Judge Ann Williams of the United States Court of Appeals for the Seventh Circuit and Exelon CEO Pamela Strobel addressed the class regarding how lawyers fulfill problem solving roles in a number of settings. The Conference was sponsored by a number of law firms who met with the students at a reception following the Program.

The Lawyer as Problem Solver Program held for the Class of 2005 was held at the Hyatt Regency Hotel in January 2003. Although the conference format was used, several changes were implemented that year. A lunch panel replaced the plenary speakers. The members of the panel represented diverse areas of practice, such as corporate, public service and law firms. Lynn Cohn led the panel members through a fast-paced lively series of questions focused on how each of them used problem solving skills in their everyday work. In addition, upper class students participated in the program as student leaders serving as role players and facilitating small group discussions.

For the Class of 2006, the Lawyer as Problem Solver program changed from a conference format to a four session program held throughout the year at the Law School. In addition the curriculum expanded to include effective presentations, professionalism, civility and ethics.

7.3.4 Student response

Students fill out evaluations after each session and the Lawyer as Problem Solver Committee has met with first years in debriefing sessions. Student response has been overwhelmingly positive to the Lawyer as Problem Solver program since its inception.

Like every other new curriculum, however, the Lawyer as Problem Solver Program has required curricular modifications in order to maintain the highest standards and to meet the needs of a sophisticated student body.

7.3.5 Benefits of the Lawyer as Problem Solver Program

1. Introduce first years to broader roles lawyers fulfill in diverse professional World.

2. Early development of essential lawyering skills.

3. Forum for diverse faculty to collaborate on curriculum and teaching.

4. Expose first year students to practicing lawyers from diverse areas.

5. Enhance reputation of northwestern law as leader in developing outstanding leaders in profession via unique curriculum.

6. Meet job market demand that students possess problem solving skills.

[Professor Lynn Cohn, Northwestern University School of Law
l-cohn@law.northwestern.edu]

7.4 PROFESSOR KIMBERLEE K. KOVACH: THE HAT EXERCISE

[**Editor's Note:** *This section is based on an article authored by Professor Kimberlee K. Kovach and is reprinted and reformatted here with permission.*]

This exercise is utilized to increase awareness of various individual approaches to problem solving and how mediators and others can facilitate better communication and understanding between and among those with different styles.

Several years ago, Edward de Bono authored a book entitled, *Six Thinking Hats*. In it, he identifies six types of thinking, each represented by a color:

The White Hat... white suggests paper... the white hat concerns information... when we wear the white hat, we ask the following questions: what information do we have/need; what is missing; how are we going to get such information.

The Red Hat... red suggests fire, thus warmth... red hat has to do with feelings, intuition and emotions; when the red hat is in use, you can describe feelings and intuitions without explanation.. can vocalize feelings.

The Black Hat... The black hat reminds us of judicial robes; it is for caution. Stops us from doing what may be harmful; risk hat; why something may not work; more pessimistic; thus should not be overused...

The Green Hat... green suggests vegetation... growth, energy, and life. Thus, the green hat is the energy hat; under the green hat, you offer proposals and suggestions; often explore and discuss new ideas and alternatives; possibilities; and even creativity.

The Blue Hat... blue is the process hat; when blue is on, you look at the thinking process itself; what have we achieved; what should we do next; could even be used to sequence the other hats...

The Yellow Hat... yellow suggests sunshine and optimism... under the yellow hat, we make a direct effort to find value and benefit in suggestions; seek out the good points; search also (and recognize) the values...

Each color is discussed and I ask the participants to identify first their dominant hat, and thereafter, the hat (or approach) they are most uncomfortable with.

We discuss that each person dons each hat at one time or another, but that often one or two hats or approaches are dominant. One is even more emphasized when the individual is in a conflict or problem situation. The individual will resort to that approach which is most comfortable. Difficulties in problem solving frequently arise, however because the two people have entirely different approaches which then creates barriers to the process. Negotiators must be aware of their own hat, but open to what the other side's approach is. Mediators or facilitators often find themselves between a red hat and a white hat, which does not make for effective communication.

The participants are then asked to select a hat that they are uncomfortable with, and put on the hat (I bring to the classroom six hats each with the color designation). I then engage the class in a discussion and debate, to which they are to respond in a way consistent with the hat they are wearing.

You can continue to change hats, and how the various hats or approaches interface with one another.

Another quick description to help keep everyone in role:

    White - Objective look at data and information

    Red - Legitimizes feelings, hunches and intuition

    Black - Logical, negative judgment and caution

    Yellow - Logical positive, feasibility, benefits

    Green - New ideas and creative thinking

    Blue - Control of the thinking process

[Professor Kimberlee Kovack, University of Texas Law School
KKovach@mail.law.utexas.edu]

7.5 PROFESSOR BERYL BLAUSTONE: "BROKEN SQUARES: AN EXERCISE DESIGNED TO DEMONSTRATE THE SHIFT FROM INDIVIDUAL TO COOPERATIVE PROBLEM SOLVING

[**Editor's Note**: *This article is reprinted with the permission of its author, Professor Beryl Blaustone.*]

7.5.1 General description of exercise

"Broken Squares" is an exercise that develops the perspective of the lawyer as problem solver. This exercise requires participants to analyze aspects of cooperative problem solving in group settings. I also use this exercise to discuss behaviors and attitudes that promote or detract from effective group problem solving activity. I attach the complete set of instructions for the manufacture and the conducting of "Broken Squares" by the original author and subsequent authorized editors/adopters.

The task for each group in "Broken Squares" is to form five squares of equal size. The instructor should emphasize and repeat this goal. "Broken Squares" involves groups of six participants each. There are five participants and one observer/judge in each group. Each of the five participants is given a set of cardboard pieces to be used for forming squares. The group has twelve minutes to solve the problem. There are rules for all participants that prohibit any communication other than a non-invasive, non-verbal offer. Any other communication results in ten-second penalties added to the group's time for solving the problem. The exercise is introduced with both instructor explanations and written instructions. The instructor should also read out loud the written instructions and entertain any questions before starting the exercise. Each group requires table space in order for the group to observe each other's pieces of the broken squares. The entire exercise, including debriefing, takes approximately no less than forty-five minutes. When possible, I prefer more thorough participant debriefing lasting another thirty to forty-five minutes depending upon the total number of participants.

I begin the exercise with a discussion of cooperative problem solving both in lawyering and mediation. I also discuss the importance of reevaluating potential solutions in group decision-making. When training law students and lawyers, I discuss the relevance of rethinking solutions as part of the expanded role of lawyers and the broader range of skills increasingly expected from lawyers. I highlight the process goals stated by the author and editors of "Broken Squares" which are:

1. Each person should understand what the overall problem is.

2. Each person should understand how s/he contributes towards the solution.

3. Each person should be aware of the potential contributions of the others.

4. Each person should recognize the difficulties of others in order to aid them in making their maximum contribution.

5. Groups that pay attention to their own problem solving process are more likely to be effective than groups that do not.

During the exercise, the instructor should keep time and keep track of the penalties on a large blackboard or a large piece of newsprint so that afterwards all groups can see all the group scores. The observers/judges should be calling out penalties for the instructor and keeping time of their respective group. As you stop the exercise after 12 minutes, you should convene the large group discussion. You should be prepared for and anticipate legitimate remarks that the communication rules are limiting and artificial. I always acknowledge these reservations and indicate that the exercise is designed to demonstrate certain issues for discussion and is thus limited in its construction. I try to take such observations and tie them back into what the exercise illustrates regarding individualistic versus group problem solving and the necessity of rethinking individual solutions. The attached complete set of instructions give you some alternative methods for conducting the exercise which you may find less confining and more effective.

As an introduction to the debriefing, I indicate that the average time for a solution by U.S. workers (dominant culture) is 6 minutes and 48 seconds. I then indicate the average time for a solution by Japanese workers is 2 minutes, 56 seconds. I then state that an average US group (dominant culture) will spend approximately three minutes in a competitive struggle before someone breaks up a completed square and commences collaborative behavior. The problem is then usually solved in another 3-4 minutes.

Some groups fail to solve the problem within the twelve minute time limit and also may have additional penalty seconds imposed. The discussion from such groups is often insightful about how the task was interpreted. The instructor should be careful to avoid giving the sense of failure to any group performance. Rather, I emphasize that success comes from the lessons learned from the exercise and that we often benefit the most from the comments from groups that did not achieve the goal of the exercise.

Debriefing this exercise often yields very rich discussion about the need to break up one's own square several times in order to achieve the group goal or to achieve the best result in these circumstances. This discussion serves as a good metaphor for the challenges of engaging in creative problem solving with others and staying open to rethinking solutions. Often, participants reflect on the difference between individualistic versus collaborative approaches to working with others. These observations are significant in discussions about the professional role of the lawyer. In my mediation/negotiation instruction and training, I find this a useful exercise to set the tone for the remainder of the semester or workshop. I continually refer to the necessity of "breaking up our squares" in discussing subsequent material later in the seminar or workshop.

7.5.2 Goals, process, and instructions for the Broken Squares exercise

[**Editor's Note:** *Reproduced from* A Handbook of Structured Experiences for Human Relations Training, Volume I, Revised *J. William Pfeiffer and John E. Jones, Editors La Jolla, Calif.: University Associates, Inc., 1974.*]

BROKEN SQUARES; NONVERBAL PROBLEM SOLVING

Goals
I. To analyze some aspects of cooperation in solving a group problem.
II. To sensitize participants to behaviors which may contribute toward or obstruct the solving of a group problem.

Group Size
Any number of groups of six participants each. There are five participants and an observer/judge in each group.

Time Required Approximately forty-five minutes.

Materials
I. A set of broken squares (prepared according to directions following) for each group of five participants.
II. One copy for each group of the Broken Squares Group Instruction Sheet.
III. One copy for each observer of the Broken Squares Observer/Judge Instruction sheet.

Physical Setting
A table that will seat five participants is needed for each group. Tables should be spaced far enough apart so that no group can see the puzzle-solving results of other groups.

Process

[Adapted with permission from Alex Bavelas, "Communication Patterns in Task-oriented Groups," *Journal of the Acoustical Society of America*, 1950, 22, 225-230. See also Bavelas, "The Five Squares Problem: An Instructional Aid In-group Cooperation," *Studies in Personnel Psychology*, 1973, 5, 29-38. Variations I-IV were submitted by Tom Isgar, Case Western Reserve University, Cleveland, Ohio.]

I. The facilitator begins with a discussion of the meaning of cooperation; this should lead to hypotheses about what is essential to successful group cooperation in problem solving. The facilitator indicates that the group will conduct an experiment to test these hypotheses. Points such as the following are likely to emerge:

1. Each individual should understand the total problem.
2. Each individual should understand how s/he could contribute toward solving the problem.
3. Each individual should be aware of the potential contributions of other individuals.

4. There is a need to recognize the problems of other individuals in order to aid them in making their maximum contribution.
5. Groups that pay attention to their own problem solving processes are likely to be more effective than groups that do not.

II. The facilitator forms groups of five participants plus the observer/judge. These observers are each given a copy of the Broken Squares Observer/Judge Instruction Sheet. The facilitator then asks each group to distribute among its members the set of broken squares (five envelopes). The envelopes are to remain unopened until the signal to begin work is given.

III. The facilitator gives to each group a copy of the Broken Squares Group Instruction Sheet. The facilitator reads these instructions to the group, calling for questions or questioning groups about their understanding of the instructions.

IV. S/He then tells the groups to begin work. It is important that the facilitator monitor tables during the exercise to enforce rules established in the instructions.

V. When all groups have completed the task, the facilitator engages the groups in a discussion of the experience. Observations are solicited from observers/judges. The facilitator encourages the groups to relate this experience to their "back-home" situations.

Variations:

I. When one member makes a square and fails to cooperate with the remaining members, the other four can be formed into two-person subgroups to make squares of the leftover pieces. They discuss their results, and the exercise is resumed.

II. The five-person teams can be given consultation assistance by the observer/judge or by one appointed member of the team. This may be a person who has done the exercise before.

III. Ten-person teams can be formed, with two duplicate sets of five squares each distributed among them. Teams of six to nine persons can be formed; in this case, prepare a broken square set with one square for each person, duplicating as many of the five squares as necessary.

IV. An intergroup competition can be established, with appropriate recognition to the group that solves the problem first. V. Members may be permitted to talk during the problem solving, or one member may be given permission to speak.

VI. Members may be permitted to write messages to each other during the problem solving.

Similar Structured Experiences: Vol. 1: Structured Experience 12; Vol. II: 29, 31,32,33; Vol. III: 54; "72 Annual: 80; Vol. IV: 102,103,105, 117. Notes on the use of "Broken Squares":

DIRECTIONS FOR MAKING A SET OF BROKEN SQUARES

A set consists of five envelopes containing pieces of cardboard cut into different patterns which, when properly arranged, will form five squares of equal size. One set should be provided for each group of five persons.

To prepare a set, cut out five cardboard squares, each exactly 6"X 6". Place the squares in a row and mark them as below, penciling the letters lightly so they can be erased.

The lines should be so drawn that, when the pieces are cut out, those marked A will be exactly the same size, all pieces marked C the same size, etc. Several combinations are possible that will form one or two squares, but only one combination will form all five squares, each 6"X 6". After drawing the lines on the squares and labeling the sections with letters, cut each square along the lines into smaller pieces to make the parts of the puzzle.

Label the five envelopes 1,2,3,4, and 5. Distribute the cardboard pieces into the five envelopes as follows: envelope 1 has pieces I, H, E; 2 has A, A, A, C; 3 has A; J; 4 has D, F and 5 has G, B, F, C.

Erase the penciled letter from each piece and write, instead, the number of the envelope it is in. This makes it easy to return the pieces to the proper envelope, for subsequent use, after a group has completed the task.

Each set may be made from a different color of cardboard.

BROKEN SQUARES - GROUP INSTRUCTIONS

Group Instruction Sheet for Problem Solving

Each of you will have an envelope, which contains pieces of cardboard to be used for forming squares.

When the facilitator gives the signal to begin, the task of your group is to form FIVE SQUARES OF EQUAL SIZE. You will have a maximum of twelve minutes to solve the problem of how this is to be done.

The task will not be completed until each member of your group has before her or himself, a perfect square of the same size as the square in front of each other group member. The task can be completed with the materials provided.

Four specific rules must be adhered to during the exercise. A penalty of ten seconds will be levied each time a rule is broken.

The rules are:

1. No member of the group may speak or communicate with any other member in any way or at any time except as allowed in the following rule.
2. Any group member may voluntarily offer one or more pieces of cardboard to any other member but may not force that member to accept them.
3. No member may take a piece or pieces from another member except as they are actually being offered.
4. No member of the group may signal in any way that another member should give a piece or pieces to her or him.

[Group instructions and Observer Instructions modified with permission by Blaine Hartford adapted by J. William Pfeiffer in *A Handbook of Structured Experiences for Human Relations Training*, (Volume I, Revised) University Associates, Inc. with permission from Alex Bacelas, "Communication Patterns in Task-Oriented Groups," *Journal of the Acoustical Society of America*, 1950, 22, 225-230.]

BROKEN SQUARES - OBSERVER INSTRUCTIONS

Your job is to be both a judge and an observer. As a judge, you need to decide when one of the following rules is being broken and then communicate this fact immediately by saying, in a flat, matter of fact voice, "A rule has been broken." Do not speak to any one person or try to force adherence to the rules. Keep an accurate count of the number of times a rule is broken…

As an observer, keep a record of the following:

1. At what time during the twelve minutes does the first person break up a completed square and offer pieces to another? Does this noncompetitive norm take hold at once, or if not, when does it take hold?

2. How long after collaboration sets in does it take to solve the problem?

3. Who struggles with nonfitting pieces yet seems unwilling to give any or all of them away?

4. Who finishes a square then withdraws from the problem-solving activity of the group? How many of the five members stay actively engaged in solving the group problem?

5. Does anyone manage to take a leadership role without breaking rules?

6. What is the feeling or tone of the group? At what points does it change?

7. Who purposefully breaks rules as a way to expedite solving the problem?

8. Try to note at what time the group seems to become collaborative, i.e., everyone begins to work together to get the task completed correctly.

9. Make note of any other observations you can share that will help the group learn from its experience.

— Be sure to indicate the exact time when the task is completed —

Be ready to share you observations with the group after it has completed its own debriefing of the experience. Also, see that all pieces of the puzzle are returned to the envelope marked with the number on the back of the piece.

[Group instructions and Observer Instructions modified with permission by Blaine Hartford adapted by J William Pfeiffer in *A Handbook of Structured Experiences for Human Relations Training*, (Volume I, revised) University Associates, Inc. with permission from Alex Bavelas, "Communication Patterns in Task-Oriented Groups," *Journal of the Acoustical Society of America,* 1950, 22, 225-230.]

[Beryl Blaustone, Professor of Law
Director, Mediation Clinic, Main Street Legal Services, Inc., CUNY School of Law
718-340-4325, blaustone@mail.law.cuny.edu]

7.6 JOHN W. COOLEY: TOOLS AND TECHNIQUES FOR TEACHING CREATIVE PROBLEM SOLVING

In my teaching in law school and in conducting creative problem solving seminars for the last twenty-five years, I have had the opportunity to experiment with numerous tools and techniques to facilitate and stimulate students to think creatively in their problem solving endeavors. Some of these tools and techniques are described below.

7.6.1 Perspective in creative problem solving

In some law school classes, I have provided the students with some experiential learning on the importance of perspective in creative problem solving. On the first day of class, prior to the students entering the tiered classroom, I place a box containing a simple sculpture that I made consisting of cones, spheres, and small cubes (about 3" on a side). I place this box (sporting question marks all over it) on about the third tier (of six) up – and in the center of all of the tiered seating. When the students come in, I ask them to spread out around the classroom and sit away from the box at a good distance. After making all the introductions and going over the course syllabus with them, I tell them that they are about to experience one of the most important teaching points in the whole course, and I encourage them to remember it throughout the course, their law school experience, and their professional careers.

I then lift up the box and expose the cones/spheres/cubes sculpture. This action is usually greeted by the students' smiles and quizzical looks. Then I ask the students to spend fifteen or twenty minutes drawing what they see. After they are finished drawing and hand them in to me, I give them a break, during which time I post their completed work so that, when they return, they can see how differently each of them has approached the subject. Because of the large size of one of the spheres and its position in relation to the students, some students only see one cone, others, two, and still others, all three (or parts of them). For the same reason, some students see one cube, others two, and some students draw cubes that are not even there! Because the classroom is amphitheater style, some students have a top view of the sculpture and others have more of a bottom view. Between those two extremes, students experience a multitude of separate angular perspectives.

Although this exercise is simple (some would say simplistic), it is a powerful learning experience for the students. It teaches each student that he or she approaches problem solving from a unique perspective, and to see the "whole picture," one must be *willing to move* from a commitment to one's own unique perspective and view the problem from the unique perspectives of others. The more perspectives experienced, the more likely one will be able to bring the whole picture of a situation into focus and resolution. This skill is basic to creative problem solving both in professional work and in personal life.

7.6.2 Perception in creative problem solving

A tool that I frequently use to demonstrate the important role that perception plays in the creative problem solving experience consists of an explanation of the three types of optical illusions and how their counterpart illusions can operate in a negotiation or mediation setting either to enhance or inhibit effective problem solving. I have found this tool to be very beneficial throughout a negotiation or mediation course or seminar as an instructional tool. In many instances, when giving feedback to the group after a role play exercise, some students will describe their role play experience in terms of a specific optical illusion. Occasionally, I also refer to optical illusions and problems of perception when giving students feedback on role play exercises that I have observed. Some of the optical illusions and related explanations appear in Section 1.7.2.

7.6.3 Word Problems (Conundrums)

I normally begin all my creative problem solving classes or seminars with a few word problem exercises. Facially, this is for ice-breaking purposes, but actually I do this to foreshadow and emphasize some of the lateral thinking principles and strategies that I will discuss in detail later. I normally begin with word problems that are not directly related to negotiation and mediation situations. Later on, I focus on negotiation/ mediation situations in simple contexts. Even later, I involve the participants in a role play exercise in which they can experiment three-dimensionally with the lateral thinking principles in real-life dispute contexts. The point that I continually make is that the principles we employ to solve word problems or conundrums are identical to many of the principles we employ to solve real-life transaction and dispute situations. In the remainder of this section, I provide you with an example of the typical escalation of problem types culminating in a dispute resolution role-play exercise (See Smullyan, 7-19).

1. A question of grammar. Those of you who are interested in questions of good grammatical usage, is it more correct to say the yolk is white or the yolk are white?

Answer: Actually, the yolk is yellow. This is an excellent example of an unchallenged assumption and a failure to focus on an underlying problem. The problem presents itself as a question of grammar, but the larger problem of definition is obscured by the problem statement.

2. Whose picture is it? An old man was looking at a portrait of a young man. Someone asked him, "Whose picture are you looking at?" Pointing to the portrait of the man, he replied: "Brothers and sisters I have none, but this man's father is my father's son." Whose picture was the man looking at?

Answer: Most people solve this problem by saying that the old man is looking at a portrait of himself. Unfortunately, that answer is wrong. The first statement of this reasoning is absolutely correct: if I have neither brothers nor sisters, then my father's son is indeed myself. But it doesn't follow that "myself" is the answer to the problem. If the second clause of the problem had been, "this man is my father's son," then the answer to the problem would have been "myself." But the problem didn't say that. It said "this man's *father* is my father's son." From which it follows that this man's father is myself (since my father's son is myself). Since this man's father is myself, then I am this man's father, hence this man must be my son. Thus, the correct answer to the problem is that the old man is looking at a picture of his son. This is an interpreting and reasoning problem and it always generates a lot of discussion. But the basic problem solving strategy here is a lateral thinking one: challenge assumptions and shifting attention areas. If you do that, you will focus first on the following statement:

(1) This man's father is my father's son.

Substituting the word "myself" for the phrase "my father's son" yields:

(2) This man's father is myself.

Convinced?

3. A Rate-Time Problem. A train leaves from Boston to New York. An hour later, a train leaves from New York to Boston. The two trains are going at exactly the same speed. Which train will be nearer to Boston when they meet?

Answer: Obviously, the two trains will be the *same* distance from Boston when they meet. Lateral thinking strategies of challenging assumptions, visualization, and fractionation can help solve this problem. Most people assume that the problem is to compare distance traveled from the two separate starting points to the meeting point. If you challenge that assumption, you see that the problem is to determine the distance between two points only – from one starting point to the meeting point – which is the same distance for both trains. Visualization by sketching also aids in solving this problem. Fractionation can be used to break the problem down into separate parts and solving them separately. Breaking the problem down, you would ask: 1) how far is the first train from Boston at the meeting point? 2) how far is the second train from Boston at the meeting point? Once you do that, you immediately recognize that both trains have to be at the same distance from Boston and they are also at the same distance from New York.

After presenting and discussing a few of these simple word problems, I then make a short presentation on Lateral Thinking principles. I then move to problems placed in the context of a mediation (or negotiation) setting. Two examples appear below:

4. A commercial dispute. You are mediating a case between Acme Manufacturing Company and Halmart Stores. Acme manufactures VCRs. Halmart contracted with Acme to purchase 10,000 VCRs wholesale for a nationwide Christmas promotion. When the shipment was delivered to Halmart, the price was $50,000 more than Halmart had anticipated. Halmart refused to pay. The pertinent part of the purchase contract read as follows:

> Acme and Halmart agree that Acme will absorb the cost of the packaging. The cost of a VCR and its packaging is $110, and the VCR is $100 more than the package.

Acme contends that, under a proper interpretation of this purchase contract, the packaging is $5.00 per VCR; Halmart contends that the packaging is $10 per VCR. How would you help them solve this problem?

Answer: You could, through questioning, engage them in a dialogue to help them see that this contract provision is subject to at least two interpretations, but that only one of them is reasonable and is mathematically valid. Acme's contention that the packaging is $5 per VCR is correct. Halmart's contention that each VCR costs $100 and packaging is $10 per VCR does not satisfy the language parameters of the contract. The lateral thinking strategy that helps here is shifting attention area. If you shift your attention and focus on the phrase "the VCR is $100 *more than* the package," then you have to conclude that the cost of each VCR is not $100, but rather some amount *more than* $100. Thus, the only amounts that satisfy the parameters of the problem are $105 for the VCR and $5 for the packaging. If you assume, as many people do, that the cost of the packaging is $10 and the cost of the VCR is $100 and the total cost is $110, you have not taken into account the "more than" language. Using an algebraic formula would be a visual way to arrive at the correct solution. In the following formula, X = the cost of packaging. The formula is: ($100 + X) + X = $110. Subtracting 100 from each side of the equation, the equation reduces to 2X = $10. Dividing both sides of the equation by 2 yields: X = $5. Thus, the cost of packaging is $5 and the cost of each VCR is $100 more than $5, or $105.

5. An employment discrimination dispute. Assume you are mediating a sexual harassment claim brought by an employee against an employer. Because of the nature of the incident, you cannot tell if either is telling the truth (both could be lying). You are justified in your belief that if the person is a liar, the person will consistently lie to you, and if the person is a truth teller, the person will invariably tell the truth. In caucus, you ask the employer, "Is either of you a Truthteller?" After the employer answers, you know the truth. What did the person say?

Answer: The employer said, "No." Hearing that answer, you know that the employer is a liar and the employee is a truthteller. If they were both liars, both truthtellers, or the employer was a truthteller and the employee was a liar, the employer would have answered, "Yes" – and you would not have known whether the employer was lying. The key here is to apply the lateral thinking strategy of fractionation. Break the problem down into separate information elements.

If they were both liars, how must the employer answer the question?	– "Yes"
If they were both truthtellers, how must the employer answer the question?	– "Yes"
If the employer was a truthteller and the employee was a liar, how must the employer answer the question?	– "Yes"

There is only one other alternative. If the employer was a liar and the employee was a truthteller, how must the employer answer the question?   – "No."
Thus, the employer was a liar.

In a creative problem solving course or training session, after completing these preliminary problem solving exercises, I normally move into a negotiation or mediation role-play exercise in which the students or participants can experiment with using the lateral thinking strategies (See Section s 7.6.9 and 7.6.10, below).

7.6.4 Puzzles

My first sensed experience with lateral thinking occurred in the early 1980s when I was teaching an "Alternatives to Litigation" course to students at Loyola University of Chicago School of Law. I had just finished reading Edward de Bono's book, *Lateral Thinking: Creativity Step by Step*, and I wanted to design what I thought would be a unique learning experience for the students. It turned out to be a unique learning experience not only for them but also *for me*.

In planning and designing the negotiation segment of the course, I thought it would be interesting to incorporate a class on lateral thinking and the importance of information as a medium in negotiation. The first part of the class was planned as a lecture on lateral thinking with examples and student discussion. The second part of the class was to be a classroom demonstration with student participation. In the demonstration I planned to use two overhead projectors side-by-side, a few feet apart, and a large projection screen. In preparing for the demonstration I had purchased four child's puzzles with fairly large-sized puzzle pieces. None of the puzzles had the same size pieces – but they were close in size. The idea of the exercise was to have two negotiating teams, each consisting of two student volunteers. Each team was to be assigned an overhead projector, in the "on" position and projecting light onto the screen. I would then give each team an envelope full of puzzle pieces representing pieces of information in a negotiation. However, neither envelope contained a complete basic puzzle. In addition to puzzle pieces for the basic puzzle, I inserted, into each envelope, puzzle pieces that were "close" but didn't exactly fit the respective puzzles. From each envelope I extracted several pieces of the basic puzzle so that the basic puzzle could not be fully completed. In short, if each team used all their basic puzzle pieces there would be some gaping holes, missing pieces in the basic puzzle; and a few puzzle pieces of the wrong size would appear on the screen located on the periphery of the basic puzzle. The puzzle pieces, and the students' work in attempting to solve the problem would be projected on the screen during the entire exercise so that all students could see. The missing pieces (which I had previously extracted from each envelope) would be distributed in the following manner. Two pieces from each puzzle were to be distributed to students in the audience and two pieces from each puzzle were placed in the opposite envelope.

The exercise had many teaching points, but the principal ones were that in negotiation:

1. Information is of the utmost importance.

2. You may not need all the information you collect.

3. Needed pieces of information to "solve the problem might be obtained from other people, including witnesses, experts, etc." (represented in the exercise by students holding puzzle pieces in the audience).

4. Needed pieces of information might be obtained from people on the other side of the negotiation.

Before conducting this exercise for the first time, I anticipated that I would at some point (when the student teams progressed as far as they could in solving the basic puzzle) suggest that they investigate whether other students in the audience possessed needed information (puzzle pieces). I also anticipated at some point that I would invite the audience to help solve the problem, and that eventually students from the audience would come down around one of the projectors and suggest to one of the teams that the other team might have the missing pieces. That was my thinking pattern going into the experiment. Needless to say, I was quite surprised how the experiment actually unfolded.

At class, the student audience and I watched the volunteer "negotiators" struggling to find pieces of the basic puzzle which fit, looking "puzzled" themselves when they found and pushed to the periphery pieces which were slightly too large or slightly too small, and scratching their heads when they went as far as they could go and still had gaping holes in the puzzle. I then suggested that they might inquire of the audience if anyone had pieces of information; which they did. They obtained puzzle pieces from the audience and simultaneously with the second negotiating team inserting the puzzle pieces supplied by the audience, I noticed in my peripheral vision a lone student moving with a quick deliberate stride from the back of the room. Before I could say anything, he moved quickly across the front of the room and took two pieces from the periphery of one basic puzzle and placed them in the other, and vice versa. In a split second he had completely solved both puzzles. Then, as briskly as he came, he returned full circle to his seat in the back of the room. I was flabbergasted! I immediately thought to myself "This student had quite boldly stolen my thunder! What nerve!" He had acted before I had even invited the whole class to participate in helping the negotiating teams solve the problem. I wanted to be the one to point out to the class that needed information might be held by the other team. After all, isn't that what a teacher is for? To teach! He had deprived me of my right to teach. That's it! I felt cheated. He had broken the rules, and he cheated me.

After thinking about it for a few moments, I realized what had happened. I had just encountered a natural lateral thinker. Here I was, teaching how to be a lateral thinker without having ever consciously viewed a real, live one. How ironic! For the next few minutes, I shared my realizations with the class. In fact, the whole thing had happened so quickly that the student audience was not aware of what had happened. But it was obvious to me what had happened. I had assumed a set of rules that really didn't exist. I had assumed that no member of the audience would participate in solving the problem that was projected on the screen unless and until they were invited by me to participate. That assumption was erroneous. In my pre-exercise instructions, I had not communicated to the class that no member of the audience could participate unless invited. In fact, I had said absolutely nothing in my introduction about audience participation. Thus, the nonparticipation rule was an assumption on my part, a cliché pattern formed by my prior experiences both as a student and as a teacher. I was a victim of my own assumption, of my dependence on logic.

Before the class session concluded, the "lateral thinker" confirmed that my analysis of what had occurred was correct. He said there was no rule against audience participation, as he perceived the situation. He also said that he immediately visualized the solution to the problem and simply solved it. In retrospect, his explanation for his behavior was completely "logical." Had I been more of a "lateral thinker" I would have anticipated, in advance of the class session, the conduct of the student "lateral thinker" in solving the problem. Incidentally, by reading this student's journal entries and in personal conversations with him later, I learned that his brain preference test revealed that his thinking was significantly right-brain dominant, that he had a visual orientation to problem solving, and that people often thought he reached solutions to problems in a rapid, unorthodox way, not logically explainable except in post-solution analysis. You probably won't be surprised to learn that this student "lateral thinker" wound up with an "A" for the course. He demonstrated an unusual, natural ability as a negotiator and mediator.

7.6.5 The design concept in creative problem solving.

To impress upon law students the importance of creativity and creative problem solving in lawyering, I sometimes involve them in a unique exercise early in the course. In particular, I have used this exercise many times in my course on appellate advocacy, but it could easily be adapted for teaching negotiation, mediation, or mediation advocacy.

Of the fifteen students in the class, I pair off twelve of them into six two-person advocate teams and designate three of the pairs as "appellant teams" and three as "appellee teams." I designate the remaining three students as "the judicial panel" and ask them to leave the room for about fifteen minutes, or until I recall them. I usually suggest that while they are outside, they should review the portion of my appellate advocacy book on "thinking like a judge." After the judicial panel has left the room, I then distribute to each advocate team a (8 ½" x 11" x 2") box which I refer to as "the record" in the case. I then ask the students to open the box, and when they do, much to their surprise they do not find a paper court record, but rather an assortment of a child's plastic snap-blocks, commonly known as LEGOS. I then explain the nature of the exercise and the related ground rules. The goal of the exercise, I explain, is for the advocate teams, using identical information (record) – i.e. plastic snap-blocks – to design an object to persuade the judicial panel to the advocates' point of view. That is, to be effective, the advocate team must successfully design an object which the judicial panel will recognize as a *particular* person, place, or thing. The two-person teams design the object in private. The teams may not allow other teams to see their works in progress, until they are before the panel of judges, and are ready to make their presentation.

The teams are told that the judicial panel members are permitted to confer with each other during the course of the presentations and to ask a total of three questions (requiring a "yes" or "no" answer) of each advocate team. Thus, if an advocate team designs the Empire State Building with their snap-blocks, and the judicial panel recognizes it as a building, but cannot identify it as the Empire State Building, the advocate team members may have designed an effective statement of facts generally, but their "argument" as to the identity of a particular building is unpersuasive and therefore fails. The students are then apprised of the exercise's three simple rules: (1) the designs cannot spell out any words in any language; (2) the plastic snap-blocks cannot be altered (melted, bent, broken, etc.); and (3) the finished design (argument) must stand on its own, without assistance.

Invariably, the advocate teams, working separately, design a variety of objects from the same set of information (LEGOS pieces). When the judicial panel reenters the room, its members are informed that the advocate teams have designed arguments which they wish to present to the judicial panel. The panel members are told that each advocate team has brought two issues before the court:

1. Whether the advocate team's design communicates a person, place or thing (i.e. whether the design is an effective statement of facts); and

2. Whether the advocate team's design communicates a *particular* person, place, or thing (i.e., whether the design is an effective argument).

Types of designs that students have produced in the past include: the American flag, the John Hancock Building in Chicago, the Sears Tower in Chicago, the "Great Chicago Fire," and, perhaps the most creative of all, a replica of the appellate advocacy instructor himself (me), complete with an overhead projector. Of course, even though the judicial panel members are not always successful in deducing the specific identity of the designs produced by the various advocate teams, the exercise has many teaching points. Aside from learning basic differences between facts and arguments, the students also learn how to collaborate in a creative and intellectual project that will be replicated later in the course when they work in two-person teams to draft an appellate brief. They get a taste, at least, of the importance to the lawyer of the artist and scientist functions and of accurately anticipating how their reviewers (judges) will think. But most importantly, the students learn the value of successful design. How to create an object (argument) that is sturdy and sound, stands on its own, communicates more than merely the sum of its parts, possesses both utilitarian and aesthetic qualities, and above all, makes a discernible, persuasive statement. In short, they become familiar with the basic design functions of a lawyer as an architect of problems and of creative solutions.

There are a variety of ways that this exercise could be adapted to negotiation, mediation, or mediation advocacy training. I will suggest only a couple of them here. Early in a mediation advocacy course, the students could be divided in groups of five. There would be two, two-student teams for a case (one team representing the plaintiff and one team for the defendant) the fifth person in each five-student group could serve as the mediator. In each group of five, one box of LEGOS would be given to each student team. These boxes would contain predominantly the same types of LEGOS pieces, *but* each box given to a team would *also contain* some LEGOS pieces (information) that were different from the opposing team's pieces (information). The exercise would teach the basic principles of how advocates can make effective opening statements in mediation. The same rules and principles that applied to the appellate advocacy exercise would apply to the mediation situation, except that the mediator would substitute for the panel of judges. The rules could be modified slightly to allow each opposing team, in addition to the mediator, to attempt to discern the *particular* person place or thing designed by the other side. This exercise would help give advocates a basic understanding of their role as problem designers and problem solvers in the mediation process, including such concepts as: (1) the differences in information available to parties in certain instances; (2) the need to think creatively to design an opening statement that has both a good statement of facts and a good argument to persuade, or at least influence, both the mediator's and the opposing team's thinking; (3) the importance of teamwork in the design of problems and solutions, which will replicate itself in later role-play exercises in the course and in life; and (4) the existence of (sometimes stark) differences in the way mediation participants look at things, their differing perceptions and perspectives.

As a stand-alone exercise, or as a final stage of the opening statement exercise described above, the five-person group could combine the LEGOS pieces from the opposing teams, and then work together to design a LEGOS solution – a set of facts and an argument (a course of action) that would be acceptable to all in the group. (In some situations the mediator might not be convinced of the "rightness" or " appropriateness" of the solution, but in the end, it would be up to the other four persons in the group to determine what is an acceptable solution for them). This exercise of course would provide the students with experiential learning. The will to understand what it feels like to collaborate in order to reach a result (a settlement) that is satisfactory to all the parties.

7.6.6 Games (Word Finding)

In teaching mediation techniques to groups as large as 200 lawyers, I have experimented with an exercise involving word finding and sentence finding. The purposes of the exercise are to quickly familiarize the audience with the concepts: conflict frames of disputants, the mediator's role in assisting the disputants to reframe the conflict situation, and the basic principles of creative problem solving.

I first give the members of the audience a list of words with scrambled spellings as follows:

CATFEF
EMOS
FLIDYFRENET
SOMT
ELEPPO
DARRYOIN
SCLOCTNIF

I then explain that the objects of the exercise are to unscramble the spellings to form words and then to use the words in a simple declarative sentence. I also explain that, if they wish, they may "collaborate" to solve the problem in teams of two persons. The audience is told that the exercise is timed, and each two-person team (or individual) is competing against all the other teams to solve the problem first. The audience is instructed that when a solution is reached, one team-member (or individual) must shout "solution" in a loud, clear voice.

In one such experiment, one team took approximately two minutes to solve the problem. After ten minutes, only about ten percent of the 200 person audience had solved the problem. Before reviewing the solution below and the learning analysis, perhaps the reader would like to test his or her prowess at solving the problem.

After ten minutes have elapsed, regardless of the progress of the audience's problem-solving efforts, I display the following list of words in unscrambled form:

AFFECT
SOME
DIFFERENTLY
MOST
PEOPLE
ORDINARY
CONFLICTS

I explain that the first list of words with scrambled spellings is analogous to disputants' perceptions of some (or possibly) all the issues involved in the conflict between them. One side of the dispute may come to the mediation with an unambiguous perception of the issue(s) or may be able to acquire such perception rapidly (as did some audience teams) as the mediation progresses. Some disputants may never timely acquire an unambiguous perception unless they receive assistance from the mediator (as when I displayed the list of unscrambled spellings). This, I suggest to the audience, is a very simple analogy to disputants' dimensions of conflict frame in a conflict setting.

I then ask for solutions (declarative sentences) from the audience. Normally, I ask the team (or individual) who had solved the problem the quickest to go first. The first two solutions from the audience might be:

MOST ORDINARY CONFLICTS AFFECT SOME PEOPLE DIFFERENTLY.
PEOPLE AFFECT SOME ORDINARY CONFLICTS MOST DIFFERENTLY.

I then ask for other solutions. Many people in the audience do not immediately realize that there are multiple solutions (declarative sentences) which satisfy the parameters of the exercise as framed. Here are three more possible solutions:

SOME CONFLICTS AFFECT MOST ORDINARY PEOPLE DIFFERENTLY.
MOST ORDINARY PEOPLE AFFECT SOME CONFLICTS DIFFERENTLY.
SOME ORDINARY CONFLICTS AFFECT MOST PEOPLE DIFFERENTLY.

I then point out that there are probably many more solutions, and I emphasize that the number of solutions is really dependent on the creativity of the disputants and the mediator. The mediator can help the parties perceive other potential solutions and can help the disputants perceive that they have complete control of the process. The disputants can go beyond the assumed rules or parameters of the exercise (or mediation process) and define new or modified rules leading to win-win or super-optimum solutions. For example, in the basic exercise described above, the mediator could point out that no rule prohibits the use of punctuation to achieve more solutions. For example:

MOST CONFLICTS AFFECT ORDINARY PEOPLE, SOME DIFFERENTLY.
SOME DIFFERENTLY AFFECT ORDINARY-PEOPLE CONFLICTS MOST.
CONFLICTS: MOST AFFECT ORDINARY PEOPLE, SOME DIFFERENTLY.

The mediator can also suggest expansion of the rules of the exercise to include consideration of the relevance and utility of other resources (words) toward achieving solutions of greatest satisfaction to the disputants. For example, suggesting the word "positively" as an additional resource for the exercise would create a whole host of new possible solutions which could not have even been contemplated initially by the disputants. The mediator could, of course, suggest that the whole exercise be redesigned to use totally new words as resources for a win-win or a possibly super-optimum solution. For example:

JOKE DESIGN: THE KEY TO ACHIEVING
SUPER-OPTIMUM SOLUTIONS IN MEDIATION.

Finally, I point out that, regardless of the solution (declarative sentence) finally agreed upon by the disputants, it is the mediator's job to ensure that each element (word) of the solution is being interpreted identically by the disputants in the context of their agreed solution. For example, if the disputants agree to resolve their conflict by adopting this last solution, the mediator would be obligated to ensure that the term "joke design" was understood by the parties to relate to creative processes in directed problem solving, as opposed to an undirected, comedy club-like joke fest.

7.6.7 Joke design

When teaching negotiation or mediation courses or seminars, I often include a segment on joke design either at the beginning of class as a warm-up exercise or later on in the class immediately preceding a negotiation or mediation role-play exercise. The purpose of the segment on joke design is to stimulate the students to think in innovative and satisfying ways. I usually have a handout sheet that contains three set-ups for jokes without punch lines. The idea is for the students to come up with punch lines for the jokes, one at a time. With regard to the first joke set-up, after a few minutes of thinking, each student individually writes down a punch line. After the students are finished writing, then each student reads his/her punch line. Obviously, some of these punch lines are hilarious. A ground rule is that if a student knows the "stock" punch line to the joke, the student must improve on it, or better yet, come up with something entirely different. There is a competitive part of this game too, in that, as to each joke, a winner is proclaimed after all punch lines have been read. The winner is determined by the loudness of the applause after I call each student's (or group's) name. After the winner is announced, I then read the "stock" punch line. Often the student-designed punch line is better than the "stock" one. This procedure is replicated with respect to the second joke set-up, except that the students work in pairs; and, as to the third joke set-up, the students work in threes. Many times the students come up with much funnier (more creative, more satisfying) punch lines when they collaborate with one or two other students in the second and third rounds. This is an important piece of learning in itself. A few examples of the joke set-ups (and their stock punch lines) that I have used appear below.

1. How many mediators does it take to change a light bulb?
   Punch line: Only one – but the light bulb really has to want to change.

2. Two frogs were sitting on a lily pad. One leaned over to the other and said, "_____."
   Punch line: Time sure is fun when you're having flies.

3. Not to be outdone by the "Snap, Crackle, and Pop" of the cereal industry a confectionary chemist invented a chocolate candy that talks when you bite into it. So when you hear Yummy, yummy, slurp, slurp, coming from the mouth of a chomping young lad, you can ask: "_____."
   Punch line: Pardon me boy, is that the chatty nougat you chew?

If there is time after the joke design segment, I might also draw a few relationships between joke design and the mediation process (see Section 6.1, above), so that the students understand that the just-completed exercises have far more significance in relation to creative problem solving in mediation than merely a class room ice-breaking tool.

7.6.8 Cartoon captioning

In teaching negotiation to non-lawyers in seminars and to law students in law school, I have experimented with cartoon captioning as a technique to quickly acclimate persons toward achieving creative solutions (win-win or super-optimum) in negotiation exercises. The procedure is as follows. After a short lecture on brainstorming and creativity, I present the participants with an unusual picture such as one where a man is shown waving to the camera while sitting at the steering wheel of a tractor which is balanced on top of what appears to be a black fifteen-foot pole.

I then ask the students, working individually, to write down a serious or "straight" caption for the picture, one which they might find in the business section of the *New York Times* and one which evokes no laughter. I tell them that they are in a competition to design the "most reasonable" caption, the one which describes the "most likely" explanation for what is represented by the picture in the real world of everyday life. Students, individually, have come up with serious captions such as: "John Deere substitutes billboard advertising with the real thing," or "New hydraulic lift may be boon to Acme Hydraulic Corp." The students then form groups of three. Taking turns, each person in the group of three plays the role of a judge and determines which of the other two captions is "more reasonable" under the ground rules. At this point I draw an analogy between what they have just done and the process of adjudication (court process or arbitration). Essentially, I explain to them their solution was designed under a number of restrictions, which included the concept of right and wrong.

Next, I ask them to work individually on another task. I tell them to look at the same picture and engage their imaginations to design a humorous caption. After they are finished designing captions individually, I ask them to form the same groups of three and share their results. They can then collaborate to achieve the "most humorous" caption for their group. They can select one of the three captions, designed individually, as the most humorous or, working collaboratively, they can create a new one. The criterion for "most humorous"" is: the one that makes the most laughter. As you can imagine, for several minutes while the students are collaborating on the humorous caption, the class turns into a din of laughter. Creative thought processes are running in high gear. Imagination is free to "run wild." After a few minutes of collaboration, I ask each group to jointly select its most humorous caption. Then each group, in turn on my cue, orally shares its best caption with the whole class. Inevitably, there is much additional laughter when these captions are read. The captions are exceptionally diverse and the students are amazed at how the same visual information (one set of facts portrayed by the picture) can, through reframing of perceptions (creative interpretation), be transformed into other sets of perceived facts (solutions). Some of the reframed perceptions have ranged from "Farmer Jones takes new 'Pogo stick' tractor on test-jumps," to "Russians, deep-drilling for oil in Siberia, produce `gusher' on Iowa farm."

After the most humorous captions are shared orally, I next explain that what they just experienced and felt is very similar to the experience and feelings in producing super-optimum solutions. The unrestricted freedom to reframe perceptions and the reframing of them are essential steps in achieving super-optimum solutions. While the super-optimum solution is not necessarily the most humorous (or most drastic) reframing, the unrestricted freedom of the process often evokes ideas or interpretations that the participants can use to design a mutually acceptable, "better than best expectation" solution. This, I explain, is the advantage of negotiated and mediated solutions over adjudicated solutions. Adjudicative solutions are restrictive and normally partially satisfy interests of the parties, and sometimes, of only one party, and occasionally, of no party. The students then engage in negotiation (or mediation) exercises as the case may be.

In my informal observations of such negotiations and mediations, I have noted that these creative acclimating and captioning exercises enhance the level of collaboration among students in the negotiation and mediation and tend to influence disputants' reaching win-win and sometimes super-optimum results.

7.6.9 Large group creative problem solving exercises

Occasionally, when teaching negotiation or mediation in law school or at seminars, I use fact scenarios involving groups of four to seven participants. The purpose of these exercises is to demonstrate the differences between individual and group decision-making and to provide the students with experience in collaborative problem solving. Often in transactional and dispute negotiation, and also in mediation, there are multiple parties at the table. These exercises are helpful in giving the students a "taste" of what it is like to negotiate or mediate in a large group setting where the participants have disagreements and differences of opinion on the issues that confront them.

One exercise, introduced to me in the 1980s by mediator and trainer Richard A. Salem, is called the NASA Moon Walk. In groups of seven the students are told they are members of an astronaut crew whose spaceship has just crash-landed on the dark side of the moon. They are further told that they were scheduled to rendezvous with a mother ship 200 miles away on the lighted surface of the moon, but their spaceship's rough landing disabled it and destroyed all the equipment on board except for fifteen items. The crew members are given a list of the fifteen items, including such things as a box of matches, food concentrate, fifty feet of nylon rope, one case of dehydrated milk, magnetic compass, and so on. The crew's survival depends on its ability to reach the mother ship. The crew's task is to rank the fifteen items in terms of their importance for survival. First, however, each crew member rank orders the fifteen items and then the crew members meet to reach a joint decision on the appropriate ranking. The crew members are then instructed to avoid arguing their views, to not change their mind simply to avoid conflict and reach harmony, to be suspicious when agreement comes too quickly and easily, to not use majority voting, averages, or coin flips, and to try to work cooperatively to find the best solution.

What makes this problem particularly interesting is that sometimes crew members with the most scientific knowledge will assume leadership of the group and lead the problem solving discussion using reasoning based on what would be an appropriate ranking *on earth.* The moon is very different from the earth in physical, atmospheric, and gravitational traits, to name just a few. Thus, a box of matches and a magnetic compass would be worthless on the moon because there is no oxygen to sustain a match's flame and there is no polarized magnetic field to allow the compass to work.

Some groups are unable to agree on the ranking, while other groups are able to reach consensus, but are often at odds with NASA's "approved solution." Invariably, most of the students are surprised when they receive NASA's ranking. Very rarely does an individual or a group rank all of the items correctly. Each group's score is virtually always better than the average of the individual scores and often better than any individual's. This exercise affords great lessons in positional versus cooperative negotiation, the effects of knowledge and interpretation of information in problem solving, the importance of both listening and evaluating, the role of persuasion in negotiation, and the benefits of collaborating to find the appropriate solution.

7.6.10 Student-developed role-play exercises

One of the best ways I have found to teach students how to solve problems creatively in negotiation and mediation is to engage them in drafting role-play exercises. There are various ways to do this, and I will suggest only a couple of them here.

Readers who have drafted negotiation or mediation role play exercises understand what a tremendously creative experience it is. Not only does the drafter have to select an interesting topic and develop a realistic plot so to speak, but he/she needs to have a reasonably good grasp of the principles of negotiation (or mediation) so that the role-players derive several gems of learning from the exercise. Drafters can build into the role-play, through the parties' confidential information, instructions to make parties behave competitively or cooperatively, with opportunities for an integrative solution, a distributive one, or both. Only the drafter has all of the information in that he/she has created the common information and two or more sets of confidential information. The drafter is in the best position to know how the negotiation should play out, and what its principal teaching points should be.

One teaching technique involving student-developed role-play exercises is to assign a role play drafting project well into a negotiation course. If students undertake such a drafting project too early in the course, they will not have a good enough grasp of negotiation principles to make the project meaningful. The project can be billed as a "creative problem solving exercise." The students can work in teams of two to enhance the creative potential of their experience. Two three-hour class periods should be set aside for this project. Each student team will create a role-play exercise and the watch two other teams actually engage in the role-play exercise they have created. The instructor can set some general parameters for the role-play exercise – i.e. no more than one page of common facts and one page of confidential information for each party, at least one ethical issue, two possible opportunities for a win-win solution, highly emotional plaintiff, and perhaps a specific law topic area (commercial, divorce, employment dispute). After observing the two student teams engage in their role-play exercise, the drafting team then engages in a discussion with the two negotiating teams, receiving the negotiating teams' reaction to the role-play and what they have learned. The drafting team can then give feedback to the negotiating teams, evaluating their performance, pointing out what the drafting team intended for them to learn, and what opportunities the negotiating teams might have missed. Then, this role-play experience is replicated twice, the drafting team becoming, sequentially, a negotiating team in two more role play exercises drafted by two other teams of students. This can result in a very creative and educational experience for all the participants.

Another way that the student-developed role-play technique can be used, is to do it orally in a classroom setting. As the instructor, you can begin the discussion by describing the basic contours of a dispute scenario. Then you ask for assistance from the students to flesh out the fact scenario. Either yourself or a student can make notes of the evolving story on a flip chart, blackboard, or transparency. Sometimes this can become a very humorous, if you allow it to be so. After the common facts are developed and you've advised the students of any special parameters, then you divide the class into two groups (plaintiff group and defendant group) out of the hearing range of the other. If the class is very large you may have to use four or six groups. In those separate groups, the students create the confidential information for the plaintiff or defendant, depending on their group assignment. In drafting the confidential information, the drafting group cannot assume that the other drafting group has knowledge of some fact unless it can be gleaned from the common facts. After the confidential information is developed the students divide into two person teams and negotiate the problem.

With a little creative thought, teachers of creative problem solving will be able to enhance the effectiveness of these techniques. For other readings on teaching creative problem solving, classroom exercises, and related topics see: Albrecht (2); Wood; Bransford and Stein, 195-212; Robertson, 173-200; and Davis and Scott.

EPILOGUE

It is fitting, I believe, to conclude Volume One of the *Creative Problem Solver's Handbook for Negotiators and Mediators* with the famous story of one of the greatest creative problem solvers of all time, the world-acclaimed Italian astronomer, physicist, and mathematician, Galileo (1564-1642). He possessed a most valuable kind of intellectual virtue, the courage to dispute "what everybody knows." As aspiring creative problem solvers, we can learn from Galileo to be appropriately curious and inquisitive, to be perseverant, and to challenge our own assumptions and those of others in our perception of problems, processes, and solutions.

In Italy some four hundred years ago there lived a young man named Galileo Galilei. He possessed an intensely inquiring spirit – that is to say, he was the kind of man who makes a point of seeing whatever he looks at, thinking about it afterward, and asking the question: "Why?" He started out as a student of medicine, but soon gave up that plan to spend time on what he really loved – physics and mathematics. He turned his whole mind to the pursuit, and by the time he was twenty-six years old, he became a professor of mathematics at the University of Pisa.

In those times, most people accepted without question the theories and statements inherited from the great thinkers of past ages. It did not enter their minds to test the truth of these statements for themselves. They regarded Aristotle, the ancient Greek philosopher, as the greatest of all authorities... Students were actually fined for disagreeing with the opinions of the ancients.

Now, one of the statements of Aristotle was this: The speed at which an object falls to earth depends upon its weight. A ten pound weight, for example, will fall ten times faster than a one-pound weight.

But Galileo had noticed different objects falling to the ground, and he thought differently. He made a few experiments and satisfied himself.

"Aristotle was wrong," he announced. "Weight has nothing to do with how fast objects fall. It is the resistance of air which affects the rate of descent. As long as two objects can overcome the resistance of the air to the same extent, they will reach the ground at the same time, no matter how much they weigh. A heavy stone and a light stone will fall at exactly the same rate of speed."

The other professors at the university were shocked and angry. They declared that of course Aristotle had been right and that Galileo was making a fool of himself. He should be quiet and stop bothering them with his silly notions, if he wanted to keep his job.

"All right," said Galileo. "We'll have a little test – my theory against Aristotle's. If I'm wrong, I'll be quiet. Meet me at the tower."

The bell tower in Pisa is known the world over, of course, as the Leaning Tower, because it stands at an angle and looks as though it might topple to the ground at any time... When it was finished [in 1174], the 179-foot tower leaned so much that any object dropped from the top story on the lower side would land some fifteen or twenty feet from the building's base.

Up climbed Galileo. A crowd of scholars, students, and interested townspeople gathered on the lawn below. With every step, he could hear their snickers and jeers.

At the top, on the uppermost gallery, he placed two iron balls. One weighed ten pounds. The other weighed just one. And the question to be answered was this: When Galileo pushed them off at exactly the same instant, would the heavier ball hit the ground first, as Aristotle had maintained, or ...?

Balancing the weights carefully on the balcony, Galileo rolled them over together.

From far below, the breathless crowd saw the two balls plunge over the edge. They came hurtling straight down. They fell at first side by side, then – side by side – and then finally –

There was a tremendous thud. One single thud. They had struck the ground together.

Galileo was right and Aristotle wrong.

Even then, some who had seen would not believe their own eyes. It is very difficult to let go of old ideas, especially ones that have persisted for centuries. Some of the professors made all sorts of excuses and continued to insist that Aristotle was correct. After all, if they were to admit that Galileo was right, how many more of the great Aristotle's principles might also be wrong? It was better, they thought, to silence this troublemaker. They booed and hissed Galileo at his Lectures, and made his life as miserable as they could.

But Galileo was not one to be browbeaten. He said goodbye to Pisa, and took a job teaching at the University of Padua, where thoughts were given a bit more freedom. There he went on searching, questioning, and discovering, and showing the world what can be done when someone dares to think for himself.

["Galileo and the Leaning Tower," as told by William J. Bennett in *The Moral Compass: Stories for a Life's Journey* (Simon & Schuster, 1995), pp. 333-335.]

INDEXES TO VOLUME ONE

Index Designation	**Index Title**
A.	General Index
B.	Index to List of Sources

INDEX A

GENERAL INDEX

Volume One

References are to sections.

Section No.

–A–

Architect,	1.1.2
Architecture,	1.1.2

–C–

Creative problem solving,	1.3.15.1
barriers,	1.7
defined,	1.3.15.1
favorable conditions,	1.3.15.2
orientation,	1.6
Creative problem solving strategies,	1.3.3.2
analogies,	2.2.8
brainstorm,	2.2.2
challenging assumptions,	2.2.3
fractionate,	2.2.5
generate alternatives,	2.2.4
random stimulation,	2.2.9
reverse thought,	2.2.7
suspend judgment,	2.2.1
visualize,	2.2.6
Creative problem solving tools and techniques,	
analytical,	3.2 (See Ch. 3, Table of Contents)
generative,	3.1 (See Ch.3 Table of Contents)
Creative skills,	1.3.16
Robert A. Creo's suggestions for breaking impasse,	See 5.3 and Table of Contents under 3.10, Vol. 2

–D–

Decision-making,	1.5
Design,	1.1.2
Designer,	1.1.2

–E–

Enneagram,	3.5.2

–I–

Impasse breaking,	Ch 5
Peter S. Adler, (Leadership)	5.1
Steven J. Brams & Alan D. Taylor, (Fair Division Procedures)	5.2
John W. Cooley, (Fair Settlement Value Formula)	5.9
Robert A. Creo, (Methods and Paradigms)	5.3
Robert A. Creo, (Bargaining Models)	5.4
Hon. Morton Denlow, (Five Techniques)	5.5

Rodney A. Max, (Closing the Deal)	5.7	Robert D. Benjamin, (Guerilla Mediation)	6.6
Robert H. Mnookin, Scott R. Peppet, Andrew Tulumello (Creating Value)	5.6	Robert D. Benjamin, (Strategic Use of Cognitive Art)	6.7
V. Michelle Obradovic, (Standard Techniques)	5.8	Robert A. Creo, (Art and the Artist)	6.8

Interdisciplinary approach, 1.2.1

defined, 1.2.1
JokeThink, 6.1
MagicThink, 6.2
MathThink, 6.3
MusicThink, 6.4

–L–

Lateral thinking, 1.3.3.2
  compared with vertical thinking, 1.3.3.2

Left-brain functions, 1.3.3.3
  compared with right-brain functions, 1.3.3.3

Practitioners' suggestions for creative problem solving, See Indexes A-E in Vol 2, Table of Contents

–M–

Mediation, 1.3.2
  defined 1.3.2

Problem, 1.3.4
  defined, 1.3.4
  design, 1.3.10
  finding, 1.3.15.3
  types, 1.3.7

Metaphor, 1.2.2
  defined, 1.2.2
  roles, 1.2.2

Problem solving, 1.3.4
  defined, 1.3.4
  different processes, 1.3.4
  group, 1.3.13.3
  individual, 1.3.13.2
  types, 1.3.13

–N–

Negotiation, 1.3.1
  defined, 1.3.1
  adversarial model, 1.3.1
  problem solving model, 1.3.1

Process, 1.3.8
  design, 1.3.11
           4.1
  Creo Blind Trust Method, 4.2.2

Neuro-linguistic programming, 3.5.1

  Creo Pie Chart tool, 4.2.1

–P–

Pracademic, 1.2.1
  defined, 1.2.1

  Rodney A. Max, (Mediation Design) 4.3

Pracademics, 1.2.1
  Robert D. Benjamin, (Physics of Mediation) 6.5

  Rodney A. Max, (Multiparty Mediation) 4.4

Rodney A. Max, (Para-mediator)	4.5	Prof. Linda Morton, (Techniques & Exercises)	7.2
hybrid ADR processes,	1.3.8, 4.1	stimulating conditions,	7.1.2

–R–

Reasoning,	1.4
deductive,	1.4.3
fallacies,	1.4.4
inductive,	1.4.2
Right-brain functions,	1.3.3.3
compared with left-brain functions,	1.3.3.3

–S–

John Settle's suggestions for breaking impasse,	See 5.13 in Vol. 2 and Table of Contents, under 5.13, Vol. 2
Solution,	1.3.9
types,	1.3.9
design,	1.3.12
off-the-shelf,	3.4

–T–

Teaching creative problem solving,	Ch. 7
Prof. Beryl Blaustone, (Broken Squares Exercise)	7.5
Prof. Lynn Cohn, (Lawyer as Problem Solver Program)	7.3
John W. Cooley, (Ten Teaching Techniques)	7.6
facilitating conditions,	7.1.1
Prof. Kimberlee K. Kovach, (The Hat Exercise)	7.4

Thinking mechanics,	1.3.4
Thinking modes,	1.3.3
abductive,	1.3.3.4
abstract,	1.3.3.5
active,	1.3.3.6
analogical,	1.3.3.7
analytical,	1.3.3.8
automatic,	1.3.3.9
body (kinesthetic),	1.3.3.10
conscious,	1.3.3.11
convergent,	1.3.3.1
creative,	1.3.3.12
critical,	1.3.3.13
deductive,	1.3.3.14
defined,	1.3.3
dialectical,	1.3.3.15
divergent,	1.3.3.2
heuristic,	1.3.3.17
holistic,	1.3.3.18
inductive,	1.3.3.19
integrative,	1.3.3.20
lateral,	1.3.3.2
reflective,	1.3.3.21
synthetic,	1.3.3.22
systems,	1.3.3.23
transformational,	1.3.3.24
unconscious,	1.3.3.25
vertical,	1.3.3.1
whole-brain,	1.3.3.3
Thinking skills,	1.3.5
Thinking styles,	1.3.6
Trees,	3.3

–W–

Whole-brain thinking,	1.3.3.3
applied,	3.5.3
lateral dominance,	1.3.3.3
lateral preference,	1.3.3.3
tests for lateral dominance,	1.3.3.3

INDEX B

INDEX TO LIST OF SOURCES

Russell L. Ackoff, *The Art of Problem Solving: Accompanied by Ackoff's Fables* (Wiley, 1978).

James L. Adams (1), *Conceptual Blockbusting* (Addison-Wesley Publishing Co., 1986).

James L. Adams (2), *The Care and Feeding of Ideas* (Addison-Wesley Publishing Company, Inc., 1986).

Peter Adler, "Leadership, Mediation, and the Naming, Framing, and Taming of Type-II and Type-III Problems," in Handbook Vol. 1.

Andrei G. Aleinikov, *Mega Creativity: Five Steps to Thinking Like a Genius* (Walking Stick Press, 2002).

Karl Albrecht (1), *Brain Power: Learn to Improve Your Thinking Skills* (Prentice-Hall, Inc., 1980).

Karl Albrecht (2), *Brain Building* (Prentice-Hall, Inc., 1984).

James J. Alfini, Sharon B. Press, Jean Sternlight, & Joseph Stulberg, *Mediation Theory and Practice* (Matthew Bender & Company, 2001).

Silvano Arieti, *Creativity: The Magic Synthesis* (Basic Books, Inc., 1976).

Thomas Armstrong, *7 Kinds of Smart* (A Plume Book, 1993).

John D. Arnold, *The Art of Decision Making* (AMACOM, 1978).

Robert Axelrod, *The Evolution of Cooperation* (Basic Books, 1984).

Jordan Ayan, *Aha! 10 Ways to Free Your Creative Spirit and Find Your Great Ideas* (Crown Trade Paperbacks, 1997).

Jonathan Baron, *Thinking and Deciding* (Cambridge University Press, 1988).

Renee Baron & Elizabeth Wagele, *The Enneagram Made Easy* (HarperCollins Publishers, 1994).

Thomas D. Barton, *Creative Problem Solving: Purpose, Meaning, and Values,* 34 CAL. W. L. REV. 273 (1997-98).

Howard Bellman, *Some Reflections on the Practice of Mediation*, 14 NEGOT J. 3 (1998).

Robert D. Benjamin (1), "The Constructive Uses of Deception: Skills, Strategies, and Techniques of the Folkloric Trickster Figure and their Application by Mediators," 12 MEDIATION Q. 3 (1995).

Robert D. Benjamin (2), "Mediation as a Subversive Activity." DCBA Brief 11 DUPAGE COUNTY ILL B. J. 2 (1998); also published by Mediation Information & Resource Center (MIRC), available at www.mediate.com. (last visited June 6, 2005).

Robert D. Benjamin (3), "The Mediator as Trickster: The Folkloric Figure as Professional Role Model," 13 MEDIATION Q. 131 (1995).

Robert D. Benjamin (4), "The Natural Mediator," Acad. of Family Mediators: 18 MEDIATION NEWS 1, (1999).

Robert D. Benjamin (5), "Negotiation and Evil: The Sources of Religious and Moral Resistance to the Settlement of Conflicts." 15 MEDIATION Q. 3 (1998).

Robert D. Benjamin (6), "The Physics of Mediation: The Reflections of Scientific Theory in Professional Mediation Practice." 8 MEDIATION Q. 2 (1990).

Robert D. Benjamin (7), "The Quest for Truth and the Truth of Lies," Acad. of Family Mediators: 18 MEDIATION NEWS, (1999).

Robert D. Benjamin (8), "Guerilla Mediation: The Use of Warfare Strategies in the Management of Conflict," (1998).

Robert D. Benjamin (9), *Effective Negotiation and Mediation: Applied Theory and Practice Handbook*, 9th Ed. (Mediation & Conflict Management Services, 2002).

Robert D. Benjamin (10), "Strategies for Managing Impasse," in Folberg, J., Milne, A. & Salem, P., eds., *Divorce and Family Mediation* (Guilford Press, 2004).

Robert D. Benjamin (11), "The Strategic Use of Cognitive Art in Problem Solving," Section 6.6 of Volume 1 of this Handbook.

Mark Bergren, Molly Cox, & Jim Detmar, *Improvise This! How to Think on Your Feet So You Don't Fall on Your Face* (Hyperion, 2002).

Michael Billig, *Arguing and Thinking* (Cambridge University Press, 1996).

Howard Bloom, *The Lucifer Principle: A Scientific Exploration into the Forces of History* (Grove/Atlantic, 1995).

Margaret A. Boden (ed.), *Dimensions of Creativity* (The MIT Press, 1994).

Daniel Bonevac, *The Art and Science of Logic* (Mayfield Publishing Co., 1990).

Daniel Bowling and David Hoffman (eds.), *Bringing Peace Into the Room: How Personal Qualities of a Mediator Impact the Process of Conflict Resolution* (Jossey-Bass, 2003).

John Brockman (ed.), *Creativity: The Reality Club 4* (Simon & Schuster, 1993).

Steven J. Brams & Alan D. Taylor, *The Win-Win Solution* (W.W. Norton & Co, 1999).

John D. Bransford & Barry Stein, *The Ideal Problem Solver: A Guide for Improving Thinking, Learning, and Creativity* (W.H. Freeman & Co., 1984).

Jennifer Gerarda Brown, *Creativity and Problem-Solving*, 87 MARQ. L. REV. 697 (2004).

Stephen I. Brown & Marion I. Walter, *The Art of Problem Posing,* 2d ed. (Lawrence Erlbaum Assoc., 1990).

Edward Brunet & Charles B. Craver, *Alternative Dispute Resolution: The Advocate's Perspective* (LexisNexis, 2001).

Guy & Heidi Burgess, "Beyond Intractability," available at http://www.beyondintractability.org/iweb/ (last visited June 6, 2005).

Robert A. Baruch Bush & Joseph P. Folger, *The Promise of Mediation* (Jossey-Bass Publisher, 1994).

Thomas Cleary, (Trans. with commentary), *Sun Tzu II, The Art of War* (HarperSanFrancisco, 1996).

Jim Collins, *Good to Great: Why Some Companies Make the Leap ... And Others Don't* (HarperCollins, 2001).

E. Jeffery Conklin & William Weil, "Wicked Associates, Inc.", available at http://www.touchstone.com/tr/wp/wicked.html (last visited January 14, 2004).

John W. Cooley (1), *Callaghan's Appellate Advocacy Manual*, Lawyer's Edition (Clark Boardman Callaghan, 1989, supplemented through 1995).

John W. Cooley (2), *The Mediator's Handbook* (NITA, 2000).

John W. Cooley (3), *Mediation Advocacy,* 2d ed. (NITA, 2002).

John W. Cooley (4), "Mediation and Joke Design: Resolving the Incongruities," J. DISP. RESOL. (1992).

John W. Cooley (5), "A Classical Approach to Mediation - Part I: Classical Rhetoric and the Art of Persuasion in Mediation," 19 U. DAYTON L. REV. 83 (1993).

John W. Cooley (6), "A Classical Approach to Mediation - Part II: The Socratic Method and Conflict Reframing in Mediation," 19 U. DAYTON L. REV. 589 (1994).

John W. Cooley (7), "Descartes' Analytic Method and the Art of Geometric Imagineering in Negotiation and Mediation," 28 VAL. U. L. REV. 83 (1993).

John W. Cooley (8), "The Geometries of Situation and Emotions and the Calculus of Change in Negotiation and Mediation," 29 VAL. U. L. REV. 1 (1994).

John W. Cooley (9), "Mediation Magic: Its Use and Abuse," 29 LOY. L. REV. 1 (1997).

John W. Cooley (10), "Joke Structure: A Source of Creative Techniques for Use in Mediation," 33 U.S.F.L. REV. 85 (1998).

John W. Cooley (11), "The Art of Clear Imaging in Legal Writing, Appellate Law Review," (Illinois Appellate Lawyers Assoc., 2000).

John W. Cooley (12), "Music, Mediation, and Superstrings: The Quest for Universal Harmony" (in process).

John W. Cooley (13), "Mediation, Improvisation, and All that Jazz" (in process).

John W. Cooley (14), "The Ethical Limits of Acceptable Deception in Mediation," 11 J. OF DUPAGE COUNTY B. ASS'N 29 (1998).

John W. Cooley (15), "Merging Minds and Microcomputers: The Coming of Age of Computer-Aided Mediation of Court Cases," in Stuart S. Nagel & Miriam K. Mills, *Systematic Analysis in Dispute Resolution* (Quorum Books, 1999).

John W. Cooley (16), *The Arbitrator's Handbook*, 2d ed. (NITA, 2005).

John W. Cooley (17), *Arbitration Advocacy*, 2d ed. (NITA, 2003).

James M. Cooper, "Towards a New Architecture: Creative Problem Solving and the Evolution of Law," 34 CAL. W. L. REV. 297 (1997-98).

J. Daniel Couger, *Creative Problem Solving and Opportunity Finding* (Boyd & Fraser, 1995).

Stephen R. Covey, *The Seven Habits of Highly Effective People: Restoring the Character Ethic* (Simon & Schuster, 1990).

Charles B. Craver, *Effective Legal Negotiation and Settlement*, 2d ed. (The Michie Co., 1993).

Robert A. Creo (1), "A Pie Chart Tool to Resolve Multiparty, Multi-Issue Conflicts," 18 Alternatives 1 (CPR Inst. for Disp. Resol., May 5, 2000).

Robert A. Creo (2), "How a "Blind-Trust Method" Resolves Multi-Defendant Cases," 17 ALTERNATIVES TO THE HIGH COST OF LITIGATION 1 (CPR Inst. for Disp. Resol., September, 1999).

Mihaly Csikszentmihalyi, *Creativity: Flow and the Psychology of Discovery and Invention* (HarperPerennial, 1996).

John S. Dacey, *Fundamentals of Creative Thinking* (Lexington Books, 1989).

John S. Dacey & Kathleen Lennon, *Understanding Creativity* (Jossey-Bass Publishers, 1998).

Antonio R. Damasio, *Descartes Error: Emotion, Reason and the Human Brain* (Grossett & Dunlap, 1994).

Gary A. Davis, *Psychology of Problem Solving: Theory and Practice* (Basic Books, 1973).

Gary A. Davis & Joseph A. Scott, *Training Creative Thinking* (Holt, Rinehart & Winston, Inc., 1970)

Edward de Bono (1), *Lateral Thinking: Creativity Step by Step* (Perennial Library, 1970).

Edward de Bono (2), *New Think* (Basic Books, Inc., 1967).

Edward de Bono (3), *The Mechanism of Mind* (Simon & Schuster, 1969).

Edward de Bono (4), *Six Thinking Hats* (Little, Brown & Company, 1985).

Edward de Bono (5), *New Thinking for a New Millennium* (New Millennium Press, 2000).

Edward de Bono (6), *de Bono's Thinking Course* (Facts on File Publications, 1985).

Daniel Dervin, *Creativity and Culture* (Fairleigh Dickinson University Press, 1990).

Franz deWaal, *Good Nature: The Origins of Right and Wrong in Humans and Other Animals* (Harvard University Press, 1996).

Jayne Seminare Docherty, "Narrative, Metaphors, and Negotiation," 87 MARQ. L. REV. 847 (2004).

Robert Epstein, *Creativity Games for Trainers: A Handbook of Group Activities for Jumpstarting Workplace Creativity* (McGraw-Hill, 1996).

Charles Farkas & Suzy Wetlaufer, "*The Ways CEOs Lead*," in *On Leadership* (Harvard Business Review Publications, 1990).

John F. Feldhusen & Donald J. Treffinger, *Creative Thinking and Problem Solving in Gifted Education,* 3d ed. (Kendall/Hunt Publishing Company, 1985).

Ronald Finke, *Creative Imagery: Discoveries and Inventions in Visualization*, (Lawrence Erlbaum Assoc, 1990).

Roger Fisher & William Ury, *Getting to Yes* (Penquin Books, 1991).

Richard Fobes, *The Creative Problem Solver's Toolbox* (Solutions Through Innovation, 1993).

Robert Fritz, *The Path of Least Resistance* (Fawcett Columbine, 1984).

Eric Galton, *Representing Clients in Mediation* (Texas Lawyer Press, 1994).

Kathleen Galvin, Carma L. Bylund, & Bernard J. Brommel, *Family Communication: Cohesion and Change*, 6th ed. (Allyn & Bacon, 2004).

Howard Gardner, *Frames of Mind: The Theory of Multiple Intelligences* (Basic Books, Inc., 1983).

Jack R. Gibb, "Managing for Creativity in the Organization," in *Climate for Creativity* (Calvin W. Taylor, ed., 1972).

Donald G. Gifford, *Legal Negotiation: Theory and Applications* (West Publishing Co., 1989).

K. J. Gilhooly, *Thinking: Directed, Undirected and Creative* (Academic Press, 1982).

Malcolm Gladwell, *Blink: The Power of Thinking Without Thinking* (Little, Brown and Co., 2005)

Friedrich Glasl, *Konfliktmanagement. Ein Handbuch für Führungskräfte, Beraterinnen und Berater* (Paul Haupt Verlag, 1997).

John A. Glover & A.L. Gary, "Procedures to Increase Some Aspects of Creativity," 9 J. OF APPLIED BEHAV. ANALYSIS 79 (1976).

John A. Glover, Royce R. Ronning, & Cecil R. Reynolds, *Handbook of Creativity* (Plenum Press, 1989).

Dwight Golann, *Mediating Legal Disputes: Effective Strategies for Lawyers and Mediators* (Little, Brown & Co., 1996).

Stephen B. Goldberg, Frank E. A. Sander, and Nancy H. Rogers, *Dispute Resolution: Negotiation, Mediation, and Other Processes,* 2d ed. (Little, Brown & Co., 1992).

Gary Goodpaster, *A Guide to Negotiation and Mediation* (TransAtlantic Publishers, 1997).

Robert K. Greenleaf, *Servant Leadership: A Journey into the Nature of Legitimate Power and Greatness* (Paulist Press, 1993).

Richard L. Gregory (1) (ed.), *The Oxford Companion to the Mind* (Oxford University Press, 1998).

Richard L. Gregory (2) (ed.), *The Oxford Companion to the Mind* (Oxford University Press, 1987).

Raymond Guindon, *Designing the Design Process: Exploiting Opportunistic Thoughts*, HUMAN COMPUTER INTERACTION, Vol. 5 (1990).

Allen F. Harrison & Robert M. Bramson, *Styles of Thinking* (Anchor Press, 1982).

Kurt Hanks & Jay Parry, *Wake Up Your Creative Genius* (Crisp Learning, 1997).

John M. & Gretchen L. Haynes, *Mediating Divorce: Casebook of Strategies for Successful Family Negotiations* (Jossey-Bass Publishers, 1989).

Ronald Heifitz, *Leadership Without Easy Answers* (Harvard University Press, 1994).

G. Nicholas Herman, Jean M. Cary, & Joseph E. Kennedy, *Legal Counseling and Negotiating: A Practical Approach* (Matthew Bender & Co., 2001).

James M. Higgins, *101 Creative Problem Solving Techniques* (The New Management Publishing Co., 1994).

David P. Hoffer, *Decision Analysis as a Mediator's Tool*, 1 HARV. NEGOT. L. REV. 113 (1996).

John H. Holland, et al., *Induction: Processes of Inference, Learning, and Discovery* (The MIT Press, 1989).

R.W. Hutchinson, S.L. English, & M.A. Mughal, "A General Problem Solving Approach for Wicked Problems: Theory and Application to Chemical Weapons Verification and Biological Terrorism," in *Group Decision and Negotiation*, Vol. 11 (Kluwer Publishers, 2002).

Susan Jarboe, "Group Communication and Creativity Processes," in Lawrence Frey, Dennis Gouran, & Scott Poole, *Handbook of Group Communication Theory and Research* (Thousand Oaks, 1999).

Andrea L. Johnson, "Teaching Creative Problem Solving and Applied Reasoning Skills: A Modular Approach," 34 Cal W. L. Rev. 389 (1997-98).

Barry Johnson, *Polarity Management: Identifying and Managing Unsolvable Problems* (HRD Press, 1992).

Vera John-Steiner (1), *Notebooks of the Mind: Explorations of Thinking* (University of New Mexico Press, 1985).

Vera John-Steiner (2), *Creative Collaboration* (Oxford University Press, 2000).

Morgan D. Jones, *The Thinker's Toolkit: Fourteen Powerful Techniques for Problem Solving* (Random House, 1998).

Donald Kagan, *On the Origins of War and the Preservation of Peace* (Anchor Books, 1995).

John A. Keegan, *A History of Warfare* (Knopf, 1993).

Lawrence H. Keeley, *War Before Civilization* (Oxford University Press, 1996).

Janeen Kerper, "Creative Problem Solving vs. the Case Method: A Marvelous Adventure in Which Winnie-the-Pooh Meets Mrs. Palsgraf," 34 CAL. WEST. L. REV. 351 (1997-98).

Paul Klee, *On Modern Art* (London, 1948).

Deborah Kolb, *When Talk Works: Profile of Mediators* (Jossey-Bass Publishers, 1994).

Stephen Kozicki, *Creative Negotiating* (Adams Media Corp., 1998).

George Lakoff & Mark Johnson, *Metaphors We Live By* (The University of Chicago Press, 1980).

Marc Leman, "A Theory of Metaphor," in L. Apostel, H. Sabbe, & F. Vandamme, *Reason, Emotion and Music* (Communication and Cognition; Ghent Belgium, 1986).

Lynne C. Levesque, *Breakthrough Creativity* (Davies-Black Publishing, 2001).

David Lewis & James Greene, *Thinking Better* (Henry Holt & Co., 1982).

Paul M. Lisnek, *A Lawyer's Guide to Effective Negotiation and Mediation* (West Publishing Co., 1993).

Jack Lochhead, *Thinkback: A User's Guide to Minding the Mind* (Lawrence Erlbaum Assoc., 2001).

Norman Maier, *Problem Solving and Creativity in Individuals and Groups* (Brooks/Cole Publishing Co., 1970).

Richard S. Mansfield & Thomas V. Busse, *The Psychology of Creativity and Discovery* (Nelson-Hall, 1981).

Sandra P. Marshall, *Schemas in Problem Solving* (Cambridge University Press, 1995).

Abraham H. Maslow, *The Farther Reaches of Human Nature* (Penguin Arkana, 1971).

Rollo May, *The Courage to Create* (W.W. Norton & Co., 1975).

Richard E. Mayer, *Thinking, Problem Solving, Cognition* (W.H. Freeman & Co., 1983).

Carrie Menkel-Meadow (1), "The Lawyer as Problem Solver and Third-Party Neutral: Creativity and Non-Partisanship in Lawyering," 72 TEMP. L. REV. 785 (1999).

Carrie Menkel-Meadow (2), "Aha? Is Creativity Possible in Legal Problem Solving and Teachable in Legal Education?," 6 HARV NEGOT. L. REV. 97 (2001).

Robert H. Mnookin, *Beyond Winning: Negotiating to Create Value in Deals and Disputes* (Harvard University Press, 2000).

Alfonso Montuori & Ronald E. Purser (1), *Social Creativity*, Vol. 1 (Hampton Press, 1999).

Alfonso Montuori & Ronald E. Purser (2), *Social Creativity*, Vol. 2 (Hampton Press, 1999).

Paul E. Moody, *Decision Making: Proven Methods for Better Decisions* (McGraw-Hill Book Co., 1983).

Brooke Noel Moore & Richard Parker, *Critical Thinking* (Mayfield Publishing Co., 1992).

Christopher W. Moore, *The Mediation Process: Practical Strategies for Resolving Conflict* (Jossey-Bass Publishers, 1986).

Linda Morton, "Teaching Creative Problem Solving: A Paradigmatic Approach," 34 CAL. W. L. REV. 375 (1997-98).

Stuart Nagel & Miriam Mills (1), *Multi-Criteria Methods for Alternative Dispute Resolution* (Quorum Books, 1990).

Stuart Nagel & Miriam Mills (eds.) (2), *Systematic Analysis in Dispute Resolution* (Quorum Books, 1991).

David G. Myers, *Intuition* (Yale University Press, 2002).

Gerald Nadler, Shozo Hibino, with John Farrell, *Creative Solution Finding* (Prima Publishing, 1999).

Stephen Nathanson, "Designing Problems to Teach Legal Problem Solving," 34 CAL. W. L. REV. 325 (1997-98).

Howard Nemerov (1), *The Collected Poems of Howard Nemerov* (University of Chicago Press, 1977).

Howard Nemerov (2), *A Howard Nemerov Reader* (University of Missouri Press, 1991).

Allen Newel & Herbert A. Simon, *Human Problem Solving* (Prentice-Hall, 1972).

Raymond S. Nickerson, David N. Perkins, & Edward E. Smith, *The Teaching of Thinking* (Lawrence Erlbaum Assoc., 1985).

Debra Niehoff, *The Biology of Violence: How Understanding the Brain, Behavior, and Environment Can Break the Vicious Circle of Aggression* (The Free Press, 1999).

Gerard I. Nierenberg (1), *Fundamentals of Negotiating* (Hawthorn/Dutton, 1973).

Gerard I. Nierenberg (2), *The Art of Creative Thinking* (Barnes & Noble Books, 1982).

Cheryl Niro, "The Decision Tree: A Systematic Approach to Settlement Decisions," 82 ILL. B. J. 3 (1994).

Alex F. Osborn (1), *Applied Imagination* (Charles Scribner's Sons, 1963).

Alex F. Osborn (2), *Your Creative Power: How to Use Imagination* (Charles Scribner's Sons, 1948).

Catherine Patrick, *What is Creative Thinking?* (Philosophical Library, 1955).

David Perkins, *Archimedes' Bathtub: The Art and Logic of Breakthrough Thinking* (W.W. Norton & Co., 2000).

Ian Robertson, *Problem Solving* (Psychology Press, 2001).

Susan Podziba, *The Human Side of Complex Public Policy Mediation,* 19 NEGOT J. 285 (2003).

Ellen S. Pryor & Will Pryor, "Concurrent Mediation of Liability and Insurance Coverage Disputes," 4 CONN. INS. L. J. 485 (1997-98).

Howard Raiffa, *The Art & Science of Negotiation* (Harvard University Press, 1982).

Michael Ray & Rochelle Myers, *Creativity in Business* (Broadway Books, 1989).

Arthur S. Reber & Emily Reber, *The Penguin Dictionary of Psychology*, 3d ed. (Penguin Books, 2001).

Leonard L. Riskin & James E. Westbrook, *Dispute Resolution and Lawyers* (West Publishing Co., 1987).

Nancy Roberts (1), "Coping with Wicked Problems," paper presented at the Third Bi-Annual Research Conference of the International Public Management Network, Sydney, Australia, March 4-6, 2000, available at http://www.inpuma.net/research/papers/sydney/nancyroberts.html (last visited June 6, 2005).

Nancy Roberts (2), "Wicked Problems and Network Approaches to Resolution," available at http://www.willamette.org/ipmn/test2/issue1/ejchapter1.htm (last visited Sept. 23, 2000).

Nancy Roberts (3), "The Transformative Power of Dialogue*," Research in Public Policy Analysis and Management,* Vol. 12 (JAI, 2002).

Robert & Michele Root-Bernstein, *Sparks of Genius: Thirteen Thinking Tools of the World's Most Creative People* (Houghton Mifflin Co., 1999).

Lee Ross & Andrew Ward, "Naïve Realism: Implications for Social Conflict and Misunderstanding," in *Values and Knowledge*, Brown & Turiel, eds. (Lawrence Erlbaum Assoc., 2001).

William Roth, James Ryder, & Frank Voehl, *Problem Solving for Results* (St. Lucie Press, 1996).

Albert Rothenberg & Carl R. Hausman, *The Creativity Question* (Duke University Press, 1976).

Edward Rothstein, *Emblems of Mind: The Inner Life of Music and Mathematics* (Times Books, 1995).

Moshe F. Rubinstein & Iris R. Firstenberg, *Patterns of Problem Solving,* 2d ed. (Prentice-Hall, 1995).

Loyal Rue, *By the Grace of Guile: The Role of Deception in Natural History and Human Affairs* (Oxford University Press, 1994).

Mark A. Runco, *Divergent Thinking* (Ablex Publishing Corp., 1991).

Mark A. Runco & Robert S. Albert, *Theories of Creativity* (Sage Publications, 1990).

Mark A. Runco & Steven R. Pritzker (eds. in chf.), *Encyclopedia of Creativity* (Academic Press, 1999).

Sandra Walker Russ, *Affect and Creativity: The Role of Affect and Play in the Creative Process* (Lawrence Erlbaum Assoc., 1993).

Peter Russell, *The Brain Book* (E.P. Dutton, Inc., 1979).

Roger Schank, *The Creative Attitude: Learning to Ask and Answer the Right Questions* (Macmillan Publishing Co., 1988).

Mark K. Schoenfield & Rick M. Schoenfield, *The McGraw-Hill 36-Hour Negotiating Course* (McGraw-Hill, Inc. 1991).

Alfred W. W. Schoennauer, *Problem Finding and Problem Solving* (Nelson-Hall, 1981).

E. F. Schumacher, *A Guide for the Perplexed* (Harper & Row, 1977).

Simon Buckingham Shum, "Representing Hard-to-Formalise, Contextualised, Multidisciplinary, Organisational Knowledge," available at http://kmi.open.ac.uk/people/sbs/org-knowledge/aikm97/sbs-paper2.html (last visited June 6 2005).

Jan D. Sinnott (ed.), *Everyday Problem Solving: Theory and Applications* (Praeger, 1989).

Steven M. Smith, Thomas B. Ward, & Ronald A. Finke, *The Creative Cognition Approach* (The MIT Press, 1995).

Raymond M. Smullyan, *What is the Name of this Book?* (Prentice-Hall, 1978).

V. Spolin, *Improvisation for the Theater* (Northwestern University, 1972).

Morris Stein (1), *Stimulating Creativity: Individual Procedures,* Vol. 1 (Academic Press, 1974).

Morris Stein (2), *Stimulating Creativity: Group Procedures,* Vol. 2 (Academic Press, 1975).

Robert J. Sternberg (1), *The Nature of Creativity* (Cambridge University Press, 1988).

Robert J. Sternberg (2), *Handbook of Creativity* (Cambridge University Press, 1999).

Robert J. Sternberg (ed.) (3), *Thinking and Problem Solving* (Academic Press, 1994).

Robert J. Sternberg & Janet E. Davidson (eds.), *The Nature of Insight* (MIT Press, 1995).

Robert J. Sternberg & Peter A. Frensch (eds.), *Complex Problem Solving: Principles and Mechanisms* (Lawrence Erlbaum Assoc., 1991).

James E. Stice (ed.), *Developing Critical Thinking and Problem-Solving Abilities* (Jossey-Bass, 1987).

Lawrence Susskind & Jeffrey Cruikshank, *Breaking the Impasse: Consensual Approaches to Resolving Public Disputes* (Basic Books, 1987).

Shunryu Suzuki, *Zen Mind, Beginner's Mind* (Francisco Zen Center, 1981).

Deborah Tannen, *The Argument Culture: Moving from Debate to Dialogue* (Random House, 1998).

Irving A. Taylor & J. W. Getzels (eds.), *Perspectives in Creativity* (Aldine Publishing Co., 1975).

Edward Tenner, *Why Things Bite Back* (Vintage, 1997).

Charles Thompson, *What a Great Idea!: The Key Steps Creative People Take* (HarperPerennial, 1992).

E. P. Torrance (1), "Group Dynamics and Creative Functioning," in *Climate for Creativity*, (Calvin W. Taylor, ed., 1972).

E. P. Torrance (2), "Creativity as Manifest in Testing," in *The Nature of Creativity: Contemporary Psychological Perspectives* (Cambridge University Press, 1988).

Martin van Creveld, *The Transformation of War* (The Free Press, 1991).

Arthur B. Vangundy (1), *Creative Problem Solving: A Guide for Trainers and Management* (Quorum Books, 1987).

Arthur B. Vangundy (2), *Techniques of Structured Problem Solving,* 2d ed. (Van Nostrand Reinhold Co., 1988).

Nigel Warburton, *Thinking from A to Z* (Routledge, 1996).

Thomas B. Ward, Steven M. Smith, & Jyotsna Vaid, *Creative Thought: An Investigation of Conceptual Structures and Processes* (American Psychological Ass'n, 1997).

Robert Paul Weiner, *Creativity & Beyond: Cultures, Values, and Change* (State University of New York, 2000).

Janet Weinstein & Linda Morton, "Stuck in a Rut: The Role of Creative Thinking in Problem Solving and Legal Education," 9 CLINICAL L. Rev. 835 (2003).

W. H. Weiss, *The Supervisor's Problem Solver* (AMACOM, 1982).

Arthur Whimbey & Jack Lochhead, *Problem Solving and Comprehension*, 5th ed. (Lawrence Erlbaum Assoc., 1991).

Jacquelyn Wonder & Priscilla Donovan, *Whole-Brain Thinking* (William Morrow & Co., 1984).

Larry E. Wood, *Thinking Strategies* (Prentice-Hall, Inc., 1986).